D1230723

EDWARD IV

EDWARD IV

Charles Ross

YALE UNIVERSITY PRESS
NEW HAVEN AND LONDON

First published in Great Britain in 1974 by Eyre Methuen Ltd
First published in paperback in 1983 by Methuen London Ltd
This edition first published by Yale University Press in 1997

Copyright © 1974 Charles Ross
New edition © 1997 The Estate of Charles Ross
New Foreword © 1997 R. A. Griffiths

All rights reserved. This book may not be reproduced in whole or
in part, in any form (beyond that copying permitted by Sections
107 and 108 of the U.S. Copyright Law and except by reviewers
for the public press), without written permission from the publishers.

Printed in Great Britain by St Edmundsbury Press Ltd

Library of Congress Catalog Card Number 97-61404

ISBN 0–300–07371–2 (hbk.)
ISBN 0–300–07372–0 (pbk.)

A catalogue record for this book is available from the British Library.

1 3 5 7 9 10 8 6 4 2

CONTENTS

LIST OF ILLUSTRATIONS   *page* vii
FOREWORD TO THE YALE EDITION (by R. A. Griffiths)   ix
PREFACE   xxv
ACKNOWLEDGEMENTS   xxvii
ABBREVIATIONS   xxix

Part I · THE ROAD TO THE THRONE

1 The Heir of York   3
2 The Yorkist Triumph, 1460–1461   22

Part II · THE FIRST REIGN, 1461–1471

3 The Defence of the Throne, 1461–1464   41
   (i) Disorder, Disaffection and Pacification   41
   (ii) The Lancastrian Resistance, 1461–1464   45
4 The Establishment of the Yorkist Regime   64
5 The King's Marriage and the Rise of the Woodvilles   84
6 The Burgundian Alliance and the Breach with Warwick,
   1465–1469   104
7 The Years of Crisis, 1469–1471   126
   (i) Warwick's Challenge and Failure, 1469–1470   126
   (ii) Edward's Deposition and Exile   145
   (iii) The Recovery of England, March–May 1471   161

Part III · THE SECOND REIGN, 1471–1483

8 Domestic Problems and Policies, 1471–1475   181
   (i) The Settlement of 1471: Rewards and Punishments   181
   (ii) The Quarrel of Clarence and Gloucester, 1471–1475   187
   (iii) Policies towards Wales, the north of England, and Ireland 193
9 The King's Great Enterprise, 1472–1475   205
   (i) Diplomacy and the Formation of Alliances: the Approach
      to War   205
   (ii) Financial and Military Preparations   214
   (iii) The Invasion of France, 1475   226

10 Family, Politics and Foreign Relations, 1475–1480   *page* 239
  (i) The Fall of Clarence   239
  (ii) Marriage Politics and Diplomacy   245
  (iii) England, France and Burgundy   249
11 Court Life and Patronage of the Arts   257
12 War, Diplomacy and Disillusion, 1480–1483   278

Part IV · THE GOVERNANCE OF ENGLAND

13 Personal Monarchy   299
14 Councillors, Courtiers and King's Servants   308
15 The King and the Community: Nobles, Commons in Parliament, and Merchants   331
  (i) Relations with the Nobility   331
  (ii) The King and the Commons in Parliament   341
  (iii) Merchants and Commercial Policy   351
16 The King's Finances   371
17 Law and Order   388
  Conclusion: The End of the Reign: Achievement and Aftermath   414

APPENDICES

I Note on Narrative Sources   429
II Edward IV's Governor   436
III Edward IV's Grants to Warwick   437
IV The Northern Rebellions of 1469: A Note on Sources and Chronology   439
V Warwick, Clarence, and the Lincolnshire Rebellion of 1470   441

SELECT BIBLIOGRAPHY   443
INDEX   457

ILLUSTRATIONS

PLATES

1   Letter from Edward, earl of March, and Edmund of Rutland
    to their father, Richard, duke of York
2   Edward IV enthroned, upon a Wheel of Fortune
3   Edward sets sail for Calais
4   Edward pardoning Henry VI after the battle of Northampton
5   William, Lord Herbert, and Anne, his wife, kneeling before
    Edward IV
6   Letter of Edward IV to the mayor of Bristol
7a Richard, duke of York
 b Edward, prince of Wales
 c Edward IV
8a Elizabeth Woodville
 b Elizabeth Woodville
9a Charles the Bold, duke of Burgundy
 b Margaret of York, duchess of Burgundy
10a Louis of Bruges, lord of Gruthuyse
 b Letter of Edward IV to the duke of Brittany
11 Edward IV as Hadrian
12a Edward IV
 b Edward IV
13a Philippe de Commynes
 b Louis XI
14 Warwick the Kingmaker and his family
15a Detail from the Rous Roll
 b Clarence, Duchess Isabel and their son, Edward, from the
    Rous Roll
16 Richard III
17a Angel with a shield of arms of Edward IV
 b Daughter of Edward IV
18 Coinage of Edward IV
19a Coins of Edward IV
 b Continental imitations of Edward IV's rose noble

20a Great Seal of Edward IV, obverse
  b Great Seal of Edward IV, reverse
21 Waurin's Chronicle: the author presents his manuscript to
     Edward IV
22 Edward IV's arms and his badge of the 'Rose en Soleil'
23a Windsor: the west front of St George's Chapel
  b Windsor: St George's Chapel
24a The ironwork grille for the tomb of Edward IV
  b Eltham Palace, Kent

MAPS

I   The North of England, 1460–1464   page 47
II   The Rebellion of 1470 and the flight of Warwick and
     Clarence   139
III The Campaign of 1471   162
IV   The English Invasion of France, 1475   227

DIAGRAMS

1 York and Lancaster   page 4
2 York and Bourchier   6
3 The Nevills   15
4 The Woodvilles   88
5 Exports and imports of dutiable commodities in the later
   fifteenth century   369

Acknowledgements and thanks for permission to reproduce photographs
are due to the British Museum for plates 1, 2, 3, 4, 5, 10b, 14, 15b and
21; to the Public Record Office for plates 6, 20a and 20b; to the Leigh
Gallery and Queens' College, Cambridge, for plate 8b; to the Society of
Antiquaries for plate 12a; to the National Portrait Gallery for plate
12b; and to the Glasgow Art Gallery and Museum, Burrell Collection,
for plate 17b. Plate 16 was reproduced by gracious permission of Her
Majesty the Queen, and plate 24a was reproduced by permission of
the Dean and Canons of Windsor.

Diagrams 1–4 were re-drawn from the author's roughs by Edgar
Holloway.

FOREWORD TO THE YALE EDITION

by R. A. Griffiths

Charles Ross died in 1986. Among those of this writings intended for a wide reading public as well as the professional historian, *Edward IV* (1974) is the finest achievement. *The Wars of the Roses* (1976) and *Richard III* (1981) are also highly successful and deservedly popular studies, and together the three volumes display the author's masterly understanding of Yorkist England and the relationship between king and realm in an age of dynastic civil war.[1] No scholarly, large-scale study of Edward IV's reign had appeared since Cora Scofield's two-volume compendium in 1923.[2] Almost a quarter of a century on, Ross's *Edward IV* remains authoritative. Couched in economical and pellucid prose (J. R. Lander found the book 'grippingly readable'), most of its judgements retain the respect initially accorded them by readers and reviewers alike, and it is likely to remain the most reliable port of call for anyone seeking to understand Edward IV and his impact on England.[3]

This is remarkable, for since 1974 the fifteenth century has continued to attract attention from a generation of scholars, many of whom have been inspired personally by Charles Ross or by his writings. Editions of original sources have appeared, and a torrent of books and essays has been published on many aspects of Yorkist England. A substantial proportion of these were part of the frenzied concentration on the quincentenary of Richard III's usurpation in 1483 and his defeat at Bosworth Field two years later, yet most could not fail to illumine Edward's reign as well, and Yorkist England more generally. In large part these writers filled *lacunae* in *Edward IV*, or substantiated Ross's conclusions in detail, rather than significantly altered them. This is a tribute to the original text of *Edward IV* and to Ross's perspicacity as a historian of the fifteenth century.

[1] A. Crawford, 'A Bibliography of Charles Ross', in *Kings and Nobles in the Later Middle Ages*, ed. R. A. Griffiths and J. Sherborne (Gloucester, 1986), 304–7.

[2] C. L. Scofield, *The Life and Reign of Edward the Fourth*, 2 vols (1923).

[3] Reviews: *Historical Journal*, 18 (1975), 879–81 (Delloyd Guth); *American Hist. Rev.*, 81 (1976), 572–3 (J. R. Lander); *EHR*, 91 (1976), 369–74 (B. P. Wolffe); *History*, 61 (1976), 105–6 (C. F. Richmond). See also K. Dockray, 'Edward IV: Playboy and Politician', *The Ricardian*, 10/131 (1995), 306–25.

Ross's acute assessment of Edward's character and personality is based on a critical yet sympathetic appraisal of the king in relation to the realities of his life and rule. This does not mean that Edward was Ross's hero: far from it for, as every reviewer noted, his was a penetrating analysis of the king, warts and all – and one that departed from the view of Edward current in 1974. On the whole, Ross's judgement has not been seriously undermined, though some scholars have not been entirely happy with his harsher colours, stressing (as these do) Edward's inconsistencies, misjudgements and failures as well as his flair, flamboyance, generosity and decisiveness. J. R. Lander, himself a distinguished interpreter of Yorkist England, sprang to Edward's defence, uneasy that Ross was too energetic in finding flaws in his character and policies; yet not even Lander ventured to find substantial fault with Ross's portrait.[4]

Edward IV is based carefully on an interpretation of those original – mostly contemporary – narrative and administrative sources available in 1974. No major narrative source has come to light since then, although a few newly-published contemporary fragments shed light on some aspects of the reign.[5] New editions of sources which Ross used tend to confirm and extend his interpretation of their content rather than alter his conclusions. On the other hand, Ross's valuable 'Note on Narrative Sources' (Appendix I) was soon supplemented by two important commentaries. First, Alison Hanham's *Richard III and his Early Historians, 1483–1535* (Oxford, 1975), was in the press when *Edward IV* was published. Despite its title, it includes extensive commentary on the strengths and deficiencies of the Crowland Chronicle and Dominic Mancini's *De Occupatione Regni Anglie per Ricardum Tercium Libellus* (known as 'The Usurpation of Richard III'), and of Polydore Vergil and Sir Thomas More among early Tudor writers, as important sources for Edward IV's reign.[6] Broader in scope, Antonia Gransden's *Historical Writing in Medieval England, II: c. 1397 to the Early Sixteenth Century* (1982), provides valuable descriptions and analyses of those

---

[4] J. R. Lander, *Government and Community: England, 1450–1509* (1980), 45, 51; cf. A. R. Myers, 'Parliament, 1422–1509', in *The English Parliament in the Middle Ages*, ed. R G. Davies and J. H. Denton (Manchester, 1981), 342–7.

[5] *The Politics of Fifteenth-Century England: John Vale's Book*, ed. M. L. Kekewich, C. F. Richmond, A. F. Sutton, L. Visser-Fuchs and J. L. Watts (Stroud, 1995), 178–80 ('Short chronicle of events, 1431–71'); L. Visser-Fuchs, 'English events in Caspar Weinreich's Danzig Chronicle, 1461–1495', *The Ricardian*, 7/95 (1986), 310–20; idem, 'Sanguinis Haustor – A Burgundian view of England, 1471', ibid., 7/92 (1986), 213–19.

[6] See also A. J. Pollard, 'Dominic Mancini's narrative of the events of 1483', *Nottingham Medieval Studies*, 38 (1994), 152–63, for a critique.

English and foreign writers who commented on the Wars of the Roses. New editions of chronicles and other sources, and reprints of older ones, reflect continuing interest in this period and a demand that classic texts be more widely available than in dusty, Victorian editions: for example, John Warkworth's brief chronicle, which is valuable for the crisis years of 1470–1, the 'Chronicle of the Rebellion in Lincolnshire' in 1470, and the propagandist 'Historie of the Arrivall of Edward IV' in 1471.[7] New editions of the Cely letters and the Plumpton correspondence, and the second volume of Norman Davis's edition of the Paston letters (the first volume was available to Ross when he wrote *Edward IV*) are, in large part, more reliable editions of letters and papers already well known; in any case, the Cely collection, for all its uniqueness as a substantial archive of merchants' business correspondence concerned with the wool trade, contains relatively little of the political comment that was Ross's prime interest.[8]

Of cardinal significance is the new edition of the Crowland Chronicle, published in 1986. In constructing his picture of Edward IV and the politics of the reign, Ross attached great importance to the anonymous political memoir that lies at the heart of the so-called 'second continuation' of this chronicle: 'by far the most important single source for the years 1471–85'.[9] The new edition prompted fevered discussion about the authorship of the continuation. Taking his cue from P. M. Kendall's *Richard III* (1955), Ross expressed a strong preference for John Russell, bishop of Lincoln, and he also reasserted the view that it was written at the Lincolnshire abbey of Crowland towards the end of April 1486. The editors of the new edition prefer Dr Henry Sharp, one of Russell's entourage, and others have championed Richard Lavender, another of Russell's associates, or have resurrected

---

[7] These three works are conveniently reprinted in *Three Chronicles of the Reign of Edward IV* (Gloucester, 1988), with a new introduction by K. Dockray; the first has been independently reprinted in facsimile by Llanerch Enterprises (1990).

[8] *The Cely Letters and Papers, 1472–1488*, ed. A. Hanham (Early English Text Soc., 273, 1975); *The Plumpton Letters and Papers*, ed. J. Kirby (Camden Fifth Ser., 8, 1996), with the greatest concentration of dated letters between 1480 and 1510; *Paston Letters and Papers of the Fifteenth Century*, Parts I and II, ed. N. Davis (Oxford, 1971, 1976). *The Stonor Letters and Papers, 1290–1483*, ed. C. L. Kingsford (Camden Third Ser., 29, 30, 1919), has been reprinted, with a new introduction by C. Carpenter (Cambridge, 1996). On the Celys, see A. Hanham, *The Celys and their World* (Cambridge, 1985). On the Plumptons, see J. Kirby, 'A Fifteenth-century Family; The Plumptons of Plumpton and their Lawyers, 1461–1515', *Northern Hist.*, 25 (1989), 106–19, and idem, 'A Northern Knightly Family in the Waning Middle Ages', ibid., 31 (1995), 86–107.

[9] *The Crowland Chronicle Continuations, 1459–1486*, ed. N. Pronay and J. Cox (1986); below p. 430.

the claims of Peter Curteis, who had been proposed by C. L. Kingsford in 1913 and was keeper of the great wardrobe under Edward IV.[10] Whilst authorship and date of compilation pose interesting historical questions, all the protagonists agree with Ross that the author was a close observer of Edward IV, with access to the corridors of his court and government, and that his 'memoir' is a first-rate source for the reign.

Ross was critical of the young Edward as he struggled to secure his grip on the realm after 1461. In particular, he felt that the king was unduly lenient towards his foes in northern England. The unreconciled Lancastrians dominated the north and its castles, yet Edward initially offered pardon to Lancastrian sympathisers who accepted the new regime; and he allowed them to retain positions of trust which they soon abused. With justification, more than one writer considers Ross to have been too hasty in condemning the new king and underestimating the strength of Lancastrian loyalties and the threat they posed so long as Henry VI, Queen Margaret and their son were at large.[11] Edward's urgent need to broaden his support in the north, rather than over-confidence, explains the king's actions. Moreover, as A. J. Pollard suggested, there was justifiable fear of a Scottish invasion after 1461, to aid the Lancastrians and cause maximum havoc in the borderland by capturing English-held fortresses. Pardons to opponents might buy time and, at best, win support; that they did not do the latter need not invalidate the attempt, for the choices facing Edward IV were difficult and their respective merits far from clear. Whether Edward used his breathing-space to best advantage is an open question, though his lieutenant, Warwick, returned to the north in 1463 and complemented Edward's diplomacy towards Scotland and France to secure the north for much of the 1460s. Norman Macdougall's 'political study' of *James III* of Scotland (Edinburgh, 1982) is unequivocal in endorsing Ross's assessment of the situation in Scotland and the course of Edward's

---

[10] H. A. Kelly, 'The Last Chroniclers of Croyland', *The Ricardian*, 7/91 (1985), 142–77; idem, 'The Croyland Chronicle Tragedies', ibid., 7/99 (1987), 498–515; A. Hanham, 'Richard Lavender, continuator?', ibid., pp. 516–19; L. Visser-Fuchs, 'A Commentary on the Continuation', ibid., pp. 520–2; D. Williams, 'The Crowland Chronicle, 616–1500', in *England in the Fifteenth Century*, ed. D. Williams (Woodbridge, 1987), pp. 371–90; M. Condon, 'The Crowland Chronicle Continuations, 1459–1486', *Hist. and Archaeology Rev.*, 3 (1988), 5–11; A. Hanham, 'Croyland Observations', *The Ricardian*, 8/108 (1990), 334–41.

[11] M. A. Hicks, 'Edward IV, the Duke of Somerset and Lancastrian Loyalism in the North', *Northern Hist.*, 20 (1984), reprinted in his *Richard III and his Rivals* (1991), ch. 8; A. J. Pollard, *North-eastern England during the Wars of the Roses* (Oxford, 1990), 228–9.

negotiations with the queen-regent. The king's desire to come to terms with the Lancastrians as part of a general settlement of the north reflects, at worst, a policy of optimism. In any case, the economic and financial difficulties facing a new king were bound to affect his ability to mount military operations in northern England. Civil war in the late 1450s and early 1460s undermined English trade, especially in cloth, and this caused unrest in southern parts of the realm and led to debasement of the coinage in 1463–4, as Ross noted.[12] Edward's attitude to the north, and his early return southwards, may be more comprehensible in the circumstances than Ross allowed.

Detailed study of the celebrated trial for treason of Sir Thomas Cook, an influential London merchant, in 1468 has also modified Ross's judgement of the king. Rather than colluding with the supposed political intrigues of his wife's relatives, the Woodvilles, against Cook, Edward seems genuinely to have believed the charges against him and felt that action was necessary at a time of Lancastrian and other plots. If the king's treatment of Cook is to be judged at all misconceived, it must be because of Edward's later generosity towards him, despite condemnation for misprision of treason.[13]

Ross did not see Edward as a great warrior-king: on occasion, the king lacked strategic judgement and decisiveness, and during the rebellions of 1469–70 he made mistakes. This latter verdict partly hinges on Edward's unwillingness to accept that Clarence and Warwick were behind the Lincolnshire disturbances in March 1470. Yet there remain doubts about the extent of their implication, and Edward, by his propaganda and military campaign, may have magnified their overt treason for his own purposes.[14] Later in the year, when Warwick and Clarence were rumoured to be planning an invasion, Edward went north to suppress Lord FitzHugh's rising, which may have seemed dangerous to those in London. The king was still in Yorkshire when Warwick and Clarence landed in the West Country, and he was forced to flee abroad. Edward faced a dilemma: to suppress

[12] R. H. Britnell, 'The Economic Context' in *The Wars of the Roses*, ed. A. J. Pollard (1995), 44, 57, and references cited there; C. E. Challis, *A New History of the Royal Mint* (Cambridge, 1992).

[13] M. A. Hicks, 'The Case of Sir Thomas Cook, 1468', *EHR*, 90 (1978), reprinted in his *Richard III and his Rivals*, ch. 23; A. F. Sutton, 'Sir Thomas Cook and his "troubles": an investigation', *Guildhall Studies in London History*, 3/2 (1978), 85–108; cf. *John Vale's Book*, ed. Kekewich et al., 89ff, which stresses official panic rather than political intrigue by the Woodvilles.

[14] P. Holland, 'The Lincolnshire Rebellion of March 1470', *EHR*, 103 (1988), 849–69.

a northern rising or await an invasion of uncertain date and destination. That he made the wrong choice does not reflect entirely badly on the king's judgement.[15] The events of 1471, on the other hand, were a triumph for Edward. He crushed his enemies separately by sound strategy and good luck: Warwick was brought to battle and killed at Barnet on 14 April, and the Lancastrian army was intercepted and defeated at Tewkesbury on 4 May. Detailed study of both engagements vindicates Ross's judgement that 'the king responded . . . with the same vigour and decision which mark all his actions in this critical year.'[16]

Other criticisms of the quality of Edward's judgement seem better founded. Ross detected the king's propensity to illegality and ruthlessness when it suited his purposes, and Michael Hicks asserts that Edward was prepared to countenance breaches of the law on retaining by those who were close to him or had responsibility for controlling distant provinces. The survival of the exceptional *cadre* of indentures of William, Lord Hastings, Edward's friend and chamberlain, led several historians to place Hastings in this category.[17] Hicks confirmed this trait in Edward's treatment of the countess of Oxford, Elizabeth de Vere. The king allowed his brother, Richard, to appropriate the countess's estates in 1473–5 by legal means but under duress; Edward declined to intervene on her behalf because he valued Richard's loyalty at a time when their brother George was proving increasingly irksome.[18] When the interests of himself or of those closest to him were involved, Edward's pliability and passivity – at worst his unscrupulousness – led him to misjudgements which ran a risk of alienating the nobility. Ross was right to draw a contrast with Henry VII; yet at least Edward did not unleash the forces of factionalism and favouritism to quite the same extent as Henry VI had managed to do.

The politics of Edward's reign were characterised as much by the

---

[15] A. J. Pollard, 'Lord FitzHugh's Rising in 1470', *BIHR*, 52 (1979), 170–5.

[16] P. W. Hammond, *The Battles of Barnet and Tewkesbury* (Gloucester, 1990).

[17] S. M. Wright, *The Derbyshire Gentry in the Fifteenth Century* (Chesterfield, 1983); I. Rowney, 'Resources and Retaining in Yorkist England: William, Lord Hastings and the Honour of Tutbury', in *Prosperity and Politics: Essays in Later Medieval English History*, ed. A. J. Pollard (Gloucester, 1984), 139–55; idem, 'The Hastings' Affinity in Staffordshire and the Honour of Tutbury', *BIHR*, 57 (1984), 35–45; C. Carpenter, *Locality and Polity: A Study of Warwickshire Landed Society, 1401–1499* (Cambridge, 1992); with an overview by M. A. Hicks, 'Lord Hastings' Indentured Retainers?', in his *Richard III and his Rivals*, ch. 12.

[18] M. A. Hicks, 'The Last Days of Elizabeth, Countess of Oxford', *EHR*, 100 (1988), reprinted in his *Richard III and his Rivals*, ch. 16.

actions of senior nobles as by those of the king. The towering figures of Warwick the 'Kingmaker' and the king's brothers, Clarence and Gloucester, alongside the Woodville family of the queen, have centre-billing throughout the reign. Beyond this group were other significant noblemen and their families. In 1974 few of either group had been studied in detail. Ross's view of the 'Kingmaker' and his part in the Yorkist collapse in 1469–70 was damning; Michael Hicks's forth-coming study will doubtless clarify the significance of this enigmatic figure. Hicks's study of *False, Fleeting, Perjur'd Clarence* (Gloucester, 1980), confirms the picture of a magnate whose 'treasons, perjury, overweening ambition, quarrelsomeness and other faults' seem un-deniable, though the duke had been thwarted in his ambitions by Edward who, in the 1470s, was inclined to favour their younger brother, Gloucester – yet who could blame him after Clarence's stark disloyalty in 1469–71?[19] Gloucester himself attracted most attention in the 1980s. This was partly with the object of rescuing his reputation, but a valuable picture has emerged of Richard's thirty-one years before he seized the crown, especially the period between 1471 and 1483 when he was usually in the north constructing a dominion for himself with Edward's indulgence.[20]

As for the Woodvilles, Ross concluded that their influence on English political life was 'malign'. Not only was Edward's marriage to Elizabeth Woodville a major blunder and a shock to contemporaries, but the patronage extended to her large family created a royal faction that courted much unpopularity. Neither the queen nor her talented brother Anthony, Earl Rivers, has received major study; but Hicks's examination of the Woodvilles as a political family underscores Ross's verdict.[21] A measure of dissent has been voiced: the king's marriage did at least present Edward with a ready-made, grown-up family which, if

[19] See also C. Carpenter, 'The Duke of Clarence and the Midlands: a Study in the interplay of local and national politics', *Midland Hist.*, 11 (1986), 23–48.

[20] Charles Ross, *Richard III* (1981); L. C. Attreed, 'An Indenture between Richard, Duke of Gloucester and the Scrope Family of Masham and Upsall [1476]', *Speculum*, 58 (1983), 1018–25; M. A. Hicks, *Richard III as Duke of Gloucester: A Study in Character* (Borthwick Paper, 70, 1986), reprinted in his *Richard III and his Rivals*, ch. 13; *Richard III and the North*, ed. R. Horrox (Hull, 1986); A. J. Pollard, 'St Cuthbert and the Hog: Richard III and the County Palatine of Durham, 1471–85', in *Kings and Nobles in the Later Middle Ages*, ed. Griffiths and Sherborne, ch. 6; R. B. Dobson, 'Richard III and the Church of York', ibid., ch. 7.

[21] M. A. Hicks, 'The Changing Role of the Wydevilles in Yorkist Politics to 1483', in *Patronage, Pedigree and Power in Later Medieval England*, ed. C. D. Ross (Gloucester, 1979), 60–86, reprinted in his *Richard III and his Rivals*, ch. 11.

deployed carefully, might have broadened his support among the nobility, and D. E. Lowe judged the aggrandisement of the Woodvilles 'a deliberate and shrewd move of royal policy'.[22] Moreover, Elizabeth's religious and cultural interests make possible a more admiring verdict than Ross allowed when viewing her as queen and politician.[23]

Several studies of the nobility have been completed since 1974, either of noble fortunes across the generations or of the environment in which individuals moved and safeguarded their interests and estates. The young Henry, duke of Buckingham played a muted role in Edward's reign, though Carole Rawcliffe's study of the Stafford family highlights the suspicion in which his royal blood was held by Edward IV, and the grudge that Henry bore against the royal family as he grew up – factors which doubtless contributed to his actions in 1483.[24] The Hollands, relatives of the Lancastrians, have been studied by Michael Stansfield. The care with which Edward supervised the last of the brood, Henry Holland, duke of Exeter, married him to his sister and, after he parted from her, kept him under restraint – until he was lost overboard when the king's expedition returned from France in 1475 – demonstrates the king's determination to control the nobility and subdue potential troublemakers.[25] The Bourgchiers, who were Edward's kinsmen, have been studied by Linda Clark: Henry Bourgchier was given the earldom of Essex by Edward IV in 1461.[26] Three of the 'new nobility' patronised by Edward at the outset of his reign – William Hastings, created Lord Hastings, William Herbert of Raglan, created Lord Herbert and, in 1468, earl of Pembroke, and John Howard, made a baron in 1470, have

[22] D. E. Lowe, 'Patronage and Politics: Edward IV, the Wydevills and the Council of the Prince of Wales, 1471–83', *Bull. Board of Celtic Studies*, 29 (1981), 568–91; Mr. T. B. Pugh saw this paper through the press after Lowe's death. See, in general, R. A. Griffiths, 'The Crown and the Royal Family in Later Medieval England', in *Kings and Nobles in the Later Middle Ages*, ed. Griffiths and Sherborne, 15–26, reprinted in his *King and Country: England and Wales in the Fifteenth Century* (1991), ch. 1.

[23] A. F. Sutton and L. Visser-Fuchs, 'A "Most Benevolent Queen": Queen Elizabeth Woodville's Reputation, her Piety and her Books', *The Ricardian*, 10/129 (1995), 214–45.

[24] C. Rawcliffe, *The Staffords, Earls of Stafford and Dukes of Buckingham, 1394–1521* (Cambridge, 1978).

[25] M. M. N. Stansfield, 'The Holland Family, Dukes of Exeter, Earls of Kent and Huntingdon, 1352–1475' (unpublished University of Oxford DPhil thesis, 1987).

[26] L. Clark (née Woodger), 'Henry Bourgchier, Earl of Essex and his Family (1408–83)' (unpublished University of Oxford DPhil thesis, 1974); idem, 'The Benefits and Burdens of Office: Henry Bourgchier (1408–83), Viscount Bourgchier and Earl of Essex, and the Treasurership of the Exchequer', in *Profit, Piety and the Professions in Later Medieval England*, ed. M. A. Hicks (Gloucester, 1990), ch. 9. For Edward's brother-in-law, see J. A. F. Thomson, 'John de la Pole, duke of Suffolk', *Speculum*, 54 (1979), 528–42.

also been studied since Ross wrote.[27] As a result, historians, can now evaluate Ross's conclusion that Edward strove to contain the disputes of the nobility and was able to remove Clarence in 1478 without arousing open hostility from them.

As Ross averred, England may have paid a high price for the advancement of the Woodvilles and Gloucester, with disastrous consequences in 1483 when noble position, royal patronage and extraordinary provincial power combined with soaring ambition. The Woodville position in Wales and the Marches, following the revival of the prince's council in 1471, has been revealed in detail by D. E. Lowe.[28] Wales, the Marches and the border shires became a Woodville fiefdom in a pragmatic act of regional delegation of royal government. Ross may have exaggerated the sinister significance of Earl Rivers's powers and, in particular, the novelty of the military authority that was confirmed to him six weeks before King Edward died. Nevertheless, by 1483 the Woodvilles were all-powerful in Wales and the west, where their authority may have been resented by Buckingham and mistrusted by Gloucester.

Ross seems also to have exaggerated Edward's responsibility for the creation of Gloucester's unique position in the north. Gloucester created his own northern affinity and extended his power beyond what the king authorised: political independence and opportunities in Scotland may have mattered more to Richard than obligations to his brother and king. In the lordship of Middleham and the city of York, and in the king's duchy of Lancaster estates in the north, he acquired land and rights, and developed ties of loyalty with gentry and citizens alike; although Ross consulted the York House Books, their publication in a new, full edition reveals Gloucester's activities with greater clarity.[29] Ross also mistook the scope of the king's most beneficent

[27] Above n. 17 and C. Kelly, 'The Noble Steward and Late-Feudal Lordship', *Huntington Library Quarterly*, 49 (1986), 133–48 (for Hastings); R. A. Griffiths and R. S. Thomas, *The Making of the Tudor Dynasty* (Gloucester, 1985) (for Herbert); and *The Household Books of John Howard, Duke of Norfolk, 1462–1471, 1481–1483*, with an introduction by A. Crawford (Stroud, 1992), a reprint of earlier editions used by Ross, with additional documents; idem, 'The Private Life of John Howard: A Study of a Yorkist Lord, his Family and Household', in *Richard III: Loyalty, Lordship and Law*, ed. P. W. Hammond (1986), 6–24.

[28] Lowe, *Bull. Board of Celtic Studies*, 29 (1981), 545–73, and idem, 'The Council of the Prince of Wales and the decline of the Herbert Family during the Second Reign of Edward IV (1471–1483)', ibid., 27 (1977), 278–97.

[29] Hicks, *Richard III as Duke of Gloucester* (reprinted in his *Richard III and his Rivals*, ch. 13); D. Palliser, 'Richard III and York', in *Richard III and the North*, ed. Horrox, 51–81; R. Horrox, *Richard III: A Study of Service* (Cambridge, 1989); Pollard, *North-eastern England*, ch. 13; *York House Books, 1461–1490*, ed. L. C. Attreed, 2 vols (Stroud, 1991).

grant to Richard, in 1483: it did not include Westmorland, and palatine powers were confined to lands which his brother might gain in southern Scotland and did not extend to his English estates too. It was Richard who made his position in the north a danger to the realm, albeit on foundations provided by Edward. Pollard goes so far as to say that Edward had no choice but to acquiesce in his brother's aggrandisement, as the price of controlling the north and protecting the Anglo-Scottish border.

With these adjustments made, Ross's conclusion is compelling: Edward created two powerful, regional affinities in the hands of ambitious individuals close to the king. Whether or not these individuals were openly suspicious of, or hostile to, one another is an open question, but Edward had inadvertently created a situation fraught with danger by the time he died – and one which Gloucester was the first to exploit.[30]

Gloucester's apologists put great store not simply by his loyalty to Edward IV but also by his command of the English forces in Scotland in the last years of the reign. Ross's account of the war has been praised by English and Scottish historians alike, though his judgement of Edward's diplomacy is controversial.[31] The king's entanglement in Scotland seems another misjudgement, with war distracting the king from more pressing continental affairs; yet once in the Lowlands, the army's retreat from Edinburgh seemed to Ross a lost opportunity, an example of Edward's indecision and even his weakening grip in his last months. Others believe that Ross over-stated his case and underestimated the significance of Anglo-Scottish relations at this juncture: the recovery of Berwick was important to his reputation and the realm's defence. A Gloucester who cherished independent power for himself in the north is likely to have appreciated these facts and he accordingly prosecuted the campaign with vigour. Once again, Edward may have had little choice – or inclination – but to support Richard's ambitions. As for the withdrawal from Edinburgh, this appears less of a puzzle (in Ross's judgement) when the king's confrontation with France and the costs of war and the garrisoning of Berwick are taken into account.[32]

[30] For an interesting pointer, C. E. Moreton, 'A Local Dispute and the Politics of 1483: Roger Townshend, Earl Rivers and the Duke of Gloucester', *The Ricardian*, 8/107 (1989), 305–7.

[31] Pollard, *North-eastern England*, 235–44; Macdougall, *James III*, 156 and n. 28; Lander, *Government and Community*, 304–5.

[32] 'Financial Memoranda of the Reign of Edward V: Longleat Miscellaneous Manuscript Book II', ed. R. Horrox, in *Camden Miscellany, Vol. XXIX* (Camden Fourth Ser., 34, 1987); *John Vale's Book*, ed. Kekewich et al., 71–2.

Anglo-Scottish relations were intimately connected with continental diplomacy, notably towards France, Burgundy and Brittany. 'The marriage of the century' in 1468 between Edward IV's sister and Charles the Bold, duke of Burgundy, and the multi-faceted significance of the Anglo-Burgundian connection in the 1460s and 1470s, continue to attract attention, adding detail to the picture painted by Ross in *Edward IV*.[33] There was a hardening of England's attitude to the Hanseatic League and even a rash of privateering clashes. Edward's negotiations for a peace with the Hanse, which provided naval assistance for his return from exile in 1471, led to the treaty of Utrecht in 1474. This treaty was an essential preliminary to his invasion of France in 1475 and may therefore be judged one of Edward's successes; in T. H. Lloyd's estimation, Ross 'authoritatively challenges the usual view of a sell-out by Edward IV'.[34]

Edward's motives in taking an army to France in 1475 continue to remain uncertain. Ross believed that his lengthy diplomatic, financial and military preparations suggest serious war plans: had it not been for Charles the Bold's ambitions and preoccupation elsewhere, the English army might have posed as serious a military threat as Lous XI feared. J. R. Lander remains unconvinced: for him the war was defensive on Edward's part, designed to pre-empt French interference in England. Likewise, whereas Ross blamed Edward for failing to support Duke Charles's heiress, Mary of Burgundy, against French aggression in 1477, Lander is inclined to interpret his caution as a fear of what Louis might do if England intervened.[35]

Ross sustained his critical view of Edward's continental relations right down to the end of the reign, when his diplomatic plans were unravelling, thereby endangering England's security. In addition to war with Scotland, he noted deteriorating relations with the Hanse and the unwelcome reconciliation between Mary of Burgundy's husband,

[33] C. Weightman, *Margaret of York, Duchess of Burgundy, 1446–1503* (Gloucester, 1989); M. H. A. Ballard, 'Anglo-Burgundian Relations, 1464–72' (unpublished University of Oxford MPhil thesis, 1993); R. F. Green, 'An Account of the Marriage of Margaret of York and Charles the Bold, 1468', *Notes and Queries*, 233 (1988), 26–9.
[34] T. H. Lloyd, *England and the German Hanse, 1157–1611* (Cambridge, 1991), 207–13. See also idem, 'A Reconsideration of Two Anglo-Hanseatic Treaties of the Fifteenth Century', *EHR*, 102 (1987), 916–33; J. B. Fudge, *Cargoes, Embargoes and Emissaries: The Commercial and Political Interaction of England and the German Hanse, 1450–1510* (Toronto, 1995), chs. 2, 3.
[35] Lander, *Government and Community*, pp. 285–92; see also *John Vale's Book*, ed. Kekewich et al., 67–72.

Maximilian of Austria, and Louis XI, leaving Edward diplomatically isolated. Lander's charge that such an assessment lacks perspective carries some weight: what were the benefits of the Scottish campaign, and should Edward be blamed for events beyond his control?[36]

French and Burgundian cultural influence on Yorkist England was great, and Ross alluded to it in his chapter on Edward IV's court. He was inclined to moderate Edward's reputation as a patron of the arts and of the printing press established at Westminster in 1477. The flurry of quincentenary studies of William Caxton confirmed that Edward had a minor role in patronising the new technology and commissioning printed books. On the other hand. Ross emphasised the Netherlandish influences on his court, especially on the magnificence and splendour that created an impressive stage for his public and private activities.[37] They may date from before his exile: visits of high-ranking Burgundians to England, the tournaments associated with them, and the marriage of the king's sister in 1468 provided a context. The surviving engraving of the king and the original of the famous portrait in The Royal Collection, which Ross used on the dust-jacket of his book – and which may date from c. 1471-5 – are believed to have been executed in England, though Netherlandish in inspiration or technique. Their purpose may have been propagandist rather than decorative, to mark Edward's restoration to the throne in 1471. Netherlandish influence on his building enterprises was also detected by Ross, and his works at Windsor, Eltham and Nottingham have been documented recently by Simon Thurley.[38]

Considerable attention has been given to the books collected by Edward, the 'first king to commission books in any quantity', most of them from abroad, especially Burgundy. His illuminated manuscripts of historical and literary works were commissioned for formal use and

[36] Lander, *Government and Community*, 301–5; Lloyd, *England and the German Hanse*, 235–6; and see C. F Richmond's and M. L. Kekewich's reassessment of Ross's pessimistic view, in *John Vale's Book*, ed. Kekewich et al., 71–2.

[37] G. Kipling, *The Triumph of Honour* (Leiden, 1977); N. F. Blake, *William Caxton and English Literary Culture* (London, 1980); *William Caxton: An Exhibition to commemorate the Quincentenary of the Introduction of Printing into England* (1976); N. F. Blake, *Caxton: England's First Publisher* (1976); G. D. Painter, *William Caxton: A Quincentary Biography* (1976).

[38] F. Hepburn, *Portraits of the Later Plantagenets* (Woodbridge, 1986), ch. 4; S. Thurley, *The Royal Palaces of Tudor England* (1993), ch. 2. On Edward's Burgundian friend, see M. G. A. Vale, 'An Anglo-Burgundian Nobleman and art patron: Louis de Bruges, Lord of La Gruthuyse and Earl of Winchester', in *England and the Low Countries in the Later Middle Ages*, ed. C. Barron and N. Saul (Stroud, 1995), 115–32.

reflect the courtly taste of the age.[39] Ross's suggestion that they are the literary and artistic dimension of his luxurious court, where they were designed to be read and admired, rather than a reflection of the king's personal interests, commends itself to recent commentators.[40]

This flair for artistic display, with its counterpart in propagandist writings, figures less prominently in *Edward IV* than in Ross's subsequent paper on 'Rumour, Propaganda and the Wars of the Roses'. Yorkist uses of propaganda have been identified in studies of genealogy, prophecy and myth, and in analyses of the propagandist accounts of Edward IV's return from exile (or 'Arrivall') which were circulated abroad as well as in England, to proclaim his victory and deter his enemies.[41]

The arts of propaganda and modes of communication (a little-studied subject) bear on the effectiveness of royal government in fifteenth-century England.[42] Ross concentrated on the relationship

---

[39] J. J. G. Alexander, 'Painting and Manuscript Illumination for Royal Patrons in the Later Middle Ages', in *English Court Culture in the Later Middle Ages*, ed. V. J. Scattergood and J. W. Sherborne (1983), 152–3; in general, see R. F. Green, *Poets and Princepleasers: Literature and the English Court in the Late Middle Ages* (Toronto, 1980). Edward's ordinances for the education of his son (February 1483) were detailed yet traditional in character: N. Orme, 'The Education of Edward V', *BIHR*, 57 (1984).

[40] J. Backhouse, 'Founders of the Royal Library: Edward IV and Henry VII as Collectors of Illuminated Manuscripts', in *England in the Fifteenth Century*, ed. Williams, 23–42; S. McKendrick, 'The *Romuleon* and the Manuscripts of Edward IV', in *England in the Fifteenth Century*, ed. N. Rogers (Stamford, 1994), 149–69, and '*La Grande Histoire César* and the Manuscripts of Edward IV', in *English Manuscript Studies, 1100–1700*, Vol. 2 (1990), 109–38; A. F. Sutton and L. Visser-Fuchs, 'Choosing a Book in Later Fifteenth-century England and Burgundy', in *England and the Low Countries*, ed. Barron and Saul, 71–98; K. Harris, 'Patrons, Buyers and Owners: the Evidence for Ownership, the Role of Book Owners in Book Production and the Book Trade', in *Book Production and Publishing in Britain, 1375–1475*, ed. J. Griffiths and D. Pearsall (Cambridge, 1989), 163–200; C. Meale, 'Patrons, Buyers and Owners: Book Production and Social Status', ibid., 201–38.

[41] C. D. Ross, 'Rumour, Propaganda and Popular Opinion during the Wars of the Roses', in *Patronage, the Crown and the Provinces in Later Medieval England*, ed. R. A. Griffiths (Gloucester, 1981), ch. 1. Cf. I. M. W. Harvey, 'Was there Popular Politics in Fifteenth-century England?', in *The McFarlane Legacy*, ed. R. H. Britnell and A. J. Pollard (Stroud, 1995), ch. 7.

[42] A. Allan, 'Political Propaganda employed by the House of York in England in the Mid-Fifteenth Century, 1450–1471' (unpublished University of Wales PhD thesis, 1981); idem, 'Yorkist Propaganda: Pedigree, Prophecy and the "British History" in the Reign of Edward IV', in *Patronage, Pedigree and Power in Later Medieval England*, ed. Ross, 171–92; R. F. Green, 'The Short Version of *The Arrivall* of Edward IV', *Speculum*, 56 (1981), 324–36; L. Visser-Fuchs, 'Edward IV's "memoir on paper" to Charles, Duke of Burgundy: the so-called "Short Version" of *The Arrivall*', *Nottingham Medieval Studies*, 36 (1992), 167–227; A. F. Sutton, L. Visser-Fuchs and P. W. Hammond, *The Reburial of*

Continued overleaf—

between the crown and the nobility, and the king in his household, court and council.[43] But throughout his career, he was alive to regional, provincial dimensions of royal rule and noble society, not least in Yorkshire and the north. Since 1974, more attention has been given to the king's government and the enforcement of its will in the shires of England, and to relations between the crown and the nobility, gentry and townsfolk. It is a shift of emphasis of which Ross approved, and it underscores his awareness of the links between the king's household and court and provincial power structures.[44] On parliament, the most formal of these links, A. R. Myers stressed the recovery of the king's initiative in legislation under Edward IV more heavily than Ross did.[45] On the other hand, Nicholas Pronay noted how the chancery changed from 'an administrative department with a certain amount of judicial business to becoming one of the four central courts of the realm', perhaps as a result of an increase in mercantile cases which Edward may have regarded as more profitable to the crown.[46] Ross's reluctance to see marked innovation in government as opposed to pragmatic change and *ad hoc* decisions offers an agenda for discussion of such subjects as the king's legislation, his treatment of the criminal and the overmighty, and continuity of administrative service from the Lan-

---

Continued from previous page—

Richard, Duke of York, 21–30 July 1476 (1994). On communication, there are interesting suggestions in A. Allan, 'Royal Propaganda and the Proclamations of Edward IV', *BIHR*, 59 (1986), 146–54; I. Arthurson, 'Espionage and Intelligence from the Wars of the Roses to the Reformation', *Nottingham Medieval Studies*, 35 (1991), 134–54.

[43] K. Mertes, 'The *Liber Niger* of Edward IV: a new Version', *BIHR*, 54 (1981), 29–39; P. M. Barnes, 'The Chancery *Corpus cum Causa* File, 10–11 Edward IV', in *Medieval Legal Records*, ed. R. F. Hunnisett and J. B. Post (1978), 429–76, for Edward's suggested pragmatic use of his council rather than government departments; *The Coronation of Richard III: The Extant Documents*, ed. A. F. Sutton and P. W. Hammond (Gloucester, 1983), ch. 3, for the great wardrobe under Edward IV.

[44] R. A. Griffiths, 'The Hazards of Civil War: The Mountford Family and the Wars of the Roses', *Midland Hist.*, 5 (1980), 1–19, reprinted in his *King and Country*, ch. 21; Wright, *Derbyshire Gentry*; Carpenter, *Midland Hist.*, 11 (1986), 23–48; idem, *Loyalty and Polity*, especially chs. 13, 14; E. Acheson, *A Gentry Community: Leicestershire in the Fifteenth Century* (Cambridge, 1992); C. Kelly, *Huntington Library Quarterly*, 49 (1986), 133–48 (Hastings and the north Midlands). On the Edwardian peace commissions and JPs, see C. Arnold, 'The Commission of the Peace for the West Riding of Yorkshire, 1437–1509', in *Property and Politics*, ed. Pollard, ch. 6; J. R. Lander, *English Justices of the Peace, 1461–1509* (Gloucester, 1989).

[45] Myers, 'Parliament, 1422–1509', in *English Parliament in the Middle Ages*, ed. Davies and Denton, ch. 6.

[46] N. Pronay, 'The Chancellor, the Chancery, and the Council at the End of the Fifteenth Century', in *British Government and Administration: Studies presented to S. B Chrimes*, ed. H. Hearder and H. R. Loyn (Cardiff, 1974), 87–103.

castrian era.[47] Ross was equally guarded in attributing administrative novelty and notable success to Edward's management of the royal finances and landed wealth. There were precedents in the 1450s for Edward's use of the household, and the chamber within it, as a more effective organ of financial administration.[48] Whatever doubts may be expressed about endorsing his contemporary reputation as a restorer of the royal finances, manifestly the near-bankruptcy of Henry VI's later years was repaired by the new king; yet when he died only modest cash reserves were left to his son.[49]

Ross's conclusion on Edward IV is an indictment of the king: 'He remains the only king in English history since 1066 in active possession of his throne who failed to secure the safe succession of his son'. Some writers have expressed reservations about this verdict; yet the anxious words of the warden of Tattershall College, Lincolnshire, in a letter to William Waynflete, bishop of Winchester, just ten days after the death of the king on 9 April 1483, have a foreboding ring of truth:

> For nowe oure soveren lord the kyng ys ded hose soule Jhesu take to his grete mercy we wet not hoo schal be oure lord noo schal have the reule a boute us . . .[50]

July 1997

---

[47] Revival of the concept of a 'new monarchy' under Edward IV and the early Tudors is premature on present evidence: ct. A. E. Goodman, *The New Monarchy: England, 1471–1534* (1988), and J. A. Guy, *Tudor England* (Oxford, 1988), 13–14 (or 'refoundation'). For a critical comment, see A. J. Pollard, 'New Monarchy renovated: England, 1461–1509', *Medieval Hist.*, 2/1 (1992), 78–82.

[48] R. A. Griffiths, *The Reign of King Henry VI* (1981), 785–90; for hints of adminstrative continuity, see Clark, 'Benefits and Burdens of Office', in *Profit, Piety and the Professions*, ed. Hicks, ch. 9.

[49] Financial Memoranda', ed. Horrox, in *Camden Miscellany, vol. XXIX*. This report does not take into account Edward IV's moveable wealth.

[50] C. F. Richmond, 'A Letter of 19 April 1483 from John Gigur to William Wainfleet', *Hist. Research*, 65 (1992), 111–16 (at p. 116).

PREFACE

This book is essentially a study in the power-politics of late medieval England. It could hardly be otherwise. The reign of Edward IV began with his forcible seizure of the throne; it is punctuated in mid-term by his deposition, exile, and his subsequent recovery of the crown, again by force; and his premature death was the prelude to two further usurpations, the first removing his heir, the second extinguishing the Yorkist dynasty itself. Any student of the reign must, therefore, be primarily concerned to provide an explanation of these violent changes of political fortune. The ways and means of gaining and keeping power are central themes of this study. For the same reason, Edward's relations with the English nobility, and especially his use of patronage, occupy a prominent place, since, as the late K. B. McFarlane once remarked, 'no one but a fool would deny that the territorial power of the nobility was the supreme factor in later medieval society'. On this crucial aspect of the reign, however, much research remains to be done, and much, fortunately, is already in progress.

Edward IV is the only fifteenth-century king whose reputation stands substantially higher today than it did a half-century ago. This modern re-appraisal of his achievement has largely been the work of a number of scholars of the present generation, notably Professor J. R. Lander and Dr B. P. Wolffe. It rests firmly on a far more informed understanding of the practical problems of government in late medieval England, and of Edward's considerable success in finding solutions, albeit highly personal solutions, to the more pressing difficulties confronting him. Yet there remains a paradox between his undoubted success in government and his serious failings as a politician, especially his failure to provide for the peaceful succession of his son – the prime duty of an hereditary king: and to this problem I have endeavoured to find some solution. Proper treatment of Edward's diplomacy, so important throughout the reign, and particularly in his later years, presents great difficulties. Reasons of space alone would prevent any attempt to unravel in detail its immensely complex threads, in an age of Machiavellian international relations, but my attempt to isolate its principal motives has necessarily involved some foreshortening, and for details one must still refer to Miss C. L. Scofield's elaborate if episodic account of Yorkist foreign policy. Finally, this is a highly personal reign, dominated by the forceful, worldly, and often contradictory character of the king. In trying to see things through Edward's eyes, I have concentrated on matters such as finance and commercial affairs which much engaged his attention, and paid correspondingly little attention to those which did not interest Edward himself.

Fifteenth-century English is often obscure, through its spelling, syntax, and the use of unfamiliar words which require constant glossing. For the convenience of readers, therefore, I have rendered in modern English all quotations in the text from vernacular contemporary sources. In spite of rather pedantic objections that the term 'The Wars of the Roses' is unhistorical, I have preferred to follow the example of K. B. McFarlane and others in retaining its use as a convenient and by now established phrase.

ACKNOWLEDGEMENTS

I owe a great deal to the work of the many scholars whose works are cited in my footnotes. In particular I must pay tribute to the remarkable pioneer work of Miss C. L. Scofield. Her two-volume study, published as long ago as 1923, was a piece of sustained and meticulous scholarship, which provided an exhaustive (and sometimes exhausting) but indispensable narrative of the reign which is unlikely ever to be superseded. To Professor David Douglas, the General Editor of this series until 1981, my thanks are due for providing me with the opportunity and the encouragement to write this book, and for much kindness over the years. I am grateful also to the Librarian and staff of Bristol University Library for their willing assistance. Dr R. A. Griffiths kindly read the early chapters of the book and saved me from a number of errors. My colleagues in the University, especially Mr J. W. Sherborne and Dr A. V. Antonovics, have shown exemplary patience in listening to my problems, and have given generously of their scholarship. I have learnt much, perhaps more than they realized, from my students, past and present, in special-subject discussions, and my post-graduate students have been generous in allowing me to make use of some of the results of their research, especially Miss M. M. Condon of the Public Record Office. Their help, I hope, has been sufficiently acknowledged in the footnotes. This book has been long in the preparation, but it would have been longer still without the vigorous encouragement and patient advice of my wife, Anne, who has also helped greatly in preparing the bibliography and the index.

ABBREVIATIONS

The following abbreviations are used in the footnotes. Full details of the works cited below, and of other books and articles referred to by short titles, will be found in the Bibliography at the end of the book. Manuscript sources are separately identified in the footnotes, usually following P.R.O. or B.M.

Annales	'Annales rerum anglicarum' (formerly attributed to William Worcester)
Arrivall	'Historie of the Arrivall of King Edward IV' (ed. J. Bruce, Camden Society, 1838)
BIHR	*Bulletin of the Institute of Historical Research*
B.M.	British Museum
CC	'Croyland Chronicle' ('Historiae Croylandensis Continuatio', being pp. 449–592 of *Rerum Anglicarum Scriptores Veterum*, ed. W. Fulman)
CCR	*Calendar of Close Rolls*
CChR	*Calendar of Charter Rolls*
CFR	*Calendar of Fine Rolls*
Commynes	Commynes, Philip de, *Mémoires*, ed. J. Calmette and G. Durville (except where other editions are indicated)
CP	*The Complete Peerage*
CPR	*Calendar of Patent Rolls*
CSP, Milan (Venice)	*Calendar of State Papers, Milan (Venice)*
DNB	*Dictionary of National Biography*
EconHR	*Economic History Review*
EHR	*English Historical Review*
Fifteenth-Century England	*Fifteenth-Century England, 1399–1509: Studies in Politics and Society* (ed. S. B. Chrimes, C. D. Ross and R. A. Griffiths, 1972)
GC	*The Great Chronicle of London* (ed. A. H. Thomas and I. D. Thornley, 1938)
Gregory	'Gregory's Chronicle' (in *Collections of a London Citizen*, ed. J. Gairdner)
Mancini	Dominic Mancini, *The Usurpation of Richard III* (ed. C. A. J. Armstrong, 2nd edn, 1969)
PL	*The Paston Letters* (1904 edn, ed. J. Gairdner, 6 vols) (except where other editions are indicated)
P.R.O.	Public Record Office
RP	*Rotuli Parliamentorum*
Rymer, *Foedera*	Thomas Rymer, *Foedera* etc. (1704–35 edn, 20 vols)

Scofield	C. L. Scofield, *The Life and Reign of Edward the Fourth* (2 vols, 1923)
TRHS	*Transactions of the Royal Historical Society*
VCH	*The Victoria History of the Counties of England*
YCR	*York Civic Records*, 1, ed. A. Raine

Part I

THE ROAD TO THE THRONE

Chapter 1

THE HEIR OF YORK

Edward of York was born on 28 April 1442 at Rouen in Normandy, the headquarters of his father, Richard, duke of York, then serving as Henry VI's lieutenant-general in France. His high birth alone would have been sufficient to secure for Edward a leading place in the politics and society of his age. By 1447, when the king's uncle, Humphrey, duke of Gloucester, died without heirs, the recently married but still childless Henry VI became the last surviving male in the direct line of the House of Lancaster. This gave Duke Richard a strong claim to the throne of England as long as Henry VI failed to produce an heir. He was not, however, the king's nearest male relative. This distinction belonged to the youthful and violent Henry Holland, duke of Exeter, a descendant of Elizabeth, daughter of John of Gaunt, duke of Lancaster, from whom the royal house derived, and his close blood-relationship to the king may have led Exeter to believe that he, rather than York, should have been made Protector of England during Henry VI's illness in 1453–4.[1] If male descent were to be preferred to female, then York's main rival, Edmund Beaufort, duke of Somerset, a grandson of John of Gaunt by his mistress (later his third wife), Katherine Swynford, might have been regarded as Henry VI's heir presumptive but for a royal addition to an act of parliament which had excluded the Beaufort family from succession to the throne. York's family connections were rather with the Plantagenet than the Lancastrian line. He was directly descended in the male line from John of Gaunt's next brother, Edmund of Langley, 1st duke of York, fourth surviving son of King Edward III and he was later to adopt the surname 'Plantagenet' as if to emphasize the purity of his royal ancestry.[2] But if descent in the female line were to be allowed, then Duke Richard's claim to the throne was better than that of Henry VI himself, for through his mother, Anne Mortimer,

[1] As suggested by R. A. Griffiths, 'Local Rivalries and National Politics: the Percies the Nevilles, and the Duke of Exeter, 1452–1455'; *Speculum*, xlii (1968), 613; and see Genealogical Tables. The male line of John of Gaunt's elder daughter, Philippa, was in 1450 represented by her grandson, King Alfonso V of Portugal.
[2] J. R. Lander, *Conflict and Stability in Fifteenth-Century England*, 73, suggests that he may have begun to use the name as early as 1450.

Table 1 YORK AND LANCASTER

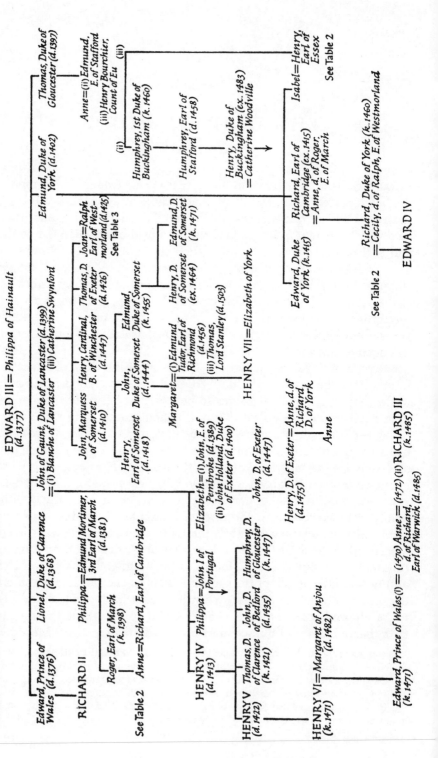

he was directly descended from John of Gaunt's *elder* brother, Lionel, duke of Clarence. But not until 1460, the year of his death, did Duke Richard, or anyone else on his behalf, raise that particularly dangerous question, and meanwhile he continued, unprovocatively, to bear the arms of Edmund of Langley. Yet York evidently thought well enough of his male descent – or was prompted by fears of Somerset – to encourage his supporter, Thomas Young, the member of parliament for Bristol, to propose in the parliament of 1451 that the duke should be recognized as heir presumptive to the throne, a suggestion so strongly resented that it landed Young in the Tower forthwith.

Richard of York was also the greatest English landowner of his day. In England proper his estates, chiefly inherited from Edmund of Langley, extended into more than twenty shires. In Yorkshire he had wide estates in the West Riding centred around his castle of Sandal near Wakefield. Fotheringhay Castle in Northamptonshire was the focus of substantial estates in the east midlands. Further south another concentration lay in Hertfordshire, Essex and Suffolk, and he had other valuable properties in Berkshire, Hampshire, Wiltshire and Somerset. But his greatest strength lay in the inheritance of his mother, Anne, heiress of the powerful Mortimer earls of March. A chain of great lordships stretched through eastern Wales and the Marches from Denbigh in the north to Caerleon and Usk in the south, and was flanked by others in the adjoining English border counties, especially Shropshire, where Ludlow Castle formed the administrative headquarters of the whole. As earl of Ulster, York was also a leading Anglo-Irish landowner. These estates together yielded the duke nearly £7,000 a year gross, and perhaps about £5,800 net.[1]

Edward's mother, Duchess Cecily, was a far from negligible person in her own right. She was a member of the powerful and numerous Nevill clan which came to play so large a part in English politics in the 1450s, and seems to have inherited the startling fecundity of that family. She herself was the eighteenth child of her father, Ralph Nevill, 1st earl of Westmorland, and his tenth by his second wife, Joan Beaufort, daughter of John of Gaunt. Before Edward was born, she had already presented Duke Richard with a daughter, Anne (1439), and a son,

[1] J. T. Rosenthal, 'The Estates and Finances of Richard, duke of York', *Studies in Medieval and Renaissance History*, ii (1965), 115–204; 'Fifteenth-Century Baronial Incomes and Richard, duke of York', *BIHR*, xxxvii (1967), 233–9. He seems, however, seriously to underestimate York's landed income: see C. D. Ross, 'The Estates and Finances of Richard, duke of York', *Welsh History Review*, iii (1967), 299–302, and the comments of K. B. McFarlane, *The Nobility of Later Medieval England* (1973), 177–8, from whom these figures are taken.

Table 2 YORK AND BOURCHIER

YORK

BOURCHIER

Edmund, Duke of York, 4th surviving son of EDWARD III (d.1402)

Richard, Earl of Cambridge=Anne, d. of Roger Mortimer
(ex.1415)   Earl of March (d.1398)
                                        See Table 1

Edmund, Earl of Stafford (ii)=Anne=(iii) William Bourchier,
                            d. of Thomas   Count of Eu
                            Duke of
                            Gloucester,
                            youngest son
                            of EDWARD III

Dukes of Buckingham
See Table 1

Richard, Duke of York=Cecily, d. of Ralph Nevill, Earl of
(k.1460)   Westmorland (d.1425)
                                  See Tables 1 and 3

Isabel=Henry, Earl   William, Lord   John, Lord   Thomas, Cardinal   Eleanor =
         of Essex   Fitzwarin   Berners   Archbishop of   John, Duke
         (d.1483)   (d.1474)   Canterbury   of Norfolk
                                                         (d.1486)   (d.1461)

William, Viscount   Humphrey, Lord   John   Thomas
Bourchier (d.1482)   Cromwell (d.1471)

Anne 1439-1475/6   EDWARD IV=Elizabeth   Edmund,   Elizabeth, 1444-1503/4   George, Duke of   Margaret, 1446-1503   RICHARD III   Ursula
=1447 (i) Henry, D.of   1442-1483   Woodville   Earl of   =John, Duke of   Clarence, 1449-1478   =(1468) Charles,   1452-1485   1455-?
Exeter (d.1475)   (1464)   Rutland   Suffolk (d.1491)   =(1469) Isabel, d.of   Duke of Burgundy   =(1472) Anne, d. of
=(ii) Sir Thomas   1443-1460   Richard,   (d.1477)   Richard,
St. Leger (ex.1483)   John, Earl of Lincoln   Earl of Warwick   Earl of Warwick
                                                              (k.1487)
Anne   Edward, Earl of   Margaret, Countess of
Anne   Warwick (ex.1499)   Salisbury (ex.1541)   Edward, Prince of Wales
                                                                                                                                          (1473-1484)

Mary   Cecily 1469-1507   EDWARD V   Margaret   Richard   Anne 1475-1510   George   Katherine   Bridget
1467-   =(i) Lord Welles   1470-?1483   b.&d.1472   1473-?1483   =(1495) Thomas,   1477-9   1479-1527   1480-1513
1482   (1487)   Duke of York   Earl of Surrey   =(1495) William,   a nun
           =(ii) Thomas Kyme   =(1476) Anne   Earl of Devon
           (1502)   Mowbray

Elizabeth 1466-1503
=(1486) HENRY VII

Henry (1441), who died an infant, leaving Edward himself as his father's heir. Between 1442 and 1452 she continued to produce children steadily: there were six more sons, of whom three died young, leaving Edward with three young brothers, Edmund, George and Richard, and two more daughters. The family was completed by the birth, on 20 July 1455, of Edward's youngest sister, Ursula.[1]

Little is known of Edward's early years. His father came home from France in the autumn of 1445 and then remained in England until he left to take up his appointment as lieutenant of Ireland in July 1449. Edward and his nearest younger brother, Edmund (born, like himself, at Rouen), were probably established with their own household at Ludlow, which was later to become the home of his son, Edward, prince of Wales, in the 1470s. Their mother spent much time at Fotheringhay, where several of the younger children, including the future Richard III, were born, and Edward may have done so too, for it was certainly later one of his favourite residences. At first the boys were in the care of a Norman nurse, Anne of Caux, who was later to be rewarded with a handsome pension of £20 a year by Edward in 1474.[2] As they grew older, the boys were placed in the charge of a governor. He is generally said to be Richard Croft, of Croft in Herefordshire, who lived on to serve Edward himself as king, and then Richard III and Henry VII, and died in 1509, plump with prosperity. But the evidence for this repeated assertion is slender and should be rejected.[3]

Equally, we have no direct information about the education received by the young Edward and his brothers. That they took their studies seriously is shown by a letter to their father from Edward and Edmund at Ludlow dated 3 June 1454.[4]

> And where ye command us by your said letters to attend especially to our learning in our young age, that should cause us to grow to honour and worship in our old age, please it your Highness to wit that we have attended our learning sith we come hither, and shall hereafter; by the which we trust to God your gracious lordship and good fatherhood shall be pleased.

Their training probably followed the pattern usual amongst the English aristocracy of the day. Something of its character and flavour may perhaps be inferred from the regulations laid down by Edward himself

[1] See Genealogical Tables. The information comes from *Annales*, 764-5, 771, and Gairdner, *Richard III*, 5.
[2] *CPR,1467-77*, 439.
[3] See Appendix II for evidence on this point.
[4] *Excerpta Historica*, ed. S. Bentley, 8-9, for text of the letter: reproduced in Plate 1.

in 1474 for the education of his own son, Edward, prince of Wales. Each day, after hearing matins and mass, and taking his breakfast, the boy was to spend his mornings 'occupied in such virtuous learning as his age shall now suffice to receive'. His midday meal was accompanied by the reading aloud to him of 'such noble stories as behoveth a Prince to understand; and know that the communication at all times in his presence be of virtue, honour, cunning, wisdom, and deeds of worship, and of nothing that should move or stir him to vices'. 'In eschewing of idleness' after his meal, he was to be further occupied about his learning, and then should be shown 'such convenient disports and exercises as behoveth his estate to have experience in'. After evensong and supper, he might be allowed 'such honest disports as may be conveniently devised for his recreation'.[1]

Despite its obvious emphasis on moral training, this traditional regimen conceals a solid element of book-learning. Recent research has suggested that the upper classes of fifteenth-century England were far from being ignorant or ill-educated.[2] The educated layman becomes increasingly prominent in all walks of life. The tone had been set by the Lancastrian kings themselves, all of whom enjoyed a distinctly bookish upbringing. Resident tutors were now common in the households of the wealthy. In the ordinances which Edward approved for his own royal household, provision was made for the education of the young 'henchmen' – the sons of nobles and gentry – who waited upon the king's person. Their master was to show them 'the schools of urbanity and nurture of England'. They were to be taught to ride, joust and wear armour, and to learn the formalities of court and household, paying special attention to their manners at table. But they were also to learn 'sundry languages and other learnings virtuous, to harping, to pipe, sing and dance'.[3] In the same way, Edward and his brothers received a grounding in Latin, and there is abundant evidence that they could both speak and write in French as well as in English.[4] Probably Edward also received some instruction in such practical

---

[1] *A Collection of Ordinances and Regulations for the Government of the Royal Household* (Society of Antiquaries, 1790), 27–8.

[2] See, especially, McFarlane's remarks on noble education in his *Nobility of Later Medieval England*, 228–47, and also J. Simon, *Education and Society in Tudor England* (1966), 7–56 *passim*.

[3] A. R. Myers, *The Household of Edward IV*, 126–7.

[4] Whilst still earl of March, Edward owned at least one Latin MS volume, containing medical treatises and a version of an Aristotelian work, now B.M. Royal MS 12 E XV. Several royal warrants of the reign contain his own autograph additions and instructions, e.g. P.R.O., C 81/1377/20.

matters as estate management and the law as it related to land. In his *Boke of Noblesse*, revised for presentation to Edward IV in 1475, the antiquary William Worcester spoke of the frequency with which men of noble or gentle birth 'learn the practice of law or custom of land'. It is perhaps no coincidence that the introduction of the methods of private estate management into the government of the royal lands comes so soon after the accession of a king who was himself brought up as heir to a great private estate. His interest in the law is reflected in his sitting in 1462 in the court of King's Bench, where no king had sat for generations, a rare enough event to be noticed in contemporary London chronicles.[1]

Edward's education, therefore, probably provided a sound training for a practical man of affairs. His later career shows that he had no marked intellectual interests. He shared to the full his contemporaries' taste for ceremony and elaborate display, for hunting, jousting, feasting, and the company of women, but his library shows that his reading habits were conventional, and largely confined to chivalric romances and to history seen as a repertory of 'deeds of virtue' and useful examples. He read for pleasure in French and English, but not in Latin.[2] Unlike one or two of his lay lords, such as John Tiptoft, earl of Worcester, or his brother-in-law, Anthony Woodville, Earl Rivers, and several of his leading churchmen, he had no interest in contemporary humanism, nor was he an active patron of the new art of printing. Nor does he seem to have been influenced by the profound piety of his mother, Duchess Cecily. Her deeply religious way of life, and her love of the writings of the great mystics, like St Catherine of Siena and St Bridget of Sweden, left their mark upon her daughter, Margaret, the future duchess of Burgundy, but her eldest son escaped them entirely.[3]

If Edward was neither scholar nor saint, he possessed many of the assets which go to make a successful king. He was clearly a man of considerable intelligence, equipped with a particularly retentive memory.[4] He had considerable personal charm and affability and by temperament was generous, good-natured and even-tempered. Consistently courageous, he had great confidence in himself and the capacity to inspire it in others, and from early in his career showed natural gifts of leadership. All this was united with remarkable physical advan-

---

[1] J. Simon, *op. cit.*, 65; *Three Fifteenth-Century Chronicles*, 175.
[2] See below, chapter 11.
[3] C. A. J. Armstrong, 'The Piety of Cecily, Duchess of York: A study in Late Medieval Culture', in *For Hilaire Belloc*, ed. D. Woodruff (1942), 73–94. But see the remarks of the Croyland Chronicler mentioned below, pp. 415–6.   [4] *CC*, 564.

tages. Like his great-great-grandfather, Edward III, he inherited to
the full the Plantagenet characteristics of great height and good looks.
When his coffin was opened in 1789, his skeleton was found to measure
6 feet 3½ inches, and to be broad in proportion.[1] His good looks were
universally acclaimed by his contemporaries, and it may be doubted
whether they would have recognized the bovine and lack-lustre
features which peer blearily from the most familiar portrait of him
(now in the National Portrait Gallery). Even his sharpest contemporary
critic, Philippe de Commynes, who met him twice, repeatedly praises
his fine appearance: 'He was a very handsome prince, and tall. . . .
I do not remember having seen a more handsome prince than he was
when my lord of Warwick forced him to flee from England.' 'A handsome upstanding man,' said a German traveller, Gabriel Tetzel, in
1466. 'A person of most elegant appearance, and remarkable beyond
all others for the attractions of his person,' said the Croyland Chronicler
at the end of the reign. Dominic Mancini, writing a few months after
Edward's death, refers to a streak of vanity which went with charm and
good looks:

> Edward was of a gentle nature and cheerful aspect: nevertheless should
> he assume an angry countenance he could appear very terrible to behold-
> ers. He was easy of access to his friends and to others, even the least
> notable. Frequently he called to his side complete strangers, when he
> thought that they had come with the intention of addressing or beholding
> him more closely. He was wont to show himself to those who wished to
> watch him, and he seized any opportunity . . . of revealing his fine stature
> more protractedly and more evidently to onlookers.

'He was a goodly personage,' adds Sir Thomas More, 'and very princely
to behold . . . of visage lovely, of body mighty, strong and clean made;
howbeit in his latter days, with over-liberal diet, somewhat corpulent
and boorly, and natheless not uncomely.'[2] As his household accounts
reveal, Edward always had a taste for the fine clothes, expensive furs,
and rich jewellery which best showed off his superb physique.[3] In an
age so prone to judge by external display, to look like a king was an
immense asset in being a king; and when Edward came to the throne
at nineteen in the full flush of his youth, he must have presented his

[1] Scofield, I, 127.
[2] Commynes, II, 64; *Travels of Leo of Rozmital*, ed. and trans. M. Letts, Hakluyt Soc.,
2nd ser., cviii (1965), 45; *CC*, 563; Mancini, 79–80; More, *Richard III*, 4.
[3] One of the two surviving letters of his boyhood, written probably 1454–5, contains
a request for fine bonnets, Ellis, *Orig. Letters* . . ., 9–10. For his expenditure on personal finery, see below, pp. 261–2.

subjects with a startling contrast to the sickly and shabby person of King Henry VI.

As Edward of York grew to manhood, the pattern of his future career was already being shaped by the political ambitions of his father. A brief account of the political conflicts of the 1450s, and Duke Richard's role therein, is an essential preliminary to understanding the circumstances which brought Edward himself to the throne, and helps to illuminate the problems with which he had to deal as king.[1]

The 1450s dawned darkly for the government of Henry VI, the best-intentioned and most ineffectual of all English kings. Against a background of renewed but increasingly disastrous war in France, two dangerous movements of protest against the regime came to a head. The first, in the spring of 1450, was the impeachment by the commons in parliament of the king's chief minister, the duke of Suffolk; the second, the outbreak in May and June of a formidable popular rebellion in Kent and the south-east under the leader known as Jack Cade. Between them the charges brought against Suffolk and the grievances of the rebels provide a damning commentary on the misgovernment of the regime; and their reliability has been very largely substantiated by modern research.[2] Both commons and rebels concentrated essentially on three issues. First, it was alleged that Suffolk and his friends had monopolized the king's ear and had excluded from his presence his natural councillors, the great lords of the realm. Secondly, they were accused of having severely impoverished the Crown and enriched themselves at the king's expense. Hence the king was heavily in debt, he did not 'live of his own', and his subjects suffered from the evils of royal purveyance and heavy taxation. Thirdly, they were charged with having perverted the course of justice for their own ends. The corruption and oppressiveness of local officials, and the difficulties of obtaining impartial justice, were specifically linked with corruption and self-seeking at the centre of government, in court and council.[3]

The Kentish rebels suggested remedies as well as advancing complaints. As a cure for the insolvency of the Crown they proposed the comparatively new idea (already popular with the commons in

[1] The fullest and best-documented account, especially of events to 1455, is by R. L. Storey, *The End of the House of Lancaster*. See also Lander, *op. cit.*, 72–80; E. F. Jacob, *The Fifteenth Century*, 490–516; Scofield, I, 12–36.
[2] Discussed by Storey, *op. cit.*, 43–8.
[3] They were also blamed for mismanagement of the French war, and the loss of English conquests in France, but these charges are less prominent than the domestic issues.

parliament) that the king should resume into his own hands the 'liveli-hood' – the royal estates and revenues – he had squandered so recklessly and apply the proceeds to the support of his household and royal estate.[1] But their chief remedy for the abuses they had outlined so forcefully was traditional enough. The king should dismiss his evil councillors and replace them with the great lords of the realm. Special mention was made of the duke of York. The king was urged[2]

> to take about his noble person his true blood of his royal realm, that is to say, the high and mighty prince the Duke of York, exiled from our sovereign lord's person by the noising of the false traitor the Duke of Suffolk and his affinity. Also to take about his person the mighty prince the Duke of Exeter, the Duke of Buckingham, the Duke of Norfolk, and his true earls and barons of this land, and he shall be the richest Christian king.

Against this background of widespread popular discontent, York himself made a forceful entry into politics in the autumn of 1450. His sudden emergence as leader of the critics of the government was prob-ably largely inspired by his own genuine personal grievances. As a likely heir to the childless king, and the greatest magnate of the realm, he could reasonably expect a place in the king's councils. This had been refused him. Supplanted in his command in France by Suffolk's ally and political successor, Edmund Beaufort, duke of Somerset, he had been shuffled off to a dignified political exile as lieutenant of Ireland, far from the centre of power at the English court. He had experienced enormous difficulty in getting any repayment of the vast sums owed him by the government for his service in France, and saw his rival, Somerset, and Somerset's friends, given preference at the exchequer; and this happened at a time when, like all great Welsh landowners, he was suffering from sharply declining revenues from his estates.[3] Despite Somerset's disgraceful record in France, he re-turned to England in 1450 to take a prominent place in the king's council, and York may even have begun to fear that Somerset might be officially recognized as heir presumptive to the throne.[4] In Septem-ber 1450, York came back to England to begin the first of a series of

---

[1] B. P. Wolffe, *The Crown Lands, 1461–1536*, 24–7.
[2] *Three Fifteenth-Century Chronicles*, 97.
[3] For the repayment of royal debts, see Storey, *op. cit.*, 72–5, though his conclusion – 'The bankruptcy of Lancaster drove York to rebellion' – is open to question: for Welsh revenues, T. B. Pugh, *The Marcher Lordships of South Wales. 1415–1536*, 176–9; C. D. Ross, *op. cit.*
[4] As suggested by Storey, *op. cit.*, 74.

attempts to oust his rivals at court and to establish himself in their place as the king's leading councillor. His efforts convulsed English politics throughout the 1450s, and an increasingly hostile reaction by the court to his ambitions ultimately provoked civil war.

Historians in general have shown scant charity to Richard of York. His entry into politics has been seen as largely inspired by a personal vendetta against the duke of Somerset. His demands for reform and retrenchment, and his professed concern for order and justice, have been regarded as no more than cynical attempts to exploit in his own interest popular resentment of the regime.[1] Such judgements may well be over-harsh. An upright and honourable man, York seems to have believed sincerely in the need for peace and good government. As protector of England, when he had solid backing from the council, he made notable efforts to come to grips with the problems of growing disorder. He showed himself vigorous and successful in Ireland.

But he had serious defects as a political leader. He lacked the panache and popular appeal of Warwick the Kingmaker, or the charm and affability of his own son Edward. He seems to have been a proud, reserved and aloof man, who was also headstrong and sadly lacking in political sensitivity. His arrogant claims to be the king's principal councillor, and later to be king himself, were selfish causes unlikely to commend themselves to his fellow-peers. Though convinced of the justice of his own case, he made little effort to win over the nobility, and his failure to attract their support is one of the main reasons for the repeated rebuffs to his schemes in 1450–52.[2]

His failures were, however, due only in part to personal deficiencies. They were also inherent in the structure of medieval English politics. As long as England remained very much a personal monarchy, it was difficult for any man or group of men to control the government against the king's will, except by the use of force. As a critic of an unpopular administration, as in 1450–51, York could expect much support from the commons in parliament, themselves in restless mood. But parliaments could not be kept in being indefinitely and the king could ignore their wishes once they had been dissolved. York failed

1 R. A. Griffiths, 'Local Rivalries and National Politics', 609 ff.; E. Curtis, 'Richard Duke of York as Viceroy of Ireland, 1447–60', *Jour. Royal Soc. of Antiquaries of Ireland*, lxii (1932), 158–66. For the hostile assessments mentioned above, see Storey, *op. cit.*, 73–4, 76–7, 92, and Lander, *Conflict and Stability*, 81–2; see also K. B. McFarlane, in *Cambridge Medieval History*, viii, 410.
2 K. B. McFarlane, 'The Wars of the Roses', *Proc. British Academy*, L, 90–1; 'what robbed him of victory was . . . the size and number of the armed retinues ranged against him'.

wholly in his attempt to drive Somerset and his friends from court or to get himself formally recognized as heir to the throne. But when, early in 1452, he tried to impose himself on the king by force of arms, he found himself even more isolated. Neither lords nor commons had much sympathy for violent action against the person of their lawful king. York's attempted *coup d'état* ended in his humiliation, and at Ludlow later in the year the young Edward may well have witnessed the unwelcome spectacle of the duke of Somerset presiding at one of a series of trials of York's tenants and retainers.[1]

It is about this time that we first hear references to Edward and his brother, Edmund, appearing on the political scene in support of their father, in spite of their extreme youth. The London Chronicles report that York himself was released from custody after the abortive field at Dartford because his son, the earl of March, was marching on London with ten thousand men. It is easy to dismiss the story on the grounds that the council had no cause to fear a ten-year-old boy but there were plenty of experienced soldiers in the Welsh March to form a powerful retinue for Edward as nominal leader, and Edmund, by then just ten years old, was attending a meeting in the great council chamber in London in February 1454.[2] We know for certain from a contemporary letter of 19 January 1454 that Edward accompanied his father to London at the head of their household troops, 'cleanly beseen and likely men', shortly before the duke was commissioned to open parliament on behalf of the invalid king.[3] This is the first directly contemporary reference to Edward by the style of earl of March. But it was probably some time before this that Henry VI had been prevailed upon to create Edward and Edmund earls of March and Rutland, though no record of the creation has been preserved; and by 13 June 1454, in a letter to their father, the boys sign themselves 'E. Marche' and 'E. Rutland'.[4]

Duke Richard's ambitions became a serious threat to the ruling court party only when certain leading magnates, for reasons of their own, quarrelled with Somerset and found in York a focus for their discontent. Between 1452 and 1455, events in the north of England changed the situation to York's advantage. For more than half a century the two great families of Nevill and Percy had competed with

[1] Storey, 102.
[2] Kingsford, *Chronicles of London*, 163, discounted by Storey, 101; J. F. Baldwin, *The King's Council in England during the Middle Ages* (1913), 197.
[3] *PL*, II, 297.
[4] *RP*, V, 346; *CP*, XI, 252 and note, *sub* 'Rutland'; and see Plate 1a.

Table 3 THE NEVILLS

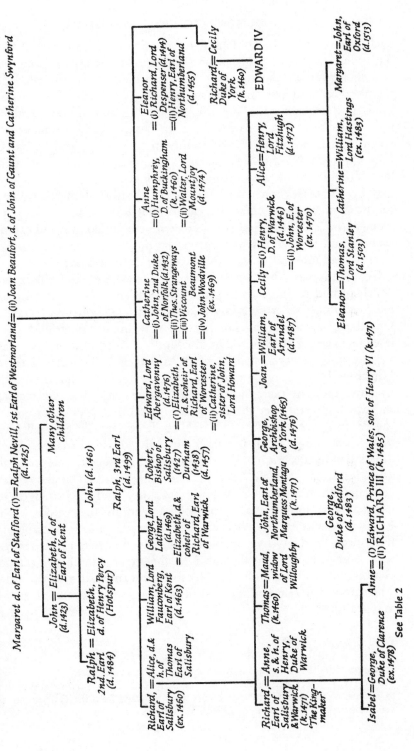

each other for office, land, and territorial influence north of Trent. This long-standing rivalry, which had been dormant for some years, was sharpened in the 1440s by the expansion of Nevill influence in Cumberland and Westmorland and on the West March towards Scotland. The senior Nevill, Richard, earl of Salisbury (York's brother-in-law), possessed to the full the drive for family aggrandizement which was the hallmark of the Nevill family in its heyday, and he had skilfully exploited his mother's Beaufort connections at court to achieve local dominance in the north-west. Percy reaction to this was led at first by Thomas Percy, Lord Egremont, the turbulent second son of the head of his family, Henry, earl of Northumberland. In 1453 the scene of the feud shifted to Yorkshire, where both families had extensive estates, and virtual private war broke out, which threw the whole county, and later other parts of the north, into upheaval.[1]

To claim that 'the Nevill–Percy feud was the chief single factor which turned political rivalry into civil war' may be something of an exaggeration,[2] but it certainly had implications, both immediate and long-term, of considerable importance. First, the bitterness and rivalries it engendered in the north of England survived the private war of 1453–4 and powerfully influenced the struggle between York and Lancaster between 1459 and 1464. As we shall see, for the north of England the true meaning of the Yorkist triumph was the victory of the Nevill interest over the Percy family and their allies. For a decade the Percy interest lay in ruins, only to be revived by Edward himself at a critical point of his fortunes. Secondly, the feud soon dragged in others beside the original protagonists and helped to determine their attitudes to the struggle between York and Somerset at the centre of government. On the Nevill side, Salisbury and his younger sons, Thomas and John Nevill, were soon joined by their elder brother, Richard Nevill, earl of Warwick. This energetic and formidable magnate, now, at thirty-five, in his prime, had quarrelled independently with Somerset over rival claims to the great Marcher lordship of Glamorgan, and was holding it by force in contempt of royal orders.[3] The earl of Northumberland and his younger sons, Egremont, Richard and Ralph Percy, were joined by his heir, Lord Poynings, by north-

[1] Storey, *op. cit.*, 114–26.

[2] Storey, 193, but cf. Griffiths, 'Local Rivalries and National Politics', 631–2 – this article provides the fullest account of the private war in the north.

[3] Storey, 134–5, 231–41. Dr Storey antedates the breach of Warwick and Somerset to summer 1452, but the evidence points to its resulting from the Glamorgan issue; see T. B. Pugh in *Glamorgan County History*, III, 196.

country barons like Clifford and Roos, and by the young Henry Holland, duke of Exeter, who was both stupid and violent, and had dangerous pretensions of his own.

Finally, the immediate result of the feud was to make possible York's re-emergence as an effective claimant to political power through a newly-formed alliance with the Nevill earls. It would be hard to exaggerate the importance of their support. Each of them commanded resources little inferior to York's own. In addition to his position as warden of the West March, which gave him the opportunity to maintain a private army at the king's expense, Salisbury had large estates in the north, especially Yorkshire, inherited from his father, Ralph Nevill, earl of Westmorland. His marriage to the Salisbury heiress, Alice Montagu, brought him further substantial estates mainly in south-central England. His income at this time may well have exceeded £3,000 a year.[1] His son, Richard Nevill, in whom Nevill greed and ambition found their most extreme incarnation, was the wealthiest of the English earls. His marriage to the principal heiress of the former Beauchamp earldom of Warwick brought him vast estates in the midlands, southern England and South Wales. He enjoyed a yearly net income from land of not less than £3,900.[2] According to a recent estimate the Nevill earls (like their Percy rivals) could put about ten thousand men in the field, and this suggestion is far from implausible.[3]

Warwick's quarrel with Somerset may well have been the key factor in drawing both him and his father away from hitherto profitable connections with the court. At least by the end of 1453 they were moving towards an alliance with York. By then the whole situation had been radically – if temporarily – changed by the breakdown of the king's health: from August 1453 until December 1454 he was incapable of conducting the government of his realm. Fearful of a regency dominated by the queen, Margaret of Anjou, other lords besides the Nevill earls gave their support to the duke of York, and his growing ascendancy culminated in his appointment as protector of England on 27 March 1454. His main achievement, even though partisan in the sense that it led to the triumph of his Nevill allies, was to put an end to the growing anarchy north of Trent. There is some truth, if also some exaggeration,

[1] Storey, 114.
[2] K. B. McFarlane, *Nobility of Later Medieval England*, 199; and for the Beauchamp lands, C. D. Ross, *The Estates and Finances of Richard Beauchamp, Earl of Warwick* (Dugdale Society, 1956).
[3] Storey, 132. According to an early Tudor estimate, the Percies could raise 11,241 men from their estates in Northumberland, Cumberland and Yorkshire: M. E. James, *A Tudor Magnate and the Tudor State* (Borthwick Papers, no. 30, 1966), 13, 27.

in a contemporary chronicler's claim that 'for one whole year he governed the entire realm of England well and nobly, and miraculously pacified all rebels and malefactors . . . without great severity'.[1] It is true that he took the opportunity to improve his own and his friends' position in other ways. The earl of Salisbury was made chancellor on 2 April 1454; York's Anglo-Irish rival, James Butler, earl of Ormond and Wiltshire, was removed from the lieutenancy of Ireland; and York himself superseded Somerset as captain of Calais. But the council records show that these measures had the approval of a large number of lords, and they must not be regarded as narrowly partisan.

Henry VI's recovery at the end of 1454 has rightly been described as a national disaster. The political pendulum swung back again from a comparatively widely-based administration, enjoying the support of a goodly number of lords, to a small partisan council dominated by the court. Somerset was released from prison and restored to his command at Calais on 6 March 1455, and Salisbury was dismissed as chancellor. Fear of reprisals from Somerset and his friends caused York, Salisbury and Warwick to leave London in haste. They were summoned to appear before what they rightly suspected to be a great council called especially to punish them, at Leicester on 21 May 1455. Instead, they gathered men in the north and came down in force to meet the king and his lords at St Albans. According to one chronicler, the young Edward joined them from Ludlow with a force of March men, but this is not confirmed in any other of the several surviving accounts of the First Battle of St Albans (22 May 1455).[2] This skirmish – for it was little more – was soon over. The fighting ceased as soon as Somerset, the earl of Northumberland and Lord Clifford had been killed. With the deaths of their leading enemies, York and the Nevills had achieved their immediate ends.

Yet their position was still far from secure. They owed their victory to their more numerous rank-and-file, but still had little committed support from most of their fellow-barons. For this reason they tried to win over moderates like Humphrey Stafford, duke of Buckingham, and his Bourchier kinsmen, Thomas, archbishop of Canterbury, and Henry, Viscount Bourchier. They also bade for support from the commons in parliament and advanced a programme to deal with the main immediate problems facing the government, the financing of Calais, the keep-

[1] 'John Benet's Chronicle', ed. G. L. Harriss, Camden Miscellany, xxiv (Royal Hist. Soc., 1972), 213.
[2] Three Fifteenth-Century Chronicles, 151; C. A. J. Armstrong, 'Politics and the Battle of St Albans, 1455', BIHR, xxxiii (1960).

ing of the seas, and the pacification of Wales. Pressure from the commons led to York's appointment as Protector for a second time, on the pretext that the king should be spared the strain of dealing with renewed disorders in the West Country.[1] During their brief period of power (19 November 1455–25 February 1456) the Yorkists helped themselves to the spoils of office, the grasping Nevills taking the richest rewards.[2] Politically, their most important gain came from Warwick's appointment as captain of Calais. Eventually, after negotiations with the Company of the Staple and the garrison over financial arrangements, this gave him control of the largest military establishment in the service of the Crown. By the summer of 1456 he was firmly established in Calais, which became a Yorkist stronghold and eventually a base for invasion of great strategic importance.[3]

But at home York's ascendancy proved short-lived. King Henry would have been willing to retain York as his principal councillor, but his masterful queen, Margaret of Anjou, who openly hated York and his friends, increasingly became the real driving force at court. Her entry into politics may have been inspired by fears for the succession of her infant son, Edward, prince of Wales (born on 13 October 1453), or that she would lose all reality of power so long as York retained his position.[4] From 1456 onwards her uncompromising hostility to York and the Nevills was the major obstacle to any genuine pacification between the rival groups of magnates. The Yorkist group felt itself increasingly insecure, and its reactions became correspondingly tense and nervous. Meanwhile, the moderates amongst the lords strove to keep the peace and lent their support to King Henry's well-meaning efforts to reconcile his great men. The results were disappointing. The Yorkists eventually agreed to pay compensation to the families of the lords slain at St Albans. But the so-called Loveday of 24 March 1458, when the rival parties marched arm-in-arm to St Paul's Cathedral, was acted out against the ominous backcloth of thousands of armed retainers quartered inside and outside the gates of London. The growing size of baronial retinues on every public occasion is a more accurate sign of the times than this classic example of a hollow reconciliation.

Even in the meagre records of the years 1457–8 we can discern the steady growth of suspicion and hostility. The queen's influence can be

[1] J. R. Lander, 'Henry VI and the Duke of York's Second Protectorate, 1455 to 1456', *Bulletin John Rylands Library*, xliii (1960), 46–69.
[2] Listed by Storey, 163–4.
[3] G. L. Harriss, 'The Struggle for Calais: An Aspect of the Rivalry between Lancaster and York', *EHR*, lxxv (1960), 30–5.   [4] Storey, 176–7.

seen in the retirement of the court to the midlands, where she strove to build up a personal government and a following based on her son's earldom of Chester and the broad midland estates of the royal Duchy of Lancaster. 'The queen,' said a Paston correspondent, 'is a great and strong laboured woman, for she spareth no pain to sue her things to an intent and conclusion to her power', and as one hostile chronicler later observed, 'the queen, with such as were of her affinity, ruled the realm, gathering riches innumerable'.[1] Two personal enemies of York, the earls of Shrewsbury and Wiltshire, held the office of treasurer of England in succession between 1456 and 1460. The court gave a warm welcome to the sons of the lords killed at St Albans, the violent young Henry Beaufort, duke of Somerset, Henry Percy, third earl of Northumberland, and John, Lord Clifford. The king's half-brothers, Jasper Tudor, earl of Pembroke, and Edmund Tudor, earl of Richmond, were working to increase royal influence in Wales and the Marches. In response, Warwick defiantly consolidated his hold on Calais and defeated an attempt by the court in November 1458 to oust him from his command in favour of Somerset. Both parties looked for foreign support. Warwick's negotiations with Duke Philip the Good of Burgundy in these years seem to have included plans for a marriage between Edward of March and the duke's niece, Katherine, daughter of the duke of Bourbon, a scheme later revived when Edward became king.[2]

What finally brought about an open breach was the evident determination of the court to crush its opponents by force. A final decision seems to have been made at a meeting of the great council at Coventry on 24 June 1459. York, Salisbury, Warwick, and Warwick's brother, George Nevill, bishop of Exeter, were not summoned. Others excluded, presumably because of their Yorkist sympathies, were Thomas Bourchier, archbishop of Canterbury, his brother, Henry, Viscount Bourchier, William, earl of Arundel (now Warwick's brother-in-law), and William Grey, bishop of Ely.[3] Facing indictments from this council, the Yorkist leaders laid plans to forgather in a strength sufficient to gain them a hearing from the king, who was personally still anxious to keep the peace. The duke of York at Ludlow was to be joined by Salisbury with his North-Country followers and by Warwick with a force of men from the Calais garrison under Andrew Trollope. The

[1] PL, III, 75; English Chronicle, ed. Davies, 79.
[2] Scofield, I, 28–9; Thielemans, Bourgogne et Angleterre, 372.
[3] 'John Benet's Chronicle', 223 – the only source to mention this great council and the exclusion of Yorkist sympathizers. See also Storey, 186–7, for further evidence that the court took the initiative.

queen's party in turn endeavoured to forestall this hostile concentration. Marching south from Middleham, Salisbury was intercepted at Blore Heath in Shropshire by a royalist force from Cheshire under Lord Audley. In the indecisive battle which followed (23 September 1459), Audley was killed and Salisbury's younger sons, Thomas and John Nevill, were taken prisoner.[1] The Yorkists managed to effect their reunion and prepared to meet the advancing royal army under Henry VI from a fortified position at Ludford Bridge, near Ludlow. Believing the court could no longer be trusted, they rejected royal offers of pardon, but the Calais soldiers now refused to fight against the king in person. Their defection was probably less important in bringing about the 'Rout of Ludford' (12–13 October) than York's numerical inferiority: 'his party was over-weak', not having mobilized its potential strength.[2] York and his friends now prudently decided on flight, leaving their troops to surrender and abandoning Ludlow to pillage by the royal army. The duchess of York and two of Edward's brothers, George and Richard, fell into the king's hands, but York himself, and Edmund, earl of Rutland, made good their escape to Ireland. Edward of March chose instead to go with Salisbury and Warwick to south Devon, where they found shelter in the house of the widowed Joanna Dinham, probably at Nutwell, near Newton Abbot.[3] With an appreciation of services rendered which was to become characteristic of him, Edward later rewarded her with the grant of the custody and marriage of a royal ward, and a present of £80 to distribute among her tenants and servants.[4] Sailing in a ship bought by her son, John Dinham, the earls eventually reached Calais in safety on 2 November 1459. At this point the seventeen-year-old Edward shook off the tutelage of his father and emerged as an independent political figure in his own right. The dramatic events of the next fifteen months were soon to place him in command of his country's fortunes.

[1] A. H. Burne, *More Battlefields of England* (1952), 140–9.
[2] Gregory, 205, and see below, pp. 23–4.
[3] This was the Dinhams' usual family home: Joanna's husband John had died there in 1458, and her son is called 'of Nutwell' in 1466 (*CP*, IV, 378–9; *CPR, 1461–7*, 476). Kendall, *Warwick the Kingmaker*, 54, mistakenly assumes they sailed from north Devon; cf. Scofield, I, 42.
[4] *CPR, 1461–7*, 75; Scofield, I, 41–2.

Chapter 2

THE YORKIST TRIUMPH, 1460–1461

Of the many sudden changes of political fortune which mark English history in the fifteenth century, none is more remarkable than the recovery of the Yorkist cause following the *débâcle* of October 1459. Within a month of Ludford its leaders were proscribed and attainted exiles. Yet by June 1460 they were able to mount a successful invasion of England and take control of London. Shortly after, they defeated the king's forces at Northampton and Henry VI became a prisoner in their hands. This made possible a period of Yorkist-controlled government lasting to the end of the year, when the disasters at Wakefield (30 December 1460) and St Albans (17 February 1461) again put all in suspense, and thrust Edward of March onto the English throne.

Why this Yorkist revival was so successful has never been properly explained. Certainly, the rebels' control of bases outside England kept these out of the clutches of the Lancastrians and allowed York and his allies to prepare their armed welcome in Ireland. His clever appeal to the Anglo-Irish lords' desire for autonomy strengthened his hold in the province and caused them to reject James Butler, earl of Wiltshire, whom Henry VI appointed to supersede him as lieutenant.[1] In Calais Warwick, Salisbury and March defeated all the efforts of the duke of Somerset to dislodge them.[2]

But the possession of useful springboards for invasion does not explain the success of the invasion itself. In England the majority of the baronage remained loyal to Henry VI and his heir. Amongst those who swore an oath of loyalty in the Coventry Parliament were several of York's kinsmen, including the dukes of Buckingham and Norfolk, Viscount Bourchier, and Edward Nevill, Lord Abergavenny. Of the gentry some former Yorkists, like Sir William Herbert of Raglan, shared the rewards as the confiscated estates of the exiles were distributed, or were confirmed in offices they already held. Such behaviour,

---

[1] For York in Ireland, see Curtis, article cited above, p. 13; A. J. Otway-Ruthven, *A History of Medieval Ireland* (1967), 386–8.
[2] Scofield, I, 42–4, 47–54, 59–65; and, for a highly-coloured account, P. M. Kendall, *Warwick the Kingmaker*, 55–61.

however, was no more than discreet and politic in the circumstances, and Bourchier, Abergavenny and Herbert, at least, were quick to join the rebel earls on their landing in England.[1] Many Yorkist sympathizers lay low and awaited a change of fortune. Those attainted in the highly partisan parliament of Coventry in November 1459 represent a small proportion of Yorkist well-wishers, especially among the gentry. They included only six peers: York himself, and his sons, Edward of March and Edmund of Rutland; the earls of Salisbury and Warwick; and the insignificant John, Lord Clinton, poorest of the English barons. Younger sons or kinsmen of peers included Viscount Bourchier's sons, John and Edward, Salisbury's cadets, Thomas and John Nevill, and William Stanley, brother of Thomas, Lord Stanley. The rest of the twenty-seven persons attainted were knights and esquires, nearly all of them already in exile with their leaders. The personal clemency of Henry VI saved some from the dread sentence of attainder, amongst them Lords Stanley and Grey of Powys, and Sir Walter Devereux, later Lord Ferrers, and was, of course, extended to the duchess of York and her younger children. Others escaped with fines or obtained pardons.[2] The government was clearly anxious to conciliate all those Yorkist servants and connections who had not fled the realm, but this did not prevent them from joining the rebels when the invasion came; and in some parts of the country, especially in Wales, they continued to defy Henry VI's authority.[3]

How much popular sympathy the rebels enjoyed is more difficult to assess. Pro-Yorkist chroniclers present a rather distorted picture of an England which was primarily Yorkist in the south and east and royalist in the north and west.[4] Nevertheless, there is a good deal of evidence to suggest considerable popular support for the rebels in Kent and some other parts of the south, including London. This was partly due to the growing reputation of the earl of Warwick, who had now emerged as the most forceful of the Yorkist leaders. His successful

[1] Bourchier and Abergavenny fought at Northampton, and Herbert at Mortimer's Cross; see below, pp. 26, 31.

[2] For the attainders, see *RP*, V, 348–9, and for the fines and pardons, *RP*, V, 349; *CPR*, *1452–61*, 526–92 *passim*. Those fined or pardoned included many prominent connections of York like Sir Walter Devereux, William Hastings and Ralph Hopton, who were at once appointed to crucial commissions after the landing of the Yorkist earls, e.g., those of 28 June 1460 (*ibid.*, 607).

[3] *CPR*, *1452–61*, 576 (lands of York and Warwick detained by their adherents), 602–6 (castles holding out); Scofield, I, 56 (for resistance of Denbigh to February 1460).

[4] E.g. *English Chronicle*, ed. Davies, 98; but cf. *PL*, III, 249–50, for similar views by Clement Paston.

attacks from Calais on Spanish and Hanseatic shipping in the Channel appealed to anti-alien sentiments and provided a rallying-point for a bruised national patriotism. Skilled in the use of propaganda, vigorous and open-handed, Warwick was already displaying that capacity to win over the common people which was later to prove so troublesome to Edward IV.

More important was the prevailing disillusion with Lancastrian government. In the ten years since Kent had risen against Henry VI's regime in 1450, little or nothing had been done to remedy the manifold abuses of which the rebels under Jack Cade had complained. Hence a list of grievances originally drawn up in 1450 could quite plausibly be refurbished and used again in 1460 to support the Yorkist cause.[1] In London, too, there was no great sympathy for the Lancastrian court, which had deserted the capital for the midlands, and had alienated some sections of London society by its commercial policy. The large number of popular recruits which joined the rebel earls as soon as they landed suggests the extent of the reaction to Lancastrian misgovernment. The unpopularity of the regime in the south-east was certainly a major asset of the Yorkists in the early stages of their campaign.[2]

The flames of disaffection were fanned by a vigorous publicity campaign conducted from Calais by the rebel earls. Before they landed in England, they sent letters all over the country, claiming that their only purpose was to remedy the sufferings of the realm. They insisted that they intended no harm to the person or title of Henry VI. Their sincerity need not be doubted, for it would have been political folly to challenge the widespread loyalty to the king's person, whatever the defects of his administration. Shortly before they left Calais they issued a manifesto, in which the name of Edward of March appears besides those of York, Salisbury and Warwick. This dwelt upon the failures of the government – the poverty of the Crown, the corruption of the law, the extortions practised upon the Commons, the loss of France.[3] All these were blamed upon evil and grasping councillors, especially the earls of Shrewsbury and Wiltshire, and Viscount Beaumont, 'oure mortall and extreme enemies'. For the most part couched in familiar

[1] *Chronicles of the White Rose of York*, lxxiv–vi.
[2] For Yorkist popularity in Kent, see *Gregory's Chronicle*, 206, and *English Chronicle*, ed. Davies, 91; the latter suggests that Kent feared that the earl of Wiltshire would repeat there the acts of judicial terrorism already carried out at Ludlow, Newbury and elsewhere. For support in the south and east of England generally, see Storey, *End of the House of Lancaster*, 196–7. In Norfolk Friar Brackley regarded the Yorkist earls, especially Warwick, as saviours of the realm (*PL*, II, 226, October 1460).
[3] *English Chronicle*, ed. Davies, 86–90.

terms, the document introduced one skilful touch in its allegation that Shrewsbury, Wiltshire and their friends had planned the attainders of the Coventry Parliament to enrich themselves: who, it asked, could know where such malice and greed for other men's inheritances might end? The property-owning classes at least were likely to be moved by any threat to the sanctity of inheritance, which has rightly been called 'one of the most deeply rooted emotions of the age'.[1] Thus the Yorkists tried to present themselves as champions of good government and as rightful claimants to the inheritances of which they had been unjustly deprived. Formal manifestos were backed by popular ballads, like that pinned on the gates of Canterbury just before the landing of the earls. It dwelt again on the misfortunes of the realm and presented the rebel lords as the saviours of the kingdom:

> Richard duk of York, Job thy servant insigne . . .
> Edward Earl of March, whose fame the earth shall spread,
> Richard earl of Salisbury named prudence,
> With that noble knight and flower of manhood
> Richard, earl of Warwick shield of our defence,
> Also little Fauconberg, a knight of great reverence. . . .[2]

By now the Yorkist leaders had gained a useful recruit in the person of the papal legate, Francesco Coppini, bishop of Terni, who had joined them at Calais. Coppini had been sent to England in 1459 by Pius II to seek Henry VI's backing for the crusade planned by the pope, but was led by his own ambition to attach himself to the earls. He now became their active partisan, and his share in their propaganda campaign lent prestige to their cause. He was also feeding back strongly pro-Yorkist accounts of events in England to his master in Rome. Pius's judgement on Henry VI – 'a man more timorous than a woman, utterly devoid of wit or spirit, who left everything in his wife's hands' – owed much to Coppini's bias.[3]

By the early summer of 1460 the earls in Calais were ready to make their descent on England. A further effort by the duke of Somerset to recapture Calais from the nearby fortress of Guines had been defeated at Newnham Bridge on 23 April. A muster of troops under Sir Osbert

---

[1] J. R. Lander, 'Marriage and Politics: the Nevilles and the Wydevilles', *BIHR*, xxxvi (1963), 125–6; *Conflict and Stability in Fifteenth Century England*, 87, where it is suggested that this factor may explain why the number of peers actively supporting the Yorkists rose from six to seventeen between Ludford and Northampton.

[2] *English Chronicle*, ed. Davies, 91–4.

[3] For a full account of Coppini's activities, see Constance Head, 'Pope Pius II and the Wars of the Roses', *Archivum Historiae Pontificiae*, viii (1970), 139–78.

Mountfort to reinforce Somerset was destroyed by a Yorkist raid on Sandwich in June, led by William, Lord Fauconberg.[1] On 26 June he was joined there by Edward of March and the earls of Salisbury and Warwick, with a force of some 1,500 to 2,000 men. They soon had the support of that staunch Yorkist Lord Cobham, and large numbers of Kentishmen. As they approached Canterbury, the 'captains' appointed to hold the town against them, John Fogge, John Scott and Robert Horne, decided to join their standard: Fogge and Scott were soon to be amongst Edward's most trusted servants.[2] From Canterbury, with a large and growing force, the earls moved on unopposed towards London. After some hesitation the city authorities decided to admit them, and a force of royalists commanded by Lords Scales and Hungerford withdrew into the Tower. On 2 July the earls entered London, and were welcomed by the mayor and by the archbishop of Canterbury. The following day they appeared before the convocation of the province of Canterbury, then in session, and once more explained that they had come to reform the realm but intended no ill to King Henry.[3]

It was no part of the rebels' plan to linger in the capital. Their main aim was to confront the king, who was now gathering his forces near Northampton. The earls spent two days in organizing horses and baggage for their army and in raising funds. They were acutely short of ready cash and borrowed eagerly from all who could be persuaded to lend.[4] A corporate loan of £1,000 from London indicates the rather reluctant commitment of the city fathers to the rebel cause.[5] On 4 July the vanguard of the Yorkist army moved out of London, the rest following the next day. Salisbury, Cobham and Wenlock were left behind to contain the still defiant Lancastrian garrison in the Tower. The earls had now been joined by several lords (Viscount Bourchier, Audley, Abergavenny, Say, and Scrope of Bolton) who represented most of their support amongst the peers, but they had with them a notable company of churchmen, including Thomas Bourchier, arch-

---

[1] Scofield, I, 61–2, 64–5.

[2] *Ibid.*, 76–7. Sir John Fogge became treasurer of the royal household, 1461–9, and was one of the grasping favourites denounced by Warwick (J. Wedgwood, *History of Parliament, Biographies*, 339–42); for Scott's career under Edward IV, see below, pp. 325–6.

[3] Scofield, I, 77–81. The London authorities were reluctant to commit themselves to either side, and were mainly concerned to prevent the destruction of property in the city (summary of the unpublished London M.A. thesis by M. I. Peake, 'London and the Wars of the Roses', *BIHR*, iv (1926–7), 45–7).

[4] E.g. £40 lent 'in our great necessity' by the prior of St Bartholomew, Smithfield, and repaid by Edward in July 1461 (P.R.O., Warrants for Issues, E. 404/72/1).

[5] E. 404/72/1, no. 23, 4 July 1460.

bishop of Canterbury, brother of the viscount, and the bishops of London, Exeter, Lincoln, Salisbury, Ely and Rochester, with the papal legate not far behind.[1]

As in 1455 and 1459, their professed aim was to parley with the king, not to fight him. Opinion in the royal camp was divided on whether to grant them a hearing, but when the duke of Buckingham threw his considerable influence against negotiation, a battle became inevitable. The king had the backing of Shrewsbury, Beaumont, Egremont and Grey of Ruthyn, as well as Buckingham, but the rank-and-file of his army were probably outnumbered by the rebels (another indication of their popular support). The royalists took up a defended position beside the River Nene outside the walls of Northampton. On 10 July the Yorkists advanced to the attack in three divisions, commanded by Fauconberg, the young Edward of March, and Warwick. Their men had orders to spare the king and commons, but to slay the lords, knights and esquires. In the event, the battle was decided largely by the timely treachery of Edmund Grey, Lord Grey of Ruthyn, commander of the Lancastrian vanguard, and the fighting seems to have been over in half an hour. Amongst the three hundred or so found dead on the field were the royalist captains Buckingham, Shrewsbury, Beaumont and Egremont.[2] The hapless king became a prisoner. Treated with every possible mark of respect, he was escorted back to London, where the victorious earls arrived on 16 July. The stubborn Lancastrian garrison in the Tower then capitulated, and many of their number were condemned to death before the earl of Warwick, who, then as later, showed scant mercy to his enemies.[3]

From the Yorkists the most important consequence of Northampton was their possession of the person of the king. They could now exercise the government of England in the king's name and in their own interests. On 25 July Warwick's brother, George Nevill, bishop of Exeter, became chancellor of England and Viscount Bourchier was made treasurer. Warwick proceeded to reward himself with a valuable and lucrative series of offices and wardships.[4] On 30 July writs were sent out for a parliament to meet at Westminster on 7 October. Its purpose was to get the sanction of the high court of the realm for this latest

[1] Scofield, I, 86–7.
[2] R. I. Jack, 'A quincentenary: the battle of Northampton, July 10th, 1460', *Northamptonshire Past and Present*, ii (1960), 21–5.
[3] *English Chronicle*, ed. Davies, 97–8; 'Short English Chronicle', 74–5; 'John Benet's Chronicle for the years 1400 to 1462', ed. G. L. Harriss (Camden Miscellany, xxiv, 1972), 227; Scofield, I, 91, 95.
[4] For Warwick's rewards, see below, p. 70, and Appendix III.

political revolution and to remove the sentences of attainder passed by the Coventry Parliament. This would formally reinstate the rebels as the king's loyal subjects and enable them to recover their inheritances; and the annulment of the proceedings at Coventry was, in fact, the first formal measure passed by parliament when it assembled.[1]

With these measures the rebel earls had achieved the immediate purpose of their invasion. It had never been part of their plans to depose Henry VI. Indeed, the stubborn sentiment of loyalty to the king's person could only be regarded as a political asset by those who had him under their control. But they had reckoned without Duke Richard of York. Some time before he returned to England, and apparently without informing his friends, he had decided to lay claim to the throne in his own right. From the moment he landed near Chester, on about 8 September, it was clear that he had renounced his allegiance to Henry VI. Documents drawn up in his name on 13 September omit any reference to the regnal year, and were dated instead by the year of grace, quite out of conformity with usual practice. Lingering in Ludlow and Hereford until parliament assembled, he then marched on London, his trumpeters bearing banners charged with the arms of England, and with his sword carried upright before him – the very mark and privilege of a king. On 10 October he reached Westminster Hall and strode through the assembled lords of parliament to lay his hand on the empty throne. His reward was an embarrassed silence, for his intervention was unexpected and unwelcome, apparently even to his closest allies, the Nevill earls.[2] Again York had miscalculated, but he did not intend to allow his claim to be ignored. On 16 October he formally asserted his title to the throne. Based essentially upon legitimism, his argument stressed his superior descent from Lionel of Clarence, elder brother of John of Gaunt, great-grandfather of Henry VI.[3] Neither the judges nor the serjeants-at-law were prepared to give an opinion on a matter which (they said) was 'above the law and past their learning', and it was left to the lords to advance objections to his claim. To the last and most practical of these – why, if he were the heir of Clarence,

---

[1] RP, V, 374; Wedgwood, Hist. Parl., Register, 267 and n. 4.

[2] For a discussion of this point, see K. B. McFarlane, 'Wars of the Roses', 9; Lander, 'Marriage and Politics', 126–8. The evidence of Waurin and Whethamstede on which they relied can now be supported by Pope Pius's statement that Warwick opposed York, derived, no doubt, from Coppini (C. Head, 'Pius II and the Wars of the Roses', 160).

[3] See Genealogical Tables. The claim, and the discussions in parliament upon it, are printed in RP, V, 375–80. For modern comment, S. B. Chrimes, English Constitutional Ideas in the Fifteenth Century, 26–30.

had he always carried the arms of his paternal forebear, Edmund of Langley? – he replied that he had abstained from bearing the arms of Clarence for reasons known to all the realm, adding forcefully: 'though right for a time rest and be put to silence, yet it rotteth not nor shall it perish'. Yet still the lords would not abandon a king to whom they had pledged solemn oaths of loyalty. Their reluctance is the more remarkable since many of the overt partisans of Lancaster were not present in this parliament.[1] The lords were, however, less attached to Margaret of Anjou and her son Prince Edward – they may even have believed in the rumours that he was not Henry VI's son – and agreed to accept York and his male issue as right heirs to the throne on the death or earlier abdication of King Henry. On 24 October a formal Act of Accord was ratified whereby York should succeed immediately on Henry's death, unless he previously decided to abdicate. 10,000 marks a year were to be provided for York and his sons, of which 3,500 marks were assigned to Edward of March and 1,500 to Edmund of Rutland. With this York had to be content.

More urgent and threatening matters now demanded the attention of the Yorkist leaders. King James II of Scotland, taking advantage of English weakness, captured Roxburgh and Wark in July 1460, and his army continued to threaten Berwick and the northern border.[2] Much more dangerous was the inability of the Yorkist-controlled government to extend its authority over large areas of the realm. Much of Wales defied it. In Devon, Hereford, Shropshire and Yorkshire bands of armed men roamed the countryside. Much of the north was under the control of the earl of Northumberland and Lords Clifford and Roos. Repeated orders to them to yield up key castles like Pontefract in Yorkshire and Penrith in Cumberland were wholly ignored. By October the government had been reduced to issuing hopeful commands to a mixed bag of Lancastrian and Yorkist partisans to expel evildoers from these castles, and to call out 'the lieges of Yorkshire and adjacent counties to storm the same' in case of resistance.[3] But there was little hope of success. The Yorkshire estates of York and the Nevills were devastated, and men were forced on pain of death to join the swelling Lancastrian resistance. In the south-west the duke of Somerset, returning from Calais in September, joined the earl of Devon in raising

---

[1] Including the dukes of Somerset and Exeter, the earls of Devon and Northumberland, and at least five North-Country barons.
[2] Scofield, I, 99–100, 117.
[3] *CPR, 1452–61,* 607–8, 610–11; *Annales,* 774–5; Gregory, 209–10; *Proc. Ord. Privy Council,* ed. Nicolas, VI, 304–5; Evans, *Wales in the Wars of the Roses,* 180–6.

troops, and early in December they marched north to rendezvous at Hull with the queen's North-Country supporters. The duke of Exeter, the earl of Northumberland, and Lords Roos, Clifford, Nevill and Dacre came in to swell the royalist army; this rapid muster took the Yorkists by surprise.[1]

In London urgent plans were made to meet the growing menace. York and Salisbury and the young Edmund of Rutland set out on 9 December for the north. Warwick and the duke of Norfolk remained behind in London. The earl of March now received his first independent command and was despatched to the Welsh Marches, probably with the dual task of curbing the activities of the Welsh Lancastrians under Jasper Tudor, earl of Pembroke, and raising troops in the areas of York family influence. He was given 650 marks for his expenses.[2] Fifteenth-century political crises were commonly decided by battles fought in the more distant parts of the realm, especially in the north and the Welsh border regions. The year 1460–61 proved no exception. In the north, Duke Richard made his final miscalculation. On 30 December 1460 he emerged from the safety of his castle at Sandal near Wakefield with an army weakened by the absence of foraging patrols, to give battle to a much larger Lancastrian force, commanded by the sons of his former enemies, Somerset, Northumberland and Clifford. In the ensuing rout York and Rutland, Salisbury's younger son, Thomas Nevill, and several of their leading supporters were killed. Salisbury was executed shortly after the battle. The severed heads of York and Salisbury were impaled on the gates of York, Duke Richard's adorned with a paper crown in macabre comment on his failed pretensions to the throne.[3]

The disaster at Wakefield was a severe blow to the Yorkist cause. The way was now open for the queen's army to march south on London. Her troops were given licence to sack and pillage along their route, and towns belonging to the duke of York, such as Grantham and Stamford, suffered severely. Such lawlessness was a grave political blunder, for the threat to property and fear of 'the malice of the Northernmen' stiffened support in the south for the rival cause. Yorkist propaganda was quick to take advantage: as one contemporary ballad, 'The Rose of Rouen', in praise of Edward, earl of March, expressed it:

[1] *Annales*, 774–5; *English Chronicle*, ed. Davies, 106; Gregory, 209–10.
[2] Scofield, I, 118.
[3] Ramsay, *Lancaster and York*, II, 237–8. The only roughly contemporary source to mention the paper crown is *Annales*, 775, but the 'Brief Latin Chronicle' (*Three Fifteenth-Century Chronicles*, 172) speaks of the heads being displayed 'obprobiose'.

All the lords of the north they wrought by one assent
For to destroy the south country they did all their entent
Had not the Rose of Rouen been, all England had been shent.[1]

Whilst Warwick prepared to resist the queen's advance, Edward had spent Christmas at Gloucester. Early in the New Year the bad news from the north reached him, and he prepared to set out for London with the troops he had raised in the Welsh Marches.[2] With him were many former servants and retainers of his father, men such as Sir Walter Devereux, one of Duke Richard's councillors, and steward of many of his Welsh lordships since 1452; Devereux's son-in-law, Sir William Herbert of Raglan, who had been the duke's steward of Caerleon and Usk as well as Warwick's sheriff of Glamorgan, and his brother, Sir Richard Herbert, and estates officials like John Milewater. There were also the young John Tuchet, Lord Audley, who had deserted to the earls at Calais in spite of his father's death at their hands at Blore Heath, Reginald, Lord Grey of Wilton in Herefordshire, another new baronial recruit to their cause, and Humphrey Stafford of Southwick, the future Yorkist earl of Devon. Many of these men were to have distinguished and successful careers under Edward IV in the 1460s.[3] But news from Wales caused Edward instead to turn north, to meet the challenge of Jasper, earl of Pembroke, and James, earl of Wiltshire, who had recently returned from the Continent with a force of French, Bretons and Irish, and, with their Welsh supporters, mainly from Pembroke and Carmarthen, were now marching on Hereford. On 2 or 3 February 1461 the armies clashed at Mortimer's Cross, a few miles from Edward's stronghold of Wigmore Castle, and there he won his first and signal victory. Pembroke and Wiltshire escaped, but many Welsh Lancastrians were killed in the battle, and several others, including Pembroke's father, Owen Tudor, formerly the husband of Henry V's queen, Catherine of Valois, were summarily executed in the market-place at Hereford.[4] A meteorological phenomenon – three

---

[1] Printed in *Archaeologia*, xxix (1842), 344. The Lancastrian pillaging, though probably exaggerated, was very widely reported at the time, see Scofield, I, 135–6.
[2] 'Short English Chronicle', 76.
[3] The fullest list of his supporters is in William Worcestre, *Itineraries*, ed. J. H. Harvey, 203–5. Despite the statement of Scofield, I, 137, there is no evidence that Hastings was in Edward's company. For Devereux's offices, see K. B. McFarlane, 'Wars of the Roses', 90, 93; J. T. Rosenthal, 'Estates and Finances of Richard, Duke of York', 181; and for further details of these men's later careers, see below, pp. 75–8, 80–1.
[4] William Worcestre, *op. cit.*; 'Short English Chronicle', 76–7; Gregory, 211; H. T. Evans, *Wales in the Wars of the Roses*, follows Gairdner, the editor of Gregory, in the belief that Owen and other prisoners were executed at Haverfordwest in Pembroke-

suns 'in the firmament shining full clear' – seen before the battle had been interpreted by Edward as a portent of victory, and is said to have provided the origin of one of his favourite badges, the 'Golden Sun of York'.[1]

Edward seems to have been in no hurry to come to the aid of the earl of Warwick, now threatened by the advance of the main Lancastrian army from the north. Not until about 19 February, when news reached him of Warwick's heavy defeat in the bloody and hard-fought battle of St Albans (17 February), did he set out with a substantial force for London.[2] Fortunately for his cause, the royalist victory proved less decisive militarily than it might have been. The Londoners' reluctance to admit into the city an army so notorious for its destruction of property and the queen's hesitation about forcing an entry together prevented her from taking control of the capital, and the news of Edward's now rapid approach helped to stiffen the citizens' resolve. Edward joined Warwick on about 22 February, either at Chipping Norton or Burford in the Cotswolds, and together they entered London on Thursday, 26 February. They were well received. Edward especially was seen as a youthful saviour; among the citizens the saying ran: 'Let us walk in a new wine yard, and let us make a gay garden in the month of March with this fair white rose and herb, the Earl of March.'[3] Margaret turned north again. Control of the capital with its departments of state, its financial power, and its symbolic prestige, was again denied to the queen's party.

Yet the second battle of St Albans, like Northampton, had important political consequences. As usual, Henry VI had been a passive spectator at the battle, and was recaptured by the queen's forces. At once all legal authority was stripped from the regime which the Yorkists had maintained since July 1460. Without control of the person of

---

shire. This seems unlikely because of the distance involved and because the Yorkists had no control over the far west of Wales until many months later (see below, pp. 48–9). It is based on a misunderstanding of the contemporary form for Hereford.

[1] As first suggested by the Tudor writer, Edward Hall, *Chronicle*, 251, followed by Scofield, I, 139. Cf. Ramsay, *Lancaster and York*, II, 244.

[2] *Annales*, 777; Evans, *op. cit.*, 130–1. For St Albans, and London's dealings with Queen Margaret, see Scofield, I, 149.

[3] Gregory, 215. Both *English Chronicle*, ed. Davies, 109, and *GC*, 194, suggest that, whatever the divisions of the city authorities, popular feeling in London was strongly in favour of the Yorkists. The date of Edward's entry into London is often wrongly given as Friday, 27 February (e.g. Scofield, I, 149; Lander, *Wars of the Roses*, 123), but it is clearly the 26th, as Gregory, 215, and 'Short English Chronicle', 77. *GC* and other London chronicles say a Thursday, which must be the 26th.

Henry VI, they had no claim on the obedience of his subjects. They now needed their own king, and, more than anything else, this explains Edward's assumption of the throne in March 1461. It has been generally assumed, especially by modern biographers of Richard Nevill, that Edward's usurpation is the first example of 'kingmaking' by his powerful cousin of Warwick.[1] But this view, which reflects the opinions of some foreign observers (who were prone to exaggerate Warwick's influence),[2] does not allow sufficiently for Edward's own role in the events of which he now becomes the central figure. The new duke of York, already calling himself 'by the grace of God of England, France and Ireland vray [true] and just heir' – as he was, under the Accord of 1460 – had a mind and will of his own and a natural capacity for leadership. His victory at Mortimer's Cross had won him personal prestige, and the larger part of the army which had followed him to London was comprised of Yorkist servants and retainers, who had come at their own expense.[3] The consent and support of the Nevill clan was necessary for Edward to assume the throne, but we have no good reason to assume that the initiative came rather from Warwick than from the confident young Edward himself.

The essential basis of his title to the throne, like that of his father, lay in the concept of legitimate inheritance. As set forth in the form of a petition from the commons in his first parliament (November 1461), his claim emphasized that, because the Lancastrian kings had all been usurpers, by God's law, man's law and the law of nature, the right title lay in Edward, as heir of Lionel of Clarence, after the death of his father; and since that day he had been in lawful possession. Under the rule of the usurper Henry VI (it continued), 'unrest, inward war and trouble, unrightwiseness, shedding and effusion of innocent blood, abusion of the laws, partiality, riot, extortion, murder, rape and vicious living have been the guiders and leaders of the noble realm of England'. Moreover, Henry had 'long before' 4 March 1461 breached the parliamentary Act of Accord of October 1460. For these reasons the usurper

---

[1] E.g. Oman, *Warwick the Kingmaker*, 112–13; P. M. Kendall, *Warwick the Kingmaker*, 85–7; see also Lander, 'Marriage and Politics', 129. Professor Kendall speaks of Warwick '*producing*' another king, and '*staging*' his elevation to the throne.

[2] E.g. Francesco Coppini, the papal legate: 'Warwick . . . has made a new king of the son of the Duke of York', *CSP, Milan*, I, 69. For examples of foreign exaggerations of Warwick's influence, see below, p. 63. It is noticeable that contemporary *English* chroniclers make no such assertions.

[3] Gregory, 215; 'the substance of his mayny [affinity or retinue] come at their own cost'. For Edward's use of the style 'heir of England', see C. A. J. Armstrong, 'The Inauguration Ceremonies of the Yorkist Kings, and their Title to the Throne', *TRHS*, 4th ser., xxx (1948), 53.

had been removed, and to the 'universal comfort and consolation' of all Englishmen, their 'rightwise and natural liege and sovereign lord' had resumed possession of his inheritance.[1]

It was important for the Yorkists that the process of kingmaking should follow precedent as closely as possible, and the ceremonies following Edward's entry into London were carefully stage-managed to that end.[2] The first step was an address by the chancellor, Bishop George Nevill, to a gathering of some three or four thousand people in St George's Fields on Sunday, 1 March. He set forth the articles of Edward's title, and the populace then acclaimed him and expressed their wish to have him as king. Their 'captains' carried this news to Edward at Baynard's Castle, the York family's London house beside the Thames. Next day the articles of his title were formally proclaimed throughout London. On 3 March a hastily-assembled 'great council' met at Baynard's Castle to 'agree and conclude' that Edward should be king of England. Those present included the archbishop of Canterbury, Richard Beauchamp, bishop of Salisbury, George Nevill, bishop of Exeter, John, duke of Norfolk, the earl of Warwick, William Herbert, Walter Devereux, and 'many others' unnamed.[3]

On Wednesday, 4 March, after hearing Te Deum in St Paul's, Edward made his way to the Palace of Westminster and into the great hall. There he took the oath, and, donning the robes of a king and the cap of estate, took his seat upon the marble chair called 'the King's Bench', with sceptre in hand. Having personally expounded his title to the throne, he was formally acclaimed by the assembled company, and at this point 'took possession of the realm of England'. His formal coronation was postponed until later.[4]

How long Edward could continue to enjoy his new office now depended on his ability to crush the still formidable Lancastrian resistance, which even now had the backing of a majority amongst the English nobility. On 6 March 1461 he issued proclamations addressed to the sheriffs of thirty-three English counties – significantly, all but one were south of Trent – and to the authorities of London, Bristol, Coven-

---

[1] *RP*, V, 463-7.
[2] For much of what follows, see Armstrong, 'Inauguration Ceremonies', 51-73.
[3] Though it is unlikely that the 'multi alii' contained many men of note, Professor Lander's comment on this assembly – 'a meagre list to make a king!' ('Marriage and Politics', 128-9) – minimizes unduly the extent of Yorkist support among the barons. Many proven Yorkists (including Viscount Bourchier and his sons, and others like Lords Abergavenny, Grey of Ruthyn, Audley, and Cobham) were absent, probably because the assembly was summoned in great haste.
[4] See below, p. 41.

try and certain other cities.[1] These called upon all men to accept him
as king. No man was to offer his adversaries help or comfort, nor to
pass 'over the water of Trent towards our said adversary' without
licence. In a second proclamation issued on the same day, he announced that any adherent of Henry VI who submitted within ten
days should have 'grace and pardon of his life and goods', except for
twenty-two men listed by name, and all others with an income of more
than 100 marks a year (which would include all barons and the richer
gentry).[2] This probably represents an attempt to win popular support,
by isolating the Lancastrian lords from the commonalty as in the orders
given to the Yorkist troops at Northampton. A reward of £100 was
offered to any man who put to death certain particular enemies of the
House of York. These included Andrew Trollope, leader of the contingent from Calais which had deserted at Ludford; Sir Thomas
Tresham, speaker of the Coventry Parliament of 1459; Thomas Fitz-
Harry from Herefordshire, who had fought against Edward at Mortimer's Cross; William Grimsby, formerly treasurer of Henry VI's
chamber, who had been at Wakefield; and the two 'Bastards of Exeter',
offspring of the duke of Exeter, one of whom is said to have executed
Salisbury after the battle of Wakefield.[3]

The Yorkist leaders now dispersed to raise troops in areas where they
had 'the rule of the country'. Edward lingered a few days longer in
London in an effort to raise funds. Once again the financial support
of London proved vital to the regime. The Londoners had already lent
the Yorkists £4,666 13s 4d since July 1460. In the first three days of
Edward's reign they were induced to advance a further £4,048.[4]
Individual merchants also made loans, and more was borrowed from
religious houses, like Holy Trinity Priory, Aldgate.[5]

By such means funds were collected to pay the troops assembled by
Yorkist captains like John Fogge and Robert Horne, and recruits who
flocked in from regions like East Anglia, generally favourable to the
Yorkist cause. On 11 March 1461 William Nevill, Lord Fauconberg,
left London with the footmen of the army, many from the Welsh
Marches and from Kent. Two days later Edward himself set out for
the north with the duke of Norfolk and the rest of the army, which
included a contingent sent by Duke Philip of Burgundy under the
banner of his protégé, the dauphin of France, the future Louis XI.

---

[1] *CCR, 1461-8*, 54-5. Northumberland was the surprising exception.
[2] *Ibid.*, 55-6.   [3] According to *Annales*, 775.
[4] P.R.O., Warrants for Issues, E. 404/72/1, no. 22.
[5] Scofield, I, 158.

Their advance northwards was deliberate, in order to allow time for contingents raised by captains like Sir John Howard in East Anglia and the earl of Warwick himself in the midlands to join the main army.[1]

When Edward eventually reached Pontefract on 27 or 28 March, he commanded an exceptionally large force by the standards of the age. The Lancastrian forces are generally agreed to have been even larger. They contained an impressive array of noblemen, including two dukes, four earls, a viscount and eight barons, mainly from the north, in addition to various baronial cadets. There was also a huge array of knights and gentry from all over England: some sixty were afterwards attainted for their part in the battle, and of these twenty-five were of sufficient substance to have sat in parliament as members.[2] By contrast, Edward's army contained comparatively few men of note – the duke of Norfolk, the earl of Warwick and his brother, John Nevill, Lord Montagu, his uncle, Lord Fauconberg, John, Lord Scrope of Bolton, and John Radcliffe, styled Lord FitzWalter. Among the gentry were several who were to become his trusted servants, and whom he knighted after the battle, such as Walter Devereux, John Howard, Humphrey Stafford, Walter Blount and William Hastings.[3] Medieval estimates of numbers are notoriously fallible and exaggerated, and most modern scholars have tended to discount the very high figures of combatants which the chroniclers supply. But, given the unparalleled number of notables present at the battle – they included some three-quarters of the surviving adult peerage – it is not at all unlikely that as many as 50,000 men were engaged.[4]

The battle of Towton, on Palm Sunday, 29 March 1461, was fought in bitter Yorkshire weather and no less bitter spirit.[5] It was the bloodiest battle of the entire civil war. On the previous day there had been a sharp clash between the Yorkist vanguard attempting to cross the River Aire at Ferrybridge and a Lancastrian force under Lord Clifford. Edward's troops turned Clifford's position by forcing a crossing at

[1] Scofield, I, 157, 159–60, 162. For the background of the dauphin's connection with Duke Philip, see P. M. Kendall, *Louis XI*, 95–102.

[2] *RP*, V, 477; Wedgwood, *Hist. Parl., Register*, 293.

[3] List in Gregory, 216. Montagu and Berners interceded for the city of York immediately after the battle (*PL*, III, 267), and were probably present there. Montagu had probably been summoned as a baron for the first time at a hitherto unknown session of the 1460 parliament; see *John Benet's Chronicle*, ed. Harriss, 229.

[4] As suggested by Lander, *Wars of the Roses*, 21 (who is elsewhere properly sceptical of large numbers). The large number of casualties also implies very large forces (see below, pp. 37–8).

[5] For accounts of the battle, see Burne, *op. cit.*, 96–107; Ramsay, *op. cit.*, II, 271–3.

Castleford slightly upstream, and, in the ensuing fighting, FitzWalter was killed and Warwick slightly wounded. But the Lancastrian holding-force was driven northwards and cut to pieces at Dingtingdale, two miles south of the main Lancastrian position. Lords Clifford and Nevill died in the action.

Early the next morning, with snow already threatening from the north-east, Edward's troops advanced towards the enemy host who were drawn up on a ridge between the villages of Saxton and Towton, with the little River Cock on their right. This bold offensive (as at Barnet and Tewkesbury) is more characteristic of Edward's generalship than the defensive tactics usually adopted by Warwick. The Yorkist vanguard under William Nevill, Lord Fauconberg, soon challenged the enemy. Taking advantage of the wind which blew the snow into their enemies' faces, his archers opened fire. The Lancastrian archers, blinded by snow and out of range, wasted most of their arrows in a vain response. Stung by the Yorkist archery, the Lancastrian infantry charged down the hill, and bitter hand-to-hand fighting followed. For hours a furious and indecisive struggle raged, until, in the course of the afternoon, the duke of Norfolk's contingent came up on the Yorkist right and began to turn the enemy left. Even then the stubborn Lancas-trians did not give up, and the day was drawing to a close before their line eventually collapsed, and they fled the field. Many were drowned in the Cock river, many more cut down on the field, and others were killed by the Yorkist cavalry as they streamed north towards the little town of Tadcaster. The slaughter was immense. The earl of Northum-berland, Lords Dacre of Gilsland and Welles, Andrew Trollope and Sir Henry Stafford, younger son of the late duke of Buckingham, were all killed in the field. According to Gregory's Chronicle, forty-two knights were taken prisoner and put to death at the end of the day.[1] A report on the battle amongst the Paston family papers states that the slain numbered 28,000, though this is likely to be exaggeration.[2] The earl of Devon was taken and executed at York on the following day, and the earl of Wiltshire soon after at Newcastle. King Henry, the

[1] Gregory, 217.

[2] *PL*, III, 268, in a newsletter appended to a letter of 4 April. The reappearance of this 'herald's estimate' in other sources (e.g. in a letter of the bishop of Salisbury, 7 April, and the Milanese ambassador in France, 12 April, *CSP Milan*, I, 64–5, 68; Kingsford, *Chronicles of London*, 175, and Edward's own statement, Burne, *op. cit.*, 104) suggests this letter was widely circulated. Many other contemporary estimates are much higher, but the figure given by *Annales*, 778, of 9,000 deaths, apparently on the Lancastrian side, seems more plausible.

queen, and the prince of Wales, who had not been at the battle, made good their escape to Scotland, where they were soon joined by the dukes of Exeter and Somerset, Lord Roos, Sir Humphrey Dacre, Sir John Fortescue and other Lancastrian stalwarts. By contrast, the Yorkists lost no men of note save Lord FitzWalter and the Kentish captain Robert Horne.[1]

Edward had won an immense victory. The particular importance of Towton is that it finally shattered the strength of the great northern lords, like Percy, Clifford, Roos and Dacre, who had hitherto been so loyal to Lancaster, and who between them could dominate England north of Trent. The way now lay open for the subjugation of Yorkshire and the regions towards the Scottish Border. As we shall see, the danger was far from over. Many die-hard Lancastrians were still at large, and even exiles might prove a menace with foreign support. Traditional loyalties to the great families were not extinguished overnight. Much of Wales remained to be brought under control. Yet, in a wider sense, Towton proved politically decisive. For most Englishmen, including a majority amongst the barons and gentry, it now became prudent and realistic to acknowledge the authority of the new king.

[1] *PL*, III, 267.

Part II

THE FIRST REIGN, 1461-1471

Chapter 3

THE DEFENCE OF THE THRONE, 1461–1464

(i) *Disorder, Disaffection and Pacification*

On Friday, 26 June 1461, Edward made his state entry into London to await his coronation two days later.[1] The citizens' applause and the splendid ceremonies of crown-wearing and banqueting did not conceal the fact that the new king was far from secure on his throne. Towton had discredited but had not destroyed the Lancastrian cause, chiefly because the defeated king and queen and many of their most active supporters were still at large and free to continue the struggle. In large areas of the country the authority of the new government remained precarious.

The firm establishment of the Yorkist regime depended on the successful resolution of three related problems. First, it was essential to restore a measure of peace and order to a disturbed and divided country. This involved not only suppressing Lancastrian-inspired disaffection, but also quelling much local disorder which was the legacy of weak government and had been encouraged by the conditions of civil war. Secondly, Edward had to prevent intervention by foreign powers tempted to benefit from English domestic discord. The danger of Lancastrian resistance would be greatly increased if backed by foreign support. Thirdly, a Yorkist regime had to be created which would carry the royal authority into the shires, especially into areas where Lancastrian sympathies were strong, including the west and north of England, large parts of the midlands, and Wales and the Marches. For the next three years these tasks provided the Yorkist leaders with their main preoccupation.

The main weakness of Edward's position in the months following his victory at Towton lay in the fact that he still possessed comparatively few really reliable supporters amongst the English nobility and gentry, and his realization of this fact is reflected in the urgency with which he

[1] For a description of the ceremonies, see Scofield, I, 181–4.

pursued a policy of conciliation towards his former enemies. Casualties in battle had thinned the ranks of loyal Lancastrians; others, less committed, hastened to make their peace with the young king, but could not be fully trusted immediately.[1] Even men with very close associations with the house of Lancaster found it prudent to make a temporary accommodation. Thus Sir Thomas Tuddenham, formerly keeper of the wardrobe and treasurer of the household to Henry VI, who had been deeply involved with the dukes of Suffolk and Somerset, escaped attainder, as did his collaborator, John Heydon, who received a general pardon in April 1462. Edward's clemency was carried so far as to arouse criticism from his own supporters. In East Anglia it was reported that the common people 'grudge and say how that the King receiveth such of this country . . . as have been his great enemies, and oppressors of the commons; and such as have assisted his highness, be not rewarded; and it is to be considered, or else it will hurt'.[2]

But many Lancastrians were not disposed to give up the fight. Among them were Jasper Tudor, earl of Pembroke, Henry Holland, duke of Exeter, and several young lords whose fathers had died in the fighting, like the sons of the duke of Somerset, the earl of Wiltshire, and Viscount Beaumont. Many prominent Lancastrian gentry remained unreconciled, and the spring and early summer of 1461 saw the appointment of a series of commissions to arrest active rebels and to enquire into treasons and rebellions.[3] The West Country was particularly disaffected, and the dangers here were increased by fears of a French invasion. Elsewhere disorder was increased by local family feuds, like the bitter strife of the Vernons and the Gresleys in Derbyshire, which flared into violence in the favourable atmosphere of civil war.[4] Gangs of 'seditious vagabonds' roamed through many midland and southern regions, accused of killing, despoiling and oppressing the king's subjects.[5] In Norfolk Margaret Paston expressed the anxious hope that 'there may be set a good rule and a sad in this country in haste, for I heard never say of so much robbery and manslaughter in this country as is now within a little time'.[6]

As Lancastrian sympathizers were rounded up or made good their escape, the tide of specifically treasonable disorders slackened during

[1] E.g., Edward's future father- and brother-in-law, Lords Rivers and Scales, both pardoned in July 1461.
[2] PL, III, 292. For the careers of Tuddenham and Heydon, see Wedgwood, Hist. Parl., Biographies, 452–3, 880–1. For commissions to Hastings, Warwick, and other trusted supporters to receive rebels into the king's grace, CPR, 1461–7, 7, 45, 190.
[3] Ibid., 28–30, 31, 102.   [4] Ibid., 31, 33, 135.
[5] Ibid., 28, 37, 66, 101, 135.   [6] PL, IV, 25.

the autumn of 1461, only to break out again during the winter and in the early months of 1462. In November followers of the dukes of Exeter and Somerset and the earl of Wiltshire were stirring up sedition in Hampshire. In January 1462 'suspicious congregations' inspired by named Lancastrians were reported from Somerset, Dorset and Wiltshire, and there was evidence too of popular disillusionment with the new king. In February reports of further disturbances came in from six counties in the north midlands and the north-west.[1] In some of the more remote parts of the realm, government control was barely nominal, and effective royal administration had collapsed.[2] Edward and his councillors clearly feared a widespread conspiracy by Lancastrian sympathizers, in league with their exiled and foreign friends, and on 12 February 1462 they appointed a powerful commission of twenty-three barons and ten judges to investigate treasons and trespasses in no fewer than twenty-five counties and eight cities.[3] At the same time they uncovered a Lancastrian plot headed by the earl of Oxford, his son, Aubrey de Vere, and Sir Thomas Tuddenham. Arrested on 12 February they were speedily convicted before the Constable of England, John Tiptoft, earl of Worcester, who was now creating his unenviable reputation for ruthlessness; and between 20 and 26 February they, and two fellow-conspirators, were executed on Tower Hill.[4]

In southern England the alarm was increased by fears of foreign invasion. The aged Charles VII of France had shown some favour to the Lancastrian cause. After Towton, he had permitted Queen Margaret's friend, Pierre de Brézé, seneschal of Normandy, to assemble a fleet for the conquest of the Channel Islands, a reward already promised to Pierre by Margaret; and in May this led to the French establishing themselves on Jersey.[5] Active preparations for war were going ahead in the last few weeks of Charles's life. In reply, Edward incited the men of the southern and western counties of England to resist the French, urging his subjects to raise a fleet at their own expense, and organizing measures for the defence of the Isle of Wight.[6] The death of Charles VII on 22 July 1461 raised Edward's hopes,

---

[1] CPR, 1461-7, 67, 101-2, 132; Storey, End of the House of Lancaster, 197.

[2] Notably in many parts of Wales (R. A. Griffiths, 'Royal government in the southern counties of the principality of Wales', unpublished Ph.D. thesis, Bristol, 1962, pp. 552-9). For the north, see below, pp. 46-7.   [3] CPR, 1461-7, 132-3.

[4] Scofield, I, 231-4, and sources there cited. According to John Benet's Chronicle, ed. Harriss, 232, the earl of Worcester and Lords Ferrers and Herbert were sent to arrest the conspirators.

[5] Scofield, I, 161, 179; Calmette and Perinelle, Louis XI et l'Angleterre, 2-3.

[6] CPR, 1461-7, 33-4, 38; Scofield, I, 180.

for the new king, Louis XI, had been on bad terms with his father, and had shown some sympathy to the Yorkist cause. At first the change of ruler seemed to work in Edward's favour: de Brézé was temporarily disgraced, and the war preparations were halted. But Louis soon began to pursue the subtle and baffling policies which became characteristic of him, playing off one side against the other in England, and rapidly creating a tension and uncertainty about his intentions. As his envoys were rebuffed, Edward's suspicions grew, especially as early in 1462 Louis seemed to move towards a definite *rapprochement* with his Lancastrian kinsmen.[1]

The fears produced in England by this apparent danger from France were exaggerated, for Louis hoped to keep England weak and divided rather than to secure the triumph of either side, but it was taken seriously enough both by government and popular opinion. Edward himself found it convenient to dwell upon the perils of the situation as a means of getting loans from the Londoners. In a letter of 13 March 1462 to the London alderman Thomas Cook, he spoke of a fearful alliance between Lancaster and England's foreign enemies, which would bring upon the realm 'such war, depopulation and robbery and manslaughter as here before hath not been used among Christian people'; they would seek to extinguish 'the people, the name, the tongue and the blood English of this our said realm'.[2] Behind such calculated alarmism his real fear was shown in extensive defence measures. In the early months of 1462 watches were set and beacons manned along the south and south-east coasts; commissions to array all able-bodied men were issued in Kent; ships were seized in the Bristol Channel to provide against a descent on Wales; and preparations were made for the earl of Warwick to go to sea with a patrolling squadron in the Channel.[3] Edward's own subjects scarcely needed their king to exaggerate their fears. Early in 1462 a contemporary writer reported a vast international conspiracy against England, involving an invasion by half the princes of Western Europe with hundreds of thousands of men at their backs.[4] Confessions made by French prisoners taken off the East Coast spoke of vast joint French and Spanish naval preparations in the Seine, and the imminent death of England's friend, Duke Philip of Burgundy, by poison.[5]

---

[1] Scofield, I, 207–14; Calmette and Perinelle, 7–16. For the mediating role of Burgundy, M. R. Thielemans, *Bourgogne et Angleterre*, 383–90.
[2] H. Ellis, *Original Letters*, I, 126.
[3] *CPR, 1461–7*, 100–1, 203; Rymer, *Foedera*, XI, 488; Scofield, I, 234.
[4] *Three Fifteenth-Century Chronicles*, 158.   [5] *PL*, IV, 35.

There are good reasons for emphasizing the extent of domestic disorder and disaffection, and the degree of alarm and apprehension felt
by Edward's subjects, during the first twelve months of his reign. The
danger lay in the explosive potential of the situation. With a disturbed
and uneasy country behind them, even a minor defeat at the hands of
the Lancastrians might have proved disastrous for the new regime.
This also provides part of the explanation for the government's difficulties in Wales and the north, and the success of limited Lancastrian
forces in maintaining themselves in these regions. Still insecure even in
the south and midlands, and unable to ignore the risk of attack from
abroad, Edward could not venture on major operations in the more
remote areas of the realm. It is against this background that the story
of Lancastrian resistance in the north and Wales must be seen.

(ii) *The Lancastrian Resistance, 1461–1464*

In spite of the strength of Lancastrian sympathies in Yorkshire, the
county offered no resistance to Edward after Towton. After a leisurely
three weeks in York, the king moved north to Durham, where he arrived on 22 April 1461. There he attempted to win the goodwill of the
bishop, Lawrence Booth, whom he appointed his confessor, although
Booth had previously had very close associations with Queen Margaret. Here again we have evidence of Edward's wish to conciliate.
Anyone who showed a willingness to cooperate was given his chance,
whatever the risks implied by his previous record. From Durham
Edward moved on to Newcastle to attend the execution of his father's
arch-enemy, James Butler, earl of Ormond and Wiltshire. Thence he
abruptly turned west for a progress through Lancashire, Cheshire, and
parts of the north midlands which had shown strong sympathy for
Henry VI and Margaret.[1] The problem of subduing the hostile county
of Northumberland, where the word of a Percy counted for more than
the king's command, was left to his Nevill kinsmen and lieutenants. Not
for the last time in these early years, Edward showed his reluctance to
be drawn away to the extreme north. Probably he felt that his presence
was more urgently needed further south, but an opportunity was missed
for asserting the royal authority in Northumberland whilst he still had
large forces at his back.

The key to the northern problem now lay in the attitude of Scotland.
King James II, attempting to exploit English weakness, had been killed
on 3 August 1460 by the explosion of one of his bombards whilst

[1] Gregory, 217–18.

besieging Roxburgh Castle. His widow, Mary of Guelders, the new regent, was pressed by her uncle, the duke of Burgundy, to support the Yorkist cause, but was dissuaded from this by the most influential person in Scottish politics, James Kennedy, bishop of St Andrews. After Towton, Scotland offered a refuge to the fleeing Henry and Margaret, and by 25 April they had reached an agreement with Mary of Guelders, whereby the Scots promised military aid in return for the cession to them of the coveted border fortress of Berwick, a bribe which even Mary could not resist. Edward's response to the Scots *démarche* was twofold. Friendly overtures in the hope of persuading the Scots government to give up the Lancastrians were matched by efforts to stir up trouble within Scotland. James II's enemies, the earl of Douglas and his brother, then in exile in England, were commissioned in June 1461 to make an approach to other disaffected lords, especially the powerful earl of Ross, lord of the Outer Isles, and his kinsman, Donald Balloch, in the hope that together they could foment a successful rebellion in Scotland.[1] But for the moment the attitude of the Scots had to be reckoned a serious threat to northern England. Early in June a combined force of Scots and Lancastrian exiles raided Carlisle: this caused great alarm in the south, but John Nevill, Lord Montagu, had no difficulty in raising the siege. The end of the month saw another surprise raid. Lords Roos, Dacre and Rougemont-Grey, taking Henry VI with them, slipped across the border to the earl of Westmorland's castle at Brancepeth in south Durham, where they raised the Lancastrian standard, but with little success. They were dispersed without difficulty by Bishop Booth of Durham and local levies.[2]

During all this time the government seems to have had no effective authority in Northumberland. Garrisons of 120 men in Newcastle under Lord Fauconberg and of 40 men in Tynemouth under Sir George Lumley marked the frontier of Yorkist control. No attempt to reduce the county to submission was made until after Warwick had been appointed, on 31 July 1461, to the wardenship of both the East and West Marches towards Scotland.[3] By mid-September the Nevill lords had managed to gain the submission of the great Percy stronghold of Alnwick, and a Yorkist constable was appointed to hold it with 100 men. Soon after, the coastal fortress of Dunstanborough submitted

[1] Scofield, I, 31–2, 99–100, 134–5, 175–7; Annie Dunlop, *Life and Times of James Kennedy*, 215–23, for relations with Scotland and the political background there.
[2] *RP*, V, 478; *PL*, III, 276.
[3] *Rotuli Scotiae*, II, 402. On 5 April 1462 he was made warden of the West March for twenty years, R. L. Storey, 'Wardens of the Marches of England towards Scotland, 1377–1489', *EHR*, lxxii (1957), 614. For the garrisons, see Scofield, I, 204.

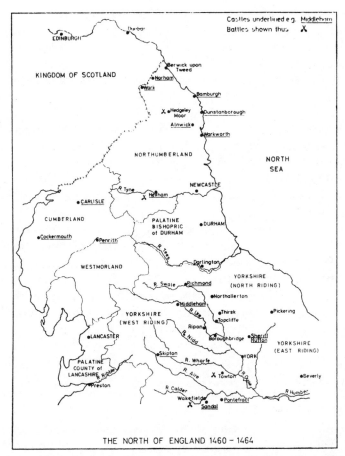

THE NORTH OF ENGLAND 1460 – 1464

also, but its Lancastrian constable, Sir Ralph Percy, was allowed to remain in command. His record scarcely inspired confidence in his future loyalty. This younger son of Henry Percy, 2nd earl of Northumberland, had seen his father killed fighting the Yorkists at St Albans in 1455, and his elder brother, the 3rd earl, killed at Towton and attainted, whilst his nephew, later the 4th earl, was a prisoner in the Tower. Ralph himself had been appointed by Henry VI in 1457 and had served on Lancastrian commissions as late as June 1460.[1] To allow a key fortress to remain in the control of a man like this shows how precarious was the royal authority in a countryside where the cooperation of the Percies and their followers was essential. The general uncertainty of the position in the far north first became clear in the winter of 1461–2 when the Lancastrian William Tailboys recaptured

[1] Somerville, *History of the Duchy of Lancaster*, I, 538; *CPR, 1452–61*, 609, 673.

Alnwick, and another unreconciled rebel, Humphrey, Lord Dacre of Gilsland, re-established himself in his family fortress of Naworth, near Carlisle.[1] The best hope of more solid success in this region seemed to lie in the growing willingness of Mary of Guelders to make a truce with Edward, and thereby cut off aid and refuge from the Lancastrians across the Border.[2]

Similar problems faced the new government in Wales. Especially in West Wales, Lancastrian loyalties were strong, and Jasper Tudor, earl of Pembroke, had considerable influence. On the morrow of Towton several strong castles, including Pembroke, Harlech and Denbigh, were still held for Henry VI. Operations for the subjugation of Wales resembled those in the north in that the king played little direct part and they were delegated to lieutenants, notably the able and ambitious William Herbert, who soon emerged as the driving-force and central figure of Yorkist government in Wales and the Marches. Attempts to bring Wales to order were delayed until the return of the king and his chief lords from the north in June 1461. On 8 July 1461, William Herbert and Sir Walter Devereux were authorized to raise men in the border counties and preparations were begun to assemble a fleet in support, and in August the king's subjects in the Marches and the south-west were urged to raise troops at their own expense against the rebels in Wales.[3] At first it was intended that the king should lead his army in person: his tents, ordnance and some ready cash were sent on ahead to await his arrival at Hereford, where an army was to muster on 8 September.[4]

Edward made his journey to the Marches the occasion for one of those royal provincial progresses which are a feature of his early years. He left London early in August, in the company of the earl of Essex, Lord Hastings, and some of the judges, and made a leisurely journey by way of Canterbury, Sandwich, Arundel and Salisbury to Bristol, where he arrived on 4 September. There he presided in person over the trial of the West Country rebel, Sir Baldwin Fulford, who was executed on 9 September: his head was to remain impaled in the market-place at Exeter until March 1463, when it was removed because 'it daily falleth down' among the feet of the citizens.[5] But already Edward had changed his mind about taking personal command of the Welsh

[1] *Annales*, 779. The appointment of commissions of array in the north, November 1461, is further evidence of disturbance (*CPR, 1461–7*, 66).   [2] Scofield, I, 207, 214.
[3] *CPR, 1461–7*, 14, 36–9, 45, 65, 98–9. Early in September sailors were being pressed in Bristol and Bridgwater for the fleet, which was to assist Herbert in the blockading of the castles in West Wales (*ibid.*, 99–100).
[4] *Ibid.*, 98–9.   [5] P.R.O., Exch., Council and P.S., E. 28/89/28; Scofield, I, 197–200.

campaign. As one of his entourage, probably the earl of Essex, reported from Bristol, his plan was now to go to Ludlow, and there to remain until it was time to return to Westminster for the opening of his first parliament on 4 November, and this forecast proved accurate.[1] Again Edward displayed a reluctance to take part in military operations in the distant parts of his realm, and the pattern was to be repeated over and over again in these early years. Some of his contemporaries believed that the king's love of ease and pleasure lay behind this distaste for campaigning, but it is much more likely that in the autumn of 1461 he was unwilling to postpone any longer the opening of parliament, where his personal presence was necessary.

In the event his absence made little difference to the conduct of the campaign in Wales. William Herbert and his friends moved with vigour to eliminate the main centres of Lancastrian resistance in the Principality. Although strongly fortified, victualled and manned, Pembroke Castle surrendered to him on 30 September 1461. Moving north, he defeated Jasper Tudor, Henry, duke of Exeter, and the main body of Welsh Lancastrians at Twt Hill just outside Caernarvon on 16 October. Denbigh Castle gave itself up by January 1462. But the country as a whole was far from reconciled to Yorkist rule, especially the west, where the castle of Carreg Cennen held out until May 1462. The great fortress of Harlech showed no disposition to surrender, and, lacking the will or the resources to mount a regular set siege, the government allowed this nest of rebels to survive and prey upon the surrounding countryside for several years. Rebellion was never far from the surface, and Wales remained an area obviously vulnerable to a Lancastrian seaborne invasion.[2]

Meanwhile, the royal government renewed its efforts to persuade the Scots to abandon their support for the Lancastrian cause. The negotiations begun in 1461 with the Scots dissidents now bore fruit. In March 1462 Edward ratified a treaty with Ross and Balogh which pledged them to make war on James III in return for annuities and a share in any conquests to be made; soon after, Ross began to devastate Atholl in northern Perthshire.[3] Freed from the embarrassing presence of Margaret of Anjou (now seeking help in France), Mary of Guelders seemed willing to negotiate, and there was even a suggestion that she might marry the young Edward of York, but the negotiations were

---

[1] Ellis, *Original Letters*, 1st ser., I, 116.
[2] *RP*, V, 478; Evans, *Wales and the Wars of the Roses*, 140–5; Griffiths, thesis cited above, p. 43, n. 2; *CPR*, *1461–7*, 100, 132 (for further disturbances in S. Wales, March 1462).   [3] Rymer, *Foedera*, XI, 483–7.

frustrated by the bishop of St Andrews. The earl of Warwick now step-
ped up the pressure by launching raids into Scotland, and recovered
one of the Border fortresses. Faced by danger both from north and south,
Mary agreed to a short truce to last from June to the end of August
1462. This in turn enabled Edward's lieutenants to strengthen his
position near the Border. Naworth was recovered from Lord Dacre,
and in July Alnwick Castle surrendered after a siege by Lord Hastings,
Sir John Howard and Sir Ralph Grey.[1]

These modest Yorkist gains were soon in jeopardy as Margaret of
Anjou made her most determined effort to challenge the rival dynasty.
Disillusioned by Scotland's uncertain support, she left for France in
April 1462 in an attempt to win the committed backing of her powerful
kinsman, Louis XI. At first she was successful. Tempted by her willingness to cede Calais to him, Louis concluded a secret agreement with
her at Chinon (24 June 1462), later amplified in the Truce of Tours
(28 June), whereby he promised to lend her money and released her
friend de Brézé to raise an army and accompany her back to Scotland.[2]
His enthusiasm soon cooled when the duke of Burgundy refused to
allow the passage of French troops through his dominions, thus preventing access to Calais, and he was further alarmed by the activities of
an English naval squadron under the earl of Kent which raided the
Breton coast in August 1462. His effective support for Margaret did
not materialize, and when she left for Scotland in October she could
take only 800 men, and even these seem to have been paid for by de
Brézé. With this modest force she eventually set sail for Scotland, to
collect Henry VI, and landed near Bamborough Castle on 25 October.[3]

Yet her mere return immediately emphasized the dangers of the
Yorkist policy of entrusting the northern fortresses to men of doubtful
loyalty. Bamborough speedily opened its gates, and Alnwick and
Dunstanborough soon followed suit, 'by the which castles' (as a
chronicler observed) 'they had the most part of Northumberland'.[4]
For lack of accurate intelligence, Edward may have overestimated the
forces at the disposal of the rebels, but his alarm is reflected in the vigour
of his reaction. He at once made preparations to leave London for the
north, and set about summoning to his side almost the entire nobility of
England: one immediately contemporary source names 2 dukes, 7
earls, 31 barons and 59 knights as being in his company.[5] There were
also substantial northern levies which Warwick had been commissioned

[1] *Annales*, 779; *PL*, IV, 44, 50–1; Dunlop, *James Kennedy*, 226–9; Scofield, I, 246–9.
[2] Calmette and Perinelle, *op. cit.*, 19–21; Scofield, I, 250–3.
[3] *Ibid.*, 254–61.   [4] Warkworth, *Chronicle*, 2.   [5] *Three Fifteenth-Century Chronicles*, 157.

to raise on 6 November. Another contemporary source claimed that 'our men be in all estimation between 30 and 40 thousand without the King and his host', and, even if we discount the usual exaggeration in such medieval estimates, it is clear that an impressive force was brought together.[1] Alarmed by these rapid preparations, and perhaps disappointed by the lack of any general support from the northern lords and gentry, Margaret decided her strength was not sufficient to risk any engagement. Leaving garrisons in the Northumbrian fortresses, she took ship for Scotland on 13 November. Winter storms scattered her fleet, and although Margaret herself, with Henry VI and de Brézé, reached Berwick in safety, some of her French soldiers were driven ashore at Lindisfarne and were there overwhelmed by Yorkist forces.[2]

Her withdrawal gave the royal army the chance to invest and blockade all three rebel strongholds. Edward himself had reached York by 19 November, and moved on to Durham, only to fall ill with measles.[3] Overall command of the sieges therefore fell to the earl of Warwick, who supervised operations by means of a daily round on horseback from a base in the Percy fortress of Warkworth. More than a dozen Yorkist noblemen were dispersed in command of the separate besieging forces. Though the royal army had ordnance in plenty, no attempt was made to bombard the three castles into surrender, and frontal assault was out of the question against formidable fortifications. Instead, the royal army relied upon blockade to starve the garrisons out. The defenders in their turn hoped for a relief army from Scotland. A Scottish force under the earl of Angus and de Brézé was already moving south shortly before Christmas, a fact known to Edward and his commanders; but this intelligence did not reach the defenders of Dunstanborough and Bamborough (by now reduced to eating their horses) in time to prevent their making a conditional offer to surrender, on Christmas Eve 1462. The leading defenders, including the duke of Somerset and Sir Ralph Percy, were then escorted to the king's presence at Durham.[4]

There now followed one of those political blunders which mars Edward's record as a statesman. Somerset and his friends were accepted into the king's obedience, and the rebel duke soon found himself assisting Warwick at the siege of Alnwick against his former allies.

---

[1] *Excerpta Historica*, ed. S. Bentley, 365; and see also Gregory, 219; *PL*, IV, 60; *CPR, 1461–7*, 231.   [2] *GC*, 199–200; Gregory, 218–19.

[3] *GC*, 200; Kingsford, *Chronicles of London*, 178.

[4] Contemporary accounts (with some discrepancies as to the names of the commanders) in *Excerpta Historica*, 365; *Three Fifteenth-Century Chronicles*, 159, and in the letter of John Paston the Youngest, who was present at the sieges, 11 December 1462, *PL*, III, 59–61.

Even more surprising is Edward's willingness to accept the demand made by the besieged garrisons, as a condition of surrender, that the turncoat Sir Ralph Percy should be restored to the command of both Dunstanborough and Bamborough as soon as he had sworn allegiance to Edward. Shortly after, Percy was commissioned to receive repentant rebels into the king's grace at his discretion, a power normally given only to men of unquestioned loyalty. This latter decision seems to have been made by the king with the advice of the council, but probably did not reflect the attitude of the earl of Warwick, whose record of ruthlessness towards his defeated enemies suggests that their fate would have been very different had the choice been his.[1] The king's treatment of Somerset and Percy can only be explained by a combination of his natural generosity and gross over-confidence in his own personal charm as a means of winning the committed loyalty of even the most hardened enemy. But nothing in the record of either Somerset or Percy seems to justify Edward in placing such trust in them; and events soon proved how serious had been his miscalculation.

With Bamborough and Dunstanborough in Yorkist hands within two days after Christmas, the royal forces, still under Warwick's command, were now re-deployed before Alnwick. But on 5 January 1463 de Brézé and the Scots earl of Angus appeared in the neighbourhood with a substantial force. For reasons which are difficult to understand, Warwick failed to offer battle, withdrew his men from their siege positions, and allowed the hard-pressed garrison under Lord Hungerford to march out of the fortress in full view of the Yorkist army. Warwick was always a defensively-minded general, but it may be that his failure to challenge the Scots was influenced by the low morale of his troops. The chronicler John Warkworth tells us that 'they had lain there so long in the field, and were grieved with cold and rain, that they had no courage to fight', and stringent measures had already proved necessary to prevent desertion.[2] As the Scots and the defenders of Alnwick withdrew unmolested over the Border, one immediately contemporary critic expressed his disillusionment:

And in all this long time, when almost all the armed force of England was assembled against our enemies, what, I ask, what action memorable or deserving of praise was done, except the capture of the aforesaid three castles?[3]

---

[1] *Annales*, 780–1; Gregory, 219; *RP*, V, 511; *CPR, 1461–7*, 262 (commission to Percy, 17 March 1463); McFarlane, 'Wars of the Roses', 101.

[2] *Chronicle*, 2; *PL*, III, 60. Conflicting accounts of the operations at Alnwick are in Warkworth, *Chronicle*, 2; *Annales*, 781; *Three Fifteenth-Century Chronicles*, 176; *GC*, 200.

[3] *Three Fifteenth-Century Chronicles*, 176.

But whatever Edward's critics might say, Margaret's great venture had failed. Neither the Lancastrian nobility and gentry of the north, who had supported the standard of Henry VI in 1460–61, nor the common people, had rallied to her cause. Probably her association with the ancient enemy of Scotland did little to commend her to many North-countrymen. Edward could now turn south to celebrate his father's obit with splendid pomp at the family house of Fotheringhay, on 30 January 1463, comfortable in the knowledge (as Warkworth remarked) that he now 'possessed all England, except a castle in North Wales called Harlech'.[1] The Nevill lords too went south for the solemn interment of their kinsmen killed at Wakefield, the earl of Salisbury and Sir Thomas Nevill, at Bisham Abbey in Berkshire. But no sooner was their vigilance relaxed than the brittle nature of Yorkist control, dependent on the suspect loyalties of men like Sir Ralph Percy and the disgruntled Sir Ralph Grey, was again revealed.[2]

In March 1463 Sir Ralph Percy turned traitor yet again, and allowed a force of French and Scots to re-occupy Bamborough and Dunstanborough. In May Sir Ralph Grey followed Percy's example and turned over Alnwick Castle to a force under Lord Hungerford.[3] Thus, for the third time since Towton, the three strongholds were again in Lancastrian hands, and all the expensive labours of the winter campaign had been in vain. News soon came of a threat to Newcastle, and John Nevill, Lord Montagu, newly-appointed warden of the East March, was despatched to its aid, only to learn that the citizens had beaten off the rebel attack, and had captured four French ships carrying victuals to Bamborough.[4] Warwick and his brother-in-law, Thomas, Lord Stanley, had meanwhile left London with a large force on 3 June. On arrival in the north they found the situation so serious that they urged the king himself to come north with reinforcements.[5] For this time the rebels were to be supported by a large-scale Scots invasion. Before the end of June a substantial army had accompanied the young king of Scotland, Queen Mary of Guelders, Henry VI and Margaret of Anjou over the Border, and early in July they laid siege to Norham Castle, a few miles inland from Berwick on the River Tweed.[6]

[1] Warkworth, *Chronicle*, 3; Scofield, I, 268.   [2] *Ibid.*, 269.

[3] Gregory, 219–20; *Annales*, 781. Grey was apparently piqued because he had not received the chief command at Alnwick, given instead to Sir John Ashley, but cf. Scofield, I, 287.

[4] Waurin, *Anchiennes chronicques d'Engleterre*, ed. Dupont, III, 159–60 (despatch to the court of Burgundy, 19 June 1463).   [5] *Ibid.*, 160.

[6] Evidence for the dating of the Scots invasion is conflicting. I have followed the version in K. Bittmann, 'La Campagne Lancastrienne de 1463: un document

In London Edward himself planned a speedy departure. The exchequer was asked to supply £5,000 in cash for his own expenses, and a further £4,800 to finance a fleet under the earl of Worcester for combined operations in the north. The convocation of Canterbury, then sitting in St Paul's, was pressed for more money for the king's urgent needs in the defence of the realm against the Scots.[1] Edward travelled no further north than Northampton. There a riot broke out amongst the citizens directed against the duke of Somerset, then high in Edward's favour, which caused the king to send Somerset to North Wales for his own safety.[2] But whilst he was at Northampton news arrived from the north of a notable success for the Yorkist arms. Warwick and Montagu, aided by the archbishop of York with a force of northern levies, had confronted the invaders, who had panicked and fled. The Nevills in their turn swept into southern Scotland, pillaging and burning for a distance of sixty-three miles, and only lack of victuals forced them to turn back. The siege of Norham Castle had been raised. Margaret and her young son, Prince Edward of Wales, made good their escape to Berwick, and soon after sailed to Sluys, where they arrived early in August. Henry VI himself stayed on in Scotland under the protection of the bishop of St Andrews.[3]

It was widely believed, both in England and on the Continent (where these events were reported as far afield as Italy), that Edward intended to follow up these successes with a major campaign directed at crushing the Scots and putting an end to Scots independence for good.[4] As Lord Hastings told the Franco-Burgundian agent, Jean de Lannoy, in a letter sent from Fotheringhay on 7 August, the Scots would be made to repent to the day of judgement the aid they had given to Henry and Margaret.[5] Edward himself told parliament, when he asked for an aid of £37,000 for the defence of the realm in June, that he planned to lead his army in person against his enemies.[6] Yet, with

---

italien', *Revue Belge de Philologie et d'histoire*, xxvi (1948), 1059–83. Cf. Scofield, I, 291–4; Dunlop, *James Kennedy*, 236–7.

[1] Scofield, I, 290–1; *Registrum Thome Bourgchier*, ed. F. R. H. Du Boulay (Canterbury and York Society, 1957), I, 100–3. The king's requests were presented by a delegation of seven royal councillors, including the earls of Worcester and Essex, and Lord Grey of Ruthyn as treasurer of England.

[2] According to Gregory, 221, who also says that the duke's men (who had formed the king's own bodyguard) were then sent to Newcastle as part of the garrison.

[3] Bittmann, *op. cit.*, 1061–5; Scofield, I, 293–4, 300–1; II, 461–2 (letter from William, Lord Hastings, to Jean de Lannoy, 7 August 1463).

[4] Bittmann, *op. cit.*, 1066.

[5] Hastings's letter, cited above.   [6] *RP*, V, 497–8.

the immediate danger over, he gave himself up to the pleasures of hunting at Fotheringhay, and later in August went south to Dover to confer with his ambassadors, led by the chancellor, George Nevill, who were about to depart for important negotiations with France and Burgundy at St Omer.[1] He was still publicly maintaining his intention to march against the Scots. From Fotheringhay he wrote on 15 August to the city fathers of Salisbury requesting that men should be sent to meet him at Newcastle on 13 September, and on 9 August orders were issued for the assembly of the king's ordnance. As late as 28 August preparations were still being made for the victualling of the 'king's fleet against Scotland'.[2] But though he moved north to York in September and remained in Yorkshire until January 1464, no further military operations of any kind were undertaken. Even the rebel strongholds in Northumberland passed the winter unmolested.

Exactly why Edward chose not to follow up the successes of the summer and to allow the Scots to go unpunished remains something of a mystery. Probably lack of money was the chief consideration: the larger part of the aid voted by parliament, and the subsidy from convocation, went to meet heavy obligations elsewhere, notably the payment of the Calais garrison.[3] In the first twenty-seven months of his reign, Edward had subsisted largely on loans, and his debts were now considerable. To mount a major military operation in the north against the rebel castles, let alone a campaign into Scotland, was almost certainly far beyond his resources. But these considerations were not apparent to his tax-paying subjects, and Edward's conduct of affairs did not escape sharp criticism. 'Gregory's Chronicle' remarks that although 'there was ordained a great navy and a great army both by water and by land', yet 'all was lost and in vain, and came to no purpose, neither by water nor by land'.[4] Still more pointedly, a clerical chronicler reported that the clergy resented the king's demands, some because they were too poor, others because the money was put to no good use. The king's great army, he adds, was intended for the subjugation of his foes by land and sea: 'but I know not what expedition it achieved'. The fleet had clung to the coast, consumed all its victuals, and achieved nothing. 'What a wretched outcome, shame and confusion!' (he concludes), reflecting a disillusion widely shared by Edward's subjects.[5] Public

[1] Hastings's letter, as above; and for the negotiations, Scofield, I, 294–307.
[2] R. Benson and H. Hatcher, *Old and New Sarum* (1843), 158; *CPR, 1461–7*, 280, 303.
[3] Scofield, I, 298, 309; and see further below, pp. 371–3.
[4] Gregory, 221.
[5] *Three Fifteenth-Century Chronicles*, 177.

resentment was sufficient to compel Edward in November to agree to a remission of £6,000 of the aid voted by parliament in the summer.[1]

Edward might also have pleaded that possession of the Northumbrian fortresses would be of little advantage to the Lancastrians if they could be deprived of foreign support; and throughout the autumn and winter of 1463 his main attention was devoted to the task of isolating the rebels diplomatically. The first improvement in England's hostile relations with her French and Scottish neighbours came in the autumn of 1463. The ageing Duke Philip of Burgundy had been endeavouring for some time to bring about a *rapprochement* between Edward and Louis XI, with himself as intermediary. Louis now saw little hope of a Lancastrian restoration, and had nothing to gain from continued hostility towards the House of York. He also wished to keep the duke of Burgundy in good humour in order to carry through his plan of buying back from Philip the strategically important Somme towns ceded to him in 1435. Early in 1463 he began to respond to Philip's overtures, and meanwhile refused to receive Jasper, earl of Pembroke, and John Fortescue, envoys sent to him by Henry VI to seek further French aid. The delay came rather from the English side. Still suspicious of Louis, and preoccupied with the events in the north, Edward did not finally give instructions to the embassy under Bishop George Nevill until 21 August. There followed a tripartite conference at St Omer, which ended in a convention between France and England signed at Hesdin on 8 October. This provided for a truce between the two countries on land, in ports and on rivers (though not at sea) to last until 1 October 1464. Each king undertook not to support the enemies of the other, and Louis specifically renounced all aid to Henry VI and the Lancastrians. He even went so far as to tell the English envoys that he would abandon the traditional French protection for Scotland. He would not object if Scotland were brought under English control, and would even help therein if it achieved a real understanding between himself and King Edward.[2]

The *détente* with France inevitably made more difficult the task of Bishop Kennedy and the party in Scotland still faithful to the Lancastrian cause. The pressure on Kennedy to come to terms with England had been mounting during the summer, when Edward's ally, the earl

---

[1] *RP*, V, 497–9, and below, pp. 348–9.
[2] Calmette and Perinelle, *op. cit.*, 40–7; Thielemans, *op. cit.*, 395–402; Scofield, I, 294–307; Bittmann, *op. cit.*, 1067–8. Louis's offer to help in the subjugation of Scotland is reported in a 'credence' from his Scots diplomatic agent, William Monypenny (Scofield, II, 469–70).

of Douglas, was doing great damage on the West March, and a full-scale English invasion was threatened. The news that Scotland had been abandoned by her chief ally caused great dismay throughout the realm, as Kennedy himself reported.[1] The bishop opened negotiations, and on 9 December a truce was concluded at York with the king of England. It was to last until 31 October 1464, and negotiations for a more permanent settlement were to begin at Newcastle in March 1464. Edward had to abandon his support for the rebel earl of Douglas, but he obtained from the Scots the all-important concession that as soon as safe-conducts then in force expired, no further aid or succour would be given to Henry VI, Margaret, Prince Edward and their adherents.[2]

The readiness with which the Scots came to terms after the conclusion of the truce with France may help to explain why Edward judged that a punitive war with Scotland was unnecessary as well as expensive, although it is unlikely that Edward's subjects saw things in the same light after the costly military preparations of the summer had come to nought. The government was now widely unpopular, and resentment was expressed in a new wave of disorder and disaffection larger in scale than at any time since the winter of 1461, particularly in regions with traditional Lancastrian sympathies. From this the die-hard rebels were not slow to profit. In January and early February exceptionally strong commissions of oyer and terminer were appointed to deal with disturbances in fifteen counties from Kent to Cornwall and northwards to Warwick and Leicester. On 26 January 1464 James Gresham reported from London to John Paston that the king had called up his retainers in all haste to ride with him through Sussex, Kent, Essex, Suffolk and Norfolk.[3]

Shortly afterwards, disturbances in Gloucestershire were serious enough to bring the king thither in person, in company with the two chief justices, to hold sessions of oyer and terminer against violators of the peace. A Gloucester annalist suggested that these sprang from a riot between the citizens of Gloucester and the men of the shire, but the government thought them treasonable: in thanking the mayor and corporation of Salisbury for their help, a royal signet letter spoke of certain persons 'blinded and deceived by the malicious labour and subtle imaginations of such as be adherent and favouring to our traitors

[1] Dunlop, *James Kennedy*, 238–9.
[2] *Loc. cit.*; *Foedera*, XI, 511. Margaret and her son had already left Scotland, but Henry VI was now transferred from the refuge Kennedy had provided to Bamborough Castle, probably by 8 December 1463, Scofield, I, 309 n. See also Kennedy's despatch in Waurin, ed. Dupont, III, 171.
[3] *CPR, 1461–7*, 303–4; *PL*, IV, 89.

and rebels'.[1] Also in February there were disturbances in Cambridge-shire. Risings in both North and South Wales and in Lancashire and Cheshire were more specifically treasonable and were very likely con-nected with the machinations of the duke of Somerset.[2] In spite of Edward's exceptional – and foolish – generosity to him, that nobleman had never abandoned his true loyalties to the House of Lancaster. From his refuge in North Wales he was already in touch with likely supporters, and reported to Henry VI in Bamborough that many of the chief men of Wales and others in the south and west were ready to rise on his behalf; and, in fact, a number of men from these regions were afterwards attainted for their treasonable activities at this time. To counter these dangers, Duke John of Norfolk was sent to Denbigh-shire to suppress traitors there, whilst in South Wales the vigorous Yorkist civil servant, John Donne, with the aid of Roger Vaughan, defeated the insurgents on 4 March 1464 at Dryslwyn, near Car-marthen.[3]

It is likely that the abortive insurrections in Wales and elsewhere were intended to coincide with military action in the north by the Lancastrian leaders. In December 1463, Somerset left North Wales with a few household retainers, and made for Newcastle, hoping to profit from the fact that Edward had placed in the garrison there many of his own men, who had been with him at Northampton in the pre-vious summer. But he was recognized and narrowly avoided arrest in Durham, escaping barefoot and in his shirt. Thus forewarned, the authorities in Newcastle were able to seize most of his supporters in the town before they could attempt any armed *coup*; but Edward now took the precaution of making Lord Scrope of Bolton captain of the town and stuffing it with more reliable men.[4] Somerset himself escaped to Bamborough, and there was soon joined by two other Lancastrians, whom Edward had hopefully pardoned and restored to favour, Sir Henry Bellingham and Sir Humphrey Nevill of Brancepeth. From Bamborough the rebels sent urgent appeals for help to the count of Charolais and the duke of Brittany. They also received a visit from Louis XI's agent, Guillaume de Cousinot, a fact which led the English government to believe that France was again actively interesting her-self in the Lancastrian cause. Henry VI told his foreign friends that he

---

[1] *PL*, IV, 88; 'Gloucester Annals', in Kingsford, *English Historical Literature*, 356, whose version is followed by J. G. Bellamy, 'Justice under the Yorkist Kings', *American Jour. of Legal History*, ix (1965), 136–7; R. Benson and H. Hatcher, *Old and New Sarum*, 159. Treason at Gloucester is also mentioned in *RP*, V, 499.   [2] *PL*, IV, 95–6.
[3] *Loc. cit.*; *RP*, V, 511–12; Waurin, ed. Dupont, III, 179 (Cousinot's memorandum of his instructions from Henry VI at Bamborough).   [4] Gregory, 223.

expected a Yorkist attack on the northern castles during the summer, but for the time being (February–March 1464) the rebels seemed to have faced no organized opposition in the north. They carried out a series of raids from Bamborough, took Norham Castle, and virtually controlled most of the country immediately south of the Scottish border. Further south again, in their homeland in the Yorkshire Dales, another staunch Lancastrian family, the Cliffords, gained possession of their chief castle at Skipton-in-Craven and declared for Henry VI.[1]

Edward had reacted to the outbreak of disaffection in the southern half of his realm with vigour and urgency, and he had no hesitation in proroguing the meeting of parliament, summoned for 20 February at York, on the grounds that his personal presence was needed in Gloucestershire. As usual, he was far less sensitive to similar developments in Wales and the far north. On leaving Cambridge in February, he had not turned north, but instead returned to London to conduct discussions with envoys from Castile and with Jean de Lannoy.[2] But the extension of rebel activities in the north, and the danger of sympathetic risings elsewhere, at last forced him to take action. Lancastrian activities also threatened the resumption of negotiations with the Scots. The meeting of envoys planned at Newcastle for 6 March was postponed to 20 April and, for safety's sake, was to take place in York. Montagu was despatched about mid-April to the Border to provide the Scots ambassadors with an escort through what had now become hostile territory. His small force successfully evaded an ambush laid near Newcastle by Sir Humphrey Nevill, but was then attacked by the main body of the rebels, led by Somerset, Lords Roos and Hungerford, and Sir Ralph Percy, at Hedgeley Moor, some nine miles from Alnwick. In this engagement (on or about 25 April) the rebels were routed and Sir Ralph Percy killed. Montagu met the Scots at Norham and brought them in safety to York.[3]

For more than a month before the fight at Hedgeley Moor, Edward had been making rather leisurely preparations to go north in person and lay siege to the Northumbrian castles. On 27 March he had publicly

<hr>

[1] Scofield, I, 312–18; Cousinot's memorandum in Waurin, ed. Dupont, III, 178–81, and additions printed by Scofield, II, 463–6. For Lancastrian control of Northumberland, E. Bateson, *History of Northumberland*, I (1893), 44–6. *Three Fifteenth-Century Chronicles*, 178 (for Cliffords).   [2] *RP*, V, 499; Scofield, I, 320–6.

[3] Gregory, 223–4. The only other contemporary source to mention the battle, the 'Brief Latin Chronicle' (*Three Fifteenth-Century Chronicles*, 178), gives 2 May as the date; but the chronology of this writer, who is critical of Edward and strongly pro-Nevill, is confused. He gives a leading role to Bishop George Nevill, who had been sent north to aid Warwick and Montagu in the negotiations (Scofield, I, 329).

announced his intention to proceed against them 'at the beginning of summer'.[1] His main problem was cash. The aid of 1463 had long since been spent, and he was forced into heavy borrowing, the pledging or sale of some of the royal jewels, and even more dubious expedients in order to raise funds.[2] He certainly showed little haste to betake himself to the north. In the middle of April he spent several days in Kent in the punishment of men responsible for further recent disturbances in the county. Parliament was then prorogued from 5 May to 26 November on the grounds of the king's preoccupation in the north. In a now familiar pattern, Warwick had already hurried on ahead, but not until 28 April did the king himself leave London. His journey was delayed for a few days by his secret marriage to Elizabeth Woodville on 1 May, and he then pushed on to Leicester, there to await the muster of his troops. Arrangements had already been put in hand to assemble a very substantial force fully equipped with siege artillery. Signet letters sent to individual lords and gentry and to borough corporations asked for the supply of troops, and the sheriffs of over thirty counties were directed to array all able-bodied men and have them ready to depart at twenty-four hours' notice.[3] As the troops converged on Leicester, good news came in from the north.

The rebels in Northumberland, probably seeking some local success before the main weight of the royal army was deployed against them, had pushed south from Alnwick into the Tyne valley, and had encamped in a meadow called the Linnels on the south side of the river some two miles from Hexham. This intelligence reached the energetic and courageous Lord Montagu twenty miles away in Newcastle. With the aid of Lords Greystoke and Willoughby, he set out at once with all available men, and on 15 May 1464 attacked the rebels in their encampment. His victory was complete, and especially welcome because almost all the leading rebels were either taken on the field or captured soon after. This was the prelude to a round of executions which virtually wiped out the surviving active Lancastrians still in England. The Nevills, left to themselves, had a far shorter way with rebels than their royal master. Somerset and four others were put to death by Montagu on the day of the battle. Lords Roos and Hungerford, Sir Thomas Findern and two others were executed at Newcastle two days later. Six or seven more were chopped at Warwick's castle of Middleham on 18

---

[1] *CCR, 1461-8*, 230.
[2] Scofield, I, 331, for his extensive borrowing; and see also below, p. 337.
[3] *PL*, IV, 101; *RP*, V, 500; Benson and Hatcher, *Old and New Sarum*, 159; *CPR, 1461-7*, 391; Rymer, *Foedera*, XI, 523.

May. A further fourteen captives had the dubious benefit of an official trial at York before the Constable of England, the earl of Worcester, and were executed in two batches on 25 and 28 May. To complete the round-up, the Lincolnshire rebel, Sir William Tailboys, was caught hiding in a coalpit on 20 July and beheaded at Newcastle, and some 3,000 marks of Lancastrian war-funds still in his possession disappeared into the pockets of Montagu's soldiers. Only Henry VI himself, who had not been at the battlefield, made good his escape from Bywell Castle and disappeared into hiding somewhere in the remote Pennines. Devoted Lancastrians were able to conceal their ageing, if not bonny, prince until his capture a year later.[1]

The defeat and decimation of the rebel forces at Hexham virtually scaled the fate of the Northumbrian castles. This time there was to be no let-off. As the victorious Montagu approached with a royal army and siege-train at his back, Alnwick capitulated without a fight on 23 June and Dunstanborough surrendered then or on the following day. Only Bamborough showed defiance. Here the two chief surviving rebels, Sir Ralph Grey and Sir Humphrey Nevill, were in command; and, since Edward was anxious to obtain the castle undamaged, an offer of pardon was made to the garrison, except its two commanders, if they surrendered at once. This Grey stubbornly refused to do, and thus provoked the only set siege with artillery and bombards in four years of fighting. The king's great guns, whose weight, value and power earned each its own name, such as *Newcastle*, *London* and *Dijon*, were brought into action, and battered the walls with their heavy fire. Grey himself was seriously wounded – *Dijon* is said to have 'smote through his chamber oftentimes' – and Sir Humphrey Nevill then arranged the surrender of the castle. This obdurate rebel even managed to win a pardon for himself, and only the injured Grey was brought for trial before the earl of Worcester at Doncaster, and paid the penalty for his sturdy defiance by execution on 10 July.[2]

Edward had played no direct part in these military successes, and was content to leave the conduct of operations in the hands of Montagu, who was now deservedly rewarded for his labours with promotion to the Earldom of Northumberland. Instead, the king preferred to remain

[1] Scofield, I, 333–4. For the executions, I have followed the details in Gregory, 225–6, and *Three Fifteenth Century Chronicles*, 79, 179, where the information suggests a common source in a newsletter of the time. Details of Henry VI's wanderings, his capture in Lancashire, 13 July 1465, and subsequent imprisonment in the Tower, are assembled by Scofield, I, 380–4.

[2] Warkworth, *Chronicle* (notes), 37–9, from a contemporary description in the College of Arms.

in York and take personal charge of negotiations with the Scots envoys escorted thither by Montagu. The fruit of his efforts was the signature on 1 June of a truce for fifteen years between the two realms, an agreement which Edward ratified on 11 June.[1] Thereafter he lingered apparently inactive in Yorkshire, whilst Montagu marched on the northern castles, but on 14 July the king appeared at Doncaster to persuade a diocesan synod to grant him a subsidy. Two days later he moved slowly south to Leicester, and the northern parts of his realm were not to see him again until he came as a prisoner to Middleham Castle five years later.[2]

The surrender of Bamborough at the end of June 1464 marks the end of the decisive phase in the Yorkist effort to master a stubborn and determined Lancastrian resistance. Henceforth, the cause of Henry VI could be of significance only when allied with powerful Yorkist dissidents. In the fighting since Towton, Edward had shown clearly that he did not cast himself in the role of conventional warrior-king. Of the four major expeditions involved – three to the north, and one into Wales – Edward had set out for all, and signally failed to arrive. The main burden of defence had been borne by Warwick and Montagu in the north and Herbert in Wales. The king's failure to take the field was criticized by some of his contemporaries and some modern writers, and seen as a sign of laziness and an excessive concern with his own pleasures.[3] But it is doubtful whether events would have been different had Edward conducted his operations in person. His lieutenants were willing and competent enough. More serious were mistakes of judgement and policy, particularly his excessive clemency to his opponents. Men like Somerset, Percy and Humphrey Nevill were not only spared their lives and repeatedly pardoned, but were given the opportunity to make more mischief. Decisions like that to return the Northumbrian castles to the care of Sir Ralph Percy in December 1462, or the failure to reduce them in the summer of 1463, remain hard to justify. They provide at least part of the explanation why a comparatively small group of rebels was able to remain active for so long, even if it never attracted much general support from the country at large, whilst the foreign backing it received was grudging and largely ineffective.

The king's absence from the campaigns and sieges of these early

---

[1] Rymer, *Foedera*, XI, 525, 527. [2] Scofield, I, 338, and below, p. 135.
[3] 'Brief Latin Chronicle' in *Three Fifteenth-Century Chronicles*, 177–8; Commynes, I, 203; II, 334; Ramsay, *Lancaster and York*, II, 305, who comments: 'The Nevills had done the work: the young King, self-indulgent and fond of pleasure, had contributed little since the day of Towton to his own success.'

years was due less to laziness or a distaste for war than to his own sense of priorities. Like his great rival, Louis XI, he saw his place as being very much at the centre of government, and already the exercise of his personal energy was doing much to revitalize the administration of the realm. For Edward the management of peers, parliament and people was an essential part of successful kingship, and the records of these years show how active he was in the conduct of business.[1] The close supervision of his foreign relations with Burgundy, France and Scotland was also very much a matter of intimate personal concern. From all this he did not wish to be distracted except in times of emergency. Above all it was important to consolidate his grip on the heartland of England, whatever the danger on the borders. Against these concerns rebel activity in the far west and north seemed less important, especially if deprived of French or Scottish assistance. Events justified this analysis of the situation.

All this contains a further implication. Bishop Kennedy's description of the mighty earl of Warwick as 'governor of the realm of England beneath King Edward' implies a certain contempt for the authority of the young king; and the belief that Warwick was the real ruler of England was shared then and later by Louis XI until he ruefully discovered his mistake.[2] The illusion has been perpetuated by recent writers. 'Warwick' (we have been told) 'governed in the saddle from the periphery of the realm.'[3] But the whole pattern of Edward's activities in these years suggests that he was very much king in fact as well as in name. Warwick remained invaluable: energetic, influential and self-important, he was allowed every freedom to act on the king's behalf. It is not altogether surprising that his prominence in the defence of the north and later in diplomatic activity gave foreigners a false impression of his importance. Informed Englishmen probably had no such illusions. Warwick's great influence was a factor of the king's permissiveness. Its continuance depended on the continuing identity of interest between the young king and his greatest subject.

[1] See below, pp. 302–7, 399–402.
[2] Waurin, ed. Dupont, III, 173–4. In March 1464 the governor of Abbeville reported to Louis that in England 'they have but two rulers – M. de Warwick and another, whose name I have forgotten' (*ibid.*, 184).
[3] P. M. Kendall, *op. cit.*, 97. In fact – so far as the witness lists to royal charters are a reliable guide – Warwick was more often at court than away from it. He attests no less than 41 of the 46 charters granted by Edward in the period 1461–6, and only William, Lord Hastings, compares with Warwick in this respect. (P.R.O., C. 53/191–194.) Elsewhere, however, Kendall allows that Edward was less of a puppet on Warwick's string (e.g. p. 146).

Chapter 4

THE ESTABLISHMENT OF THE
YORKIST REGIME

An important and necessary consequence of the change of dynasty in 1461 was a large-scale redistribution of political power at the regional and local level. Successful government in the localities depended upon the active cooperation of the nobility and their connections and well-wishers among the knights and gentry; but at Edward's accession a majority of these, especially amongst the higher nobility, was more or less Lancastrian in sympathy. The local influence and traditional loyalties commanded by these families had to be challenged, and political authority in the shires placed in reliable hands. The problem was the more acute because aristocratic influence had increased sharply during the weak rule of Henry VI.

Characteristically, Edward IV saw the solution to this problem essentially in terms of men and not of institutions. He never contemplated any systematic attack on private power as such, and was not concerned with the potential dangers of 'bastard feudalism' which have so alarmed some modern scholars.[1] In his eyes no subject could be over-mighty so long as he enjoyed the royal confidence. An expectation of loyalty and a readiness to serve were the conditions upon which he gave his confidence and delegated local authority. For key positions (as we shall see) something more was required, generally an association with the House of York going back before 1461, or a combination of ability and personal friendship with the king. High birth, or even a close connection with the royal family by blood or marriage, was not in itself a sufficient recommendation, as may be seen from the meagre employments and rewards given to men such as Edward's brother-in-law, John de la Pole, duke of Suffolk, and to some members of the queen's family. At a lower level of political responsibility, however, Edward was quite willing to make use of men whatever their past political record had been.

From the outset of his reign Edward invested a heavy political capital

[1] On this point, see below, pp. 412–13.

in a policy of conciliation. Even men who had had close personal association with the households of Henry VI and Margaret of Anjou were given a chance – often more than one – to enter the service of the new king. So, too, were the trimmers, the doubters, and the passive Lancastrian sympathizers. Past loyalties were ignored in the hope of future commitment. Such clemency fits well with what we know of Edward's easy-going temperament, and was continued even after 1471 when he had far more provocation to indulge motives of revenge with much less risk.[1] His record of mercy to his enemies is quite remarkable in a ruthless age. But clemency was also dictated by policy, by the need to widen the basis of support for his regime, especially among the baronage. On the whole the policy was only partially successful. We have already seen, in the careers of men like Sir Ralph Percy and Sir Humphrey Nevill, the risks involved in trusting active Lancastrians. The behaviour of Henry Beaufort, duke of Somerset, is a prime example of ingratitude. Following his surrender at Bamborough in December 1462, Edward made every effort to win over this prominent rebel, whose conversion would have an obvious propaganda value. He became the king's close companion, sharing the royal chamber, and going out hunting with him when three out of his six attendants were the duke's retainers. Later, he was made captain of the king's bodyguard. Edward even mounted a great tournament at Westminster so that Somerset might 'see some manner sport of chivalry after his great labour and heaviness'. In March 1463 he was given a general pardon, and later, in parliament, was restored to his 'name, state, title, and dignity', and recovered all his lands, together with money advanced by the king for his immediate needs, and an annuity of £220.[2] But none of this prevented Somerset from defecting at the earliest opportunity.

Nor did Edward have any better success with the de Vere family, earls of Oxford. Following the execution for high treason of the 12th earl, John, and his eldest son, Aubrey, in February 1462, the latter's younger brother, John, was allowed to succeed; and in January 1464 had licence to enter on all his lands without making proof of his age. In May 1465 he was made a Knight of the Bath at the queen's coronation. Committed to the Tower in November 1468, on suspicion of plotting against the king, he was nevertheless released, and pardoned in April 1469, only to join Warwick and Clarence in their rebellion in July.[3] Edward's generosity to the Courtenay and Hungerford families

---

[1] See below, pp. 183-4.
[2] Gregory, 219; *RP*, V, 511; Scofield, I, 273-4, 292.
[3] *CP*, X, 239-40; Lander, 'Attainder and Forfeiture', 131.

met a similar response. Henry Courtenay, brother of the attainted earl of Devon, was allowed a generous share of the forfeited estates.[1] Thomas Hungerford, son of the attainted Robert, Lord Hungerford, who continued in arms against the king, not only escaped attainder himself, but was pardoned in November 1462, knighted not long after, and permitted to recover some of his lands. Provision was also made for his mother, Eleanor, and her three younger children, and for his grandmother, Margaret.[2] But both the young lords became involved in conspiracy in 1468, and were eventually executed for treason in the king's presence at Salisbury in 1469, though rumour had it at the time that their downfall owed something to the machinations of Edward's favourite, Humphrey Stafford.[3] William, Viscount Beaumont, was yet another defector. After his father had been killed fighting for Henry VI at Northampton, he was allowed to enter on his inheritance. He then joined Margaret at Towton, and on 21 December 1461 was attainted. But two days later, 'in consideration of the approach of Christmas', he was pardoned, an act of personal generosity by the king. This time, however, he was not permitted to recover his lands, which passed to buttress the midland influence of the powerful William, Lord Hastings. In 1470 this disinherited lord joined the Lancastrians, and remained a die-hard exile until imprisoned in 1474 for the remaining few years of Yorkist rule.[4] The unreliability of such men was at least one of the reasons why in the first years of the reign Edward was compelled to delegate extensive authority to a comparatively small group of Yorkists on whose loyalty he could depend.

The extent of Edward's desire for general conciliation emerges clearly from his treatment of the baronage at the outset of the reign. In the parliament of 1461 sentences of attainder were passed against 113 persons for their share in the fighting of 1459–61.[5] These included fourteen lay peers. Seven of them had already died in battle or under the executioner's axe. Six others were still actively hostile and in arms with Margaret of Anjou.[6] Much more remarkable, however, is the

---

[1] CPR, 1461-7, 119, 429; and 533, 572, for his appearance on commissions of array and piracy in 1466.
[2] CP, VI, 621; Cal. Inquisitions Post Mortem, IV, 344, 348; CPR, 1461-7, 181, 284, 363-6; CFR, 1461-71, 216.
[3] See below, pp. 123-4.   [4] CPR, 1452-61, 632; 1461-7, 86.
[5] Lander, 'Attainder and Forfeiture', 124 (excluding the defenders of Harlech and those provisionally attainted).
[6] The dead were the earls of Devon, Northumberland and Wiltshire, and Lords Clifford, Nevill, Dacre of Gilsland and Welles; the active rebels were the dukes of Somerset and Exeter, the earl of Pembroke, and Lords Hungerford, Roos and Rougemont-Grey. The other peer was William, Viscount Beaumont, for whom see above.

number of peers who were not attainted, even though they had fought against Edward. Among them were the young John, earl of Shrewsbury, whose father had been killed on the wrong side at Northampton, and had himself been at Towton; John, Lord Lovel, who had fought against the Yorkists in 1459 and 1460; Edward's future kinsmen by marriage, Richard, Lord Rivers, and Anthony, Lord Scales, both taken prisoner at Towton, but pardoned in July 1461, and Lords Grey of Codnor and Willoughby, with similar records. Two North-Country lords, FitzHugh and Greystoke, who seem to have been rather unwilling Lancastrians in spite of their presence in Margaret's army in January 1461, soon came to enjoy Edward's confidence; and a third, Thomas, Lord Scrope of Masham, whose record was also rather dubious, likewise escaped attainder, but was evidently not trusted for some years.[1]

Edward was no less generous to his non-noble opponents. In 1461 sentences of attainder were passed against ninety-six men of the rank of knight or below. Many were quite humble people, yeomen or clerks who had held minor offices in the household of Henry VI, but they include at least twenty-four who had sat in parliament, and a number of other prominent gentry. Some were already dead, others were to lose their lives in the fighting of the next three years, and others again remained die-hard Lancastrians in exile. But even prominent Lancastrians who continued in arms against the king could make their peace if they wished. A good example is the Northamptonshire knight, Thomas Tresham, whom Edward had every reason to view with disfavour. In 1455 he had been blamed by the Yorkists as one of 'the solicitors and causers' of the First Battle of St Albans; he had served as controller of Henry VI's household; and in 1459 he had been speaker of the vindictive Coventry Parliament which had attainted Edward himself and the Yorkist group. On 6 March 1461, two days after

[1] For the political activities of these peers, see *CP*, V, 428 (FitzHugh); VI, 130-1 (Grey of Codnor), 198 (Greystoke); VIII, 223 (Lovel); XI, 20, 22 (Rivers and Scales), 569 (Scrope of Masham), 706 (Shrewsbury). John, 2nd earl of Shrewsbury, killed at Northampton, was several times described in official documents as a rebel (e.g. *CPR, 1461-7*, 30), but his son, John, 3rd earl, was allowed whilst still a minor to enter on all his lands in August 1464, except those granted to and retained by William, Lord Herbert (below, p. 78, n. 2). Lancastrian suspicions of the loyalties of FitzHugh (who had married Warwick's sister, Alice Nevill) and of Greystoke (FitzHugh's brother-in-law) are recorded by *Annales*, 775-6, but though both seem to have marched south with Margaret and fought at St Albans, they were soon trusted by Edward (e.g. commission to Greystoke, 13 May 1461, to arrest and try rebels, *CPR, 1461-7*, 30) and they acted as triers of petitions in the 1461 parliament. Willoughby (whose father was killed at Towton) and Grey of Codnor had alsc fought with the queen at St Albans, but both were soon serving King Edward.

Edward's accesssion, a price of £100 was set on his head.[1] Yet in March 1464 he was pardoned his life, and in 1467 was elected to parliament as knight of the shire for Northamptonshire. There he secured the reversal of his attainder on the ground that he had been brought up in the service of Henry VI since his early youth, and knew no other loyalty, and (as he further pleaded) his official position gave him no choice but to fight at Second St Albans and Towton.[2] But he was not restored to his estates, and had to work his way back into the king's favour. The process of recovering his lands by purchase left him saddled with debt and disillusionment, and he became involved in Lancastrian plots which landed him in prison in 1468.[3]

Yet as with the lay peers, the number of gentry attainted is less remarkable than the many who might have been but were not. In May 1461, for example, Edward ordered the seizure of the lands of twenty lords and gentry of Northamptonshire on grounds of their treason, but only six of these were later attainted or finally deprived of their lands.[4] Nor was anything done to disinherit the heirs of several men who had died fighting against the Yorkists at Towton or elsewhere.[5] It was also very much easier for families to secure the reversal of sentences of attainder, and hence to recover their estates, under Edward IV than it was to be under Henry VII, who used attainders as a system of political control.[6]

The parliamentary attainders of 1461 brought into the king's hands

[1] CCR, 1461–8, 56.

[2] J. S. Roskell, 'Sir Thomas Tresham, Knight', *Northamptonshire Past and Present*, ii, no. 6 (1959), 313–23, and his *Commons and their Speakers in English Parliaments, 1376–1523* (Manchester, 1965), 110–11, 263–6, 270, 282–3, 368–9.

[3] Lander, 'Attainder and Forfeiture', 139–40; Roskell, *Speakers*, 282. Inevitably, Tresham supported the Readeption in 1470–71, and was executed after the Battle of Tewkesbury.

[4] CPR, 1461–7, 35. Of those not attainted, some remained under suspicion: e.g. Richard III's future councillor, Sir William Catesby, who fought with Henry VI at Northampton and Towton, did not obtain a pardon by making a fine until 22 December 1461 (*ibid.*, 35, 120), and does not reappear on the Northamptonshire commissions of the peace until 1465. For his close Lancastrian associations before Edward's accession, see J. S. Roskell, 'William Catesby, Councillor to Richard III', *Bull. John Rylands Library*, xlii (1959), 145–74.

[5] E.g. Sir Ralph Bygod, sometimes styled Lord Mauley, was killed at Towton, and might therefore have been attainted, but his son was allowed to succeed to his estates (*CPR, 1461–7*, 228–9). Bygod and Catesby (see previous note) appear with many others in a list of attainted persons quoted by *Annales*, 778–9: this was probably a draft list from which names were afterwards removed – hence his total of 150 names.

[6] Lander, 'Attainder and Forfeiture', 144–5; 'Bonds, coercion, and fear', 333–5. See also 'Attainder and Forfeiture', 141, for Edward's generosity to the wives and families of attainted persons.

a great conglomeration of lands and offices, together worth many thousands of pounds annually.[1] Along with the hundreds of offices of which Edward could dispose as king, or as duke of Lancaster or duke of York, these provided the means for Edward to enrich and aggrandize his supporters and thereby to strengthen their own and his influence in the shires. The early months of the reign saw the beginning of a series of grants which continued almost undiminished for the first four years of the reign until the resources of patronage had almost been used up. From the pattern of this flow of patronage it is possible to derive some indication of Edward's political objectives and of his relationship with particular individuals or groups within the baronage and gentry.

Most of his supporters expected some kind of reward in proportion to their rank or the value of their services, and few went wholly unsatisfied. Yet some had long to wait or got surprisingly little. For example, Edmund, Lord Grey of Ruthyn, whose opportune treachery had done much to bring about the Yorkist victory at Northampton, got no lands from Edward, and, although briefly enjoying the lucrative office of treasurer of England from June 1463 to November 1464, had to wait until May 1466 before the king created him earl of Kent. Similarly, Richard Fiennes, Lord Dacre of the South, received little tangible reward for his services, even though in 1462 he was said to be, along with Hastings, 'now greatest about the the king's person', and was clearly then and later close to Edward. The king's cousin, William FitzAlan, earl of Arundel, and his brother-in-law, John de la Pole, duke of Suffolk, likewise received virtually nothing from their royal kinsman.[2] It may be said in criticism of Edward that a disproportionately large amount of his patronage went to a comparatively small group of men. Some, already powerful, were made even more so; others, of relatively humble origins, were newly elevated into magnate status by royal policy. It is arguable that Edward might have obtained

[1] Professor Lander's guess that they were worth nearly £18,000 a year (*op. cit.*, 147) is certainly too low. My own estimate, the evidence for which cannot be detailed here, would be of the order of £30,000.

[2] *PL*, IV, 61. All Dacre received in the early years of the reign were the lands claimed by his wife, Joan, as heir general of her attainted grandfather, Thomas, Lord Dacre. Although initially substantial (12 manors in Cumberland, 2 in Westmorland, 4 in Lancashire, and 1 in Lincolnshire), this grant was eroded by properties given to her sister-in-law, Eleanor, and the claims of the heir male, Humphrey Dacre; and ultimately Fiennes got only 4 manors (*CPR*, *1461-7*, 140; *1467-77*, 26, 96; *RP*, VI, 43-5; *CP*, IV, 8). For the meagre rewards of Arundel and Suffolk, see *CPR*, *1461-7*, 15, 42, 435, 512, 547: compare the rewards of Warwick and Hastings mentioned below, pp. 70-1, 75.

better dividends from his investment of political capital if his patronage had been spread more widely and evenly. He was dangerously dependent on a Yorkist aristocratic group, which was ultimately torn to pieces by quarrels amongst its members, whilst the rank-and-file of the nobility had been given little tangible inducement to support his rule.[1]

To some extent Edward's deployment of patronage may have been influenced by his personal likes and dislikes, but for the most part its purpose was primarily political, in that it was aimed at securing future service rather than rewarding past loyalty. His generosity to his principal supporter, Richard Nevill, earl of Warwick, however, set that nobleman's rewards in a class apart. His debt to his political mentor and ally was clearly great, but it was munificently repaid. To list Warwick's dignities and rewards in detail would involve an excessively lengthy catalogue. The more important, however, included the great chamberlainship of England; the office of captain of Calais, Guines and Hammes; the constableship of Dover Castle and wardenship of the Cinque Ports (with a fee of £300); the wardenship of both the East and West Marches towards Scotland; the chief stewardship of the Duchy of Lancaster in both north and south parts, and the stewardship of the Duchy Honours in Lancashire and Cheshire, Pontefract, Knaresborough and Pickering in Yorkshire, and Tutbury in the midlands; and the office of Admiral of England, Ireland and Aquitaine. In addition, he was granted eight substantial manors and lordships forfeited from the Percy family in Yorkshire, and all the Westmorland estates of John, Lord Clifford, together with other lands in the counties of Buckingham, Worcester and Warwick. He was also given custody of the lands of his idiot uncle, George Nevill, Lord Latimer, and of important lordships in the Marches of Wales belonging to the duke of Buckingham and the earl of Shrewsbury. Further valuable grants to the earl continued to be made until the very eve of his rebellion in February 1469.[2] Some of these grants did no more than confirm Warwick in offices which he or his father had held under Henry VI, or had acquired during his period of control of government in 1460. Others can be seen as a means of strengthening his position in the vulnerable north of England, in line with Edward's policy of entrusting great power in the regions to his chief supporters. Such justifications, how-

[1] T. B. Pugh, 'The Magnates, Knights and Gentry', in *Fifteenth-Century England*, 107–9. For the lack of a strong Yorkist affinity amongst the gentry, see below, pp. 329–30.
[2] For details and references, see Appendix III.

ever, do not dispel the impression that Edward was excessively generous and Warwick excessively greedy. For the earl was already by far the richest of Edward's subjects in his own right. Yet he appropriated for himself a disproportionately large share of the most valuable offices at the king's disposal and continued to acquire more as the reign wore on. No wonder contemporaries, even on the Continent, commented on his wealth and rapacity: 'his insatiable mind could not be content and yet before him was there none in England of the half possessions that he had', as one chronicler roundly remarked.[1]

Even by the standards of an acquisitive age Warwick appears exceptionally grasping. His private greed is well illustrated by his efforts to expand his territorial influence not merely in the north of England but also in South Wales, where he sought to get control of the duke of Buckingham's lordships adjoining his own Marcher holdings of Glamorgan and Abergavenny. Here, however, his ambitions ran counter to Edward's own plans. Once the king had decided to make William, Lord Herbert, his principal lieutenant in South Wales, he did not hesitate to override the grants to Warwick. Only four days after custody of the Buckingham lordships had been given to the earl, effective control was transferred to William Herbert. This rebuff may well have marked the beginning of the enmity between the earl and the rising Welshman who had once served him as sheriff of Glamorgan and who soon became the dominant force in South Wales.[2] Similarly, Edward had no scruple in replacing Warwick by William, Lord Hastings, as steward of the Duchy of Lancaster's Honour of Leicester, in order to strengthen the latter's influence in the midland shires.[3] These actions, so early in the reign, are a very clear indication that Edward intended to be master where his own plans for government were at stake, and that his indulgence to his powerful cousin's ambition had definite limits.

The remarkable series of grants to Warwick by no means exhausted the king's generosity to the Nevill family. The earl's brother, George Nevill, was the only prelate to benefit substantially from the change of

[1] 'Hearne's Fragment', in *Chronicles of the White Rose of York*, 23; Commynes, I, 192–3.
[2] For details, see T. B. Pugh, *Glamorgan County History*, III, 197–8. It is worth noticing that Warwick took care to grant himself the wardship of these Stafford lands when the chance came during the Readeption, and rewarded himself with most of Herbert's Welsh offices after the latter's death at Edgecote (*CPR, 1467–77*, 165; and below, p. 133).
[3] Somerville, *History of the Duchy of Lancaster*, I, 564. This and other offices had been given to Warwick for life on 10 November 1460, but were granted to Hastings for life on 4 July 1461, and in tail male 7 March 1466.

dynasty. The young and talented bishop of Exeter had been appointed chancellor in July 1460, during the period of Warwick's dominance, but was confirmed in office six days after Edward's accession. On 15 March 1465 he was translated to the archbishopric of York, the first major see to become available to the king. He was also given a series of valuable wardships, notably of nineteen manors belonging to John de Vere, earl of Oxford, in July 1463.[1] Warwick's uncle, William Nevill, Lord Fauconberg, was promoted to the earldom of Kent on 30 June 1461, and appointed steward of the royal household on the same day. On 1 August 1462 he was granted some fifty-six manors in the West Country forfeited from the earls of Devon and Wiltshire.[2] Only Warwick's youngest surviving brother, John Nevill, remained for a time something of a poor relation. Though created Lord Montagu in 1461, it was not until his northern victories of 1464 that he was rewarded with the title of earl of Northumberland (27 May) and a grant of almost all the Percy estates in Northumberland, which were worth in excess of £700 yearly.[3]

The Nevills apart, it is possible to distinguish a group of about a dozen peers who came to enjoy the king's special confidence in the early years of the reign, and were the chief props of his power. His confidence was not, of course, confined to lords alone, and the vital part played in government and administration by non-noble laymen will be discussed elsewhere.[4] The distinction between lords and gentry is, in any case, blurred by the fact that so many of the new Yorkist nobility had risen from the ranks of the gentry, and were promoted and enriched by Edward himself. But it was the lords whose support was politically decisive, especially in terms of regional and local influence and the capacity to raise troops when needed. Some were important chiefly for the regional power entrusted to them. Others held major official positions. Nearly all were prominent members of the royal council. It is significant that the majority of them were Edward's own creations. In 1461 he created seven new barons and six more were summoned to parliament as barons before his deposition in 1470. Four of these new titles were for the benefit of the sons of existing peers, but the remainder were promotions of gentry.[5] Amongst these latter, all

[1] *CPR, 1461–7*, 25, 105, 122, 151–2, 287.   [2] *Ibid.*, 225.
[3] *Ibid.*, 332, 340–1. He had previously been given custody of the king's mines in Devon and Cornwall, and nine manors forfeited from the Beaumont family (*ibid.*, 19, 195).
[4] See below, pp. 322–8.
[5] The peers' sons were Humphrey Bourchier, Lord Cromwell (son of Essex), Thomas FitzAlan, Lord Maltravers (son of Arundel), William Herbert, Lord Dunster (son of

of whom had some previous connection with the House of York, were several who were to become Edward's most powerful and trusted lieutenants. These were the core of the new Yorkist nobility, the king's friends against whom the dissident Warwick fulminated in 1469. A brief consideration of their careers will show what manner of men Edward chose to rely upon and how they rose to power in the uneasy politics of his first decade.

Of all Edward's councillors, none stood closer to him personally than Sir William Hastings. Their relationship was based on mutual trust and affection and compatibility of taste. Royal confidence in Hastings was repaid by a lifetime of personal devotion. Hastings left behind him an enviable reputation for loyalty and uprightness: he was, according to Sir Thomas More, 'an honourable man, a good knight and a gentle . . . a loving man, and passing well-beloved', a man who preferred to be buried at Westminster alongside his royal master rather than beside his wife near his home at Ashby de la Zouch. Despite his wealth and the high favour he enjoyed throughout the reign, he made remarkably few enemies. Those who intrigued against him, like the queen and some of her kinsmen, were moved primarily by his influence over, and intimacy with, his royal master.[1]

There is abundant contemporary testimony as to his special standing with the king throughout the reign. In part this derived from his appointment as king's chamberlain in the summer of 1461 (an office he held until Edward died), which gave him control over all who wished to have access to the king.[2] Already in 1462 the Pastons believed him to be greatest in influence with the king, an opinion repeated in 1470 by Philippe de Commynes, and afterwards echoed by Sir Thomas More.[3] Writing in 1483, Dominic Mancini placed him with Archbishop

---

Lord Herbert), and William Lovel, Lord Morley (son of William, Lord Lovel). The gentry ennobled were William, Lord Hastings, William, Lord Herbert, Humphrey, Lord Stafford of Southwick, Walter Devereux, Lord Ferrers, John, Lord Wenlock, Robert, Lord Ogle, Thomas, Lord Lumley (all in 1461), Walter Blount, Lord Mountjoy (1465), John, Lord Dinham (1467) and John, Lord Howard (1470). See T. B. Pugh in *Fifteenth-Century England*, 116–17, for a useful list of Edward's peerage creations.

[1] For Hastings's character, see More, *Richard III*, 10–11, 52, 226; Mancini, 69, 89, *CC*, 564–5; *GC*, 231; for his will, W. H. Dunham, *Lord Hastings' Indentured Retainers*, 17–18.

[2] A. L. Brown, 'The Authorization of Letters under the Great Seal', *BIHR*, xxxvii (1964), 149. His constant presence at court is revealed by the frequency with which he witnesses royal charters (P.R.O., C. 53/191–4).

[3] *PL*, IV, 61; Commynes, I, 201; More, *Richard III*, 10–11 ('for the great favour the king bare him').

Rotherham and Bishop Morton of Ely in a triumvirate which 'helped more than other counsellors to form the king's policy, and besides carried it out', and even goes so far as to describe him as 'the author of the sovereign's public policy' as well as being 'the accomplice and partner of his privy pleasures'.[1] In 1472 a Paston correspondent remarked that 'what my said lord chamberlain may do with the King and with all the lords of England, I trow it be not unknown to you most of any one man alive'.[2] This view was shared by many shrewd and hard-headed contemporaries. An impressive list of English lords and ladies, bishops, abbots and gentry paid him annuities or gave him profitable sinecures, and thought it money well spent to engage his influence with the king. The company includes even the earl of Warwick himself in the first decade of the reign. In cash alone these annuities yielded Hastings well over £200 a year after 1471.[3] It is also worth noticing that Hastings was able to engage the services of a powerful retinue without (as was usual) paying them cash fees: the promise of his 'good lordship' was sufficient.[4] Hastings heads the list of English notables whom Louis XI of France thought it prudent to have in his pay in 1475, with a pension of 2,000 crowns, and he was by then already receiving a pension of 1,000 crowns from Duke Charles of Burgundy.[5]

Born about 1431, Sir William came of a substantial gentry family with lands in Yorkshire and Leicestershire, which had a remarkable record of service to the House of York over four generations.[6] William followed his father, Sir Leonard, in the retinue of Duke Richard and was with him at the Rout of Ludford. He joined Edward on his march from Mortimer's Cross to London, and, along with two other new barons of 1461, Humphrey Stafford and Walter Devereux, was knighted by him on the field of Towton. Edward soon showed his high regard for Hastings, and his determination to increase the power of a trusted

[1] Mancini, 69.

[2] PL, V, 148 (James Arblaster, writing on behalf of the duchess of Norfolk).

[3] Dugdale, Baronage of England, I, 581–3 (from the Hastings family papers); Hist. MSS Comm. Reports, MSS of R. R. Hastings, I (1928), 99, 271–2, 302; Lander, 'Council, Administration and Councillors, 1461 to 1485', BIHR, xxxii (1959), 163. Warwick's appointment of Hastings on 2 April 1468 as steward of all his lordships in Leicester, Rutland and Northampton may have been an attempt to salvage something of his waning influence with Edward.

[4] Dunham, op. cit., 41, 47 ff.

[5] Calmette and Perinelle, Louis XI et l'Angleterre, 215; Hist. MSS Comm. Reports, Hastings, I, 301 (wrongly dated to 1461 instead of 1471).

[6] For the family background and early career of Hastings, see Dugdale, op. cit., I, 579–80; CP, VI, 370–71; Dunham, op. cit., 19–21, and references there cited.

supporter in the troubled and disaffected midland counties. As early as 5 April 1461 he was a member of the king's council, and on 13 June he was summoned to parliament as a baron.[1] On 8 May he was made receiver-general of the Duchy of Cornwall for life; a fortnight later he received the profitable position of master of the mint for twelve years; and he was already king's chamberlain when appointed chamberlain of North Wales on 31 July.[2] Before February 1462 he was of sufficient importance to make an advantageous match with Warwick's sister, Katharine Nevill, widow of William Bonville, Lord Harington.

Meanwhile, his territorial power in the midlands was being built up steadily. In July 1461 Edward appointed him for life to an important group of Duchy of Lancaster offices in the shires of Leicester, Warwick and Northampton, and, with his brother Ralph, he was already constable of the royal castle of Rockingham and held other offices in Northamptonshire.[3] On 17 February 1462 he was given very large estates in Leicestershire, Lincolnshire and Rutland, from the newly-forfeited lands of James, earl of Wiltshire, William, Viscount Beaumont, and Thomas, Lord Roos, and further substantial grants of land in the midlands followed in 1464 and 1469.[4] His local influence was increased by the several stewardships of land given him by private persons, and his own purchases of property in this area.[5] The value of this midland connection was to be proved during the troubles of 1469–71, especially in Leicestershire, formerly a strongly Lancastrian area, but where Hastings now had 'the whole rule' of the county: it was from these regions that Hastings produced the three thousand retainers who were the first substantial reinforcements to join Edward in his bid to recapture the throne.[6]

The rise of Sir William Herbert is even more spectacular than that of Hastings. This son of Sir William ap Thomas of Raglan Castle in Monmouthshire, by Gwladys Ddu, daughter of Sir Dafydd Gam, was the first Welshman since the Edwardian conquest to achieve a high

---

[1] The creation is discussed in *CP*, V, 370 n., where it is assumed that he (and William Herbert) were specially created some time before their summons to parliament on 26 July 1461. In fact, his creation seems to date from his summons by individual writ on 13 June (*CCR, 1461–68*, 61).

[2] Lander, 'Council, Administration and Councillors', 168; *CPR, 1461–7*, 9, 26, 130.

[3] Somerville, *op. cit.*, I, 564; *CPR, 1461–7*, 13. Both grants are wrongly dated in *CP*, V, 471.

[4] *CPR, 1461–7*, 103–4 (Roos lands, etc.); 353 (honours of Peverell, Boulogne and Haughley, 1464); *ibid.*, *1467–77*, 154 (stewardship of Fotheringhay, Northants, 1469).

[5] Dugdale, *op. cit.*, I, 180–3; *Hist. MSS Comm. Reports, Hastings*, I, 296.

[6] *Arrivall*, 8–9; *VCH, Leicestershire*, III, 100.

position in English politics and to penetrate the upper ranks of the
English aristocracy. He came to command a power in Wales never
seen before, and only briefly matched again. As one Welsh poet aptly
described him, he was 'King Edward's master-lock' in Wales.[1] His
employment as a virtual viceroy in Wales marks a departure from the
policy of earlier English kings in relying on an alien and largely absentee
English aristocracy for the government of that country.

In the 1450s Herbert had been both the earl of Warwick's sheriff of
Glamorgan and the duke of York's constable and steward in his
Marcher lordships of Usk, Caerleon, Dinas and Ewyas Lacy.[2] Wooed
by the Lancastrian government in its attempt to increase its influence
in the Marches, Herbert had actually benefited from the Rout of
Ludford, but never abandoned his Yorkist sympathies. After Northampton he joined the rebel earls and sat in the parliament of 1460 as
MP for Herefordshire. In February 1461 he rallied to Edward's
standard at Gloucester, fought at Mortimer's Cross, and marched with
him to London. Like Hastings he was summoned as a baron by writ of
13 June 1461.

At this time the opportunities for a redistribution of power in South
Wales were quite exceptional. The attainder of the Lancastrian Prince
of Wales brought into Edward's hands all the lands of the Principality,
and that of Jasper Tudor brought the earldom of Pembroke. For the
first time the lordships of the House of York were at the Crown's
disposal, whilst the accident of three minorities (of Henry Stafford,
duke of Buckingham, John Mowbray, duke of Norfolk, and John Talbot, earl of Shrewsbury) placed every other important lordship in
South Wales under the king's control, save for Warwick's possession of
Glamorgan and Abergavenny. Beginning with his appointment as
chief justice and chamberlain of South Wales on 8 May 1461, Herbert
was soon invested by Edward with a tremendous agglomeration of
land, office and influence in South Wales. After 1463 his power was
gradually extended into North Wales also.[3] Not even Warwick enjoyed
so complete a delegation of royal power in any one region. So great
was Edward's confidence in Herbert that (as we have seen) he was even
prepared to cross Warwick's hopes of family aggrandizement in South

---

[1] *Gwaith Lewis Glyn Cothi*, ed. E. D. Jones (1953), 4.
[2] For Herbert's early career, see the articles in *DNB*, XXVI, 218–20; *Dictionary
of Welsh Biography*, 354; T. B. Pugh, ed., *Glamorgan County History*, III, 259–61;
D. H. Thomas, 'The Herberts of Raglan as supporters of the House of York in the
second half of the fifteenth century' (Univ. of Wales M.A. thesis, 1968).
[3] His principal offices and land-grants in Wales were as follows: chief justice and
chamberlain, South Wales, 8 May 1461; constable of Cardigan, for life, 2 August

Wales, a decision which may partly reflect Herbert's already considerable influence with the king.[1]

Nor were Lord Herbert's rewards confined merely to the exercise of
royal stewardship. His own family interests were admirably provided
for. Outside Wales, he secured, in June 1463, a grant of the lordship of
Dunster and all the possessions of its attainted lord, James Luttrell, in
Somerset, Devon and Suffolk, and his eldest son, William, though still a
minor, was recognized as Lord Dunster in 1466, in view of his approaching marriage to the queen's sister, Mary Woodville.[2] In 1462 he obtained
the wardship and marriage of Henry Tudor, heir to the earl of Richmond, and in 1467 was given the wardship of the estates and the marriages of the heirs of Viscount Lisle and Lord Grey of Powys.[3] In July
1463 Crickhowell and Tretower were separated from the earldom of
March and made into a full Marcher lordship for Herbert's benefit, and
in March 1465 his own paternal inheritance, the lordship of Raglan,
was given similar status: this creation of two new independent Marcher
lordships was a remarkable sign of royal favour.[4] Finally, Herbert's
services in reducing the obstinate stronghold of Harlech to obedience
brought him promotion to the earldom of Pembroke on 8 September
1468. 'In less than ten years this grossly ambitious and grasping Welsh
country squire had turned himself into an English magnate, with an
annual income of some £2,400.'[5]

Without doubt, Herbert gave excellent service in return. From the
successful campaign of 1461 to the fall of Harlech on 14 August 1468 he

---

1461; grant in tail of the castle and lordship of Pembroke, Kilgerran, Castle Martin,
etc., 3 February 1462; chief justice of Merioneth and constable of Harlech, 17 June
1463; chief justice of South Wales, and steward of Usk, Caerleon and other Duchy
of York lands in South Wales, in tail male, 26 September 1466; chief justice of North
Wales and steward of lordships of Denbigh and Montgomery, etc., for life, 28 August
1467; constable of Conway and master-forester of Snowdon, 11 November 1468
(*CPR, 1461-7*, 7, 42, 114, 271, 526-7; *1467-77*, 22, 41, 113). In addition to the
custodies of the Stafford lordships in South Wales and the Talbot lordships in Hereford mentioned elsewhere, he acquired the custody of the duke of Norfolk's lordship
of Gower on 12 February 1462, and soon converted temporary control into ownership;
by September 1468 the 4th duke of Norfolk conveyed both Gower and Chepstow to
Herbert, an act confirmed by the king on 3 May 1469 (*CPR, 1467-77*, 112; *Glamorgan
County History*, III, 258-9).
1 T. B. Pugh, *Glamorgan County History*, III, 198, believes that the incident demonstrates that Herbert's influence with the king was superior to Warwick's. But Edward
had his own ideas about regional authority (*v.* the similar transfer of offices from
Warwick to Hastings noted above, p. 71), and a more likely explanation is that
advanced in *Glamorgan County History*, 261.
2 *CPR, 1461-7*, 286, 366.   3 *Ibid.*, 114; *1467-77*, 25, 51, 62.
4 *Ibid.*, *1461-7*, 268, 425-6.   5 T. B. Pugh, *The Fifteenth Century*, 92.

was responsible for military operations in Wales, and contributed to keeping the peace in that unruly land. His Welsh birth and upbringing inspired much respect in contemporary Welsh literature, where he appears as a national hero. His countrymen followed him in very large numbers to the battle of Edgecote in 1469, and many died there. His large family and numerous kinsmen provided a core of loyal servants in Edward's Welsh service.[1] Hence Jasper Tudor's repeated efforts to raise the standard of rebellion in Wales met with little success, and the absence of any support for Warwick in South Wales, despite his Marcher interests, testifies to the success of Herbert's labours in establishing Yorkist control in that region. In the first few years of the reign he spent very little time at court, but he commanded considerable influence with the king and queen, especially after his son's Woodville marriage.[2]

The pattern of delegation of local authority which benefited Hastings in the east midlands and Herbert in Wales was repeated in the West Country, also an area of strong Lancastrian sympathies. Here William Nevill, earl of Kent, seems to have been designated as the king's chief agent, but, with his death in 1463, his influence passed to another of the new men, Humphrey Stafford, created Lord Stafford in 1461. Local offices, forfeited estates and wardships were showered upon him, and in return he served on a large number of political and administrative commissions in the south-west.[3] A greedy and ambitious man, he achieved the height of his ambition when he was raised to the earldom of Devon in 1469, shortly before his death in the Edgecote cam-

---

[1] R. A. Griffiths, 'Wales and the Marches', in *The Fifteenth Century*, 159, and references there cited; and see below, p. 131. For his work on Welsh commissions, see *CPR*, *1461-7*, 30, 38, 45, 65, 98, 100, 132, 280, 355; *1467-77*, 29, 54, 58, 102, 103.

[2] His absence from court is reflected in the fact that he did not attest a single royal charter before 1466: P.R.O. Charter Rolls, C. 53/191-4. The Croyland Chronicler, p. 551, specifically links the growth of his influence at court with the Woodville marriage: on this point, see T. B. Pugh, *The Fifteenth Century*, 93. For examples of his presence at court after 1466, see Scofield, I, 417, 443-4; *CPR*, *1461-7*, 529; *1467-77*, 127; *CCR*, *1461-8*, 456-7. A good example of his influence with the king may be seen in the inability of the young earl of Shrewsbury to recover his lordships of Goodrich and Archenfield, co. Hereford: though never forfeited to the Crown, these had been granted to Herbert in 1461, and were specifically excluded when John Talbot was given licence to enter on his inheritance in August 1464 (*CPR*, *1461-7*, 329).

[3] No good account of Stafford's career exists, but see the article in *DNB* and Wedgwood, *Hist. Parl., Biographies*, 793-4. He was granted virtually all the former Courtenay estates in Devon, and amongst other offices held the stewardship of the Duchy of Cornwall for life, the custody of the forest of Dartmoor, the stewardship of the Duchy lands in Devon, and was constable and steward of the lordship of Bridgwater, Somerset (*CPR*, *1461-7*, 25, 116, 120, 129, 360, 438-9; *1467-77*, 22-3, 124, 156).

paign.[1] Thereafter his mantle fell on another Westcountryman, John, Lord Dinham. As a Devonshire esquire, Dinham had come to Edward's attention when he gave refuge to the young earl of March and his Nevill kinsmen after the Rout of Ludford, and engineered their escape to France. Although active in the royal service in Devon and Cornwall, his advancement was relatively slow. He was a councillor as early as 1462, but was not created a baron until 1467, and he becomes really prominent only after the fall of Humphrey Stafford.[2]

Others amongst this group of king's friends served Edward primarily at the centre of government. Amongst them were the two or three members of the established nobility who (apart from the Nevills) enjoyed the king's confidence in the first decade of his reign. The senior member of the group in age and experience was Henry Bourchier, Viscount Bourchier. Uncle by marriage to Edward himself, and brother of Thomas Bourchier, archbishop of Canterbury, Henry was an experienced soldier and statesman, who had already acted as treasurer of England in the Yorkist administration of 1455–6. Raised to the earldom of Essex in June 1461, he was Edward's first treasurer (until April 1462), steward of the royal household from 1467 to 1471, and then treasurer again until his death in 1483. He was therefore constantly about the king's person and was a leading member of the royal council. Hence he served on few local commissions and his local influence, chiefly in Essex, was exercised from a distance. Perhaps because of his wealth, he received few rewards from the king.[3] Bourchier was also important as head of a family which had early declared for the House of York and remained consistently loyal to it. His two brothers, William, Lord FitzWarin, and John, Lord Berners, and his younger son, Humphrey, created Lord Cromwell in 1461, had all married baronial heiresses. FitzWarin was a useful supporter of the Crown in the West Country, as was his son, Fulk Bourchier; and both Lord Cromwell and Berners's son, Humphrey, were later to die fighting for Edward at the battle of Barnet.[4]

[1] See below, pp. 129–32.
[2] R. P. Chope, 'The Last of the Dynhams', *Trans. Devonshire Association*, 1 (1918), 431–92; *CP*, IV, 378–9; Lander, 'Council, Administration and Councillors', 168. Before 1467 his only substantial grant consisted of 8½ manors forfeited from the Hungerfords in Devon and Somerset (*CPR, 1461–7*, 359–60, 1 October 1464).
[3] For his career, see *CP*, V, 137–8; Dugdale, *Baronage*, II, 129. He had already been treasurer of England, 1455–6. The only reward of substance he received was the grant to him and his wife, Isobel, the king's aunt, in 1462, of 18 manors, in belated fulfilment of the will of Edward's great-uncle, Edmund Mortimer, earl of March (d. 1425), to the value of 500 marks (*CPR, 1461–7*, 145).
[4] See below, pp. 167–8.

Bourchier was succeeded as treasurer of England in April 1462 by one of the more unusual members of the Yorkist peerage. John Tiptoft, earl of Worcester, Edward's first cousin by marriage, had spent four years travelling and studying in Italy and returned to England in September 1461, with many of the civilized and scholarly interests of the Renaissance, and is rightly remembered as an early lay patron of humanist studies and a noted collector of books. He had also imbibed some of the political ruthlessness of contemporary Italy. As Constable of England (1463–7 and again in 1470), he earned an evil reputation for cruelty, and was branded 'the Butcher of England' soon after his death. He also served Edward as steward of the royal household (1463–7), admiral (1463) and deputy-lieutenant of Ireland (1467–8). He was clearly much trusted by Edward, and appears as a member of the royal council within two months of his return from Italy. Like Bourchier, he was often with the king, and was not active in the counties of Cambridge and Huntingdon where most of his lands lay.[1]

The remaining members of the group may be introduced more briefly. John, Lord Audley, who had defected to the Yorkist earls after being taken prisoner in Calais in 1460, became one of Edward's most active supporters in the shires, chiefly in Somerset, Hampshire and Wiltshire, where his estates were situated; and in the first decade of the reign he served on an impressively large number of local commissions. Although denounced by the rebels in 1469 as one of the king's grasping favourites, his rewards had in fact been quite modest.[2]

The others were all new Yorkist lords. Sir John Wenlock had risen from quite obscure origins to become chamberlain to Queen Margaret of Anjou, but in 1455 he attached himself to the Yorkists, and was attainted by the Coventry Parliament. He had shared the exile of the earls in Calais, and fought at Towton. He already had much diplomatic experience, and it was chiefly in this capacity that he served Edward. From 1461 to 1470 he was abroad for some part of every year as an ambassador. But he was also a royal councillor as early as Sep-

[1] For his career, see the biography by R. J. Mitchell, *John Tiptoft*, and further below, p. 155, for his death and reputation. The phrase 'Butcher of England' first occurs in the early-sixteenth-century versions of the London Chronicles (e.g. *GC*, 212–13), but he was already called 'the harsh hangman and executioner' (*Trux carnifex et hominum decollator*) in the immediately contemporary *Brief Latin Chronicle*, 183.

[2] See Wedgwood, *Hist. Parl.*, *Biographies*, for an account of his career. He served on 31 commissions before 1471, excluding commissions of the peace. His only rewards consisted of his appointment, 2 May 1461, as steward and keeper of royal lands and forests in Dorset, with the custody of Wardour Castle, and a grant in July 1467 of two Surrey manors, valued at £37 5s a year, forfeited from the earl of Wiltshire (*CPR, 1461–7*, 8, 87; *1467–77*, 22).

tember 1461, was created a baron in the first parliament of the reign, and was rewarded with offices of profit and dignity and grants from forfeited Lancastrian estates, chiefly those of the ex-chief justice, Sir John Fortescue.[1] Sir Walter Blount, of Elvaston in Derbyshire, had been a servant of Duke Richard of York, and in 1459–60 was probably with the earls in Calais. On 21 June 1461 he was appointed treasurer of Calais, and on 24 November 1464 he became treasurer of England. In 1465 he was created Lord Mountjoy. Though his two offices may have given him some opportunities for profit, they also involved him in heavy lending to the Crown, and he had to wait a long time for repayment.[2] He also waited long for any other reward for his services. He had no grant of any substance until August 1467, about the time he married the king's aunt, Anne, dowager duchess of Buckingham, when he was given a group of Courtenay lands in Devon and Hampshire. No attempt was made to increase his local influence in Derbyshire. But he was clearly a member of the inner circle at court, more particularly after his marriage.[3] Sir Walter Devereux, whom Edward created Lord Ferrers of Chartley in 1461, had long-standing and close connections with the House of York. His seat at Weobley in Herefordshire gave him an interest in the Welsh Marches, and he served on a number of commissions on Welsh affairs and was appointed captain of Aberystwyth Castle in 1463. In 1462 he had a substantial grant of lands, partly in the Marches, and partly in Berkshire and the east midlands, where the estates of his wife, heiress of the Ferrers family, chiefly lay.[4] Finally, Sir John Howard, one of the most active of Edward's gentry servants, and a man with extensive influence in East Anglia, was raised to the peerage as Lord Howard early in 1470. In the second half of the reign he was to become one of the king's closest and most trusted councillors.[5]

[1] His career is fully described by J. S. Roskell, 'John, Lord Wenlock of Someries', *Bedfordshire Historical Record Society Publications*, xxxviii (1957), 12–48; *The Commons and their Speakers in English Parliaments, 1376–1523*, esp. pp. 258–62, 370–1.

[2] For his loans to the Crown, see below, p. 379. For his career, see Wedgwood, *Hist. Parl., Biog.*, 86 and *CP*, IX, 344–9. In Wedgwood he is misleadingly treated as being primarily an associate of the earl of Warwick, but before 1460 Richard, duke of York, calls Blount his servant, and he was already a king's knight by 13 August 1461 (Ellis, *Original Letters*, 2nd ser., i, no. 40; *CPR, 1461–7*, 41); and see the next note.

[3] *Ibid., 1467–77*, 24–5 (for the Courtenay lands). He went with Edward to relieve George Nevill of the Great Seal in June 1467, and his later service on commissions was largely confined to the special commissions of oyer and terminer to which other members of the court party were appointed; and Edward's confidence in him is also shown by his being empowered to receive rebels into the king's grace, 25 April 1470 (*CCR, 1461–8*, 456; *CPR, 1461–7*, 490, 554; *1467–77*, 102, 171, 207).

[4] *CP*, V, 322–3; Wedgwood, *Hist. Parl., Biog.*, 272–3.

[5] For Howard's career, see below, pp. 324–5.

Several points emerge from this survey of the careers of this inner ring of Edward's supporters. First, there is a clear distinction between the rewards gained by men like Hastings, Herbert and Stafford, on the one hand, and those who served Edward at the centre of government on the other. The heaping of material rewards on members of this group was largely confined to men who were expected to have special responsibilities in certain regions and was inspired by essentially political considerations. None of the others was given land, local office, or wardships on any significant scale. Even to those who stood high in his favour and were his intimate friends and councillors, Edward did not dispense patronage without discrimination. Men of established wealth like the earls of Essex and Worcester were rewarded only with offices of dignity or profit or with promotion within the peerage. Secondly, it seems clear that in promoting, aggrandizing and delegating great authority to his new men, Edward was inspired by a wish to offset the excessive power of the Nevills, under whose power he had begun his reign. To be master in his own realm, he needed his own men to execute his policies. It is significant that, save for Worcester and Audley, all owed their titles (or, like Essex, their promotions within the peerage) to Edward's favour. Only Essex and Worcester had ever held high office or enjoyed royal confidence before 1461, and even they were more powerful and prominent under York than they had ever been under Lancaster. The rest owed their entire advancement to Edward's favour.

The emergence of this group of king's men, soon to be reinforced by some of the queen's Woodville relatives, is the most important factor in the politics of Edward's first decade. The king's reliance on this 'new court party' led by the Woodvilles, Herbert, and Humphrey Stafford has recently been branded as a singular error of judgement on Edward's part, on the grounds that these newly-created magnates were unpopular upstarts, who could not withstand the enmity of Warwick because they were unable to attract any binding loyalty from the gentry.[1] This view seems rather perverse. In the crisis of 1469, Herbert and Stafford were able to raise very considerable forces from Wales and the West Country, and there seemed to be no lack of support for them from their home regions. Herbert's defeat at Edgecote on 26 July was at least in part due to his quarrel with Stafford the night before, and the battle itself proved a close-fought affair, which might easily have gone the other way. Similarly, William, Lord Hastings, was able to build up a powerful and durable connection in the midlands which proved of great value in helping his master to recover the throne in 1471. That he still com-

[1] T. B. Pugh, *Fifteenth-Century England*, 93.

manded much support amongst the lords, including quite important families like the Bourchiers, is shown by Warwick's inability to rule through a captive king for more than two months.[1]

As a group, the king's men showed considerable loyalty and political homogeneity. They are to be found at Edward's side in moments of political crisis. Thus in June 1467, when the king decided to override publicly Nevill obstruction of his policy, he took the unusual step of making a personal visit to Archbishop George Nevill's lodgings in order to relieve him of the Great Seal. Ten of the twelve notables whom he chose to accompany him in this act of self-assertion belonged to the group of men whose careers have been discussed above.[2] Not only were they willing to support him in his widening breach with the Nevills, they also showed themselves more ready than the Nevills to accept the consequences of the king's ill-advised marriage, and to tolerate and cooperate with the queen's Woodville relatives.[3] Finally, they remained conspicuously loyal to Edward during the recurrent crises of 1469–71. Three of them – Worcester, Pembroke and Devon – lost their lives on his behalf. Others shared his Netherlands exile. Those who remained behind in England were viewed with deep suspicion by the Readeption government, and quickly rallied to Edward's standard on his return.[4] Only one, John, Lord Wenlock, deserted to Warwick and the Lancastrians. Whether for reasons of self-interest, gratitude, or personal respect and affection for their royal master, they displayed a capacity for sustained loyalty, although some of them at least might have made a good bargain with Warwick's regime. But in 1469 they remained a minority amongst the baronage. They failed to preserve their master's throne because his rule had not yet commended itself to the remainder of the baronage, a majority of the gentry, and to popular opinion in general. The Yorkist regime was not yet widely enough based to withstand a combination of Warwick's ambition, Clarence's disloyalty, and the revival of Lancastrian sentiment which had been weakened but not destroyed.[5]

[1] See below, pp. 133–5.
[2] CCR, 1461–8, 456. The others were his brother, Clarence, and his cousin by marriage, William FitzAlan, earl of Arundel.
[3] The heirs of the earls of Essex, Pembroke and Kent all married Woodvilles; see further below, p. 93.
[4] Essex, Mountjoy and Cromwell were temporarily arrested during the Readeption, and Audley, Devereux and Howard were removed from the bench of JPs. See below, pp. 157–8.
[5] See below, pp. 122–5, 127–8.

Chapter 5

THE KING'S MARRIAGE AND THE
RISE OF THE WOODVILLES

In the spring of 1464 Edward of York was Europe's most eligible bachelor. Young, handsome and genial, he was also increasingly secure on his throne. His marriage could now be used as a useful weapon in England's dealings with her continental neighbours, and as a means of establishing his dynasty amongst the ruling houses of Europe.

Plans of various kinds for his marriage had been discussed since his infancy. In 1445, when he was no more than three years old, his father had proposed a grandiose match with Madeleine, the eighteen-month-old daughter of King Charles VII of France. After exchanges of letters and envoys, the king had agreed, and then the scheme was dropped.[1] In the summer of 1458 his name had been mentioned again as part of an elaborate proposal (which may have been part of Henry VI's peace-making activities) for a triple marriage alliance between the prince of Wales, 'a son of the Duke of York' and the duke of Somerset with three ladies of the ducal house of Burgundy. Meeting no response, the English envoys made a similar proposal to the king of France, but again it was never seriously discussed.[2]

The notion of a marriage alliance with Burgundy was revived soon after Edward's accession. In October 1461 an English mission headed by Lord Wenlock proposed a match between the young king and the beautiful Mademoiselle de Bourbon, a niece of Duke Philip and sister-in-law of his heir, Charles, count of Charolais. This union represented for Edward a means of consolidating his dynasty, and, he hoped, of

[1] Apparently because King Charles would not agree to substitute an elder daughter, Jeanne, for the infant Madeleine; J. Stevenson, *Letters and Papers Illustrative of the Wars of the English in France*, I, 79–82, 83–6, 160–3, 168–70; G. Du Fresne de Beaucourt, *Histoire de Charles VII*, IV, 142–3. In 1452 and again in 1455–6 there were further proposals for a marriage between Edward and a daughter of the dissident French conspirator, Jean, duke of Alençon (*ibid.*, VI, 41, 52–4).
[2] *Ibid.*, VI, 260–1; Thielemans, *Bourgogne et Angleterre*, 372; Scofield, I, 28–9. Ramsay, *Lancaster and York*, II, 210–11, wrongly represents this as a wholly Yorkist-inspired negotiation.

detaching Charolais from his strong support for the Lancastrian cause. Philip, however, was not then willing to commit himself definitely to a dynasty still very insecure on its throne, and no progress could be made.[1] Then in 1462 Warwick proposed that Edward should marry the Scottish regent, Mary of Guelders, despite her age and dubious reputation – the Lancastrian duke of Somerset was reckoned amongst her lovers – but this was blocked – if ever seriously meant – from the Scots side.[2] In 1464, according to diplomatic rumours, the Burgundians were willing to revive the proposed Bourbon marriage, as a counter to the French marriage now being negotiated for Edward IV, but apparently it was never seriously pressed.[3] At the same time another suitable claimant for Edward's hand made her appearance, when, in February 1464, Henry the Impotent of Castile proffered his sister and eventual heiress, Isabella. Though the match would have aided Edward's plans for an alliance with Castile, the offer was declined. Twenty years later, the slight still rankled with Queen Isabella, especially since Edward had chosen to marry a mere 'widow of England'.[4]

Any prospect of a continental marriage alliance, however, was soon wrecked by Edward's own impulsive action, the first major blunder of his political career. On his way north to meet the threat from the Lancastrians, Edward stopped at Stony Stratford on 30 April 1464. Very early the next morning, he slipped away from his entourage and rode over to Grafton Regis, the home of Richard Woodville, Lord Rivers, and his wife, Jacquetta of Luxembourg, widow of John, duke of Bedford. There, on May Morning, in the presence of Jacquetta and no more than four or five others, he married her daughter, Elizabeth Woodville, who was herself a widow: her former husband, Sir John Grey, son of Edward Grey, Lord Ferrers of Groby, had died fighting for Henry VI at St Albans in February 1461. Immediately after the ceremony (if we can trust the details given much later by Robert Fabyan), Edward went to bed for a short time, and then returned to Stony Stratford, pretending that he had been hunting, and complaining sorely of fatigue, and went to bed again. Shortly afterwards he returned to Grafton for three days, where Elizabeth was brought secretly to him each night, before resuming his journey to the north.[5]

No one knows when Edward had first met and become enamoured

---

[1] Scofield, I, 211.
[2] Dunlop, *James Kennedy*, 227, 241; and above, pp. 40–50.   [3] Scofield, I, 327.
[4] J. Gairdner, *Letters and Papers Illustrative of the Reigns of Richard III and Henry VII*, I, 31; Scofield, I, 320.
[5] R. Fabyan, *The New Chronicles of England and of France*, 654.

of Elizabeth, still less why he should have chosen to make her his queen.[1] The best explanation may also be the simplest – that it was the impulsive love-match of an impetuous young man. This was evidently the belief of the chronicler, Gregory, writing between 1468 and 1470; he uses Edward's marriage to point the moral: 'Now take heed what love may do, for love will not nor may not cast no fault nor peril in no thing.'[2] But another explanation was popular both at the time and later – that Edward married her as the only way to obtain her favours. He came to enjoy a very considerable reputation as a successful womanizer. Commynes went too far in ascribing Edward's loss of his throne in 1470 to his excessive devotion to pleasure.[3] But there is ample testimony from other and less critical sources. In his flattering portrait of Edward – deliberately heightened by contrast with Richard III's villainy – Sir Thomas More was emphatic on this point: 'He was of youth greatly given to fleshly wantonness' (from which, More tolerantly adds) 'health of body in great prosperity and fortune, without a special grace, hardly refraineth. This fault not greatly grieved the people. . . .'[4] The shrewd Mancini had the same impression: 'he was licentious in the extreme. . . . He pursued with no discrimination the married and the unmarried, the noble and lowly: however, he took none by force.'[5] The Croyland Chronicler, no less observant or well informed, remarked on the astonishment of Edward's subjects that he was able to combine a grasp of business with a passion for 'boon companionship, vanities, debauchery, extravagance and sensual enjoyments. . . .'[6] Equally, Edward's reputation for lechery was well known on the Continent in his own lifetime.[7]

If much of this evidence comes from Edward's later years, there is no good reason to suppose his tastes had changed very much. Indeed, Gregory's Chronicle, the most immediately contemporary narrative, remarks that 'men marvelled that our sovereign lord was so long without any wife, and were ever feared that he had not been chaste of his living'.[8] More certainly believed that he had bastard children, and tells

---

[1] Scofield (I, 177–8) suggested that they met early in June 1461, when Edward spent three days at Stony Stratford on his way back to London, and pardoned Lord Rivers as he left there (12 June), but, apart from this coincidence, there is no evidence to support this conjecture.
[2] Gregory, 226, and Kingsford, *English Historical Literature*, 97, for the date of the chronicle.
[3] Commynes, I, 203.   [4] More, *Richard III*, 4.
[5] Mancini, 67.   [6] *CC*, 564.
[7] See below, p. 232, for Commynes's story about the ladies of Paris.
[8] Gregory, 226.

a neat – if apocryphal – story to prove it.[1] This is the background against which reports of Elizabeth's virtuous resistance to the king's advances must be judged. The successful philanderer, confronted by a rejection of his suit so obstinate as to survive threats at the point of a dagger, concedes marriage as the only means to achieve his ends. Hitherto this story has been known to us from later authorities, such as Mancini, More and Edward Hall, but a recent discovery has shown that it was already current on the Continent as early as 1468, when a Milanese courtier-poet, Antonio Cornazzano, made it the basis for a tale of virtue triumphant.[2] It has a certain plausibility.

Modern attempts to read a political motive into the marriage are very unconvincing.[3] Edward scarcely needed to marry this unsuitable widow in order to assert his independence of Warwick and the Nevills: had he wished to avoid the French marriage advocated by Warwick, there was no shortage of suitable brides, even amongst the higher ranks of the English nobility. Still less did he need to promote her relatives to create a counterpoise to the Nevills: a court party was already being formed before 1464, and the promotion of the Woodvilles added rather to its unpopularity than to its strength.

If Edward's motives in making this remarkable misalliance remain a matter for awestruck speculation, its consequences were a matter of high political concern, and ultimately contributed largely to the downfall of the Yorkist dynasty.[4] The immediate disadvantages were obvious to all. Elizabeth had nothing to recommend her except her obvious physical attractions. Her rather cold beauty was not offset by

[1] More, *Richard III*, 64. Edward is said to have told his mother that Elizabeth 'is a widow and hath already children, by God's Blessed Lady I am a bachelor and have some too: and so each of us hath a proof that neither of us is like to be barren'.
[2] Mancini, 61 (and the editor's notes, p. 109); More, 60–1; Hall, *Chronicle*, 264; C. Fahy, 'The Marriage of Edward IV and Elizabeth Woodville; a new Italian Source', *EHR*, lxxvi (1961), 660–72. J. R. Lander, 'Marriage and Politics', 131 n., dismisses the Italian narrative as 'essentially a pleasant tale', but, as Fahy points out, its inaccuracies do not detract from the fact that it is an independent and unadulterated source nor from the general line of the story.
[3] E.g. B. Wilkinson, *Constitutional History of England in the Fifteenth Century*, 146–8, who suggests it was 'both a love match and a cold and calculated political move' and that 'his immoderate promotion' of the queen's relatives also had strong political motives.
[4] The whole subject has been fully discussed in a valuable study by J. R. Lander, 'Marriage and Politics: the Nevilles and the Wydevilles', *BIHR*, xxxvi (1963), 119–52, on which much of what follows is based. Lander, however, whilst arguing convincingly against attaching too much importance to the marriage and its consequences in Yorkist politics, goes too far in the other direction. In particular, as indicated below, he underestimates the unpopularity of the queen's family, and their role in the feuds which led to the deposition of Edward's heir in 1483.

Table 4 THE WOODVILLES

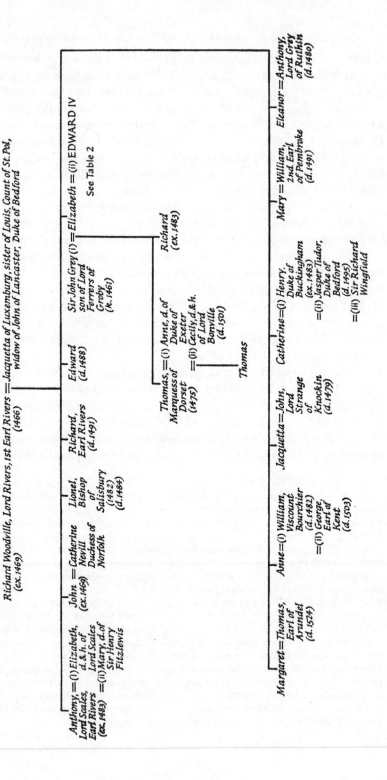

Richard Woodville, Lord Rivers, 1st Earl Rivers = Jacquetta of Luxemburg, sister of Louis, Count of St. Pol,
(1466)   widow of John of Lancaster, Duke of Bedford
(ex.1469)

Anthony, =(i) Elizabeth,   **John** = Catherine   **Lionel,**   **Richard,**   **Edward**   Sir John Grey (i) = **Elizabeth** = (ii) EDWARD IV
Lord Scales,   d.&h. of   (ex.1469) Nevill   Bishop   Earl Rivers   (d.1488)   son of Lord
Earl Rivers   Lord Scales   Duchess of   of   (d.1491)   Ferrers of   See Table 2
(ex.1483) =(ii) Mary, d.of   Norfolk   Salisbury   Groby
       Sir Henry   (1482)   (k.1461)
       Fitzlewis   (d.1484)

                                       Thomas, =(i) Anne, d.of   **Richard**
                                       Marquess of   Duke of   (ex.1483)
                                       Dorset   Exeter
                                       (1475) =(ii) Cecily, d.&h.
                                                   of Lord
                                                   Bonville
                                                   (d.1501)

                                         Thomas

Margaret = Thomas,   **Anne** =(i) William,   **Jacquetta** = John,   **Catherine** =(i) Henry,   **Mary** = William,   **Eleanor** = Anthony,
         Earl of   Viscount   Lord   Duke of   2nd Earl   Lord Grey
         Arundel   Bourchier   Strange   Buckingham   of Pembroke   of Ruthin
         (d.1524)   (d.1482)   of   (ex.1483)   (d.1491)   (d.1480)
                  =(ii) George,   Knockin   =(ii) Jasper Tudor,
                     Earl of   (d.1479)   Duke of
                     Kent   Bedford
                     (d.1503)   (d.1495)
                                       =(iii) Sir Richard
                                          Wingfield

any warmth or generosity of temperament. She was to prove a woman of designing character, grasping and ambitious for her family's interests, quick to take offence and reluctant to forgive.[1] For the present, however, her personal defects were less important than the political problems arising from her marriage.

This impoverished Lancastrian widow might have made a fitting wife for a member of the Northamptonshire gentry, or even for one of Edward's newly-created barons. She was far from suitable as a queen. Too much should not be made of her Lancastrian connections. Although her father, Richard, Lord Rivers, and her brother, Anthony, Lord Scales, had fought with Margaret at Towton, both had been quickly pardoned, and received minor grants from Edward, and Rivers was a member of the royal council by March 1463. The advancement of her family at the Yorkist court did not begin with Elizabeth's marriage.[2] On her father's side, she was of relatively humble origin, for Sir Richard had been no more than the son of the duke of Bedford's chamberlain when he married the duke's wealthy widow. Jacquetta herself, however, belonged to the high nobility of Europe. Her father, Pierre, count of St Pol, was a powerful French magnate, and through him she could claim descent from the Emperor Charlemagne himself. Her first husband, Sir John Grey of Groby, was related to the Greys of Ruthyn, and by marriage to the Berkeleys, the Bourchiers and the Mowbrays. A recent writer has rightly emphasized that the social status of the family 'was not as lowly as many historians have assumed'.[3] But any temptation to argue that by birth and social degree she was a suitable queen must be resisted. The Burgundian chronicler, Jean de Waurin, however unreliable as to details, can be trusted for his sense of contemporary social nicety, and his account of the council's reaction to the news probably puts the point fairly enough:

> ... they answered that she was not his match, however good and however fair she might be, and he must know well that she was no wife for a prince such as himself; for she was not the daughter of a duke or earl, but her mother, the Duchess of Bedford, had married a simple knight, so that though she was the child of a duchess and the niece of the count of St Pol, still she was no wife for him.[4]

Edward scarcely needed anyone to point out this truth to him, for he

[1] See below, pp. 97 ff., 336–7.   [2] *CPR, 1461–7*, 81, 97, 188; Lander, *op. cit.*, 130–1.
[3] Lander, *op. cit.*, 134. For Elizabeth's descent, D. MacGibbon, *Elizabeth Woodville*, 45 n., and genealogy at p. 225. In a pageant presented at Coventry in 1474 she was said to have been descended from the Magi (*Coventry Leet Book*, 393).
[4] Waurin, ed. Dupont, II, 327–8.

had taken part at Calais in 1460 in the 'berating' of the captured Rivers and Scales by the Yorkist earls. In a display of aristocratic snobbishness, Warwick had roundly told Rivers that

> his father was but a squire and brought up with King Henry the Fifth, and sithen himself made by marriage, and also made lord, and that it was not his part to have language of lords, being of the king's blood.[1]

In an age of sharpening social distinction, for a king to marry at this level was both impolitic and unprecedented.[2]

That Edward was painfully conscious of his problem is proved by the extreme secrecy of his marriage and the long delay before it was made public. Even William, Lord Hastings, perhaps his closest friend, seems to have been kept in the dark.[3] Edward could expect trouble on three counts. First, there were obvious repercussions for the negotiations for a French marriage now in progress. Secondly, he might expect some hostile reaction from Warwick and the lords in general, not only for his choice of wife but also for his having married without consultation and advice, as would have been normal practice in an affair of such public concern. Thirdly, he had to find provision for Elizabeth's horde of relatives. The new queen brought with her formidable liabilities – two sons by her first marriage, five brothers, and seven unmarried sisters, all of whom might expect some improvement of their rather lowly condition, as befitted the kinsfolk of a queen.

Edward increased his difficulties by his refusal to face these issues squarely and without delay. Instead of making an immediate declaration of his marriage, he hung on, waiting for a favourable moment, until the diplomatic events of the summer of 1464 finally forced his hand.[4] Louis XI of France was now anxious for a closer *rapprochement* with England, and had already begun a systematic flattery of the earl of Warwick, through whom he hoped to bring about an Anglo-French alliance. Warwick himself was taking an increasing interest in foreign policy. In March 1464 he and Wenlock had pushed forward the negotiations which led to the signing of a truce with France at sea on 14 April. He planned to attend a conference arranged in the previous autumn to meet at St Omer on 21 April, to discuss a longer truce with

---

[1] *PL*, III, 203–4.

[2] For the growth of demarcations within the peerage, and a sharp separation of peers from others, see K. B. McFarlane, *The Nobility of Later Medieval England* (1973), 122–5.

[3] Lander, *op. cit.*, 132.

[4] For the negotiations of spring and summer 1464, see Scofield, I, 320–9, 343–51; Calmette and Perinelle, 49–54.

France and perhaps a marriage treaty and alliance. The news that Edward was looking for a wife had first reached the sharp ears of the Milanese ambassador in France in September 1463. King Louis, he reported, had been asked to give his daughter, Anne, as bride to the English king. Louis refused, for the child was only three years old, but he offered his sister-in-law, Bona, daughter of the duke of Savoy, in her place.[1] This was the marriage alliance which Louis and Warwick were now anxious to bring about. Though Louis had expected him, the earl was kept in England by the disturbances in the north and the negotiations with the Scots, and the conference at St Omer was postponed until 8 June, when only Lord Wenlock and Warwick's lieutenant at Guines, Richard Whetehill, appeared for England. The conference was further postponed until 1 October 1464.

During September Edward met his council at Reading to discuss, among other things, English policy at the forthcoming conference.[2] Warwick and Wenlock had been authorized to lead the English delegation, and were now in urgent need of instructions. His councillors pressed Edward to make clear his intentions about the French marriage. Clearly Edward could keep silent no longer. By 4 October rumours had begun to reach King Louis, who was in Picardy awaiting the arrival of the English embassy, and by 10 October he had learnt the truth. The English envoys never came, and the St Omer conference was abandoned. Yet Edward's marriage in itself had little effect on Anglo-French relations. Louis XI was not discouraged in hoping for a treaty with England, and, despite his chagrin, Warwick also continued to press actively for a French alliance. It was rather the gradual decline of Warwick's influence over his master, and Edward's wish for a closer association with Burgundy and Brittany, which finally wrecked their plans.

Immediate English reactions to the news of the king's marriage cannot be readily assessed. The accepted view that it caused considerable displeasure amongst the lords and angered Warwick especially has recently been challenged on the grounds that the evidence is either biased or late.[3] There is, however, no good reason to suppose that it

---

[1] *CSP, Milan*, I, 109.

[2] The date of this council meeting is given as 14 September (Scofield, I, 354; cf. Calmette and Perinelle, 61, who give 28 September). Since Elizabeth's official presentation as queen took place on 29 September (*Annales*, 783), and on 3 October Wenlock wrote to Lannoy to inform Louis of the marriage (Waurin, ed. Dupont, II, 326-7), it is unlikely that either of these would have been so long delayed if the announcement took place as early as 14 September.

[3] Lander, 'Marriage and Politics', 133 and n., where contemporary references to the marriage are collected.

was received without dismay. Edward's lords could scarcely have been other than astonished at the news, and probably resented his failure to consult even his closest advisers on an important matter of state.[1] Their confidence in his political judgement probably received a sharp shock. Edward had shown himself willing 'to be led by blind affection, and not by rule of reason'.[2] Warwick, too, had good reason for annoyance. Even if he had not been made to look a fool in the eyes of the French,[3] he could justifiably resent Edward's failure to confide in him, who had contributed so much to the success of the Yorkist cause. It may have been as much Edward's secretiveness as the affront to his foreign schemes which aroused the earl's anger.

The strength of Edward's position lay in the fact that the marriage was an accomplished fact, and could not be undone. Even his sharpest critics could accept it only with as good grace as possible unless they wished to forfeit the king's goodwill: as Warwick's friend, John, Lord Wenlock, remarked, 'We must be patient despite ourselves'.[4] Warwick was certainly not too angry to join Clarence in escorting the new queen into the chapel of Reading Abbey on Michaelmas Day 1464, when she was first publicly introduced to the royal court. It is hardly likely that there was enough initial disapproval of Edward's marriage to alienate any section of his supporters, not even Warwick himself. Yet the whole episode inevitably raised doubts in political circles about the future of a king who could so rashly indulge himself. Nor did the further implications of the marriage strengthen confidence in Edward as 'the man to give nervous politicians the political stability they desired'.[5]

Edward has been accused of making matters worse by his inordinate promotion of the queen's relatives. The prominence at his court of so many grasping *parvenus*, it has been argued, served only to alienate the aristocracy and was especially offensive to Warwick. Recent re-examination of the evidence, however, has shown these criticisms to be excessive in many respects.[6] Promotion of the Woodvilles was

[1] This point was stressed by Lord Wenlock in his letter to Lannoy (Waurin, ed. Dupont, II, 326–7).   [2] Polydore Vergil, 117.
[3] It has generally been accepted on the authority of Miss Scofield, I, 344–5, 347, and in *EHR*, xxi (1906), 732–7, that Warwick was on the Continent negotiating for the marriage between 17 June and 5 August and 10–30 August 1464; it is now clear that he was in the north negotiating with the Scots (A. L. Brown and B. Webster, 'The Movements of the Earl of Warwick in the summer of 1464: a correction', *EHR*, lxxxi (1966), 80–2).   [4] Letter to Lannoy, cited above.
[5] K. B. McFarlane, 'The Wars of the Roses', 114.
[6] See especially J. R. Lander, 'Marriage and Politics', 135–43, whose interpretation I have largely followed except where otherwise indicated. For a list of the marriages, see MacGibbon, *Elizabeth Woodville*, 222–5.

achieved largely by a series of advantageous marriages – so rapid and numerous as temporarily to corner the aristocratic marriage market. These began immediately after Edward's public recognition of Elizabeth as his wife. In October 1464 Margaret, the queen's next sister, was betrothed to Thomas, Lord Maltravers, son and heir of the Earl of Arundel, and a nephew of Warwick. In January 1465 the queen brought off a less suitable match – the marriage of her younger brother, John Woodville, then aged about twenty, to the very wealthy dowager duchess of Norfolk, Katherine Nevill, who was then 'a slip of a girl' (*juvencula*) of at least sixty-five, who had already survived three husbands. The marriage of elderly widows to much younger men was not without precedent, but this was an extreme example, and even a chronicler hostile to the Woodvilles had some justification for calling it a *maritagium diabolicum*.[1] There is a certain irony in the fact that the old lady (who was last seen alive at the coronation of Richard III in 1483) was to survive her youthful bridegroom by more than fourteen years.

Aristocratic husbands were soon found for three more of the queen's sisters. Their betrothals or marriages seem to have taken place soon after the baptism of the royal couple's first child, Elizabeth of York, who was born on 11 February 1466. Katherine Woodville married Henry Stafford, grandson and heir of the duke of Buckingham; Anne became the wife of William, Viscount Bourchier, eldest son and heir of the earl of Essex; and Eleanor married Anthony Grey, son and heir of the earl of Kent. Then, in September 1466, Mary Woodville was betrothed to William Herbert, son of William, Lord Herbert, and the young man was allowed to assume the style of Lord Dunster. Finally, in October 1466, the queen paid 4,000 marks to Edward's sister, Anne, duchess of Exeter, for the marriage of her elder son, Thomas Grey, to the duchess's daughter and heiress, Anne Holland, who was already betrothed to Warwick's nephew, George Nevill, son and heir of John Nevill, earl of Northumberland.

Two points emerge from this remarkable series of marriages. First, three of them are said to have given direct offence to the earl of Warwick.[2] He could reasonably resent the exploitation of his aged aunt, Duchess Katherine.[3] The Holland match was a direct affront

---

[1] *Annales*, 783. Her wealth derived from a disproportionately large share of the ducal inheritance of Norfolk, which she had held since her first husband's death in 1432.

[2] *Ibid.*, 783-5.

[3] For a different view, see Lander, 'Marriage and Politics', 136 and notes. Lander appears to assume that the old lady herself was anxious for a new husband. See also his comments on the Holland marriage (p. 137), which seem prejudiced against the Nevills.

to his family's dignity, no less so since the king presumably assented to it. The Buckingham marriage is also said to have caused him secret displeasure. Moreover, he was reported to have taken offence at the elevation of the young William Herbert to the title of Lord Dunster: he had wanted the lordship of Dunster for himself when it was given to the Herberts in 1461. More generally, he could justly feel aggrieved about the implications of these marriages for the prospects of his own heirs, his two daughters, Isabel and Anne Nevill, now both approaching marriageable age.[1] Warwick was England's premier earl and greatest magnate; his daughters were the wealthiest heiresses in the realm. Suitable husbands for them could come only from the major English families, and the marriages of the queen's kinswomen had preempted all likely candidates. This probably explains the earl's anger at the appropriation of the young Henry Stafford, duke of Buckingham, who might otherwise have made an admirable husband for Isabel Nevill. Only the king's brothers, the dukes of Clarence and Gloucester, could now provide fitting consorts for the Nevill girls. Warwick's plan to marry his elder daughter to Clarence was a logical consequence of the series of Woodville marriages. The king's persistent refusal to approve this match merely added further to Warwick's mounting grievances.[2]

Secondly, it is worth noticing that other Yorkist noblemen had no scruple about allowing their sons or daughters to marry the queen's kinsfolk. Henry, duke of Buckingham, who was a minor in the king's wardship at the time of his marriage, is said to have complained later that he had been 'disparaged' by being wedded to an upstart Woodville.[3] Such sentiments do not seem to have been voiced by the several other peers who had a free choice in their children's marriages. It is reasonable to infer that the Yorkist nobility accepted the consequences of the king's marriage without difficulty, and some saw a Woodville connection as a useful link with power in high places. Warwick, the chief sufferer, is also the chief exception.

Provision for the Woodvilles was largely achieved without impoverishing the Crown. Apart from the seven great marriages, the queen's kinsfolk got little in the way of tangible rewards. Certainly, Edward made every effort to do honour to the new queen and her family. No

[1] Isabel was born on 5 September 1451, Anne on 11 June 1456. Their marriages eventually took place in 1469 and 1470.
[2] Lander, op. cit., does not mention this quite legitimate grievance of Warwick's. T. B. Pugh, Glamorgan County History, III, 199, suggests that Edward's opposition to the match 'may well have been decisive' in determining the earl to rebel.
[3] Mancini, 75 ('whom he scorned to wed on account of her humble origin').

expense was spared to make Elizabeth's coronation on Sunday, 26 May 1465, an especially impressive and splendid occasion. Large sums were spent on cloth-of-gold, costing £280, cups and basins of gold, jewellery, scarlet and crimson robes for the kings of arms and heralds, and bay and white coursers for the queen's chairs. In January the duke of Burgundy had been invited to send over the queen's uncle, Jacques de Luxembourg, to represent him at the coronation and to call attention to her high connections on her mother's side. On 23 May at the Tower of London Edward created forty or more new Knights of the Bath, a larger number than had been knighted at his own coronation.[1] Amongst them were the queen's brothers, Richard and John Woodville, and three of her new brothers-in-law, Buckingham, Maltravers and Anthony Grey. The City of London mounted pageants in her honour. Her coronation by the archbishop of Canterbury was conducted with pomp. Nearly all the high nobility of England, together with their ladies, took part in this and later ceremonies. The only notable absentees were the earl of Warwick and Lords Hastings and Wenlock, who had departed a fortnight before on an embassy to Burgundy. The occasion was rounded off with banquets, and a tournament in which Burgundian knights in the train of Jacques de Luxembourg took part, though the honours of the day were carried off by Thomas, Lord Stanley. Arrangements had already been made for a further tournament between the queen's brother, Anthony, Lord Scales, and Anthony, Bastard of Burgundy, who had a great chivalrous reputation, though it did not actually take place until June 1467. This too represents a calculated use of chivalric pageantry to impress the people and focus attention on the high connections of the Woodville family.[2]

Yet Edward did little to advance the material interests of the queen's relatives. Certainly, with the partial exception of her father, they never enjoyed the lavish patronage in land, wardship and profitable offices which had so benefited the Nevill family and men like Hastings and Herbert in the early years of the reign.[3] On 4 March 1466, Richard, Lord Rivers, replaced Sir Walter Blount in the highly lucrative office of treasurer of England. On 24 May 1466 he was created Earl Rivers, and on 24 August 1467 he succeeded the earl of Worcester, who was

[1] Numbers vary according to source; see Scofield, I, 376. In 1461 Edward had created 32 KBs (ibid., I, 182). A contemporary account of the coronation is published in G. Smith, The Coronation of Elizabeth Woodville (1935); see also MacGibbon, Elizabeth Woodville, 45–55; Scofield, I, 375–7.

[2] A contemporary herald's account of this tournament is printed in Bentley, Excerpta Historica, 176–212; and see below, pp. 110, 259.

[3] Above, pp. 70–77.

leaving for Ireland, as Constable of England, the office being granted
to him for life, with remainder to his son Anthony. Together these
offices, and his position as a member of the king's council, provided
him with an income of £1,330 per annum. But he was given no land,
since the king probably judged him rich enough already from the very
extensive dower revenues of Duchess Jacquetta.[1] His eldest son, the
talented and cultivated Anthony, Lord Scales, already had a respectable income in right of his wife, Elizabeth, heiress of Thomas, Lord
Scales. In November 1466 he was given the lordship of the Isle of
Wight, with the castle of Carisbrooke, and a year later was made
keeper of the castle of Portchester in Hampshire. Otherwise, he received
nothing of value until he became head of the family following the death
of his father in 1469.[2] His younger brothers, Sir Edward and Sir
Richard Woodville, got very little from Edward either before or after
1471, and neither seems to have enjoyed the king's confidence at any
time during the reign.[3] The fourth brother, Lionel, became arch-
deacon of Oxford at nineteen and dean of Exeter at twenty-five, but
had to wait until he was twenty-nine before he was promoted to the
bishopric of Salisbury in 1482. Of the queen's two sons by her first
marriage, the elder, Thomas Grey, had already been provided with
the rich marriage of Anne Holland, and nothing more was done for
him in the first decade of the reign.[4] No grants to the second son,
Richard Grey, are recorded during Edward's reign, and he was never
given any important office or appointment. Finally, the dower estate
assigned to Queen Elizabeth herself for the maintenance of her household was on a modest scale, and smaller than that given to Queen
Margaret of Anjou. Edward was careful to see that it was allotted to
her with the advice of a council of great lords. Her household was also
more economically administered than her predecessor's.[5]

The cost of providing for the queen's kindred had not, after all,
proved high. No more had been done for them than they might reasonably expect. Edward had not given away much in terms of cash

[1] Lander, *op. cit.*, 140; Pugh, *Fifteenth-Century England*, 91.
[2] The grants to Scales and other Woodvilles are analysed by Lander, 141–2.
[3] According to the *Annales*, 517, Edward tried to provide for Richard in 1468 by
pressing him on the Knights Hospitaller as their Prior in England, but without
success.
[4] See below, pp. 98, 336–7, for his career after 1471.
[5] A. R. Myers, in 'The Household of Queen Margaret of Anjou, 1452–3', *Bull. John
Rylands Library*, xl (1957–8), 1–21, and his 'The Household of Queen Elizabeth
Woodville, 1466–7', *Bull. John Rylands Library*, l (1967–8), 207–35, 443–81, compares
the income and expenditure of the two queens.

revenue, nor used royal resources to increase the local influence of the Woodvilles in competition with other families. Grants to other families continued, and some, like the Nevills themselves and the Herberts, probably received more from the king during the years after 1464 than did any member of the queen's family. None of Edward's nobles could justly complain that he had been starved of royal patronage by the rise of the Woodvilles, if we except Warwick's grievance about the seven great marriages. When, in July 1469, the rebel manifesto inspired by Warwick accused several members of the court of having impoverished the realm, 'only intending to their own promotion and enriching', the charge had far more substance as applied to Herbert, Humphrey Stafford or Audley than it did to the Woodvilles held guilty – and could equally well have applied to Warwick himself.[1]

Yet the Woodvilles soon became – and remained – highly unpopular. Much of the evidence for this comes from prejudiced or later sources (perhaps in part reflecting their increased power and influence after 1471), but it is too persistent and general to be disregarded.[2] Dislike of the Woodvilles is so prominent as an element in Yorkist politics that it requires some discussion and explanation. Some initial resentment may have been caused by the speed rather than the scale of their promotion. The seven marriages, Rivers's appointment as treasurer and his creation as earl, and Scales's grant of the Isle of Wight, all fall within a period of two years after the announcement of Edward's marriage. No month seemed to pass without further evidence of Woodville advancement. There was also a continuing snobbish resentment of people regarded, whether rightly or wrongly, as *parvenu*.[3]

More important in creating their unsavoury reputation was their own behaviour. As a family, the Woodvilles were not conspicuous for charm and amiability. Like his daughter, Earl Rivers seems to have been greedy and grasping, and the duchess of Bedford was not much better. They could also be vengeful and overbearing.[4] Their eldest son, Anthony, Lord Scales, is a more attractive figure. His literary interests and his early patronage of Caxton have won for him a certain posthumous esteem. The earliest products of Caxton's printing press in

---

[1] See above, pp. 70 ff., for the grants to the Nevills, Herbert, Stafford and Audley.

[2] *CC* (First Continuation), 542; Waurin, ed. Dupont, II, 331–3; *CSP, Milan*, I, 131; Mancini, 61–5, 69; *GC*, 202–3; More, 7, 9, 15; *Annales*, 783 ff.

[3] Especially emphasized by Mancini, 69 ('certainly detested by the nobles, because they, who were ignoble and newly made men, were advanced beyond those who far excelled them in breeding and wisdom'), with reference to the younger male Woodvilles.

[4] For examples, see below, pp. 100–1.

England were made from Anthony Woodville's translations of 'The Dictes and Sayings of the Philosophers' and the *Moral Proverbs* of Christine de Pisan, published in November 1477 and February 1478. He was later to travel widely in Italy, Spain and Portugal, mainly to make pilgrimages to Rome, Compostella and shrines in southern Italy, and also had a considerable reputation for his knightly feats of arms. He is unusual (though not unique) amongst fifteenth-century laymen for a strange streak of melancholy and asceticism, reflected both in his 'death-day ballad' and his practice of wearing a hair-shirt beneath the silken clothes of the courtier.[1] Alone among the Woodvilles, he earned the approval of Mancini: 'a kind, serious and just man, and one tested by every vicissitude of life. Whatever his prosperity he had injured nobody, though benefiting many'; and Commynes saw him as 'ung tres gentil chevalier'.[2] Edward thought well enough of him to appoint him 'governor and ruler' of the young prince of Wales in 1473. Yet he too could be unscrupulous and overbearing. According to More, when balked by Hastings of the office of captain of Calais, he spread slanders about his rival, and temporarily brought him into disfavour with Edward.[3] He was also very much a realist in politics. As the recent discovery of some of his business papers relating to the last few months of the reign has shown, he was concerned to exercise the very considerable power which his control of the prince of Wales gave him, and his activities in Wales may have contributed to the fears which led Richard of Gloucester to seek power by force in 1483.[4] Less is known of the other male members of the family, but Thomas and Richard Grey and Sir Edward Woodville appear later in the reign as playboy-courtiers, enjoying a generally unsavoury reputation as the profligate companions of Edward's drinking and wenching. Thomas Grey, however, was also emerging as a serious political figure in the later part of the reign. Like Rivers, he had a personal feud with Hastings, and in 1482 the rivals were busy suborning informers and spreading incriminating stories about each other. Their quarrel gave the king much worry in the last months of his life.[5]

---

[1] For accounts of Scales, see *DNB* (*s.n.*, Woodville); Bentley, *Excerpta Historica*, 240–5; *CP*, XI, 22–4; J. Rous, *Historia Regum Anglie*, ed. T. Hearne, 212. The death-day ballad was printed incompletely in Rous, *op. cit.*, 214, and more fully in J. Ritson, *Antient Songs* (1790), 87–8.

[2] Mancini, 67–9; Commynes, II, 14. See also the approving remarks of More, 14.

[3] More, 51.

[4] E. W. Ives, 'Andrew Dymmock and the Papers of Anthony, Earl Rivers, 1482–3', *BIHR*, xli (1968), 216–25.

[5] More, 10–11; Mancini, 69; Ives, *op. cit.*, 221–2, who mentions that Dymmock's

1. Letter from Edward, earl of March, and his brother, Edmund of Rutland (with their autograph signatures), to their father, Richard, duke of York, complaining of 'the odious rule and demeaning of Richard Croft and his brother'. Written from Ludlow Castle, 'Saturday in Easter week', probably in 1454. (*B.M., Cottonian MS., Vespasian F. III.*) (See Appendix II)

2. Edward IV enthroned, upon a Wheel of Fortune. From an illuminated roll showing events in Edward's early life juxtaposed with scenes from biblical history. Executed by English artists before 1465. (*B.M., Harleian MS. 7353*)

3. Edward sets sail for Calais, probably in 1459. (*B.M., Harleian MS. 7353*)

4. Edward pardoning Henry VI after the Battle of Northampton, 1460.

5. William, Lord Herbert, and Anne, his wife, kneeling before Edward IV. Probably before 1462. (*John Lydgate*, Troy Book, *B.M., Royal MS. 18 D II, fol. 6*)

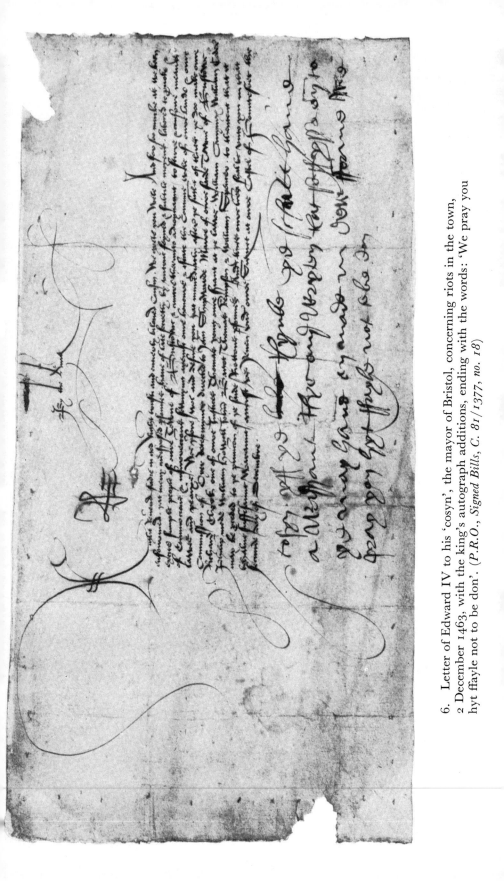

6. Letter of Edward IV to his 'cosyn', the mayor of Bristol, concerning riots in the town, 2 December 1463, with the king's autograph additions, ending with the words: 'We pray you hyt ffayle not to be don'. (*P.R.O., Signed Bills, C. 81/1377, no. 18*)

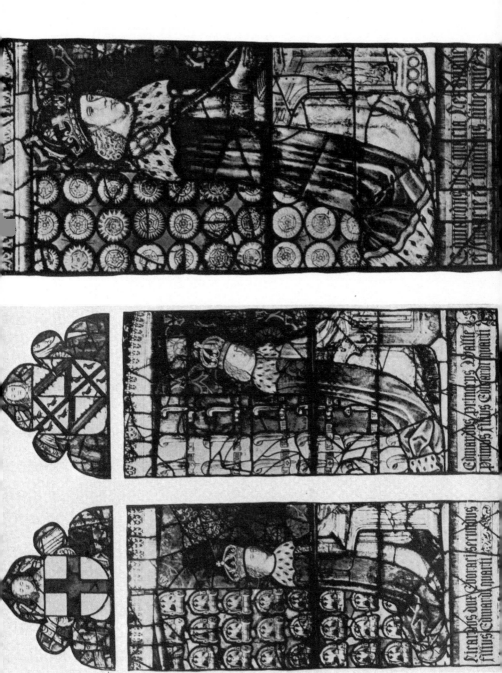

7 (a) Richard, duke of York, (b) Edward, prince of Wales and (c) Edward IV, from the series of family portraits in stained glass presented by the king to Canterbury Cathedral about 1482. In the North (Royal) window of the North-West Transept.

8a. Elizabeth Woodville, stained glass portrait from Canterbury Cathedral. The right-hand background shows the broomcods which were the Woodville device.

8b. Elizabeth Woodville. Panel portrait, probably contemporary, from Queens' College, Cambridge.

Yet the main source of Woodville unpopularity was undoubtedly the contemporary belief that they exercised an excessive and malign influence upon the king. They were essentially a courtier family, and their very numbers and closeness to the king made them a very conspicuous element in the royal entourage. In 1469 a court jester told the king that in some places the 'Ryvers' were so high that he could scarce escape through them.[1] The introduction of a new and favoured group into the malicious and competitive atmosphere of a royal court was likely to produce exaggerated reports of its influence. How great was the political weight of the queen and her family is not easy to determine, but there are good reasons for believing that it was much more considerable than some scholars would allow.[2] There is no need to rely upon a prejudiced chronicler for early evidence as to the powerful influence the Woodvilles had upon the king. T. B. Pugh has recently pointed out how revealing is the sober evidence of a marriage contract, between Lord Herbert's heir and the queen's sister, Mary Woodville, made on 20 March 1466. In 'this treaty of alliance between two upstart magnate families', Lord Herbert, whose own influence with the king was not negligible, stipulated that his existing lease of the lordship of Haverfordwest should be converted into a grant to him and his heirs, and he also sought to acquire from the king the reversion of Kilpeck (Herefordshire) and certain other lands. Rivers promised to arrange that these grants took place before the young couple were married, and they were all duly made on 26 September 1466.[3]

This evidence puts a different perspective on the participation of the Woodvilles in a famous episode – the persecution in 1468 of a former Lord Mayor of London, Sir Thomas Cook, as related in the *Great Chronicle of London*.[4] The author of the Chronicle, probably Robert Fabyan, states that he was himself an apprentice in Cook's household at the time, and his description is so circumstantial as to make this probable. Cook was accused of treason and imprisoned. Whilst he was still in gaol, the servants of Rivers and Sir John Fogge (who was

---

papers contain no fewer than four copies of an informer's confession, specially prepared for circulation. It should be noticed, however, that the supposed bad relations between Hastings and the queen's family did not prevent their doing business together; for examples, see below, p. 336.

[1] *GC*, 208.   [2] Especially Lander, *op. cit.*, 139 and *passim*.

[3] T. B. Pugh, *The Fifteenth Century*, 92–3.

[4] *GC*, 204–8, and below, Appendix I. See also below, pp. 100–1, for the misrepresentation of the legal aspects of the case by the chronicler. Apart from Fabyan's *Chronicle*, which has a common origin with the *Great Chronicle*, the only source to mention illegal despoliation by Rivers and Fogge is *Annales*, 790.

treasurer of the royal household, and a kinsman of the queen) ransacked his town house, drinking all they could from the wine in his cellars and letting the rest run to waste, and carrying away two hundred broadcloths, together with jewels and plate worth £700, and a valuable arras much desired by Jacquetta, duchess of Bedford, and said by Cook's foreman to have cost £800. The duchess is said to have borne a grudge against Cook because she had not been able to purchase this arras 'at her pleasure and price'. Cook was eventually brought to trial, and found guilty not of high treason but of the much lesser offence of misprision of treason (that is, being aware of treason but not revealing it). This verdict, according to the chronicle, did not entirely please the king, but so angered Rivers and his wife that they procured the dismissal from office of John Markham, chief justice of the king's bench, who had presided over the trial.[1] Cook was condemned to pay the enormous fine of 8,000 marks, and although (as the chronicle admits) an independent tribunal of merchants was appointed to assess the damage done to his property by Rivers and Fogge, the amount of which was to be deducted from his fine, he now had to face further demands from the queen. Under her ancient right of 'queen's gold', she claimed a further 800 marks, to which Cook had to agree, besides giving 'many good gifts' to her council. In his petition to the Readeption parliament (for, not surprisingly, Cook was a vigorous supporter of the restoration of Henry VI), Cook is said to have estimated the damage done to his property in London and to his country house in Essex, also ransacked by the servants of Rivers and Fogge – and clearly not paid for – at the vast sum of £14,666.[2] Recent attempts to maintain that the whole affair was conducted by due process of law lack conviction.[3] The legal records themselves show that, whilst the London juries of presentment were willing to indict known Lancastrian agents, such as Hawkins, whose evidence under torture involved Cook, they would not accept charges of treason against prominent and respectable London citizens. The first jury of presentment would not even allow that Cook and other Londoners accused with him were guilty of concealing treason. It became necessary for the commissioners to dismiss

[1] Markham was, in fact, dismissed from his post soon after 23 January 1469 (Foss, *Judges of England*, 435). Though accepted by Foss and others, the story that Rivers procured his dismissal probably derives from the *Great Chronicle* via the Elizabethan antiquary, John Stow (*Annales*, 420). But dismissals of chief justices were very rare in Edward's reign.

[2] *GC*, 207–8, 213. The details of gifts to the queen's council are in Fabyan, *Chronicle*, 656–7.

[3] Particularly by Bellamy, 'Justice under the Yorkist Kings', 143–5.

this jury, and empanel a new one. On the third day this second grand jury was prevailed upon to indict Cook and the others of the full charges, but the trial juries entirely acquitted the others – a London mercer named Portaleyn and Hugh Pakenham 'late of Southwark, gentleman' – and found Cook guilty of misprision. Clearly the juries were acting under extreme pressure.[1] Though the chronicler's version of these events is obviously partisan, it cannot easily be set aside. It may well be, as Miss Scofield observed, that 'the truth of the whole ugly story seems to be that Earl Rivers and his wife, who for some reason wanted to get rid of Cook, played upon the cupidity of the king . . . in order to accomplish their purpose'. In the wider context of Edward's courting the goodwill of the Londoners, this persecution of Cook, who had been created a knight of the Bath at Queen Elizabeth's coronation only three years before, seems ill-judged and impolitic in the extreme.[2]

It is unlikely that the influence of the queen and her family diminished in the second decade of Edward's reign, especially as other contenders for power were removed, with the fall of the Nevill family in 1471, the overthrow of Clarence in 1478, and Gloucester's virtual withdrawal to the north of England about the same time.[3] The records of the London Mercers and Merchant Adventurers contain a number of revealing entries which show that the queen's influence, at least, had not diminished with the passage of time. In 1479 they incurred the royal displeasure through being in arrears in the payment of their subsidy, and the king demanded a 'recompense' of £2,000. The merchants lobbied the queen, the marquis of Dorset, the earl of Essex, and Lord Hastings to 'labour the king' on their behalf. Hastings, whose own influence at court was very considerable, promised to be 'their very good and special lord', but advised them, nevertheless, to apply their labour still 'unto the queen's grace and to the lord marquis', and he (Hastings) would help also 'when the time cometh'. It was especially through the queen that 'we trust in God to have help and comfort'.

[1] P.R.O., K.B. 9/319/mm. 7, 35-7, 40, 49–51. Another prominent Londoner, Sir John Plommer, who, like Cook, had been made a Knight of the Bath in 1465, was also found not guilty of any treason.

[2] Scofield, I, 461. For Edward's relations with London, see below, pp. 353–6. There is, however, no truth in the later story that Elizabeth Woodville procured the death of the Irish earl of Desmond on the grounds that he had urged against Edward's marrying her, and thought a divorce desirable. It can be dismissed as a Tudor fabrication (E. Curtis, *Hist. of Medieval Ireland, 1110–1513*, 378–9; G. H. Orpen, *EHR*, xxx (1915), 342–3; and see also below, pp. 203–4).

[3] For their alleged share in the fall of Clarence, see below, p. 244.

Further labouring of Earls Rivers, Dorset and Hastings followed, but in the end it was 'at the instance of the queen's good grace' that Edward agreed to forgo a part of his demand. Nor was this the only example of her ability to protect the interest of the adventurers.[1] The corporation of Bristol likewise found comfort in Woodville influence when their mayor was maliciously accused of treason by one Thomas Norton. After the king, who personally heard the case, had decided in their favour, they sent off a series of letters of thanks for 'good and favourable lordship' to Rivers, Dorset, his brother, Richard Grey, Lord Dacre, the queen's chamberlain, John Alcock, bishop of Worcester, who was president of the prince of Wales's council, and Sir Thomas Vaughan, treasurer of the prince's chamber, and a close Woodville associate.[2] Nor were the queen's relatives neglectful of their own interests. Promoting a landed endowment for the queen's sons by her first marriage, Thomas and Richard Grey, involved the king in one of the more shabby inheritance deals of the reign, and Rivers's position as governor of the Prince of Wales gave him and other Woodville associates considerable political power in Wales and the Marches. Not only had he control of the prince's revenues but also the right to remove the person of the prince from place to place at his discretion, which provided him with important political initiative in the event of any mishap to the king, and apparently also power to raise troops in Wales if need be.[3]

The prominence of the Woodvilles at court, even their control of the heir to the throne (and his younger brother, Richard of Shrewsbury), would have been less politically dangerous if they had not been at once so widely unpopular and so jealous of their own influence as to be on bad terms with possible rivals for power, among them Gloucester and Hastings. Amongst contemporary writers, Dominic Mancini is the most forthrightly critical of the Woodvilles. He may have exaggerated their influence, but as a foreigner, with no political axe to grind, he is probably accurately reflecting contemporary opinion in reporting how unpopular they were, especially among the nobility.[4] A year later, in his attempt to blacken his brother's regime, Richard III did not need to name the 'persons insolent, vicious and of inordinate avarice' whose evil counsel had misled Edward IV.[5] Mancini is supported by

[1] *Acts of Court of the Mercers' Company*, ed. L. Lyell and F. D. Watney, 118–27.
[2] *Great Red Book of Bristol*, ed. E. W. W. Veale (Bristol Record Society Publications, xviii, 1953), iv, 84–6.
[3] Ives, 'Andrew Dymmock . . . and Earl Rivers', 223–4; and for the Greys and the Exeter inheritance, see below, pp. 336–7.
[4] Mancini, 65, 69.   [5] *RP*, VI, 140.

the more temperate testimony of the Croyland Chronicler. In the vital council meeting which took place shortly after Edward's death, he tells us (and he was probably present in person), all the councillors were anxious to secure the untroubled succession of Edward V, but the more prudent councillors believed that it would be utterly wrong to entrust the government of the young king to 'the uncles and brothers of the queen's blood'.[1] Apart from the queen's jealousy of Gloucester, her animosity towards Hastings, and the latter's feud with the marquis of Dorset, were unfortunate in persuading the powerful and much-respected Hastings to lend his support to Gloucester against the Woodvilles, until, too late, he began to suspect Gloucester's intentions towards the young princes. Hastings told the same council meeting that he would withdraw to Calais if the young king came to London at the head of a Woodville army, for he 'feared that if supreme power fell into the hands of those of the queen's blood, they would most bitterly revenge themselves on himself for the injuries which they claimed he had done to them'.[2] Mancini was probably right in his belief that an important factor in the revolution was the dissension between Hastings and Dorset, for despite the king's attempt to reconcile them on his deathbed, the latent jealousy between the two remained.[3] Edward had created a real risk to the future political peace of his realm in allowing his heir to be surrounded by Woodvilles from infancy, educated under their guidance, and necessarily under their influence. When Edward died prematurely in April 1483, the likelihood of a regency dominated by the queen's unpopular family was a prospect which commended itself to no one.

[1] *CC*, 564.   [2] *CC*, 565.   [3] Mancini, 69.

Chapter 6

THE BURGUNDIAN ALLIANCE AND THE BREACH WITH WARWICK, 1465–1469

In England's domestic politics the later 1460s are dominated by Edward's growing estrangement from Richard, earl of Warwick, and the latter's gradual drift into open rebellion. In foreign affairs the key issue in England's increasingly active involvement in European politics was whether she should enter into a firm alliance with either France or Burgundy against the other. Between these two themes there is a more than casual connection. For it was essentially over the direction of foreign policy that the differences between the king and the earl were most sharply apparent, within the wider context of Edward's continuing assertion of his political independence.[1]

From the beginning of 1465, certain factors in England's foreign situation begin to stand out more clearly. First, the expansionist and centralizing policies of King Louis XI of France produced a growing tension between the French Crown and many of its greatest subjects, especially the dukes of Burgundy and Brittany. In 1465 this feudal and provincial reaction erupted into civil war, but the princely coalition – the League of the Common Weal – was soon broken up by Louis at the cost of concessions to some of its leaders. Continuing pressure by Louis on Burgundy and Brittany combined to maintain a state of constant unease on the Continent. In this situation England, with Edward increasingly secure on her throne, assumed a new importance. Neither side across the Channel wished to see her actively committed to the other, and first France, and then Burgundy and Brittany, actively sought her alliance. Next, and of great importance in Anglo-French

[1] This was the explanation adopted by the most perceptive of contemporary observers, the Croyland Chronicler, 551: 'the earl continued to show favour to all the queen's kindred, until he found that all her relatives and connections, contrary to his wishes, were using their utmost endeavours to promote the other marriage, which, in conformity with the king's wishes, eventually took place between Charles and the lady Margaret, and were favouring other designs to which he was strongly opposed'.

relations, is the attitude of Warwick himself. We can probably never know how far his advocacy of an Anglo-French alliance was based upon principle rather than self-interest, but there is no doubt that King Louis's systematic courting of the earl's goodwill, treating him as the arbiter of English policy, tempted his ambition and increasingly involved his prestige. As he was drawn more deeply into Louis's schemes, it became increasingly difficult and humiliating for him to accept the obvious decline of his influence over his royal master. His dilemma was sharpened, since (as there is good reason to believe) Woodville influence was being exerted equally strongly towards an English alliance with their Burgundian kinsmen.

Finally, the diplomatic situation was complicated by questions of commercial interest and national sentiment. The duke of Burgundy's dominions formed England's most important overseas market, especially for cloth. But the dukes had to take account of pressure from their own cloth-manufacturing interests, anxious to keep out competition from much cheaper English goods; and in October 1464, Duke Philip was persuaded to place an embargo on the import of English cloth into his territories.[1] For the well-organized mercantile lobby in England, one advantage of a treaty with Burgundy would be the restoration of free trade. But commercial considerations were not wholly on the side of a Burgundian alliance. France, too, was potentially a great market for English exports, and Louis was at pains to dangle before English eyes the advantages of a favourable commercial treaty. These were probably greater than most Englishmen realized, as the treaty of 1475 was to prove. Protagonists of a French alliance had, however, to reckon with the deep and strong popular feelings in England which still regarded France as the ancient and traditional enemy. War with France had become almost the only cause for which the commons in parliament were ready to vote money. Though Burgundy might not be wholly popular with the merchant class, there was a legacy of wider prejudice against France; and, in inclining towards a Burgundian connection, Edward, rather than Warwick, proved a better judge of popular opinion.[2]

In the early months of 1465 the diplomatic situation was still full of

[1] This was partly in response to English protectionist statutes in 1463. The English in their turn responded with a ban on all Burgundian imports except foodstuffs in 1465 (*Statutes of the Realm*, II, 395-9, 411-13). For the context of this, see below, pp. 358-60.

[2] See below, pp. 158-9, for the unpopularity of Warwick's French alliance in 1470-1471, and for English popular nationalism in general, V. J. Scattergood, *Politics and Poetry in the Fifteenth Century*, 35-106 *passim*.

uncertainty for England. During the illness of Duke Philip, Burgundy was temporarily under the control of his heir, Charles, count of Charolais, who still retained strong Lancastrian sympathies.[1] King Louis was urging an active alliance between France and England against Burgundy. In Brittany, Duke Francis II, who had earlier shown sympathy towards the Lancastrians, was now being forced by Louis's provocative policies, aimed at undermining the independence of the Breton duchy, into a posture hostile to France. Friendship with England was a natural consequence of his sense of insecurity, and here too commercial considerations played a part, for England was Brittany's most important market.[2] On 8 May 1465, Edward appointed a powerful embassy, headed by Warwick, Hastings and Wenlock, with a very wide brief. It had instructions to treat at will with the king of France, the duke of Burgundy, and the duke of Brittany for treaties of peace, friendship or commerce. In other words, it was intended as a means of finding out what these princes might offer for English support without committing her to anything definite.[3] But it had little chance to achieve anything, for France was now convulsed by the War of the Public Weal, begun in the spring by an attack from Brittany led by Louis's dissident brother, Charles. Louis was able to confront his opponents one by one; Charolais was checked at the battle of Montlhéry (16 July 1465) and soon afterwards the League broke up. Louis, however, had to surrender to Burgundy Boulogne, Guines and the 'Somme towns' by the treaties of Conflans and St Maur (October 1465), and to install his brother Charles as duke of Normandy.[4]

From all this England remained carefully aloof. Probably Edward was wary of a league which included Margaret of Anjou's brother, Duke John of Calabria, as well as Charolais, whom he could not yet trust. He may have feared that any attempt to exploit Louis's difficulties would lead the French king to give aid to Queen Margaret, who

[1] John of Gaunt, duke of Lancaster, was his great-grandfather on his mother's side; his affection for the House of Lancaster is mentioned by Commynes and Chastellain, both of whom knew him well; and he was paying pensions to the exiled dukes of Somerset and Exeter (J. Calmette, 'Le Mariage de Charles le Téméraire et de Marguerite d'York', *Annales de Bourgogne*, I (1929), 194–5).

[2] B. A. Pocquet du Haut-Jussé, *François II, Duc de Bretagne, et l'Angleterre*, 1–3, 60–1, 70 ff.

[3] For the diplomacy of autumn 1464 and 1465, Scofield, I, 355–60, 378–80; Calmette and Perinelle, *Louis XI et l'Angleterre*, 63–72; Thielemans, *Bourgogne et Angleterre*, 415–17.

[4] P. M. Kendall, *Louis XI*, 142–86. The 'Somme towns' were the domains of the French Crown on either bank of the Somme and between that river and Flanders, originally ceded to Burgundy in 1435 and since repurchased by Louis.

was in Paris in October 1465, trying to unite the adversaries in France in a plan to restore Henry VI.[1] Above all, he had not the sinews of war to hand. He did not react when Louis boldly ejected his brother from Normandy and resumed possession of the duchy. He had been encouraged to do this by what has been called 'an undoubtedly treasonable message' from the earl of Warwick, telling him that England would not attempt any offensive at this time.[2]

1466 saw Edward moving steadily closer to a firm connection with Burgundy. Charles of Charolais's mistrust of Louis, and his wish to prevent an Anglo-French alliance, led him to take the initiative. A widower since the death in August 1465 of his second wife, Isabel of Bourbon, he now overcame his Lancastrian sympathies sufficiently to revive the notion of an Anglo-Burgundian marriage alliance. Late in 1465 or early in 1466 he sent his agent, Guillaume de Cluny, to England to make a tentative proposal that he should marry Edward's nineteen-year-old sister, Margaret of York. This young lady was already virtually betrothed to Don Pedro of Portugal, who had recently been proclaimed king by the Catalan independence movement.[3] Edward's response was the appointment of an embassy on 22 March 1466, again headed by Warwick, Hastings and Wenlock, to negotiate with both Burgundy and France.[4] With Charolais it was to discuss the restrictions on commerce, to treat regarding the marriage of Margaret of York, and to propose a further marriage between Charles's daughter, Mary of Burgundy, and George, duke of Clarence. Warwick can scarcely have relished this part of his task. Not only did he prefer the French connection in general but he also had plans to marry Clarence to his elder daughter, Isabel. It was possibly at this meeting with Charolais at Boulogne on 15 April 1466 that he first conceived the violent dislike he later had for Charles.[5] It is not surprising that no agreement was reached. To Louis the English envoys were to make offers for a truce or a peace treaty, and perhaps to sound him about an alternative

<hr>

[1] Calmette and Perinelle, 69.
[2] So described by E. F. Jacob, *The Fifteenth Century*, 551. It is known only from a despatch by the Milanese ambassador in France, printed in Calmette and Perinelle, 72, n. 2.
[3] Calmette, *op. cit.*, 195–6; Scofield, I, 404. Don Pedro died on 29 June 1466.
[4] Rymer, *Foedera*, XI, 562–6 (for the instructions); Scofield, I, 405–7; Calmette and Perinelle, 72–3.
[5] P. M. Kendall, *Warwick the Kingmaker*, 189, claims that 'at first sight the two men hated each other, politically, viscerally'. But both *CC*, 551, and Polydore Vergil, 118, merely say that Warwick hated Charolais because of Charles's marriage to Margaret of York in 1468.

marriage for Margaret of York. No difficulty was found in agreeing, on 24 May, the terms of a truce to last until March 1468. Although he could offer no marriage for Margaret as attractive as the match with Charolais, he may already have been prepared to bid high for an English alliance.[1] News of Louis's activities seems to have reached the ears of Charolais, and his fears of a league between France and England merely served to make his own approaches more vigorous. On 23 October 1466 he concluded with Edward a secret treaty of amity and mutual assistance. Whilst committing neither side to anything very specific, this is of interest as a sign of Edward's intentions and of Charolais's now active interest in an English alliance.[2]

During 1467 London became the centre of an increasingly vigorous competition for English support. A series of dual negotiations followed. In December 1466 a Burgundian embassy came to England to discuss the problems of 'intercourse of merchandise', and negotiations on the English side were led by Earl Rivers, Lord Hastings and Bishop Stillington of Bath and Wells, but progress was slow because of Burgundian reluctance to revoke the ban on the import of English cloth. Then, in February 1467, safe-conducts were granted for a French embassy led by the Bastard of Bourbon to come to London. It arrived with plans to extend the truce and for mutual aid against each other's rebels, but more important were Louis's proposals for a French-sponsored marriage for Margaret of York and his offer to pay Edward a regular pension of 4,000 crowns annually.[3] Tempting as this last offer might have been, Edward was not to be diverted. He carefully avoided all contact with the French embassy, leaving Warwick to deal with it. But he was also anxious to keep alive the negotiations with France, partly to avoid an open breach with Warwick, and partly to get better terms from Burgundy. The negotiations with Charolais were continuing. In April 1467 an English embassy was sent to Bruges to talk further about the marriage and the conclusion of an alliance. Arrange-

[1] Scofield, I, 406, and Jacob, *The Fifteenth Century*, 551, both wrongly attribute to this year French proposals apparently first advanced in 1467. Charolais's fears of an Anglo-French *rapprochement* are set forth in the document printed in Calmette and Perinelle, 298–9.
[2] Thielemans, *op. cit.*, 420–1, and documents cited there.
[3] Calmette and Perinelle, 79–80. *Annales*, 787, gives the pension as 4,000 marks (£2,666 13s 4d): cf. Scofield, I, 406, and Jacob, *op. cit.*, 551, for the figure of 40,000 gold crowns (about £8,000). Edward was also in touch with various other foreign princes at this time. The chronicler, Gregory, 235, mentions under 1467 the arrival of ambassadors from Castile, Scotland, Naples, the duke of Ferrara, the Emperor Frederick III, and the pope (as well as France, Burgundy and Brittany) – a sign of the growing international acceptance of the Yorkist regime.

ments had been made for the long-awaited tournament between Anthony, Bastard of Burgundy, and Anthony, Lord Scales, to take place in London in May or early June, and it was convenient for Edward to have Warwick out of the way during the ceremonial flattery of Burgundy which would accompany the Bastard's visit. For these reasons, therefore, Edward commissioned Warwick and Wenlock on 6 May 1467 to lead an embassy to France for further discussions of Louis's proposals, and on 28 May they sailed from Sandwich in company with the returning French ambassadors.[1]

Louis's warm reception of this embassy marks the high peak of his efforts to bid for an English alliance through the medium of Warwick's influence. Everything possible was done to flatter the ambassadors and win their goodwill; expensive presents were lavished upon them, including a great jewelled gold cup costing 2,000 livres for the earl, and no fewer than twelve silver cups for his steward. The benefits of a French alliance, especially the commercial advantages, were firmly placed before them. Louis offered to create free fairs for English merchants to supplant those in Burgundian territory at Antwerp, and to reduce the tolls and restrictions which had hampered the trade in wine and cloth between England and France for many years. He also commanded the merchants of Rouen to supply the English party with all they wanted of silk, damask and velvet free of charge, as an advertisement for fine French textile manufactures. In public he had already professed high hopes for the future of Anglo-French cooperation. Together they would destroy the Burgundian state and partition its territories. Holland, Zeeland and Brabant might form a dowry for the marriage of Duke Richard of Gloucester and Louis's second daughter, Jeanne, and Margaret of York should marry Philip of Savoy, brother of Queen Charlotte of France.[2] In private, he was probably less sanguine. The Milanese ambassadors believed that it was now, for the first time, that Louis put forward his scheme for a *rapprochement* between Warwick and Margaret of Anjou, and the subsequent restoration of Henry VI.[3]

The events of the summer and autumn of 1467 made it entirely clear that where foreign policy was concerned Warwick could no longer maintain the illusion of influence over his royal master. There is a striking coincidence between Warwick's absence abroad and the events

---

[1] Rymer, *Foedera*, XI, 578; Scofield, I, 412–13.
[2] For details of the embassy, Calmette and Perinelle, 81–7; Scofield, I, 424–6; and for Louis's hopes, *CSP, Milan*, I, 118–20.
[3] *Ibid.*, 120.

in London during the first fortnight of June. The ceremonies which
followed the arrival of the Bastard of Burgundy in London prominently
featured the Woodvilles and their new connections by marriage, like
the earls of Arundel and Kent, and men from the king's personal circle,
such as Lords Herbert, Stafford and Mountjoy.[1] On 3 June, after
having audience with the king, the Bastard was among the spectators
at the opening of parliament in Edward's presence in the Painted
Chamber at Westminster. A notable absentee was the chancellor,
George Nevill, archbishop of York, who may have been ill at the time.[2]
On 8 June, however, he was dismissed from office. The chancellor had
probably acted as his brother's spokesman during Warwick's absence;
he is said to have tried to obstruct the Bastard's visit to England; and
he was intriguing in Rome for a cardinal's hat.[3] Probably Edward was
no longer prepared to be lectured by him. But his dismissal was the
most direct and unequivocal blow at Nevill power the king had hitherto
allowed himself, and his action was made the more pointed by the
way it was done. For Edward rode in person, with Clarence and eleven
of his closest supporters in his company, to George Nevill's inn at
Charing Cross, to demand the surrender of the Great Seal, and he
stayed there until it had been handed over to the keeping of Robert
Kirkham.[4] Finally, and as another indication that in matters of foreign
policy he intended to have his own way, on 9 June he concluded a
thirty-year truce with Duke Francis of Brittany, and undertook to help
him against whatever enemy might attack him.[5]

The death of Duke Philip of Burgundy on 15 June 1467 put an end
both to the Bastard's visit to England and Warwick's mission to France.
Louis appointed a substantial embassy under the archbishop of Narbonne to accompany Warwick on his return to England, where both
arrived on 24 June. Although not entirely cold-shouldered by the king,
they saw little of him, and evidently felt themselves ill-used.[6] Quartered
in apartments just vacated by the Bastard and his train, receiving only
the most meagre of the customary presents given to ambassadors (in

---

[1] *Excerpta Historica*, ed. S. Bentley, 171–212 (Chester Herald's account); Scofield, I,
414–20. Not a single Nevill is mentioned as playing any part.
[2] *Annales*, 786, which claims that he was ill a week later when dismissed from office.
[3] Scofield, I, 407; *Annales*, 789.   [4] *CCR, 1461–8*, 456–7.
[5] Pocquet du Haut-Jussé, *op. cit.*, 123; Calmette and Perinelle, 88.
[6] The circumstantial account in Waurin, ed. Dupont, II, 346–9, though followed by
Calmette and Perinelle, 89, exaggerates the hostility of Edward's reception; cf.
Annales, 787, and Scofield, I, 426. Apart from Clarence, however, their reception at
Westminster was handled by strong supporters of Burgundy, Hastings, Scales and
his brother, John Woodville.

pointed contrast to Louis's generosity to Warwick's mission), they could get no answer to any of their proposals, except that Edward promised to send an embassy to France bearing his final answer. Moreover, during their stay in London, Edward renewed his treaty of friendship with Burgundy, and also, on 6 July, concluded an alliance with King Henry of Castile, equally a potential threat to France.[1] On 14 July the French ambassadors, aggrieved and empty-handed, left for home, whilst Warwick, having escorted them to the coast, withdrew to his estates in the north. As the arbiter of English foreign policy, his credibility was now wholly destroyed in the eyes of Louis XI.

Edward now pressed forward his plans for a firm alliance with Burgundy and Brittany. With the new Duke Charles the bargaining was hard and the English got the worse of it. Edward, risking considerable unpopularity, cleared the way for commercial settlement by annulling the statutes of 1463 and 1465 which had prohibited Burgundian imports into England. A commercial treaty was drawn up on 24 November 1467, which provided for free 'intercourse of merchandise' between the subjects of the two princes for the next thirty years, but it specifically reserved the problem of the 'enlarging' of English cloth for discussion at a diet to be held at Bruges on 15 January 1468.[2] There was less difficulty in agreeing upon a truce for thirty years and pledges by the two princes to give each other aid against their enemies.[3]

The marriage treaty, settled at Brussels on 16 February and ratified by Edward on 14 March 1468, raised its own problems. Edward had to bid high for Charles's hand. The bride's dowry was fixed at 200,000 gold crowns (£41,666 13s 4d), of which 50,000 were due on the wedding day. Further, Charles insisted that Edward's bond for this sum should be guaranteed by responsible groups of English or Italian merchants. It was essentially his difficulties in raising this money which caused the marriage day to be postponed from 4 May to 3 July 1468. With the commercial treaty unpopular among English merchants, he did not dare ask parliament for money to be sent to Burgundy. Eventually he raised the down-payment by loans chiefly from Staple and London merchants, on the security of grants voted by parliament for the pur-

---

[1] Rymer, *Foedera*, XI, 580–1 (Charles's ratification of the treaty, 15 July; for Edward's, 17 July, Scofield, I, 427); Rymer, *Foedera*, XI, 583–90 (for Castile). Edward had already concluded a treaty with an enemy of France, King Ferdinand I of Naples (Scofield, I, 401–2), and was in active negotiation with another, John II, king of Aragon (Calmette and Perinelle, 98–9).
[2] Rymer, *Foedera*, XI, 591–600; Scofield, I, 430–2; and below, p. 364 and n. 2.
[3] Calmette and Perinelle, 95–6 (dates as for marriage-treaty below).

pose of war with France.[1] Margaret of York finally left London on 18 June, crossed from Margate to Sluys, and on 3 July, amidst 'the most splendid and extravagant festivities ever contrived in the entire annals of Burgundy', was married at Damme to Duke Charles.[2]

Negotiations with Brittany were much easier, for her relations with France had been deteriorating steadily, and her need of English support was correspondingly greater. Duke Francis's main need was for English troops to help him when his six-month truce with France, signed on 6 January 1468, expired. On 2 and 3 April 1468 an Anglo-Breton conference at Greenwich agreed on the main features of an offensive–defensive treaty of alliance. England was to supply 3,000 archers to Brittany at two months' notice, and to pay half their wages for six months; arrangements were made for the division of conquered territory in the event of an English invasion of France; there was to be a truce for thirty years between the two, complemented by an elaborate commercial treaty, on much the same lines as that between England and Burgundy.[3] Since Brittany and Burgundy were already bound to each other by agreements for mutual aid, the diplomatic triangle pointed at France now seemed complete.

By midsummer 1468, therefore, Edward had completed his first major series of diplomatic manœuvres. From the wholly defensive posture of his early years, imposed by insecurity and internal conflict, he had moved into the classic anti-French stance of late-medieval English kings, exploiting opposition within the kingdom of France, and the malice of her external enemies, for their own aggressive purposes; and this pattern was to be repeated in 1472 and 1475. On 17 May 1468 the new chancellor, Bishop Robert Stillington of Bath and Wells, was able to inform parliament that the king had now concluded, or was about to conclude, treaties with Castile, Aragon, Denmark, Scotland, the Empire and Naples, but especially with the dukes of Burgundy and Brittany; and that he now felt secure enough in his alliances to invade France. The commons responded by voting him a substantial grant of taxation for war purposes. All this was done in the teeth of continuing opposition from the earl of Warwick.[4]

[1] Scofield, I, 446–50, 450–3.
[2] Vaughan, *Charles the Bold*, 48 ff., for a good modern description. Lengthy contemporary accounts of the marriage and the subsequent festivities are in Olivier de la Marche, *Mémoires*, III, 101–20, IV, 95–144, and *Excerpta Historica*, ed. Bentley, 227–39; and see *PL*, IV, 198–9, for the great impression made on John Paston the younger, who was in Margaret's retinue.
[3] Rymer, *Foedera*, XI, 618–25; Pocquet du Haut-Jussé, *op. cit.*, 128–36.
[4] *RP*, V, 622–4; and for Warwick's attitude, below, p. 118.

In the event, the new anti-French coalition proved brittle. Brittany was its weakest link. King Louis persuaded Charles of Burgundy, still engaged in his fortnight-long wedding celebrations, to agree to a truce with France to last until 1 August, and then ordered his troops to strike at Brittany immediately after the expiry of the Franco-Breton truce on 15 July. Edward showed no haste to come to the aid of his ally. In London haggling continued over the diplomatic details of his treaty with the duke, and not until 3 August did he ratify the clause committing him to send troops to Brittany. There was further delay before indentures were signed with the commanders of the English forces. On 10 September Lord Mountjoy undertook to lead the expeditionary force of 3,000 archers, and Lord Scales to command a naval force of 3,000 soldiers and 1,100 sailors serving at Edward's own cost and under English control, and intended, apparently, to descend upon France.[1] But on the very same day Duke Francis, unable to resist the French invasion any longer without immediate aid, came to terms with France, and by the Treaty of Ancenis agreed to abandon his allies.[2] Edward now united a much reduced force under Mountjoy with the fleet under Scales and seems to have projected a landing in southern France.[3] Diverted from this plan by reports that Margaret of Anjou, with a small force collected at Harfleur, was preparing to invade England in October, the English fleet set out to patrol the Channel. It encountered no enemies except heavy storms and eventually retired ingloriously to the Isle of Wight in November. All Edward had to show for the expenditure of about £18,000 was some help in the reconquest of Jersey from the French.[4] Nor did Charles of Burgundy prove a satisfactory ally. He soon made a separate settlement with Louis, and by the Treaty of Péronne (14 October 1468) he promised not to aid the English if they invaded France, and agreed to a truce. Clearly nothing more could be expected of him for the time being.[5]

1 Rymer, *Foedera*, XI, 626–30; Pocquet du Haut-Jussé, *op. cit.*, 138–41; Calmette and Perinelle, 101–2; Scofield, I, 472–3.
2 Pocquet du Haut-Jussé, *op. cit.*, 142; Scofield, I, 473.
3 This was the belief of the Milanese agents in France, one of whom reported (November 1468) an improbable English landing on the French Mediterranean coast (*CSP, Milan*, I, 126–7).
4 The evidence for Margaret's plan is a statement in *Annales*, 792; although dismissed by Scofield, I, 477, it is supported by a Milanese report that Louis had given her seven ships at Rouen, cited by Calmette and Perinelle, 104 n. 3. For the fleet at sea, *Annales*, 792; *Three Fifteenth-Century Chronicles*, 182; and for the reconquest of Jersey (where the castle of Mont Orgueil had been in French hands since 1461), Scofield, I, 478–80.
5 Kendall, *Louis XI*, 196–224, esp. 213–14.

Whether Edward seriously intended to invade France in 1468 on any substantial scale is very doubtful, despite his grandiose statement to parliament. There was no plan for a direct frontal assault under his own command on the lines of the grand expedition of 1475. He seems to have thought primarily in terms of assistance to allies who would bear the main burden of war with Louis. His commitment was at best of a very limited character, and the defection of his allies soon put an end to his hopes. Yet not all was lost from his diplomatic labours. Close relations with Burgundy and Brittany were soon renewed, and on 20 October 1468, after months of negotiations, a treaty of alliance with John II, king of Aragon, complemented England's treaty with Castile, and completed the diplomatic encirclement of France.[1]

An active anti-French policy, however, carried its own inherent risks. Support for the Lancastrians was Louis's obvious response to Yorkist hostility. The revival of Lancastrian plots made 1468 a year of alarm and intrigues.[2] In June Louis gambled, in rather miserly fashion, on Jasper Tudor's chances of raising insurrection in Wales. His tiny expedition of three ships and some fifty men reached West Wales in July, only to find the garrison of Harlech Castle now closely invested by Lord Herbert. Marching towards the north coast, Jasper had more success, and roused enough support to sack and burn the town of Denbigh, before meeting defeat at the hands of a royal force under Lord Herbert and his brother, Sir Richard. Though Jasper made good his escape to France, disappointment at his failure drove the defenders of Harlech to capitulate on 14 August 1468.[3] But the danger of active French assistance to the exiled government of Henry VI remained real enough. Official Lancastrian spokesmen were now commending their cause to Louis by proposing to enlist the aid of the earl of Warwick.[4] Growing unrest in England and the prospect of support from abroad were a dangerous combination in the winter of Richard Nevill's discontent.

It is far from easy to trace with precision the development of the breach between the king and his most powerful subject. Some modern critics

[1] Rymer, *Foedera*, XI, 631–5; and, for the relations of England with Brittany and Burgundy, Scofield, I, 483–5; Pocquet du Haut-Jussé, *op. cit.*, 142–4. In 1469 Edward was presented with the collar of the Burgundian order of the Golden Fleece, and Duke Charles was made a Knight of the Garter.

[2] See below, pp. 122–4.

[3] *Annales*, 791; Gregory, 237; and below, p. 120.

[4] Calmette and Perinelle, 303–5 (Memoir presented to the chancellor of France by Henry VI's chancellor, Sir John Fortescue, after 17 May 1468).

have accused Edward of tactless and provocative behaviour towards the Nevills. His worst rudeness seems to have been directed rather at Archbishop George Nevill than at his brothers. The king and queen were conspicuously absent from the vulgarly ostentatious ceremonies accompanying his installation as archbishop of York in September 1465.[1] The way in which he was dismissed from the chancellorship in June 1467 was equally pointed. According to one report, Edward mocked the archbishop's ambitions for a red hat by sending to him the pope's letter announcing that Archbishop Bourchier of Canterbury had been made a cardinal in September 1467.[2] The earl himself was more directly affected by Edward's refusal to consider Warwick's wish to marry one of his daughters to Duke George of Clarence. No one knows when Warwick first conceived this scheme, but it was probably during 1466 as the Woodville marriages were being completed, and it was certainly being discussed at the French court by April 1467.[3] The fact that Warwick had to negotiate secretly at Rome in order to obtain the necessary papal dispensation for the marriage shows that Edward was not to be diverted from his opposition to a plan which would link the Nevill interest to the succession to the throne, for Clarence was still Edward's heir male presumptive.[4]

But it would be false to suppose that by a series of calculated insults Edward deliberately drove Warwick into a position from which rebellion was the only honourable escape. In spite of his already massive gains from the Yorkist victory, Richard Nevill continued to bask in the golden sun of royal patronage. His rewards included further forfeited lands in the north, the profitable office of justice of the royal forests north of Trent, which carried a fee of 100 marks yearly, the valuable wardship of the estates of the baronial family of Lovel, with the marriage of the heir, Francis, and (with his brother, John) the profits of all royal mines of gold, silver and lead north of Trent. Further grants were made to him as late as February 1469.[5]

[1] *Annales*, 785 (the only chronicler to mention it). For details of the great feast provided, see Scofield, I, 399–400. Sixty-two cooks were employed to prepare (amongst a host of other things) 104 oxen, 1,000 sheep, 500 deer, 400 swans, 2,000 geese, 2,000 chickens, and 13,000 jellies, tarts and custards, at what must have been the biggest festivity of the entire fifteenth century.   [2] *Annales*, 789, and above, p. 110.
[3] *CSP, Milan*, I, 119 (reported as an accomplished fact); Waurin, ed. Dupont, II, 334, places it immediately after the Woodville marriages of 1464–6, and claims (in a circumstantial story) that Edward heard of it immediately afterwards.
[4] *Annales*, 788, for the dispensation. Edward now had two daughters by Elizabeth Woodville – Elizabeth, to whom Warwick stood godfather, born 11 February 1466, and Mary, born August 1467.
[5] For details, see Appendix III.

Nor was royal goodwill confined to an attempt to pacify Warwick's ill-humour through a series of profitable favours. In spite of the earl's truculent opposition to his foreign policy, and accumulating evidence of his dissidence, Edward still wished to allow Warwick an honourable, if not a dominant, place in government. The earl was offered a series of opportunities to share in the work of the council. In general, the king showed remarkable patience with his angry and overbearing cousin. Eventually this forbearance became an almost culpable failure to believe him guilty of treason. The breach with Edward was essentially of Warwick's own making, and was the product of his inability to accept anything less than domination over the king.

The earliest evidence that Warwick was actively turning to treason comes from a rather suspect source. This is the circumstantial account of events in London during the visit of the French ambassadors in June and July 1467, written by the Burgundian chronicler, Jean de Waurin.[1] According to Waurin, the earl was already engaged in suborning the young duke of Clarence from his allegiance. Warwick alleged that Rivers and his children controlled everything at court, and, on being asked by Clarence how this might be remedied, told the duke that he would make him king of England or governor of the realm, and he had little doubt but that most of the country would support him. He also spoke openly to the French ambassadors of the traitors around the king who had caused his brother to be deprived of the office of chancellor. Waurin's account may be highly coloured, but it is quite likely that Warwick was already exploiting the young duke's temperamental weaknesses and incipient discontent. Contemporaries credited the eighteen-year-old Clarence with much of the charm and ability of his brothers, Edward and Richard. Like Edward, too, he was very good looking, was possessed of a silver tongue, and not without a sarcastic wit.[2]

[1] See p. 110, n. 6, above. Though Waurin is demonstrably inaccurate as to detail and can (as Scofield showed, I, 426) be misleading, he had access to much first-hand information. He had been in England during the Bastard's visit, and in 1469 had personal conversations with Warwick at Calais, apart from drawing upon the considerable amount of material on English affairs which reached the court of Burgundy (Dupont's Introduction to her edition of Waurin, III, xxxii–iv).

[2] CC, 557, says that the three brothers were possessed of such outstanding talents that if they had been able to live without dissensions, 'such a threefold cord could never have been broken without the utmost difficulty'; Mancini, 63, for his comeliness, 'worthy of the crown', and his eloquence; GC, 206, for his remark at the trial of Sir Thomas Cook: when the mayor of London 'being a replete and lumpish man' fell into a doze, Clarence 'said openly in his derision, Speak softly, sirs, for the mayor is asleep'. See also the remark of the contemporary antiquary, John Rous of Warwick (The Rows Roll, ed. W. Courthope, no. 59) that he was 'right witty and well-visaged'

But his character was neither strong nor sensible, and, as his later career proved, he could be ambitious, jealous and grasping. Heirs presumptive to an hereditary throne often became a focus for discontent, and Clarence was no exception.

Duke George had no obvious reason to be dissatisfied with his brother. Provision for him had been made on an exceptionally generous scale – in August 1464 he was even given the lands of the earldom of Chester, part of the traditional inheritance of the prince of Wales – and by 1465 he was in possession of a very considerable appanage. Two years later his lands were worth about £3,666 in net annual value (only a little less than was allowed to the queen), and he had expectations of another 1,000 marks a year.[1] On 28 February 1462 he had been appointed king's lieutenant in Ireland for seven years, an office which he could execute by deputy, and from June 1465 he begins to appear on several important commissions.[2] Perhaps his only genuine reason for discontent lay in the matter of his marriage. None of the various foreign matches proposed for him (like that projected in 1466 with the heiress, Mary of Burgundy) had materialized, and Edward had blocked his union with the most suitable English bride, Isabel Nevill. But this scarcely justified him in plotting treason. The key to his disaffection lies in his own ambition and instability, which made him easy prey to the wiles of Warwick. Although he went with the king to relieve George Nevill of the Great Seal in June 1467, from then on he seems to have come increasingly under Warwick's influence. By the autumn he had clearly lent his support to the earl's secret manœuvres at Rome to obtain the necessary dispensation for his marriage to Isabel, and by Christmas Edward thought it necessary to summon him to Coventry in order to keep an eye on him.[3]

[1] Extensive provision was made for Clarence between August 1462 and January 1463 including forfeited Percy lands – some forty-two manors and lordships – in Northumberland and Yorkshire, the Honour of Richmond in Yorkshire, taken from his brother, Richard, and large estates in the west, forfeited from the earl of Wiltshire. These arrangements proved unsatisfactory for various reasons, and fresh provision was made in August and September 1464, which gave Clarence the lordship and county of Chester during pleasure, some lands in Kent and Surrey, and St Briavels and the Forest of Dean for life. Apart from these he retained the Yorkshire lands of the Percies and the Wiltshire lands mentioned above, and some important reversions. His holdings are detailed in a definitive grant of 2 July 1465 (*CPR, 1461-7*, 198-90, 212-13, 226-7, 327-8, 331, 362, 454-5). The valuation comes from *RP*, V, 578, where his lands to the *net* value of 5,500 marks a year (£3,666 13s 4d) were exempted from the 1467 Act of Resumption, exclusive of reversions worth 1,000 marks extra.
[2] *CPR, 1461-7*, 142, 488-9, 529; *1467-77*, 55. From 1466 onwards he was appointed to the commissions of the peace in eighteen counties, chiefly in south-west and south-central England. [3] *Annales*, 788-9.

Warwick's sulky retreat to his Yorkshire estates in the autumn of 1467 indicates his anger with Edward's policies and advisers, but he was not yet ready to translate this resentment into openly hostile action. Polydore Vergil believed that he was merely dissembling his fury, whilst continuing to foment discord through months of intrigue;[1] but he may still have hoped for a change of heart in Edward, or was perhaps himself unsure of the extent of support he could collect against the king. His mood, however, was prickly and resentful. When, in the autumn of 1467, Lord Herbert captured a messenger from Margaret of Anjou to the garrison of Harlech, this man implicated Warwick (amongst others) in charges of treason, and more particularly alleged that he was in league with Margaret of Anjou. Since similar rumours were already in circulation (at least on the Continent) Edward was not prepared entirely to discount the allegations, and summoned Warwick to come and explain himself. This the earl refused to do, even under safe-conduct. Edward made the concession of sending the accuser to the earl at his castle of Sheriff Hutton, whereby Warwick was able to dispel the charges as frivolous. Edward's suspicions were no more allayed than was Warwick's anger, and on 7 January 1468 a second summons to Warwick to come to the king was met by a curt refusal, so long as Rivers, Herbert and Scales were with Edward. But through the mediation of George Nevill, who had had a meeting with Rivers, the earl eventually agreed to go to Coventry to attend a council meeting.[2]

At Coventry Edward proved far more conciliatory than Warwick. The earl was cordially received and unbent sufficiently to go through a form of reconciliation with Lords Herbert, Audley and Stafford, though not with the Woodvilles. He refused, however, to help under-write the cost of Margaret of York's dowry, or to assist in raising archers for Brittany, and continued to urge upon the king the dangers of making alliances with such self-interested princes as the dukes of Burgundy and Brittany. But Edward was not to be deflected from his chosen policy. It was clear that he wanted Warwick's friendship, but would not take his advice, and the earl was now openly hostile.[3]

Warwick's discontent was far from being Edward's sole cause for anxiety about the internal state of his realm. The years 1467 and 1468

---

[1] Polydore Vergil, *English History*, 118.
[2] *Annales*, 788–9; Waurin, ed. Dupont, III, 193 (report from England to Louis XI by his agent, William Monypenny, 16 January 1468).
[3] *Annales*, 789; second report from Monypenny, 8 March 1468, printed in H. Morice, *Mémoires pour servir de preuves à l'histoire de Bretagne*, III, 159–61; *CSP, Milan*, I, 122.

saw a disturbing growth in the incidence of local lawlessness, strengthened, as the months went by, with reports of treason and disaffection.
At the end of their first session (June–July 1467), the commons in
parliament called the king's attention to the increase in murders, riots
and other outrages, and asked for urgent measures for the enforcement
of the law.[1] These disturbances sprang from a variety of causes. Some
were the product of the 'heavy lordship' of great men in good standing
with the king: against such powerful offenders it was hard to get redress, as the unhappy experiences of the Paston family at the hands of
the king's brother-in-law, John, duke of Suffolk, amply illustrate.[2]
Still more dangerous were quarrels between the king's great men
themselves, as they intervened in local disputes on behalf of their
retainers and followers. In 1467, for instance, trouble broke out in
Derbyshire. A feud between Henry, Lord Grey of Codnor, and Henry
Vernon, esquire (who was supported by the earl of Shrewsbury), led to
the murder of one of the Vernons. On 3 January 1468 a powerful
commission of oyer and terminer was appointed, headed by Clarence,
Rivers and Hastings, to deal with these and other local disturbances.
But peace was not easily enforced, for as late as June 1468 Shrewsbury,
Grey and Vernon all had to be bound over in large sums not to do
violence towards the jurors – local Derbyshire esquires – who had been
directed to investigate the facts and report to the commission. The
dispute found a reflection in ill-feeling at the royal court, where Clarence was said to favour Vernon (later one of his retainers) whilst 'the
king's men' favoured Lord Grey.[3] It was a sign of the deterioration of
royal control that such disputes became more numerous as time went
on. 'Great riots and oppressions done to our subjects' were widespread
enough at the end of 1467 to cause the appointment of commissions of
oyer and terminer in six midland counties, and to persuade Edward to
surround himself with a bodyguard of two hundred chosen valets and
archers when he went to Coventry to spend Christmas.[4]

Elsewhere there were signs of growing discontent with the Yorkist
regime, which may have been inspired partly by Nevill dissidence. In
January 1468 one of Earl Rivers's estates in Kent was attacked by a
mob and pillaged, whilst in Yorkshire there was a gathering of malcontents around a captain named Robin who are said to have offered

---

[1] *RP*, V, 618.
[2] See below, pp. 406–7.
[3] *Annales*, 788–9; *CPR*, *1467–77*, 55; *CCR*, *1468–76* (for the bonds, which show Lords
Mountjoy and Dudley standing surety for Shrewsbury, and Hastings for Lord Grey).
[4] *CPR*, *1467–77*, 55; *Annales*, 788.

their services to Warwick.[1] More alarming was the recrudescence of
Lancastrian activity. Rebels were taken in the Isle of Wight in 1466;
the stubborn rebel Humphrey Nevill of Brancepeth was again active in
Northumberland; and the Yorkist hold on Wales was being threatened
by rebel activity. In 1466 the garrison of Harlech sallied forth on a raid
which took them seventy miles away to Wrexham, and the nervous
captains of Beaumaris, Caernarvon and Montgomery Castles had to be
assured that they should have adequate reinforcements 'for the safe-
guarding of our strongholds considering our rebels be daily in the said
country'.[2] Successive attempts to reduce Harlech to obedience had met
with no success, nor had an expedition led by the earl of Worcester
into North Wales in 1466 brought that area under control. Large parts
of the revenues due from Caernarvon and Anglesey were still in 1466
unpaid from the beginning of the reign. It was this still very nominal
control over an area of Lancastrian sympathy which explains the
success of Jasper Tudor in June 1468, when he could march from Barmouth to Denbigh without meeting serious resistance. His subsequent
failure, however, and the vigorous siege pressed by William, Lord
Herbert, led to the final surrender of Harlech on 14 August 1468.[3]

Meanwhile, the king's relations with Warwick and his kinsmen
appeared to improve. Whatever his objections to the marriage of
Margaret of York and the plans for war against France announced in
May 1468, the earl concealed his feelings sufficiently to make a graceful
appearance at the ceremonial departure of the Lady Margaret from
London on 18 June. She rode out of the city behind him on the same
horse. Although surrounded by an entire pride of Woodvilles, he
accompanied her to the abbey of Stratford by Bow, where she spent
several days, and then on through Canterbury to the coast at Margate.[4]
There is much evidence to show that, both then and for some months
later, Warwick and his brothers were prominent at court and in the
king's council.[5] In council meetings they were probably outnumbered

[1] Waurin, ed. Dupont, III, 193–4 (Monypenny's letter of January 1468).

[2] Scofield, I, 423; *Hist. MSS Comm. Reports*, 54 (Beverley Corporation MSS), 142, and
15th Report, App. Part X (Shrewsbury Corporation MSS), 30; R. A. Griffiths,
thesis cited above (p. 43).

[3] Scofield, I, 423; *CPR, 1461–7*, 529 (for enquiries into unpaid revenues, 20 March
1466); Evans, *Wales in the Wars of the Roses*, 165–6. The earl of Worcester had been
chief justice of North Wales since 25 November 1461 (*CPR, 1461–7*, 62), until replaced by William, Lord Herbert, who was also appointed constable of Harlech, on
28 August 1467 (*CPR, 1467–77*, 41). For Jasper's invasion, see above, p. 114.

[4] *Excerpta Historica*, ed. Bentley, 227–8. Scofield, I, 456, and Kendall, *Warwick*, say
wrongly that they stayed at Stratford Langthorne, Essex.

[5] Apart from the evidence cited below, Richard and George Nevill appear regularly

and outweighed by 'king's men'. Apart from those 'evil councillors' like Rivers, Scales, Herbert, Audley and Stafford, whom they denounced in 1469, most of the other active councillors are not likely to have had much sympathy with the Nevills. The Bourchier group led by the archbishop of Canterbury and the treasurer, the earl of Essex; household officers like Sir John Fogge and Sir John Scott; that rising royal servant, Sir John Howard; and the chamberlain, William, Lord Hastings (even though he was Warwick's brother-in-law), were all men closely attached to the king, and owed little to the Nevill interest. Only Lord Wenlock and Thomas Kent may be classed as Warwickites.[1]

Yet the Nevills had not lost all influence. During July 1468, Warwick, Northumberland and the archbishop of York seem to have been active in the council deliberations which led to the disastrous 'verdict of the council' against the Hansard merchants; and it is significant that all three were prominent among the English shipowners whose vessels had been seized. Probably Warwick pressed for a tough policy against the Hanseatic League, which eventually led to a war at sea, and was in line with the rather irresponsible nationalism he had previously shown the Hansards in the 1450s.[2] That Warwick and the archbishop were active at court in October 1468 is known from the evidence of a Paston correspondent, who hoped to enlist their aid against the duke of Norfolk. They had, he reported, spoken to the duke on the Pastons' behalf 'in the king's chamber'. The archbishop, it was expected, would also tackle Earl Rivers and his wife, and William Herbert, earl of Pembroke, on the same matter – evidence of apparently civil relations between the rival factions at court. It was even rumoured that George Nevill might become chancellor again.[3]

The Pastons and their agents were shrewd and hard-headed men of business, with a keen, practical interest in unravelling the strands of power at court. That they thought it worthwhile to cultivate Nevill influence shows that Warwick and his brothers still commanded a respectful hearing at court. It also shows how the earl, and still more the clever and plausible archbishop, had been able to convey an impression of political amiability by dissembling their hostility to the

on the witness lists to royal charters throughout 1468, John Nevill less frequently (P.R.O., Charter Rolls, C. 53/195/mm. 6–16). In June and July 1468, Richard and John were appointed to major commissions of oyer and terminer (for the trial of Thomas Cook and others) in the city of London, Middlesex, Surrey and Essex (*CPR, 1467–77*, 102–3).

[1] Lander, 'Council, Administration and Councillors, 1461–1485', 159–60.
[2] For the breach with the Hanse, see below, pp. 361–2, 365–6.
[3] *PL*, IV, 303–5.

king's men. Unfortunately for himself, the king also chose to believe that they had come to accept an honoured and profitable place at court even if their influence was no longer what it had been, and that they were prepared to tolerate the Woodvilles and the 'king's men'. That he continued too long to cling to this belief may have owed much to Nevill skill in deceit, but also reflects his own defects of political judgement. His easy-going nature, persistent optimism, and confidence in his personal charm prevented him from taking a hard and suspicious line. Even if he suspected them of treasonable plans, there was little to indicate that Warwick would command any measure of support amongst the baronage, some of whom now owed a good deal to a generous king. Warwick himself was aware of his political isolation amongst the magnates, and, before he could come into the open, he had to wait upon and foment popular discontent with Edward's rule.

In the latter half of 1468 Edward's troubles again multiplied. The realm was filled with reports of intrigue, disaffection and Lancastrian conspiracies. Already in the summer there had been alarms following the capture of the Lancastrian agent, Cornelius, whose confessions eventually involved not only Sir Thomas Cook and other prominent Londoners but also Sir Gervase Clifton, a former treasurer of Calais, and even John, Lord Wenlock, himself. The trial and punishment of some of the accused continued into the autumn.[1] In November came a fresh wave of arrests. For some time past the king had been allowing money to the sheriffs to organize a spy service, and now, as information flowed back, yeomen of the royal household were sent down 'into divers counties to arrest men that be appeached'.[2] Among the first to come under suspicion were the heirs to two Lancastrian baronies. Henry Courtenay, esquire, brother and heir of the former earl of Devon, and Thomas Hungerford, son of the rebel Lord Hungerford executed after Hexham, were both arrested in Wiltshire before 11 November, and imprisoned in Salisbury to await the king's arrival before being brought to trial. Both appear to have been living quietly enough on their estates, but they were obvious targets for a nervous government which thought them likely sympathizers with the exiles in France.[3] Soon after, an equally vulnerable figure, John de Vere, earl of Oxford, whose father and brother had already been executed for treason, was apprehended and committed to the Tower. Others arrested as a result

[1] Scofield, I, 454–5, 457, 459–62.
[2] Ramsay, Lancaster and York, II, 326 and n. 1; Plumpton Correspondence, 20.
[3] Loc. cit.; Hist. MSS Comm. Reports, Various Collections, IV, 206–7 (Salisbury Corporation MSS); and above, pp. 65–6.

of Oxford's turning king's evidence included two former Lancastrians, Sir Thomas Tresham and Sir John Marney. Another, a London skinner named Richard Stairs, who had been a former servant of the duke of Exeter and was 'one of the cunningest players of the tennis in England', was charged with carrying treasonable correspondence on behalf of Queen Margaret and was beheaded on Tower Hill on 28 November. So too were Poynings and Alford, servants of the duke of Norfolk, who were alleged to have been in contact with Lancastrian exiles at Bruges whilst attending the wedding ceremonies of the Lady Margaret.[1]

Of the others accused of treason only Courtenay and Hungerford were ever brought to trial. Oxford (who had recently married the earl of Warwick's sister, Margaret) talked his way out of trouble and was soon released. Sir John Marney was pardoned in April 1469, whilst Tresham was simply held in jail.[2] On 12 January 1469, Hungerford and Courtenay were brought before a special commission of oyer and terminer at Salisbury, headed by Duke Richard of Gloucester, Arundel, Scales, Audley, Stafford and Stourton.[3] They were charged with having conspired on 21 May 1468 and on other occasions, with having plotted, in league with Margaret of Anjou, the 'final death and final destruction . . . of the Most Christian Prince, Edward IV'. Both put themselves 'upon the country' (that is, on the verdict of a local jury), and Courtenay pleaded in addition a general pardon granted to him on 25 July 1468. The king's attorney, Henry Sotehill, then said they were guilty, and the jury of sixteen agreed with him. They were then subjected to the fullest and protracted horrors of a fifteenth-century political execution. John Warkworth reported that their downfall had been brought about by the malice of Humphrey Stafford (who was created earl of Devon in May 1469), but the presence of the king at Salisbury when the verdict was pronounced is significant of his personal concern in the case.[4] How far Edward was seriously threatened at this time by any extensive or organized Lancastrian conspiracy is difficult to judge, especially since so little direct evidence was ever produced.

[1] *Plumpton Correspondence*, 19–20 (for the arrests and executions); *GC*, 207 (for the tennis); for Tresham, see above, pp. 67–8.
[2] Oxford may have been at liberty by 7 January 1469 (*PL*, V, 5) and was pardoned all offences on 15 April (*CPR, 1467–77*, 155; also for Marney's pardon); for Tresham, Roskell, *The Commons and their Speakers*, 282–3.
[3] The original record of the case is among the Ancient Indictments in the P.R.O., K.B. 9/320, from which the quotation comes. Clarence and Warwick were members of the commission, appointed on 12 December 1468 (*CPR, 1467–77*, 128), but did not serve; it also included eleven judges and professional lawyers. See also Bellamy, *The Law of Treason in the Later Middle Ages*, 164–5.
[4] Warkworth, *Chronicle*, 6. For the king's presence, *Hist. MSS Comm. Reports*, as above.

Much of this may merely have been the over-anxious reaction of a government alarmed by persistent rumours of treason, and concerned to remove the likely leaders of a Lancastrian rebellion.

More serious was the growth of popular discontent with Edward's government, some of it probably actively fostered by Warwick. The most direct evidence comes from the *Chronicle* of John Warkworth, written not later than 1483. This North-Country scholar, who became Master of Peterhouse, Cambridge, in 1473, was in no sense a Nevill sympathizer, and his criticisms of Edward IV therefore carry more weight.[1] The common people, he claims, had been weary and disgusted with Lancastrian government, and were 'full glad to have a change'. But they had been disillusioned in their hope that the new king would 'bring the realm of England in[to] great prosperity and rest'. There had been battles, heavy taxes, and still the need to serve far from home at their own cost; and 'many men said that King Edward had much blame for hurting merchandise'. Some of these grievances were echoed by the rebel manifesto of 1469. This was clearly a propaganda document, carefully angled against the Woodvilles and the 'king's men' whom Warwick wished to destroy, but to be plausible it also had to appeal to real grievances amongst the common people.[2] This, too, complains of heavy taxation, in spite of Edward's having 'as great livelihood and possessions as ever had king of England', and its references to the prevalence of disorder reiterate the remarks of the speaker in the parliament of 1467. It especially emphasized the malignant effects of the power of the king's great men in the localities. By their maintenances, and those of their servants, it alleged, the king's laws could not be executed upon those to whom they owed favour; and there were impeachments of treasons brought against men to whom the king's favourites 'owe any evil will'. There had been borrowing without repayment, purveyance for the royal household without payment, and money raised for the pope had been held back by the king.

How far these alleged grievances reflect widespread popular discontent is not easy to judge. The commercial treaty with Burgundy in 1467 seems to have been unpopular; in January 1468, William Monypenny could report to King Louis that the talk ran in London taverns that men who had advised the king to refuse an alliance with France for one with Burgundy deserved to lose their heads.[3] Even if

[1] Warkworth, *Chronicle*, 11–12; Kingsford, *English Historical Literature*, 171–3.
[2] Wilkinson, *Constitutional History of England in the Fifteenth Century*, 151. The manifesto is printed in the notes to Warkworth, *Chronicle*, 47–9.
[3] Waurin, ed. Dupont, III, 191.

the Hansards, like other alien merchants, were unpopular with England, the ill-advised breach with them in 1468 probably did not commend itself to the bulk of popular opinion, and, in general, royal policy might well seem to have done more to 'the hurting of merchandise' than to the helping of it.[1] Royal taxation had not been especially heavy, but the way in which the king had extracted money in 1463 and in 1467, and then failed to carry out his promises, was scarcely likely to endear him to his people.[2] The failure to provide impartial justice had been one of the strongest complaints against the government of Henry VI, and here, too, Edward's government had done little to improve matters.[3] There may well have been a general disillusionment with Yorkist government by 1469. Edward seems to have lost ground in popular esteem, whilst Warwick, partly by reason of his open-handed generosity to the populace wherever he went, retained their favour. No doubt Monypenny exaggerated when he observed that, as the earl passed on his way to London, the people had cried out as if with one voice 'Warwick! Warwick!' and had behaved as if God himself had descended from the skies; but Commynes was later to report that by 1471 Edward had conceived a great hatred against the ordinary people, 'for the great favour which he saw the people bore towards the earl of Warwick, and also for other reasons'.[4] The commons were far from indifferent to political issues, and (as K. B. McFarlane rightly observed) 'with little to lose and grievances that were real enough, [they] were easily incited to rebellion by magnates they admired'.[5] In the spring of 1469 Nevill agents were already at work in Yorkshire exploiting popular grievances. With the rising of the northern commons in the summer of 1469 the way lay open for Warwick's attempt to reassert his former dominance.

[1] M. M. Postan, 'The Economic and Political Relations of England and the Hanse from 1400 to 1475', in E. Power and M. M. Postan, Studies in English Trade in the Fifteenth Century, 133, 139–41; and below, pp. 362–6.
[2] Above, pp. 55–6, and for a similar reaction in 1475, below, p. 236.
[3] Below, pp. 393–4, 404–13.
[4] Monypenny's letter of 8 March 1468 (Morice, op. cit., III, 159–61); Commynes, I, 214–15. The Great Chronicle, 207, is one of several sources which mention Warwick's generosity: 'The which earl was evar had in great favour of the commons of this land, by reason of the exceeding household which he daily kept in all countries . . .'.
[5] 'The Wars of the Roses', 112.

Chapter 7

THE YEARS OF CRISIS, 1469–1471

(i) *Warwick's Challenge and Failure, 1469–1470*

The two years from June 1469 to May 1471 form a period of political instability without parallel in English history since 1066. Control of the government changed hands three times, and two of these changes involved the crown itself. Warwick's successful rebellion enabled him for a time to overpower Edward and rule in his name (July–October 1469). Then Edward's recovery of power led to Warwick's second rebellion, and his expulsion from the realm in April 1470. His invasion turned the tables on Edward, who had to flee to the Continent and see his throne restored to Henry VI (October 1470–March 1471). Lastly, Edward's return led to the final overthrow of his Nevill and Lancastrian enemies, the deposition of Henry VI, and his recovery of the throne (March–May 1471). For Edward – the only king of England ever to lose his throne and then recover it – these were the decisive years. His personal triumph in 1471 contributed largely to the greater strength and security of his rule during his second, and more peaceful and prosperous, decade.

In spite of their importance, we know little of the risings in the north which heralded two years of renewed civil war in England. Contemporary narrative accounts are meagre, confused and contradictory, and both the character and chronology of these rebellions remain obscure.[1] Trouble first broke out in Yorkshire late in April 1469, when a large assembly of malcontents gathered round a captain calling himself Robin of Redesdale or Robin Mend-All. They appear to have been dispersed by John Nevill, earl of Northumberland, only to regroup later in Lancashire.[2] Immediately after, the earl was called upon to deal with another and separate movement of discontent originating in the

---

[1] For comment on these difficulties, see Appendix IV.

[2] Men were sent from Beverley on 26 April 'pro repressione Rob. de Redesdale et aliorum inimicorum Domini Regis', and returned home after nine days (*Hist. MSS Comm. Reports, Beverley Corporation MSS*, 144). This provides some independent confirmation for a rising at this early date, which otherwise depends on 'Brief Latin Chronicle' (*Three Fifteenth-Century Chronicles*, 183), and a Cambridge fragment,

East Riding of Yorkshire under a leader known as Robin of Holderness, who has been identified (rather uncertainly) as Robert Hillyard, from Winestead, near the Percy family lordship of Pocklington.[1] Historians have generally followed the suspect authority of Polydore Vergil in explaining this second rising as a movement of protest against the much-resented claim by the Hospital of St Leonard at York to take a thrave (or twenty-four sheaves of corn) from each ploughland in the four northern counties. This demand had caused trouble for over a century, and as recently as the previous summer it had been under review by the king and council: after an investigation conducted by Warwick himself and the two chief justices, they had pronounced for the hospital against the 'withholders' amongst the East Riding gentry.[2] Yet the only really contemporary source to mention this rebellion says nothing of the hospital's claim, but asserts that the rebels were followers of the Percy family, seeking to bring about the restoration of the young Henry Percy to the earldom of Northumberland.[3] Whatever its nature, the rising was efficiently suppressed by John Nevill, who scattered a disorderly force marching on York and beheaded the leader. By the end of May all seems to have been over, though some of the rebels may have joined the much more dangerous movement now taking shape (or reviving) under Robin of Redesdale during June. As he moved southwards from Yorkshire towards the end of June, Robin began to attract large numbers of recruits.[4]

Redesdale's rebellion has generally been seen as essentially a movement inspired by the Nevills, and consisting largely of Nevill retainers, tenants and well-wishers.[5] Certainly it had strong Nevill connections,

---

apparently of very contemporary date, which puts the rising 'at the end of April and in the month of May' (*Abbreviata Cronica*, ed. J. J. Smith, Cambridge Antiquarian Soc., no. 11, 1840, p. 13).

[1] Modern scholars, following Ramsay, *Lancaster and York*, II, 339, have accepted this identification. But 'Robin of Holderness' was executed (as below), whilst Robert Hillyard the elder was still alive in March 1470 when appointed to a commission (*CPR, 1467–77*, 199), and his son, 'yong Hilyard of Holdrenes', submitted to Edward in the same month, after having taken part in the Yorkshire rising of that year (*Chronicle of the Rebellion in Lincolnshire*, 17). John Stow, *Annales*, 421, identified him with Robin of Redesdale.

[2] Polydore Vergil, *English History*, 121–2, followed by Scofield, I, 490–1; Ramsay, *op. cit.*, II, 338–9; Kendall, *Warwick the Kingmaker*, 241. Polydore also says it was stirred up by Archbishop Nevill at Warwick's instigation. For the dispute with St Leonard's, *VCH, Yorkshire*, III, 336, 342; *RP*, IV, 249–50; *CPR, 1467–77*, 131–2.

[3] *Three Fifteenth-Century Chronicles*, 183.

[4] For the dating of Robin of Holderness's rebellion, see Appendix IV.

[5] For a different view, see Jacob, *The Fifteenth Century*, 555; J. Gairdner, *PL*, I, 246; Roskell, *The Commons and their Speakers*, 281.

especially among the leaders. Robin himself was probably Sir John Conyers of Hornby in north Yorkshire, Warwick's cousin by marriage; and amongst those afterwards killed in the battle of Edgecote on 26 July were his nephew, Sir Henry FitzHugh, son of Lord FitzHugh, another cousin, Sir Henry Nevill, son of George Nevill, Lord Latimer, and a son of Lord Dudley, who had married Latimer's daughter.[1] But contemporaries also speak of the rebellion as a large-scale popular rising, 'a whirlwind from the north . . . a mighty insurrection of the commons', as one chronicler put it.[2] Although it would be naive to deny its Nevill inspiration, the rebellion probably drew upon popular disillusionment, and attracted support on a scale not even the mighty Warwick influence could have commanded alone (for no other magnate openly lent his backing). Like the well-supported rising of the Bastard of Fauconberg in Kent in 1471, men probably joined it from a variety of motives, whatever its overall political complexion.[3]

The government was slow to react to the dangers from the north, and slower still to link them with Nevill treason. Warwick had so far done nothing to show his hand. He seems to have received some sort of naval command, and threw himself with energy into preparations for the war at sea which might be expected to follow upon the previous autumn's breach with the Hanseatic League.[4] After attending a Garter ceremony at Windsor on 13 May, when the order was conferred on Duke Charles of Burgundy, he went to Sandwich to supervise the fitting-out of his great ship, the *Trinity*, in harbour there. He was still being appointed to important commissions, including an exceptionally strong commission of oyer and terminer issued on 22 May 1469 for the counties of York, Westmorland and Cumberland, which seems to have been the government's first official reaction to the disturbances in the north.[5] Clearly Edward did not yet suspect treason.

Early in June the king set out on a pilgrimage to Bury St Edmunds and Walsingham in East Anglia, in company with Gloucester, Rivers, Scales and other Woodvilles. By 18 June he had decided to go to the

---

[1] Warkworth, *Chronicle*, 6–7. Warkworth is the only contemporary to identify Redesdale by name, and calls him William Conyers, but see *DNB*, XLVIII, 433, for the view that he was John.

[2] *CC*, 542 (First Continuation); Warkworth, *Chronicle*, 6; *Three Fifteenth-Century Chronicles*, 182, which speaks of 'many . . . petitioners seeking the reform of many things in the realm'.

[3] Below, pp. 173–4.

[4] Scofield, I, 489; Ramsay, *op. cit.*, II, 336.

[5] *CPR, 1467–77*, 170. The commission also included the dukes of Clarence, Gloucester and Suffolk, 6 earls, 12 barons, 12 judges and 2 knights.

north and deal with the disorders in person, for from Norwich he ordered the royal wardrobe to supply banners, standards, coat-armour, forty jackets of velvet and damask with roses, and a thousand jackets in the York colours of murrey and blue, 'together with such other stuff for the field as must needs be had at this time'.[1] But even then his preparations lacked any urgency. Joined now by the dukes of Norfolk and Suffolk, he eventually made his leisurely way to Fotheringhay Castle, where, at the end of the month, he rested for a week or so, and awaited the arrival of more troops and war material. Continuing north, he reached Stamford on 5 July and Grantham two days later, and thence, by way of Nottingham, to Newark.[2] Here reports from further north became suddenly menacing. Robin of Redesdale was said to have three times as many men as the king disposed of, and the common people were not coming in to Edward as quickly as he had hoped. The urgent demands for men which follow reflect his sudden alarm. On 5 July he had already written to the city of Coventry asking for a hundred archers; now from Newark (on 10 July) came another demand for these troops, 'with more if ye godly may', to be despatched at once, 'without failing, all expenses laid apart, upon the faith and ligeance ye owe unto us'.[3] Meanwhile, Edward hastily turned back to Nottingham to wait for more men, especially the Welsh and West-Country forces which he had called upon William Herbert, earl of Pembroke, and Humphrey Stafford, the new earl of Devon, to collect. For safety's sake, the unpopular Woodvilles were now sent away, Rivers and his younger son, Sir John, to Wales, and Scales to Norfolk.[4] By now the rebels were dangerously close, and preparing to outflank the king by slipping south towards Coventry. By now, too, he could no longer ignore the growing rumours of treason surrounding Warwick, Clarence and the archbishop of York; and on 9 July he wrote hopefully to each of them, calling upon them to show that they were not 'of any such disposition towards us, as the rumour here runneth'.[5]

Warwick's plans were now nearing completion. With his brother George and Clarence already in his company, he wrote from London on 28 June to his supporters in Coventry, announcing the duke's forthcoming marriage to his daughter, Isabel, and it was probably this news which had reached the king at Nottingham. The three were joined at

---

[1] P.R.O., Warrants for Issues, E. 404/74/2; Scofield, I, 491–2. On 20 June orders were sent out for the mobilization of the royal artillery (*CPR, 1467–77*, 163).
[2] *PL*, V, 28–33; *CC*, 542; Scofield, I, 492.
[3] *CC*, 542; *Coventry Leet Book*, ed. M. D. Harris, II, 341–2.
[4] Waurin, ed. Dupont, II, 405–6; *CC*, 542.   [5] *PL*, V, 35–6.

Sandwich on 4 July by Warwick's brother-in-law, John, earl of Oxford, and then crossed to Calais. On 11 July the archbishop performed the wedding ceremony in the presence of a considerable company.[1] Immediately after, they abandoned all pretence of loyalty, and directly associated themselves with the northern rebels. From Calais on 12 July they issued a manifesto in the form of an open letter attached to a copy of the rebels' petition.[2] After setting forth certain general grievances, this document then specially emphasized the exclusion of the princes of the blood royal from the king's secret council in favour of 'the disceivable covetous rule and guiding of certain seducious persons'. These were named as Earl Rivers and his wife, Scales, Sir John Woodville and his brothers, the earls of Pembroke and Devon, Lord Audley and Sir John Fogge, which persons, they claimed, 'have caused our said sovereign lord and his realm to fall in great poverty of misery, disturbing the ministration of the laws, only intending to their own promotion and enriching'. But the most original feature of their proclamation was the ominous analogy drawn between the misdeeds of Edward II, Richard II and Henry VI, which had cost these kings their thrones, and the mistaken policies of Edward himself. Finally, they announced their intention to lay their proposals for 'a remedy and reformation' before the king, and called upon all their supporters to join them in arms at Canterbury on 16 July.

The rebels were well received on their landing in Kent, and left Canterbury about 18 July to march on London with a growing force. The city government found itself in a dilemma. Self-interest capitalized in extensive royal debts, and perhaps the fear of later retribution, may have inclined it towards the distant king, but the mayor and council had to reckon with Warwick's popularity among the common people and the danger of pillage and bloodshed if they resisted him. In the event they would not take the risk. The rebels were admitted to the city, and even supplied with a modest loan of £1,000. They soon set off towards Coventry to join the forces under Robin of Redesdale, now threatened by the advance of the royalists under Pembroke and Devon.[3]

The military manœuvres leading to the battle of Edgecote on 26 July 1469 caused total confusion amongst contemporary chroniclers, and are certainly far from clear today.[4] It is hard to find any sensible

---

[1] The movements of Warwick and Clarence are reconstructed in detail in Kendall, *op. cit.*, 244–6.

[2] Printed in the notes to Warkworth, *Chronicle*, 46–9. For a discussion of the rebel grievances, see above, pp. 124–5.   [3] Scofield, I, 495–6.

[4] E.g., 'Hearne's Fragment', in *Chronicles of the White Rose of York*, 24–5, which says

explanation for the total inactivity of the king. Perhaps he still accepted
Warwick's protestations of innocence, and could not believe that his
own brother, Clarence, could have risen against him, for such family
disloyalty, even in this ruthless age, was quite exceptional.[1] Perhaps,
cut off by the rebels to the south from his own supporters, he had no
up-to-date information, and too readily took no news for good news.
At all events, he sat idle at Nottingham until it was too late. Meanwhile,
Pembroke, with a powerful force of Welshmen, and Devon, with his
followers from the west, were marching together towards Northampton.[2] On 25 July, when near Banbury, they seem to have quarrelled
about billeting arrangements in the town. As a result, they made
separate camps, with Devon, who had most of the archers with him,
several miles away from Pembroke at Edgecote. Early the next day the
rebels fell suddenly upon the Welshmen, who were hampered by lack
of archers but put up a brave fight. The heavy casualties amongst the
rebel leaders bear witness to a fierce struggle. Devon's troops either
arrived too late to turn the tide of battle or were never fully committed.
The royalists seem to have been finally demoralized by the appearance
of a small force under one of Warwick's supporters, John Clapham,
which they mistook for the vanguard of a separate enemy army under
the earl's command. The Welshmen were finally overwhelmed. Devon
escaped, but Pembroke and his brother, Sir Richard, were taken
prisoner, and carried off to Northampton, where Warwick had them

that *Edward* sent the army which defeated Herbert. Polydore Vergil, *English History*,
122, which does not mention Devon at all, has two battles, one between Pembroke
and the Yorkshiremen, and one between Pembroke and Warwick and Clarence. The
very confused account in Waurin, ed. Dupont, II, 406–9, places the battle at Tewkesbury.

[1] The propaganda put out by Warwick and Clarence as to their intentions certainly
confused some contemporary chroniclers, as pointed out by Kendall, *Warwick the
Kingmaker*, 349, but his suggestion (pp. 349–50) that Edward never intended to fight
at all, and was confident enough of his hold on the kingdom to confront Warwick in
person, rests on unconvincing evidence – a sixteenth-century marginal note to the
text of the *Great Chronicle*, 208–9, and Polydore Vergil's very contrived and unreliable account. For the rarity of family disloyalty, K. B. McFarlane, 'The Wars of
the Roses', 105.

[2] What follows is based upon *CC*, 446; Warkworth, 6–7; *GC*, 209; 'Hearne's Fragment', 24; Edward Hall, *Chronicle*, 273–4. Though writing much later, Hall is acknowledged to have information on the battles of this period not found elsewhere, and
there may be some truth in his story that the main battle was preceded by a preliminary engagement, when the advance force of the earls was repulsed by the
northerners; this is confirmed by the evidence of the Welsh poets, who bewailed the
battle as a national calamity (Evans, *Wales in the Wars of the Roses*, 174–85). See the
valuable list of Welsh casualties in William Worcestre, *Itineraries*, ed. J. H. Harvey,
339–41, which also claims that 1,500 northerners were killed there.

beheaded on the following day. For this he had no legal justification, for they had not been in arms against a king whom Warwick himself recognized; and (like the execution of Rivers and Sir John Woodville soon after) it was an act of private revenge against men who had come to supplant the earl in royal favour and had thwarted his ambitions in South Wales.

The defeat of the royalist earls need not have been decisive for Edward's fortunes if he himself had remained at liberty, but the rebel triumph was soon completed by his capture. Still apparently unaware of the fate of Pembroke and Devon, the king left Nottingham on 29 July, heading south to Northampton to meet them. Nearing the city, he heard news of the battle, and was thereupon deserted by almost all his men.[1] At Olney, on the road to London, he fell into the hands of Archbishop Nevill, who had been sent to take him as soon as Warwick learnt of his whereabouts. Although treated with formal respect, he was now a prisoner, and was sent to Warwick Castle for safe-keeping. The ruin of Warwick's enemies was now quickly completed. Rivers and Sir John Woodville were captured beyond the Severn and executed outside Coventry on 12 August. Sir Thomas Herbert was beheaded in Bristol, and on 17 August the earl of Devon was taken and executed by the common people of Bridgwater in Somerset.[2] By mid-August Warwick was fully in control both of the king's person and the government of the realm.

King Edward was himself largely to blame for the humiliating *débâcle* of July 1469. A mixture of complacency and inactivity characterizes his behaviour, in marked contrast to the vigour and decision he was to display in the spring of 1470 and the summer of 1471. Throughout he seems to have underestimated the extent to which he had lost popular sympathy and was loath to accept the fact of treachery within his own family circle. His reaction to the news from the north was tardy and half-hearted. No general commissions of array seem ever to have been issued, and most of his supporters amongst the magnates were not summoned to his side.[3] He relied too heavily and exclusively on the ability of Pembroke and Devon alone to crush the

[1] Warkworth, *Chronicle*, 6–7; *CC*, 453 (First Continuation). What happened to the lords in his company is not recorded. His letter to Coventry on 29 July (*Coventry Leet Book*, II, 345) shows that he still had no news of Pembroke's defeat.
[2] Scofield, I, 497–8. For the manner of Devon's death, Warkworth, *Chronicle*, 7. The statement in *Complete Peerage*, IV, 328, that he was beheaded on Edward's orders because he had deserted the field at Edgecote derives from a later fabrication by Holinshed.
[3] Kendall, *Warwick*, 247, conjectures that only Gloucester and Hastings were with

northern rebels. Bad intelligence can only be a partial explanation for his hopeful loitering at Nottingham for almost three weeks between 10 and 29 July, whilst the rebel plans came to completion, and he finally blundered into a captivity he might have avoided. Above all he failed to appreciate how little his government had succeeded in winning popular support when confronted by a rival with Warwick's reputation. The earl's success is the more remarkable because, in spite of his skill in exploiting the discontent of the commons, he had no significant support amongst the baronage. The significance of this political isolation soon became apparent.

Lack of committed support from his fellow-magnates severely limited Warwick's freedom of action from the start. Though he speedily helped himself to the earl of Pembroke's vacant offices of chief justice and chamberlain of South Wales (17 August), and tried to win over his brother-in-law, William, Lord Hastings, by appointing him chamberlain of North Wales (12 August), he did not attempt to dispose of many other offices and wardships formerly held by Pembroke, Devon and Rivers, nor to grant out custody of their estates to his supporters, as Edward was able to do when he recovered power.[1] Hence Warwick had no fund of patronage at his disposal. There were no rewards for Clarence, Oxford or the archbishop of York. Of offices of state, only the treasurership vacated by Rivers had to be filled, and this was given on 16 August to Warwick's supporter, Sir John Langstrother, Prior of the Hospital of St John of Jerusalem in England. The other ministers and members of Edward's council continued to serve, including such strong royalists as Lord Ferrers and Sir John Howard.[2] But Warwick needed more backing for his illegal usurpation of authority than a reluctant council could provide. Following the precedents of the Yorkists in 1455 and 1460, he hastily sent out writs (on 10 August) for a parliament to assemble on 22 September at York, near the strongholds of Nevill power and away from a London which was proving highly troublesome. Whether he intended to get the assent of parliament for Edward's replacement by Clarence remains uncertain, though on 8 August the Milanese ambassador in France reported that he planned to have Edward declared a bastard and give the crown to Clarence instead.[3]

him when he was taken at Olney, though Norfolk and Suffolk had been with him earlier. But many other strong royalists (e.g. Mountjoy, Dinham, Ferrers and Howard) were still in London (Scofield, I, 499).
[1] *CPR, 1467-77*, 165 (grants to Warwick and Hastings), and below, pp. 136-7, for Edward's grants.   [2] Scofield, I, 499.
[3] *CCR, 1468-76*, 85-7; Calmette and Perinelle, *op. cit.*, 108, and Pièce Justificatif no. 30.

Nothing better illustrates the limitations of Warwick's authority than his difficulties in keeping order. In London the populace regarded Warwick's triumph as a licence for violence: there was serious rioting and pillaging, held in check only by the combined efforts of the king's council and the city authorities, backed by the duke of Burgundy's ambassadors, who published a message from their master promising his goodwill if the citizens remained loyal to Edward and the Burgundian alliance.[1] Some of the nobility also saw their chance to pursue their private quarrels without official interference. In August the duke of Norfolk tried to take the castle of Caister by force from the Paston family. Efforts by Clarence, Archbishop George Nevill, and the lords of the council, to reach a compromise were rejected by the duke, and it is significant that Sir John Paston then tried in vain to get a writ from the king in person, as the only authority whom Norfolk might respect. After a regular siege of more than five weeks, the little Paston garrison, 'for lack of victuals, gunpowder, men's hearts, lack of surety of rescue', was driven to surrender on 26 September.[2] In Gloucestershire there was trouble between the Berkeley and Talbot families, and in Lancashire between the Stanleys and the Harringtons, and in Yorkshire a quarrel between Thomas, Lord Stanley, and Richard, duke of Gloucester, led to outbreaks of violence before March 1470.[3] The government also feared a Lancastrian incursion or rebellion in South Wales.[4]

The danger that Yorkist dissensions might encourage unregenerate Lancastrians was more clearly revealed in August, when Sir Humphrey Nevill of Brancepeth and his brother, Charles, suddenly raised the standard of revolt on behalf of Henry VI along the northern border. Though his cause apparently attracted little support, Warwick judged the situation serious enough to countermand the summoning of parliament on grounds of the 'great troubles in divers parts of this our land not yet appeased', and so that he might take personal command of operations in the north. But he discovered that he could get no response to proclamations calling for troops to be raised so long as the people believed the king to be a prisoner.[5] Clearly the common people in the north who had supported Redesdale's rebellion were bewildered by Warwick's policy. The unpopular favourites against whom they had

[1] Scofield, I, 500–1. On 2 September 1469 a proclamation was issued in London against riots and affrays and against all those who did anything contrary to the Burgundian alliance (CCR, 1468–76, 78–9).
[2] PL, V, 40–52, 55–7, and discussion by Gairdner, PL, I, 250–4.
[3] Below, pp. 138, 408–9; CCR, 1468–76, 138.
[4] Scofield, I, 503; CPR, 1467–77, 172 (commission of array to Lord Ferrers, 13 September).   [5] CC, 552; Scofield, I, 501–2.

campaigned were dead or out of power, and they were suspicious of the continued restrictions on the liberty of the king. Only the moral authority of the king in person could now command their obedience. Earl Richard now had no choice but to release Edward from his confinement in Middleham Castle in Yorkshire (where he had been taken from Warwick Castle late in August). He appeared in public and apparently his own master soon after 10 September at York.[1] With the king's help, Warwick raised the troops he needed, and put down the northern rising without difficulty. Humphrey and Charles Nevill were taken and executed at York on 29 September, in the king's presence.[2]

But this episode gave Edward his chance. From York or nearby Pontefract he seems to have summoned his brother, Gloucester, and his brother-in-law, Suffolk, together with the earls of Arundel, Northumberland, and Essex, Hastings, Mountjoy, and other members of the council then in London to come north and join him. Once surrounded by his own men, he announced his intention to return to his capital. By mid-October he was approaching London in full state, with his lords in attendance, to be met by the mayor and aldermen in scarlet, and two hundred men of the city crafts in blue. Warwick's attempt to repeat the Yorkist tactic of 1460 and rule through a captive king was at an end.[3]

'The King himself,' wrote Sir John Paston on Edward's return to London, 'hath good language of the Lords of Clarence, of Warwick, and of my Lords of York and Oxford, saying they be his best friends', but, he added ominously, 'his household men have other language'.[4] Certainly, Warwick's ruthless revenge upon his enemies, and the humiliations he had imposed upon Edward himself, had made a lasting reconciliation with the earl and his friends seem unlikely. Yet, in public at least, the king seemed bent on reconciliation, as Polydore Vergil remarked:[5]

> He regarded nothing more than to win again the friendship of such noble men as were now alienated from him, to confirm the goodwill of them that were hovering and inconstant, and to reduce the mind of the multitude,

---

[1] For dates of his imprisonment, Scofield, I, 497, 503. For a useful discussion of the contradictory evidence surrounding his 'liberation', see Kendall, *Richard III*, 445–7; cf. Scofield. It is more likely that he simply asserted his freedom of action (as the Croyland Chronicler says, p. 552) rather than that he escaped from custody.

[2] Warkworth, *Chronicle*, 7.

[3] *PL*, V, 62–3 (for the entry into London); *ibid.*, 50, a letter written before 26 September, which speaks of 'divers of my Lords [of the council] be at the King's high commandment hastily departed unto his highness'; also p. 53.

[4] *PL*, V, 63. [5] *English History*, 125.

being brought by these innovations into a murmuring and doubtfulness what to do, unto their late obedience, affection and goodwill towards him.

He was careful to take no punitive action against Warwick. The replacement of his minion, Langstrother, as treasurer by William Grey, bishop of Ely, on 25 October, was to be expected; so too was the transfer to Duke Richard of Gloucester in February 1470 of the Welsh offices which Warwick had granted to himself in the previous summer. The exclusion of Warwick and Clarence from commissions of array issued on 29 October for twenty-six English counties was probably also to be expected. When Edward restored Henry Percy to the earldom of Northumberland, Warwick, along with Clarence and John Nevill, had to surrender the Percy estates he had held, but otherwise his private gains of earlier years were respected.[1] The king even took the initiative in a programme of formal pacification. Warwick and Clarence were prevailed upon to attend a series of meetings of the Great Council which began in London in November and lasted until mid-February 1470, where all parties agreed to 'peace and entire oblivion of all grievances upon both sides'. He also arranged the betrothal of his eldest daughter, Elizabeth, to John Nevill's son, George, who, on 5 January 1470, was elevated to the dukedom of Bedford, a substantial peace-offering to Nevill pride.[2]

Another problem which confronted Edward in the autumn of 1469 was to devise a new political settlement in Wales. To fill the vacuum left by the death of the all-powerful and respected earl of Pembroke, he now chose to rely upon Richard of Gloucester, who first emerges at this time as Edward's trusted and responsible lieutenant. Appointed Constable of England for life on 17 October (in spite of the claims of Scales), in November he became chief justice of North Wales and chief steward and surveyor of the principality of Wales and the earldom of March, and, on 7 February 1470, he replaced Warwick as chief justice and chamberlain of South Wales during the minority of Pembroke's heir.[3] Lesser offices in Wales were entrusted to Lord Ferrers, Sir Roger Vaughan, Sir William Stanley and John Donne, who was now made especially responsible for West Wales.[4] Edward also had at his disposal

[1] *CPR, 1467–77*, 176, 195–6; below, pp. 144–5.
[2] *CC*, 552; P.R.O., C. 53/195, m. 2.
[3] *CPR, 1467–77*, 178–80, 185. Reversion of the office to Scales had been included in the grant of the constableship to Rivers on 24 August 1467 (*ibid.*, 19). For grants of land to Richard, including Sudeley Castle and lordship, Gloucestershire, *CCR, 1468–76*, 102; Kendall, *Richard III*, 78, 447.
[4] Ferrers: constable and steward of Brecon, Hay and Huntington, 16 November;

a variety of lands and offices which had been accumulated by Humphrey Stafford, earl of Devon. Some were given to John, Lord Dinham, who gradually took Devon's place as the government's chief supporter in the far west, and to the young John Stafford, younger son of the duke of Buckingham killed at Northampton, whom Edward was to create earl of Wiltshire in January 1470.[1] The largest share, however, went to John Nevill, earl of Northumberland. On 27 February 1470 most of the estates of the former Courtenay earls of Devon were granted to him, apparently as compensation for the extensive Percy lands in the north which he had to surrender when Edward gave them to Henry Percy on 1 March, three weeks before he was restored to his ancestral earldom.[2]

Warwick's brief triumph in the summer of 1469 had not solved his problems. He had destroyed some of the royal favourites, and temporarily reduced the influence of the Woodvilles. Through his son-in-law, Clarence, and his nephew, Bedford, he had brought the Nevills closer to the throne if Edward had no male heir. Yet he had not succeeded in re-establishing himself as the king's principal councillor with a great influence on the formulation of policy. Warwick now returned to the pattern of 1460. Government through a puppet king having failed, he turned to the more desperate remedy of replacing Edward by a king of his own making, George, duke of Clarence. Warwick's contumacious ambition lies at the root of the upheavals to follow. The degree of miscalculation which this scheme implied is telling evidence of his want of political judgement. Even if Edward were not very popular, the events of the summer and early autumn had shown that public opinion in general was not anxious to see him driven from the throne. Nor was Clarence an especially attractive substitute for his elder brother. Moreover, the opposition to the king stood out as nakedly selfish and factious, for in 1470 there was no pretence of championing popular grievances, and no programme for the reform of government. Above all, Edward was now on his guard. Although he went to considerable lengths to give Warwick and Clarence the chance to avoid charges of

---

Vaughan, constable of Cardigan Castle, 16 February; Stanley, steward of Denbigh, 14 February; Donne, steward of Haverfordwest, Pembroke, Llanstephan, Cilgerran; CPR, 1467–77, 173, 183, 185. West Wales was largely out of control in the autumn of 1469, and about the same time there was a campaign of civil disobedience and refusal to pay rents and dues in north-west Wales (ibid., 180, 198; Evans, op. cit., 188–90).

[1] CPR, 1467–77, 173, 175–6.   [2] Below, pp. 144–5.

treason, he was far less complacent about the dangers of popular disturbances or their connection with the treachery of great men. In contrast to his actions in 1469, he responded to the crisis of spring 1470 with energy and decision.

The spark-point of the renewed upheavals was provided by a series of disturbances in Lincolnshire in the early months of the year. According to the contemporary but official narratives of these events, they were fomented from the first by Warwick and Clarence. Some modern writers have regarded these narratives as wholly propaganda attempts by the king to brand them with treason.[1] Others, more reasonably, have doubted whether the 'great rebels' actually instigated the risings, but believe that they were ready enough to exploit them;[2] and there can be no question but that Warwick and Clarence soon began to behave in a treasonable fashion (as we shall see). Other historians have chosen to regard the risings as essentially Lancastrian in character; but, although Lincolnshire was a county with strong former Lancastrian connections, especially among the great landowning families, this view can be discarded as having no justification in the evidence.[3]

The trouble sprang from a private feud between Sir Thomas Burgh, of Gainsborough in Lincolnshire, who was Edward's master of the horse, and a former knight of the body, and Richard, Lord Welles and Willoughby, whose chief estates lay in the south-east part of the county. Welles, his son, Sir Robert, and his brothers-in-law, Sir Thomas de la Lande and Sir Thomas Dymmock, attacked and destroyed Burgh's manor house, carried off his goods and chattels, and drove him from the shire.[4] Such incidents were far from rare in fifteenth-century England, and only a month later Berkeley and Talbot supporters clashed in a minor pitched battle near Nibley Green in Gloucestershire, which ended in the death of Thomas Talbor, Viscount Lisle, and many of his men.[5] What gave the Lincolnshire affair a wider importance was the king's decision to intervene, in order to restore the peace and demonstrate the royal authority in person. On 4 March he announced in a letter to Coventry that he intended to leave at once for the north, and asked them to send troops to join him at Grantham on 12 March. Welles and Dymmock had already been summoned to appear before

[1] For a discussion of this view, and the evidence, see Appendix V.
[2] E.g., S. B. Chrimes, *Lancastrians, Yorkists and Henry VII*, 103; J. R. Lander, 'The Treason and Death of the Duke of Clarence: a Re-interpretation', *Canadian Journal of History*, ii (1967), 4 n.   [3] See Appendix V.
[4] Warkworth, *Chronicle*, 8; R. L. Storey, 'Lincolnshire and the Wars of the Roses', *Nottingham Medieval Studies*, xiv (1970), 64–82.
[5] J. Smyth, *Lives of the Berkeleys*, II, 111–12.

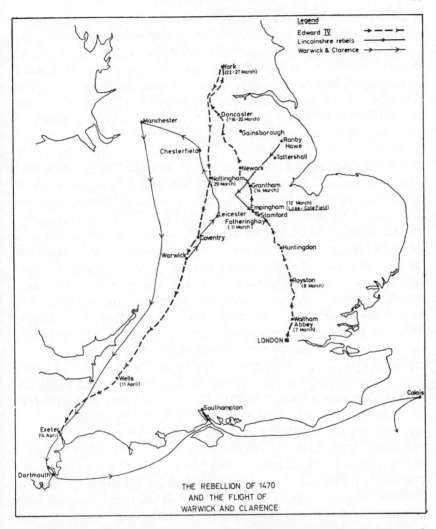

Legend
Edward IV
Lincolnshire rebels
Warwick & Clarence

York (22-27 March)

Doncaster (?16-20 March)

Manchester

Gainsborough

Ranby Hawe

Chesterfield

Tattershall

Newark

Nottingham (29 March)

Grantham (14 March)

Empingham (12 March) (Lose-Cote Field)

Leicester

Stamford

Fotheringhay (11 March)

Coventry

Huntingdon

Warwick

Royston (8 March)

Waltham Abbey (7 March)

LONDON

Wells (11 April)

Southampton

Calais

Exeter (14 April)

Dartmouth

THE REBELLION OF 1470
AND THE FLIGHT OF
WARWICK AND CLARENCE

the king at Westminster.[1] News of the king's descent upon the north
produced widespread rumours in Yorkshire that he did not intend to
honour the general pardon granted earlier to all former rebels, and
that his intent was to 'come thither and utterly destroy those that late
made commotion there'.[2] Similar fears of a Bloody Assize were also
strong in Lincolnshire, a county which had sent many men to join

[1] *Coventry Leet Book*, II, 353; Scofield, I, 511. Welles and his son were pardoned on
3 March, Dymmock on 6 March.
[2] According to Edward's proclamation from Newark on 16 March, *CCR, 1468–76*,
137–8.

Redesdale's rebellion; it was reported that 'the king's judges should sit, and hang and draw a great number of the commons'.[1] Whether or not under the influence of agents sent by Warwick and Clarence, Sir Robert Welles now set himself up as 'great captain of the commons of Lincolnshire', and on 4 March he caused proclamations to be made throughout the county for an assembly to meet at Ranby Hawe near Lincoln two days later to resist the king, who was 'coming to destroy the commons of the said shire'.[2]

When the news of Welles's call to arms reached him, Edward was already at Waltham Abbey in Essex (7 March), in company with Arundel, Hastings, Henry Percy and other lords.[3] As he moved north to Royston, on 8 March, he received further and more alarming news, from Lord Cromwell's steward at Tattershall Castle in Lincolnshire, that the rebels were making for Stamford, where they were to be joined by assemblies from Yorkshire and other counties to the number of 100,000 men. He still seems to have had no great suspicion of Warwick and Clarence, for, on the same day, letters arrived from the duke, saying that he and the earl would join the king on his journey north, to which Edward responded by sending them commissions to array troops in Warwickshire and Worcestershire. The next day he pushed on twenty-one miles north to Huntingdon, where he was joined by the captive rebels, Welles and Dymmock, who had been sent on after him from London; and he then caused Welles to write to his son, Sir Robert, demanding his submission, otherwise his father and Dymmock would be put to death.

By Sunday, 11 March, Edward was a further twenty-one miles north at Fotheringhay. There he received news that the rebels were heading for Leicester for a rendezvous on the following day with a force under Warwick's command. The rebels, directed by Warwick, planned to allow the king to proceed northwards: he would thus be cut off from London and threatened from two sides by the Yorkshire insurgents and the troops of Warwick and Welles. But on the Monday Sir

---

[1] 'Confession of Sir Robert Welles'. For the support for Redesdale, see the pardon to Richard FitzWilliam, sheriff of Lincolnshire, November 1468–November 1469, for great losses 'through the insurrection of divers lieges', CPR, 1467–77, 185.

[2] Chronicle of the Rebellion in Lincolnshire, 6.

[3] The narrative which follows is based, except where otherwise stated, on Chron. Lincs. Rebellion, 6–16, from which the quotations come; 'Confession of Sir Robert Welles'; Warkworth, 8–9; Kingsford, Chronicles of London, 180–1; Flenley, Six Town Chronicles, 164 (names of lords with Edward); Polydore Vergil, English History, 126–8; CPR, 1467–77, 218 (commissions of array to Warwick and Clarence, 7 March, issued verbally).

Robert Welles received his father's letter and turned back towards Stamford. Edward now moved confidently against the Lincolnshire men. Reaching Stamford on the same day (12 March), he discovered that the rebels lay at Empingham, some five miles west, and were disposed to fight; after ordering the summary execution of Lord Welles and Dymmock, he then 'incontinent took the field'. The result was more a rout than a battle, with the rebels discarding clothing as they fled to give the engagement the name of 'Lose-Cote Field'. By nightfall they had been dispersed, and the king was safely back in his lodgings at Stamford.

The official chronicle tells us that the complicity of Warwick and Clarence in the rising first became obvious during the battle, when the rebels had advanced crying 'A Clarence! A Clarence! A Warrewike!'; some of them, including Sir Robert Welles, wore the duke's livery; and treasonable messages from the duke and earl were found in an abandoned helmet. Whether or not he was now convinced of their defection, Edward still hoped to avoid an outright breach, calculating perhaps that the failure of the rising might bring them to a timely and discreet submission. Messages were sent directing them to disband the forces they had raised under their commissions of array, and come to the king only 'with convenient number for their estates'. They told Edward's messenger, John Donne, that they would do so, but were observed by him to set forth in the direction of Burton-on-Trent.

On 14 March the royal army reached Grantham, where Sir Robert Welles and other leaders of the Lincolnshire rising were brought before the king. Upon examination, they confessed openly (at least according to the official chronicle) that Warwick and Clarence were 'partners and chief provokers of all their treasons', and that their purpose had been to put Clarence on the throne. News now came in of hostile gatherings in Richmondshire, where John, Lord Scrope of Bolton, Sir John Conyers ('Robin of Redesdale'), and other kinsmen and friends of Warwick were raising his Wensleydale connection. Probably about the same time he heard news of a separate rising in the West Country, almost certainly stirred up by Clarence, and led by six members of the Courtenay family. John Nevill, earl of Northumberland, was commissioned to array the king's lieges in Cumberland and Westmorland against the northern rebels, and orders were issued for the arrest of the Courtenay dissidents. But when news of Edward's victory in Lincolnshire reached them, the Yorkshire rebels dispersed.[1]

[1] *CPR*, *1467-77*, 217, for commissions 16 March to FitzWarin, Dinham and the sheriff of Devon against the Courtenays. For the close connections of Sir Hugh

Edward was now in position to take a firmer though still diplomatic line with Warwick and Clarence. In reply to further 'pleasant writings' from them, saying they would join him at Retford, he despatched Garter King of Arms to command their appearance before him. Clarence was told that the king would 'entreat you according to the nighness of our blood and our laws', but if he and Warwick did not cease 'that unlawful assembly of our people in perturbation and contempt of our peace and commandment', Edward would proceed to punishment. The rebel lords replied by demanding a safe-conduct for themselves and their fellowship, together with pardons for themselves 'and all the lords and others that had taken their party'. After consulting his own lords, Edward replied in angry tones. He would treat them 'as a sovereign lord oweth to use and entreat his subjects, for his ancient enemies of France would not desire so large a surety for their coming to his royal presence'. He could not be too liberal of his pardons, for 'it should be too perilous and too evil example to all other subjects in like case'. They must now come to his presence or face the consequences.

Edward had every reason for confidence. The royal army had now been swelled by the retinues of the dukes of Norfolk and Suffolk, the earl of Worcester and Lord Mountjoy, who had joined him as he moved north, and probably by the great midland connection of Lord Hastings; and local levies were coming in under the commissions of array sent to twelve eastern and south-eastern counties between 8 February and 2 March.[1] When Edward left Doncaster in pursuit of the rebels on Tuesday, 20 March, it was reported that 'were never seen in England so many goodly men, and so well arrayed in a field'.[2]

In contrast, the political isolation of Warwick and Clarence now became apparent. After their flight to France, Edward ordered the seizure of the lands and property of fifty-three of their supporters.[3] An analysis of this list shows that they had commanded the support of a number of substantial country gentry. Apart from the four leaders of the Lincolnshire rising, all then dead, they included eleven knights and sixteen esquires, of whom no fewer than seventeen sat in parliament either before or after 1470, many as knights of the shire.[4] But many

Courtenay of Boconnoc and Sir Philip Courtenay of Powderham and his several sons with Clarence, see J. A. F. Thomson, 'The Courtenay Family in the Yorkist Period', *BIHR*, xlv (1972), 234–8.
[1] These lords were with the king at York on 25 March, P.R.O., C. 53/195, m. 1; for the commissions, *CPR, 1467–77*, 199–200.
[2] *PL*, V, 71.   [3] *CPR, 1467–77*, 218–19 (25 April 1470).
[4] The details which follow are derived mainly from Wedgwood, *Hist. Parl., Biog.,*

had ties of professional self-interest with either the duke or the earl, such as Sir Walter Wrottesley of Staffordshire or Sir Edward Grey, who were members of Warwick's council. Others, like Sir Hugh Courtenay (whose son, Edward, was restored to the earldom of Devon in 1485), were men of Lancastrian sympathies who remained loyal to the cause of Henry VI during the Readeption and later. Others were former Lancastrians like Sir Nicholas Latimer who turned to rebellion for reasons of private discontent. Some may have been inspired by bitter memories from the past, like the Surrey esquire, George Browne, whose father, Sir Thomas, had been executed by the Yorkist leaders when they entered London in 1460. Of those charged with treason, at least nine were able to obtain pardons from Edward soon after.[1] Some fell into the king's hands at Southampton in April 1470, and were nastily put to death by the earl of Worcester. Many escaped with their leaders to France. But it is a sign of Edward's persistent generosity to his opponents that most of these men survived both this crisis, and their later support of Henry VI, to prosper in Edward's second decade.

A more significant feature of the rebellion of 1470 is the failure of Warwick and Clarence to attract any support from their fellow-peers. The earl's brother-in-law, John de Vere, earl of Oxford, though he had taken no active part in the rising, found it prudent to flee to France. The loyalty of John Talbot, earl of Shrewsbury, was suspected at the time, but he seems to have made no overt move.[2] Warwick certainly hoped for help from another brother-in-law, that shifty trimmer, Thomas, Lord Stanley, for, on 20 March, as Edward took up their pursuit, they left Chesterfield for Manchester to seek his aid. But he had no wish to commit himself to a discredited cause, and may, in any case, have been prevented from supporting them by a clash with Richard of Gloucester, coming up from Wales to his brother's aid.[3] Even John Nevill, earl of Northumberland, showed no disposition to risk life and fortune for his brother's sake, and indeed gave valuable

---

s.n. For Wrottesley, see G. Wrottesley, 'A History of the Family of Wrottesley', *Collections Hist. Staffs.*, vi (ii), (1903), 220; for Courtenay, Thomson, *op. cit.*, 234–5.

[1] *CPR, 1467–77*, 208–9, 212.

[2] According to *CSP, Milan*, I, 137, quoting information received from an English knight on his way to Jerusalem, Talbot, Stanley and John, Lord Scrope, were named as lords in the company of Warwick and Clarence, and he found it prudent to take out a pardon on 26 April (*CPR, 1467–77*, 210).

[3] *PL*, V, 71; Polydore Vergil, *English History*, 128; *CPR, 1467–77*, 211 (pardon, 2 June); Kendall, *Richard III*, 83–4, 448 n.

help in suppressing the Yorkshire rising.[1] The English baronage in 1470 showed little sympathy for a cause based on nothing more appealing than personal ambition and wounded pride. Faced by this lack of response, Warwick and Clarence now had no choice but to flee the realm and seek safety (as they hoped) in Calais.

Meanwhile, the king, after ordering the execution of Sir Robert Welles and Richard Warin, captain of the Lincolnshire footmen, before the entire army at Doncaster on 19 March, set out the following day in pursuit of Warwick and Clarence. Finding them flown from Derbyshire, he checked his march and turned towards York, partly because he feared a lack of supplies for his large army in the Pennine uplands, and partly to place himself between the rebel leaders and 'the strongest of the north part, whereupon they hoped and would have been fain joined with'. At York he received the submission of Scrope, Conyers and the other northern insurgents, and on 24 March issued a proclamation against Warwick and Clarence. If they appeared before him by 28 March, he would have them in his grace and favour. If not, they were to be treated as rebels and traitors, and a reward of £1,000 in cash or £100 yearly in land was offered to their fortunate captor. This much-publicized patience was, however, a little specious, for the previous day he had written to his deputy-lieutenant in Ireland, Edmund Dudley, announcing that he had replaced Clarence as lieutenant by Worcester, and that he was to refuse all obedience, aid and comfort to the duke and earl as rebels and traitors. Similar orders were sent to Calais.[2]

Edward's final act during his five-day stay at York was the restoration on 25 March of Henry Percy to his father's forfeited earldom of Northumberland. The king had obviously contemplated this move for some time, for on 27 October he released the Percy heir, who had been in custody since 1464, from his imprisonment in the Tower. He then swore fealty to Edward: 'I faith and truth shall bear to you as my sovereign liege lord . . . of life and limb and of earthly worship, for to live and die against all earthly people.'[3] John Nevill was compensated on the same day by promotion to the marquessate of Montagu. The lands he had been given in south-western England on 27 February were a good deal more than a 'magpie's nest', as he scornfully described

---

[1] Archbishop George Nevill, however, was less trustworthy, and his arrest was ordered on 3 April (CPR, 1467-77, 217).

[2] Chron. Lincs. Rebellion, 16-18; CCR, 1468-76, 137-8.

[3] Rymer, Foedera, XI, 648. He also gave bonds for £5,000 for his good behaviour in the next six months, and the bishop of Ely, Arundel, Kent and Ferrers stood surety for him in a further £3,000 (CCR, 1468-76, 100-1).

them, but they were not an adequate compensation for the great Percy estates in the north which he had to surrender; and on 24 June he had to give up his office of Warden of the East March to the new earl.[1] This move is the more surprising in view of the admirable service which John Nevill had rendered to Edward, and his conspicuous loyalty to the king, even against the pull of family ties. Presumably Edward had come to the conclusion that only the traditional influence of the Percy family, now wielded by a man who owed much to Edward, could command the turbulence of the north. Presumably, too, he hoped that Montagu's new title, the dukedom given to his son, George of Bedford, and a royal bride for the latter, might mollify him for the loss of his princely northern earldom. Percy's restoration, though it forfeited the loyalty of Montagu, was to prove invaluable to Edward in the critical period following his landing in 1471, but ultimately it contributed to the downfall of his dynasty.[2]

(ii) Edward's Deposition and Exile

About 27 March 1470, Edward left York in pursuit of his 'great rebels'. Calling troops to join him on the way, he moved through Nottingham, Coventry and Wells to Exeter, where he arrived on 14 April – a ride of 290 miles in 18 days. By now the birds had flown. Taking with them the countess of Warwick and her daughters – with Duchess Isabel of Clarence now heavy in pregnancy – they sailed from Devon for Calais. Warwick had not forgotten that a navy could be as vital a political asset as an army. His first thought was to increase his strength by securing his great ship *Trinity*, and perhaps others, berthed at Southampton. But Anthony Woodville, the new Earl Rivers, whose naval squadron was fitting out there for service in the Channel, was not to be caught unawares, as he and his father had been at Sandwich in 1460, and the rebel attack was beaten off with the loss of both ships and men.

At Calais a further disappointment awaited the refugees. Entry was refused, and they had to withdraw out of range of the guns of the fortress. Actual command in Calais at this time was in the hands of

---

[1] Warkworth, *Chronicle*, 10; J. M. W. Bean, *The Estates of the Percy Family*, 109–10. The West-Country estates may have compensated for the Percy lands in Northumberland, but he received nothing in exchange for the rest of the Percy inheritance placed in the custody of the new earl on 26 March 1470 (*CPR, 1467–77*, 206). For the wardenship, see R. L. Storey, 'Wardens of the Marches', 615.

[2] Below, pp. 163–4, 202–3.

Warwick's deputy, John, Lord Wenlock, but the garrison as a whole remained loyal to Edward, partly through the efforts of a Gascon exile, Gaillard, Lord Duras, and partly through promises of aid from the duke of Burgundy. Wenlock may have felt that to admit Warwick would have been dangerous both to the earl and to his own position. At Warwick's insistence, wine was sent out to the ships for the comfort of the duchess of Clarence, who was now in childbirth – the mother survived, though not the child – but there was nothing else to encourage the rebels. Privately advised by Wenlock that Calais was a mousetrap, Warwick now decided to seek the aid of the king of France.[1]

This discomfiture was, in part, offset by the defection to Warwick of a naval squadron commanded by a kinsman, the Bastard of Fauconberg – Thomas Nevill, a natural son of William, Lord Fauconberg and earl of Kent – which had detached itself from Lord Howard's fleet in the Channel.[2] With these reinforcements, Warwick fell upon a large Flemish convoy outside Calais on 20 April and carried off all the ships as prizes – a major naval disaster in the eyes of Duke Charles of Burgundy. Though the vigilant Howard pursued Warwick along the coast of Normandy and successfully recaptured some of the Burgundian ships, Warwick and Clarence still had a substantial flotilla, laden with booty, when they finally dropped anchor in the mouth of the Seine about the beginning of May.

Warwick's arrival in France provided that arch-intriguer, Louis of France, with a supreme opportunity to effect the ambitious scheme already canvassed at the French court for some years past.[3] With French help, a reconciliation between Warwick and Margaret of Anjou might be used to promote a Lancastrian restoration, and so serve the double purpose of destroying his enemy, King Edward, and gaining a grateful ally for war on the duke of Burgundy, whose overthrow was

---

[1] For these events, and the summary account of Warwick's activities in France which follows, see in general Scofield, I, 518–36; Calmette and Perinelle, *Louis XI et l'Angleterre*, 109, 120; Kendall, *Warwick*, 259, 275; and for the naval operations, C. de la Ronciere, *Histoire de la marine française*, II, 339–46. The chief contemporary sources are Commynes, I, 192–200; Waurin, ed. Dupont, III, 28–46; 'The Manner and Guiding of the Earl of Warwick at Angers', in Ellis, *Original Letters*, 2nd ser., I, 132–5, also printed in *Chron. White Rose of York*, chronology as revised by Calmette and Perinelle, 114; Chastellain, *Chronique*, V, 467–8; *CSP, Milan*, I, 137–43; *Lettres de Louis XI*, ed. Vaesen, IV, 110–31.

[2] According to La Ronciere, *op. cit.*, II, 340, the English fleet was commanded by Rivers, not Howard; but Rivers's appointment was not sealed until 23 June, and part of his squadron was still being mustered on 27 June (*CPR, 1467–77*, 217, 221; T. Carte, *Catalogue*, II, 361).

[3] Above, p. 109. Kendall, *op. cit.*, 261, suggests that the idea was Warwick's.

Louis's most persistent and dearest ambition. The difficulties and dangers involved were considerable. Apart from the risk of English naval attacks on the French coast, Louis risked the hostility of Burgundy and Brittany, angered by the continuing indiscriminate piracy of Warwick's fleet. He was soon faced by the threat of combined Anglo-Burgundian naval operations. Nor were his proposed allies exactly eager partners. Warwick wanted assurances of effective French help, and would not be a mere cat's paw for Queen Margaret. The stubborn queen herself, brought up from the Anjou family home at Bar in eastern France at the king's expense, was even more recalcitrant at the prospect of cooperating with the man who had done so much to overthrow the house of Lancaster; and the presence of the Yorkist king's brother was an embarrassment to all. Eventually, after discussions at Amboise, a meeting was arranged at Angers on 22 June between Warwick and Margaret, in the king's presence. Their agreement centred round a marriage treaty between her eighteen-year-old son, Edward, prince of Wales, and Warwick's younger daughter, Anne, now seventeen, and on 25 July they were solemnly betrothed in Angers Cathedral.[1] Plans were laid for the invasion of England with French aid. Even then Margaret refused to let her high-spirited son take part in any wildcat venture. He must remain in France with Margaret herself until the greater part of England had been secured for King Henry, a decision which later proved unfortunate for the new alliance.

Warwick then departed to prepare his fleet for the invasion of England, but it was several weeks before they could set sail. The admiral of France, with the escort squadron, and part of Warwick's fleet, was pinned down at Honfleur by a joint Anglo-Burgundian blockade, and the rest of the earl's ships were similarly held at La Hogue and Barfleur in the Cotentin peninsula by another Burgundian squadron. Only when these forces were dispersed by a great storm in early September did a crossing become possible. With the earls of Pembroke and Oxford, Warwick and Clarence embarked at La Hogue on 9 September, and some four days later landed safely in Devonshire.[2] What plans had Edward made for the defence of his realm against

[1] They could not be formally married, since a dispensation for their relationship in the fourth degree could not be obtained at such short notice: they had a common great-grandfather in John of Gaunt, duke of Lancaster. They were later married at Amboise, probably on 13 December 1470 (Calmette and Perinelle, 139–40).
[2] Though early Tudor sources say they landed at Dartmouth (e.g. Polydore Vergil, *English History*, 132; *GC*, 211; Kingsford, *Chron. London*, 181), more contemporary writers say Devonshire or the West Country (Warkworth, *Chronicle*, 10; *Three Fifteenth-Century Chronicles*, 183; *CC*, 553).

the expected invasion? Contemporary Burgundian chroniclers, echo-
ing the opinions current at the court of Duke Charles, roundly accused
him of negligence and insane over-confidence. Commynes relates how[1]

> the duke of Burgundy, who presently perceiving that there were great
> transactions in England in favour of the earl, gave frequent information
> thereof to king Edward. But he never heeded it, which seems to me a fine
> example of folly, not to fear one's enemy and to refuse to believe anything,
> considering the preparations against him.

The duke, he continues, gave Edward precise indications about Warwick's coming invasion, and urged him to put his kingdom in a posture
of defence:

> But he never was concerned at anything, but still followed his hunting,
> and nobody was so trusted by him as the archbishop of York and the
> marquis of Montagu, brothers of the said earl of Warwick. . . .

Chastellain's criticisms are rather different but no less firm:[2]

> . . . he was a valiant prince, and he was always confident that he would be
> able to recover against him quickly enough . . . for he was certain that once
> he found himself on the field of battle with Warwick, the latter would
> not oppose him, for he was a faintheart and a coward.

Burgundy's good advice did not profit Edward,

> since he never knew how to put into effect what would be for his salvation.
> He promised many things and said he would do them, but he never did
> any of them.

Although echoed by some modern scholars, these charges, especially
Commynes's, are largely without foundation.[3] He did not respond to
Burgundy's suggestions that he should seize Calais in person, and
thereby frighten Louis and Warwick, and that he should deliver
Henry VI to Burgundy's custody, and 'thereby deprive Warwick of
the instrument on which he relied to aid his return into England'.[4]
But he did take every reasonable precaution for the protection of his
realm, and the mistakes he made sprang from miscalculation rather
than negligence or over-confidence.

Edward had already taken measures to secure Ireland and Calais so
as to ensure that they could not be used as springboards for invasion
after the pattern of 1460.[5] Wenlock was at first rewarded for turning

---

[1] Commynes, I, 197, 200.   [2] *Chronique*, V, 486, 492–3.
[3] Calmette and Perinelle, 117, 119; Scofield, I, 523; Jacob, *Fifteenth Century*, 560.
[4] Chastellain, *Chronique*, as above.   [5] Above, p. 22.

away Warwick and Clarence by an appointment as lieutenant of the town and marches of Calais on 26 May, but on 11 June the king put Calais under Rivers's control as 'general governor and lieutenant', and then, becoming even more suspicious of Wenlock's loyalties, replaced him altogether by the reliable John, Lord Howard, who was made lieutenant on 2 July.[1] Dover and the Cinque Ports had been put in charge of the earl of Arundel as constable and Sir John Scott as lieutenant, and in June the king made a personal visit to Dover and Sandwich to inspect their defences, perhaps with memories of 1460 in mind. In the same month commissions of array were issued to several counties along the south coast and the Welsh border.[2]

The invasion scares of 1461 and 1462 had called forth an elaborate series of measures for watch and ward and coastal defence. In 1470 these were not repeated, for he was able to rely primarily on naval defences. The preparations which had been going on for some time for Channel patrol against the Hansards helped him here, for Howard's fleet, aided by further squadrons from Southampton and Sandwich under Earl Rivers, was already at sea and these forces could be turned against Warwick and the French. Further, thanks to the vigilance of Rivers and several ships' captains, Warwick had been denied, and Edward acquired, the use of the earl's own private navy which had already been of great value in previous years. With his usual generosity, Edward rewarded the good service of nine shipmasters, including at least one of Warwick's captains, with sizeable annuities for life on 1 May.[3] Finally, and as a direct result of Warwick's indiscriminate piracy, Edward had the advantage of powerful assistance from a Burgundian fleet, which put to sea on 11 June and was thereafter almost continuously in operation until September. Together these factors gave the Anglo-Burgundian alliance supremacy at sea. Being first at sea they put the French on the defensive, exposed the French coast to raids and pillage, and neutralized the French and rebel naval forces by almost continuous blockade.[4]

But there were limits to the effectiveness of naval power in these days

1 T. Carte, *Catalogue*, II, 361; where Howard's name is given as Thomas, but John Howard was deputy for Hastings in July 1471; Scofield, I, 521 (for Rivers); II, 11.
2 *CPR, 1467-77*, 206, 209, 220; *Chronicle of John Stone*, ed. W. G. Searle (Cambridge Antiquarian Soc., 1902), 113.
3 *CPR, 1467-77*, 208. John Porter, master of the *Trinity*, was given an annuity of £20.
4 La Ronciere, *op. cit.*, II, 341-4; Scofield, I, 526. For the importance of this element of priority, which had been clearly put before parliament in 1454 by Edward's father, Duke Richard, see C. F. Richmond, 'English Naval Power in the Fifteenth Century', *History*, lii (1967), 1-4, 12.

of small ships overcrowded with fighting men and mariners. A blockade could be maintained only for a period of a few weeks before ships
had to return to port for revictualling and often for repair. This happened to the Burgundian ships blockading the Seine in July 1470,
whilst the English flotilla had to withdraw at the same time to protect
the English coast against attack from a Hanseatic naval force.[1] But
the blockade was later successfully resumed, and only the final ill-
fortune of an autumn storm scattered the Anglo-Burgundian ships and
provided the invaders with a favourable wind. Warwick and his French
allies were lucky indeed, for wind and weather conditions could often
keep an invasion fleet in French harbours for months on end, as
Margaret of Anjou soon discovered to her cost.[2]

In all these measures Edward showed clearly that he had learnt
much from his own experience as a political exile, and, in his awareness
of the value of sea-power, had benefited from the practice and perhaps
the advice of his great enemy Richard Nevill.[3] In matters of internal
security his judgement was perhaps more open to question. A single act
of savagery, when Worcester as Constable of England was allowed to
add impalement to the usual horrors of execution against the rebels
taken in the naval attack on Southampton, was probably designed as a
warning and example to others, but for the most part Edward followed
his customary policy of generous clemency to his opponents. On
25 April the earl of Wiltshire and Lord Mountjoy were empowered to
pardon any rebels who submitted before 7 May, and many took advantage of this offer.[4] There were no reprisals and no confiscations. Stanley,
Shrewsbury and Scrope were pardoned, and Montagu (though not his
brother, the archbishop) continued to enjoy the king's confidence.[5]
Though Edward has often been criticized for his apparent naiveté in
trusting him, nothing in Montagu's record suggested he was likely to
be less loyal than in the past, and it is doubtful whether Edward felt
he had treated Warwick's brother badly. Further grants and rewards
may well have been planned for him.

Late in July Edward faced a difficult decision when news reached
London of further risings in the north on behalf of the Nevills. The
chroniclers mention only a rebellion led by Warwick's brother-in-law,

[1] La Ronciere, II, 344; Richmond, *op. cit.*, 4.   [2] Below, p. 169.
[3] Richmond, *op. cit.*, 8, for Warwick's use of sea-power.
[4] *CPR, 1467–77*, 207.
[5] *Ibid.*, 209–11. Montagu was present at a meeting of the Great Council at Canterbury
in June, went north later, was appointed to a large commission of oyer and terminer
for Lincolnshire on 11 July, but was omitted from that for Yorkshire on 21 August
(*ibid.*, 221; *Chron. John Stone*, 114).

Lord FitzHugh of Ravensworth, in the North Riding of Yorkshire, but there is other evidence of hostile assemblies in the neighbourhood of Carlisle.[1] Here the leaders included some local gentry whose families had close associations with the Nevills, among them Richard Salkeld, until recently constable of the castle of Carlisle. How substantial or well supported these risings were is difficult to assess. The list of pardons granted to the rebels on 10 September suggests they were on a very small scale. Only 101 persons were pardoned with FitzHugh, including his five sons, eleven women and four chaplains; almost all the people named came from Ravensworth, and are described as gentlemen or yeomen. This probably represents the retinue or affinity of a baron of modest status, reinforced by some of his local tenants. In Cumberland a mere 97 persons thought it prudent to take out pardons. Reports reaching London, however, suggested something much more serious. On 7 August Sir John Paston told his brother that 'so many folks be up in the north' that the new earl of Northumberland could not resist them; and so, he added, 'the king hath sent for his feedmen to come to him, for he will go to put them down'.[2]

Why did Edward allow himself to be drawn away to the north at a time when the risk of invasion from the Continent was daily becoming greater? He could scarcely have been unaware of Warwick's doings in France, for warnings and advice reached him from the duke of Burgundy, as well as information from his own agents, like the lady whom he sent overseas to make contact with Clarence and persuade him to desert the Lancastrian alliance.[3] Even common rumour had it that invasion was imminent, and Sir John Paston clearly believed that Edward was unwise to go north at all, and even less so to linger there.[4] On the analogy of 1469, the rebel movements in the north were likely to be little more than a diversion to get Edward away from London and leave the south clear for an invasion. But this was a risk the king had to balance against the proven dangers of northern insurrections spreading unchecked, especially in the presently excitable state of the country. In 1469 he had been slow to move, with disastrous results; the prompt action of 1470 had brought handsome rewards. The silence of Montagu and the apparent lack of success of the new

[1] GC, 211; Chron. White Rose ('Hearne's Fragment'), 29; CPR, 1467–77, 214–16 (pardons to rebels on 10 September).
[2] PL, V, 80.
[3] Chastellain, Chronique, V, 492; Commynes, I, 198–200; Scofield, I, 523, citing accounts of the treasurer of Calais.
[4] PL, V, 80, a view echoed by Scofield, I, 535; Oman, Warwick, 205; Ramsay, Lancaster and York, II, 335.

earl of Northumberland, may have been a further cause for concern. Nor could he know in advance where the invasion, if and when it came, would descend. Fifteenth-century pretenders were to assault the coast from as far apart as Spurn Head in Yorkshire to Milford Haven in West Wales, and, as an area of potential support for Warwick and Henry VI, the north was a more likely area than most. In the event, he took the wrong decision.

With many of his lords, he left London for the north at the end of July. Reaching York on 14 August, he then went on to Ripon, only to find that FitzHugh had fled to Scotland and his men had returned to their homes. By 12 August he was back in York. Since a pardon was issued to the northern rebels on 10 September, the north may be presumed quiet by this time. But the king lingered on in Yorkshire, even though he now clearly anticipated a landing in Kent; on 7 September he had sent instructions to his people there on what to do when it came, and told them he soon hoped to be back in London. Nevertheless, he was still in Yorkshire when news came, about the middle of the month, of Warwick's landing in the West Country.[1]

Immediately they arrived, Warwick and Clarence declared openly for Henry VI. With Jasper Tudor, earl of Pembroke, and Oxford, they issued proclamations in the old king's name calling on all able-bodied men to support them. Soon the earl of Shrewsbury and Lord Stanley joined them with substantial retinues, and, gathering in popular levies as they came, they approached Coventry with a large force. When the news of their landing reached the south-east, there were violent outbreaks in Kent, and bands of Kentishmen broke into Southwark and other London suburbs south of the river, looting and plundering chiefly at the expense of Flemings and Dutchmen, whose beerhouses they destroyed. Meanwhile, King Edward set out from York for London but checked his march (near either Doncaster or Nottingham) to await the arrival of troops whom Montagu was assembling on his behalf. Suddenly news reached him that Montagu had defected to his brother and carried most of his men with him, and that he was now in pursuit of the king. Although Edward still had a number of loyal noblemen in his company, including Gloucester, Rivers, Worcester, Hastings, Howard and Say, he decided that the only safety lay in urgent flight. A rapid dash across Lincolnshire brought him to the Wash, where he narrowly escaped drowning, and thence to King's Lynn, where Rivers had influence. There the party found shipping and set

---

[1] *GC*, 211; *Chron. White Rose*, 28–9; *CPR, 1467–77*, 214–16; *PL*, V, 83 (Edward's letter of 7 September).

sail on Tuesday, 2 October, for the Low Countries.[1] It proved a risky voyage, for they were sighted by a hostile squadron of Hanseatic ships. These gave chase and almost captured them, and were still pursuing closely when the king's ships touched the Dutch coast near Alkmaar. Having no money, Edward was reduced to rewarding the master of his ship with a fine furred gown, but he was fortunate to fall into the hands of Duke Charles's governor of Holland, Louis of Bruges, Lord of Gruthuyse, a friend of the house of York who had several times been ambassador to England and knew the king personally. Gruthuyse took charge of the English party, providing food, clothes and money, and escorted Edward and his lords and their small company of followers to his house at The Hague, where they arrived on 11 October.[2]

Barely three weeks separate the rebel landing in Devonshire from Edward's flight from King's Lynn. This short period saw the total collapse of Edward's position in face of men who had been unable to find any backing for their rebellion against him only a few months before. A revolution so sudden and bloodless drew from Commynes an exclamation of astonishment at the mutability of human fortune, but he blamed it, none the less, on Edward's sloth and negligence.[3] This, as we have seen, is scarcely convincing. Most contemporary accounts suggest that Montagu's defection was the decisive factor in bringing about Edward's overthrow, but the story as told by the chroniclers raises a number of questions. Montagu had been ordered to raise large numbers of men; Edward had very few, and could not face him in the field.[4] But this seems very unlikely, for the retinues of the magnates who surrounded him were probably considerable, and Commynes, who met Lord Hastings soon after, reported that the latter had said he had a body of 3,000 of his men with the king.[5]

A more probable explanation for the *débâcle* is that Edward faced a sudden crumbling of his authority, a loss of popular support such as happened in the summer of 1469. All contemporary sources emphasize

---

[1] The date of Edward's sailing is established precisely by the records of King's Lynn, quoted in W. I. Haward, 'Economic Aspects of the Wars of the Roses in East Anglia', *EHR*, xli (1926), 179; not 29 September, as Scofield, I, 542, and other modern writers, following Warkworth, 11. For the events described above, *CC*, 553–4; *GC*, 211; Waurin, ed. Dupont, III, 46–8; Commynes, I, 201–5; Chastellain, *Chronique*, V, 501–3, 508; *Chron. White Rose of York*, 28–9.

[2] Chastellain and Commynes, as above; the latter says (I, 205) that Edward had 500 men in his company.

[3] *Ibid.*, I, 204.   [4] Thus, for example, Warkworth, 10–11.

[5] Commynes, I, 202. The King's Lynn records (cited above, in Haward, *op. cit.*, 179) say Edward had 3,000 men with him when he reached there.

that popular sympathy had swung to Warwick, and that large numbers
of people flocked to his standards from the outset.[1] Even those who
might have preferred to support the king found it politic to abstain.
For example, at their council meeting on 21 September, the city
fathers of Salisbury found themselves in a predicament. It was announced that Warwick and Clarence had entered England with a
large army, and their agent, John Pike, esquire, came to demand the
services of forty armed men; at the same time Thomas St Leger, one
of Edward's esquires of the body, appeared ordering them to resist
the invaders. An attempt to compromise by offering Warwick's agent
40 marks was refused, and one John Hall, 'who had already volunteered
to serve the king on horseback', offered to find the men if paid 40 marks,
and the city's little contingent marched out to join the rebels.[2]

Edward's remoteness in the north probably made loyalty no easier.
Here too he was isolated in a countryside which, to judge from the
events of 1469 and 1471, was either apathetic or hostile. This in turn
doubtless influenced the attitudes of the gentry and yeomen who made
up the retinues of his lords, for a magnate could not always *command*
the loyalty of his following against their own disposition, as the earl of
Northumberland discovered in 1471. Probably the real reason for
Edward's decision to flee the realm is that given in the summary
account of these events in the official record of Coventry:[3]

> So then there drew to them [Clarence and Warwick] much people or
> they come to Coventry they were 30 thousand. King Edward lay at
> Nottingham, and sent for lords and all other men, but there come so
> little people . . . to him that he was not able to make a field against them . . .
> and then he . . . went to Lynn.

Finally, the cause of Warwick and Clarence probably owed something
to surviving Lancastrian loyalties. In the circumstances, Edward was
right to take flight to the dominions of his brother-in-law. Certainly
he could not risk falling into the hands of an enemy whose record (unlike his own) was not conspicuous for clemency to the defeated.

Edward's political future now depended on two things: the ability
of the restored government of Henry VI to consolidate its position in
England, and the attitude of Duke Charles of Burgundy, confronted
by a regime which had already pledged itself to join the king of France

---

[1] E.g., Commynes, I, 200–1; Warkworth, *Chronicle*, 10; Calmette and Perinelle, 317–
318 (a letter written from Bruges, 11 October).
[2] Benson and Hatcher, *Old and New Sarum*, 175.
[3] *Coventry Leet Book*, II, 358–9.

in making war upon him. From the first the so-called Readeption government of Henry VI depended upon an uneasy cooperation between Warwick and his personal following, former Lancastrians, and moderate Yorkist lords. These last, who had mostly benefited substantially from Edward's rule, and who now formed the largest group amongst the peers, had to be placated if the new regime were to survive, and Warwick went to some lengths to win their support. There could be no extreme measures and no recriminations against them. Certain prominent Yorkists, including Archbishop Bourchier, Norfolk, Essex, Wiltshire, Cromwell and Mountjoy, were at first placed under arrest, but soon released; and when writs were sent out on 15 October for a parliament to meet at Westminster on 26 November, only seven Yorkist peers did not receive a summons. Four of these (Gloucester, Rivers, Hastings and Say) were in exile with Edward; of those still in England the only notable omissions were the earl of Wiltshire and Lords Dudley and Dinham.[1] The solitary victim of prominence was the highly unpopular earl of Worcester, whose cruelties would later win for him the title of 'Butcher of England'. Arraigned before the earl of Oxford as constable of England, he was sentenced to die on 17 October, but such large crowds came to 'gaze and gawre' at this hated man that his escort could not get through to Tower Hill, and the execution was postponed until the following day.[2] Since the official records of the Readeption parliament have disappeared, we cannot know for certain what measures of political reprisal it approved, but it would appear that only Edward himself and his brother, Gloucester, were attainted. If any of the acts of attainder against former Lancastrians were reversed, this was certainly not taken to involve the restoration of their estates, for any such action would have involved a head-on clash with all the Yorkist lords who held forfeited estates.[3]

Moderation was imposed on the new government by necessity, and

---

[1] For the arrests, *Hanserecesse von 1431–1476*, ed. G. von der Ropp, II, 416; Norfolk at least was at liberty by 16 October, *CPR, 1467–77*, 245. For the writs, Wedgwood, *Hist. Parl., Reg.*, 378–82. What follows on the Readeption concerns only matters relevant to Edward's invasion; for general accounts, see Scofield, I, 543–65; Kendall, *Warwick*, 281–308; Jacob, *Fifteenth Century*, 561–6.

[2] Warkworth, *Chronicle*, 13; *GC*, 212–13; Kingsford, *Chronicles of London*, 182–3.

[3] Scofield, I, 555, and Ramsay, *op. cit.*, follow the authority of Warkworth and Polydore Vergil for the view that Lancastrian attainders were reversed, and Yorkists other than Edward and Gloucester were attainted; cf. Wedgwood, *op. cit.*, 375, for a more likely view. The absence of any grants on the Patent and Fine Rolls from forfeited estates, and the respect for the rights of heirs, show conclusively that none of Edward supporters was attainted, and that his grants by letters patent were respected.

was not a sign of enlightened statesmanship. But Warwick's problems were not solved thereby; they were merely postponed. In one important respect his position was far weaker than Edward's had been ten years earlier. He could not reward his supporters or buy support with lavish distributions of land and office from extensive forfeitures. There were few pickings for anyone, and the earl himself took most of what was available – the offices of captain of Calais, chamberlain of England, and admiral, and the wardship of part of the duke of Buckingham's lordships in South Wales which he had been forced to surrender to Herbert in 1461.[1] There were no rewards for supporters like Oxford, Shrewsbury and Stanley. Fortunately for Warwick, his bitterest enemies amongst the disinherited Lancastrian loyalists did not return with him in September 1470. Not until the following February did the duke of Exeter, or Edmund Beaufort, duke of Somerset, return from exile. But other Lancastrians, such as Jasper Tudor, earl of Pembroke, who had suffered exile and forfeiture for their Lancastrian loyalties, got little from Henry VI's restoration. Obviously this situation could scarcely continue indefinitely. The return of Queen Margaret and Prince Edward was likely to weaken Warwick's influence and strengthen that of unreconciled Lancastrian elements. Their supplanters, Edward's men, many occupying their inheritances, probably viewed the future with suspicion.

Especially vulnerable was George, duke of Clarence. Though rather tardily reappointed lieutenant of Ireland, he was not associated with Warwick as joint lieutenant of the realm, and it is highly unlikely that he was recognized as heir to the throne in the event of the failure of Henry VI's male line.[2] Moreover, on 23 March 1471 he was compelled to give up part of his possessions in favour of Queen Margaret and her son, and accept instead a less secure provision of fee-farm rents, 'notwithstanding' (say the letters patent, reflecting the duke's obvious protest) 'the agreements made between the said queen and prince and himself and Richard, earl of Warwick and Salisbury, that he should retain all his possessions until duly recompensed, the honour and lord-

---

[1] *CPR, 1467–77*, 233; *CFR, 1461–71*, 293, 295. Montagu was restored to his wardenship of the East March, which had been given to Henry Percy, earl of Northumberland, on 24 June, and was given the wardship of the estates of the earl of Worcester during the heir's minority, and of those of John, Lord Clifford (d. 1461); R. L. Storey, 'Wardens of the Marches', *EHR*, lxxii (1957), 615. For grants to Pembroke (including custody of lands of William Herbert and Lord Grey of Powys during minority, *CPR, 1467–77*, 236, 243; *CFR, 1461–71*, 283–4.

[2] J. R. Lander, 'Treason and Death of the Duke of Clarence', esp. pp. 14–15; and below, pp. 242–3. He may have been recognized as heir to the Duchy of York.

ship of Tutbury excepted'. Though confirmed at the time in possession of his earldom of Richmond, his title to it was obviously threatened by the presence at court of its Lancastrian heir, Henry Tudor, son of Henry VI's half-brother, Edmund Tudor, earl of Richmond.[1] Clarence found himself

> held in great suspicion, despite, disdain, and hatred, with all the lords, noblemen, and other, that were adherents and full partakers with Henry the usurper . . . he saw also, that they daily laboured amongst them, breaking their appointments made with him, and, of likelihood, after that, should continually more and more fervently intend, conspire, and procure the destruction of him and all his blood.[2]

No wonder Edward thought it worthwhile to bring pressure upon Clarence – through his mother, the duchess of York, his sisters, the duchesses of Burgundy, Suffolk and Exeter, Cardinal Bourchier, Bishop Stillington, and the earl of Essex to persuade him to defect whenever opportunity arose. Clarence's position may have been particularly invidious, but his feelings were probably shared by many other Yorkist lords. The Lancastrian–Nevill misalliance could offer them little but unease and insecurity.

How narrowly based was support for the government amongst the barons as a whole can be seen from its defence measures. When, towards the end of 1470 and in the early months of 1471, Warwick began to fear invasion, he trusted only a very small group of men with the task of raising troops – Montagu alone in the whole of the north, Clarence, Oxford, Lord Scrope of Bolton and himself in the rest of England, and Pembroke, again with Clarence and himself, in Wales and the Marches.[3] Never had commissions of array for national defence been placed in the hands of so few. A similar caution appears in other government measures. Many of Edward's barons were removed from the commissions of the peace. Despite his Lancastrian record, the new earl of Northumberland, Henry Percy, did not appear on a single commission, whilst the heir to the Lancastrian earldom of Devon was confined to a solitary commission of the peace in Devon.[4] Attempts by Warwick to win over the earl of Essex seem to have been a failure, and on the eve of Edward's landing the duke of Norfolk and probably other

---

[1] *CPR, 1467–77*, 241–3; Rymer, *Foedera*, XI, 693; Scofield, I, 543.
[2] *Arrivall of Edward IV*, 10 (for this source see below, p. 162); it also details the pressures mentioned below.
[3] *CPR, 1467–77*, 251–2.
[4] *Ibid.*, 611–12. Yorkists removed from the bench include Howard, Dudley, Dinham, Mountjoy, Audley and Ferrers (*ibid.*, 607–38).

lords were arrested for safety's sake.[1] Even Montagu's loyalty was not above suspicion, and, according to one report, he had to apologize to parliament for his previous support of King Edward.[2] Most of the barons were unsympathetic if not actively hostile to the new regime.

How far the new government commended itself to the mass of Englishmen is not easy to assess. Some gentry families had private reasons for welcoming the change. The Pastons, for example, found a new and powerful patron in John de Vere, earl of Oxford, in their efforts to recover Caister Castle from the duke and duchess of Norfolk, and clearly relished the temporary fall of their mighty and oppressive neighbours, 'who now' (wrote Sir John) 'sue to him [Oxford] as humbly as ever I did to them', and, he went on, 'as for my Lord of Oxford, he is better lord to me, by my troth, than I can wish him in any matters'.[3] Self-interest and local politics explain the presence of both Sir John and his brother on Warwick's side at the battle of Barnet.

Contemporary chronicle evidence suggests that the restoration of King Henry, for whom there still existed much personal respect and sympathy, was generally welcomed, 'whereof', says one writer, 'all his good lovers were full glad, and the more part of people'.[4] Nor had Warwick lost all his popularity. Even that enthusiastic Yorkist, the author of the *Arrivall*, the official chronicle of Edward's 1471 campaign, had to admit that there was little sign of popular welcome for his king in March 1471.[5] Baronial support for Edward, and to some extent the self-interest of the merchant classes, rather than any change in popular esteem, were to prove his principal assets.

The most difficult problem facing Warwick's administration sprang from the commitment made at Angers to join King Louis in making war upon Burgundy. Earl Richard was no unwilling partner in this venture. Sentiment and self-interest – he had been promised the provinces of Holland and Zeeland if the war were a success – combined to make him press forward his plans. On 16 February 1471 a ten-year truce with France, with provision for freedom of commerce, was signed. Already, on 5 February, he had told the French ambassadors that he would be ready to begin operations against Duke Charles within a few days, that he was sending troops to Calais, and that he would later go there himself, in command of 8,000 to 10,000 prime English archers. On 12 February he gave orders to the Calais garrison to begin hostili-

---

[1] *Arrivall*, 2, 10.
[2] Polydore Vergil, *English History*, 112. The *Arrivall*, 6, also implies that his loyalties were ambivalent in March 1471.
[3] *PL*, V, 84–5.　　　　[4] Warkworth, *Chronicle*, 11.　　　　[5] *Arrivall*, 3–4.

ties against adjacent Burgundian territories.[1] None of this was likely to commend itself to mercantile interests, already suffering from the commercial war with the Hanse, and for a government still precariously in control at home to risk even a limited military venture abroad seemed unwise. War meant taxation, for the government was already very short of funds. It could draw upon the revenues of the royal estates and upon the profits of the customs, but these sources probably provided less than £15,000 a year, and Warwick had been compelled to provide finance for the royal household out of his own resources for some time.[2] His difficulty in raising loans is a sharp indication of how little confidence the propertied classes had in his regime. London had lent him only £1,000 (to be compared with the £11,000 it had advanced to the Yorkist earls in 1460–1), and was already pressing for repayment of an earlier loan made in 1469.[3] Funds were simply not available for heavy military spending, and attempts to raise troops by other means were likely to prove unpopular. Entries in the Coventry records make it clear that Warwick was expecting the town to supply men for service overseas at its own expense, an unwarrantable demand, for the crown had long since recognized that local militia could be used only for the internal defence of the realm.[4]

The chief short-term danger of Warwick's policy of aggression lay in its effect upon Duke Charles of Burgundy. The earl was to some extent the victim of Louis XI's impatience. In December 1470 he had denounced the Treaty of Péronne, declared war on Burgundy, and moved French forces into Picardy to threaten the duke's northern dominions. But the effect of English support for these offensive moves by France was to change Duke Charles's attitude to the Lancastrian regime. From an embarrassed but careful neutrality it was now transformed into positive hostility. His immediate reaction was to give his support to a Yorkist invasion.

Edward IV's arrival in his domains had not elicited any welcome from Duke Charles. He was well aware of Louis's intention of using England against him, and therefore exerted himself to avoid any

---

[1] Calmette and Perinelle, 128–33; Scofield, I, 555–63; A. R. Myers, 'The Outbreak of War between England and Burgundy in February 1471', *BIHR*, xxxiii (1960), 114–15.
[2] Scofield, I, 542 n. The figure of £15,000 is a likely guess by Kendall, *Warwick*, 288 n.
[3] *Ibid.*, 288–9, citing *London Journal* 7, ff. 225, 230b–231; and for 1460–61, above, p. 35.
[4] *Coventry Leet Book*, II, 362; the nature of local militia service is discussed at length by M. R. Powicke, *Military Obligation in Medieval England*, 182–210, 216–20. Internal defence might include war against the Welsh and Scots.

action against England which might be seen as providing a *casus belli*. He repeatedly expressed his friendship for the House of Lancaster.[1] But Anglo-French hostility gradually forced him to change his attitude. For more than two months Edward had been compelled to depend on the hospitality of Louis of Bruges, and not until 26 December 1470 was he finally summoned to a meeting with the duke himself. A conference between the two at Aire on 2–4 January 1471 was followed by another at St Pol on 7 January, where Edward had been invited to stay with his queen's kinsman, Jacques de Luxembourg. Even then the duke would not commit himself publicly to Edward, and officially forbade his subjects to give him aid, but in private he supplied Edward with 50,000 florins (£20,000) and gave orders for three or four Dutch ships to be fitted out for him at Veere on the island of Walcheren.[2]

Meanwhile, Edward himself had not been inactive. He was in touch with Clarence and with other loyal or potential supporters in England, including Henry Percy, earl of Northumberland, who had reason to fear that if the Readeption proved lasting he might again lose his earldom in favour of Montagu.[3] He also appealed for aid to Duke Francis of Brittany, and entered into negotiations with the Hansards, who were promised great privileges when he recovered his kingdom. The Hansards eventually provided fourteen ships to aid his crossing and to serve him for fifteen days after his landing in England. In Bruges Earl Rivers was bargaining for the hire of more ships. Two sea-captains from England, John Lyster and Stephen Driver, brought their vessels over to join the small invasion fleet which began to assemble at Flushing during February. English merchants trading in Bruges lent Edward modest sums of money. On 19 February he left for Flushing and on 2 March embarked upon the *Antony*, a ship belonging to the Burgundian admiral, Henry of Borselle, lord of Veere. The invasion force now consisted of 36 ships and about 1,200 men, some English, some Flemings, the latter including a number of gunners. Held back for nine weary days by contrary winds, they finally set sail from Flushing on 11 March 1471.[4]

[1] Commynes, I, 207–11; Commynes, ed. Dupont, III, 271–2 (for the duke's instructions to Commynes on his mission of friendship).
[2] Commynes, I, 211–12; Scofield, I, 562.
[3] Warkworth, *Chronicle*, 11; Pugh, *The Fifteenth Century*, 109 and n.
[4] Calmette and Perinelle, Pièces Justificatives, nos 40 (Edward's letter to Brittany) and 41 (letter from Bruges to the earl of Ormond, 19 January 1471); *Hanserecesse*, II, 404–5; Commynes, I, 212; *Arrivall*, 2; the size of the forces is estimated at 1,200 by Warkworth, 13 (900 English, 300 Flemings with hand-guns) and by Waurin, ed. Dupont, III, 97, probably from French version of the *Arrivall*; at 2,000 by *Arrivall*, 1, and *Hist. MSS Comm., Rutland MSS*, I, 3–4 (Warwick's letter to Henry Vernon); at 1,000 by *GC*, 214 (500 English, 500 Flemings).

(iii) *The Recovery of England, March–May 1471*

It was a highly risky venture on which Edward now embarked. Considering his limited resources, Warwick deserves every credit for his vigilant precautions against invasion. All along the coast of eastern England, where a landing was held to be likeliest, Warwick's agents had scoured the countryside, threatening and exhorting local authorities to be on guard. The king's friends were closely watched and his enemies correspondingly active. For some time past an English fleet under the command of the Bastard of Fauconberg had been patrolling the Channel. Warwick overcame the problem of financing these naval operations by allowing his ships to indulge in profitable and successful piracy, and large numbers of Spanish, Portuguese and Breton ships had been captured. Help could be expected also from Louis XI, who had made extensive naval preparations for the war with Burgundy. In spite of the secrecy with which the invasion force had been assembled in the creeks of Walcheren Island, the English government was not caught off its guard. But in one respect Edward was fortunate. The English fleet was diverted by the activities of a Breton naval squadron in the Channel as well as by continuing hostilities with the Hansards, and the French ships were lying in the Seine waiting to escort Queen Margaret and her company from Honfleur to England. Like Edward's fleet, they had been held in port by continuing bad weather during February. Edward's chances of a safe crossing of the North Sea were better than he could have known.[1]

The invaders' plan was to make for the coast of East Anglia. Here they might hope for help from the dukes of Norfolk and Suffolk, and Rivers had lands and friends in northern Norfolk. After an uneventful voyage, they put in at Cromer on 12 March, and Edward sent off two of his company with local knowledge, Sir Robert Chamberlain and Sir Gilbert Debenham, to make enquiries. They returned with warnings from the archbishop of Canterbury and Thomas Rotherham, bishop of Rochester, that it would be quite unsafe to land. Norfolk and other friends were in custody, and Oxford and his brothers had been raising men and were very much on the alert. The king then decided to sail north to Yorkshire. But his fleet was hit by storms and scattered. Edward himself eventually came ashore on Thursday, 14 March, at

---

[1] *CPR, 1467–77*, 250 (naval preparations); for naval operations, Scofield, I, 554; Calmette and Perinelle, 129; La Ronciere, *op. cit.*, II, 347–50. The letter from Bruges cited in the previous note shows that precise information of Edward's preparations was reaching a Lancastrian supporter in Rouen.

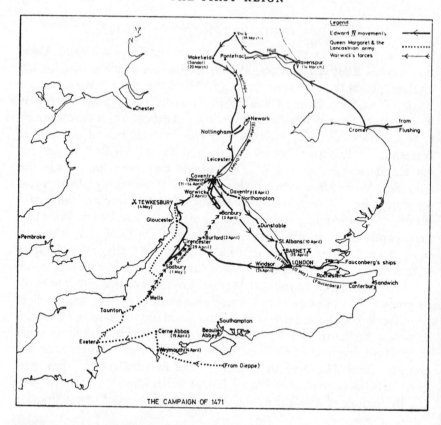

THE CAMPAIGN OF 1471

Ravenspur on the Humber, where Henry Bolingbroke, duke of Lancaster, had landed on a similar mission seventy-two years before. The other ships all made land within a few miles of the *Antony*, and on the next day 'the whole fellowship' was reunited.[1]

'It is a difficult matter to go out by the door and then try to enter by the windows. They think he will leave his skin there.'[2] Such was the Milanese ambassador's comment from France on early reports of

---

[1] For these events, and those of the next six weeks, the principal source, on which the following narrative of Edward's campaign is largely based, is the official account known as the *Arrivall of Edward IV*. Despite its partisan nature, it is an invaluable narrative, written by one of Edward's servants who was an eye-witness of much that he describes. It was completed, at least in its shorter form, by 29 May 1471 (Kingsford, *English Historical Literature*, 174–5). Three French versions of it exist, one of which was used by Waurin (ed. Dupont, III, 96–147), and these have some independent value; see J. A. F. Thomson, ' "The Arrival of Edward IV" – The Development of the Text', *Speculum*, xlvi (1971), 84–93. Other useful narratives are in Warkworth, *Chronicle*, 13–20; Polydore Vergil, *English History*, 136–54; *CC*, 554–6.

[2] *CSP, Milan*, I, 151 (letter from Beauvais, 9 April).

Edward's landing; and probably few men in England rated his prospects much higher. As the author of the *Arrivall* emphasized, Yorkshire was essentially a hostile countryside. The government had many supporters in the region. Large bands of armed men were afoot lying in wait for Edward, notably one under a local gentleman, Martin de la See, from Barmston in Holderness, and the nearest town, Kingston on Hull, which had Lancastrian sympathies, refused to admit Edward. He was reduced to attempting what might be called the king's gambit by repeating the tactic used by Henry Bolingbroke in 1399 – that he had come back to claim not the throne but his own ducal inheritance. He also displayed letters from Henry Percy, earl of Northumberland, saying he had come there by his advice; and this helped in a region where Percy influence was strong.[1] But it was still a risky gamble in the early stages. He was able to gain admission to York on 18 March only by leaving his troops outside the walls and chancing his safety in the city with no more than sixteen or seventeen men at his back. According to Warkworth, he also pledged loyalty to Henry VI and wore the white ostrich feather (the prince of Wales's badge) in his hat. From York he went on to the family castle of Sandal, near Wakefield, the scene of his father's death ten years before; but even here he did not find much support; there 'came some folks unto him, but not so many as he supposed would have come'.[2]

But popular sympathy – or lack of it – was not to be a decisive factor in 1471. Much more now depended on the attitude of the magnates and local gentry. Two men in Yorkshire – Montagu and Northumberland – could easily have snuffed out Edward's chances by a prompt move in these early days of his invasion. His first clear stroke of luck came when Montagu failed to move against him from Pontefract Castle, as Edward marched nearby from York to Wakefield. He 'suffered him to pass in peaceful wise' (says the *Arrivall*) 'whether it were with good will or no, men may judge at their pleasure; I deem yea'; but the author goes on to advance other reasons why Montagu remained inactive. The most important of these was that Henry Percy held the greatest influence over gentry and people in that region, and they 'would not stir with any lord or noble man other than with the said earl, or at least by his commandment'. The earl, however, though loyal to Edward, could make no positive move on his behalf, for memories of Towton were too strong hereabouts: men who had lost fathers, sons, or kinsmen a decade before

---

[1] Warkworth, 14; *Arrivall*, 3-7.
[2] *Arrivall*, 7. This lack of support even on York estates is in marked contrast to that aroused by Henry of Lancaster in 1399; see T. B. Pugh, *The Fifteenth Century*, 109.

were still unwilling to fight for a Yorkist king. But merely by taking no action, the earl 'did the king right good and notable service'. Edward's decision to restore him in the previous year now paid a handsome dividend.[1]

The failure of the government's supporters in the north to attack Edward whilst still weak saw him through the first critical days, and now his own friends began to come into the open. As he pushed south, his forces grew. At Doncaster he was joined by a small band under William Dudley, later dean of his chapel; at Nottingham Sir William Parr and Sir James Harrington came in with 600 men from Lancashire and the north-west; and at Leicester his force was swelled by 3,000 men of Lord Hastings's midland connection, led by Sir William Stanley and Sir William Norris. But the enemy was also gathering his forces. When Edward arrived at Nottingham, news reached him that the duke of Exeter, the earl of Oxford, and William, formerly Viscount Beaumont, were in Newark with a great fellowship. When Edward boldly turned east to Newark, he found they had fled south during the night to rendezvous with Warwick. The earl himself was in Warwickshire raising men. Other Lancastrians gave him little support. Edmund Beaufort, duke of Somerset, and John Courtenay, the heir of Devon, came up to London, but then, early in April, they left for the south coast to await the landing of their true leaders, Queen Margaret and Prince Edward.

The duke of Clarence was in the West Country when news first reached him that Edward had landed. Though probably now disposed to defect if opportunity offered, he was also anxious not to back a losing cause, and began cautiously to test the wind. On 16 March he wrote to his Derbyshire supporter, Henry Vernon, asking for news not only of Edward's doings but also of the activities of Northumberland, Shrewsbury and Stanley. The latter two soon proved themselves fair-weather friends of Warwick. Shrewsbury's connections were with Clarence rather than the earl, and he made no move on his own initiative. The shifty Stanley – whose family motto 'Sans Changer' has a splendid historical irony – was busily engaged in his private feud with the Harringtons, and was now besieging their castle of Hornby in Lancashire with some official backing; and he too had not moved to help Warwick. This lack of action by men whose aid he hoped for may help to explain the earl's cautious behaviour during the later days of March 1471, and he is also said to have been deceived by messages

[1] *Arrivall*, 6–7.

from Clarence exhorting him not to risk a battle with Edward before the duke arrived.[1]

Yet Edward's position was dangerous enough. As he lay at Nottingham, Montagu, now in action at last, was moving south behind him; ahead lay Warwick; and on his flank the forces of Exeter and Oxford. Had his opponents moved with decision, he might have been trapped between these enemy forces, probably much larger than his own. But again he made the bold move and kept the initiative. He marched straight on Coventry, where Warwick withdrew within the walls, and refused repeated challenges to come out and give battle, and even the promise of a pardon for himself and his followers. Meanwhile, the Yorkist forces beat off an attack by Exeter and Oxford.[2] Warwick's timidity gave Clarence his chance to defect. On 2 April, Edward, who by then was at Warwick, heard that Clarence was coming up from Burford, and on the next day he and Gloucester rode out to meet him on the Banbury road. The three brothers were reconciled, and there was 'right kind and loving language betwixt them'. Strengthened now by Clarence's contingents, Edward again challenged Warwick to leave Coventry and give fight. Again Warwick refused. Nor would he discuss terms of surrender, although Clarence was despatched as mediator to offer 'a good accord'.[3]

Once more Edward faced a critical decision. He could not besiege Coventry, and food supplies in the area were running short. Risky as it was to leave enemy forces intact in his rear, he decided to strike for London. Control of the capital would have great advantages, as the author of the *Arrivall* appreciated. He would gain

> the assistance of his true lords, lovers, and servants, which were there, in those parts, in great number; knowing also that his principal adversary, Henry, with many his partakers, were at London, there usurping and using the authority royal, which barred and letted the king of many aids and assistances, which he should and might have had, in divers parts, if he might once show himself of power to break their authority.

On 5 April he began his march. The news of his approach threw the mayor and council of London into a state of deep uncertainty, especially since they had just heard that Queen Margaret and her company were daily expected to land in England. Messages from Edward were

---

[1] *Hist. MSS Comm., Rutland MSS*, I, 3 (Clarence's letter to Vernon); for Shrewsbury's connections with Clarence, above, p. 119; and for the Stanley–Harrington feud, below, pp. 408–9.
[2] According to the French version of the *Arrivall*, cited by Thomson, *op. cit.*, 91.
[3] *Arrivall*, 7–12.

matched by others from Warwick. The mayor, John Stockton, prudently took to his bed and refused to exercise his authority. The only
Lancastrians of note in the city, Archbishop Nevill and the aged Lord
Sudeley, a veteran of Henry V's French campaigns, tried to rally support by parading King Henry through the streets. Dressed in 'a long
blue gown of velvet as though he had no more to change with', he had
to be held 'by the hand all that way' by Archbishop Nevill. The poverty
of his attire and the meagreness of his retinue was 'more like a play than
the showing of a prince to win men's hearts', and did his cause more
harm than good.[1] Moreover, there were influential Yorkists in the
city, including the archbishop of Canterbury and the earl of Essex.
Their presence, according to Commynes, was one of the reasons
why the ruling oligarchy inclined to favour Edward, the others being
their hope of recovering the large loans made to him in earlier years,
and the influence of many of their ladies, who had enjoyed Edward's
friendship and favours. In any case they were anxious to prevent the
destruction of property. The Common Council prudently resolved
that[2]

> as Edward late king of England was hastening towards the city with a
> powerful army, and as the inhabitants were not sufficiently versed in the
> use of arms to withstand so large a force, no attempt should be made to
> resist him.

By way of Daventry and Dunstable Edward had reached St Albans
on 10 April, and the next day he entered London in triumph, his army
led by a 'black and smoky sort of Flemish gunners to the number of
500'.[3] After offering at St Paul's, he made his way to the bishop's
palace to secure the person of Henry VI. The two kings shook
hands, and Henry, now far gone in simplicity, is reported to have
said: 'My cousin of York, you are very welcome. I know that in your
hands my life will not be in danger.'[4] The archbishop of York and
several other Lancastrian bishops were placed, along with Henry VI,
in the Tower. Edward now went on to Westminster, and, after a brief
crown-wearing ceremony, was reunited with his queen in the abbey's
sanctuary, where she had spent the entire period of his exile. There,
for the first time, he could see the son and heir she had borne him on
2 November.[5]

The next day – Good Friday, 12 April – Yorkist supporters began to

---

[1] GC, 215.   [2] Cited by Scofield, I, 575; Commynes, I, 213.   [3] GC, 216.
[4] According to a letter from Duchess Margaret of Burgundy to the dowager duchess
of Burgundy, April 1471, Waurin, ed. Dupont, III, 210–15.
[5] Loc. cit.; Arrivall, 17; GC, 216; letter of Gerhard von Wesel, Hanserecesse, II, 416.

flow into the city, among them John, Lord Howard, Humphrey Bourchier, Lord Cromwell, and Hastings's brother, Sir Ralph. The same day news reached London that Warwick, with Montagu, Exeter, Oxford and Beaumont, was approaching the city with a powerful force, and had already reached St Albans. Perhaps, as the *Arrivall* suggests, he hoped to take Edward unprepared during the Easter celebrations. If so, he was to be disappointed, for Edward reacted at once. The next day, taking Henry VI with him, he marched out of London on the Great North Road towards Barnet. With him were Gloucester and Clarence, Hastings, Rivers and some five or six other lords, and an army of about 9,000 men.[1] Towards evening, as he neared Barnet, his scouts reported that Warwick's army was drawn up along a ridge of high ground about half a mile north of the town, astride the main road to St Albans. Not wishing to be caught in the town, Edward ordered his men forward in spite of the gathering darkness, and they quietly took up position on an east–west line facing the enemy. This rather unusual night-manœuvre had two consequences. Because the king's army could not see its opponents clearly in the dark, the lines overlapped, each army's right extending beyond the enemy's left. For the same reason, Edward's troops were much closer to the enemy lines than they supposed. During the night Warwick tried to distress the Yorkists by harassing fire from his guns, but, because the lines were so close, the cannon overshot the royalists and achieved nothing. Edward sensibly ordered his troops to maintain silence and not to return the fire, in order to conceal their positions from the enemy gunners.[2]

Easter Sunday morning dawned thick with mist. Even before it was fully light, 'betwixt four and five of the clock', Edward decided to attack at once on foot:

> he committed his cause and quarrel to Almighty God, advanced banners, did blow up trumpets, and set upon them, first with shot, and, then and soon, they joined and came to hand-strokes.

[1] This is the figure given by the *Arrivall*, 21; cf. Warkworth, *Chronicle*, 15 (7,000), Duchess Margaret's letter (12,000). Estimates of the size of the Nevill–Lancastrian army vary from 20,000 to 30,000 in these same sources, but they agree that it was larger.

[2] Contemporary accounts of the battle are in *Arrivall*, 18–21, from which the quotations below are taken; Warkworth, 15–17; Duchess Margaret's letter, as above. Later and less reliable versions are in *GC*, 216–17, and Polydore Vergil, *English History*, 144–7. For modern reconstructions, with plans, see Ramsay, *Lancaster and York*, II, 370–3, and with a more plausible topography, Burne, *Battlefields of England*, 108–16, Kendall, *Richard III*, 93–9, 449–50, and *Warwick the Kingmaker*, 317–22. Burne was misled by later sources into making the duke of Somerset commander of the Lancastrian centre, though he was not present at the battle at all.

But in the mist the fact that the armies were not directly aligned front to front began to tell. On the Lancastrian right, 'the west end', the earl of Oxford's troops rolled up the Yorkist left, which gradually broke and fled, pursued by Oxford's men. Some of the refugees poured south through Barnet and even got as far as London, announcing that all was lost for Edward, and this news was despatched to the Continent before it could be corrected. Some of Oxford's men began to pillage in the streets of Barnet, but eventually their captains regrouped some 900 of them and marched them back towards the battlefield. Because of the continuing mist the other divisions of the armies knew little of all this and fought on fiercely in a hand-to-hand *mêlée*. In the centre of his own battle, Edward used his great height and strength to perform prodigies of valour. But the disintegration of the Yorkist left and the pressure of Edward's overlapping right wing on Warwick's left caused the battle lines to swivel until they lay almost parallel with the Barnet–St Albans road. This caused Oxford's returning men to make contact with their own troops instead of the enemy. They wore the De Vere livery badge of a star with streams, easily confused with the Yorkist rising sun ('the sun with streams'). Mistaking them in the mist for Yorkists, Warwick's men opened fire on Oxford's troops, who broke and fled with cries of treason, which demoralized their fellows. Meanwhile, Montagu had been slain, and, seeing that the Yorkists were gaining the upper hand, Warwick decided on flight, and took to his horse. But as he galloped off towards Barnet wood, he fell into the hands of some of Edward's men, and was killed and 'spoiled naked' before Edward, hurrying up, could save his life.

So 'the perfect victory' went to Edward. After a hard-fought battle lasting three or more hours, there were substantial casualties on both sides. The Yorkists lost Lords Say and Cromwell, Sir Humphrey Bourchier and Sir William Blount, Lord Mountjoy's heir. On Warwick's side, only the earl and his brother were killed amongst the leaders. Exeter was seriously wounded and left for dead on the field, but afterwards recovered, and spent the next four years a prisoner in the Tower. Oxford, his two brothers, and Viscount Beaumont escaped to Scotland. On his return to London the king had the bodies of Warwick and Montagu displayed in St Paul's so that people should not be deluded by 'fained seditious tales' that they were still alive, but with his usual generosity he spared them the customary indignities of quartering and impalement on some bridge or town-gate, and sent off the corpses for decent burial in the family vault at Bisham Abbey.[1]

[1] *Arrivall*, 20–1, and other sources cited above. Sir John Paston, who was present and

Edward was given little leisure to relish his victory or to savour the delights of his return to his capital. On 16 April news arrived that Queen Margaret had landed at Weymouth two days before, the evening of the fatal day at Barnet. With her son and his new wife and the countess of Warwick, Margaret had arrived at Dieppe in January 1471. Thereafter her arrival in England was constantly expected but, for a variety of reasons, constantly delayed. Eventually her party had boarded its ships at Honfleur on 24 March, but was driven back again and again by contrary winds until finally they made a safe crossing, leaving France on 13 April. Hearing the news of her husband's death, the countess of Warwick took sanctuary at Beaulieu Abbey. Queen Margaret was joined at Cerne Abbey on 15 April by Duke Edmund of Somerset and John Courtenay. They assured her that, in spite of the defeat at Barnet, all was not lost, and their cause might indeed be stronger. The whole company then departed for Exeter.[1]

There she and her friends had immediate success in raising a considerable force. Beaufort and Courtenay influence helped her to rally 'the whole might' of Devon and Cornwall, 'districts presumably primitive and ignorant', as Sir James Ramsay quaintly described them. There was support, too, in Somerset, Dorset and Wiltshire, where her followers had been hard at work preparing the ground.[2] There is some evidence also of disturbances in her favour elsewhere in England, especially in the north.[3] With a growing army, the queen and the Lancastrian lords moved up in the later days of April through Taunton and Wells to Bath.

The king responded to this new challenge with the same vigour and decision which marks all his actions in this critical year. It was essential to crush Margaret before support for her spread into new local risings. Edward at once set about raising fresh troops. Between 18 and 26 April commissions of array were sent to fifteen counties, and requests for men to various towns. Orders were given for the assembly of the royal artillery train. Spies were sent westwards to report on the enemy's movements. If the Lancastrians seemed likely to march on London by way of the southern counties, Edward planned to march out and

---

wounded at the battle, put the casualties on both sides at 'more than 1,000' (*PL*, V, 100); cf. Commynes, I, 215 (1,500 on Edward's side).
[1] For this paragraph, see *Arrivall*, 22; Warkworth, *Chronicle*, 16; Scofield, I, 558-9, 563-4, 582-3; Calmette and Perinelle, 133-42.
[2] *Arrivall*, 23; Ramsay, *op. cit.*, II, 376.
[3] *Arrivall*, 31; *CPR.*, *1467-77*, 285-8.

meet them as far from the capital as he could, to prevent their drawing strength from these regions as they advanced. On the other hand, they might make for the Welsh border regions and effect a junction with Jasper Tudor and his Welsh supporters, and thence they could make for Cheshire and Lancashire, with their strong traditional ties with the prince of Wales and the descendants of John of Gaunt. If this were their plan, it was important to head them off from the Severn crossings, at either Gloucester or Tewkesbury or Worcester. The king rightly interpreted information from his agents that Lancastrian troop movements south-east into Somerset towards Yeovil were a feint, and concluded that the main force was marching for the Severn.[1]

On 24 April the king set out from Windsor, and his forces reached Cirencester on the 29th. News that Margaret was about to attack him proved false and he pushed on to Malmesbury in Wiltshire. Here he learned that the queen had succeeded in obtaining men, money and artillery from the citizens of Bristol, and, being 'greatly refreshed and relieved thereby', was again advancing upon him, and that her vanguard lay at Sodbury, on the road between Bristol and Malmesbury. On 1 May Edward took up position on Sodbury Hill, only to discover that Margaret's force was already pushing hard towards the Severn, and had reached Berkeley, twenty-four miles north of Bristol. After a few hours' rest, her men set out again and marched on through the night a further fourteen miles to Gloucester. This news reached the king in the early hours of the morning of 3 May.

He set off at once in pursuit. His army took the ancient road running along the high western scarp of the Cotswold ridge, and had better marching conditions through this 'champain country' than the Lancastrians in the 'foul country' of the Severn Vale below. But the day was very hot, and, high up on the sheepruns of the wold, his men suffered from hunger and thirst. The enemy had troubles of their own. Edward had sent messages ahead to Sir Richard Beauchamp, governor of the castle and town of Gloucester, to hold the gates closed against them, and, encouraged by the proximity of Edward with his 'mighty puissance', Gloucester kept them out and barred the Severn bridge to them. They had no choice but to push on to the next crossing, the ford at Tewkesbury, where they finally arrived in the evening, weary after a twenty-four-mile march from Berkeley, and took up position

[1] This account of the campaign up to the eve of Tewkesbury is based very largely on the *Arrivall*, 23–8. For a useful table of times and distances, Burne, *Battlefields of England*, 117–25. For the raising of troops, *CPR, 1467–77*, 259, 283–5; *Coventry Leet Book*, II, 367–9; Benson and Hatcher, *Old and New Sarum*, 178–9.

in the ruins of the ancient castle destroyed during the wars of Stephen and Matilda's reign about half a mile south of the town, and close to the ford. Later that day the king's troops came down from the wold at Cheltenham, marched on to Tewkesbury, and made camp some three miles from the enemy, after a mighty march of thirty-six miles.

The next day, Saturday, 4 May, Edward advanced to the attack.[1] The Lancastrian position was strong. From the high ground of their camp they looked down over a confused stretch of wooded ground: in 'front of their field were so evil lanes and deep dykes, so many hedges, trees and bushes, that it was right hard to approach them near, and come to hand', as the *Arrivall* observed. Through this area the royal army moved forward in the customary three 'battles', with young Gloucester commanding the van, Edward the centre, and Hastings the rear. Before moving off, the king had taken the precaution of posting a 'plomp' of 200 spears at the corner of Tewkesbury Park to the left of his own line of advance to prevent any ambush prepared amongst the trees. These men had instructions to engage in battle at their discretion, if the wood proved to be clear of enemy troops. The battle began with an exchange of fire, from the king's guns, and from Gloucester's archers, who gave the enemy 'right-a-sharp shower' of arrows. Had the Lancastrians maintained their defensive positions, the result of the battle might have been different. But, whether because his men were sorely harassed by the Yorkist fire, or because he hoped to strike the Yorkists before they could fully deploy in battle positions, Somerset, commanding the Lancastrian vanguard, now ordered his forces to move down the hill under cover of the trees and lanes. This manœuvre brought his men into contact with the flank of the king's battle, but they were themselves 'somewhat aside-hand' Gloucester's division. Fierce hand-to-hand fighting now broke out. Pressed by the superior weight of the two royal divisions, Somerset's soldiers were gradually driven back up the hill. Now the 'plomp' of 200 spears saw their chance to engage, and charged the flank of Somerset's hard-pressed forces. These now broke and fled. Many were cut down as they tried to escape into the park or the meadows beside the river. Edward immediately pressed his advantage and fell upon the Lancastrian centre commanded by Edward, prince of Wales, which was routed in its turn.

[1] The only detailed contemporary account of the battle is in *Arrivall*, 28–30. The best modern reconstruction of the terrain, followed here, is by J. D. Blyth, 'The Battle of Tewkesbury', *Trans. Bristol and Gloucs. Arch. Soc.*, lxxx (1961), 99–120. Cf. Burne, *op. cit.*, 125–36; Kendall, *Richard III*, 101–3; Ramsay, *op. cit.*, 378–81.

Soon this entire division was in full flight, north towards the town. There was heavy slaughter among the fugitives, the most prominent casualty being Prince Edward himself.[1] Finally, the Lancastrian left was overpowered, and John Courtenay, earl of Devon, Somerset's brother, John Beaufort, and John, Lord Wenlock, were slain on the field.

There remained the problem of the many fugitives who had taken refuge in the abbey of Tewkesbury and hoped to find sanctuary behind the skirts of Holy Church. Probably Edward broke into the abbey and took them out by force. On Monday, 6 May, they were brought to trial before the duke of Gloucester as Constable of England and the duke of Norfolk as marshal. Duke Edmund of Somerset, Sir John Langstrother, prior of the Hospitallers, Sir Gervase Clifton and some nine or ten other die-hard Lancastrians were sentenced to death and summarily executed in Tewkesbury market-place, though they were spared any of the usual indignities and given honourable burial afterwards. Not too much should be made of this incident as a lapse from Edward's record of clemency to his opponents. The victims were all men who had shown themselves irreconcilable, and nearly all had been pardoned by Edward in the past, only to abuse his generosity. Given their records, they could have expected little else, and, by contemporary standards, deserved little else. But it is worth noticing that the king also spared a number of Lancastrian captives. These included not only some lawyers and civilians, like the former Chief Justice John Fortescue, who had been Henry VI's chancellor in exile, but also soldiers like Sir Henry Roos and Thomas Ormond, who had been guilty of nothing but sturdy loyalty to their king, and who had not defected after a pardon from Edward.[2]

Tewkesbury completed the ruin of the Lancastrian cause as Barnet had destroyed the Nevills. The arch-enemies of the house of York, the Beauforts, had now been entirely eliminated in the male line. The House of Lancaster itself was on the verge of extinction, with Prince Edward dead, and Henry VI soon to perish in the Tower. Only Jasper Tudor,

---

[1] All immediately contemporary sources agree that he was killed in the fighting: see *Arrivall*, 30; *PL*, V, 104; 'Brief Latin Chronicle', in *Three Fifteenth-Century Chronicles*, 184; 'Yorkest Notes, 1471' and 'Tewkesbury Abbey Chronicle', both printed in Kingsford, *English Historical Literature*, 374, 377; Warkworth, *Chronicle*, 18, which adds that he called to Clarence for succour. Cf. *CC*, 555. The elaborate scene in Shakespeare, *Henry VI*, Part III, V, v, is based essentially on Tudor sources, see *GC*, 218; Polydore Vergil, *English History*, 152; Hall, *Chronicle*, 301.

[2] For a list of those spared, Warkworth, *Chronicle*, 19; cf. *Arrivall*, 30–1; Waurin, ed. Dupont, III, 140; 'Tewkesbury Abbey Chronicle', as above, for this paragraph.

earl of Pembroke, and his young nephew, Henry of Richmond, remained
even of the half-blood branch of the family. Soon after the battle, Queen
Margaret, who had taken refuge in a nearby house of religion, fell into
Edward's hands, and at last her capacity for trouble-making was at an
end.

Yet Edward's trials were not yet over. Immediately after the battle,
reports reached him of further dangers at opposite ends of his realm.
From Kent came news that the Bastard of Fauconberg, reinforced by
300 men sent to him by the pro-Nevill command at Calais, had brought
his fleet ashore and was now stirring Kent to rebellion.[1] From the north
there was news of large-scale risings of Lancastrian partisans, stimulated by the news of Queen Margaret's landing three weeks before.
These Edward judged to be the more serious threat, and, as in 1470, he
did not wish to risk northern rebellions getting out of hand. He therefore left Tewkesbury on 7 May, heading for Worcester and the north,
and relying on Rivers, Essex, Arundel, Sir John Scott and the London
authorities to resist Fauconberg. But when he reached Coventry, where
he awaited the arrival of fresh troops from 11 to 14 April, the earl of
Northumberland came in person to inform him that as soon as the news
of Tewkesbury reached the north, the insurrections there had collapsed. Since there was now no Nevill to lead them, and Northumberland himself was loyal, the local captains had laid down their arms
and come in to beg Percy's good offices with the king.[2]

The news from the south-east was much less reassuring.[3] The Bastard
of Fauconberg had already attracted much support not only from
Calais and the Cinque Ports but more generally in Kent, a county
much given to rebellion in the later middle ages. The rebel force included a substantial element of gentry and yeomen, drawn from almost
every hundred in Kent, nor were they in any way deterred by the news
of Edward's victory at Tewkesbury: they may still have hoped to get
the good government which was such a strong and general feeling in

[1] *Arrivall*, 33; *Warkworth*, 19. Calais proper was controlled at this time by Sir Walter
Wrottesley and Sir Geoffrey Gate, who had rebelled with Warwick in 1470, and
the subordinate castles of Guines and Hammes by Richard Whetehill and John
Blount, both Nevill appointees. The Bastard seems to have landed before 3
May, when commissions were issued to check insurrections in Kent (*CPR, 1467–77*,
285).
[2] *Arrivall*, 32–3. Scofield, I, 589, shows that Edward heard of the northern risings
before he left Tewkesbury, not, as the *Arrivall* suggests, when he reached Worcester.
[3] The following summary account of the attack on London is largely based upon the
recent discussion by C. F. Richmond, 'Fauconberg's Kentish Rising of May 1471',
EHR, lxxxv (1970), 673–92, and the contemporary accounts in *GC*, 218–20, and
Arrivall, 33–9 (from which the quotation comes).

the fifteenth century from someone other than Edward IV. There was backing too from Essex and Surrey. Not all this support need be seen as evidence of Edward's unpopularity. The rising contained its element of needy and lawless men, attracted by the hope of plunder in London, and, within the city, according to the *Arrivall*, many of the poorer sort were ready to join them, for they would 'have been right glad of a common robbery, to the intent that they might largely have put their hands in rich men's coffers'. This fear of pillage deeply alarmed the mayor and council, and strengthened their will to resist, as few other towns, including London itself, resisted an army during the Wars of the Roses. Some of the rebels had local grievances, like the men of Essex who donned their wives' smocks and wore cheese-cloths to show resentment of the low prices paid by London buyers for their dairy produce. Others again are said to have been forced by fear to join the Bastard's host. It was a substantial force, backed by the Bastard's ships in the Thames, which demanded entry into London on 12 May. But the citizens stoutly resisted an attempt to force an entry over London Bridge. The next day an effort by the rebels to cross the river at Kingston and then ravage Westminster and the western suburbs was finally abandoned. On 14 May the rebels renewed their assault. Bombardment from the ships' guns; another attack across London Bridge; and an assault on the gates on the east side of the city north of the river – all were beaten off by the city levies led by the recorder of London, Thomas Urswick, stiffened by the knights and gentry in the retinues of the lords in the city, Rivers, Essex and Dudley, who was lieutenant of the Tower. The rebel discomfiture was completed when Rivers, with a picked band of troops, sallied forth from a postern in the Tower, and drove the enemy across the fields to Poplar and Stepney, where many were killed or taken prisoner. The rest withdrew to their ships and crossed to the south side of the river.

Even after this reverse the Bastard was reluctant to abandon his attempt on London, though he gradually withdrew his men to Black-heath. But the arrival of an advance-guard of 1,500 men from the king's army, and the news that Edward himself was nearing the city, greatly demoralized the rebels. Leaving his ally, Nicholas Faunt, mayor of Canterbury, and the Kentishmen to fend for themselves, Fauconberg took his Calais soldiers and his sailors first to Rochester and then to Sandwich. The Calais men sailed on across the Channel, but the Bastard stayed in Sandwich, apparently still confident that he could extract a pardon from the king.

On Tuesday, 21 May, Edward entered his capital in triumph.[1] The mayor and aldermen went out to meet him in the meadows between Islington and Shoreditch. Never neglectful of good service to his cause, Edward halted, and there and then knighted the mayor, John Stockton, eleven aldermen, and Thomas Urswick, the recorder, who was soon promoted chief baron of the exchequer – a distribution of civic knighthoods hitherto without parallel. He then made his way into London at the head of a great force, with banners and standards unfurled, and trumpets and clarions playing. With him rode his brothers, Clarence and Gloucester, the dukes of Norfolk, Suffolk and Buckingham, six earls and sixteen barons, 'together with other nobles, knights, esquires and a host of horsemen larger than had ever been seen before'. The carriage of the captive Queen Margaret provided the symbol of his victories on this day of Roman triumph.

Effective resistance to Edward's authority was now virtually at an end. The truculent Calais garrison soon made its submission in the confident hope of pardon. Only far away in West Wales, where Jasper Tudor held out in Pembroke Castle, were men still in arms against the king.[2] The death of Henry VI in the Tower on the very night of Edward's return to London took place in circumstances altogether too convenient for Edward for anyone to believe that he died a natural death. Though Richard of Gloucester, as its constable, may have been present in the Tower at the time – and has often been blamed for Henry's death – the responsibility lies clearly enough with the king himself. It is very likely, as the Milanese ambassador in France reported, that 'King Edward caused King Henry to be secretly assassinated . . . he has, in short, chosen to crush the seed'.[3] Thus was removed the last threat from the House of Lancaster; as another contemporary observed, 'no one now remained in the land of the living who could now claim the throne from that family'.[4] How decisive and complete was

---

[1] Accounts of Edward's entry are in Warkworth, *Chronicle*, 21; *Arrivall*, 38; *Three Fifteenth-Century Chronicles*, 184–5; and the very contemporary record in 'Yorkist Notes, 1471', printed in Kingsford, *op. cit.*, 375, which names twenty-seven of the lords in Edward's company, and from which the quotation comes.

[2] Below, p. 182.

[3] *CSP, Milan*, I, 157. Apart from the *Arrivall*, 38, which not unexpectedly attributes his death to 'pure displeasure and melancholy' arising from the collapse of the Lancastrian cause, the sources all agree that Henry VI met a violent end. For discussions of the evidence, see Kendall, *Richard III*, 451–2; Gairdner, *Richard III*, 16–19. As Gairdner – no friend to Richard III – commented, it is very unlikely that he would have been put to death except after a decision by the king personally, or the king and council.

[4] 'Yorkist Notes, 1471', as above.

the Yorkist triumph in 1471 may be seen from the twelve years of domestic peace which it introduced. Apart from the earl of Oxford's abortive descent on St Michael's Mount in 1473, there was to be no further fighting on English soil for the rest of Edward's reign. The House of York was at last firmly and unquestionably established on the English throne.

'The Recoverie of England' in 1471 was very much Edward's personal triumph. As Polydore Vergil observed, he had been fortunate: 'Truly King Edward was in these last wars the happiest man in the world, in that his adversaries assailed him at several times.'[1] If Margaret had landed earlier, before Warwick's defeat, or if the Bastard's attack on London had not come too late, things might have been very different. More decisive action by Warwick in the early stages of Edward's landing might have nipped the whole enterprise in the bud. But at least Edward had taken full advantage of the opportunities offered him. In the Tewkesbury campaign he showed again the qualities which had brought him victory over Warwick – self-confidence, initiative and speed of movement. His success owed much to the extraordinary energy he showed in pursuing and crushing Margaret before she could join with Pembroke or her friends in the north. His modern admirers have made rather exaggerated claims for Edward's military ability. Only in a very limited and domestic sense can he be regarded as 'the greatest general of his age'.[2] Barnet was essentially 'a soldier's battle', where success owed nothing to tactics or generalship. Both at Barnet and Tewkesbury the king had attacked boldly under conditions which could easily have brought disaster. In both battles smaller royal armies were able to defeat larger forces under Warwick and Margaret, and these successes probably owed something to the extent of baronial support which Edward enjoyed. The baronial retinues which fought for Edward are likely to have been more professional and disciplined than the popular levies which formed much of the rank-and-file of his enemies' armies. The campaigns of 1471 demonstrated the importance of committed baronial support against wide popular backing.

Yet it remains true that the challenge of 1471 brought out the best in Edward. He showed an energy and a determination at other times conspicuously lacking in him. Perhaps, like Charles II, his experience of exile made him unwilling to go on his travels again, but the greater ruthlessness and decision which marks his actions in 1471 suggests a man shaken out of his normally rather easy-going ways, driven along

---

[1] *English History*, 154.
[2] The phrase is Burne's, *Battlefields of England*, 114.

by a righteous anger against the ingratitude and treachery of men who had repeatedly abused his trust. In 1471 he was determined on the final defeat of his enemies. His leadership in these difficult days not only did much to secure the Yorkist dynasty on the throne, it also greatly increased his personal authority. More fully than before, Edward was now master in his own house.

Part III

THE SECOND REIGN, 1471–1483

Chapter 8

DOMESTIC PROBLEMS AND
POLICIES, 1471–1475

(i) *The Settlement of 1471: Rewards and Punishments*

Edward's first concern on recovering his capital was to complete the pacification of the realm. Two days after his entry into London, he set forth again for Kent with a strong force at his back. Duke Richard of Gloucester had already been sent in advance to receive Fauconberg's submission and take custody of his ships. This was achieved at Sandwich on 27 May, whilst Edward was in Canterbury. Fauconberg received the pardon he had been promised, on 10 June, and went off to serve with Duke Richard in the north, only to be executed in September, probably by Gloucester, for some new offence. His head was set upon London Bridge, 'looking into Kent ward'.[1] Some of his lieutenants were dealt with more summarily. The petty captains from Essex, Spicing and Quint, who had led the attack on the gates of London, were beheaded, and on 29 May, with Edward still in Canterbury, the rebel mayor, Nicholas Faunt, was hanged, drawn and quartered in the Buttermarket opposite the cathedral gate.

Not until July were measures taken to deal with the contumacious garrison of Calais. On the 17th Lord Hastings took over as lieutenant of Calais from Earl Rivers, who wished to go abroad to fight the Saracens. The king's anger at Rivers's wishing to go abroad when so much remained to be done at home is said to have led to this replacement, and later to have caused bad blood between the two.[2] Soon after, Hastings and his deputy, Lord Howard, crossed over to Calais with a force of 1,500 men. Equipped as they were with pardons for Warwick's followers, Wrottesley and Gate, and with money to pay the garrison's wages, they had little difficulty in securing a submission. Richard Whetehill and John Blount were reappointed as captains of Guines and Hammes in the Calais Pale, but Wrottesley, Gate and

---

[1] *PL*, V, 113, and, for the events in this paragraph, C. F. Richmond, 'Fauconberg's Kentish Rising', 681–3.   [2] *PL*, V, 106, 110; More, *Richard III*, 11, 51.

Montagu's heir, George Nevill, duke of Bedford, who had been sent there for safety, were brought home to London.[1]

More time was needed to restore Yorkist authority in Wales. For some time after Tewkesbury large parts of the country were out of royal control. Soon after the battle Roger Vaughan of Tretower was sent out against Jasper Tudor, whose father, Owen Tudor, he is said to have led to the block after Mortimer's Cross. But Jasper avenged himself by taking and summarily executing Roger at Chepstow. He then gradually withdrew west to Pembroke Castle, taking with him his nephew, Henry Tudor, earl of Richmond, whom he had found in the Herbert household at Raglan Castle. Even then a royalist siege of Pembroke had to be raised when a force of Jasper's Welsh supporters came to his aid. Commissions to deal with rebels to William Herbert, 2nd earl of Pembroke, the earl of Shrewsbury and Lord Ferrers, show that much of Wales was still defiant at the end of August and during September. Towards the end of that month, as the Yorkists slowly gathered strength, Earl Jasper's position became more precarious, and he and his nephew took ship for France. Bad weather brought them to Brittany, where they became the object of rival moves by Edward IV and Louis XI to obtain possession of their persons. But considerable violence and disorder survived Jasper's departure from Wales, and highlighted the need for a new political settlement to fill the vacuum left by the death of the 1st earl of Pembroke.[2]

Meanwhile, Edward had turned his attention to meting out punishment to those who had resisted him in south-eastern England. Most of the work fell to two commissions appointed on 15–16 July, one for Kent, Sussex and the Cinque Ports under Arundel and Dinham, the other for Essex under the earl of Essex and Sir William Bourchier.[3] They executed the royal displeasure with vigour, but though many were arrested and some executed, punishments were mainly in the form of fines – a method later taken up and extended by Henry VII. The *Great Chronicle* remarked that 'such as were rich were hanged by the purse, and the other that were needy were hanged by the necks, by means whereof the country was greatly impoverished and the king's coffers some deal increased', but the records of the commissioners and

[1] *PL*, V, 111; *CC*, 557; *CPR*, *1467–77*, 270–1, 290–2 (pardons for Calais garrison); Scofield, II, 11–12.

[2] *CPR*, *1467–77*, 281, 283, 289, 293 (commissions against rebels); Polydore Vergil, *English History*, 154–5; Evans, *Wales and the Wars of the Roses*, 194–5. For the career of Roger Vaughan, see R. A. Griffiths, *The Principality of Wales in the Later Middle Ages; The Structure and Personnel of Government*, I, 220–1, and, for the settlement in Wales, below, pp. 193–8.   [3] *CPR*, *1467–77*, 287–8.

the exchequer show that John Warkworth was more correct in his belief that even the poorest could buy their pardons if they could scrape the money together; 'and so,' he adds, 'the king had out of Kent much good and little love'.[1] Lump sums paid over as communal fines amounted to some £250 for Essex and over £1,700 for Kent.[2]

Nor were the penalties confined to the common people. The city of Canterbury and the Cinque Ports forfeited their liberties, which had to be bought back. A few powerful individuals who had been implicated in the Bastard's activities also had to purchase the king's grace with heavy fines. Reginald West, Lord de la Warr, who was pardoned on 15 October, was made to enter into bonds to pay a fine of 1,000 marks to Thomas Vaughan, treasurer of the chamber, for the king's use. Outside the south-east similar fines were extracted from William Tournay, the new prior of St John's, and three of his fellow-Hospitallers (£300), from Sir William Eure and other Yorkshire gentry (£400), and probably also from Sir John Arundell, the Cornish knight who had helped to raise the West Country for Queen Margaret.[3] It is likely that other 'gifts' were extracted from the several Lancastrian bishops who had been placed in the Tower after Barnet, and who obtained pardons during the summer and autumn. The city of Coventry also had to pay considerable sums to the king, including 400 marks to secure the restoration of its liberties, and other towns which had shown undue favour to the Lancastrians may have suffered the same fate.[4] How much money Edward raised by these means is not known, especially since it may have been paid to the chamber rather than the exchequer, but it is likely to have been considerable.[5]

Yet even now Edward showed himself neither ruthless nor vindictive in the punishment of political disaffection. His unchallenged authority would have allowed him greater latitude for a policy of vengeance than had been possible in 1461, but he still preferred clemency. Only thirteen sentences of attainder followed the upheavals of 1469–71, and at least six of those sentenced were already dead.[6] Twenty-three of the

[1] *GC*, 220–1; Warkworth, *Chronicle*, 21–2.
[2] Richmond, 'Fauconberg's Kentish Rising', 686–7.
[3] *CCR, 1468–76*, 217, 226–7; for Arundell, *Arrivall*, 13, and Ramsay, *Lancaster and York*, II, 391; Richmond, *op. cit.*, 683.
[4] Ramsay, *op. cit.*, II, 390–1; *CPR, 1467–77*, 287; *Coventry Leet Book*, II, 367–9.
[5] Ramsay, *op. cit.*, II, 391, citing Tellers and Receipt Rolls, Michaelmas term, 1471, lists 'gifts' totalling £12,904, including 1,000 marks from John Arundell, sums from Lancastrian bishops, and the fines levied on Kent and Essex mentioned above.
[6] *RP*, VI, 144–9; Lander, 'Attainder and Forfeiture', 128–30, who suggests that there were special reasons why Warwick and Montagu were not attainted, and 'the immunity of the Nevilles provided an umbrella for others'; see also below, pp. 190–1.

attainders passed earlier in the reign were reversed during the parliament of 1472-5.[1] Many more people were pardoned rather than punished. Even if their loyalty had not been seriously in doubt, many men probably thought it prudent to take advantage of the general pardon proclaimed by Edward during October 1471, but the long list of several hundred pardons on the bulky Pardon Roll of Edward's eleventh year includes a considerable number for men who had been deeply implicated in opposition to the House of York over the previous two years. Eight bishops, all originally appointed under Henry VI, had supported the Readeption, and six of these were pardoned before the end of the year, although two holders of Welsh sees, Hunden of Llandaff and Tully of St David's, had to wait until February and September 1472.[2] A great many formerly committed Lancastrians were now received into the king's grace. Some of these were men who had been especially loyal and close to the ex-king and queen, such as John Fortescue, chancellor in exile to King Henry, Dr John Morton, the future cardinal, who had also shared Margaret's exile and held the office of keeper of privy seal to Henry, Henry Lowys, 'ruler and governor' of Henry VI's household during the Readeption, and several members of such hostile families as Roos, Ormond and Courtenay. Some now began a new career in Edward's service. Sir Richard Tunstall, the brave and stubborn defender of Harlech, who had been master of the mint in 1470, became a royal councillor. Morton soon came to enjoy the king's 'secret trust and special favour'; already in 1472 he was master of the rolls and was promoted to the see of Ely in 1478. His rapid rise in the royal service is a good example of Edward's political realism in making use of talent wherever he found it. There was only one exception to this record of clemency. Edward did not trust the most prominent of the surviving Lancastrians still in England: Henry Holland, duke of Exeter, was removed from sanctuary at Westminster late in May 1471, and joined Margaret of Anjou as a prisoner in the Tower, and his wife, the king's sister, Anne, was allowed to divorce him in order to marry her lover, Thomas St Leger.[3]

[1] *RP*, VI, 16–22, 24–33, 43–8; they include many of the former Lancastrians mentioned below.

[2] The prelates were the archbishop of York and the bishops of Winchester, Lincoln, London, Coventry and Lichfield, Chichester, Hereford and St Asaph; for their pardons, *CPR*, *1467–77*, 258–9, 261, 267, 280, 294, 299; Scofield, II, 22. Another 224 pardons are entered on the Patent Roll (*CPR*, *1467–77*, 258–313 *passim*).

[3] For Morton, *CPR*, *1467–77*, 261; More, *Richard III*, 90–1; A. B. Emden, *Biographical Register of Members of the University of Oxford Before A.D. 1500*, II, 1318–20; for Holland, *CP*, V, 215; Scofield, II, 22–3.

Generous with pardons, Edward was no less lavish with rewards. No one who had rendered him or his family good service during the 'late troubles' went unnoticed. Mark Symondson, master of the *Antony* which had brought him to England in March, and her helmsman, Robert Michelson of Hull, both got annuities. His host in Holland, Lewis of Bruges, was created earl of Winchester, with an annuity of £200, during his diplomatic mission to England in October 1472. Many of the humbler gentlemen and yeomen of the household who had shared his exile were given appropriate preferments.[1] Thomas Milling, abbot of Westminster, who had sheltered the queen and her family during Edward's absence abroad, and had stood godfather to the infant prince, was appointed prince's chancellor on 8 July, and was eventually promoted to the see of Hereford in 1474.[2] The young clerk, William Dudley, one of the first to join Edward in March 1471, became dean of the chapel royal and dean of Windsor, as well as chancellor to Queen Elizabeth Woodville, and was later preferred to the very rich see of Durham in 1476.[3] Sir Richard Beauchamp, whose loyalty as constable of Gloucester had been so vital during the Tewkesbury campaign, got rather less than he deserved with an annuity of 40 marks. There were many other rewards for men like Sir William Parr of Kendal, Sir William Stanley, Sir John Fogge, and others below baronial rank who had rendered useful service to the Yorkist cause.[4]

As might be expected, however, the largest rewards went to the magnates who had done so much to aid Edward's restoration, and especially to the royal dukes. Provision for his family and his aristocratic supporters in fact absorbed almost all the quite considerable gains in forfeited land and wardships which came into Edward's hands as a result of the political upheavals of 1471.[5] Already lieutenant of Calais, Hastings was further repaid for his unswerving devotion with the offices of constable of Nottingham Castle and steward and keeper of Sherwood Forest, and the custody of most of the estates of the West-Country heiress, his stepdaughter, Cecily Bonville, together with her marriage.[6] The earl of Essex became treasurer of England again on 22 April 1471, and was to hold that very remunerative office until the end

---

[1] *CPR, 1467–77*, 265, 266, 300; P.R.O., C. 53/196, m. 3.

[2] For his career, Emden, *op. cit.*, II, 1282–3.

[3] *Ibid.*, I, 599–600, and above, p. 164. He was appointed queen's chancellor on 26 October 1471, P.R.O., D.L. 29/39/1117, mm. 3–4, and held the office until June 1474. I am indebted to Mr M. A. Hicks for this information.

[4] *CPR, 1467–77*, 264, 272, 297, 315.

[5] On this point, see further below, pp. 187–91.

[6] *CPR, 1467–77*, 310–11.

of the reign, and there were rewards for Suffolk, Northumberland, Arundel and Wiltshire.[1] Only Norfolk and Rivers amongst the magnates seem to have been overlooked, though Earl Rivers, like Hastings, now obtained a thousand-pound annuity from Duke Charles of Burgundy.[2]

The chief beneficiary of Edward's restoration was certainly his younger brother. Duke Richard had shown ability as well as a solid loyalty during the upheavals of the previous two years, and the extent of his rewards showed how far the nineteen-year-old duke had come to enjoy his brother's confidence. Apart from recovering the offices of constable and admiral of England which he had held before the Readeption, he was made great chamberlain of England in place of Warwick on 18 May. At the same time Edward took the opportunity to provide him with a landed appanage far more generous than he had enjoyed in the 1460s, and, by making him essentially the heir to Warwick's power and influence in the north of England, marked him out for special responsibility in the government of that hitherto rebellious and lawless region.[3] By contrast with Clarence, Richard had few estates of his own before 1470. In the early 1460s he had been given some lands forfeited from the Hungerfords and de Veres, the lordship of Richmond, and the earldom of Pembroke, but for various reasons – among them the jealousy of Clarence – these grants had been cancelled or withdrawn, and he had received only modest compensation.[4] Now,

[1] *Handbook of British Chronology*, ed. Powicke and Fryde, 103; *CPR, 1467–77*, 260, 310 (Arundel, warden Cinque Ports); 261 (wardship of Lovell lands to Suffolk and his wife); 258 (Northumberland, justice of forests north of Trent, constable of Bamborough Castle); 262 (Wiltshire, chief butlership of England).
[2] Scofield, II, 7; *Hist. MSS Comm., Hastings*, I, 301 (the duke's letters patent to Hastings).
[3] See further below, pp. 198–203.
[4] The large grant to Richard made on 24 August 1462 (*CPR, 1461–7*, 197) comprised the lordships of Richmond and Pembroke, many de Vere lands (20 manors in Essex, 6 in Suffolk, and 4 in Cambridge) and certain offices and farms, but was largely nullified because Richmond was given to Clarence on 20 September 1462 (*ibid.*, 212–13), the de Vere estates were restored to John, 13th earl of Oxford, on 18 January 1464 (*CP*, X, 240), and there is no evidence that Richard ever obtained control of Pembroke, which had been granted in tail to William, Lord Herbert, on 3 February 1462 (*CPR, 1461–7*, 114), and which continued in his possession. On 9 September 1462 Richard was given all the Hungerford estates, but this grant was cancelled by oral order of the king, 30 March 1463 (*ibid.*, 228). On 20 December 1463 he had a grant of the lands of Henry Beaufort, duke of Somerset, but these were not extensive and were encumbered by the interests of two dowager duchesses, Margaret (d. 1482) and Eleanor (d. 1477): *ibid.*, 292; *CP*, XII, 47, 53. He had to wait until 25 October 1468 for a second grant in tail of the Hungerford estates (*CPR, 1467–77*, 139).

on 29 June 1471, he was granted in tail male Warwick's lordships of Middleham and Sheriff Hutton in Yorkshire and Penrith in Westmorland, together with the rest of the earl's entailed estates in those counties. This complex of lands – Warwick's paternal inheritance – was the only part of his estates of which Edward could quickly dispose, for the remainder, in southern and central England and the Welsh Marches, belonged to his widowed countess, Anne Beauchamp.[1] In December 1471 the king rounded off Richard's endowment with a grant of the forfeited estates of John de Vere, earl of Oxford, and of the leaders of the Lincolnshire rebellion, lying chiefly in Essex and the eastern counties, a considerable endowment totalling some eighty manors in all, and probably worth well over £1,000 yearly.[2]

Despite his timely desertion of Warwick in April 1471, Clarence's record of treachery and ambition stood out in sharp contrast to his younger brother's loyalty, and he could expect correspondingly less from the king. Nevertheless, he was allowed to retain the lieutenancy of Ireland, and, on 28 August 1471, was amply rewarded for the loss of the Percy estates he had held until 1470 by a grant of all the forfeited lands of the Courtenay family in Devon and Cornwall, which confirmed his position as the greatest landowner in the West Country.[3] With this, however, he was far from content.

(ii) The Quarrel of Clarence and Gloucester, 1471–1475

The bitter rivalry which developed between his two brothers provided Edward with his most tiresome domestic problem in these years. Dissension between them was not altogether new. Even in his adolescence Clarence had shown himself jealous at any hint of undue favour to his brother. The very generous provision which Edward made for Clarence did not prevent the latter's resenting the grant to Richard of the great North-Country Honour of Richmond, and this apparently persuaded the king to revoke his grant and give it to Clarence instead.[4] Nor was Duke George in any way chastened by the events of 1469–71. A more judicious man might have thought himself lucky to be alive and at liberty after his attempts to take his brother's

---

[1] Ibid., 260, 266; and below, p. 189. [2] Ibid., 297.
[3] Ibid., 279–80, 335–6. On 16 March 1472 he was reappointed lieutenant of Ireland for twenty years.
[4] As suggested by Kendall, Richard III, 50–1. In 1478 the charges against Clarence dwelt upon the very generous endowment made by the king: 'so large portion of possessions, that no memory is of . . . that any king of England gave so largely to any of his brothers' (RP, VI, 193).

throne. Common prudence dictated a quiet acceptance of whatever favours Edward chose to bestow on Richard. How far he took exception to the grants made to Richard in 1471 is not known, but he could not control his anger as soon as he heard that Gloucester wished to marry his sister-in-law, the widowed Anne Nevill, now sixteen years of age.

Clarence's interest seems to have been as much greed as jealousy, for he had already shown that he wished to keep the whole great Beauchamp–Despenser inheritance of the earls of Warwick for himself, in right of his wife, Isabel, and to deny the rights of her younger sister.[1] That Gloucester should have wished to marry the lady is scarcely surprising, for she was the most eligible heiress in England. Anne's self-interest was equally engaged, for Gloucester was probably the only husband who could enforce her rights against Clarence, and we do not need to suppose any romantic attachment between the two.[2] According to one account, Clarence tried to frustrate his brother by concealing Anne as a disguised kitchen-maid in London, but Richard sought her out and carried her off to sanctuary at St Martin's. She seems to have become his wife between 12 February and 18 March 1472, without even waiting for the necessary papal dispensation.[3]

Even before the marriage took place, the strife between the royal dukes had become open and bitter, and during the winter of 1471–2 Edward felt compelled to intervene. The brothers were summoned to put their dispute before the royal council. There each argued his case with a skill and eloquence which won the approval of the professional lawyers present, and the Croyland Chronicler took occasion to remark on 'the surpassing talents' which George and Richard had in common with their royal brother. During a meeting at Sheen palace in February 1472, the king pleaded with Clarence on Richard's behalf, only to receive the angry reply that he might have the Lady Anne but not her lands.[4] Royal pressure forced a settlement, though it was very much a surrender to Clarence's arrogance. In return for giving up a portion of the Warwick inheritance to Richard, Clarence was promised, on 18 March 1472, full security in all the remainder and in the lands of the Courtenay earldom of Devon, previously granted to him, and Edward went so far as to promise that if any of these should be recovered against him, then the king would provide recompense. A week later Clarence

---

[1] T. B. Pugh, *Glamorgan County History*, III, 200.
[2] *Loc. cit.*; cf. Kendall, *Richard III*, 105–9.
[3] *CC*, 557. For the date of the marriage, usually given as 12 July, see Pugh, *op. cit.*, 200, 613.   [4] *CC*, 557; *PL*, V, 135–6.

was formally created Earl of Warwick and Salisbury, and was given a group of the Kingmaker's Nevill manors in Essex and the midlands, together with his town house, the Erber, close to London Stone. Finally, Duke Richard, who had shown considerable moderation throughout, resigned the office of great chamberlain of England in his brother's favour.[1]

But the transfer to the royal dukes of the Kingmaker's vast estates was beset by problems other than their competing claims. There were serious legal difficulties to overcome. Firstly, the larger part of the inheritance, especially Clarence's share, belonged in law to Warwick's widow, as heiress of her father, Earl Richard Beauchamp, and her mother, Isabel Despenser.[2] From her sanctuary at Beaulieu Abbey in Hampshire, Countess Anne tried desperately to protect her rights, appealing to Edward, Clarence, Gloucester and other members of the royal family, and petitioning parliament in the winter of 1472.[3] Secondly, many of the Nevill estates of Warwick's paternal inheritance had been held by him in tail male, and the heir-at-law was his nearest surviving male relative, George Nevill, duke of Bedford, Montagu's young son. If Clarence and Gloucester were to be secure, it was essential to extinguish his claims.[4] Thirdly, there was the general problem of their title. If Warwick and Montagu had been attainted, Clarence and Gloucester could have held their lands only by royal grant. This would have made them vulnerable to acts of resumption, and hence dependent on continuing royal favour. Clarence was especially anxious on this point, for, under the resumption act passed in 1473, Gloucester was exempted, but he was not, and had to sacrifice the Honour of Tutbury and other lands and offices granted to him from the Duchy of Lancaster. The Croyland Chronicler believed that he strongly resented this, and his testimony is confirmed by the need to appoint a special commission to take possession, in January 1474, of all the properties in four midland counties resumed against Clarence – clearly a special measure to overcome the duke's opposition.[5]

The solution to these problems, imposed upon the king by pressure from his brothers, was eventually carried through with a high degree

---

[1] *CPR, 1467–77*, 330, 344–6; *Cal. Charter Rolls*, VI, 239–40.
[2] For the complex descent of this inheritance, see R. L. Storey, *End of the House of Lancaster*, 231–41, and, for a list of the estates, C. D. Ross, *The Estates and Finances of Richard Beauchamp, earl of Warwick* (Dugdale Soc., 1956).
[3] Scofield, II, 27.
[4] Below, p. 190. Cf. Lander, 'Attainder and Forfeiture', 130 and n., for a different explanation of this point.
[5] Lander, *op. cit.*, 130; *CC*, 561; *CPR, 1467–77*, 428.

of callousness and disregard for the laws of inheritance. It was not achieved without further disputes between Clarence and Gloucester. In June 1473 the countess of Warwick was at last allowed to leave sanctuary, and was taken off to the north by one of Gloucester's retainers, Sir James Tyrell. This move seems to have been inspired by Gloucester, with the king's approval, and led to rumours that her estates might be restored to her, so that she could convey them to Duke Richard.[1] Clarence was displeased and suspicious. In November 1473 Sir John Paston reported that he was again behaving aggressively. The duke, he said, 'maketh him big in that [*i.e.*, so far as] he can, showing as he would but deal with the duke of Gloucester', but, he added, the king intended to be 'as big as they both, and to be a stifler atween them'. Soon after he expressed the hope that the two dukes would be 'set at one' by award of the king.[2]

During the fifth session of the parliament of 1472–5 (9–28 May 1474) a settlement was finally achieved. That assembly submissively accepted an act recognizing the right and title of the dukes and their wives to the inheritance of Richard, late earl of Warwick, and providing for its partition between them. The widowed countess was wholly barred from any claim or interest in her own patrimony, and was regarded as if she 'were now naturally dead'. Since Gloucester's marriage had not yet been confirmed by papal dispensation, it was provided that he should retain control of Anne Nevill's share of the estates in the event of their divorce, so long as he did not remarry.[3] A second act of parliament of 23 February 1475 expressly barred the claims of any male heir of the late Marquis Montagu to any portion of Warwick's Nevill inheritance, a measure which chiefly concerned Gloucester as possessor of these North-Country estates.[4] In the preamble to this act, it was rehearsed that the king had intended to attaint Montagu and his heirs, but had been dissuaded by a request from Clarence, Gloucester and other lords of the blood royal, which clearly indicates why Warwick and his brother, the arch-offenders of 1471, had not been attainted.[5] The whole

---

[1] *PL*, V, 188–9; *Hist. MSS Comm.*, *11th Report*, App. VII, 95.   [2] *PL*, V, 199.
[3] *RP*, VI, 100–1; *CPR*, *1467–77*, 455–6, 550. Details of the partition do not survive, but Gloucester is known to have secured the Welsh Marcher lordships of Glamorgan, Abergavenny and Elfael (Pugh, *op. cit.*, 200–1).
[4] *RP*, VI, 124–7; *CPR*, *1467–77*, 487, 557.
[5] Common law proceedings against Warwick and Montagu for treason had been instituted *posthumously* before special commissions in Hertfordshire and Middlesex in May 1472 (P.R.O., K.B. 9/41, mm. 38 ff.); these were often a preliminary to parliamentary sentences of attainder. See Judith B. Avutrick, 'Commissions of Oyer and Terminer in Fifteenth-Century England' (unpublished London M.Litt. thesis, 1967).

purpose had been to allow Clarence and Gloucester to succeed to the Warwick inheritance in right of their wives and by inheritance, not royal grant.[1]

The whole episode shows Edward, as well as his brothers, in an unattractive light. By any standards it was a shabby and sordid operation. In its shameless disregard for the rules of inheritance, it set precedents for similar and later transactions in favour of Edward's younger son, Richard, duke of York, and members of the queen's family.[2] But it also provides a measure of the contrast between Edward IV and his feeble predecessor. In this vital sector of high politics, the management of great men, Edward had succeeded in stifling their disputes and keeping the peace of the realm. But it is clear that Clarence's behaviour placed a severe strain on his brother's patience. Already he had shown himself to be incorrigible, the main charge in the indictment which brought about his downfall and death in 1478.

Another reason for Edward's growing hostility to Clarence may have lain in the suspicion that he was involved in treasonable designs with his wife's kinsmen, Archbishop George Nevill and John de Vere, earl of Oxford. The archbishop had apparently remained in the king's favour since his brother's death, and was expecting Edward for a hunting party at his manor of The Moor in Hertfordshire, when, on the night of 25 April 1472, he was suddenly placed under arrest, and sent across the Channel for imprisonment in the castle of Hammes in the Calais marches. The king lost no time in making his action the occasion for financial as well as political profit. Two senior officials of the royal household, its controller, Sir William Parr, and Sir Thomas Vaughan, treasurer of the chamber, were sent down to The Moor to take possession on the king's behalf of Nevill's large personal treasure, amassed 'through his great covetousness', and his splendidly jewelled mitre was broken up and made into a new crown for Edward. The king seems to have made some effort to get George Nevill deprived of his see, but, failing in this, contented himself with drawing the revenues of the see of York for the next two and a half years. The archbishop's household was dispersed: among its members were some 'great clerks and famous doctors' whom the scholarly George had patronized, and who, Sir John Paston tells us, 'go now again to Cambridge to school' – reluctantly, we may suspect.[3]

Since no formal or public charges were ever brought against the archbishop, we cannot know the reasons for Edward's sudden action. He was not much given to capricious acts of revenge, even against a

[1] Lander, *op. cit.*, 130.   [2] Below, pp. 248–9, 335–7.
[3] *PL*, V, 137; Warkworth, *Chronicle*, 24–6; *CSP, Milan*, I, 165; *CPR, 1467–77*, 346.

man he clearly disliked, and John Warkworth was probably correct in his belief that George Nevill was in communication with his brother-in-law, John, earl of Oxford, who had now arrived in France and was raiding the marches of Calais. It is likely that Edward struck first to avoid further intrigue. No contemporary source claims, or even implies, that Clarence was involved, but the suspicion remains, especially since it was widely believed that the duke was in touch with Oxford a year later; and Clarence was the most obvious focus for any plot to overthrow Edward now that the Lancastrian cause had been extinguished.[1]

Oxford had been getting help from Louis XI and the Hansards, both of whom had good reason for wishing to embarrass Edward, and he further hoped to exploit the temporary discord between England and Scotland. His hopes of support from James III of Scotland failing, he decided to attempt a landing in England, and on 28 May 1473 he landed at St Osyth's in Essex, near the centres of his family power. Frustrated in this by the earl of Essex and Lords Dinham and Duras, he took his ships to sea again, and during the summer months roamed the Channel as a pirate. On 30 September he suddenly descended on Cornwall and seized St Michael's Mount. This rocky off-shore fortress was virtually impregnable and could easily be held even by the tiny force under Oxford's command if properly victualled. But the military threat from Oxford was negligible, and royal measures to deal with him were at first confined to preventing provisions reaching the Mount. Men, ships and cannon were eventually sent down to blockade and besiege it in December, and after a month Oxford eventually capitulated, largely because his men were defecting in response to Edward's promise of pardon. The earl himself was pardoned on 1 February 1474, and sent off to prison at Hammes Castle, where he was to remain until his escape ten years later.[2] It is hard to believe that Oxford's adventure caused the king much concern. But it is clear that Oxford hoped to get support in England, and Louis XI is said to have been presented by him with the seals of twenty-four knights and esquires *and one duke* who had promised to rise with him against the king. This apart, evidence of Clarence's collusion with Oxford is confined to some necessarily veiled statements in the Paston family correspondence, but many people, both on the Continent and in England, believed that Clarence was treasonably involved with Oxford, and, through him, with Louis XI.[3]

[1] Warkworth, *Chronicle*, 25; Scofield, II, 22.
[2] *PL*, V, 188–9; Warkworth, *Chronicle*, 26; Scofield, II, 59–61.
[3] *PL*, V, 184, 186, 195; *CSP, Milan*, I, 176; Calmette and Perinelle, *op. cit.*, 161 (for

With Oxford under lock and key, Edward thought it safe to release George Nevill in November 1474, and he died in England on 8 June 1476, a broken man, though not yet forty-five years of age. Probably few mourned his passing. Intelligent, smooth-tongued, and unprincipled, he is the supreme example in his age of the aristocratic political bishop, whose only loyalty lay in the cause of Nevill family aggrandizement. He possessed to the full the Nevill characteristics of acquisitiveness and ruthless ambition. As a churchman little can be said in his favour. Himself well educated, he was a considerable patron of scholars and scholarship, but this scarcely offsets his long neglect of his province or the example of worldly pomp and ostentation – worthy of a Wolsey – which he offered to his fellow-churchmen.[1] With Oxford behind bars, and George Nevill in his grave, the last dangers of Nevill–Lancastrian intrigue against the Yorkist throne died away, for only the political feuds following on Richard III's usurpation were to make that obscure exile, Henry Tudor, a serious contender for the crown. Except for the rumbling discontents of Clarence, the political peace of England was not to be threatened again by conspiracy, rebellion or invasion as long as Edward lived.

(iii) *Policies towards Wales, the north of England, and Ireland*

The upheavals of 1469–71 presented Edward with the opportunity to devise new political settlements for the most rebellious and lawless regions of his realm. The death in battle of William Herbert, 1st earl of Pembroke, had created a power vacuum in Wales and the Marches which had to be filled, and a similar situation had arisen north of Trent, and especially in Yorkshire and the north-western counties, with the overthrow of Richard Nevill, earl of Warwick. The policies which Edward gradually introduced for the government of these regions were to have far-reaching though very different consequences.

In the fifteenth century Wales had become a by-word for lawlessness, and the problem was equally acute in both of the areas into which the country was divided by two distinct forms of government.[2] Much of

---

rumours on the Continent); Scofield, II, 29, 58–9. Amongst the charges of treason made against Clarence in 1478 was that he had intended since 1471 to bring about the destruction and disinheriting of the king 'by might to be gotten outward as well as inward' (*RP*, VI, 193–5).

[1] For accounts of his career, see Emden, *Biog. Reg., Univ. Oxford*, II, 1347–9, and the article by James Tait in *DNB*, XL, 252–6.

[2] For a lucid account of the problems of governing Wales and the Marches, on which much of what follows is based, see R. A. Griffiths, 'Wales and the Marches', in *Fifteenth-Century England*, 145–72.

west and north-west Wales made up the shires of the principality, organized in two groups centred on Carmarthen and Caernarvon. These were governed by a justiciar and chamberlain for each group, appointed by the prince of Wales or by the king when there was no adult prince, but these officers, especially in the reign of Henry VI, tended to be absentee English magnates with little direct interest in their task. The remainder, and larger part, of Wales was divided into numerous Marcher lordships, where 'every function of government was the sole responsibility of its marcher lord', and the king's writ did not run. By 1450 the majority of these lordships had fallen into the hands of great English magnates, like the dukes of York and Buckingham and the earl of Warwick, to whom their Welsh possessions were chiefly valuable as a source of profit. Effective control at the local level passed into the hands of deputies drawn from the more thrusting members of the Welsh squirearchy. Neither king, prince, Marcher lord, nor gentry had much interest in law and order, and the endemic violence of Wales was intensified by the general practice of suspending the great sessions or sessions in eyre in each lordship (both within and without the principality) in return for a financial contribution, the 'general fine' from the community.[1] Such judicial paralysis meant that lawlessness went wholly unpunished. Not only the Welsh themselves, but also the English border counties suffered from the lack of any effective peace-keeping machinery in the Marches of Wales. Criminals from one lordship could only too easily take refuge within another. Methods did exist to deal with this problem – there were 'love days' and 'days of redress' when the men of each lordship could meet their neighbours to compose their differences, and arrangements could be made for extradition; but such devices were frequently frustrated for a variety of reasons. Ultimately, responsibility for law and order rested with the English Crown, but attempts by Henry VI's government to tighten up the existing machinery met with little success, and were overtaken by the struggle for power which led to civil war in 1459.

Edward's primary concern in Wales and the Marches lay, however, far more in the assertion of political control than in any problem posed by the daily violence of Welshman against Welshman. In this he had been greatly aided by the fact that civil war brought an exceptional number of Marcher lordships under his control, either temporarily or permanently, among them twenty-three lordships belonging to his own earldom of March, and by the invaluable services of an able lieutenant,

[1] T. B. Pugh, *The Marcher Lordships of South Wales, 1415–1536*, 36–43.

whose personal interests lay in Wales, in William Herbert, 1st earl of Pembroke.[1] Immediately after the earl's death, he had entrusted Duke Richard of Gloucester with primary responsibility for Wales, but this arrangement could not continue when, in 1471, the duke's energies were committed to the north of England.[2] The king then turned in the first instance to the youthful William Herbert, 2nd earl of Pembroke, who, on 27 August 1471, was allowed to enter upon the offices of justiciar and chamberlain of South Wales, and a series of other offices in Wales and the Marches, which had been granted in tail male to his father in 1466. The office of justiciar in North Wales was given on 11 September to another young magnate, John Talbot, earl of Shrewsbury, whose own landed interests lay in the English border counties.[3]

Unfortunately, the 2nd earl of Pembroke was not the man his father had been, and proved ineffective and uninterested in his duties. The once paramount Herbert influence in South and West Wales rapidly declined, and in 1479 William Herbert was compelled to surrender his earldom of Pembroke to the prince of Wales, receiving only slender compensation in the title of earl of Huntingdon and a few manors in Somerset and Dorset.[4] Meanwhile, the problem of disorder in Wales seemed to grow worse rather than better. In the parliament of 1472 there were bitter complaints from the English border counties about 'the outrageous demeaning of Welshmen', and requests for special counsel to be taken with the Lords Marcher to deal with the problems of that region. In response, Edward was driven to intervene. In June 1473 he held a meeting with the Marcher lords at Shrewsbury, and entered into agreements with them. Though these introduced no new peace-keeping machinery, they did commit the lords to a formal promise to carry out their traditional responsibilities.[5] Disorder and even open defiance of the government was not thereby checked immediately. In 1474, for example, three bastard sons of the 1st earl of Pembroke and two sons of Roger Vaughan refused to appear before the king's council when summoned to answer for various offences: they fled to Wales and there began stirring up insurrection. Strong commissions appointed to deal with them evidently had little effect, for these

[1] Above, pp. 77-8.   [2] Above, pp. 186-7.

[3] CPR, 1461-7, 526; 1467-77, 275, 277.

[4] RP, VI, 202-4; D. H. Thomas, 'The Herberts of Raglan as supporters of the House of York in the second half of the fifteenth century' (University of Wales M.A. thesis, 1967), chapter VII.

[5] RP, VI, 8-9; P.R.O., E. 315/40/75 (indenture with the duke of Buckingham); Griffiths, op. cit., 160.

rebels were still at large in 1478 when they attacked and seized Pembroke Castle, and held it by force.[1]

By this time, however, a new machinery to exercise continuous supervision over Wales and the Marches more effectively than the distant king could do was slowly coming into being. The idea of a regional authority did not spring from any carefully-conceived plan, but was a piece of improvisation typical of Edward's rather opportunist methods of government. The notion came from the need to provide a suitable household for the king's infant son, Edward, who, at the age of six months, was formally created prince of Wales and earl of Chester on 26 June 1471, and duke of Cornwall on 17 July. At the same time a body of fifteen councillors was appointed to administer the principality until the prince reached the age of fourteen.[2] At first this council had little power, and not until 20 November 1472 was the prince allowed to draw the revenues of the principality and the counties of Chester and Flint. This led to a reorganization of his council, which was increased in number from fifteen to twenty-five members on 20 February 1473. The new members included two Marcher lords, Shrewsbury and Ferrers, and four professional lawyers. This council was given general power to administer the prince's possessions in Wales, Cornwall and Chester, but as yet had no special judicial authority in the Welsh Marches. Following the request made by the commons of 1472, Edward sent his son and a body of councillors to Hereford to represent the majesty of the Crown. Both then and in February 1474 they were given instructions to deal with disturbances in the border counties; but these were for specific purposes and do not represent any clear intent to transform the council 'from a body for administering estates into a court for enforcing the law'.[3]

Further developments followed from the king's decision that the prince should take up permanent residence in the Marches. In the winter of 1473–4 an inner council was created through the appointment of Anthony, Earl Rivers, as 'governor and ruler' of the prince's household, and of John Alcock, bishop of Rochester, as president of his council, and also as his teacher 'that he may be brought up in virtue and cunning', and Thomas Vaughan, treasurer of Edward's chamber,

[1] *CPR, 1467–77*, 429; R. A. Griffiths, 'Royal Government in the Southern Counties of the Principality of Wales' (unpublished Ph.D. thesis, University of Bristol, 1962). [2] *CPR, 1467–77*, 283; and for the development of the prince's council generally, P. Williams, *The Council in the Marches of Wales under Elizabeth I*; C. A. J. Skeel, *The Council in the Marches of Wales*; Griffiths, *The Fifteenth Century*, 159–62. [3] As claimed by Williams, *op. cit.*, 7; for the enlarged council and its instructions, *CPR, 1467–77*, 361, 365–6, 429.

was confirmed in his position as prince's chamberlain also.[1] Elaborate ordinances for the government of the household were drawn up on 27 September 1473, which regulated the prince's daily life in minute detail as well as providing for the size of the household and the conduct of its officers.[2] Towards the end of the year the prince and his officers began to reside regularly at Ludlow Castle, the principal York family residence in the Welsh Marches. From then on it was natural that the princely council should become a focal point for the exercise of royal authority in the area, and should gradually acquire larger though rather ill-defined powers.

In January 1476 the prince was given a general commission of oyer and terminer within the principality, the Marches, and the adjacent English shires of Gloucester, Hereford, Shropshire and Worcester, with power to array men if necessary, and authority to appoint others in his place. In March further power was given to him and some of his council to enquire into all liberties and franchises in the Marches and the English border counties which might be resumed into the king's hands, and into all escapes of criminals in those areas. This was all preliminary to a meeting arranged at Ludlow in March 1476 between the prince's council and the Marcher lords to discuss the best methods of suppressing crime, and Edward backed this up by announcing his intention to visit the region in person after Easter.[3] Probably as a result of the discussions in March, the prince's council was given authority in December 1476 to appoint judicial commissions in Wales, the Marches and the border shires, to array men if necessary in pursuit of criminals, and to enquire into official negligence.[4] Clearly a serious effort was being made to coordinate the administration of justice in the entire region, with the king's sovereign powers semi-permanently delegated to a resident council at Ludlow. Its responsibilities were further increased in December 1477, when the lordships of the earldom of March began to be put under its direct control, and in 1479, when William Herbert was compelled to give up his earldom of Pembroke to the prince 'for the reformation of the weal public, restful governance, and ministration of justice in the said parts of South Wales'.[5] All this did not mean that the prince's council could interfere in the day-to-day government of the many Marcher lordships still in private hands, but at least it had a supervisory authority both there and in the border

---

[1] *Ibid.*, 401, 414, 417. [2] *Collection of Ordinances . . . of the Royal Household*, 27–33. [3] *CPR, 1467–77*, 574, 605; Skeel, *op. cit.*, 26–7. Worcestershire was omitted from the March commission. [4] *CPR, 1476–85*, 5; Williams, *Council in the Marches*, 9. [5] *CPR, 1476–85*, 59–60, 94, 339; *RP*, VI, 202–4.

counties to deal with failures of justice or official negligence, as well as complete power in the principality, the earldom of March, and other lordships belonging to the Crown. Unfortunately, little information has survived about the activities of this regional council during the later years of Edward's reign, and we cannot know how effective it proved. But the problem of disorder within the Marcher lordships remained intractable, as Henry VII was to discover, and its only real solution lay in the abolition of Marcher privileges eventually undertaken by Henry VIII.[1]

The problem of violence and lawlessness was scarcely less acute in the north of England than in Wales and the Marches, and in the twenty years before 1471 it had proved even more dangerously prone to rebellion and political disorder. The Wars of the Roses themselves had been at least in part the outcome of quarrels between great North-Country magnates, and the condition of the north was a matter of great political concern to the government of the day.[2] Here the difficulties did not spring primarily from the existence of areas of privileged jurisdiction like the Welsh Marcher lordships. It is true that the north contained two great franchises in the county palatine of Lancaster and the palatine bishopric of Durham, but the former was permanently under the control of the king as duke of Lancaster, and the immunity of the latter could be interfered with when the king chose, quite apart from his ability to select the successive bishops of this princely northern see.[3] Northern lawlessness derived from a combination of factors – a chronically disturbed border region; a long tradition of self-help in areas remote from the central courts at Westminster; and the dominance of northern society by an independently-minded nobility, many of whom retained a centuries-old grip on the loyalties and military resources of their retainers and tenantry.[4] Not surprisingly, any assertion of royal authority in this region during the 1460s had remained dependent to an alarming degree on the goodwill and cooperation of its aristocratic supporters, and even more than in Wales Edward's concern lay rather in the political peace of the region than in impartial governance, although the two were not unconnected problems.

[1] See the valuable discussion of this subject by T. B. Pugh, *Glamorgan County History*, III, 555–81, and for Henry VII's policies, S. B. Chrimes, *Henry VII*, 244–57.
[2] R. A. Griffiths, 'Local Rivalries and National Politics', 589–90, 631–2.
[3] R. L. Storey, 'The North of England', in *The Fifteenth Century*, 138–42.
[4] R. L. Storey, *op. cit.*, 129–44; *The End of the House of Lancaster*, esp. chapter VII; and for the persistence of traditional loyalties into Tudor times, see M. E. James, 'A Tudor Magnate and the Tudor State: Henry 5th Earl of Northumberland', Borthwick Inst. of Hist. Research, Papers, no. 30.

These considerations are reflected in two major policy decisions – to restore Henry Percy to the earldom of Northumberland in 1470, and to transfer Warwick's northern offices, estates and influence intact to his brother, Richard of Gloucester, in 1471. These measures hark back to the arrangements of the 1460s, notably the delegation of power in Wales and the Marches to William, Lord Herbert, and show Edward's tendency to rule wherever possible through trusted individuals rather than to develop new institutions. By contrast with Wales, no special powers of supervision or jurisdiction were given to Gloucester or Northumberland in the north. Indeed the ultimate direction of Edward's policy here was in a sense reactionary, leading to the creation of a complex of private power in Gloucester's hands, even greater than that wielded by Warwick, rather than towards the establishment of an embryo council of the north. Nevertheless, it represented an effort to bring the north under some sort of supervision and control ultimately derived from the king.

The chief beneficiaries of the fall of the House of Nevill had been Duke Richard of Gloucester and Henry Percy, 4th earl of Northumberland. As wardens of the Marches and holders of land and office in the north, they were established as the main supports of royal authority north of Trent, Gloucester more especially in Cumberland and Westmorland, Percy in Northumberland, whilst they shared considerable influence in Yorkshire. It has often been claimed that from 1473 onwards Gloucester was given supervisory authority over Percy, but this is not true.[1] Differences between the two led to their appearing before the king's council at Nottingham on 12 May 1473. There the duke pledged himself not to accept or retain into his service any of the earl's servants, past or present. A year later (28 July 1474), the earl entered into a contract of retainer with the duke, to do him all lawful service (saving his duty to the king, the queen, and the prince of Wales); in return the duke undertook to be the earl's good lord at all times, and to sustain his right against all persons. But any subordination implied thereby was essentially private rather than official, and the duke had to confirm again that he would not retain any of Percy's servants, with one exception, nor ask for or claim any office held by the earl, nor interrupt him or his servants in the exercise of any such office. Northumberland's independence of action was assured.[2]

In Yorkshire, the most vital area for the stability of the north, the

---

[1] E.g. by Scofield, II, 5; Kendall, *Richard III*, 107.
[2] This indenture is printed in Fonblanque, *Annals of the House of Percy*, I, 549, and W. H. Dunham, *Lord Hastings' Indentured Retainers*, 140.

duke's influence gradually increased during the 1470s, as royal grant brought more land and offices. Part of his reward for surrendering to Clarence's demands was the keepership of the royal forests north of Trent (18 May 1472), taken from the earl of Northumberland, and from 4 July 1471 he held the office of chief steward of the Duchy of Lancaster north of Trent, which gave him influence in Yorkshire through the three great Duchy honours of Pontefract, Knaresborough and Pickering within the shire.[1] In 1475 Edward gave him the Pennine lordship of Skipton-in-Craven, homeland of the attainted Lords Clifford, and their hereditary sheriffdom of Cumberland, and, in exchange for some of his wife's lands, he acquired the castle and lordship of Scarborough on the Yorkshire coast. In 1478 the death of Clarence brought him the castle of Richmond, and he was also given the reversion (on the death of Margery, Lady Roos) of the North Riding castle and lordship of Helmsley.[2] By then he had become the greatest lord in Yorkshire, and only in the East Riding did Percy's local influence compare with his. He very largely took over the Nevill influence in the shire: in 1473–4, for example, of thirty-six men who were receiving fees charged upon the lordship of Middleham from the duke, no fewer than twenty-two had been in Warwick's service in 1465–6.[3]

But Northumberland remained a force to be reckoned with, and indeed his support was essential to ensure Gloucester's dominance of the north, for other northern families, such as Dacre, Scrope of Bolton, and Greystoke, were essentially of the second rank. The correspondence of the Yorkshire family of Plumpton, whose interests lay in the Knaresborough area of the West Riding, reveals that the earl was by no means under Gloucester's control. About 1475 Sir William Plumpton was advised by one Godfrey Grene not to try to 'labour' either Gloucester or the king to persuade Northumberland to confirm Sir William in the office of bailiff of Knaresborough which he held from the earl as steward.[4] Sir, he was told,

> as long as my lord of Northumberland's patent thereof stands good, so long will he have no deputy but such as shall please him, and can thank him for the gift thereof, and no man else.

[1] *CPR, 1467–77*, 338; Somerville, *History of the Duchy of Lancaster*, I, 422.
[2] *RP*, VI, 125; *CPR, 1467–77*, 485, 507, 549, 556; *1476–85*, 90. Lady Roos was the widow of John, Lord Roos (d. 1421), not Thomas, as stated in the Patent Roll; she died a fortnight later, 20 April 1478 (Dugdale, *Baronage*, I, 552).
[3] Gladys M. Coles, 'The Lordship of Middleham, Especially in Yorkist and Early Tudor Times' (Liverpool M.A. thesis, 1961), App. B.
[4] *Plumpton Correspondence*, 31–3.

And on another matter, Plumpton was advised not to risk anything

to the disworship of the earl of Northumberland, that hath the chief rule there under the king.

Even the powerful Lord Hastings totally declined to interfere in recommending Plumpton to the earl, and roundly told Grene that

we would make a jealousy betwixt my Lord of Northumberland and him, in that he should labour for any of his men, he being present. Sir, I took that for a watchword for meddling betwixt lords.

The care which Gloucester took to ensure that Northumberland was publicly associated with him in all matters requiring joint action, the evidence of Northumberland's independence on several occasions, and the deference which the citizens of York, Beverley and Hull showed to the earl as the most powerful man in the East Riding, are evidence that in Yorkshire 'the chief rule of the shire' remained a condominium. Not until 1482, during the war with Scotland, was Gloucester appointed king's lieutenant in the north and so given general precedence over the earl beyond the Trent.[1]

Whether singly or in collaboration, the duke and the earl and their private councils had come to wield a quasi-royal authority in the north by the mid-seventies. The city of York sought and obtained Gloucester's backing to enforce legislation about unlawful fishing in the Yorkshire rivers, and thereby brought pressure to bear on powerful offenders like the bishop of Durham. At the citizens' request, the duke discharged a corrupt town clerk and sought licence from the king after the event. In 1480, when a Scots invasion was threatened, the duke and the earl both wrote to the city seeking men for the defence of the north, 'charging' them on the king's behalf, 'desiring and praying' on their own authority. In 1482 it could be said in York that offenders were punished 'according to the king's high commandment and the Duke of Gloucester'.[2] Gloucester was also called upon to use his influence within the palatine bishopric of Durham: in 1475 the prior of Durham thanked him for his 'good lordship' and asked him 'to desire the archbishop of York to be good and gracious lord and tender father' to the prior and convent.[3]

Together Gloucester and Northumberland contributed towards the keeping of the peace, the administration of justice, the arbitration of private disputes and the enforcement of legislation. Much of this work fell upon the two magnates' private councils, which, in the pattern of the day, included local gentry and professional lawyers. Among the members of Gloucester's council were his cousins, John, Lord Scrope of Bolton, and Ralph, Lord Greystoke, retainers and estates officials like Sir William Parr of Kendal and Sir James Harrington, justices from the northern circuit like Brian Nele, and lawyers such as Guy Fairfax and Miles Metcalfe, successively recorders of York.[1] In 1482 commissions of oyer and terminer to deal with all criminal offences in Yorkshire were staffed essentially by councillors of the duke and the earl, as the principals prepared to depart to Scotland, and of the twelve men who served Yorkshire as sheriffs between 1470 and 1483, six were Gloucester's retainers and four more Northumberland's.[2]

The advantages which derived from having the royal will implemented by two such dominant and influential lords were obvious enough. Men who might ignore a distant government in Westminster could not afford to risk the displeasure of powerful magnates acting in the king's name on their very doorsteps, and the resident ducal and comital councils could do something to check the characteristic northern indifference to the authority of the law. But the dangers of this policy were also conspicuous. The powers of the duke and the earl derived not from the delegation to them of specific functions of royal authority, but from their position as great private magnates and leaders of northern society, commanding huge estates, reserves of patronage, and private affinities. Nothing better illustrates the direction of Edward's policy in this region than his decision in January 1483 to carve out for Gloucester a great hereditary palatine lordship comprising Cumberland, Westmorland and whatever parts of south-west Scotland he might conquer, where he was to enjoy virtually the same high immunities as the bishop of Durham. With this Gloucester and his heirs were to enjoy the wardenship of the West Marches, which was thus alienated from the control of the Crown for the first time.[3] No man had ever enjoyed such independent power in north-western England. Potentially at least Gloucester and Northumberland were over-mighty subjects on the grand scale, and only the unexpected development of Gloucester's

[1] Reid, *King's Council in the North*, 44–6.
[2] *CPR, 1476–85*, 343; Reid, *op. cit.*, 46; M. A. Hicks, 'The Career of Henry Percy, 4th earl of Northumberland, with special reference to his retinue' (Southampton M.A. Dissertation, 1971).
[3] *RP*, VI, 204–5; Storey, 'Wardens of the Marches', 608; Reid, *King's Council*, 46.

becoming king led to the conversion of his private council into a royal regional council on the model of the prince's council in Wales and the Marches. The underlying dangers of Edward's policy in the north of England need no emphasis, for in 1483 it was Gloucester, with the implicit support of Northumberland, and the backing of North-Country barons and gentry, who was able to depose Edward's heir and take over the government of England for himself.

Late medieval Ireland was if anything even more perennially lawless and disturbed than either Wales or the north of England. Edward IV, however, was one of those few fortunate rulers of England for whom Ireland presented no serious political problems. Immunity from an 'Irish problem' was bought at the price of virtual surrender of effective royal control. The rare occasions when Edward tried to assert his authority produced trouble, from which he hastily retreated. In effect, Yorkist policy in Ireland amounted to little more than a sell-out to the interests of the Anglo-Irish aristocracy, more especially to the Fitz-Gerald family represented by the earls of Desmond and Kildare.[1]

The foundation stone of Edwardian policy towards Ireland was laid by Duke Richard of York in the late 1450s. His desire to entrench himself in Ireland led him to appeal to the desire of the Anglo-Irish lords for virtual autonomy, and in a meeting of the Irish parliament he allowed them to adopt what has been termed 'a frankly revolutionary programme', which stated, in essence, that 'the land of Ireland is and at all times has been corporate of itself, by the ancient laws and customs used in the same, freed of the burden of any special law of the realm of England'.[2] This brought him the support of the Anglo-Irish, and the eventual victory of the Yorkists in England also entailed the overthrow of one of the great families, the Butlers, represented by James, 5th earl of Ormond, and earl of Wiltshire, who, with his brothers, John and Thomas, was attainted in Edward IV's first parliament. Power in the English Pale passed thereafter to the Geraldines, Thomas FitzGerald, who succeeded his father as 7th earl of Desmond in 1462, and Thomas FitzMaurice, 7th earl of Kildare, and, after his death in March 1478, to his son, Gerald, the 8th earl. Edward IV appointed a series of

[1] For Yorkist Ireland, see E. Curtis, *History of Medieval Ireland*, 361–91, and 'Richard Duke of York as Viceroy of Ireland', *Jour. Royal Soc. Antiquaries of Ireland*, lxii (1932), 158–86; A. J. Otway-Ruthven, *History of Medieval Ireland*, 377–400, on which the following very brief summary is based. For the problem after 1485, see S. B. Chrimes, *Henry VII*.

[2] Otway-Ruthven, *op. cit.*, 387.

nominal and largely absentee lieutenants of Ireland; George, duke of Clarence (1462–70, 1472–8), John Tiptoft, earl of Worcester (1470), his third son, George (1478–9), and his second son, Richard, duke of York (1479–83), but any attempt to impose an effective deputy of his own choice on the Anglo-Irish proved unavailing.[1]

Only two such attempts were made. In 1463 Edward proved willing to accept as deputy the versatile and attractive earl of Desmond, 'a renaissance magnate with an Irish tinge'.[2] Like other Anglo-Irish deputies of the period, he was allowed to use the meagre authority and financial resources of the English Crown in Ireland to maintain his own position, and to further his family interests. But quarrels between Desmond and other Anglo-Irish, and his excessive contacts with the native Irish, brought severe disturbances, and in 1466 he was heavily defeated in an expedition against Offaly, a setback which permanently weakened the defences of the Pale. This led Edward to replace Desmond as deputy by the earl of Worcester, who, early in 1468, proceeded to attaint Desmond and Kildare in a parliament held at Drogheda: soon after the former was murdered, and the latter imprisoned. Worcester managed to survive the Anglo-Irish reaction which followed, but was recalled to England to succeed Clarence as lieutenant in March 1470. The Irish lords showed little disposition to support the Lancastrian cause during the troubles of 1470–71, and the earl of Kildare, elected justiciar of Ireland by the Irish Council, declared his loyalty to the House of York. Thereafter Kildare and his son, Gerald, had little to worry about, and ruled Ireland for the rest of the reign, either as justiciars elected by the Irish or as deputies appointed by the king. Edward's second attempt to interfere proved abortive, for when in 1478 he sent over Henry, Lord Grey, as deputy, he encountered such general resistance from the Anglo-Irish that he was quite unable to wield any authority, and returned to England in the following year. The 8th earl of Kildare steadily strengthened his position in Ireland, and was so strongly entrenched that not even Henry VII was able to remove him. Edward had to be content with an almost totally nominal lordship of Ireland, but, if it brought him little profit, equally it gave little pain.

[1] For a list of 'Chief Governors of Ireland', see *Handbook of British Chronology*, ed. Powicke and Fryde, 154–5. John de la Pole, duke of Suffolk, was appointed lieutenant in March 1478, but never took office.
[2] Otway-Ruthven, *op. cit.*, 389.

Chapter 9

THE KING'S GREAT ENTERPRISE,
1472–1475

(i) *Diplomacy and the Formation of Alliances: the Approach to War*

England's foreign relations in Edward's second reign do not possess that intimate relationship with domestic affairs which marks the 1460s. The attitude of continental powers no longer seriously threatened the security of the Yorkist dynasty.[1] Yet English foreign policy in these years has a considerable interest. It came close to involving England in a ruinous foreign war, which might profoundly have changed the character of Edward's later years, and from which only good fortune rescued him. Secondly, the settlements made with Scotland and the Hanseatic League, and eventually with France, went far towards determining the main lines of English foreign relations for the rest of Edward's reign, and the latter two were of considerable importance in the country's commercial history.

Following his restoration in 1471, Edward was full of resentment against the recent hostility of King Louis of France, 'the principal ground, root, and provoker of the King's let and trouble', who, he claimed, still endeavoured by 'subtle and crafty means' to disturb the realm of England.[2] This attitude found a ready response in the continuing restlessness of the great French feudatories. Before the year ended, both Burgundy and Brittany were trying to engage him in anti-French schemes. But Edward's experiences in exile had given him

[1] A very different interpretation from that which follows has recently been advanced by J. R. Lander, 'The Hundred Years War and Edward IV's Campaign in France', in *Tudor Men and Institutions: Studies in English Law and Government*, ed. A. J. Slavin, 70–100. Lander argues (p. 81) that the campaign of 1475 should be seen 'not as a revival of the genuinely aggressive policies of Henry V, but as ... a somewhat defensive reaction to the development of Anglo-Burgundian-French relationships over the past two decades'. My reasons for differing from this view will appear generally below, but see especially pp. 211–14, 223–4.
[2] *Literae Cantuarienses*, ed. J. B. Sheppard (Rolls Series, 1889), III, 277, 279 – the official address on the king's behalf to the parliament of 1472.

cause to doubt the depth and sincerity of Duke Charles of Burgundy's friendship for him: Charles's chilly treatment of him until necessity changed his mind had left a certain legacy of mistrust, assiduously fostered by Louis XI.[1] For the time being he was not to be drawn, and in September 1471 ratified a truce with France to last until May 1472.

Early in 1472, however, he began to respond to further overtures from Duke Francis of Brittany, for whom his feelings were a good deal warmer than for his brother-in-law of Burgundy.[2] Alarmed by the hostile moves of Louis of France, Francis appealed to Edward in March for 6,000 archers for the defence of his duchy, and in response the king sent Earl Rivers and his brother, Sir Edward Woodville, to Brittany with 1,000 archers, where they arrived early in April. At the same time he made a renewed approach to Burgundy, both for a political cooperation and the settlement of commercial differences, and, as Dukes Francis and Charles were already discussing an alliance, the prospect of an anti-French coalition began to take shape.[3] To forestall this, Louis XI struck at Brittany, as the weakest of the three, but the Bretons, with Rivers's aid, resisted his invasion, and the French withdrew early in August 1472. Further aid for Brittany was approved by Edward, and a force of 2,000 archers under the Gascon, Gaillard, Lord Duras, was assembled by the end of July, and landed in Brittany probably early in September. At the same time an English fleet was equipped for service in the Channel. Burgundy, too, was seeking English aid: there is evidence that the duke offered Edward the county of Eu in Normandy as the price of a descent on France, and that he wanted the services of 3,000 English archers for war against King Louis.[4]

But Edward was not anxious for England to be used as a mere recruiting ground for foreign princes, nor to assist them in any sub-

---

[1] Commynes, I, 139, says Charles and Edward disliked each other in 1471, and CSP, Milan, I, 161, speaks of Edward being 'ill-content with the savage treatment' he had received from the duke. According to Commynes, Edward and his council also became 'unnecessarily worked up' about reports that Charles planned to marry his daughter Mary to Louis's brother, Charles (op. cit., 221–5). For these negotiations, see Scofield, II, 15–17, 24–5; Calmette and Perinelle, Louis XI et l'Angleterre, 146–9.
[2] B. A. Pocquet du Haut-Jussé, François II, Duc de Bretagne, et l'Angleterre, 155–7. Francis had sent money to Edward in exile, and in 1475 Edward was at pains to include Brittany in the treaty; see below, p. 233.
[3] Pocquet du Haut-Jussé, op. cit., 166–9; Scofield, II, 19–20; Calmette and Perinelle, 148.
[4] Rymer, Foedera, XI, 737–40; Scofield, II, 33–4; CPR, 1467–77, 339–40, 356. For Charles's offer, Calmette and Perinelle, 152–4, and also for evidence that the 3,000 archers were actually sent to Burgundy, supported by Pocquet du Haut-Jussé, 171. Cf. Vaughan, Charles the Bold, 83.

sidiary role. His negotiations with Brittany in the summer of 1472 show clearly the direction of his policy – the conclusion of firm alliances leading to an invasion of France, in which England should be the dominant partner. An embassy headed by Earl Rivers in July 1472 laid down the conditions for an English attack on France which were eventually accepted by Duke Francis, and became the basis for the Treaty of Châteaugiron agreed on 11 September 1472. In essence, it provided for an English invasion, either in Gascony or Normandy, by 1 April 1473. The English army was to be financed by Edward but was to receive all possible assistance from Brittany, including the use of Breton ports and passage through the duke's dominions. Any territory conquered from France should remain in Edward's hands unless he chose to make cessions to Brittany. Aid to Brittany, if needed for the duchy's defence during the war, should be paid for by Francis and meanwhile he should have the services of 1,000 archers.[1]

At the same time Edward was seeking to make similar arrangements with Burgundy. In response to English overtures, the duke sent over Lord Gruythuyse, who came in part to enjoy Edward's splendid hospitality and to receive the earldom of Winchester as reward for his services to Edward during the king's Burgundian exile.[2] But he also carried with him Charles's conditions for an offensive alliance against France. If the war were successful, the duke expected Edward to grant him, in full hereditary right, the counties of Champagne, Nevers, Rethel, Eu and Guise and the duchy of Bar, which would have provided him with territories linking the northern and southern halves of his divided dominions, together with the French possessions of his enemy, the count of St Pol, and the Somme towns to which he had already laid claim.[3]

Armed with these indications that Burgundy was ready to enter into active negotiations, Edward was now ready to go before parliament, when it assembled on 6 October 1472, in search of money to finance the war. It has recently been shown that the idea of an aggressive foreign war was a good deal less popular than it had once been.[4] Edward could also expect to be viewed with some suspicion by his taxpayers, since he

---

[1] Rymer, *Foedera*, XI, 760; Morice, *Mémoires de Bretagne*, III, 246–9 (for text of treaty); Pocquet du Haut-Jussé, 172–3.
[2] For a contemporary account of his visit, see 'The Record of Bluemantle Pursuivant', in Kingsford, *English Historical Literature*, 380–8.
[3] *State Papers, Henry VIII*, VI, pt v, 1–8 (instructions to English embassy, January 1473).
[4] Lander, 'The Hundred Years War and Edward IV's 1475 Campaign in France', 70–7.

had twice defaulted on promises of military action – in 1463 and 1468 – in return for taxation. For both these reasons, his spokesman – probably the chancellor, Bishop Robert Stillington – in a long address to parliament advanced a whole battery of arguments to justify the invasion of France.[1] Some were familiar, like the king's claim to his 'right inheritance' in France, and the argument that external war would be a safeguard against internal commotion by diverting the energies of the unruly elements in the population, and had not the most successful kings in England been those who engaged in war? The misdeeds and machinations of Louis XI deserved to be met and punished. Finally the king tried to appeal on a more practical plane. The conquest of Gascony and Normandy, by giving control of an enemy coast, would greatly reduce the burden of keeping the seas, and would provide a place to settle for all the landless lads of England, 'younger brothers or other'. These political persuasions do not necessarily give a true indication of Edward's war aims, and they were certainly less than candid.[2] The king told parliament that he now had alliances with Burgundy and Brittany, purchased at an expense of more than £100,000, and other princes could be expected to join in a league against France. But at this very moment Edward's supposed allies were preparing to withdraw from their warlike posture towards King Louis.

Brittany was the first to falter. Though Edward had quickly ratified the Treaty of Châteaugiron on 24 October, the Breton government, frightened by the threat of a French invasion, and by the extent to which the treaty seemed to put her in the power of the English, decided they had made a rash bargain. The irresolute duke was persuaded to sign a brief truce with France on 15 October, which was soon extended for a year. He then sent ambassadors to England to persuade Edward to postpone his invasion until November 1473. He also put pressure on Burgundy, which followed Francis's example, and on 3 November signed a truce with France to last until 1 April 1473. The English troops in Brittany, badly hit by epidemics, were brought home during October and November, and a force of 400 archers intended for Burgundy never left the country.[3] By 30 November, the day the commons made the desired grant of war taxation, any prospect of an immediate anti-French coalition had disappeared. As in 1468, the defection of Brittany, its most vulnerable member, ruined the triple alliance.

---

[1] *Literae Cantuarienses*, 274–85; and for 1463 and 1468, below, pp. 348–9.
[2] Cf. Lander, *op. cit.*, for a different view.
[3] *CPR, 1467–77*, 363; Scofield, II, 40–1; Pocquet du Haut-Jussé, *op. cit.*, 174–5.

For Edward, however, this implied a postponement, not an abandonment, of his warlike plans. He, too, found it prudent to sign a truce with Louis on 22 March 1473, to last until 1 April 1474, though he did not find it convenient to tell parliament of this when he asked for more money during its second session (February–April 1473). But he was still pressing hard for a firm alliance with Burgundy as well as a settlement with the Hansards. On 19 January 1473, William, Lord Hastings, left England at the head of an embassy armed with the considered views of Edward and his council on the way the war should be waged and on the subsequent partition of France. Their terms were specific and practical and clearly indicate Edward's serious intent to make war. They may be summarized briefly as follows:

1. Edward was willing to land in Normandy or nearby in April, May or June 1473, to begin the war 'on which his affection was now greatly set'.
2. He would cede to Charles all the French territory he had asked for, but he wanted to have at least the diocese of Rheims, which lay within Champagne, for his coronation as king of France.
3. Charles was to aid the English with 10,000 men for a year, the cost to be met from England's share of the conquests.
4. General direction of the operations should be under English control, but the two armies were to attack the French from different points, not to act as a unified force.

The English ambassadors met Duke Charles at Ghent on 26 January 1473, but they soon discovered they could make little progress, for he was now preoccupied with exploiting a favourable opportunity to seize the Duchy of Guelders, and it was this realization which made Edward conclude the truce with France in March 1473.[1]

Undeterred, he pressed on his negotiations with Scotland and the Hansards, and resumed his discussions with Burgundy as soon as the duke could be persuaded to show an active interest. In May an embassy under Lords Hastings and Howard was commissioned to treat further with the duke for 'the great enterprise which by them both is intended against their common adversary', and on which they were now said to be well-nigh agreed. The purpose of the mission was to give Edward's replies to various questions raised by the duke, especially the nature of English military commitment. Edward now told Charles that he would ship to France in April 1473, with an army of more than

1 *State Papers, Henry VIII*, VI, pt v, 1–8; Scofield, II, 46–9.

10,000 men, but he did not wish to be obliged to land in Normandy, but 'wherever might be most convenient for the weal of the conquest'.[1]

Charles's preoccupations with other matters prevented any discussion of these issues until August 1473. Then, in a series of meetings at Bruges, they reached agreement with the duke on what they called 'the forms and numbers of all the minutes of pactions' touching the invasion of France, but no formal or precise treaty of alliance was signed. In fact, the negotiations with Burgundy now began to reach a stalemate, largely through the intrusion of Charles's imperial ambitions. In return for the marriage of his daughter and heiress, Mary of Burgundy, to the Archduke Maximilian, heir to the Emperor Frederick III, he was persuaded to believe that he might himself be elected King of the Romans and elevate his duchy into a kingdom – a prospect which dazzled him more than a combined Anglo-Burgundian onslaught on France. The pursuit of his plans for aggrandizement in the east was to prove henceforward a major hindrance to his final commitment to England. He raised his terms for an offensive alliance; he extended his truce with France by successive instalments until 1 May 1475; and increasingly his attention and his resources became bogged down in Alsace, where a war with the Swiss was imminent.[2] These difficulties forced Edward to confess to parliament, when it met for its sixth session on 6 June 1474, that he could not invade France before Michaelmas, as the terms of its grant of war taxation required him to do, and the further extension of the duke's truce with France eventually made it obvious that he could not go at all in 1474.[3]

Suddenly, when all hope had been abandoned for the year, Burgundy came to terms. A formal alliance against France was finally signed by the Treaty of London of 25 July 1474. Edward undertook to land in France before 1 July 1475, upon substantially the same conditions as had been agreed in August 1473. Charles recognized him as king of France, and in return Edward agreed that Charles should hold all his share of a dismembered France, together with his existing dominions, in full sovereignty, save that Edward should have free access to Rheims

---

[1] Rymer, *Foedera*, XI, 778; Scofield, II, 64–5.
[2] For Charles's imperial schemes, see J. Bartier, *Charles le Téméraire*, 150–203; J. Calmette and E. Deprez, *Les Premières Grandes Puissances* (*Histoire du Moyen Age*, ed. G. Glotz, VII, pt 2), 89–100; Kendall, *Louis XI*, 254–73. The most recent and valuable discussion of his eastern policies, and of his diffusion of aims, is now to be found in Vaughan, *op. cit.*, chapters 8–9.
[3] Scofield, II, 91–4. In February 1474 Charles agreed to a truce with France which was extended to last until 1 May 1475.

on the day of his coronation.[1] Edward's negotiations with Burgundy have a considerable bearing on the problem of his true intentions concerning the invasion of France. Some modern authorities have maintained that he had little serious intention of making war, and used the difficulties in coming to terms with Burgundy as a pretext for successive delays and postponements of his undertaking.[2] This view seems to make a nonsense of his dealings with parliament over war-finance, and it is also clear from his later actions that he regarded the active and committed cooperation of the duke of Burgundy, whose army was regarded as unquestionably the best in Europe, as an essential prerequisite for a major attack on France.[3] His inability to tie the duke down to a specific time-table is less the excuse than the main reason why the whole enterprise hung fire. As if to prove that this was all he had been waiting for, Edward began, within a month of signing the Treaty of London, to enter into contracts with his captains for an invasion in the following year.[4]

If the invasion of France were to succeed, it was also essential for England to neutralize in advance any actual or potential enemies who might be tempted to exploit her continental involvement. Chief amongst these were the Hanseatic League and the king of Scotland. In 1471 the Hansards had given Edward valuable assistance in return for his promise to restore their former privileges. Unfortunately Edward did not see fit to honour his pledges, and when, on 6 July 1471, he again granted to the dissenting merchants of Cologne exclusive enjoyment of all the privileges formerly enjoyed by the League as a whole, a return to hostilities was inevitable. Naval war was resumed, and the League closed its ranks against England and Cologne. But as soon as the invasion of France became a serious prospect, Edward became anxious for a reconciliation. Through the good offices of Burgundy, a series of conferences was held at Bruges to discuss terms for a settlement. The road to peace was long and hard. Throughout 1472 the Hansards remained uncompromising in their demands that 'the verdict of 1468' must be annulled, full compensation paid for all their goods seized at that time, and complete restoration made of all their privileges in England. The English would not consider these conditions. Eventually negotiations were resumed at Utrecht in June 1473. The instructions

---

[1] Rymer, *Foedera*, XI, 804–14; Scofield, II, 95–6.
[2] E.g., Calmette and Perinelle, 161, 164, 168, and see further below, pp. 223–4.
[3] For the strength of the Burgundian army, J. Bartier, *op. cit.*, 173 ff.; Vaughan, *op. cit.*, 197–227.
[4] Rymer, *Foedera*, XI, 817–19 (indenture 20 August 1474 with Sir Richard Tunstall).

given to Edward's ambassadors reveal the extent of his anxiety to achieve a full settlement even at the cost of substantial concessions: he was prepared to concede nearly all the Hansard demands, but still hoped to get reciprocal privileges granted to English merchants in Hanseatic regions such as they had enjoyed under a treaty of 1437.[1] But the English soon discovered that, in spite of the latitude given them by their master, they would have to make further and unpalatable concessions. There was bitter bargaining about the amount of the compensation to be made – the Hansards were eventually knocked down from £25,000 to £10,000 – and the League insisted firmly that Edward should totally abandon his Cologne friends until such time as they had been re-admitted to it. Agreement was eventually reached between the delegations at Utrecht on 19 September 1473, and a formal treaty was signed at a further conference at Utrecht on 28 February 1474. Its terms represented a surrender by England to all the Hansard demands, and in return her envoys got only the limited concession that the English should enjoy their former privileges in Hanseatic territories, but without any exemption from taxes.[2] It is to Edward's credit that he did not abandon the men of Cologne and, through a series of evasions, avoided depriving them of their status in England until they had made peace with the League. Commercially, it was a blow to English merchants and shipping: unable to make good their claim to reciprocity, they saw their share of trade with Germany and the Baltic dwindle, whilst the Hanseatic trade with England soon surpassed its previous high point.[3] Edward had put political before commercial advantage, but at least England was now free of a damaging and expensive commercial war and could feel much more secure in the task of conveying a large army with all its transport, artillery and baggage across the Channel.

A settlement with Scotland proved much easier. King James III was tempted by the blandishments of Louis XI, and dallied with the notion of keeping Edward at home, either by invading England or supporting him against his own subjects, who were thought likely to rebel as soon as he abandoned his plans for an invasion of France.[4] But nothing came of it, and the truce between England and Scotland was prolonged by successive instalments to last until 10 April 1475. By September 1473, James was beginning to look favourably upon an English proposal

[1] For a detailed survey of these negotiations, see Scofield, II, 63, 67–84.
[2] Rymer, *Foedera*, XI, 793–803; *Hanserecesse*, II, 7, 341–353.
[3] Power and Postan, *Studies in English Trade in the Fifteenth Century*, 137–8.
[4] Scofield, II, 53–4.

for a marriage alliance between his infant son, James, born on 17 March 1473, and Edward's third daughter, Cecily, now four years old. Preliminary agreement was reached in July, and on 8 October an English embassy led by the bishop of Durham arrived in Edinburgh to sign the marriage-treaty. On 26 October the formal betrothal of the young couple was accompanied by a treaty between the two kings. James and Cecily were to marry within six months of their reaching marriageable age, and other suitable offspring were to be substituted in the event of the death of either of them. Edward was to provide a dowry of 20,000 crowns, payable over a period of seventeen years, and in return Cecily was to be given a suitable jointure in land whilst her father-in-law was alive; and there was to be a truce between the two kingdoms until 21 October 1519. These arrangements ensured good relations between England and Scotland for the next few years.[1]

By the end of 1474, therefore, Edward's diplomacy had achieved some very useful results – a firm alliance with Burgundy and settlements with his two principal potential enemies. But already he was reaching further afield in the hope of completing the diplomatic encirclement of France. The king's Gascon-born agent, Barthelot de Rivière, was sent in August 1474 to seek the aid of King Ferdinand I of Naples, with whom he had already a treaty of friendship; and at the same time the duke of Urbino, Federigo da Montefeltro, was elected a knight of the Garter, as a preliminary to winning the services of this noted captain of condottiere, perhaps in the hope of promoting a Neapolitan invasion of France through the duchy of Savoy under the duke's command.[2] In December 1474 the embassy sent to Alsace under Dr John Morton to hold discussions with Duke Charles of Burgundy was also given instructions to seek treaties of alliance with Matthias Corvinus, king of Hungary, and with the Emperor Frederick III, both of whom he believed to be Charles's allies.[3] But nothing practical emerged from these distant diplomatic forays. Serious efforts were made to clear up outstanding differences with Ferdinand and Isabella of Spain, mainly arising out of questions of compensation for English piracy, and in May 1475 this led to a renewal of the treaty of alliance between the two countries originally signed in 1467; but the attitude of the Peninsular rulers to the hostility between France and England remained essentially neutral, for they were preoccupied with the

---

1 Rymer, *Foedera*, XI, 820–34; Scofield, II, 62–3, 101–4; and below, pp. 278–9.
2 C. H. Clough, 'Relations between the English and Urbino Courts, 1474–1508', *Studies in the Renaissance*, xiv (1967), 202–18; Scofield, I, 369, 401–2 (for Naples).
3 Rymer, *Foedera*, XI, 834–6.

struggle for the succession in Castile.[1] Already, on 1 May 1475, a treaty of friendship had been concluded between England and King Christian I of Denmark.[2]

This diplomatic build-up now began to affect the attitude of some of Louis's domestic enemies. The head of the powerful south French house of Armagnac, Jacques, duke of Nemours, was in negotiation with Duke Charles, whilst the count of St Pol, unaware of the arrangement between England and Burgundy to overthrow him, was making treasonable offers to both, and promised to admit English troops into Amiens, Peronne and Abbeville if he were given Champagne as reward.[3] More important was the attitude of Brittany. Friendly contacts between England and Brittany continued after the *débâcle* of 1472, and there was much active negotiation over the problem of piracy. In May 1475 the duke, who had hitherto fought shy of an alliance, suddenly sent ambassadors to England to discuss a treaty similar to those of 1467 and 1472. On 16 May a treaty was drawn up which committed Francis to help Edward with 8,000 troops in the attack on France, and on 19 May Lords Audley and Duras undertook to serve with 2,000 archers under the duke of Brittany, and to be ready to sail from Weymouth on 23 June. Edward also promised aid from the English fleet under Lord Dinham if the duke needed help against Louis. Both England and Burgundy now regarded Brittany as a firm ally, but Duke Francis, a prey to conflicting factions amongst his advisers, never ratified the treaty (though he took the archers) and when war came he made no move.[4]

(ii) *Financial and Military Preparations*

The intensive efforts of the English government to prepare the way to war in the diplomatic field between 1472 and 1475 were matched by equally long-term preparations at home. When Edward first announced his intention of invading France to the parliament of October 1472, he found a generous response from an assembly which included an unusually high proportion of royal servants and followers of the court nobility.[5]

---

[1] Rymer, *Foedera*, XI, 841–2; XII, 2–3; *CPR, 1467–77*, 480. For Peninsular neutrality, Calmette and Perinelle, 173–5.
[2] Rymer, *Foedera*, XI, 775.
[3] Commynes, ed. Lenglet, III, 457 (St Pol's confession); ed. de Mandrot, I, 283 n.; Calmette and Perinelle, I, 179.
[4] *CPR, 1647–77*, 542, 551–2; Scofield, II, 99–101, 124; Pocquet du Haut-Jussé, *op. cit.*, 190–4; Calmette and Perinelle, 177.
[5] Below, pp. 342–3.

Whilst the lords voted a special tax of one-tenth of their incomes from lands, annuities and offices, the commons, following a precedent set in the parliament of 1453, undertook to provide the king with revenue sufficient to pay the wages of a force of 13,000 archers for one year, the equivalent of £118,625. But instead of voting the money in the form of the traditional tenths and fifteenths levied on the value of personal property (under the terms of a long-outdated assessment), they chose to follow the lords and granted as a first instalment an income tax of 10 per cent. This represented an attempt, along lines already tried without much success, to shift the burden of taxation to those best able to pay, who often escaped under the traditional system. The grant was not made, however, without conditions. Edward now paid the penalty for having twice defaulted upon his promises to make war in return for taxation. This time the commons were determined to ensure that the money would be spent only for its prescribed purpose. The proceeds of the tax were to be paid over not to the exchequer but to four commissioners (the archbishop of Canterbury, the bishop of Ely, the prior of St John's and Lord Dudley), and then deposited for safe-keeping in St Paul's until such time as the king was ready to sail for France. If he had not set forth by Michaelmas 1474, the money was to be returned to the taxpayers.[1]

Payment of the income tax became due on 2 February 1473. On 8 April, however, the commons had to tell the king that the collection was not complete; some counties had not yet sent in their certificates; and they had no notion of how much the tax would yield. But, recognizing the urgency of the king's needs, they now granted a further subsidy of a fifteenth and tenth of the ordinary kind, with the now customary remissions of £6,000. Again the tax was not to be paid to the king when it became due on 24 June, and was to be kept in local repositories until he had proclaimed the muster of his army. The lords, however, allowed him to make use of the proceeds of their tax for the purchase of equipment – bows, arrows and ordnance – which had to be assembled long before the expedition set sail. Having just failed to make an alliance with Burgundy, and signed a truce with France, the king was now in no hurry for the money, and deferred the date of its collection from June to Michaelmas 1473. A later indenture discloses that, in fact, the subsidy was never collected as planned.[2]

[1] RP, VI, 4–8. For a useful analysis of the financial measures of the 1472–5 parliament, see H. L. Gray, 'The First Benevolence', in *Facts and Factors in Economic History Presented to J. F. Gay*, ed. A. E. Cole, A. L. Dunham and N. S. B. Gras, 90–113.
[2] RP, VI, 39–41; Gray, *op. cit.*, 103.

As prospects for the attack upon France began to improve in the following summer, Edward approached parliament again. On 18 July 1474 an indenture drawn up in parliament revealed that the 10 per cent income tax of 1472 had so far yielded £31,410 14s 1½d. Returns from five northern counties were not in even yet, and no collection had been made of the fifteenth and tenth voted in 1473. The commons therefore confirmed their grant of the fifteenth and tenth, to be paid by 1 November, and devised special arrangements for contributions from the northern counties. This new fifteenth and tenth was calculated to yield £30,684; together with the income tax, the commons had now provided £62,094, to which they hoped to add £5,383 from the northern counties. This left a gap of £51,147 if the full cost of the 13,000 archers were to be met, and the money had to be raised from areas which had already contributed to the income tax and were about to pay the fifteenth and tenth. The commons therefore devised a new method of assessment expressly designed to extract money from those who 'were little or not charged' to ordinary subsidies, to relieve those already burdened. Since it was now clear that the king could not invade France during the summer of 1474, and the taxpayers were already burdened with the fifteenth and tenth, it was agreed that half of the £51,000 should not become payable until St John's Day (24 June) 1475, and the remainder at Martinmas; and the king was given until St John's Day 1476 to start for France.[1]

All this represented a considerable charge on Edward's subjects. Including the income tax of 1472, it amounted to no fewer than 3¾ subsidies, and thus substantially more than the total taxation levied in all the previous years of the reign. Of Edward's predecessors, only Henry V, with six subsidies in the four years 1413–17 yielding £216,868, had extracted more in the short term for war purposes.[2] No wonder John Paston expressed the fervent hope that they should rather have the devil in the parliament house than that they should grant any more taxes.[3] Nor did the clergy escape their share. In the same period of three years, the convocation of Canterbury granted three and a half clerical tenths, each worth about £13,000, and the York convocation two tenths, worth £1,400 each, a total of some £48,000.[4]

Yet Edward felt that even these large sums were inadequate. Between November 1474 and March 1475 he launched upon an extensive

[1] RP, VI, 113–19.
[2] Jacob, The Fifteenth Century (Oxford History of England), 204.
[3] PL, V, 178 (26 March 1473).
[4] Ramsay, Lancaster and York, II, 401, 463.

campaign to raise further sums without parliamentary consent. This was the notorious first benevolence – supposedly free gifts in lieu of military service – aimed mainly at those wealthier elements in the population who escaped the burden of ordinary taxation. The king, observed a Milanese correspondent, 'has been very active, and has discovered an excellent device to raise money. He has plucked out the feathers of his magpies without making them cry out.'[1] Much of this activity involved the personal exercise of the royal charm. Likely contributors were summoned before the king and cajoled or perhaps bullied into promising payments. According to the *Great Chronicle*, one rich Suffolk widow raised her contribution from £10 to £20 in return for a kiss from the king. By such methods considerable sums were raised – at least £21,656 according to the incomplete surviving returns.[2] One reason why Edward wanted money urgently was that, under the contracts of service signed during the previous summer and autumn, the payment of the first quarter's wages (about £17,696) became due on 31 January 1475, quite apart from heavy expenditure on ordnance, stores and naval preparations.[3] The government was obviously anxious if possible to meet these costs out of ready cash rather than by resort to heavy borrowing, and its difficulties were increased by deficiencies and complications in levying the £51,000 voted by parliament in July 1474.

When parliament reassembled at Westminster for its seventh and final session on 23 January 1475, the commons confessed that there was likely to be delay in payment, 'the form of the levy being so diffuse and laborious' – a clear indication that the machinery could not cope with a new and more sophisticated form of taxation. Even the income tax of 1472, now to be handed over to the king on 4 May, was found to be short because of peculation by the official guardians of the money, and there was a clear danger that the king might lack 'a great part of such sums of money as he should pay at this time to the lords, knights, squires, and others retained with his Highness . . . to the great let and hurt of his said lords, knights, squires and others so retained, and to the great displeasure of our said sovereign lord'.[4] The commons therefore fell back on traditional methods 'as the most easy, ready and prone

[1] *CSP, Milan*, I, 193–4 (letter from London, 17 March 1475).
[2] *GC*, 223; Gray, *op. cit.*, 90–9. Much of the work was done by special commissioners each answering for one or two counties; the amounts paid in by fifteen of these receivers are preserved, but eleven are missing.
[3] Gray, *op. cit.*, 105; Rymer, *Foedera*, XI, 844–8, and for the artillery and naval preparations, below, pp. 218–20.   [4] *RP*, VI, 121, 151.

payment', and on 14 March 1475, to replace the special tax of 1474, they voted the king a whole fifteenth and tenth payable within a fort- night after Easter Day (26 March), and a further three-quarters of a subsidy payable at Martinmas following. Even then Edward was told he could not have the money until he was ready to sail, and the grant would be void if he had not set forth by St John's Day 1476.[1] By this time Edward had received or been promised by his subjects the sub- stantial sum of £180,000 to finance the expedition now in its final stages of preparation.

Whatever their reluctance to pay for the war, English taxpayers could not complain that the king's preparations were on a niggardly scale. No pains were spared to ensure that the English army should be the 'finest, largest, and best appointed force that has ever left England'.[2] Arrangements to provide a suitable commissariat and proper naval and artillery support were begun many months before the date of the invasion. As early as 4 December 1474 the king issued a proclamation forbidding the export from the realm of all cereals, beans, peas, sheep, oxen, cattle and mares. During May and June supplies of wheat, beef, mutton, fish, wine and ale were being organized, and shipping and sailors provided to transport them, and even before Easter the trea- surer of the household, John Elrington, who now became treasurer of war, had already paid out £2,584 12s 9d for wheat and other pro- visions.[3]

The naval preparations, like all other aspects of the war organization, were handled by members of the royal household staff. In December 1474, Avery Cornburgh, a squire of the body, was directed to search out and examine all ships of more than sixteen tons' burthen in the ports of Bristol and the south-west and to requisition them at his discretion for the king's use, and he was also empowered to impress crews for them at the king's wages. Similar commissions were issued to other household men all along the south and east coasts of England. From January onwards a stream of orders went out to shipmasters directing them to find crews and carry out necessary repairs on a num- ber of ships – among them the old king's ship, the *Grace Dieu*, built as long ago as 1439–40, and a handful of other royal ships bought since 1471, including the *Antony* which had brought him back from exile.

[1] *RP*, VI, 149–53.
[2] *CSP, Milan*, I, 197–8 (Thomas de Portinari writing from Bruges, 28 June). See also Commynes, II, 27, for similar remarks.
[3] *CPR, 1467–77*, 515–16, 526–7, 529, 537; Scofield, II, 106, 118; Calmette and Perinelle, 167 n. 3.

Others were hired, their names revealing their home-port or their owner, such as the *Mary Redcliffe* of Bristol, the *Margaret Howard, George Howard* and *Thomas Howard*, and the *Katherine Rivers*. In March the king commissioned the earl of Arundel as constable of Dover and warden of the Cinque Ports to equip and put into service the fifty-seven ships which those ports were traditionally required to supply at their own expense, and to have them before the Downs between Dover and Sandwich by 26 May: the port of Dover found itself paying the wages of the sailors of fourteen ships.[1]

From quite early in 1475 Edward seems to have had small squadrons on sea-patrol: for example, two Bristol shipowners had five ships at sea in the king's service from 3 February until 10 July, at a cost of £190.[2] The nature of their service is not specified, but it was probably connected with Edward's evident concern about the activities of English pirates and possible attacks on the shipping of friendly powers; for during these months he was paying out large sums in compensation to Hansards, Bretons and Castilians who had suffered from English piracy.[3] It was essential to maintain peaceful conditions in the Narrow Seas whilst the English army was in transit to France. For this purpose a fleet was organized under John, Lord Dinham, with the *Grace Dieu* as his flagship, and eight more ships and 3,000 men under his command: this force was being mustered on 10 April in the port of London. But all this placed very heavy demands on the English merchant marine, and, in spite of the careful preparations, it was still necessary to obtain transports for the army from Holland and Zeeland through the good offices of the duke of Burgundy on the eve of the expedition's departure.[4]

Ashore in England men were everywhere busy with military preparations. In December 1474 proclamations were made throughout the country to ensure an abundant supply of England's most renowned weapon, essential in an army nine-tenths composed of archers. The craftsmen involved in the making of bows and arrows were each to

[1] *CPR, 1467-77*, 493-6, 515, 525-6; Rymer, *Foedera*, XI, 839, 843-4, 850-1; XII, 4-5; Calmette and Perinelle, 346-7; and for the king's ships, Richmond, 'English Naval Power in the Fifteenth Century', 13-15.

[2] *CPR, 1467-77*, 543, 545.

[3] *Ibid.*, 480, 511, 521; and for Edward's policy towards piracy in general, see below, pp. 366-7.

[4] Rymer, *Foedera*, XII, 1; *CPR, 1467-77*, 527 (for Dinham's appointment as admiral, 15 April); Scofield, II, 122; Calmette and Perinelle, 168 and n. Commynes, II, 30, gives an estimate of 500 flat-bottomed boats hired from Holland and Zeeland – probably an overestimation; but the exchequer paid out £663 to charter them (Calmette and Perinelle, 168 n. 4, citing Tellers's Rolls).

follow their own particular craft with all possible speed, and commissioners appointed on 8 December were to make purchases of these supplies as they became available: no fewer than 10,000 sheaves of arrows found their way back later to England when the invasion was over.[1] The king was especially concerned to equip his army with a sumptuous artillery train, and here also preparations were begun early. On 18 December 1474 the assistants of the controller of the royal ordnance, William Rosse, were directed to impress carpenters, stone-cutters, smiths, plumbers and other workmen, and to acquire bombards, cannon, culverins, fowlers, serpentines, powder, sulphur, salt-petre, stone, iron, and lead, longbows, crossbows, pikes, hammers and other necessary equipment. The preparations eventually produced a siege and artillery train which one surprised Italian observer pronounced to be even finer than the duke of Burgundy's, and much of the work was done under the daily supervision of the king.[2] At least thirteen great guns, some with their own names – the *Messenger*, the *Edward*, the *Fowler of Chester* and the *Megge*, for example – together with chariots for their transport, gins for loading and unloading, 779 stone cannon balls, and quantities of powder, were later shipped to France.[3]

The army also included a number of specialist craftsmen, who had been commissioned in advance to recruit men of their own trade into the king's service. Amongst them were arras-makers and tapestry-weavers, armourers, saddlers, goldsmiths, chariotmen and carters for the ordnance, pavilioners for the tents, bowyers and fletchers, 'miners' and 'manyoners' who formed a pioneer unit to dig trenches and tunnels. Some of these were there to serve the king's personal comfort – he had ordered the construction of a portable wooden house covered in leather for his use on campaign – but he was also determined not to be outdone in splendour by his brother-in-law of Burgundy. This was an occasion for prestigious display. Over £400 was spent on cloth-of-gold, part of which was made into a robe lined with red satin, probably intended to serve as a coronation garment when he became king of France, and he had already been at pains to find out from the Burgundian master of ceremonies, Olivier de la Marche, the degree of estate kept by Duke Charles at home and on campaign.[4]

[1] Rymer, *Foedera*, XI, 837–9; *CCR, 1468–76*, 376–7; Calmette and Perinelle, 358–61, for indenture of returned equipment, 29 September 1475.
[2] Rymer, *Foedera*, XI, 840–1; *CPR, 1467–77*, 474, 492; *CSP, Milan*, I, 201. An Italian visitor to London, writing on 17 March 1475, remarked on Edward's personal interest in his ordnance: *ibid.*, I, 194.
[3] Scofield, II, 119–20; Calmette and Perinelle, 184, 358–61.
[4] *CPR, 1467–77*, 495–6, 514, 524, 526; Rymer, *Foedera*, XI, 847–8; Scofield, II, 116.

Because of defective exchequer records, the exact size of the army of 1475 cannot be known, but, according to the most recent calculation, it included at least 11,451 combatants, apart from technical personnel, and exclusive of the 2,000 archers sent separately to Brittany.[1] This figure bears out Commynes's claim that it was the largest army with which any English king had ever invaded France.[2] His statement that Edward was attended by almost all the English nobility is also borne out by the facts. The army included all five dukes and the solitary marquis (Dorset); of the seven earls, three accompanied the king, two (Essex and Arundel) were members of the council left behind in England, one (Kent) was represented by his son, Anthony Grey, with a sizeable retinue, and only the old and inactive earl of Westmorland had no share in the expedition; and all except three or four of the sixteen barons available for foreign service were also present.[3] It has recently been stressed, in support of a claim that the war was not generally popular, that a high proportion of the army was raised and commanded by the 'court peers' – kinsmen of the king or those closely connected with the royal service: 11 such peers led 516 men-at-arms and 4,080 archers, with the royal dukes (Clarence with 120 men-at-arms and 1,200 archers, Gloucester with an even larger number) especially prominent.[4] By contrast, 12 'country' peers produced only 231 men-at-arms and 1,619 archers. But the presence of virtually the entire nobility of England certainly impressed a contemporary like Commynes and is telling testimony to the strength of Edward's authority. Only very rarely can so high a proportion of the English peerage have followed their king overseas. Of the non-noble captains, members of the royal household were very conspicuous, some 50 royal officials raising nearly

[1] The fullest analysis of the available material is by Lander, 'The Hundred Years War and Edward IV's Campaign', 91–3 and tables. See also F. P. Barnard, *Edward IV's French Expedition of 1475: the Leaders and their Badges* (from College of Arms, MS. 2 M. 16). The host also included a large number of non-combatants. Edward IV himself told the Milanese ambassador to Burgundy that his force mustered almost 20,000 men (Calmette and Perinelle, 188 n. 1), a point overlooked by Lander.

[2] Commynes, II, 27. Henry V's largest army, in 1417, numbered some 10,000 fighting men (Jacob, *The Fifteenth Century*, 171).

[3] Of the twenty-six barons summoned to the 1472–5 parliament, five were already dead, and one (de la Warr) died soon after; Dacre and Dudley were members of the council in England; Audley was captain of the Breton force, and Dinham was at sea. Two eldest sons of peers (Dacre of the South and Grey of Wilton) also served. There are discrepancies between the lists of those who contracted to serve and those present with the king in France on 13 August 1475, e.g. the duke of Buckingham (Rymer, *Foedera*, XII, 14–15).

[4] Lander, *op. cit.*, 94–5.

3,000 men between them, appreciably more than the various bannerets, knights and esquires without close court connections.[1]

The final muster of the army was originally planned to take place at Portsdown near Portsmouth on 26 May, and orders were sent to all the captains to that effect on 1 February. This rendezvous implied a descent upon Normandy. Very probably because of the singular behaviour of his chief ally, the duke of Burgundy, Edward changed his mind, and some time after 21 April ordered the army to assemble at Barham Downs near Canterbury, a likely place to embark at Dover or Sandwich for a crossing to Calais.[2] As the English captains and their retinues converged on Kent, the king busied himself with his final preparations for departure. The prince of Wales had been brought up from Ludlow on 12 May and was made official head of state, with the title of keeper of the realm during Edward's absence, on 20 June. The actual management of affairs in England was placed in the hands of our great council in England', headed by Cardinal Bourchier of, Canterbury and Bishop Alcock of Rochester, the latter being appointed temporary chancellor during the absence of Bishop Rotherham with the king in France. About the same time he drew up a last will and testament, following the usual practice of kings and great lords going overseas to war.[3] On 30 May he left London by boat for Greenwich and arrived at Canterbury on 7 June, where the army was waiting for him, though the first contingents were already on their way to Calais. In the next three weeks the transhipment of many thousands of men, and even more thousands of horses, proceeded steadily and without interruption from the French. This says a good deal for the efficiency of English naval preparations, but also owed much to the fact that the French, misled by a deceitful message from the count of St Pol, were still expecting a descent upon the coast of Normandy, and their naval forces were still patrolling in that region. Not until late in June, when

---

[1] Lander, 95. E.g. Sir Thomas Burgh, master of the horse, had 16 spears and 160 archers, and three other knights of the body had each 10 spears and 100 archers.

[2] Cf. Scofield, II, 120–1, for a different and unconvincing account of the reasons for this change of plan. It is very unlikely, as she believed, that Edward changed the rendezvous to Barham Downs on the advice of Duke Charles, for Charles wanted Edward to invade Normandy, not to land at Calais. With a great question-mark still hanging over Charles's intentions and ability to help with the required forces, it became essential to land at the English-controlled port of Calais.

[3] CPR, 1467–77, 534–5; Scofield, II, 125–6; Bentley, Excerpta Historica, 366–79 (for the will; for its terms, see below, p. 417). He also made concessions to many of his chief supporters waiving his rights to wardship in the event of their deaths on active service (J. M. W. Bean, The Decline of English Feudalism, 1215–1540, 240–2).

an English herald fell into his hands, did Louis know for certain that Calais was the objective of the English army.[1]

The king himself had hoped to be in Calais by 22 June, but was delayed by shortage of cash. Some he needed for the archers going to Brittany under Audley and Duras, some for his personal spending. The Medici bankers lent him £5,000, and the former Florentine agent, Gerard Caniziani, a further 1,000 marks, but attempts to raise further benevolences from Londoners who had not previously contributed met with disappointing results.[2] At last on 4 July Edward crossed to Calais, fifteen years after his last visit as an exile in Warwick's tutelage.

What were Edward IV's war aims in 1475? Philippe de Commynes – writing after the event – believed that he never intended a serious invasion of France: his love of ease and pleasure made him temperamentally unsuited to the labour involved in a war of conquest.[3] Some continental observers shared this view. In August 1474, soon after signing his alliance with Burgundy, Edward sent Falcon Herald to Louis to demand the formal surrender of Normandy and Gascony, and to threaten war if this were refused. According to Christopher Bollati, then Milanese ambassador, his true intention was to suggest a marriage alliance between the dauphin of France and an English princess and he might even join Louis in an attack on Burgundy, but it is far more likely that this was another example of the dual diplomacy characteristic of the age, and was designed merely to lull or distract Louis's suspicions. This was certainly the sense in which Louis viewed the gesture.[4] Even as late as March 1475 an Italian visitor to London, who had first-hand knowledge of English military preparations, including the date of the army's muster, could still express doubts about whether the English would actually sail for France.[5] But more realistic observers on the Continent had no such reservations. Louis XI himself had no doubt about English intentions. Even before the end of 1474 he had embarked on a series of expensive and unpopular defensive measures, which multiplied as news of English mobilization began to reach France, and he was already working hard diplomatically to make things as difficult as possible for the Anglo-Burgundian alliance.[6]

---

[1] CC, 558; Commynes, II, 30–1; Jean de Roye, Journal, I, 334; Scofield, II, 130–1.
[2] Rymer, Foedera, XII, 7–11; CCR, 1468–76, 388–9; Halliwell, Letters of the King of England, I, 144; Scofield, II, 127–8.
[3] Commynes, II, 76, 241, 245–6, a view of Edward's actions reproduced by some modern scholars, e.g. Calmette and Perinelle, 161; CSP, Milan, I, 178.
[4] CSP, Milan, I, 182–3; Calmette and Perinelle, 164.
[5] CSP, Milan, I, 194.
[6] Calmette and Perinelle, 168–73, 178, and further below.

Louis was right to take Edward seriously. All the lengthy diplomatic, financial and military preparations which have been reviewed strongly suggest that Edward hoped that in combination with the powerful forces of Burgundy he could inflict a substantial defeat upon King Louis. We may perhaps agree with Commynes that Edward was not the man to contemplate anything like the long, patient war of sieges and piecemeal occupation which had been the basis of Henry V's strategy in France. But with aid from Burgundy, and other disaffected elements in France, the invaders might hope to force substantial territorial concessions from Louis in the course of a single campaign. The recovery of Normandy and Gascony for the English Crown would have been a substantial achievement, though whether we are justified in regarding this as 'a defensive reaction to the complications and dangers of the international situation' seems disputable.[1]

That Edward regarded the full and active cooperation of Burgundy as an essential feature of his war plans seems beyond serious dispute. But in the months before he crossed to France the strange behaviour of the duke of Burgundy had begun to cause him serious concern. Not content with his existing problems in the east, Charles had involved himself in a struggle for the control of the Rhineland archbishopric of Cologne, and, on 30 July 1474, laid siege to the small but well-fortified city of Neuss. Help for the citizens poured in from neighbouring towns, and the besiegers suffered heavy losses, whilst an active French diplomacy drew into the war against Burgundy the Emperor Frederick III, the young Duke Réné of Lorraine, and, most formidable of all, the Swiss, who defeated a Burgundian army at Héricourt on 13 November. The siege dragged on into the winter months.[2]

At first Edward seemed unconcerned by his ally's behaviour, and even allowed a force of English archers (said by Commynes to be 3,000 strong) to serve in the Burgundian army.[3] But when, about the end of January, as orders to muster the English army were being sent out, English envoys headed by Dr John Morton returned from Neuss with reports that Duke Charles was still persisting stubbornly in the siege, the English king and council became more anxious. In March Lord Dacre and Edward's secretary, William Hatcliffe, were sent to Duchess Margaret to seek her good offices with her husband, and, when this

---

[1] Lander, *op. cit.*, 100.

[2] Bartier, *Charles le Téméraire*, 167 ff.; Kendall, *Louis XI*, 262–73.

[3] Commynes, II, 8. Rymer, *Foedera*, XI, 791, prints a commission to Sir John Parr and William Sturgeon to muster a force of 13 men-at-arms and 1,000 archers for service with the duke.

failed, Earl Rivers was sent directly to Neuss to remind the duke of his treaty obligations to England. He reached Charles's camp on 29 April, only a month before the final mobilization of the English army was due; but the duke proved deaf to arguments that the campaigning season was slipping away and threats that Edward might not come at all. Only King Louis's two-pronged invasion of the duke's dominions (north into Picardy and the Somme valley, and east into Burgundy proper and Franche-Comté) finally compelled the obstinate Charles to abandon the siege, although he hung on there until 13 June. His funds were exhausted and, it was said, his army was so battered that he did not wish the English to see it. A month later he was back in Flanders to meet his ally, but instead of the splendid army Edward had hoped for he was accompanied by only a small personal retinue.[1]

The king of France seems to have hoped that his pre-emptive invasion of Picardy and Burgundy's immobilization at Neuss might deter Edward from crossing to France at all, but this time he was to be disappointed. They did, however, cause Edward to change his plans. Instead of landing in Normandy, as Charles wished him to do, Edward chose Calais, since a safe port for disembarkation of the army was now essential. But the duke's defaulting on his treaty obligations also brought into question the whole purpose of the campaign. Without effective cooperation from Burgundy, Edward might have preferred not to go at all. This, however, was out of the question. To disband his army tamely after so much public money had been spent would have been extremely unpopular, even politically dangerous, as well as outraging the sentiments of the rank-and-file of his troops.[2] English public opinion and his own prestige demanded that he should go. But even before he sailed for Calais Edward and his advisers were probably considering ways and means of extricating themselves from this risky commitment.

Some indication of how they were thinking comes from the proposals put to Garter Herald whom Edward sent to France shortly before the invasion began. The main authority for the confidential aspects of his mission is the testimony of Philippe de Commynes, then a

---

[1] Commynes, II, 14–16, 17–19, 26–7; T. Basin, *Histoire de Louis XI*, ed. Samaran, II, 233 ff.; *CSP, Milan*, I, 195–6; Scofield, II, 122–4; Calmette and Perinelle, 180–1. Vaughan, *op. cit.*, 344–5, has shown recently that the effects of the siege of Neuss for the Burgundian army have been exaggerated, and that Charles's joining Edward with only his household men was part of a deliberate plan.

[2] Commynes, II, 76–7, who also suggests that Edward wanted to keep the war-taxes for himself. James III of Scotland told Louis XI that Edward would face rebellion if he gave up his expedition to France and disbanded the army (Scofield, II, 53–4).

confidential councillor of King Louis, whose narrative of the events of 1475 possesses a quality rare in late medieval historians – the inside knowledge of political decisions at a high level.[1] Garter's official mission was to present Edward's formal defiance and to demand the surrender of the kingdom of France. But in private audience Louis told Garter that he knew Edward was coming to France under pressure from Burgundy and the commons of England, that the campaigning season was already well advanced, and that he could hope for little from an impoverished Burgundy or a treacherous St Pol. Should Edward not consider the advantages of a settlement with France? Garter is said to have made the significant admission that his master would be very ready to listen to any French overtures, but only after he had landed in France. Louis should then send envoys, and also make approaches to two men high in Edward's confidence, John, Lord Howard, who had emerged in recent years as one of Edward's principal diplomatists, and Thomas, Lord Stanley, then steward of the household. It is unlikely that an envoy of Garter's status would have said as much without instructions from the king and his close advisers in England. Since there is no good reason to suppose that Commynes invented the story, the episode strongly suggests that Edward's prime intention on reaching France was to seek a settlement with King Louis, and to end the whole adventure with profit if not with honour.

(iii) The Invasion of France, 1475

The 'great enterprise of France' began inauspiciously, with ten days' loitering in Calais to await the coming of Duke Charles of Burgundy. His arrival with no more than a bodyguard at his back caused consternation in the English army. Some of the lords were for abandoning the invasion forthwith, but many of the rank-and-file, 'studying glory rather than their own ease', declared that they could manage perfectly well without Charles's troops, and that they should carry on with the campaign they had come for.[2] However much Edward may have shared his captains' sentiments, he would have faced an uproar at home if he had given up his venture without ever leaving Calais. As with Henry V after his eventual capture of Harfleur in 1415, some military gesture was necessary to satisfy English public opinion. Probably mainly for this reason, he agreed to the duke's proposal that the English should advance eastwards through his own territories to Péronne, then into France to the town of St Quentin, which the count of St Pol was still

[1] Commynes, II, 36–7.   [2] CC, 558.

9b. Margaret of York, duchess of Burgundy, sister of Edward IV. Her collar is composed of red and white marguerites, and the pendants have alternating letters C (for Duke Charles) and interlinked Vs, to form the capital M. A contemporary portrait by an anonymous Franco-Flemish artist.

9a. Charles the Bold, duke of Burgundy. Painted about 1474. From his collar hangs the ram, the insignia of the Burgundian Order of the Golden Fleece.

10a. Louis of Bruges, lord of Gruythuys, wearing the collar of the Golden Fleece. Painted 1472–82. (*Musée Groeninge, Brussels*)

10b. Letter of Edward IV in exile, written from St Pol, 9 January 1471, to the duke of Brittany, requesting his aid in the recovery of his realm. The letter is in a secretary's hand, with Edward's autograph signature: Voster cousyn Edward R. (*B.M., Add. MS. 21, 404, fol. 5*)

11. Edward IV, as Hadrian, kneeling before Trajan. Margaret of York stands to his right. From a French version of the Romuléon of Roberto della Porta, executed about 1480 by a Flemish artist for a manuscript commissioned by Edward IV. (*B.M., Royal MS. 19 E V*)

12b. Edward IV. Panel portrait, c. 1530.
(National Portrait Gallery, London)

12a. Edward IV. Panel portrait, c. 1516.
(Society of Antiquaries of London)

13b. King Louis XI. Limestone head from Toul, now in the Art Institute of Chicago.

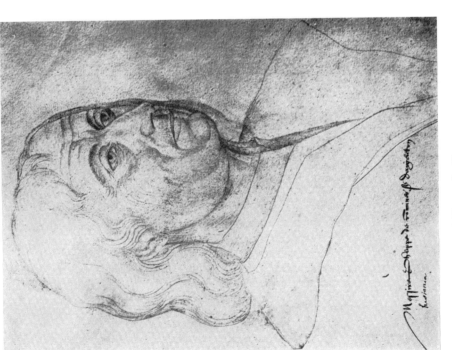

13a. Portrait of Philippe de Commynes.

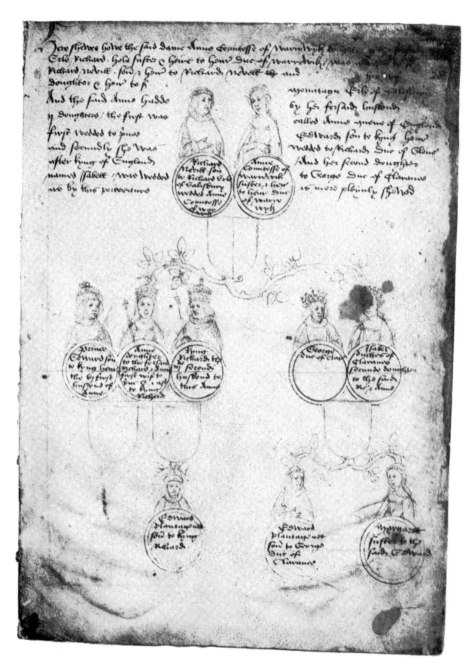

14. Warwick the Kingmaker and his family, showing below, left, his younger daughter, Anne, and her two husbands, Edward, prince of Wales, son of Henry VI, and Richard, duke of Gloucester, and, right, the elder daughter, Isabel, and her husband, George, duke of Clarence. From the Beauchamp Pageant, written and illustrated in England, c. 1472–85.

(*B.M., Cottonian MS., Julius E IV, fol. 2d*)

15a. Enlarged detail of the figures of Clarence and his wife, Isabel. Modern drawing from the Rous Roll below.

15b. Section from the Rous Roll (*B.M.*, *Add. MS. 48976*), showing Clarence, Duchess Isabel, and their son, Edward, with their emblems, the bear of Warwick and the bull of Clarence. English, probably 1483–5.

16. Richard III. Panel portrait, probably the earliest surviving, by an unknown artist. Before 1485.

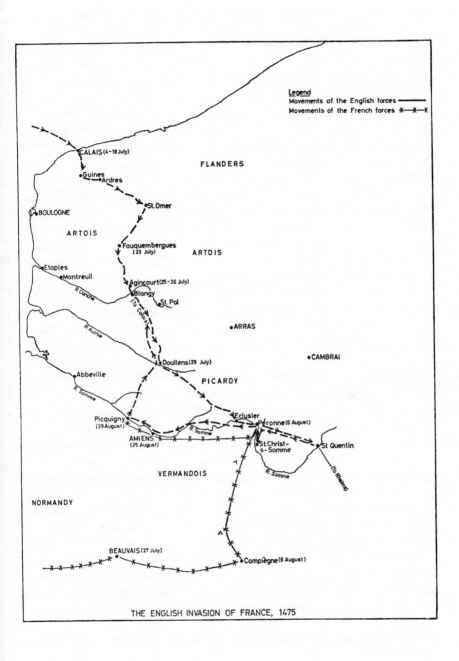

Legend
Movements of the English forces ━━━━━
Movements of the French forces ✕━✕━✕

CALAIS (4 – 18 July)

FLANDERS

●Guines
●Ardres

●St.Omer

●BOULOGNE

ARTOIS

●Fauquembergues
(23 July)

ARTOIS

●Etaples
●Montreuil

R. Canche

Agincourt (25 – 26 July)
Blangy
St.Pol

(To Calais)

●ARRAS

R. Authie

●CAMBRAI

Doullens (29 July)

●Abbeville

PICARDY

R. Somme

Eclusier

Picquigny
(29 August)

Péronne (6 August)

AMIENS
(25 August)

St.Christ-
s-Somme

●St Quentin

R. Somme

VERMANDOIS

R. Somme

(To Bretms)

NORMANDY

BEAUVAIS (27 July)

Compiègne (6 August)

THE ENGLISH INVASION OF FRANCE, 1475

offering to deliver, and thence by way of Laon to Rheims. Charles himself promised to rejoin his army in the east, crush the duke of Lorraine, and meet the English forces in Champagne. The allies were fortunate in that King Louis's main forces were in Normandy, and, even after he had learnt that the English had landed at Calais, Louis still believed that their principal attack would be directed southwards against Normandy, and took measures accordingly. Charles argued that the French army could cover only Normandy effectively and that St Quentin was the key to Champagne. Once in Rheims Edward might be crowned king of France and would soon win recognition as the country's legitimate ruler.[1]

On 18 July, therefore, the king and the duke led the English army from Calais through Ardres and Guines to St Omer, and thence, on 23 July, to Fauquembergue. Then two nights were spent at the historic site of Agincourt, and by way of St Pol they reached Doullens on 28 July. By now King Louis had divined the English plan, and, leaving a holding force in Normandy, set off with his main army on a route roughly parallel with the English line of advance. By the end of July, with some 6,000 men, he had reached Beauvais. On 1 August Edward and his army resumed their march in a south-easterly direction. Crossing the Somme they encamped on 5 August at Eclusier, a few kilometres from Péronne, with the river at their backs, and on the next day Duke Charles arrived in Péronne. There a messenger came in from the count of St Pol, expressing his continued willingness to deliver up St Quentin. But when an English detachment moved forward to the town, they were surprised to be met with cannon-fire from the walls and an attack from skirmishers. After losing a few men, the English withdrew and marched back through heavy rain to the army's main camp, which was now (by 12 August) at St Christ-sur-Somme, just south of Peronne. As if this were not enough, there was now ill-feeling between Edward and Charles over the refusal of the duke to admit the English into any of his towns. Even the gates of Péronne, where the duke lay in comfort, were closed to his allies.[2]

For Edward these irritations probably provided the final touch of disillusionment. His position gave little encouragement to pursue a bold policy. Behind him the French were already devastating Artois and Picardy, and provisions for the English army would soon become a

---

[1] CSP, Milan, I, 196–7; Gingins la Sarraz, Dépêches, I, 154–60, 192–5; Calmette and Perinelle, 185–7.
[2] This account of the movements of the English army follows the reconstruction of Calmette and Perinelle, 187–90; cf. Scofield, II, 132–3.

problem. Ahead, Rheims and other French towns were now strongly garrisoned and fortified and on the alert. From a military standpoint, any further advance into France would be dangerous unless Duke Charles could guarantee much more active help. Summer was drawing to a close, but where were the English to find winter quarters if Burgundy denied them entry to his towns? Edward himself, who had little natural taste for campaigning, probably viewed the prospect of wintering in France with little relish. Nor had he the funds to keep his army in the field indefinitely. His captains, who had enjoyed no chance to enrich themselves or their men with plunder, may already have been chafing. The king later told the duke of Burgundy that, although they had been paid for six months, they were complaining that they had been at great expense for a variety of reasons, and were reluctant to serve much longer without a further instalment of wages, especially if they were to organize winter quarters.[1]

These logistic arguments were reinforced by Edward's political disappointments. Brittany had made no move. The count of St Pol, as Louis had predicted, had defaulted on his promises. There was no sign of the hoped-for rising of the French feudality. Burgundy himself had failed to carry out his part of their contract. To proceed with the agreed plan involved gambling on the duke's good faith and his ability to deal with his enemies in distant Lorraine; but they had no means of knowing how long this might take, or whether the now almost bankrupt duke could raise an army to take the field. There seemed to be every prospect that the English might be left to fight the French alone, something which Edward had always wished to avoid. The French were numerically far superior, and the English troops were not the seasoned warriors trained in continental warfare who had been available a generation previously.[2] No doubt these were the arguments of discretion rather than valour. Perhaps they would have held less appeal to an Edward III or a Henry V. But to Edward and most of his noble captains they were cogent reasons for making terms with the French as soon as possible. When Duke Charles – rather unwisely, considering the temper of his allies – left Péronne about 12 August to join his own men in Bar, the English lost no time in entering into negotiations with King Louis.

---

[1] Some of these arguments are set forth in a memorandum sent by Edward to Duke Charles at Namur on 26 August (*CSP, Milan*, I, 202–4; Calmette and Perinelle, 356–8); others derive from the comments of the Milanese correspondents and Commynes (II, 38–9, 76).

[2] *Ibid.*, II, 28–9; Lander, *op. cit.*, 97–8 (who, however, too readily dismisses the military experience of the English gained in their own civil wars).

Their first approach was a diplomatic finesse worthy of King Louis himself. They released a French prisoner, a valet in the service of one of Louis's household gentlemen, Jacques de Gracay, and he was given a crown each by Lords Howard and Stanley and told to recommend them to the king of France. Remembering what Garter King of Arms had told him of these two noblemen, Louis interpreted the signs correctly. In reply he sent back a young valet of his household who was briefed by Commynes personally. He was instructed to tell the king of England that Louis had always wished for peace with England, and that any apparently hostile acts he had committed were, in reality, directed against the duke of Burgundy, a prince concerned only with his own interests. He was to say that Louis knew that Edward had been at great expense, and that many of his subjects in England wanted war with France. Nevertheless, if Edward would consider a treaty, then Louis could offer terms which might please both the king and his people. A meeting could be arranged, either for French envoys to visit the English camp, or half-way between the armies with delegates from both sides. After consultation with his advisers, Edward agreed.[1]

On 13 August he drew up instructions for his delegates, John, Lord Howard, Sir Thomas St Leger, Dr John Morton, master of the rolls, and William Dudley, dean of the chapel royal, and he took care to have them witnessed by his brothers, Clarence and Gloucester, and the other leading members of his company.[2] King Louis similarly empowered his own representatives, headed by the admiral of France, Jean, bastard of Bourbon, and the next day the two parties met in a village not far from Amiens. The English proposals were precise and practical. The king of France was to undertake to pay Edward 75,000 crowns (£15,000) within fifteen days, and 50,000 crowns (£10,000) yearly thereafter for as long as they both lived. His heir, the dauphin, was to marry Edward's first or second daughter, and to provide her with a livelihood of £60,000 yearly in French values. If this were agreed upon, Edward would take his army back to England as soon as possible, leaving behind hostages who should be released as soon as the larger part of the army was safely home. Edward also wanted a 'private amity' binding himself and Louis to aid each other in case either was 'wronged or disobeyed' by his subjects, and a truce and an 'intercourse

---

[1] Commynes, II, 39–45, for a detailed account of all this.
[2] Rymer, *Foedera*, XII, 14–15. Buckingham was not present on this occasion, which confirms the entry against his retinue in Barnard, *op. cit.*, 'Returned Home'. In view of his relations with Edward (below, p. 335), it would be interesting to know why.

of merchandise' for seven years.[1] Louis, anxious to come to terms before the duke of Burgundy returned, or any other dangers developed, agreed at once to the English offer, and urgent instructions were sent out to his agents to raise the sums necessary to meet the English demands and further monies intended as bribes to win the goodwill of some of the English lords.[2] By 18 August the terms of the truce had been decided, and plans made for a meeting between the two sovereigns on the Somme near Amiens. To satisfy the pride of the English soldiers, both armies should march to the rendezvous in battle-array, before the leaders met on a convenient bridge with the river separating the two forces.

Neither the fury and contempt of Duke Charles, who returned to the English camp from Valenciennes on 19 August, nor the pleadings of St Pol, had any effect upon the resolve of Edward and his captains. Both were told, in effect, that they had forfeited all claim to consideration. Charles was also informed that he could be included in the truce with France if he gave three months' notice, but he angrily refused the offer and withdrew to Namur.[3] On 25 August the French and English armies both appeared near Amiens. Anxious to win the goodwill of the English rank-and-file, Louis provided food and wine in great quantities and instructed the innkeepers of Amiens to issue free drink to any English soldier who cared to ask for it. No English army is, or ever has been, proof against this temptation. For three or four days the English troops drank happily at French expense, and Amiens was full of thousands of sodden men-at-arms and archers. Eventually Edward himself was forced to eject his men from the city and post a guard at the gate.[4]

Arrangements went ahead, meanwhile, for the meeting of the two kings. At Picquigny, three miles down-river from Amiens, where the Somme was narrow but not fordable, a bridge was built with a screen across the centre, pierced by a trellis through which conversation could be carried on: these precautions were taken to prevent any repetition of the treachery which had cost the life of John, duke of Burgundy, at a similar meeting on the bridge of Montereau in September 1419. For what followed we have the invaluable eye-witness testimony of Philippe de Commynes.[5] Impressed by the apparent size of the English army

---

[1] Rymer, *Foedera*, XII, 14–15. Cf. Commynes, II, 46.

[2] Commynes, II, 47–8, 52–3; Vaesen, *Lettres de Louis XI*, VI, 12; Calmette and Perinelle, 196–8.   [3] Commynes, II, 52–4; *CSP, Milan*, I, 204–9.

[4] Commynes, II, 54–9, for details of the English spree.

[5] *Ibid.*, 63–7 (my translation: that of A. R. Scobie, Commynes, II, 274–7, is often misleading: e.g. Edward did not speak 'very good French', merely 'assez bon français').

drawn up in order ('an incredibly large number of horsemen'), the French royal party first took up their position on the bridge, and then, says Commynes:

> The king of England came along the causeway which I mentioned and was well attended. He appeared a truly regal figure. With him were his brother, the duke of Clarence, the earl of Northumberland, and several lords including his chamberlain, Lord Hastings, his Chancellor and others. There were only three or four others dressed in cloth of gold like King Edward, who wore a black velvet cap on his head decorated with a large fleur-de-lis of precious stones. He was a very good-looking, tall prince, but he was beginning to get fat and I had seen him on previous occasions looking more handsome. Indeed I do not recall ever having seen such a fine-looking man as he was when my lord of Warwick forced him to flee from England.
>
> When he was within four or five feet of the barrier he raised his hat and bowed to within six inches of the ground. The King, who was already leaning on the barrier, returned his greeting with much politeness. They began to embrace each other through the holes and the king of England made another even deeper bow. The King began the conversation and said to him, 'My lord, my cousin, you are very welcome. There's nobody in the world whom I would want to meet more than you. And God be praised that we have met here for this good purpose.'
>
> The king of England replied to this in quite good French.

After an address by the English chancellor, Bishop Rotherham, articles of the treaty were exchanged, and the two kings solemnly swore to observe them. The French king then fell to banter, and jokingly told Edward that

> he ought to come to Paris, that he would dine him with the ladies and that he would give my lord the cardinal of Bourbon as confessor, since the latter would very willingly absolve him from sin if he should have committed any, because he knew the cardinal was a jolly good fellow.

The escorts then withdrew and the two monarchs conversed privately for a while. Commynes noted as evidence of Edward's good memory that, when Louis asked Edward if he remembered Commynes, the latter said he did, and 'mentioned the places where he had seen me and that previously I had put myself to much trouble in serving him at Calais'. The kings then discussed the position of Burgundy and Brittany, with Edward replying that he did not care what happened to Burgundy if he did not choose to keep the truce, but pleading that Brittany should be included in the truce, saying he did not want to make war on the duke of Brittany, for 'in his moment of need he had never found such a good friend'. After further polite exchanges, the meeting broke up. Commynes records that Duke Richard of Gloucester and several others were not pleased by the peace, but became reconciled to it, and Gloucester visited Louis at Amiens, and received from him some very fine presents.

The practical outcome of this meeting was a group of diplomatic instruments which have come to be called collectively the Treaty of Picquigny of 29 August 1475. Its terms, which were to govern Anglo-French relations until almost the end of Edward's reign, may be summarized as follows:

1. A truce between the two kings and their allies to last for seven years, until sundown on 29 August 1482.

2. Freedom of mercantile intercourse for the merchants of each realm in the other's countries, with the abolition of all tolls and charges imposed upon English merchants during the previous twelve years, and similar privileges for Frenchmen trading in English territory.

3. Edward was to depart peacefully from France as soon as he had received the 75,000 crowns, promised by the French king, leaving behind him John, Lord Howard, and Sir John Cheyne as hostages for his speedy return.

4. Any differences between the two countries were to be referred to four arbitrators, Cardinal Bourchier and the duke of Clarence for England, and the archbishop of Lyons and the count of Dunois for France.

5. A treaty of amity and marriage. Neither king should enter into any league with any ally of the other without his knowledge. As soon as they reached marriageable age, the Dauphin Charles should marry Elizabeth of York, with a jointure of £60,000 yearly provided by King Louis, and her sister, Mary, should take her place should Elizabeth die. Further, if either king found himself confronted by armed rebellion, the other must lend support.

6. An undertaking by King Louis to pay Edward 50,000 gold crowns each year in the city of London, by equal instalments at Easter and Michaelmas, and a guarantee for the payment of this pension either in the form of a bond by the Medici bank or a papal bull imposing interdict on his realm if he defaulted.[1]

---

[1] Rymer, *Foedera*, XII, 15–21. The crown was defined as 33 'grand blancs' of French money, of which the English equivalent was given by Fabyan as 4s. Hence the down-payment was worth £15,000 sterling, and the annual pension £10,000 as correctly stated by the Croyland Chronicler, 558.

Edward lost no time in carrying out his first commitment under the Treaty. Having collected 55,000 crowns of his initial Danegeld, he accepted a bond under the great seal of France for the remainder, and at once the English army began its march to Calais, which it reached without serious incident on 4 September. Its transshipment to England began forthwith. Edward himself lingered in Calais until 18 September, and he did not return to London until 28 September, to be escorted through the city by the mayor and aldermen and 500 members of the guilds. The 'great enterprise' was over.[1]

It was scarcely to be expected that the inglorious outcome of the 1475 expedition would be popular with the mass of Edward's subjects. His leading captains and councillors had solid inducements to approve their master's policy. Like Edward, they were quite ready to accept pensions and gifts from the French king. John, Lord Howard, and Sir Thomas Montgomery got pensions of 1,200 crowns (£200), the chancellor, Bishop Rotherham, had 1,000 and John Morton, master of the rolls, 600. According to Commynes, further pensions were paid to the Marquis of Dorset, Sir John Cheyne and Sir Thomas St Leger.[2] The largest pension of all went to the most influential of Edward's councillors, William, Lord Hastings, who now received an annual fee of 2,000 crowns. But Hastings displayed a remarkable independence of mind, and even this large sum did not buy his goodwill, for he afterwards took a notably individual line on the problem of the Burgundian succession.[3] Nor was this all. Sparing no expense to win the good offices of influential Englishmen, Louis loaded them with presents of money and plate. Howard is said to have received as much as 24,000 crowns (£4,000) in this fashion within two years; Hastings had 1,000 marks' worth of plate in a single gift, and many other English captains were among the beneficiaries.[4] It would perhaps be too cynical to suggest that these were the only reasons why these royal advisers and servants so readily agreed to the abandonment of the campaign. The Croyland Chronicler, himself a councillor, regarded the treaty as 'an honourable peace' and observed that 'in this light it was regarded by the higher officers of the royal army'.[5]

But many outside the royal circle took a very different view. Amongst

[1] Commynes, II, 75; GC, 224; PL, V, 237; Calmette and Perinelle, 206.
[2] Commynes, II, 52, 241–2. Record evidence survives to confirm that pensions were paid to Hastings, Howard, Montgomery, Rotherham and Morton (Calmette and Perinelle, 214–16, 374–5: quittances given by them to Louis's agents), but not for the other three.
[3] Commynes, II, 242–3.
[4] *Ibid.*, 241–2; Scofield, II, 147.   [5] *CC*, 559.

the soldiers of the army there was indignation at what they regarded as their leaders' tame surrender to the French offers. Some took service with the duke of Burgundy to get the plunder and fighting for which they had come to France.[1] A sense of disgrace and injured martial pride is reflected in the bitter words of Louis de Bretelles, a Gascon in the service of Earl Rivers, when he told Commynes that Edward had won nine victories and lost only one battle, the present one; and that the shame of returning to England in these circumstances outweighed the honour he had gained from the other nine. The king of France realized how sensitive were the English on this issue. He had jested incautiously that he had easily driven them from France with venison pasties and fine wines, and then became greatly concerned lest news should leak to the English of this mockery. But there was little he could do to check the jeers of his people. A version of the royal jibe became the theme of a popular French song:[2]

> J'ay vu le roy d'Angleterre
> Amener son grand ost
> Pour la françois terre
> Conquester bref et tost.

> Le roy voyant l'affaire
> Si bon vin leur donna
> Que l'autre sans rien faire
> Content s'en retourna.

Similar taunts were thrown at the two hostages, Howard and Cheyne, who, after being royally entertained in Paris, accompanied King Louis to Vervins for the signing of a truce with Burgundy. When one of them commented on the large numbers of men in Charles's train, the vicomte de Narbonne, who was standing nearby, remarked on the simplicity of the Englishmen in supposing that the duke had no troops at his disposal, but, he went on, 'you English were so anxious to return home that 600 pipes of wine and a pension which the king gave you sent you post-haste back to England'. The angry Englishman replied that it was tribute-money, not a pension, and threatened that the English army might return. Even the count of St Pol, now desperate between the grindstones of Louis and Duke Charles, both of whom he had betrayed, could call Edward a poor, dishonourable and cowardly king.[3]

1 Calmette and Perinelle, 209; Scofield, II, 148.
2 Calmette and Perinelle, 207 (for the verse); Commynes, II, 70–1.
3 *Ibid.*, II, 78–9.

Reactions in England were coloured not only by outraged national pride but also by resentment that so much public money had been spent to produce such an inglorious outcome. That Edward feared the hostility of his subjects is shown by his failure to make public much of the Treaty of Picquigny, especially the undertakings for mutual aid which he had exchanged with Louis, though news of both the French pension and the marriage alliance found its way into contemporary English chronicles.[1] Rumours were rife on the Continent about the dangers which awaited Edward on his return home. Duke Charles was confidently predicting revolution when the English learnt what had happened. It was even said that Edward dared not let his brothers reach home before him, 'as he feared some disturbance, especially as the duke of Clarence, on a previous occasion, aspired to make himself king'. The Milanese ambassador at the Burgundian court, Panicharolla, reported that the people of England were extremely irritated at the accord, 'cowardly as it is, because they paid large sums of money without any result'.[2]

In practice, these predictions proved to be wide of the mark, so far as may be judged from the meagre English sources of the time. Certainly, there was no outburst of resentment beyond Edward's capacity to suppress. The Croyland Chronicler reports criticisms of the peace with France, and that disturbances following on the disbandment of the army forced Edward to make a judicial progress through Hampshire and Wiltshire in November and December 1475. He also expressed the opinion that it was as well that Edward acted speedily and vigorously to put an end to 'this commencement of mischief', for otherwise

> the number of people complaining of the unfair management of the resources of the kingdom, in consequence of such quantities of treasure being abstracted from the coffers of everyone and uselessly consumed, would have increased to such a degree that no one could have said whose head, among the king's advisers, was in safety; and the more especially those, who, induced by friendship for the French king or by his presents, had persuaded the king to make the peace previously mentioned.[3]

There was enough resentment on this issue of waste of taxpayers' money for Edward to feel compelled to remit the three-quarters of the fifteenth and tenth due for collection at Martinmas. With Louis's cash in his pocket, and more to come, he could afford this gesture of pacification.

[1] CC, 558; GC, 224; Kingsford, Chronicles of London, 187.
[2] CSP, Milan, I, 211, 217.   [3] CC, 559.

But it is unlikely that he made any profit out of the war-taxation, as some continental critics suggested, and even more unlikely that (as Commynes believed) the hope of reserving to himself large sums from the proceeds of the taxes had been a major reason for his abandoning the campaign.[1]

If Edward had failed to realize his proffered schemes of foreign conquest, he could at least claim that the settlement of 1475 brought substantial advantages for his countrymen. The implementation of the commercial agreement at Picquigny, and the removal of all the irksome and expensive restrictions on English trade with France, brought considerable benefits to English merchants and producers, especially those of the south-west, and made a contribution to the commercial prosperity of Edward's later years no less important than the treaties with the Burgundians and the Hansards.[2]

Indirectly, Englishmen also benefited from Edward's French pension, which helped to make him largely independent of parliamentary taxation for the rest of the reign. Louis XI was at pains to ensure that the pensions to Edward and his councillors were promptly and regularly paid, despite the fact that they represented a heavy annual charge of 56,000 crowns – for he had not, in fact, bought peace with the English for the price of a few venison pies and consignments of wine.[3] The royal revenue was further augmented by the somewhat cynical bargain between the two kings over the person of Queen Margaret of Anjou. Whether or not the question of her ransom was discussed at Picquigny we do not know, but arrangements were soon put in hand for her release from captivity. In September 1475, Sir Thomas Montgomery was sent to France to discuss terms. Edward was to surrender all rights over her, and transfer them to Louis in return for a ransom of 50,000 crowns (£10,000), of which sum the first 10,000 should be paid when Margaret was handed over, and the rest in annual instalments. She was also to agree to renounce formally all title to the Crown of England, to her dower lands, and any other claims she might have against Edward. The transfer was completed at Rouen on 22 January 1476, after she had signed the necessary instruments of renunciation. But the unfortunate queen had merely exchanged one captor for another, and to obtain her liberty she had to give up all claims to the Angevin inheritance of her father, King Réné of Anjou, and her mother, Isabella of Lorraine. For the last six years of her life – she died

1 Commynes, II, 76. For the remission of the tax, see *Records of the Borough of Nottingham*, II, 388-9.
2 Below, pp. 368-70.   3 Calmette and Perinelle, 208, 214-16.

on 25 August 1482 – she was wholly dependent on the modest pension paid her by the king of France.[1]

Both the king and his subjects benefited substantially from the peaceful outcome of his French adventure. Its satisfactory if somewhat inglorious conclusion should not, however, be seen as any great tribute to Edward's statesmanship. He had fully intended to mount a major military attack upon France, and, with Burgundian aid, to extract considerable territorial concessions from her king. Even if he did not seriously seek to make himself king of France, the defence of any continental conquests would surely have involved him in years of expensive warfare, as English experience under Edward III and Henry VI had proved. The days when England, even in alliance with Burgundy, could seriously challenge the most powerful and wealthy state in Europe were long since past. But only the unexpected failure of Burgundy to cooperate effectively in Edward's plans enabled him to extricate himself sensibly and profitably. Peace with France, and the avoidance of expensive foreign entanglements, was achieved largely through good fortune rather than good judgement. Moreover, as the events of the next few years were to show, there was a price to be paid for the benefits won at Picquigny. Edward's desire to retain his French pension and the French marriage planned for his daughter severely limited his freedom of diplomatic manœuvre after 1475. They purchased English acquiescence in the partial dismemberment of the Burgundian state by Louis of France.

[1] Calmette and Perinelle, 210–12; Scofield, II, 157–9.

Chapter 10

FAMILY, POLITICS AND
FOREIGN RELATIONS, 1475–1480

The five years following the Treaty of Picquigny saw Edward at the peak of his career. Peace at home and abroad brought his realm an interlude of quiet and prosperity all too rare in fifteenth-century England. The Crown had benefited not only from the tactful accommodation with France but from the rising profits of customs duties and the absence of any extraordinary demands on income. With his debts paid, and a handsome reserve in his treasury, Edward's accounts at last showed a substantial credit. He now had the money and the leisure to indulge freely his taste for private pleasure, to finance his building schemes, to enlarge his collection of manuscripts and jewels, and to maintain a splendid court. With a large and growing family to provide for, he could set out on the search for suitable dynastic marriages. Abroad, France and Burgundy competed for his alliance, or at least his benevolent neutrality. Amidst all this confident security, only his final breach with Clarence, and the duke's attainder and death in February 1478, provided an unhappy epilogue to the political strife of his earlier years.

(i) *The Fall of Clarence*

Clarence soon showed that he had failed to learn any lessons from his previous experience of intrigue and treachery, and eventually he tried his brother's patience too far. Contintental gossips believed that there was still mistrust between them, and that the duke would be the natural leader of any rebellion.[1] That Edward himself had little confidence in his brother became clear soon after the death of Duke Charles of Burgundy in January 1477. Clarence's wife, Duchess Isabel, had died at Warwick Castle on 22 December 1476, having never fully recovered from the birth of her second son, Richard, in the previous

---

[1] Above, p. 192.

October. The duke was thus free to marry again, and his sister, the dowager duchess Margaret of Burgundy, is said to have urged Edward to allow him to wed Charles's daughter and heiress, Mary of Burgundy. But Edward would not hear of it. The dangers were obvious, for the ducal house of Burgundy had a respectable claim to the English throne.[1] Backed by its great resources, Clarence might easily have been tempted to try again to overthrow his brother. He was also believed to be circulating stories that Edward was a bastard with no right to rule.[2] Louis XI fanned Edward's suspicions by reporting remarks credited to Duchess Margaret about what Clarence would do in England if he became master of Burgundy. Nor would Edward countenance an alternative marriage for Clarence when James III of Scotland proffered the hand of his sister, Margaret.[3]

Clarence and the king were now on thoroughly hostile terms. Re-buffed over the Burgundian match, the duke behaved with typical petulance, appearing rarely at court, saying nothing in council, and showing a reluctance to eat or drink in the king's house, as though he feared poison. It is more than likely that he and his councillors were involved in a variety of treasonable plots, though no specific proof survives. Edward now resolved to teach him a sharp lesson, which anyone less foolish than Clarence might have taken to heart. The arrest of an Oxford astronomer, Dr John Stacey, who was suspected of using his magic arts for evil purposes, led to his confession under torture that he was involved with a member of Clarence's household, Thomas Burdett, esquire, of Arrow Park in Warwickshire, and another astronomer, Thomas Blake, a chaplain of Stacey's college of Merton, Oxford. On 12 May 1477 the king appointed an especially powerful commission of oyer and terminer, whose members included five earls, twelve barons and six justices, to try these men on charges of having 'imagined and compassed' the death of the king and the prince of Wales, of using the magic arts to accomplish this, and of predicting their early deaths. Burdett was further charged with having circulated treasonable writings inciting men to rebellion. On 19 May all were found guilty and ordered to be drawn to Tyburn and hanged. Blake was saved at the eleventh hour by the intercession of one of Edward's

[1] Duke Charles's mother, Isabella of Portugal, was a granddaughter of John of Gaunt, father of Henry IV, and his claim had been set forth in a secret instrument drawn up at Arras on 3 November 1471 (Calmette and Perinelle, 149).
[2] This was amongst the charges made against Clarence in 1478 (*RP*, VI, 194, and below, p. 242).
[3] Calmette and Perinelle, 376–7 (Louis's instructions to his envoy, Olivier le Roux, September 1477); Scofield, II, 188; *Cal. Documents Scotland*, IV, 474.

councillors, James Goldwell, bishop of Norwich, but the other two were put to death on the following day.[1] This was clearly a staged political trial, and the fate of Burdett had obvious implications for Clarence. But he chose to ignore the warning. Whilst Edward was at Windsor, the duke burst into a council meeting at Westminster, and directed his spokesman, Dr John Goddard, to read out the declarations of innocence which Burdett and Stacey had made. His choice of Goddard was deliberately tactless, for this Franciscan preacher had expounded Henry VI's claim to the throne at St Paul's Cross in September 1470. This act of defiance merely angered Edward further. Returning to Westminster, he summoned Clarence before him, and, in the presence of the mayor and aldermen of London, personally charged the duke with having violated the laws of the realm and having threatened the security of judges and jurors. His accusation referred, in all probability, to Clarence's high-handed action shortly before against one Ankarette Twynho, a former servant of Duchess Isabel, whom he suspected of having poisoned her. Taken by force from her home in Somerset, she was carried off to Warwick, brought before the justices of the peace, found guilty and hanged on 15 April 1477. The jury claimed that 'for fear [they] gave the verdict contrary to their conscience'. In all this, it was now alleged, the duke had acted 'as though he had used a king's power', not to mention the 'inordinate hasty process and judgement' which had followed. On these charges Clarence was arrested towards the end of June 1477, and committed to the Tower. There he remained until parliament met at Westminster on 19 January 1478. The chief reason for its being summoned was to arraign the duke on charges of high treason.[2]

Opening the session, the chancellor, Bishop Rotherham, took as his theme the text, 'The Lord is my ruler, therefore I shall not want', and ominously quoted the words of St Paul, 'For he beareth not the sword in vain'.[3] The king then introduced his own bill of attainder against

---

[1] *CC*, 561; Scofield, II, 190–1; *Dep. Keeper, 3rd Rept*, II, 214; *CPR, 1476–85*, 50 (for the commission of oyer and terminer); L. W. Vernon-Harcourt, 'The Baga de Secretis', *EHR*, xxiii (1908), 508–29; and for Stacey and Blake, Emden, *Biog. Reg., Univ. of Oxford*, I, 197; II, 776; III, 1749.

[2] *CC*, 561; *RP*, VI, 173; *CPR, 1476–85*, 172–3 (petition to parliament of 1478 by Ankarette's grandson and heir, Roger Twynho, enrolled on the Patent Roll two days after Clarence's death).

[3] The opening verse of the 23rd Psalm, which appears in the Authorized Version as 'The Lord is my shepherd', appears in the Latin Vulgate then in use as 'ruler' – *Dominus regit me*.

his brother. He reminded parliament of his notable record of clemency to former opponents, even the 'great movers, stirrers, and executors of . . . heinous treasons', but his leniency had been ill-repaid. He was now threatened by 'a much higher, much more malicious, more unnatural and loathly treason, than at any time hath been compassed, purposed and conspired'. What gave this new treason its special heinousness, he explained, was that it sprang from his own brother, who, of all earthly creatures, owed him loyalty and love, 'beside the duty of ligeance, by nature, by benefit, by gratitude, and by gifts and grants of goods and possessions'. To further his evil aims of destroying the king and his family, the duke had tried 'by might to be gotten as well outward as inward' (an echo of King Louis's insinuations about the Burgundian marriage) and by many 'subtle contrived ways' to alienate Edward's subjects. The duke's servants had gone round the country claiming that Burdett had been unjustly put to death; stories had been put about that the king was a bastard; the duke had demanded oaths of loyalty and claimed that the king had disinherited him; he had tried to send his son overseas to Flanders or Ireland and replace him by a double at Warwick Castle; and he had secretly preserved an exemplification under the great seal of an agreement made in 1470, during the Readeption of Henry VI, which recognized him as heir to the throne if Henry VI's issue failed in the male line.

Nevertheless, the king concluded, he could still have found it in his heart to forgive Clarence, on account of their nearness of blood and the tender love he had felt for him in his youth, if only the duke had not continued in his evil ways. He had clearly shown himself to be 'incorrigible', and the safety of the realm demanded his punishment. The king therefore asked for a sentence of high treason, and that the duke should be deprived of all his titles and of all estates and other properties granted to him by the Crown.[1]

Very little serious effort was made to substantiate the king's accusations, and a recent enquiry has shown that one major charge – that concerning the exemplification of 1470 – may well have been invented by Edward himself.[2] It is true that witnesses were produced in parliament in support of the royal indictment, but, according to the Croyland Chronicler, they behaved more like accusers. The duke was allowed to make an answer: he denied all the charges, and demanded that he might prove his innocence by the ancient method of wager of battle.

[1] RP, VI, 193–5.
[2] J. R. Lander, 'The Treason and Death of the Duke of Clarence', esp. 27–8.

No one spoke in his defence. Parliament then declared itself satisfied of the truth of the allegations, and the duke of Buckingham was appointed on 7 February as steward of England to pronounce the formal sentence of death. In all this due forms of law had been observed. The most unusual feature of these proceedings was the dominant role played by the king personally.[1] If it was without precedent for the indictment to be brought by the king himself, rather than by the lords or commons, this could be defended on the ancient legal maxim that the king's word, so long as it was based on his own personal knowledge of the facts, was 'the most perfect of records'. As such it was accepted by a complacent assembly which contained an exceptionally high proportion of royal servants and retainers of court peers.[2]

Even after the death sentence had been pronounced, Edward seemed to hesitate before taking the final step. Clarence was returned to the Tower and there remained for a further ten days until the commons' speaker, William Allington, came into the house of lords to ask that the verdict be duly carried out. On 18 February the duke was privately put to death in the Tower, partly to spare him the shame of a public execution, and partly to lessen a scandal which reflected on the whole York family. Very probably, as many contemporaries believed, and as later tradition has it, he met his death by drowning in a butt of malmsey wine.[3]

Not surprisingly, Edward's reputation has suffered from this act of judicial fratricide. Some contemporaries roundly condemned this 'fact most horrible', and claimed that Edward himself bitterly repented it. Modern historians have tended to echo their disapproval of what Bishop Stubbs rather unjustly called 'the crowning act of an unparalleled list of judicial cruelties which those of the next reign supple-

---

[1] It is worth noticing that the official record of the process against Clarence (*RP*, VI, 193–5) carries the royal sign-manual, the interlocked RE, at top and bottom: this, however, was not part of the Parliament Roll proper, but comes from 'an original in the Tower of London', and was probably the council's draft of an 'official bill' to be put through parliament. For the witnesses, *CC*, 562.

[2] For the legal aspects of the trial, see J. G. Bellamy, *The Law of Treason in England in the Later Middle Ages*, 170–1, and his 'Justice under the Yorkist Kings', 146–7. For the composition of this parliament, see below, pp. 343–4.

[3] Thus Mancini, 63, and the sources cited by his editor on p. 111. Scofield, II, 209, follows the Burgundian chronicler, Olivier de la Marche, for the story that Clarence met his end in a bath. The only contemporary English source to mention the affair, *CC*, 562, is curiously guarded, and speaks only of 'the execution, whatever its manner may have been'. Otherwise, the story of the malmsey does not appear in English sources until early Tudor times, e.g. Polydore Vergil, *English History*, 167; More, *Richard III*, 7.

ment but do not surpass'.[1] Certainly Edward alone must bear full responsibility for his brother's execution. There is no evidence at all to support later charges that Duke Richard of Gloucester brought about his brother's downfall, even if we need not believe Dominic Mancini's story that Gloucester mourned Clarence's death.[2] Nor is it at all likely that, as the same author alleged, Edward yielded to pressure from his queen; she was thought to believe that her son's succession to the throne was threatened by Clarence, who was spreading stories that she was not the king's legitimate wife. Such tales reflect rather the general unpopularity of the Woodvilles and the rumours current in the poisoned political atmosphere of 1483.[3]

Yet in fairness to Edward it should be remembered that he had already shown exemplary patience with his brother. It is doubtful whether he would have been allowed to remain at liberty for so long in any other fifteenth-century state. To his shameful record of treason against his sovereign, he had added the crime of treachery against his own brother, which was significant because it was exceptional; and Edward was merely reflecting contemporary opinion when he declared that this was the special 'heinous, unnatural and loathly' aspect of Clarence's behaviour. It is hard not to believe that Clarence was guilty of treasonable activities even after his pardon in 1471, and in this, as the king claimed, he had shown himself to be incorrigible. He had learned no lesson and would take no warning. By 1478 the removal of Clarence had become a political necessity. It is not wholly convincing to argue that it was a political misjudgement, a symptom of a decline in Edward's grasp of affairs brought by an untrammelled power which blurred his sense of caution.[4] Certainly, some contemporaries saw

---

[1] Polydore Vergil, 167, for the 'fact most horrible'; CC, 562, for condemnation and later repentance; W. Stubbs, Constitutional History of England (2nd edn, 1878), III, 220.
[2] Mancini, 63. For later charges, see More, Richard III, 8–9. Kendall, Richard III, 125–6, 454–5, even goes so far as to suggest that Gloucester 'pleaded with King Edward for George's life'.
[3] The charge against the Woodvilles is made by Mancini, 63, and, less specifically, by More, Richard III, 7. It is doubtful whether Clarence was circulating the story of the 'precontract' which made Edward's marriage invalid, later used by Richard of Gloucester in his claim to the throne, in 1478: see M. Levine, 'Richard III – Usurper or Lawful King?', Speculum, xxxiv (1959), 391–401, rejecting the claim made by Kendall, op. cit., 217–18, on this point. For the unpopularity of the Woodvilles, see above, pp. 97–9, 102–3.
[4] Thus S. B. Chrimes, Lancastrians, Yorkists, and Henry VII, 122, where it is argued that Clarence's death set a precedent for slaughter within the Yorkist family, with evil consequences in 1483. But, had Clarence been alive then, he would surely have been a competitor for the throne.

Clarence's downfall as an ominous sign of potential despotism. The Croyland Chronicler remarked that[1]

> After the perpetration of this deed, many persons left king Edward, fully persuaded that he would be able to lord it over the whole kingdom at his will and pleasure, all those idols being removed . . . [to whom] . . . the multitude, ever desirous of change, had been in the habit of turning in times past. The king . . . after this period performed the duties of his office with such a high hand, that he appeared to be dreaded by all his subjects, while he himself stood in fear of no one.

Yet, he added, so firmly was the realm in the grip of Edward's trusted servants that no man could risk starting trouble without being 'immediately charged with the same to his face'. He was a king to be feared as well as loved, and Clarence's overthrow was a convincing assertion of his power.

(ii) *Marriage Politics and Diplomacy*

By the end of 1475 Edward had already sired two sons and five daughters by Queen Elizabeth Woodville.[2] They were later to have three more children. Of these ten, one daughter, Margaret, died in infancy, as did their third son, George of Windsor (1477–9). The two youngest daughters, Catherine (born 1479) and Bridget (born 1480), were still too young when their father died to be the objects of serious marriage plans. But schemes for the marriages of the six elder children constantly preoccupied Edward and his queen in the years following 1475. The search for suitable dynastic marriages forms a prominent theme in fifteenth-century continental diplomacy, and, if successful, they might change the political map of Europe, like the Hapsburg–Burgundian and Burgundian–Spanish marriages which created the Empire of Charles V. Edward IV was no less concerned than his foreign contemporaries to win recognition for his dynasty and to advance his diplomatic schemes by means of judicious marriage alliances. These, therefore, loom large in English foreign policy between 1475 and 1483, but it will be convenient, and certainly less confusing, to consider separately here his efforts to provide for his growing family. They proved highly successful in the six years between Picquigny and the end of 1481.

[1] *CC*, 562, echoed by Polydore Vergil, *English History*, 168 ('many were persuaded . . . that he would from thenceforth prove an hard and severe prince . . . he perceived that every man feared him, so now he feared nobody').
[2] See Genealogical Table, p. 6.

Like most English medieval kings, Edward looked abroad for a suitable bride for his heir, Edward, prince of Wales. During the winter of 1476 the court was considering the advantages of a marriage between the six-year-old prince and the Infanta Isabella, daughter and at that time heiress apparent of Ferdinand of Aragon and Isabella of Castile. This plan was still under discussion in 1478, but the birth of a son to the Spanish rulers made the match less attractive to Edward, who was already beginning to look elsewhere. Towards the end of that year Maximilian of Austria proposed a marriage alliance between an English prince and his sister, daughter of the Emperor Frederick III, but Edward was more interested – because of her family's great wealth – in marrying the prince of Wales to a daughter of Duke Galeazzo Maria of Milan, who had been murdered in 1476. His widow, Bona of Savoy, whose hand had been offered to Edward himself in 1474, was hostile to the match, and also to a scheme for the new duke of Milan to marry an English princess. Though her brother-in-law, Louis of France, deigned to write to her on Edward's behalf, nothing came of it. The shrewd Milanese ambassador in France, Giovanni Andrea Cagnola, commented on the avarice which is a marked feature of Edward's dynastic diplomacy in his later years. In April 1479 he was reporting to his employers that

> the chief difficulty which they speak of will be owing to the great quantity of money which the king of England will want from your Excellency for the dowry and for presents, as they say he knows you have a great treasure, and he proposes in this way to obtain a good share of it, as being in any case one who tends to accumulate treasure.

Edward soon turned elsewhere.[1]

During 1479 and 1480 England was moving rather warily and uncertainly towards closer ties with her traditional allies, Burgundy and Brittany. An important feature of his negotiations with Duke Francis II was a proposal that his elder daughter and eventual heiress, Anne of Brittany, should marry Prince Edward. This was already under discussion in September 1480, and Edward was to ratify the final agreement on 10 May 1481. Again the bargaining was marked by greed on Edward's side. Anne, then four years old, was to marry Edward as soon as she reached the age of twelve; if she died, her sister Isabella

[1] Rymer, *Foedera*, XII, 36, 42; Scofield, II, 238-40, 267-70; M. G. Perinelle, 'Dépêches de Nicholas de Roberti, ambassadeur d'Hercule I, duc de Ferrare, auprès du Roi Louis XI', *Mélanges d'Archaeologie et d'Histoire*, xxiv (1904), 425-79; *CSP, Milan*, I, 235-7.

should take her place, and similarly Edward should be replaced if necessary by his brother, Richard; her dowry should be 100,000 crowns. But if the duke had a son before the marriage, this would be increased to 200,000 crowns. If he had a son after the marriage, this child was to marry one of Edward's daughters, who herself should have a dowry of 100,000 crowns provided by the duke, whilst Anne's dowry was to be the same. One Breton scholar commented that it seemed that 'to marry his daughters without dowries was the objective which this miser set before himself in the last years of his life'.[1] Had it taken place, this match might have kept Brittany out of the hands of France, but would surely have involved war with the French king, who could not afford to see such a major fief pass into English hands.

Meanwhile, Edward was driving an even harder bargain with Duke Maximilian and Duchess Mary of Burgundy. Two of his daughters, the eldest, Elizabeth, and the third girl, Cecily, had already been provided with suitable prospective husbands, the heirs of France and Scotland. The second daughter, Mary, occupied the rather unfortunate position of first reserve for her elder sister as bride to the dauphin Charles, and no special provision was made for her until she was affianced to King Frederick I of Denmark in 1481. Mary herself died prematurely on 23 May 1482. For the fourth daughter a much more brilliant match was proposed, with the infant Philip (born in 1478), only son and heir of Maximilian and Mary. Edward quite ruthlessly exploited the duke's desperate need of English support to get Anne's marriage on the cheap. Maximilian had wanted a dowry of 200,000 crowns with Anne; Edward, on the other hand, regarded paying no dowry as part of the price of signing an alliance with Burgundy. When Maximilian argued that it was quite unreasonable for the bride of one of the wealthiest heirs in Europe to have no dowry at all, he still had small success in persuading her father to release the purse-strings. The original marriage-treaty, signed on 5 August 1480, was modified by supplementary agreements on 14 and 21 August, which effectively released Edward from paying any dowry on condition of releasing to the duke the first year's instalment of the pension of 50,000 crowns which he was demanding from Burgundy.[2]

For only one of his children did Edward seek a marriage within the

---

[1] Pocquet du Haut-Jussé, *op. cit.*, 229–33; Scofield, II, 300–1; Rymer, *Foedera*, XII, 142–5.

[2] Above, pp. 213, 233, for the marriage plans of Elizabeth and Cecily; Scofield, II, 337, for Mary's betrothal to Frederick of Denmark; Rymer, *Foedera*, XII, 123–35, for the Burgundian marriage-treaty, and see further below, pp. 283–4.

ranks of the English nobility. Here again the avarice which contemporaries saw as a growing feature in Edward's character in his later years played its part. In January 1476, John Mowbray, 4th duke of Norfolk, earl of Nottingham and Warenne, and earl marshal of England, died, leaving an infant daughter, Anne (born on 10 December 1472), as his sole heir. Though many of the lands of the dukedom were then in the hands of her aged great-grandmother, Katherine, widow of the second duke, eventually she would be among the wealthiest heiresses of England, and she was immediately marked out as a bride for Edward's second son, Richard, born in August 1473, and created duke of York in May 1474. Even before the marriage took place, he was given the titles of earl of Nottingham on 12 June 1476, and duke of Norfolk and earl Warenne on 7 February 1477. The marriage of the two children took place in St Stephen's Chapel, Westminster, on 15 January 1478, in the presence of the many lords assembling for the parliament which was soon to attaint the young duke's uncle of Clarence.[1]

Unfortunately, the young bride did not live to taste the joys of marriage. She died at Greenwich on 19 November 1481, a few days short of her tenth birthday.[2] Since there was no issue of the marriage, her estates should have descended to the heirs at law, William, Viscount Berkeley, and John, Lord Howard, co-heirs of the last duke's great-aunts. But Edward had no intention of letting slip this rich inheritance. Where the interests of his family were concerned, he had already shown himself capable of extinguishing the rights of widows, notably the countesses of Warwick and Oxford in 1475.[3] He was now prepared to override the laws of inheritance. An act was put through the parliament of January 1483 which vested the Mowbray inheritance in Duke Richard for his life, with reversion first to his heirs, and then, if he had none, to the heirs of Edward himself. The claims of William, Lord Berkeley, presented no problem, for as long ago as 1476 this financially embarrassed peer had surrendered his rights to the king in return for being released from bonds totalling £37,000 which he owed to the king

---

[1] *CP*, IX, 609–10; *Lords' Report, Dignity of a Peer*, V, 406; Scofield, II, 205–6. A contemporary description of the marriage and the ceremonies which followed is in W. H. Black, *Illustrations of Ancient State and Chivalry* (Roxburghe Club, 1840), 27–40.
[2] This is the date given on her memorial plaque, found on her coffin during excavations at the Minories in London, 1965, now in Westminster Abbey; cf. *CP*, IX, 609–10.
[3] For the countess of Warwick, above, pp. 190–1. The widowed countess of Oxford, Elizabeth Howard, was forced to surrender all her property to Duke Richard of Gloucester in 1475; *CCR, 1468–76*, 334–5; *RP*, VI, 281–2; *CP*, X, 238.

and to the Talbot family. Rewarded with the title of Viscount Berkeley in April 1481, he confirmed this renunciation in the 1483 parliament. But no attention whatever seems to have been paid to the rights of Edward's hard-working and valued servant, John, Lord Howard: the act of 1483 silently disinherited him.[1]

Not one of Edward's many children was actually married when he died in April 1483. This was partly a consequence of their youth: even the eldest, Elizabeth of York, was then only seventeen. Partly it resulted from the setbacks which the king's foreign policy experienced in his last years. The war with Scotland and the Treaty of Arras of 1482 between King Louis and Maximilian of Austria temporarily extinguished the brilliant matrimonial prospects of Elizabeth, Cecily and Anne.[2] But these temporary reverses would no doubt have been overcome had their father lived longer, for arranged dynastic marriages were often repudiated when political or diplomatic advantage demanded it.[3] The real reason why only Elizabeth of York, as queen of Henry VII, eventually married according to her station, was the failure of the House of York to survive its founder by more than two years. Once the Tudors had mounted the throne, the rest of Edward's daughters, for all their surpassing beauty, had to be content with an earl, a viscount and a gentleman, a knight and a nunnery.[4]

(iii) *England, France and Burgundy*

The fifteen months separating the Treaty of Picquigny from the death of Duke Charles of Burgundy were a golden summer of harmony in the relations between England and France, with nothing at issue beyond a leisurely approach to the questions left unsettled at Picquigny. Edward's irritation with Duke Charles soon evaporated, and relations with both Burgundy and Brittany were friendly enough. This diplomatic calm was shattered by Charles's death at the siege of Nancy on

---

[1] Smyth, *Lives of the Berkeleys*, 118–19; *RP*, VI, 205–7. For comment on this case, see T. B. Pugh in *Fifteenth-Century England*, 110–11, where it is assumed that Berkeley also was disinherited.

[2] Below, pp. 290–3

[3] E.g. the dauphin Charles of France rejected Elizabeth of York to be betrothed to Margaret of Austria, daughter of Maximilian and Mary of Burgundy, only to repudiate her to marry Anne of Brittany, formerly betrothed to Edward, prince of Wales.

[4] *CC*, 563, for their beauty at the Christmas festivities, 1482; for the marriages of Anne, Cecily and Catherine, see Genealogical Table, p. 6; Bridget, the youngest daughter, became a nun at Dartford (Scofield, II, 299).

5 January 1477, leaving his daughter, Mary, as his heir. Louis XI at once set about exploiting the succession crisis in Burgundy, invading Picardy, Artois and the Duchy of Burgundy. He was clearly committed to a decisive attempt to extinguish the independence of the Burgundian state once and for all. The revival in this new form of Franco-Burgundian hostility was to dominate Western European politics for the rest of Edward's reign, and presented him with a series of acutely difficult decisions.

Edward now had to balance the relative advantages of competing claims for his support. At the centre of his policy lay his wish to retain the French pension and the French marriage arranged in 1475. Against this was the danger of allowing Louis a free hand in his efforts to destroy the Burgundian state. With the English alliance sought by both sides, Edward was in a good bargaining position so long as some balance of power between France and an independent Burgundy could be maintained. But as French pressure on Burgundy increased, Edward found it more and more difficult to avoid a decision. Should he consent to a firm alliance with Burgundy to prevent her extinction, but at the cost of losing his pension and the dauphin's marriage, and at the risk of renewed French intervention in affairs on this side of the Channel; or should he continue to rely upon Louis XI, whose good faith he was coming to doubt, and whose promises in England might soon be forgotten if he achieved his ends in Burgundy and no longer had need of English support? Between these unpalatable alternatives England wavered uneasily. Eventually Edward allowed his own avarice and Louis's diplomatic skill to render him little more than a passive spectator of developments on the Continent and unable to exploit them to his own advantage.

The Burgundian succession crisis presented Edward with his first dilemma. The dowager duchess, Margaret of York, and her stepdaughter, Mary, appealed for help to Edward, and Mary would have welcomed a suitable English husband. There were good political and economic arguments in favour of intervening to protect Burgundy against French aggression. If France could annex Artois, Picardy and Flanders, the position of Calais would be endangered, and a French presence on the North Sea coast might become a permanent menace to England. The English mercantile interest was also sharply conscious of the threat to its important trading connections in the Netherlands, and there were many influential persons in England whose dislike of France disposed them to favour Burgundy, including William, Lord Hastings. Against this was the difficulty that England really had no suitable husband to offer Mary of Burgundy, other than the duke of Clarence, a choice which Edward himself would not permit. He would have approved of Anthony, Earl Rivers, but this was hardly practical, since, as Commynes observed, 'Rivers was only a petty earl and she the greatest heiress of her time'.[1]

The whole problem was discussed by a great council at Westminster in February 1477, where it was decided that England should not intervene directly, but that Lord Hastings should be sent to Calais with 500 men to reinforce the garrison. On the other hand, Edward clearly hoped that something might be got from Louis XI as the price of English non-intervention. The nature of his demands emerges from the instructions given on 16 February 1477 to his ambassadors, John Morton and Sir John Donne. They were to seek immediate payment of an instalment of 10,000 crowns of the ransom of Margaret of Anjou, already five months overdue; early deposit of the guarantees promised by Louis for the continued payment of the pension; further pledges that the dauphin would marry Elizabeth of York; assurances that the lands held by Duchess Margaret of Burgundy as part of her jointure would not be threatened by the French invasion; and that a major discrepancy in the arrangements made at Picquigny should be eliminated. The truce and the commercial treaty, which were to last for seven years, should now be extended to conform with the treaty of amity, which was to last for the lives of the two kings.[2] Louis gave comforting assurances and concessions on most of these issues, and himself sent an embassy, which reached England in June 1477, to discuss certain outstanding commercial questions: this, however, proved little more than a time-wasting device. Opportunities to intervene directly in Burgundy were now slipping away. Though Edward sent an envoy to Flanders to offer the hand of Earl Rivers in marriage and a promise of military assistance from England, Mary had already decided, despite his lack of funds and resources, to accept Maximilian of Austria, son of the Hapsburg Emperor, Frederick III, as her husband; and on 18 August 1477 the couple were married at Ghent.[3]

The direct result of the Burgundian succession crisis was to place Edward in a position of diplomatic importance, for both sides now sought to involve him in the Franco-Burgundian rivalry. Confronted by French

---

[1] Commynes, II, 248. The arguments for and against intervention are discussed by Commynes, II, 245–8, who stressed both Edward's love of a life of pleasure and the attachment of him and his queen to the French marriage; see also Calmette and Perinelle, 219–21. For Edward's opposition to Clarence's marriage, CC, 478.
[2] Scofield, II, 176–82; Calmette and Perinelle, 221–3.   [3] Scofield, II, 184–6.

attacks, economic as well as military, and hampered by an unwarlike population and a severe shortage of funds to buy mercenary troops, Maximilian was in urgent need of support, and was soon prepared to bid high for effective assistance from England. Louis, on the other hand, tried to tempt Edward with the idea of a joint Anglo-French partition of the Burgundian dominions, proffering Edward Holland and Zeeland as his share. When Edward refused to be drawn, Louis told his envoys to propose that a *de facto* partition of the Burgundian dominions should be made, leaving the vexed question of title to be decided later; that England should be compensated for any trading losses she might suffer in warfare against the Netherlands, and that the truce between England and France should be extended to last at least 100 years.[1] Edward responded by sending John, Lord Howard, Sir Richard Tunstall and Thomas Langton to France to say that, if he were to aid Louis, he must have Brabant as well as Holland and Zeeland, and that the French king must bind himself to aid Edward by furnishing him with 2,000 lances until the conquest was complete. These demands were accepted by Louis, who now also agreed informally to extend the truce with England to last for 101 years, and to pay the existing pension throughout that period to Edward and his successors. At the same time a new covenant was signed on 7 April 1478 to settle differences still outstanding under the treaty of 1475.[2]

Edward's bargaining position with Louis was now improved by the counter-offers made by Burgundy. In response to overtures from Flanders, an English embassy was sent to Burgundy to negotiate a new commercial treaty, signed at Lille on 12 July 1478, which cleared up outstanding difficulties in the commercial relations of the two countries.[3] At the same time, the birth of an heir, Philip, to Maximilian and Mary opened up the prospect of an attractive marriage alliance for one of Edward's daughters. The threat of an Anglo-Burgundian *rapprochement* enabled Edward to step up his demands on France. On 13 July 1478 he extracted from Louis's resident ambassador in England, the bishop of Elne, an agreement in principle that the Anglo-French truce and treaty of amity should be further extended to last for 100 years from the date of death of whichever of the two kings should die

---

[1] Calmette and Perinelle, 223–7, 376–82; cf. Scofield, II, 191–9, for a slightly different version of these negotiations.
[2] Scofield, II, 200–2, 225–9; Calmette and Perinelle, 229–31.
[3] Rymer, *Foedera*, XII, 67–86, for the text of the treaty; and see further below, pp. 368–9.

first, and that the pension should be paid throughout that period, but the bishop, under instructions from Louis, evaded enshrining the agreement in formal diplomatic documents.[1]

In August Edward raised an entirely new issue. At thirteen, Elizabeth of York had now reached marriageable age, though the dauphin was still only eight years old, and Edward now demanded that their formal betrothal be carried through, and that Elizabeth should immediately enjoy the jointure of 60,000 crowns a year which had been agreed upon at Picquigny. But Louis, who was far less committed to the match than Edward and his queen, temporized again. Elizabeth, he argued, could have her jointure only when the marriage took place, but the dauphin was still too young.[2] Edward's response was to continue his dealings with Maximilian. At the end of 1478, following discussions with the archduke's envoy, he pointedly told the bishop of Elne that Maximilian's father, the emperor, wanted not only a marriage alliance with England but also an alliance against France, and that Maximilian was ready to pay Edward a pension of 60,000 crowns and to supply troops to assist in the conquest of France. This was not altogether bluff. On 18 December 1478 English envoys in Flanders renewed various articles of the treaty between England and Burgundy of 1474, and thereby virtually committed Edward to a secret treaty of friendship and alliance with Mary and Maximilian.[3]

In spite of growing English irritation with France, and mounting Francophobia among Englishmen in general, Louis continued to prevaricate. A French embassy which arrived in London in December 1478 told Edward that he could not expect immediate payment of Elizabeth's jointure. The proposal, it was said, was contrary to reason, contrary to the custom of France, and essentially conditional on the consummation of the marriage. This unsatisfactory response produced great indignation in the entire English council, which advised the king to break off all relations with France. This he would not do, but he was angry enough to take up a much more determined line. Early in 1479 Bishop Stillington of Bath and Wells, Bishop Morton of Ely, and Earls Rivers and Essex, were directed to treat with the bishop of Elne to obtain a formal agreement about the payment of the pension and the extension of the truce, as agreed provisionally in the previous June. Morton roundly told the bishop that England would stand no more prevarication. Unless English demands were immediately ac-

---

[1] Scofield, II, 236; Calmette and Perinelle, 232-3.
[2] Calmette and Perinelle, 234-5; Scofield, II, 236-7.
[3] Rymer, *Foedera*, XII, 95-7; Scofield, II, 240-1.

cepted, England would break off the negotiations and make a formal alliance with Maximilian. The bishop had little choice but to accept, though protesting that he was exceeding his powers (which enabled Louis to disavow his actions later on), and in February 1479 preliminaries of agreement for the extension of the truce, and the treaty of amity and payment of the pension, were signed on the terms dictated by the English.[1]

Throughout the spring and summer of 1479 discussions continued between England and France on a variety of issues, with the English getting little beyond fair words and prevarications, particularly as regards the ratification of the preliminaries and Elizabeth's jointure. A Burgundian victory at Guinegatte over the French (7 August 1479), and an agreement by Mary and Maximilian not to betroth their heir to anyone except Edward's daughter, Anne (18 July), slightly weakened Louis's position, and he now decided some concession was desirable. Late in the year his envoys offered 10,000 crowns (they had secret instructions to go as high as 25,000 if necessary) as a maintenance grant for the Princess Elizabeth, but the offer was angrily refused. This manœuvre reflects Louis's shrewd calculation that Edward could best be kept in line by playing upon the greed which increasingly coloured Edward's foreign policy. He was well aware that the jointure question was little more than a means of raising the price to France of England's avoiding an active commitment to Burgundy. But it was becoming more and more difficult for Louis to keep the English on the hook unless he made much more generous concessions than he had done so far. For his procrastination about the marriage of the dauphin and Elizabeth was beginning to raise doubts in England about his sincerity. A perceptive observer at the French court, the Milanese ambassador, Cagnola, correctly believed that Edward was not deceived by French delays and was aware that time was not on his side; and he accurately forecast that the marriage alliance depended intimately on Maximilian's continued ability to make head against French aggression. In January 1480 he reported that English envoys had been instructed

> to press in and out of season for the conclusion of the marriage . . . while the king here stands in fear of the king of England, on the supposition that if he will not pay him any heed while the Flemings still flourish, England

[1] Rymer, *Foedera*, XII, 101–8; Calmette and Perinelle, 236–8; Scofield, II, 245–8. The evidence for growing anti-French feeling comes mainly from the reports of the bishop of Elne, summarized by Scofield, II, 222–5, 238.

will not be able to get his desire when this king has accomplished his purpose; and so diamond cuts diamond.

Edward's continuing dilemma could not be more neatly analysed.[1] Throughout 1480 the diplomatic tussle between the two courts continued, to Edward's growing disenchantment. His envoys could get no satisfactory reply to their questions. French ambassadors were told to try to distract Edward by proposals about the time, place and manner of Elizabeth's coming over to France; if she did not come, then Louis would pay 20,000 crowns for her maintenance. These met with a cold response from Edward, who roundly told the French he would accept nothing less than 60,000 crowns for Elizabeth's jointure, and he repeated his inconvenient offer to negotiate between Louis and Maximilian. Meanwhile, the bishop of Elne, a cleric of nervous temperament, was telling Louis of his alarm at Edward's obvious hostility and growing anti-French feeling in England. To counter a deteriorating situation, Louis tried to buy goodwill amongst Edward's advisers by a series of lavish presents to Hastings, Langton and Howard, who was described by Hastings, in a letter of May 1480, as Louis's 'very good servant'; even the duke of Gloucester's good offices were sought by the gift of a great bombard.[2] But the failure of a further mission to France under Howard and Langton in May 1480 to obtain satisfaction about the ratification and the jointure could have done little but increase Edward's mounting anger.

Edward now faced a critical decision. Since 1475 he had failed signally to reach any of his diplomatic objectives. Any French concessions to his increased demands had been no more than partial or preliminary. His show of intransigence towards Louis had misfired, and his attempts to blackmail the French king had foundered (if Commynes can be believed) on Louis's belief that Edward was too wedded to a life of ease and a regular pension to risk an outright rupture of the Picquigny agreement.[3] On the other hand, the arguments for a breach with France were becoming stronger. If Maximilian and Mary were to be deprived of English assistance, then either the Burgundian state might be overwhelmed, or they might seek a separate accommodation

[1] *CSP, Milan*, I, 243–4; Scofield, II, 270–3; Calmette and Perinelle, 241; for the agreement with Maximilian and Mary, Rymer, *Foedera*, XII, 110.
[2] Scofield, II, 274–8; Calmette and Perinelle, 242–5 and 389–90 (for Hastings's letter).
[3] Commynes, II, 245–6; Calmette and Perinelle, 244, also suggest as a factor the influence on Edward of those of his councillors who were in French pay, notably John, Lord Howard.

with France: in either case Edward would lose any lever to make Louis carry out his contracts to England. Moreover, the attractions of a Burgundian alliance began to improve as Maximilian increased his offers for Edward's committed support. In the summer of 1480 English foreign policy moved gradually towards firm agreements with her traditional allies against France, the dukes of Burgundy and Brittany.

Chapter 11

COURT LIFE AND PATRONAGE OF THE ARTS

A fifteenth-century king was expected to maintain an estate appropriate to his royal dignity. Sir John Fortescue expressed the common sentiment of his time when he urged the monarch to accumulate treasure, so that he might spend freely on the proper objects of royal magnificence – new buildings, rich clothes, furs, fine linen, jewellery, ornaments for his palaces, plate and vestments for his chapel, expensive horses and 'other such noble and great costs as suiteth his royal majesty'. If, he warned, 'a king did not so, nor might do, he lived then not like his estate, but rather in misery, and in more subjection than a private person'.[1]

This attitude of mind sprang less from a mere vulgar admiration for ostentatious display than from the sharp contemporary sense of order and degree. Society was competitive and fluid: therefore it needed the social cement of an acknowledged social hierarchy. The conspicuous splendour of his court was a direct yardstick to measure a king's wealth and power. The maintenance of a proper royal estate became for this reason a political necessity rather than a matter of personal whim or indulgence. Such display was designed in part to impress foreign visitors and representatives, 'by the which your Adversaries and Enemies shall fall into the dread wherein heretofore they have been'.[2] But of greater concern was the need to impress the king's own subjects with evidence of his majesty, and to outshine the opulence of great seignorial households. To ignore this rule was to risk losing respect. As the author of the *Great Chronicle* noted, parading the shabby person of Henry VI through the streets of London in 1471 with only an insignificant company merely damaged his cause, especially since he gave the impression he had not even a new gown to his name.[3]

There was never any danger that Edward would make the same mistake. He was shrewd enough to appreciate the advantages, especially

[1] J. Fortescue, *The Governance of England*, 125.
[2] So phrased in the 1485 act of resumption, *RP*, VI, 336.   [3] *GC*, 215.

for a new and relatively unknown king, of calculated display in court ceremonies and public spectacles, just as he appreciated the value of the royal progress through the different regions of his realm. This was an area where policy was nicely married to personal inclination, for Edward was vain of his handsome person, fond of fine clothes, and loved feasts, entertainments and ceremonies.[1] This awareness of the political value of display is evident from the very beginning of his reign. In his early months as king he was poor indeed; yet no expense was spared to make his coronation ceremonies, spread over the three days from 28 to 30 June 1461, an opportunity to project a splendid image of the new king. On the third day, when Edward, 'wishing to pile glory upon glory', again wore his crown in St Paul's, the occasion attracted as great a multitude of people 'as ever was seen afore in any days'. No less than £1,000 was allotted to George Darell, the keeper of the wardrobe, for 'ready money necessary for our coronation'.[2]

Even in Edward's needy early years, the splendour of his court made a most favourable impression on foreign visitors. The Bohemian gentleman, Gabriel Tetzel, who came to England with his master, Leo of Rozmital, in February 1466, was drawn into a series of superlatives by the quality of their reception at the English court. The visitors were invited to attend the churching of Queen Elizabeth, following the birth of her first child by Edward, Elizabeth of York; and he relates how the queen

> went to church in stately order, accompanied by many priests bearing relics and by many scholars singing and carrying lights. There followed a great company of ladies and maidens from the country and from London . . . then came a great company of trumpeters, pipers, and players of stringed instruments. The king's choir followed, forty-two of them, who sang excellently. Then came twenty-four heralds and pursuivants, followed by sixty earls and knights. At last came the Queen escorted by two dukes. Above her was a canopy. Behind her were her mother and maidens and ladies to the number of sixty . . . [afterwards] she returned to her palace in procession. Then all who had joined the procession remained to eat. They sat down, women and men, ecclesiastical and lay, each according to rank, and filled four great rooms.

Everything was supplied, he continues, 'in such costly measure that it is unbelievable that it could be provided'. Rich gifts were made to

[1] CC, 563, and below, pp. 259–62, 354–5, 414.
[2] Kingsford, *Chronicles of London*, 176; cf. GC, 198; P.R.O., Warrants for Issues, E. 404/72/1 (21 June).

the trumpeters, pipers, jesters and heralds, the heralds alone receiving 400 nobles. 'All those who had received gifts went about the tables crying out what the king had given them.' The visitors were then taken to

> an unbelievably costly apartment where the queen was preparing to eat. My lord and his gentlemen were placed in an alcove so that my lord could observe the great splendour. . . . The meal lasted for three hours. The food which was served to the queen, the queen's mother, the king's sister and the others was most costly. Much might be written of it.

In all, concluded Tetzel, Edward IV 'had the most splendid court that could be found in all Christendom'.[1]

This testimony, though perhaps exaggerated, is the more striking since the Bohemian party had just left the ducal court of Burgundy, then the great exemplar of courtly magnificence. The extraordinary development by the Valois dukes of the outward trappings of an elaborate code of chivalry, the inventive use of allegory, pageant and symbolism in entertainments and public spectacles, and the sheer lavishness of display had made their court famous throughout Europe.[2] Nor was the English court ashamed to emulate the Burgundian model. It was only in part the wish to foster good relations with Burgundy which explains the lavish ceremonies mounted for the Bastard of Burgundy's visit to England in 1467. There was also a desire to show the visitors a standard of magnificence in no way inferior to their master's.[3] The same concern is apparent in the preparations for the marriage of Margaret of York to Duke Charles in the following year. King Edward was already involved in very heavy expense under the terms of the marriage treaty, and had been reduced to borrowing several thousand pounds from Italian bankers, and to pawning some of the royal jewels to the London goldsmith, Hugh Brice; this apart, there were heavy military expenses to meet. Yet the king did not hesitate to authorize the issue on 8 June 1468 of sums totalling £2,450 6s 8d for his sister's entourage and trousseau as she crossed to Bruges for the wedding, including £100 for her bedding, carpets and

[1] The Travels of Leo of Rozmital, ed. and trans. M. Letts (Hakluyt Soc., 2nd ser., cviii, 1957), 46–7.
[2] For an admirable description of the contemporary Burgundian court, see R. Vaughan, Philip the Good, 127–63.
[3] Myers, The Household of Edward IV, 4–5. For contemporary accounts of the tournaments of June 1467, see S. Bentley, Excerpta Historica, 171–213; Sydney Anglo, 'Anglo-Burgundian Feats of Arms at Smithfield, June 1467', Guildhall Miscellany, II, vii (1965).

cushions, and £500 in ready cash. The bride was not to be a poor
relation at her own wedding.[1]

Burgundian influence on the English court was strengthened not
only by this marriage alliance but also by Edward's own experiences
in exile as the guest of the Seigneur de Gruthuyse, who had amassed
in his house at Bruges one of the finest libraries in Europe. It is no
coincidence that Edward began the systematic purchasing of expensive
Flemish illuminated manuscripts soon after his return to England in
1471.[2] It was in response to an English request for information that
Duke Charles's master of ceremonies, Olivier de la Marche, compiled a
lengthy and elaborate account of the organization of the ducal court
and household in 1473–4; and the desire to compete with Burgundy
may have been one of the reasons for the re-ordering of the English
royal household which was enshrined in the *Black Book of the Household*
drawn up in 1471–2.[3] It is not known in detail how far Burgundian
fashions influenced English court festivals and ceremonies in Edward's
later years, for the latter are rather poorly documented, but the lavish
tournament mounted to celebrate the marriage of Richard of York
and Anne Mowbray in January 1478, with its pageant displays, dis-
guisings, and chivalric inventions, seems to have been directly inspired
by contemporary Burgundian tournaments.[4] If English ceremonies
lacked the ingenuity and fantasy of their counterparts at the ducal
court, they were certainly both lavish and expensive.

One of the few surviving contemporary descriptions of the English
court in the years of Edward's prime was compiled by a herald, Bluemantle Pursuivant, to record the festivities provided for Gruthuyse's
visit to England in 1472 on the occasion of his being created earl of
Winchester. It supplies a vivid picture of the royal court in holiday
mood at Windsor. On the evening of his arrival there, Gruthuyse dined
with the chamberlain, Lord Hastings, in the two chambers provided
for him, 'richly hanged with cloths of arras and beds of estate'. He was
then taken into the presence of the king, who led him to the queen's
apartments, where she sat playing with her ladies at the 'morteaulx'
(a kind of bowls), whilst other ladies danced or played ninepins with
ivory pins. The king himself danced with his eight-year-old daughter,
the princess Elizabeth. The next day Edward took his visitor to hear
mass, 'which was melodiously sung', as befitted a country with a high
international reputation for music, and where the court was the chief

---

[1] P.R.O., Warrants for Issues, E. 404/74/1, no. 35.
[2] Below, pp. 264–6.   [3] Myers, *op. cit.*, 4.
[4] Anglo, *The Great Tournament Roll of Westminster* (Oxford, 1968), 32–4.

centre of patronage.[1] After mass, Gruthuyse was presented with a gold cup garnished with jewels and containing a seven-inch piece of unicorn's horn, with a great sapphire on the cover. After breakfast Edward took him hunting in Windsor Park, riding on the king's own horse. This animal was later given to him as a present, together with a crossbow, with silken strings and a velvet cover embroidered with the royal arms and badges, and gilt-headed quarrels. Lunch was taken in a hunting lodge in the park, and the party then returned to its sport, six bucks being slain in the afternoon. As it grew dark, the king took his guest to see his garden and his 'vineyard of pleasure'. Evensong was followed by a state banquet in the queen's chambers, with dancing afterwards. About nine o'clock both king and queen escorted Gruthuyse to three specially prepared 'chambers of pleasaunce', hung and decorated with white silk and linen. The bed had fine sheets from Rennes in Brittany, a counterpane of cloth-of-gold furred with ermine, the headframe and canopy in shining cloth-of-gold, and curtains in fine white silk. Baths stood ready, and when the king and queen had withdrawn, Lord Hastings remained behind to share Gruthuyse's bath and joined him in a final collation of green ginger, syrups, sweetmeats and spiced wine.[2]

> Rich cloths, rich furs . . . rich stones . . . and other jewels and ornaments . . . rich hangings and other apparell for his houses; vessels, vestments, and other ornaments for his chapel.

There was little need for Sir John Fortescue to urge Edward of York to spend money on such objects of conspicuous kingly consumption, for they account for a significant part of his annual expenditure from the very beginning of the reign. Between April 1461 and September 1462, a period which includes the coronation, his keeper of the great wardrobe, George Darell, spent £4,784 2s 10½d on clothes, linen, furs and other fine fabrics for the king, his household and his family, exceeding his receipts by £1,481 11s 5¾d. Between September 1462 and April 1465 he spent another £5, 201, an average of some £2,000 a year.[3]

The king never stinted himself on his personal finery. In 1471, for example, amongst other things he was supplied with a jacket of cloth-of-gold, lined and trimmed with satin, linen and damask, at a cost of £13 6s 8d; another containing 5½ yards of gilt cloth at nearly £18;

---

[1] See below, p. 275.
[2] 'The Record of Bluemantle Pursuivant', in Kingsford, *English Historical Literature*, 385–8.
[3] Scofield, I, 283; Myers, *op. cit.*, 45–6.

a robe made from 14 yards of black damask, trimmed with velvet; 15 yards of crimson velvet and 14 yards of black damask, 'for the king's person'; a cloak of black and crimson velvet lined with satin; and a robe of gilt tawny satin lined with velvet and costing £32 6s 8d, with yards of velvet to line it at 12s a yard. In 1480 the great wardrobe account lists twenty-six gowns, doublets and jackets for the king's person, many in the richest materials – blue cloth-of-gold upon a figured satin ground and lined with green satin, black velvet lined with purple, white damask furred with sable, purple cloth-of-gold upon a satin ground and furred with ermine. There were several dozen pairs of boots, shoes and slippers, hats, bonnets and other clothing, including forty-eight handkerchiefs. The king's clothes were as modishly up to date as they were lavish. At Christmas 1482, for instance, he appeared at court 'clad in a great variety of most costly garments, of quite a different cut to those which had usually been seen hitherto in our kingdom'.

Furnishings for the royal houses and palaces were also provided on a lavish scale. In June 1468, for example, £397 was paid for a collection of gilt plates, saucers, spoons, basins, cups and wash-basins, for 'the king's private use in his chamber', and the further huge sum of £984 was spent on some sets of arras representing scenes from the History of Nebuchadnezzar, the History of Alexander, the Passion, and the Judgement, together with two dozen green cushions and some lengths of green velvet.[1] The money came from part of the fine levied upon the former Lord Mayor of London, Sir Thomas Cook. There is no reliable way of translating these sums into meaningful modern equivalents, but it is worth remembering that the *Black Book of the Household* of 1471-2 put the annual cost of a viscount's household at £1,000, a baron's at £500, and a knight's at £100. Modern calculations suggest that in the early sixteenth century there were in the whole country only 200 knights with an average income of £200, and that the average income of 50 peers was about £800. The normal daily wage of the labouring class was about 5d. In these terms, the royal arras represented the fruit of some 45,000 working days.[2]

By these standards royal expenditure on plate and jewellery is even

[1] F. Devon, *Issues of the Exchequer*, 491; 493-4, for 1468 above; N. H. Nicolas, *Privy Purse Expenses of Elizabeth of York: Wardrobe Accounts of Edward the Fourth*, 145-52, for 1480; *CC*, 563, for Christmas 1482.

[2] Myers, *op. cit.*, 102-4, 108-9; J. P. Cooper, 'The Social Distribution of Land and Men in England, 1436-1700', *EconHR*, 2nd ser., xx (1967), 419-21; Thorold Rogers, *Six Centuries of Work and Wages*, 327.

more impressive, although it also represented a useful form of investment which could be pawned or used as security for loans in times of
need. Thus, on 27 July 1461, the king redeemed from the executors of
Sir John Fastolf two valuable jewels, one of which had probably belonged to an earl of Warwick. They were described as 'an ouche [a
jewelled clasp] of gold set with a great pointed diamond set upon a
rose, enamelled white, and an ouche of gold in the fashion of a ragged
staff [the Warwick badge] with two images of a man and woman
garnished with a ruby, a diamond, and a great pearl': together they had
been pledged by the king's father, Duke Richard, to Sir John for £437.[1]

On important family occasions expenditure was on a lavish scale. In
1465 no less than £108 5s 6d was paid to Matthew Philip for a cup
and basin for the queen's coronation. In the following year £125 was
spent on a jewelled ornament 'against the time of the birth of our most
dear daughter Elizabeth'. In 1478 the king bought from the duke of
Suffolk an elaborate jewel, with 'an image of Our Lady of gold with
Our Lord in her arms and the images of Saint John Baptist and Saint
Katharine on either side of Our Lady and two other images with seven
angels thereto pertaining', garnished with great numbers of precious
stones, at a cost of £160. This may have been intended as a gift to the
chapel at Windsor. On one occasion Edward is reported to have bid
as high as £3,000 for a huge diamond and ruby ornament, but without
being able to meet the price demanded by the Italian importer, Luigi
Grimaldi of Genoa.[2]

Such special purchases apart, routine expenditure on jewellery was
considerable. In June 1469, for example, when short of cash and pawning some jewels to raise money, the king nevertheless paid out £930
for jewels supplied to him by John Barker and Henry Massey, goldsmiths of London.[3] Some idea of the nature of these regular purchases
can be gained from a surviving bill, presented on 5 September 1478
by one 'Cornelius the goldsmith', which included the following items:[4]

    1 cross of gold garnished with a diamond, 4 rubies and 7 pearls, £4.
    A flower of gold garnished with a fleur-de-lys diamond, £6.

[1] *CPR, 1461-7*, 96.
[2] Scofield, I, 375 (for 1465); II, 433 (1478); P.R.O., E. 404/74/2 (Elizabeth's
ornament, not paid for until 1470); A. A. Ruddock, *Italian Merchants and Shipping in
Southampton, 1270-1600* (Southampton, 1951), 74. This huge sum may be no exaggeration, for Edward's father, Duke Richard, had owned a jewelled collar valued at
£2,666, and Henry V had one worth £5,162 (McFarlane, *The Nobility of Later
Medieval England*, 98).
[3] P.R.O., E. 404/74/1; and, for financial difficulties at the time, pp. 372-3 below.
[4] P.R.O., E. 28/91.

Another flower, with a pointed diamond, 4 rubies and 4 pearls, £4.
Another flower, with a great sapphire, 40s.
A tooth-pick of gold, garnished with a diamond, a ruby and a pearl,
                                                              £8 6s 8d.
4 rings of gold, garnished with 4 rubies, at 10s each, 40s.

Much of the treasure which contemporaries believed Edward had accumulated by the time of his death was probably in the form of collected plate and jewels, though it is doubtful whether he spent nearly so heavily on either as did the avaricious Henry VII.[1]

Edward IV seems to have been the first English sovereign to accumulate a substantial and permanent royal library.[2] His interest in collecting manuscripts, as we have noted, was stimulated by his exile in Bruges, and copies of many of the works afterwards commissioned by Edward were already in the library of his host, Louis de Gruthuyse. Soon after his return he began to order a series of illuminated manuscripts from Flemish artists and scribes working mainly in Bruges, and his collection grew with the years, especially around 1479–80. These huge volumes, often measuring nineteen inches by twelve, and containing some three to four hundred parchment folios, were generously illustrated with miniatures and decorated with the royal arms, the Garter insignia, and a number of Yorkist badges, especially the 'rose en soleil'. Apart from these specially commissioned works, of which a score or more survive among the Royal MSS in the British Museum Edward certainly acquired a number of other manuscripts and printed books. Soon after his death this royal collection, then at Richmond, was large enough to be shown to the French ambassador as one of the sights which a distinguished foreign visitor ought to see.[3]

Edward's tastes as a book-collector closely resembled those of the

---

[1] Wolffe, *Royal Demesne in English History*, 223–4. Henry spent £200,000 on plate and jewels in 1491–1509.
[2] G. F. Warner and J. P. Gibson, *Catalogue of Western Manuscripts in the Old Royal and King's Collections in the British Museum*, I, xi–xii. Most of what follows is based upon this work, esp. vol. II, 54, 139–41, 170, 173–6, 258, 261–2, 313–16, 347, and on Margaret Kekewich, 'Edward IV, William Caxton and Literary Patronage in Yorkist England', *Modern Language Review*, lxvi (1971), 481–7. Both Henry V and Henry VI had considerable collections of books, of a much more strongly patristic and theological character than Edward's, but these were largely dispersed by gift or by will; see K. B. McFarlane, *Lancastrian Kings and Lollard Knights*, 115–17, 233–8; R. Weiss, 'Henry VI and the Library of All Souls College', *EHR*, lvii (1942), 102–6; and, for aristocratic book-collecting in general, K. B. McFarlane, 'The Education of the Nobility in Later Medieval England', in *The Nobility of Later Medieval England*, 228–47.   [3] Warner and Gibson, I, xii.

Burgundian court circle. The earlier Valois dukes had accumulated a substantial library, which was almost quadrupled by Duke Philip the Good, and his kinsmen and servants included several noted bibliophiles, among them the Bastard of Burgundy as well as Gruthuyse.[1] Though much smaller in scale, Edward's collection resembled theirs in a preference for showy and lavishly-illuminated volumes, in the predominance of French over Latin works, except for service books, and in the absence of any interest in contemporary Italian humanism. He shared, too, their liking for histories and historical romances – the two are not always clearly distinguishable. These formed the largest group among the surviving works known or presumed to have belonged to him. They included several histories of the ancient world, in medieval French versions, such as Raoul le Fevre's *Receuil des Histoires de Troyes*, the anonymous *La grant hystoire Cesar*, and works by Josephus and Livy. General histories included Vincent de Beauvais's *Speculum Historiale* in the French of Jean de Vignay and the compendium by Jean Mansel, the *Fleur des Hystoires*, and amongst recent histories were a chronicle of Flanders, two volumes and a continuation of William of Tyre's *History of the Crusades*, and portions of Froissart's Chronicles. There were also two volumes, part of a set of seven, of Jean de Waurin's *Anchiennes et nouvelles cronicques dangleterre*. Of Flemish work, these were almost certainly executed for Edward IV, and among their sixty-seven miniatures is a picture of the king seated on his throne, wearing the collar of the Burgundian Order of the Golden Fleece, and receiving the book from its kneeling author.[2]

Late medieval royal and aristocratic patrons had a decided taste for didactic and moralistic works, drawing upon history and legend for a series of *exempla*. A good specimen in Edward's library is a work very popular in Burgundy, *Les IX malheureux et les IX malheureuses*, consisting of eighteen ten-line stanzas put into the mouths of such figures as Priam, Hercules, Saul, Pompey, Hannibal, Helen and Medea. Bound up in the same volume (Royal MS. 14 E II) were other works of a similar character, like Boccaccio's *Des Cas des Nobles hommes et femmes malheureux* and Alain Chartier's *Le Breuiaire des Nobles* (thirteen poems in ballad form spoken by 'Noblesse' and twelve other Virtues). He also owned a copy of Boccaccio's *Decameron*, though this can scarcely

[1] R. Vaughan, *Philip the Good*, 155–7; L. Van Praet, *Recherches sur Louis de Bruges, Seigneur de Gruthuyse* (Paris, 1831), 84–264, and, for the Bastard, A. Boinet, 'Un bibliophile de XVIème siècle. Le Grand Bâtard de Bourgogne', *Bib. de l'École des Chartes*, lxvii (1906), 225–69.
[2] For this, and Waurin's dedication, see Kekewich, *op. cit.*, 485; and see Pl. 21.

be included among the moral treatises. Relatively few religious and devotional works survive in the Old Royal Library, probably because most were given away or deliberately disposed of at the time of the Reformation. Edward gave all the books of his chapel to the queen under his will, except some destined for the canons of Windsor. Amongst those remaining are a French version of St Augustine's *City of God*, three volumes of a *Bible Historiale*, and the theological allegory called *La Forteresse de la Foy*.

Probably, like the Burgundian collectors, Edward owned a number of chivalrous romances, but much depends on the attribution of one beautiful manuscript (British Museum MS. 15 E VI). This was originally produced for John Talbot, earl of Shrewsbury, for presentation to Margaret of Anjou, and may have been taken over among the chattels of Henry VI: it was certainly in the Royal Library in 1535. It contains a number of romances of Alexander, Charlemagne, Ogier the Dane, Guy of Warwick, *Le Livre des fais darmes et de chevalerie* and *le ordre du gartir*, some of which were afterwards printed by Caxton.[1] Queen Elizabeth owned a romance of the Holy Grail and a *Morte d'Arthur*, parts of a work by the twelfth-century author Walter Map.

Apart from books specially commissioned or bought by the king, his library probably also contained several works presented to him by their authors. These include John Harding's *Chronicle* in its second version, Capgrave's *Chronicle*, and William Worcester's rather carelessly revised version of his *Boke of Noblesse*, originally intended for Henry VI and urging a renewal of the French wars. All these were dedicated to Edward.[2] He may also have possessed a few printed books, the early products of William Caxton's new printing-press established in 1477 in the precinct of Westminster Abbey. Caxton's emergence, first as a translator and then as printer, undoubtedly owed a good deal to encouragement from members of Edward's family and the court circle. His first printed work, published at Bruges in 1474, was, as Caxton himself records, 'Translated and drawen out of frenshe in to englisshe by William Caxton mercer of ye cite of London at the comaundement of the right hye myghty and vertuouse Pryncesse hys redoubtyd lady Margarete . . . Duchesse of Bourgoyne.'[3] Upon arriving in London, Caxton attracted the valuable support of the king's brother-

[1] Kekewich., 485–6.
[2] Kingsford, *English Historical Literature*, 39, 142, 144; K. B. McFarlane, 'William Worcester: A Preliminary Survey', in *Studies Presented to Sir Hilary Jenkinson*, ed. J. Conway Davis, 210 ff.
[3] W. Blades, *The Life and Typography of William Caxton*, I (1861), 130.

in-law, Anthony, Earl Rivers, whose own translation of the *Dictes and Sayings of the Philosophers* became the first book to be printed in England (1477). With Rivers's continued encouragement, Caxton went on to print the earl's translations of Christine de Pisan's *Moral Proverbs* and the *Cordyale* (1478 and 1479). Hugh Brice, the London goldsmith, who had close court connections, commissioned *The Mirror of the World* in 1481 for presentation to his superior at the Royal Mint, William, Lord Hastings.[1] Edward's cousin, William, earl of Arundel, was another of Caxton's early patrons, the *Golden Legend* (1483) being undertaken at his command and request.

From all this Edward himself seems rather noticeably absent. Much of Caxton's output reflects the tastes and interests of his aristocratic patrons and consists of English versions of the moralities, histories and romances which they had hitherto been purchasing in manuscript and in French.[2] His books might have been expected to appeal to the king in person. Indeed, Caxton directly sought royal patronage. In three of his works he claims to have enjoyed 'the umbre and shadowe' of the king's protection, and two (*Tully of Old Age* and *Godefroy of Bologne*, both printed in 1481) were dedicated to Edward, who was asked to receive a copy, 'and not to desdeyne to take it of me so poure and ignoraunt & symple a persone'.[3] Edward has often been reckoned amongst Caxton's patrons.[4] But there is no reason to suppose that his protection or his interest was anything more than passive. Caxton's own prologues and epilogues show that the king never directly commissioned or encouraged any of his printed works. There is a revealing sentence in the prologue to his *Life of Jason*, which was dedicated to the young prince of Wales, 'to thentente that he may begynne to lerne rede Englissh': Caxton did not, however, he tells us, presume to present it to the king, 'for asmoch as I doubte not his good grace hath it in frensh, which he well understandeth'.[5] Since Edward continued to commission manuscripts from Bruges, he may well have preferred the more splendid artefacts of the illuminator to the less colourful productions of the printer.

The royal library, we are told, 'tended rather to entertainment and

[1] *Ibid.*, 141, 149, 156; *CPR, 1467–77*, 149–50.
[2] H. S. Bennett, *Chaucer and the Fifteenth Century*, 206–8.
[3] Blades, *op. cit.*, 161, 165.
[4] In 1479 Caxton received a payment of £20 for unspecified services to Edward, which may be unconnected with his printing; and in two of his prologues he was working under the king's 'protection and sufferance'; W. J. B. Crotch, *The Prologues and Epilogues of William Caxton* (Early English Text Soc., Original Series, 176, 1928), cix, cxi–cxii, cxiv.   [5] *Ibid.*, cix.

edification rather than to study and the advancement of learning'.[1] If so, the fault was one common to most princely libraries of the day outside Italy. Edward's Lancastrian predecessors, Henry V and Henry VI, had been exceptional in the range of their scholarly and theological interests.[2] Edward's own court circle contained amongst its lay members one or two like John Tiptoft, earl of Worcester, and Anthony, Earl Rivers, with an interest in classics and contemporary Italian humanism. They were, however, rather unusual in this respect. The lay aristocrats of fifteenth-century England were neither illiterate nor uneducated, but they did not as yet form part of the intelligentsia: and this was the class in which Edward himself had grown up.[3] But within the limits of his literary interests Edward, like Duke Philip of Burgundy, may well have enjoyed being read aloud to, as fifteenth-century authors assumed their works would be. If he rarely dealt with Latin works, he was clearly very much at home in French as well as English. The value he attached to his books is shown not only in the expensive bindings of velvet and silk with gold clasps which he ordered for them but also in the fact that some of them at least followed him round from palace to palace carefully packed in 'coffins of fir'.[4]

Unlike Henry VI, but in common with his brothers, Clarence and Gloucester, Edward IV had no wish to be remembered by posterity as a patron of learning. It is true that the Croyland Chronicler informs us that he was 'a most loving encourager of wise and learned men'. His councillors and servants included a number of influential and learned churchmen who, after the fashion of the age, did much to promote scholarship and found schools and colleges. Of the four men who served him as chancellors, Archbishop George Nevill was a noted patron of scholars and of humanist studies as well as a considerable book-collector; Bishop Stillington of Bath and Wells founded a college at Acaster in Yorkshire; and Thomas Rotherham, archbishop of York, established a college at Rotherham in Yorkshire, on the lines of Eton and Winchester, and was an active benefactor of Lincoln College, Oxford, and of the university of Cambridge. The only clerical treasurer of the reign, William Grey, bishop of Ely, had himself studied in Italy under the humanist Guarino da Verona, was a patron of humanists, and presented a notable collection of philosophical and humanist works to his own Oxford college, Balliol. Bishop John Russell of

---

[1] Warner and Gibson, *op. cit.*, I, xii.
[2] McFarlane, *Nobility of Later Medieval England*, 243-4.
[3] *Ibid.*, 228-47; and for Worcester, R. J. Mitchell, *John Tiptoft*.
[4] Nicolas, *Privy Purse Expenses . . .*, 125-6, 152.

Rochester and Lincoln, who was keeper of the privy seal from 1474 to the end of the reign, was reputed 'one of the best learned men undoubtedly that England had in his time'. This list could easily be extended further.[1]

Very little of their interest in scholarly and educational patronage rubbed off on their royal master. Unlike Philip the Good of Burgundy, he did not maintain writers or official historians at his court.[2] He was never tempted to follow the example of educational foundations set by Henry VI at Eton and King's College, Cambridge. Indeed, his vindictive antipathy towards these institutions because of their Lancastrian associations came near to wrecking their future. Shortly after his accession, he ordered King's College to pay all its revenues into the exchequer. Though the college itself was exempted from the general resumption in the parliament of 1461, its estates were not allowed to escape. Some were restored in 1462, but much of the founder's endowment was permanently lost, and the number of fellows had to be substantially reduced in consequence. Eton came even closer to extinction. In Edward's first parliament, all grants made to it by Henry VI were revoked. For a time the king contemplated suppressing it altogether and annexing it to St George's Chapel at nearby Windsor. To this end a bull was procured from Pope Pius II in 1463 authorizing its abolition, and in 1465 orders were given for the removal to Windsor of Eton's bells, jewels and furniture. Though the provost and three or four fellows continued to live there, building operations stopped – the chapel being left without a roof – and it is doubtful whether the school continued. But in 1467 the king relented, restored lands to the college, and in 1469 petitioned Pope Paul II to revoke the bull annexing it to Windsor. After 1471 he even gave Eton a few inexpensive favours. His queen may have given even more, but there is no evidence to support the legend dating back to the seventeenth century that the college was saved by the intervention of Edward's favourite mistress, Jane Shore. Even the portraits of her which hang at Eton and King's College, Cambridge, are in fact sixteenth-century versions of paintings of Diane de Poitiers, mistress of King Henry II of France.[3]

The university of Oxford, which in 1479 was prudent enough to

---

[1] Full references to the scholarly activities of these men can be found in Emden, *Biog. Reg., Univ. Oxford, s.n.*

[2] Vaughan, *op. cit.,* 157–8.

[3] J. Saltmarsh in *VCH, Cambridgeshire,* III, 379, for King's; Scofield, II, 435–8; H. Maxwell Lyte, *History of Eton College,* 59–80; Nicolas Barker and Robert Birley, 'Jane Shore', *Etoniana,* nos 125 (June 1972) and 126 (December 1972), esp. Part III, 'Jane Shore and Eton', 408–10.

choose the queen's brother, Lionel Woodville, dean of Exeter, as its chancellor, fared rather better at Edward's hands. In September 1481, on one of his frequent visits to Oxford from nearby Woodstock, he was splendidly entertained at Bishop Waynflete's new college of Magdalen, along with his company of three bishops and several lords and ladies, including his mother-in-law, the duchess of Bedford, and his sister, the duchess of Suffolk. The following day he attended a public disputation in the university and listened to a formal address, presumably in Latin, to which it is reported that he replied *satis feconde et faconde* (fluently and inventively) to every article of the address. Soon afterwards he founded a free lectureship in divinity. This seems to have been his sole significant educational benefaction.[1] His queen, on the other hand, was a notable patron of Queens' College, Cambridge, which had been begun by Margaret of Anjou: in 1475 the college received from her a set of statutes as its 'true foundress'.[2]

After 1471, and still more after 1475, security at home, increased leisure, and above all the possession of ample funds, enabled Edward to indulge his leanings towards magnificence on a far greater scale than before. In the later years of the reign the court became an important centre of patronage for architects and masons, sculptors and glaziers, goldsmiths and jewellers, dealers in fine fabrics and tapestries, and illuminators of manuscripts. Among these varied activities the king's taste for building was the most important and certainly the most expensive.

Edward fully deserves the reputation of being a great builder credited to him by the contemporary antiquary, John Rous of Warwick.[3] Even in his impecunious early years he pushed ahead with such building schemes as he could afford, and in the second decade of the reign he was in a position to finance much more ambitious and costly projects. The nature of his patronage was largely dictated by two considerations – his own personal tastes and the movements of the court. It is

---

[1] R. Chandler, *Life of William Waynflete*, 150–1. It is often said (e.g., *VCH, Oxfordshire*, III, 17; Scofield, II, 440) that Edward's death soon after prevented his endowment of the lectureship being realized, but the university's letter of thanks to the king specifically says that he had founded it, and refers to the great increase in the number of students in the faculty of theology as a consequence (H. Anstey, *Epistolae Academiae Oxon.* (Oxford Hist. Soc., xxxvi, 1898), 478–9).

[2] R. G. D. Laffan in *VCH, Cambridgeshire*, III, 408.

[3] J. Rous, *Historia Regum Angliae*, ed. T. Hearne (Oxford, 1745), 211; *The Rows Roll*. Edward's building works are also celebrated in John Skelton's elegy on his death (*Complete Poems*, ed. P. Henderson (1959), 2–4).

characteristic of him that, except at Windsor – the spiritual centre of the regime – his attention was devoted essentially to secular buildings, and that the main objects of his patronage were his favourite residences in south-eastern England, whose embellishment, improvement and modernization closely concerned a monarch with strong ideas of personal comfort.

After 1475 there was far less need for the king to tour his country to check rebellion and disorder. The more distant parts of his realm saw him but rarely. In 1476 an act of family piety took him on one of his infrequent visits to the north of England. This was for the transfer of the bodies of his father, Duke Richard, and his younger brother, Edmund, earl of Rutland, from the humble graves at Pontefract priory, where they had been buried after their deaths at Wakefield in 1460, to the family vault at Fotheringhay Castle. This was carried out with suitable splendour. A large company of lords and ladies accompanied Edward on his solemn progress south to Fotheringhay, and the final ceremonies took place on 29–30 July in the presence of the whole royal family, ending with a funeral feast in which some thousands of people are said to have shared and which cost the very large sum of £300. The king stayed on there – his favourite home outside the Thames valley – until the middle of August 1476, and then made a progress through the counties of Nottingham, Worcester and Oxford before returning to Windsor on 8 October. In August 1478 Edward visited Nottingham, returning to Windsor and Greenwich later in the month. In September he went north again to Pontefract and York, coming back to Greenwich for the hunting in October.[1]

Thereafter he rarely moved from the vicinity of his capital, except for visits to his hunting lodge at Woodstock. 1479 was a year of plague, causing many deaths, among them probably that of his third son, George of Windsor, who was little more than a year old. The pestilence was especially virulent in London, and the king lay low at Eltham and Sheen, enjoying a dispensation from the pope to eat meat, eggs and food prepared with milk during Lent, since (it was claimed) fish was injurious to his health.[2] In 1480 much of the summer was spent in entertaining his sister, Duchess Margaret of Burgundy, on a suitably lavish scale, but Edward was not far from London throughout the year.

[1] Scofield, II, 166–91, 237–8, 245. A contemporary description of the re-interment is in B.M., Harleian MS. 48 ff. 78–91.
[2] Scofield, II, 249–50; *Calendar Papal Registers*, XIII, 626; he had a similar indult on 11 September 1481 (*ibid.*, 260–1, and for one on the same grounds to James III of Scotland, *ibid.*, 224).

In 1481 his proclaimed intention to lead his army in person against the Scots proved, as usual, little more than a public-relations exercise. His journey north did not begin until September, was delayed by a fortnight's stay at Woodstock, and a visit to Oxford, and ended comfortably enough with a three-week sojourn in his new apartments at Nottingham Castle. Thereafter a journey north to Fotheringhay in May–June 1482 in connection with the Scottish war was to be his only move outside the south-east. Yet even during this later part of his reign the court was far from stationary. The household accounts for September 1478 to September 1479 show that the king changed the place of his night's lodging about sixty times within the twelve month.[1]

Edward was not primarily interested in military architecture. Even so, large sums were spent on certain key fortresses, especially on work which reflects his interest in artillery. On the defences of Calais and the Pale castles he spent more heavily and continuously than any king before him: the works there cost between £1,000 and £2,000 a year throughout the reign. His extensive transformation of the castle of Guines, completed under the early Tudors, made it one of the earliest fortresses under English control to be fully adapted to the needs of artillery warfare. Likewise at the Tower of London he built a new brick barbican or bulwark for gun emplacements. At the end of the reign large sums were spent on repairs to the castle and town walls of Berwick, damaged during the sieges of 1481 and 1482. But at Nottingham and Fotheringhay Castles, the only northerly places where he spent much time after 1471, his building works were intended for residential purposes. At Nottingham, where £3,000 was spent between 1476 and 1480, he built a new polygonal tower, with 'marvellous fair' windows and chambers, which was much admired by John Leland when he visited it during Henry VIII's reign: he described Edward's new tower as 'the most beautifullest and gallant building for lodging ... an exceeding fair piece of work'. At Fotheringhay extensive building was going on from the early years of the reign, and new chambers, latrines, turrets and a kitchen were erected. Further building there was in progress in 1478 when a royal purveyor visited Cambridge in search of masons, and accepted a bribe of 2s 6d from the Fellows of King's College to refrain from impressing the men at work on their still unfinished chapel. Similar work may have been in hand at Dover

---

[1] Scofield, II, 283–4, 293–5, 319–20, 337–8; Myers, *Household of Edward IV*, 236. Further details of his itinerary for July 1481–June 1482 are in B.M., Add. MS. 24512.

Castle, for which two million bricks were purchased in 1480, but the precise nature of the operations is not known.[1]

Edward's chief love was for the pleasant palaces of the Thames valley, just as his great rival, Louis XI, loved the smiling valley of the Loire. Here – at Windsor, Sheen, Westminster, Eltham and Greenwich – the court spent most of its time after 1475. Large sums had been spent on Sheen (which, like Greenwich, formed part of the queen's jointure) by Henry V and Margaret of Anjou, so only minor repairs were needed there during Edward's reign, but at Greenwich, formerly Margaret of Anjou's manor of La Plesance, he made various enlargements and improvements. As at Westminster Palace, these were aimed primarily at greater comfort and privacy. Considerable sums were spent on Westminster, including the making of a great chamber 'unto our dearest wife the queen in her lodging, and for a privy kitchen of new to be made within the said palace'. His major building work of this kind, however, took place at Eltham Palace in Kent. Here the magnificent new hall was begun soon after November 1475, when Roger Appleton was appointed master and surveyor of the king's works, and it was probably complete before the king's death. It ranks with Westminster Hall and Hampton Court as one of the three surviving royal halls of first-class size.[2]

It is characteristic of Edward that his rather sparse patronage of religion was expressed in close connection with his favourite residences, where colleges or religious houses could be used by the royal family. Both Edward and his queen patronized the Carthusian monastery at Sheen, founded by Henry V in 1414. In August 1479 they obtained a licence from Pope Sixtus IV to attend divine services in a chapel separate from the monastic choir.[3] At Greenwich the king was directly responsible for the introduction into England of the admired continental order of Observant Franciscans. The moving spirit in this venture was probably his sister, Duchess Margaret of Burgundy, who had strong connections with the Order, and who spent much time at Greenwich during her visit to England between July and September 1480: she may well have felt that her brother's soul stood in need of prayer. Soon after her return, he sent for the vicar-general of the

---

[1] R. A. Brown, H. M. Colvin and A. J. Taylor, *The History of the King's Works*, I, 241, 452–3; II, 570–1, 650, 729, 764–5; John Leland, *Itinerary*, I, 95–6; Devon, *Issues of the Exchequer*, 500; and, for building at Hertford Castle (new brick gatehouse) and other castles not mentioned above, Brown, *et al., op. cit.*, 656, 680–1, 732, 804.

[2] Brown, Colvin and Taylor, *op. cit.*, I, 536–7; II, 936–7, 949, 1001; also 1017, for work at Woodstock; and see Pl. 24 b.

[3] *Cal. Papal Registers*, XIII, 8, 582.

Observants, and offered him a site for a new house adjacent to his palace at Greenwich, and in January 1481 he obtained papal approval for his scheme. The site was formally transferred on 2 July 1482 by the bishop of Norwich, and the new house begun.[1] None of this, however, compares in importance with his much more ambitious patronage of the college of St George at Windsor.

Edward is said to have had a special affection for Windsor Castle, and also took a great interest in the Order of the Garter, for which the chapel of St George within the castle had been re-founded by Edward III.[2] Like the dukes of Burgundy with their order of the Golden Fleece, Edward used membership of the Garter as a diplomatic weapon. Foreign rulers or princes whose friendship he wished to win were elected from time to time, among them Ferdinand I, king of Naples, Francesco Sforza, duke of Milan, Duke Charles of Burgundy, King Ferdinand of Castile and Aragon, and John II, king of Portugal. They also included Federigo da Montefeltro, duke of Urbino, commander of the papal troops, elected in 1474: his influence at Rome helped to procure from Sixtus IV a grant of indulgences and remission of sins to all visitors to the Garter Chapel at Windsor on 1 October 1476.[3] But for Englishmen, election to the Order remained very much a mark of Edward's personal favour. Neither high birth nor even kinship with the king automatically gained a man entry into this charmed circle. Thus his cousin, John Mowbray, duke of Norfolk, and his brother-in-law, John de la Pole, duke of Suffolk, had to wait until 1472 before being elected, but personal friends like William Hastings and William Herbert were made knights as early as 1462. Even relatively obscure men such as Sir John Astley (1462) and Sir Robert Harcourt (1463) were preferred to established and prominent servants like Lords Ferrers, Mountjoy and Howard (1472). The king himself, whenever possible, kept the feast of St George (22 April) at Windsor. It was there, for example, that he was girded with the sword and cap of maintenance sent him by Pope Sixtus IV, a ceremony which ushered in seven days of feasting.[4]

Part of Edward's plan for the greater splendour of Windsor was to

---

[1] *Cal. Papal Registers*, XIII, 737; A. G. Little, 'The Introduction of the Observant Friars into England', *Proc. British Academy*, x (1921–3), 455–71. He also founded two chantries in the church of Allhallows, Barking, in the city of London, and the queen built the chapel of St Erasmus at Westminster Abbey (Scofield, II, 430).

[2] A. K. B. Roberts, *St George's Chapel, Windsor Castle, 1348–1416* (Windsor, 1947), 1–14.

[3] For the Golden Fleece, see Vaughan, *Philip the Good*, 160–2; and for Urbino, above, p. 213.

[4] G. F. Beltz, *Memorials of the Order of the Garter* (1841), lxx–lxxi, lxxiii, clxii–clxvi.

increase 'the number of ministers daily serving Almighty God in the said chapel'. Edward III's foundation had provided for a warden and twelve canons, thirteen priest-vicars, four clerks and six choristers, but when the collegiate establishment was incorporated by act of Parliament in 1483 this had been complemented by a further thirteen clerks and thirteen choristers. Windsor was one of the three Chapels Royal – the others being St Stephen's, Westminster, and the Chapel of the Royal Household – which upheld England's considerable reputation for music in the fifteenth century. The Royal Free Chapel of the Household was also incorporated in 1483, with a dean and three canons, and twenty-four chaplains and 'gentleman clerks', selected especially for their musical ability, both in singing and organ-playing. Already by 1471 this courtly musical establishment was of such repute that the duke of Milan sent his chapel master to seek out English singers and musicians and retain them for the duke's service.[1]

At the centre of all this activity at Windsor was the building of the new chapel of St George, Edward's supreme achievement as a patron of architecture. To 'daily serve Almighty God in the said chapel' was only part of his purpose. It was also intended as a monument to the splendour of the House of York in this world, and as a fitting royal mausoleum in which his own bones should find their rest. Building work on the new chapel was heralded by the appointment on 19 February 1473 of Richard Beauchamp, bishop of Salisbury, a prelate already associated with the Order of the Garter, and soon to become its dean and first chancellor, as master and surveyor of 'the king's new works' at Windsor Castle and in the chapel of St Mary and St George. He was given power to take stonecutters, carpenters and other workmen, and to acquire stone, timber, glass, lead and other necessaries.[2] Before the new chapel could be begun, a number of existing buildings had to be demolished, chiefly the great hall and lodgings of the vicars choral. This had advanced sufficiently by 1477 for Edward to appoint a clerk or controller of the works, Thomas Chanceller, and his senior staff. The true architect of the chapel (apart from its west front and vaults,

---

[1] F. L. Harrison, *Music in Medieval Britain* (1958), 20–5. The king also maintained a company of minstrels to play at court festivals, using trumpets, woodwind instruments called shawms, and small pipes (Myers, *Household of Edward IV*, 131–2).
[2] *CPR, 1467–77*, 368, 554; *Cal. Papal Registers*, XIII, 668–9. For Edward's many benefactions to Windsor, see *CPR, 1467–77*, 461, 484, 551; *1476–85*, 142, 172, 178, 181, 219, 222, 228, 242, 255, 260, 285, 333. For the building of the chapel, Scofield, II, 431–4; Brown, Colvin and Taylor, *op. cit.*, II, 875, 884–8, correcting in some particulars, W. J. St John Hope, *Architectural History of Windsor Castle* (1913), esp. 398–406, 429–44; M. R. James, *The Woodwork of St George's Chapel, Windsor* (Windsor, 1933).

which were later additions) was probably the master-mason, Henry Janyns, who had worked at Eton College, and whose father, Robert, had built the beautiful bell-tower at Merton College, Oxford.

Thereafter the work was pushed on apace. By March 1478 so many stonecutters had been drawn into the king's service that at Oxford the chancellor of the university had difficulty in finding men to work on the new Divinity School. Money to finance the building came partly from the profits of baronial estates in the king's hands during minority, and partly from exchequer drafts. The choir and aisles were the first parts of the chapel to be carried to their full height and roofed in, but the stone vault had not yet covered the timber roof when Edward died. Carving of the choir stalls and canopies was in hand in 1478–9, and soon after work was proceeding on Edward's great tomb on the north side of the choir.[1] Though the nave was yet unfinished, and the lantern-tower (later omitted from the plan) not even begun, the choir was ready to receive the body of its royal patron in April 1483.

Meanwhile, Edward had been lavishing money on rich vestments and hangings, on statues in precious metals, and on fine service books for the embellishment of the chapel. These were an essential part of the whole concept of sumptuous and dignified luxury so much admired in the later middle ages, providing a colourful match for the decorative panelling of the walls, the intricate carving of vault, screen and stalls, and the stained glass of the windows. The king's reward was a triumph, even in this great age of English architecture and craftsmanship, a building which ranks with Henry VII's Chapel at Westminster and King's College Chapel at Cambridge among the last and most perfect achievements of the English Gothic style.[2]

Deficiencies in the documentary evidence forbid any precise calculation of the total cost of Edward IV's building schemes. Even in his impecunious early years, however, the annual expenditure of the clerk of the king's works was about £600 as compared with a rate of about £400 under Henry VI. The scale of spending certainly rose considerably after 1471, and higher still after 1475. Windsor alone cost £6,572 in the years 1478–83, a period when large sums were also being spent on the substantial works at Calais, Nottingham Castle, Eltham Palace and elsewhere. It seems likely that Edward devoted more money to building than any other English king since Edward III.[3]

[1] For further details on this, see below, pp. 417–18.
[2] J. H. Harvey, *Gothic England*, 114.
[3] Brown, Colvin and Taylor, *op. cit.*, I, 198–9, 241, 425, 472, and Appendix A, II, 1024, for comparisons.

There was an element of pardonable pride in the Croyland Chronicler's comments on the splendour of Edward's later years:[1]

> for collecting vessels of gold and silver, tapestries, and decorations of the most precious nature, both for his palaces and for various churches, and for building castles, colleges, and other distinguished places . . . not one of his predecessors was at all able to equal his remarkable achievements.

And, he added,

> you might have seen, in those days, the royal court presenting no other appearance than such as fully befits a most mighty kingdom.

[1] *CC*, 559, 563.

Chapter 12

WAR, DIPLOMACY AND DISILLUSION, 1480–1483

From 1480 onwards Edward's mounting difficulties on the Continent were compounded by a new problem, the deterioration of his relations with Scotland into open war. More than anything else this distraction on his northern borders weakened his diplomatic position elsewhere, and made it more difficult for him to intervene effectively in the Franco-Burgundian rivalry, though it also provided him with an excuse for not doing so when importuned for help by Maximilian of Austria. To a considerable degree the Scottish problem explains the growing hesitations which mark Edward's relations with his continental neighbours in these closing years of his reign.

Yet Edward himself was largely to blame for the outbreak of the war with Scotland. Since the treaty of October 1474, relations between the two countries had remained generally cordial. Edward continued to pay the instalments of the marriage portion of his daughter, Cecily, as they fell due, and both sides had avoided any significant breach of the truce. In 1478 James III proposed to strengthen the friendship between the two dynasties still further by offering his sister, Margaret, as a bride for Anthony, Earl Rivers, whose first wife, Elizabeth Scales, had died five years before. With Edward's approval a marriage-treaty was drawn up in December 1478, and the king himself planned to attend the wedding, to take place at Nottingham in October 1479.[1]

Soon after, these amiable relations were transformed. The Scots government began to commit or condone serious breaches of the truce, and there was much raiding and pillaging on the English side of the border. Edward also had reason to suspect that Louis XI was now attempting to distract England from any potential commitment to Burgundy by encouraging James III to cause trouble for England, in the traditional pattern of the 'Auld Alliance'.[2] James was unresponsive to enquiries about the reasons for the truce-breaking, and blamed the

[1] Rymer, *Foedera*, XII, 171 (misdated to 1482); *YCR*, 31.
[2] Commynes, ed. Lenglet, IV, 7 (letter of a Breton spy, June 1480).

English. Edward's reaction was sharp. Early in 1480 Alexander Legh was sent to Scotland to demand reparations for breaches of the truce. If these were not forthcoming, he was to tell James that Edward, on the advice of his council and with the consent of his people, had determined to make rigorous and cruel war on Scotland. Old claims were revived by Legh's instructions to serve notice on James that he was unlawfully in occupation of Berwick, Roxburgh and other places, which of right belonged to the king of England, that he had not done homage to Edward, and that he had wronged the earl of Douglas, who had appealed to Edward as Scotland's sovereign lord. However, to avoid the effusion of Christian blood, Edward would rest content if James handed over his son and heir as a guarantee of his intention to carry through the proposed marriage with Cecily of York, and would surrender Berwick forthwith.[1]

The English government now prepared to back this Palmerstonian manifesto with military preparations. Duke Richard of Gloucester was appointed lieutenant-general on 12 May 1480, with power to call out the levies of the northern counties, and on 20 June commissions of array for the defence of the border were issued in Yorkshire, Cumberland and Northumberland. These preparations were probably defensive at first and designed to discourage further Scots incursions. But during the summer of 1480 the earl of Angus carried out a large-scale and successful raid across the East March which ended in the burning of Bamborough, twenty miles inside English territory. Gloucester and Northumberland called out their retainers and the northern levies, and late in the summer carried out a counter-raid.[2]

Now Edward and his council took the crucial decisions which led to open war. In spite of heavy pressure from Louis XI, James III was not really anxious for war. Himself a man of pacific temperament, he suffered, as did so many Scottish kings, from the chronic turbulence and violence of his nobility, whom he was quite unable to dominate.[3] He therefore sent a herald and a pursuivant to London to suggest a discussion of common grievances. This overture was rudely brushed aside, and at a Westminster council meeting in November 1480 Edward

1 *Cal. Docs Scotland*, IV, 412–15.
2 *CPR, 1476–85*, 205, 213–14; Scofield, II, 279; 'Brevis Cronica', in Pinkerton, *History of Scotland*, I, 503. The evidence for the counter-raid rests upon Edward's own statements in a signet letter to Salisbury and on a report from James III to Louis XI, mentioned in a despatch of 29 October 1480 (Benson and Hatcher, *Old and New Sarum*, 199; *CSP, Milan*, I, 244).
3 For a useful summary of James's character and difficulties, see R. L. Mackie, *King James IV of Scotland*, 8–21.

resolved to go north in person the following year, and teach the Scots a punishing lesson.[1]

By the end of the year preparations for a summer invasion of Scotland had already begun. Much attention was given to the deployment of naval power to support the land forces. Since 1471 the king had been much concerned with the creation of an effective royal navy, so neglected since the days of Henry V. A small nucleus of king's ships existed in the 1460s, and this was increased by systematic purchases after the restoration. Thus the *Antony*, which had brought him home from exile, was bought from her master, Mark Symondson, for £80 in 1472; a Spanish ship known as the *Falcon* was bought in 1475 for £450; in 1481 £1,000 was paid to Genoese merchants for the *Carvel of Portugal*; John, Lord Howard, sold the *Mary Howard*, which was to serve as his flagship on the 1481 campaign, for either 500 or 1,000 marks; and these and other purchases brought the total to fifteen or sixteen ships. Payments for repairs and maintenance to these ships accounted for regular and substantial expenditure in these years.[2] In December 1480 the able and experienced Thomas Rogers, who had been one of Warwick's captains, was appointed as Edward's first Clerk of the King's Ships, and his supervision of the maintenance and organization of the royal vessels enabled them to go out regularly and speedily on patrol. John, Lord Howard, was appointed captain of the main fleet, to serve from mid-May to the end of August 1481, with 3,000 men under his command, and on 14 May Sir Thomas Fulford, with 300 troops, was appointed to command an independent squadron patrolling off the west coast of Scotland. By May, bombards and no fewer than 250 brass handguns were being delivered from the artillery storehouses in Calais for use on the king's ships, and Edward took the prince of Wales with him to Sandwich for a royal inspection of the fleet.[3]

Preparations for the land campaign were going ahead at the same time. A stream of royal mandates was issued between February and April to procure victuals and transport for the king's household and the army going to the north. Rivers undertook to supply a force of 3,000 men, the marquis of Dorset another 600, and Lord Stanley was to bring 3,000 archers from Lancashire. The king's usual concern for his own well-being appears in the purchase of eighty butts of the sweet

[1] *Acts Parl. Scotland*, II, 138; Benson and Hatcher, *op. cit.*, 198–200 (for the council decision).
[2] Richmond, 'English Naval Power', 9–15; P.R.O., E. 28/91–2.
[3] Richmond, *op. cit.*, 9–15; Scofield, II, 303–4; J. Payne Collier, *Household Books of John, Duke of Norfolk, and Thomas, Earl of Surrey*, 3, 9, 274; *CPR, 1476–85*, 240, 264.

and expensive malmsey wine 'for the use of the king and his army against the Scots'.[1] On the useful precedent of the 1460s attempts were also made to foment dissidence in Scotland. The exiled earl of Douglas was still on hand to act as an *agent provocateur*, and two payments of 100 marks each were made to him for 'his divers services and diligences' in this connection. How much success he had is not known, but he failed to win over Edward's former ally, John MacDonald, Lord of the Isles, who now supported James III.[2]

All this cost a great deal of money. More than £2,500 was spent on buying ships; Howard was paid £5,500 as an advance for the wages of his soldiers and sailors; and a further £10,000 was provided for Gloucester's men in the north. To find the necessary finance for these forces and for the army which he proposed to lead in person, Edward first had recourse to the device used in 1475, the levy of benevolences on all who could be bullied or persuaded into making contributions. This seems to have produced a satisfactory response, including 5,000 marks from the city of London. The king also called for payment of the three-quarters of a subsidy (about £24,000) which had been voted to him as part of the war-taxation of 1475, and then remitted after his return. The people of Lancashire were excused from contributing to this in return for a promise to supply 1,000 archers at their own expense; and the city and county of York were likewise exempted because of their services in the past year and what was expected of them in the future. Finally, the king obtained a clerical tenth from the province of Canterbury.[3]

It is important to realize that by the early summer of 1481 England's resources were fully committed to war with Scotland, with the inevitable corollary that nothing serious could be undertaken on the Continent. Both Edward III in the past and Henry VIII later, at the time of Flodden, successfully conducted defensive operations against Scotland whilst campaigning in force in France. But it was unthinkable in military terms to contemplate offensive ventures both across the border and across the Channel, and the expense would in any case have been far beyond Edward's resources without extensive and unpopular parliamentary taxation. The Scottish entanglement was thus to hamper Edward's continental diplomacy to a serious degree.

[1] *CPR, 1476–85*, 249–50; Scofield, II, 305, 316.
[2] *Cal. Docs Scotland*, IV, 299–300; Rymer, XII, 140; John Lesley, *History of Scotland*, 45. John MacDonald's earlier treasonable compact with Edward had come to light in 1475, and in 1476 he had been forced to give up his earldom of Ross and other lands and offices to the king (*Acts Parl. Scotland*, II, 113).
[3] Scofield, II, 304–5; Benson and Hatcher, *op. cit.*, 198–200 (for one of Edward's requests for benevolence).

Though England's public attitude remained uncompromising, with Edward telling the pope of his intention to punish the Scots for their treacherous attacks upon his realm, in practice all this military preparation produced remarkably little.[1] In the late spring John Howard and the fleet made a damaging raid on the Firth of Forth, carrying off several large vessels and destroying others, and burning the township of Blackness. Radcliffe's squadron kept watch off the west coast of Scotland, fending off warships and privateers, whilst a third flotilla patrolled the Channel to protect against French intervention – all evidence of a well-conceived naval strategy.[2] Late in July or early in August, Howard reappeared in the Forth, but this time he achieved little, and by 18 August his fleet was back in port at Sandwich.

The movements of the English land force remain obscure. Since the king himself eventually decided not to go north, in all probability captains like Rivers and Hastings, who normally accompanied the king, and whose contingents formed the main field army, also stayed in the south. So Gloucester and Northumberland had to rely on what forces they could raise in the north, although (judging from the events of 1482) these could easily constitute an invasion army. It is doubtful whether they attempted anything more than a raid in force, since they did not know until late in the year that the king had decided not to join them. James III, however, raised troops and three Scots forces crossed the border, causing 'great burning, hardship and destruction' before withdrawing.[3]

What paralysed the English invasion plans in 1481 were Edward's own delays and his final decision not to lead his army in person. As late as 22 June he ordered the adjournment of sessions in the court of king's bench on account of the war against the Scots, but he lingered, nevertheless, in the neighbourhood of London. Not until September did Edward move to Woodstock, where he stayed a fortnight, reaching Nottingham only at the end of October: there he lodged a further three weeks.[4] It was now too late for full-scale campaigning on the border, and the English commanders in the north settled down to a lengthy and wearying siege of Berwick. But intermittent warfare continued all along the border during the winter of 1481–2, and the

---

[1] CSP, Venice, I, 142–3 (letter of 20 May 1481).
[2] Richmond, 'English Naval Power', 10.
[3] Acts Parl. Scotland, II, 138, and Lesley, op. cit., 45, for the Scots raids; also YCR, I, 34–6, for aid from York against the invasion, adopting suggestions of Kendall, Richard III, 457, as to date of these letters.
[4] Scofield, II, 319.

destruction of crops and cattle added to the suffering caused by a bad harvest and a hard winter.[1]

Perhaps there was some truth in the taunts of Edward's continental critics that he now preferred the bed to the battlefield and the banqueting-table to the tent. But it is more likely that he wished to keep contact with his complex foreign diplomacy, and one specific reason for his staying so long in the south was his plan to visit Calais in order to meet Maximilian of Austria.[2] He later justified his decision not to march in person against the Scots in a letter to the pope on the grounds of 'adverse turmoil' in England, brought about by his demand for the remitted subsidy combined with the high price and shortage of corn. But it is hard to believe that he really thought the security of his throne was threatened or the patience of his subjects sorely tried.[3] The whole affair suggests a certain irresolution in Edward's mind. He could easily have placed the Scots campaign entirely in the charge of Gloucester and Northumberland, or he could have gone north while the season lay before him. But, after much money had been spent and so many preparations made, he did neither: and his lingering in the south effectively destroyed the chances of a vigorous campaign for that year.

When he finally left Nottingham in October 1481 to make his way towards London, Edward's embroilment with Scotland was already reacting unfavourably on his continental diplomacy. Here the major event of 1480 had been the signing of a treaty of alliance with Mary and Maximilian of Burgundy. The chief intermediary was his sister, the dowager Duchess Margaret, whose visit to England between June and September 1480 was made the occasion for the customary ceremonies and display. But her serious diplomatic purpose was to get Edward's aid against France, and, if possible, a full treaty of offensive alliance. To achieve this the hard-pressed Burgundian government was prepared to go to considerable lengths, but the negotiations were hampered by Edward's intention of driving the hardest possible bargain. Not only did he demand that Maximilian should replace the French pension which Edward could expect to lose if he made an alliance, he also wanted to marry his daughter, Anne, to the heir of Burgundy, without paying any dowry for this wealthy husband.[4]

---

[1] Chandler, *Life of Waynflete*, 150–2; 'Brevis Cronica', in Pinkerton, *Hist. Scotland*, I, 503.
[2] Commynes, ed. Lenglet, IV, 38–40.
[3] Cf. Scofield, II, 320; *CSP, Venice*, I, 145–6, for the papal letter.
[4] Maximilian's instructions to Margaret, Commynes, ed. Lenglet, III, 577–83; details of Margaret's visit in Nicolas, *Wardrobe Accounts*, 126, 141–5, 163–6, 241, and Scofield, II, 283–97; and for the marriage, above, p. 247.

Maximilian's protests were overborne, and his bargaining position was weak. The result was a handsome diplomatic triumph for Edward. In a series of instruments sealed between 1 and 5 August 1480, Maximilian pledged himself to pay Edward 50,000 crowns' pension annually if he lost his pension from the king of France, as well as promising Philip of Burgundy to marry Anne of York on terms entirely favourable to the English king. All he got in return was permission to recruit 6,000 archers in England to serve in the war against France at Burgundian expense, and Edward's undertaking that if his attempts to mediate in the struggle between France and Burgundy did not succeed, he would openly declare for the duke.[1]

This Burgundian treaty of 1480 is a notable monument to the theme of avarice in the foreign policy of Edward's later years. His main concern seems to have been to exploit Burgundy's desperate straits to guarantee himself a continued foreign pension, as well as getting an advantageous marriage on the cheap. How far he regarded himself as now committed to Burgundy is not altogether clear. French scholars have argued that the *rapprochement* with Maximilian was intended as nothing more than a means of blackmailing the king of France.[2] But before the treaty was signed Edward personally told his sister Margaret that Lord Howard had reported to him that Louis was now prepared to concede almost all he asked relative to the truce and the marriage of the dauphin and Elizabeth of York, and was even prepared to spend half the yearly revenues of his kingdom to accomplish this purpose; nevertheless, she reported to Maximilian, Edward was willing to go ahead with the treaty. This may indicate either that Edward was exaggerating Louis's pliancy in order to get better terms from Burgundy, or that he had really ceased to have faith in Louis's promises. Certainly Louis took the threat of an English attack seriously enough. In a letter written on 5 November 1480, he declared that the English had shown they intended to make war, and his defence preparations included the stationing of Swiss troops in Normandy and the concentration of Scots ships at Dieppe. On the other hand, Edward would not agree to participate openly in Maximilian's scheme to revive the old triple alliance of England, Burgundy and Brittany, though he did encourage negotiations between the two dukes, conducted in London, which led eventually to the Breton–Burgundian treaty of alliance of

[1] Rymer, *Foedera*, 123–39, for the treaty. Margaret could afford to recruit only 1,500 archers and 30 men-at-arms, whose wages were paid out of a loan of 10,000 crowns made to her by Edward (Commynes, ed. Lenglet, III, 587–9).
[2] E.g. Calmette and Perinelle, 246–7.

16 April 1482.[1] With Brittany herself, England's relations became closer. Plans for a marriage between Edward, prince of Wales, and Anne, the heiress of Brittany, were already under discussion in the summer of 1480, and some kind of treaty of amity was drawn up in November. In May and June of 1481, agreements were reached on the marriage and on a treaty of mutual aid. Edward was to provide Brittany with 3,000 archers at his own expense for three months, and up to 4,000 more at the duke's expense, should Brittany be attacked by France. If Edward decided to invade France himself, the duke was to assist him with 3,000 archers for three months. But it is significant that there was no precise commitment from England on whether or when England might invade.[2]

For these reasons it would not do to assume that English diplomacy in 1480 and early 1481 was merely a manœuvre to twist the arm of the king of France.[3] If this really were his intention, his plan misfired. The first result of Edward's treaty with Burgundy was Louis's pointed failure to pay the instalment of the English pension due at Michaelmas 1480. It also provoked him into stirring up the Scots against England. Finally, it encouraged him to explore the idea of a direct settlement with a weakened Maximilian, which would enable him to jettison his commitments to England. Meanwhile, his annoyance with Edward was intense: he brushed aside English offers to mediate between France and Burgundy, and a peace conference planned for October 1480 broke down.[4]

The early months of 1481 saw increased pressure from Maximilian for more active English measures against France. A Burgundian mission led by the prince of Orange came to England in February to urge that Edward should invade France in the coming summer. The duke's plans for joint action were similar to those adopted for 1475, but Maximilian showed himself far more accommodating than ever Charles had been. If an invasion should prove impossible, then at least, he asked, England should supply more archers to buttress his own war effort.[5] It was here that the Scottish entanglement began decisively to limit England's

---

[1] Commynes, ed. Lenglet, III, 576–7, 603–8 (letters of Duchess Margaret of 27 July and 14 September 1480); Vaesen, *Lettres de Louis XI*, VIII, 295; Pocquet du Haut-Jussé, *op. cit.*, 226–9, for the Anglo-Breton-Burgundian negotiations.

[2] *Ibid.*, 231–4; Rymer, *Foedera*, XII, 142–5, and, for the marriage-treaty, above, pp. 246–7.

[3] Cf. Calmette and Perinelle, 247: 'a blackmail . . . from which he planned to extract the maximum profit'.

[4] *Ibid.*, 246.

[5] Commynes, ed. Lenglet, IV, 10–19, 32–5.

freedom of action. As English resources were mobilized against James III, it became clear that Edward could venture nothing substantial on the Continent, despite reassurances from Edward and his councillors that, war with Scotland permitting, he would either invade France or at least send sizeable contingents to Maximilian's aid. The duke had to be content with a promise from Edward to meet him personally in Calais at Michaelmas.[1]

This was the more necessary since Edward himself was now seeking a *rapprochement* with France. In March 1481, whilst the prince of Orange was still in London, and the negotiations for the Breton aid treaty were in process, he sent Thomas Langton to France to explain to Louis that such troops as he had already sent to Maximilian were intended to help the duke to suppress rebellion in Guelders, and were not to be used against France. Although Louis had failed to ratify the preliminaries of 1479, England would continue to respect the truce agreed in 1477, on condition that Louis immediately resumed payment of the English pension and also sent an embassy to London to regulate arrangements for the marriage of Elizabeth of York and the dauphin. If Louis accepted these terms, then the great army now being assembled in England would be sent against the Scots, and not to the Continent. Louis agreed with alacrity, since Edward's offers implied his abandoning any attempt to get the preliminaries of 1479 ratified as well as any active support for Maximilian. Edward's reward was the appearance in London on 14 August 1481 of Louis's agent, Pierre le Roy, bearing 25,000 crowns, the Easter instalment of his pension.[2]

Amidst the conflicting alternatives of a complex diplomatic situation in 1480–81, Edward's shift off course towards a reconciliation with France and away from an anti-French coalition may have been influenced, as contemporaries on the Continent believed, by his avarice for French gold and his stubborn hope of carrying through the French marriage. Nor could he seriously contemplate war on France without help from parliament, and his difficulties in raising money between 1472 and 1475, combined with the unpopular outcome of the 1475 expedition, made it unlikely that such help would be readily forthcoming. But the decision to make war on Scotland was more important than either of these considerations. His further decision to continue the war in 1482 proved entirely conclusive in forcing him to abandon any idea of an active anti-French policy on the Continent and deprived him of any lever to force King Louis to make his promises good.

[1] Scofield, II, 318–20.
[2] Calmette and Perinelle, 248–50.

Even to continue the war against Scotland was not without its problems. Money was short and large drafts of cash to Gloucester and Northumberland on the Marches had to be raised in part by a return to borrowing. The high price and scarcity of grain following on the bad harvest of 1481 made it difficult to victual the troops in the north. During the winter of 1481–2 there were signs of a revival of disorder and unrest, especially in the northern counties.[1] But in April 1482 a new prospect was opened by the arrival in England of a suitable pretender to the Scottish throne. James III's brother, Alexander, duke of Albany, was a kind of Scots Clarence, restless, ambitious and unprincipled. His plots against King James led to his flight to France in 1479, where Louis provided him with a wife, Anne de la Tour, daughter of the count of Boulogne and Auvergne. Edward's agents got in touch with him late in 1481 and he responded to Edward's offers to promote his claim to the throne of Scotland. At Fotheringhay on 11 June 1482 a treaty drawn up in the Scots vernacular set forth the terms of Edward's contract with Albany. In return for recognition as lawful king of Scotland, and English aid to make good his claim, Albany admitted England's claim to Berwick and the disputed borderlands, promised to deliver Berwick to Edward within a fortnight after his installation in Edinburgh, to do homage and fealty to him, and to break off all Scots confederations or alliances with the king of France. Finally, he was to marry Cecily of York, 'if the said Alexander can make hymself clere fro all other Women, according to the Lawes of Christian Chyrche' – a cynical reference to his recent French marriage. Edward now had his puppet-king to focus opposition to King James in Scotland.[2]

Active preparations for war had been afoot for some time before this treaty was signed. Edward again announced his intention to lead his army in person, and in company with Albany reached Fotheringhay on 3 June, where they were joined by Richard of Gloucester, fresh from a successful raid into south-west Scotland, during which he was said to have taken and set fire to Dumfries and many other towns. But after the signing of the compact with Albany, Edward changed his mind, and decided to return to London, possibly for reasons of ill-health.[3] On 12 June Gloucester's commission as lieutenant-general

---

[1] *CPR, 1476–85*, 343; *YCR*, I, 52–3; Somerville, *Hist. Duchy Lancaster*, I, 252; Scofield, II, 334.

[2] Rymer, *Foedera*, XII, 156–7 (for the treaty with Albany); Scofield, II, 334–9.

[3] According to an entry in the records of the city of Canterbury, William, Lord Hastings, told the mayor that the king's health was not good, and the mayor feared

was renewed, and effective command of the operations against Scotland now passed into his hands. In order to keep the king informed of the progress of the war, a courier system was instituted – the first example of its use in England – with riders stationed at intervals of twenty miles, so that a letter passed at the rate of two hundred miles in two days through a chain of messengers. This arrangement operated successfully from 4 July until 12 October.[1]

Whilst Edward went south again to Dover, probably to oversee the outfitting of his fleet under Robert Radcliffe, Gloucester and Albany moved rapidly northwards. By 18 June they were in York, where they were handsomely received by the mayor, aldermen and guildsmen of the city. By mid-July a very sizeable English army, numbering perhaps 20,000 men, began to assemble on the Border under Gloucester's command, with the earl of Northumberland, the marquis of Dorset, Lord Stanley, Sir Edward Woodville and several northern barons as his lieutenants. Faced by this imposing force, the town of Berwick opened its gates to the English, though the citadel still held out, and the invasion had begun.[2] The political situation in Scotland scarcely favoured a vigorous or united resistance to the English assault. James III was on hostile terms with many of his barons, who resented his low-born favourites. Aristocratic discontent with his rule exploded as the Scots army advanced south from Edinburgh to confront the English. James III himself was seized on 22 July, and many of his courtiers were hanged at the Bridge of Lauder; the king was taken back to Edinburgh and placed under guard in the castle. The English army, which had moved forward pillaging and devastating over a large area of Roxburghshire and Berwickshire, was thus able to enter Edinburgh without resistance before the end of July.

The Scots lords and their forces had withdrawn from the capital and were lying at Haddington, fifteen miles to the east, and were only too willing to negotiate. The changeable Albany lost no time in renouncing his new-found claim to the Scots throne in return for a

---

another revolution which would threaten the city's charter. This may, however, refer either to 1481 or 1482. (*Hist. MSS Comm., 9th Report*, 145). For Gloucester's raid, see *YCR*, I, 54–5, and H. E. Malden, 'An Unedited Cely Letter of 1482', *TRHS*, 3rd ser., x (1916), 159–65, and, for Edward's movements, Scofield, II, 336–8.

[1] Rymer, *Foedera*, XII, 157–8 (Gloucester's commission); C. A. J. Armstrong, 'Some Examples of the Distribution and Speed of News in England at the Time of the Wars of the Roses', in *Studies in Medieval History Presented to F. M. Powicke*, ed. R. W. Hunt and others, 429–54, and Scofield, II, 339–40, for the courier system.

[2] *YCR*, I, 56; Scofield, II, 344, correcting Ramsay, *Lancaster and York*, II, 442, for size of army.

promise that he should be restored to his position and property. This breach of his agreement with Edward seems to have been accepted without objection by the duke of Gloucester.[1] The Scots leaders then asked for a treaty of peace with England, and the renewal of former agreements between the two realms, including the proposed marriage of James, duke of Rothesay, and Cecily of York. In reply, Gloucester said that he had no authority from Edward to make any peace settlement upon these terms, but he demanded, as essential preconditions for any settlement, the surrender of Berwick Castle and the repayment of all monies so far paid for the dowry of Cecily. He seems to have obtained no guarantee about Berwick, but on 4 August the city authorities of Edinburgh entered into a pledge that James's son should marry Cecily, if that were still Edward's wish, otherwise they would guarantee the repayment in yearly instalments of all that part of her dowry already paid. They further promised to send James's sister, Margaret, to England for the long-delayed marriage to Earl Rivers.[2]

With this undertaking Gloucester seems to have been content, and he now made the very strange decision to leave Edinburgh and return to Berwick, where, on 11 August, all but some 1,700 men of his army were disbanded. He may have been influenced by worry about his long lines of communication and lack of victuals for his troops. Albany's defection had changed the situation politically, since the only definition of the objectives of the campaign was that contained in the compact with Albany. Fourteenth-century experience had shown that whilst England could launch powerful armies into the Scottish Lowlands, which the Scots could not meet on equal terms, any occupation of Scots territory was likely to prove unstable and highly expensive and too dependent on the weather-cock loyalties of the Scots nobility.[3] Yet Gloucester's precipitate withdrawal from Edinburgh threw away a great advantage: as commander of a powerful army installed in the capital he could surely have dictated far more satisfactory terms to a distracted Scots government. He may have felt, following Albany's defection, that he lacked instructions on major issues, but he seems to have made no attempt to await further direction from the king in

---

1 Hall, *Chronicle*, 334; Rymer, *Foedera*, XII, 160–1. According to Hall, who draws upon documentary material which has not survived, Albany pledged himself to Gloucester, by a secret deed of 3 August, to abide by his undertaking of 10 June to Edward, in spite of his temporary accommodation with the Scots.

2 Hall, 335–6; Rymer, *Foedera*, XII, 161–2.

3 J. Campbell, 'England, Scotland and the Hundred Years War in the Fourteenth Century', in *Europe in the Late Middle Ages*, ed. J. R. Hale, J. R. L. Highfield and B. Smalley, 184–216, esp. p. 191.

England, with whom the courier system ensured rapid communication. Gloucester's lack of resolution meant that the only practical outcome of an expensive campaign was the recovery of Berwick-upon-Tweed – the castle finally surrendered after a siege on 24 August – and the signing of a short truce to last until 4 November.[1]

However much Edward might choose to exult over Berwick's recapture in a letter to the pope on 25 August, it was but small return for the expenditure of so much money and effort. At least one well-informed contemporary believed that Edward was angry at the outcome of the campaign, and criticizes Gloucester for his premature retreat:[2]

> What he effected in this expedition, what sums of money, again extorted under the name of benevolences, he uselessly squandered away, the affair in its results sufficiently proved . . . [after relating the capture of Berwick]. This trifling, I really know not whether to call it gain or loss – for the safe-keeping of Berwick each year swallows up ten thousand marks – at this period diminished the resources of the king and kingdom by more than a hundred thousand pounds.

The chronicler exaggerated, but his point was valid. Whatever might have been achieved in Scotland after Albany's defection, the advantage had been lost and nothing was settled. Perhaps the fault was not wholly Gloucester's, for there are marked signs of indecision and lack of grasp in Edward's conduct of policy in these last few months of the reign. Not until October 1482 did he decide to call off Cecily's marriage with the future James IV, and demand the promised repayment of the marriage portion. About the same time the marriage planned for Rivers and Margaret of Scotland was also dropped. During the autumn he made no attempt to come to terms with King James, and the short truce was not renewed. By mid-November he seems to have decided to renew the war with Scotland in the coming year.[3]

If the invasion of Scotland had caused Edward little satisfaction, events on the Continent brought him even greater disillusion. In January 1482 a Burgundian mission under the Comte de Chimay arrived in England bearing an urgent appeal from Maximilian. He again urged

[1] Devon, *Issues of the Exchequer*, 502; Hall, *Chronicle*, 344–5; Lesley, *op. cit.*, 49–50. Cf. Kendall, *Richard III*, 143, for a more indulgent view of Richard's conduct of the campaign.
[2] *CC*, 563.
[3] This decision is implicit in the issue of writs on 15 November to summon parliament, the main purpose of which was to vote money for 'the hasty defence of the realm'. For the dropping of the marriage schemes, Rymer, *Foedera*, XII, 164–9; Scofield, II, 353.

Edward to invade France in the coming summer, and on no account must he fail to send the 5,000 or 6,000 troops he had promised. Edward was to be reminded again of his past undertakings, and to be told that, if reports that he had signed a new truce with France proved true, this would mean total ruin and destruction for Maximilian's cause.[1] Yet Edward proved merely evasive. His war with Scotland, he said, prevented him from invading France that year and even from sending any troops to aid Maximilian. The best he could advise was that Maximilian should make a truce with France, and wait for the expected death of Louis XI (who had suffered two strokes in March and September 1481, and was now clearly a deeply ailing man).[2] Only if Louis refused a truce and then invaded Burgundian territory would England send the promised troops. A further mission in March from Maximilian's agent, Pierre Puissant, got no more satisfactory answer from Edward, in spite of the duke's warnings that he could hold out little longer, since the Members of Flanders were already pressing for peace, and he doubted his ability to hold them in line. A further peace conference had been arranged to meet at Arras and he was proposing to send representatives.[3]

This was Edward's last chance, for on 27 March 1482 Mary of Burgundy died from injuries received in a riding accident. The estates of Flanders and Brabant, loyal to her dynasty but dissatisfied with Maximilian, took charge of her children and opened peace negotiations with King Louis. From the French standpoint this opened new opportunities, for a marriage between the dauphin of France and Mary's baby daughter, Margaret, could bring with it, as her dowry, Artois and the county of Burgundy or Franche-Comté. Any lingering hope Maximilian might have of aid from England was finally destroyed in September 1482, when Louis published the hitherto secret truce he had signed with Edward in the previous autumn. Maximilian could no longer control the representatives of Flanders and Brabant, and on

---

[1] This refers to the renewal on 25 October 1481 of the truce between England and France originally agreed in 1477, which was to last for the duration of the lives of Edward and Louis, and for a year after the death of whoever died first (Rymer, *Foedera*, XII, 46–50). See also below.

[2] Commynes, ed. Lenglet, IV, 20–5 (Maximilian's instructions to Chimay); III, 616–17 (Edward's reply). Calmette and Perinelle, 248, mistakenly assign Edward's letter advising a truce to the spring of 1481, following Louis's first stroke, but since it refers to Chimay's mission, it must belong to the latter year and was based upon knowledge of Louis's second stroke: *v.* Scofield, II, 320–1, 325. For the date of Louis's first attack, see Kendall, *Louis XI*, Appendix III.

[3] Commynes, ed. Lenglet, IV, 40–2 (Maximilian's instructions).

23 December France and Burgundy came to terms at the Treaty of Arras. Its conditions included the marriage of Margaret of Austria and the dauphin Charles and the transfer of Artois and the county of Burgundy, and Maximilian's allies, England and Brittany, were excluded from the peace. For Edward this meant not only the loss of his long-cherished French marriage but also of his French pension. Louis now had no further need to humour him, and the next instalment of the pension, due at Michaelmas 1482, was never paid.[1]

Edward was deeply angered and chagrined by the news of the Treaty of Arras. We have the considerable authority of the Croyland Chronicler for the belief that he was so enraged that 'he thought of nothing else but taking vengeance', and Polydore Vergil expressed a similar view. It seems more than likely (as they claimed) that in the last months of his life he was actively planning an invasion of France to punish his great rival.[2] On 18 February parliament granted him a subsidy 'for the hasty and necessary defence' of the realm; money was demanded from the clergy; measures were taken for the strengthening of the fortresses in the Calais Pale, since Artois, which surrounded it, was now to be in French hands; and in February 1483 Edward tried to stir Brittany into action against Louis XI with a promise to send 4,000 archers to serve at English expense for three months, though there was no mention in his offer of a proposed English invasion of France.[3] This impulsive reaction on Edward's part to the news of the Treaty of Arras again suggests a certain lack of grasp of reality in his conduct of affairs, but if an immediate attack upon France was seriously contemplated for a time, the mood did not last long. By March 1482, when relations at sea between France and England had deteriorated badly, there are clear signs that Edward had changed course and was making every effort to preserve the truce with France.[4]

On the other hand, he was clearly determined to maintain his

---

[1] For Louis's publication of the truce, see W. Webster, 'An Unknown Treaty between Edward IV and Louis XI', *EHR*, xii (1897), 521–3; for the treaty of Arras and its background, C. A. J. Armstrong, 'The Burgundian Netherlands, 1477–1521', in *New Cambridge Modern History*, i (1957), 228–32.

[2] *CC*, 563; Polydore Vergil, *English History*, 171. For a contrary view, see Scofield, II, 357, 363.

[3] *RP*, VI, 197; Scofield, II, 363; Calmette and Perinelle, 253; Pocquet du Haut-Jussé, 239. But, as noted above (p. 290, n. 3), parliament was not originally summoned with this purpose in mind.

[4] As shown in his efforts to put an end to seizures and reprisals against French shipping, Gairdner, *Letters and Papers . . . Richard III and Henry VII*, I, 18–19. The mission of Garter King of Arms to France in February 1483 (Scofield, II, 363) may have been connected with this.

aggressive policy towards Scotland. Perhaps the influence of Gloucester may have strengthened his resolve, for the duke stood to gain directly from any conquest north of the border, and continued to be hostile to Scotland when he became king himself.[1] A further inducement was provided by Albany's fresh defection. That unstable nobleman had been appointed lieutenant-general of Scotland by a parliament meeting at Edinburgh in December 1482, but he remained uneasy and dissatisfied. He was certainly in touch with English agents by then, and perhaps even earlier. On 12 January 1483 he formally opened negotiations with Edward to confirm and implement the pact made at Fotheringhay in the previous June, and on 11 February a new agreement was reached. Albany was to attempt to secure the throne of Scotland for himself; Gloucester and Northumberland, as wardens of the Marches, were to hold themselves ready to provide him with up to 3,000 English archers serving for six weeks at Edward's expense; and even larger forces would be supplied if needed. In return, Albany, once established on the throne, was to break any treaty with France, and to give aid to England against 'the occupiers of the crown of France' with all his power and at his own expense. He promised further to marry one of Edward's daughters, to recognize Edward's right to Berwick, and to restore his Scots friend, the earl of Douglas, to his estates.[2] Thus the prospect of collaborating with a Scots faction to overthrow James III, and, less probably, of getting Scots aid against France, could be used to justify the renewal of hostilities against Scotland in 1483. But in contrast with the elaborate military preparations of 1482, no serious war plans were put in hand in 1483. No sooner had Edward begun to collect the money voted by parliament in February than the brittle nature of his deal with the shifty Albany was revealed. On 19 March the duke came to terms with James III, and renounced his treaty with England, although he promised to try to obtain peace with Edward and to encourage the marriage of Cecily of York with the future James IV. If Scotland were to be invaded again, there would now be scant legal cover for a war of aggression.[3]

Historians in general have been harshly critical of Edward's conduct of foreign affairs in the years between 1475 and 1483. French scholars

[1] The palatine grant to Gloucester made in the January 1483 parliament gave him control over any lands conquered north of the West March (above, p. 202); for his policy as king, Gairdner, *Richard III*, 177–80.
[2] Rymer, *Foedera*, XII, 172–6; *Acts Parl. Scotland*, II, 142–3; Gairdner, *op. cit.*, 176–7.
[3] *Acts Parl. Scotland*, II, 31–3.

have tended to perpetuate the prejudices of Edward's own foreign contemporaries, especially those under the influence of the French court, like Commynes and the Italian ambassadors, and have stressed Edward's avarice, in combination with his indolence and his inability to match the cleverness of Louis XI, as the reasons for the eventual collapse of his foreign policies. One even goes so far as to claim that Edward's attitude was wholly dominated by the desire for foreign marriages for his family obtained on the cheap.[1] But even the sympathetic Miss Scofield – in a rare burst of emotion – roundly condemned Edward for a foreign policy she called at once shameful and impossible. It was shameful because he allowed himself to be outwitted and outmanœuvred by the king of France, and it was impossible because the abandonment of the alliance with Burgundy and the search for friendship with the ancient and increasingly powerful enemy of France was 'conceived, as he knew so well, in opposition to his people's best interests and best wishes'.[2] On the contrary, it would be easy to argue – with the advantage of historical hindsight – that England's interests were best served by avoiding expensive military entanglements on the Continent, that the opportunities for effective intervention against a very strong and now united France were already past, with the weakening of the Burgundian state after the death of Duke Charles, and that in practice Edward gave his country eight years of relative peace and prosperity and freedom from the vastly expensive taxation which war involved. But to use such arguments would be to import into the discussion modern criteria which Edward and his contemporaries would either have failed to understand or would have rejected, and to credit him with achievements which he certainly never intended.

Certainly Edward does not emerge with any distinction in his direction of foreign affairs. The entanglement with Scotland was a major misjudgement which greatly weakened his position in relation to continental powers. A foreign policy based upon the continuing good faith of Louis XI was always likely to end disastrously. He was irresolute in that he would neither take the steps necessary to put real pressure on King Louis nor exploit the alternative advantages of a definitely anti-French policy. From his own standpoint his foreign and dynastic policies had been ruined by the time he died, and the chagrin and depression wrought in him by the Treaty of Arras were believed, both

---

[1] Pocquet du Haut-Jussé, op. cit., 232, and see also above, p. 247; see also Calmette and Perinelle, 245–60; and for contemporary criticisms of Edward, Commynes, II, 241, 245–7 ('His greed [for the French pension] deadened his spirit'); CSP, Milan, 235–6, 244. [2] Scofield, II, 357.

by Commynes and by his own keeper of the privy seal, Bishop John Russell, to have been one of the reasons for his death soon after.[1] Yet it would be unfair to overlook his difficulties. In the Machiavellian phase in European power-politics which marks his lifetime he was dealing with opponents who were notably unprincipled, self-interested and shifty, above all with Louis XI, who was too clever for all his opponents (and sometimes too clever for his own good). Edward had neither the financial and military resources nor the backing of popular enthusiasm to enable him to indulge freely in ambitious schemes on the Continent. Moreover, it should not be forgotten that the failure of Edward's foreign policies might have appeared as no more than a temporary setback had he lived longer. The conflicts between France, Burgundy and Brittany were not ended by the Treaty of Arras, and a secure and resolute English king could have taken advantage of them. Major changes in the structure of European politics followed soon after Edward's death, with the death of Louis XI himself on 30 August 1483, his son's involvement in Italy, and the long rivalry between France and the newly-developed power-bloc, based upon dynastic marriages, of Spain, the Hapsburg dominions, and the Burgundian territories in the Low Countries. But in this changing situation England was seriously weakened by two successive usurpations in 1483 and 1485; these placed her on the defensive against foreign rulers who could support pretenders to the English throne, and prevented her from exploiting the Breton succession crisis of 1491–2, or even the Franco-Imperial rivalry for many years to come. Finally, it is worth noticing that, if for rather different reasons, Henry VII chose to follow the essential principles of Edward's foreign policy towards France and the Low Countries. He pursued them, however, with a cleverness, a consistency, and a grasp of reality notably absent from Edward's later years.[2]

[1] Commynes, II, 231; *Grants of Edward V*, ed. J. G. Nichols, liii. See below, p. 415.
[2] For assessments of Henry VII's foreign policy, see R. B. Wernham, *Before the Armada*, 11–50; R. L. Storey, *The Reign of Henry VII*, 66–91; S. B. Chrimes, *Henry VII*, 272–97.

Part IV

THE GOVERNANCE OF ENGLAND

Chapter 13

PERSONAL MONARCHY

Edward of York's approach to the tasks of kingship was essentially pragmatic. Under his rule England shared in the general European tendency towards a strengthening of the princely authority, but this was not accompanied by any interest on the king's part in theories of kingship. His reign saw no significant additions to the law of treason such as had accompanied Richard II's flirtations with absolutism. In contrast with Henry VII, he was in no way concerned to encourage the lawyers to expand the theoretical scope of the royal prerogative by subtly transforming antiquated rights into a new definition of the king's rights over the property of his subjects.[1] Towards the church, it is true, he continued the tendency of his predecessors to claim that the king was emperor in his realm. In 1482 it was held in the royal courts that the authority of convocation must give way to the authority of the royal prerogative, and precedents from his reign were quoted in 1486 to justify the idea that the pope could not act to the detriment of the royal authority.[2] In general he was content with the practical exercise of the still very extensive powers vested in the person of the king. If, on occasion, he acted arbitrarily and without the law, he either dispensed with theoretical justification or, more commonly, sought to persuade his parliaments to give *ad hoc* ratification to particular acts.[3]

This does not mean that the House of York was insensitive to its image, as the survival of a large number of genealogical rolls showing the real or mythical descent of Edward, and of a body of partisan popular ballads, bears witness. Yet the tone of these, like the claims to the throne of 1460 and 1461, is essentially conservative and legitimist, stressing the notion of the restoration of the right line of kings, the true heirs of Richard II. The author of the carol *Edward, Dei Gratia* (probably 1461–4) refers to him as 'Of the stock that long lay dead / God hath caused thee to spring and spread', but combines this with the notion that his success in battle reflects divine assistance ('God hath

---

[1] Robert Constable, *Prerogativa Regis*, ed. S. E. Thorne, v–vii.
[2] S. B. Chrimes, *English Constitutional Ideas in the Fifteenth Century*, 41–2, 52–3.
[3] See the examples of disinheritance cited above, pp. 190–1, and below, pp. 336–7.

chose thee to be his knight'). The same idea recurs in a skilful piece of partisan verse, known as 'A Political Retrospect, 1462':

> A great sign it is that God loveth that knight
> For all those that would have destroyed him utterly
> All they are mischieved and put to flight.[1]

It reappears in a royal proclamation of 27 April 1471 (between Barnet and Tewkesbury), where Edward claims to be lawful king of England 'both by judgement given in parliaments and by authority of the same, as also by Victory given unto us by our Lord Almighty God in divers battles', especially lately in the field beside Barnet, whereby 'the Truth, Right, and Will of God appeareth evidently . . . for our party'. Margaret of Anjou is disparagingly referred to as 'a Frenchwoman born', and daughter of England's mortal adversary.[2]

The 'Political Retrospect' of 1462 also develops the theme of the illegitimacy of Lancastrian rule, and, in doing so, interestingly anticipates the main features of what became (with elaborations) the Tudor view of fifteenth-century history. It contrasts the good king, Richard II, with the perjured Henry IV, struck by God with leprosy for his sins; Henry V, though he upheld the honour of England, was nevertheless a usurper; Henry VI's folly had brought all to langour. Margaret of Anjou is again attacked as an evil-disposed woman, 'And to destroy the Right line was her intent'. England had become a garden full of weeds: Edward of Rouen was 'our comforter' who would 'keep Justice and make weeds clear'.[3]

The genealogical rolls present a rather different propaganda dimension. For the benefit of his Welsh supporters, great play was made with Edward's British descent (through the Mortimers from a daughter of Llewellyn the Great, or to Cadwallader) in contrast with the English descent of Henry VI; and it has been claimed that Edward made more consistent use of this ancient ancestry than did his successors the Tudors. The Welsh bardic poets present him as a royal Welshman, come to rid the land of oppression.[4] Other rolls take the royal ancestry back through the Trojans to Adam, or back to the kings of Judah, and in one mythical pedigree illuminated scenes of his exploits are

---

[1] R. H. Robbins, *Historical Poems of the Fourteenth and Fifteenth Centuries*, 221–6; J. Scattergood, *Politics and Poetry in the Fifteenth Century*, 189–96.
[2] Rymer, *Foedera*, XI, 709–10; *CCR, 1468–76*, 188–9.
[3] Robbins, *op. cit.*, 222–5.
[4] Sydney Anglo, *Spectacle, Pageantry, and Early Tudor Policy*, 44–5; 'The *British History* in Early Tudor Propaganda', *Bull. John Rylands Library*, xliv (1961–2), 20–4.

juxtaposed with appropriate corresponding scenes from the Bible.[1] All this was distinctly outmoded by comparison with the court of Burgundy, which, for all its inflation of the chivalrous concept, was more receptive to Renaissance ideas. Charles the Bold sought to emulate the heroes of classical antiquity – Hercules, Alexander, Cyrus and Hannibal; Philip the Good chose Jason as the patron of his new chivalrous order; and Olivier de la Marche derived the descent of the dukes from a marriage between Hercules and Alice, queen of Burgundy.[2] The Yorkist dynastic attitude was essentially traditionalist, even old-fashioned.

If the advent of a new dynasty presaged no new theory of monarchy, this should not be allowed to obscure the strong element of practical innovation in Edward's government. His reign saw a series of responses to the urgent need of reasserting the royal authority. To accomplish this end, he thought more in terms of new men rather than new institutions, or even the reform of old ones. He was no doubt well aware of the inefficiency and clumsiness of the exchequer, but he made little attempt to reform it. Instead he by-passed it by the use of a more flexible, but by no means new, system of household finance, where much depended on the personal activity of Edward himself and on the work of a small group of royal servants whose importance stemmed not from the offices they held but from the confidence placed in them by the king. It was a system so highly personal that it broke down when an inexperienced king (like Henry VII in his early years) came to take charge of it. Even innovations like the council in Wales and the Marches were essentially *ad hoc* developments suggested by the existence of a prince of Wales surrounded by experienced councillors whom the king knew and trusted, and only to a limited degree did it ever become institutionalized. In the north of England Edward preferred to rule even more informally through the medium of his brother, Duke Richard, and a ducal council which never acquired any special or official powers. Similarly his use of special commissions of oyer and terminer as a means of enforcing law and order at the local level is characteristic: they were immediate and personal; and his reign saw no significant increase in the power of regularly-instituted and permanent agencies such as the justices of the peace.[3] The legislation of

---

[1] B.M., Harleian MS 7353; Lancashire Record Office, Crosse of Shaw Hill Papers, D D Sh. 15/2; cf. D. A. L. Morgan, 'The King's Affinity in the Polity of Yorkist England', *TRHS*, 5th ser., xxiii (1973), 21–2. For a similarly antiquarian interest, see J. W. McKenna, 'The Coronation Oil of the Yorkist Kings', *EHR*, lxxxii (1967), 102–4.

[2] J. Bartier, *Charles le Téméraire* (1944), 271 ff.　　　[3] Below, pp. 398–9.

the reign did little to alter the laws or the institutions of the realm. It could be said of his rule (as of Henry VII's) that it represented 'essentially a rejuvenated personal monarchy, able to instil vigour into the old administrative agencies'[1] – or to supersede them by informal devices.

Effective government in fifteenth-century England still depended largely on the personal activity of the reigning king. The development over several centuries of an established bureaucratic machinery had in no way removed the need for vigorous direction and constant personal supervision by the monarch. Nor was this need much reduced by the development of certain legal and practical limits on the exercise of the royal power. He might not make laws without the assent of his subjects; he could not tax them without their consent; he could not dispense with statute law on his own authority. Yet the powers inherent in the royal prerogative remained extensive, and they were inseparable from the king's own person.[2] Some important areas of government had always been regarded as highly personal, notably the conduct of foreign affairs and decisions as to peace and war. The exercise of the royal patronage directly concerned the king, as did the use of the king's power to pardon or punish and give grace and favour. Yet the king was also expected to make innumerable decisions on all matters of policy and administration, as well as on a host of minor matters, the trivia of day-to-day routine government. As Dr A. L. Brown has shown recently, the most striking impression left by the surviving records is of 'the dominant and burdensome role that the king was expected to play in government'.[3] The need for 'a more obsessive and personal rule than was otherwise normal' was especially acute in 1461, following on the years of disintegrating royal authority during Henry VI's last decade.[4] Neglect or mismanagement of his royal duty to govern had been one of Henry's major failings as king, and the result had been laxity, weakness and corruption at the very centre of power.

In contrast, it was a major asset of Edward IV that he never needed to be taught this lesson. From the start of the reign a new spirit pervaded the administration, as the king bent his energies to make his will felt and to demonstrate to his people his close concern for the welfare

[1] S. B. Chrimes, *The Administrative History of Medieval England*, 261–2.
[2] Chrimes, *English Constitutional Ideas*, 1–62, and an admirable short summary of the king's position in government, pp. 342–9.
[3] A. L. Brown, 'The Authorization of Letters under the Great Seal', *BIHR*, xxxvii (1964), 154.
[4] G. L. Harriss, in 'A Revolution in Tudor History?', *Past and Present*, no. 31 (1965), 91.

of his realm. His first parliament was greeted by the first recorded speech from the throne, by a remarkable declaration by the chancellor of the will of the sovereign, and by the king's promise to tour the country and do justice in person. We have evidence too from this parliament of the attention paid by king and council to the business of the assembly.[1] Two areas of government which especially interested the king were the maintenance of law and order and the commercial affairs of England, and ample evidence has been cited below to show how direct and continuous was Edward's supervision of these matters.[2] Occasionally the records reveal in some detail the nature and extent of royal activity. For example, a summons to appear before king and council usually involved facing the king in person. In 1471, for instance, the mayor and corporation of Nottingham sought action against rioters who, they alleged, had been supported and maintained by Henry, Lord Grey. On their appearance in the Star Chamber, 'in plain council, the King's Highness being present', the king's decision about the rioters was first declared by the chancellor of England, and 'over this, our said sovereign lord by his own mouth asked and questioned' Lord Grey about his connection with the accused, and then 'gave the same Lord Grey in strait commandment and injunction' that he should not support or favour any persons within the town of Nottingham.[3] In 1479 the mayor and corporation of Bristol found themselves in a quandary. They had suffered from the activities of one Thomas Norton, gentleman, the leader of a riotous gang, who was himself a man of evil life – a 'common haunter of taverns', who lay in bed to nine or ten in the morning, and during the afternoons, when sermons and evensongs were in progress, was seen 'playing at the Tennis and other such frivolous disports'. This Norton, out of malice, accused the popular mayor of Bristol of high treason, and the corporation appealed to the king. Eventually the parties appeared 'before the king in his honourable council' at the palace of Sheen, and there Edward examined Norton and required him to substantiate his charge. This he could not do, 'but demeaned himself as a person run into frenzy as the King had since said to the said John Twynho Recorder [of Bristol] and to divers other persons'. Like a 'rightwise natural Sovereign Lord and a verray Justiciar' Edward then dismissed the case against the mayor.[4] Such examples could be multiplied.

[1] Below, pp. 341–2, 346.   [2] Below, pp. 353–6, 399–402.
[3] *Records of the Borough of Nottingham*, II, 384–7.
[4] The full record of the case is printed in *The Great Red Book of Bristol*, ed. E. W. W. Veale (Bristol Record Soc., xviii, 1953), 57–92, esp. 69, 72–3.

The records of the London Company of Mercers also reveal how often they felt the force of the king's will. In 1479, when they were late in paying their subsidy, Edward demanded of them a recompense of £2,000, and said he would be answered and paid. When they appeared before the lords of the council and offered instead 500 marks, they were told that the council had no authority or power to diminish any penny of the king's demand. Only after much 'labouring' by the queen on their behalf were they summoned 'before the king's good grace at his wardrobe', and Edward consented to accept a payment of 2,000 marks. In 1480, when they complained about the activities of the Hansards, Edward asked them to produce a memorandum on the subject, which he would show to his council to oversee and understand. Soon after, hearing of the king's displeasure, they decided to prohibit the practice of going on pilgrimage to the tomb of King Henry VI. In January 1483 the king again expressed displeasure about recent attacks on Dutchmen in London, 'which it liked the king's highness to show unto the mayor'. These examples may serve to show that the mercers were dealing not with an impersonal government but with a king whose variable temper and sharp oversight was a matter of immediate concern to the entire company.[1]

The king's interest did not cease with the affairs of wealthy London companies or the corporations of the larger boroughs. His burden of work was considerably increased by the contemporary idea that no matter was too small for his attention, and that he must be accessible to the complaints or requests of even the humblest of his subjects.[2] Like all medieval kings, he was beset by a flood of petitions from his people for grace and pardon, promotion or reward. A few examples from among many documents bearing the royal sign-manual – and therefore reflecting his personal oversight – show how insistently his attention was demanded on small matters: they relate to the spring of 1462, during his tour north to Lincoln and back to London. At Stamford in March he was beset by petitions from Cambridge students. Typical of them was one Nicolas Silvester, 'scholar of divinity, which hath no livelihood nor friend to support him towards his finding and must of necessity without your good grace depart fro his said learning': the king granted his request to be made a scholar of the royal founda-

---

[1] *Acts of Court of the Mercers Company*, 106, 118–27, 136–7, 139–40.
[2] A. L. Brown, *op. cit.*, 154, showed that in Henry IV's reign the king was dealing with at least 2,000 and perhaps as many as 4,000 petitions in a given year, as well as ordering the issue of some 1,500 letters under the great seal, and hundreds of signet and privy seal letters.

tion of King's Hall, Cambridge. At Huntingdon he is found instructing one of the squires of the body, Thomas Grey, to attend diligently to the lands of the rebel, Sir Thomas Tuddenham, which had been placed in his keeping 'under a certain form declared by us unto you' – very likely an oral instruction. At Leicester he accepted John Delves, esquire, as his true liege man and subject, and ordered the sheriffs to refrain from taking any of his goods or livelihood. Also at Leicester he granted a request from John Mason, for the good service he had done to Duke Richard of York, to be master-mason of Chester Castle; he confirmed to Sir John Astley an annuity he had held from John Mowbray, late duke of Norfolk; and he released John Fletcher of Nottingham from the death sentence imposed on him. Back at Westminster he told the chancellor that he had commanded Lord Montagu and Sir James Strangways to find out whether the former rebel, Humphrey Nevill, was now 'of good and faithful disposition towards us', and, if they found in his favour, he was to be pardoned his life, land and goods. None of these was a matter of much importance except to the individuals concerned, but they were very much part and parcel of the daily routine of a busy king.[1]

The Paston family correspondence likewise reveals how burdensome could be the subjects' demands for the king's personal attention to their private affairs. In the first eight years of the reign the Pastons successfully persuaded the king to intervene in their concerns on no fewer than three occasions; on two others they tried without success to get his support; and on another Edward intervened on his own initiative. The letters also illustrate the fact that Edward's handling of such matters was based upon a wide knowledge of the personalities and issues involved. In dealing with the quarrel between the Pastons and the duke of Norfolk over the Fastolf lands in 1469, Edward was evidently well aware of the influence which Norfolk's councillor, Sir William Brandon, had over his master, in urging him to violent measures. 'Brandon,' said the king, 'though thou can beguile the duke of Norfolk, and bring him about the thumb as thou list, I let thee witt thou shalt not do me so; for I understand thy false dealing well enough', and he went on to say that if Norfolk did anything contrary to the laws then he (Edward) 'would know well enough that it was by nobody's means but his' and Brandon 'would repent it, every vein in his heart'. Such examples lend support to the claim made by the author of the Croyland Chronicle that in spite of his love of boon companion-

[1] P.R.O., E. 28/89; C. 81/1377/9.

ship, debauchery, extravagance and sensual enjoyments, Edward nevertheless

> had a memory so retentive, in all respects that the names and estates used to recur to him of nearly all the persons dispersed throughout the shires of this kingdom, just as though he were in the habit of seeing them daily; and this even, if, in the districts in which they lived, they held the rank only of a private gentleman.[1]

There is ample evidence amongst the records of his reign that Edward took his kingly duties very seriously. Beyond all doubt the business of state was his main preoccupation. A very large number of warrants, letters and petitions bear the royal sign-manual, in the form of the monogram 'R.E.'. Occasionally the king added further instructions written in his own hand to an official mandate. In 1479, for example, he wrote to 'our beloved squire', John Harcourt, rebuking him for delays in supplying money from the lands in his charge, and adding in autograph: 'John we pray you fail not this our writing to be accomplished' – a small matter, perhaps, but one which illustrates the personal nature of the king's control and of his attention to detail.[2] Of the thousands of letters patent on the bulky Patent Roll for the first year of the reign (the second largest of the fifteenth century) about one-third were authorized 'By King' or 'The King by word of mouth', that is, on Edward's personal instructions; even more, about one-half of the whole, were issued on the authority of privy seal warrants, which normally came also from the king in person.[3] The four acts of resumption passed during the reign included no fewer than 817 special clauses of exemption. Each of these was the result of a special petition, and each was signed by Edward himself.[4] There is evidence of his scrutinizing and signing the accounts of royal officials, of his acknowledging the receipt of money delivered 'unto our own person in the Chamber', and of payments made 'by our commandment to him given by our mouth'.[5] The disappearance of all the financial records of the king's

[1] *PL*, I, 202–3, 231–2, 242–3; III, 301–2, 313; IV, 113–15; V, 30–3. The king's remarks to Brandon are in *PL*, V, 31. *CC*, 564.
[2] D. A. L. Morgan, 'The King's Affinity', 21. Documents signed by the king survive in profusion in the P.R.O. classes C. 81 (Signed Bills and Warrants under the Signet) and E. 28 (Exch. T.R., Council and Privy Seal).
[3] *CPR*, *1461–7*, 6–171, collated with the original Patent Roll. On the question of authorization, see A. L. Brown, 'The Authorization of Letters', 127–55.
[4] B. P. Wolffe, *The Royal Demesne in English History*, 156–7.
[5] *Ibid.*, 168. A number of accounts by John FitzHerbert and others, tellers of the exchequer, for 19 and 20 Edw. IV, bear the royal sign-manual: e.g. P.R.O., E. 28/91–2.

chamber makes it difficult to know how extensive was the king's super-vision of his finances, but a modern authority had no hesitation in describing him as 'a king with a forceful personality, great energy and thoroughly conversant with his affairs, especially in matters of finance'.[1]

One of the clearest indications of Edward's close personal control of the work of government comes from the increased use of letters and warrants issued under the signet – the seal kept by his own secretary – and therefore emanating directly from the king. The number of war-rants to the chancellor under the signet increases greatly after 1461, and there was a marked tendency to draw up the warrant in the exact form in which letters under the great seal were to be issued, thus leaving the chancellor no discretion. Letters under the signet immedi-ately become of greater importance than they had been under Henry VI, and were used for a wide variety of purposes – for instructions to local authorities or individuals to put down disturbances or to raise troops, for example, or to summon men to appear before the king and council. The signet letter became one of the most frequently used means of communication between the king and the authorities of the towns in particular (though they are more likely to have survived in borough archives than amongst the more vulnerable records of private families). This increased use of the signet is the main reason why the office of king's secretary became noticeably more important. For the first time, it has been claimed, it became an essential part of the administration, and the way lay open for the great development of the secretaryship under the Tudor kings. For the secretaries themselves, the office now came to provide (as it had not done before) a direct stepping-stone to a bishopric.[2]

It is no longer possible to give credence to the reputation created for Edward by Philippe de Commynes that he was a lazy king, pre-occupied by wine, women, food and hunting, and spurred to energy only in times of crisis.[3] The author of the Croyland Chronicle, who must have known Edward well, shared the interest which many men felt in the paradox of the king's character – that a man so given to debauchery could still retain so great a grasp of business – but the two facets of his character were not mutually exclusive.[4] If he made mis-takes, they sprang from the errors of judgement to which he was prone, not from inattention to the kingly business of governing.

[1] Wolffe, op. cit., 174; and for further evidence, see below, Chap. 16.
[2] J. Otway-Ruthven, The King's Secretary and the Signet Office in the Fifteenth Century, 17–18, 48–9, 56, 59; and below, pp. 320–1.
[3] Commynes, I, 203; II, 5, 153–8, 239–40, 334; and see also J. R. Lander, 'Edward IV: The Modern Legend: and a Revision', History, xli (1956), 40 ff.   [4] CC, 564.

Chapter 14

COUNCILLORS, COURTIERS AND KING'S SERVANTS

No fifteenth-century king, however energetic or strong-willed, could hope to govern without expert advice and assistance. For matters of high policy, administrative and judicial decisions, and the general day-to-day functioning of the administrative machine, the king relied heavily on the collective wisdom, specialized knowledge and advice of his council. Recent research has gone far to show that the Yorkist council was a more vigorous and significant element in government than was formerly believed. It has also tended to stress the essential continuity in the work of the council throughout the fifteenth century, whichever king happened to be on the throne. Even under a king so personally active as Edward of York, the council 'remained that central coordinating body necessary to every governmental system'.[1]

The composition of the council was governed solely by the king's choice and need, and was in no way determined by ordinance or custom. Although its members were sworn and salaried, it never had a definite or nominated membership. In spite of the rather fragmentary evidence surviving today, we know the names of 105 persons described as councillor during Edward's reign, but in practice the working council was a small body. The few known attendance lists – only thirty-nine have come to light for the entire reign – show that as many as twenty people might attend a particular council, but the average was much lower, normally between nine and twelve.[2] The core of the

[1] A. L. Brown, 'The King's Councillors in Fifteenth-Century England', *TRHS*, 5th ser., xix (1959), 95–118, and for recent work on the Yorkist council, see especially the two valuable papers by J. R. Lander, 'The Yorkist Council and Administration', *EHR*, lxxxiii (1958), 27–46, where the problems of the evidence are fully discussed, and 'Council, Administration and Councillors, 1461–85', *BIHR*, xxxii (1959), 137–78. These largely supersede the discussions in such older works as J. F. Baldwin, *The King's Council in England in the Middle Ages* (1913), 419 ff. For some comment on the judicial work of the council, see below, pp. 402–3.

[2] Lander, 'Council, Administration and Councillors', 151, 158; Brown, *op. cit.*, 116. The figure of 105 excludes 19 persons named as councillors only in connection with diplomatic negotiations.

council, which did most of the work, was formed from the chief officers of state (chancellor, treasurer and keeper of the privy seal), together with one or two bishops, who were usually themselves ex- or future ministers. In Edward's first reign these were often men of high birth who had been promoted early to bishoprics and became great figures in government, notably Archbishop Thomas Bourchier of Canterbury and Archbishop George Nevill of York. After 1471, when the bench of bishops tended more to reflect Edward's own choice, they tended rather to be men of more humble origin promoted for their value to the king in the secular government of the realm, men like Rotherham of York, Russell of Lincoln and Morton of Ely.[1] Their regular associates were the successive treasurers, who normally acted as presidents of the council in the king's absence, and of these the most prominent was Henry Bourchier, earl of Essex, who held the office from July 1460 to April 1462, and then from 1471 until his death three days before the king's, and who seems to have been something of an elder statesman amongst the king's advisers. The treasurership was a valuable office, which offered opportunities for profit beyond the £1,330 a year it was worth to Earl Rivers (1466–9), and in Edward's reign it was held by a nobleman throughout the reign, except for eight months between October 1469 and July 1470.[2]

This small group was strengthened by varying numbers of magnates, barons, gentry, lesser ecclesiastics and officials. Magnates (apart from the treasurers) were never very prominent on Edward's council, and their importance certainly becomes less after 1471, as the king's security on his throne increased, and he came to rely more on 'new' or lesser men. This was certainly not due to any deliberate policy of exclusion: only fourteen peers are not known to have been summoned to council meetings some time during the reign. But it is a striking fact that his cousin, the duke of Norfolk, and his brother-in-law, the duke of Suffolk, were never councillors, probably because the king thought them troublesome or had a low opinion of their abilities. Nor probably were many magnates prepared to give that regularity of attendance which was the key to continuous influence in the council.[3] Many had demanding private affairs to engage their attention or had offices or duties under the Crown which made it difficult to attend regularly.

1 Below, pp. 319–22; and on the general point, Brown, *op. cit.*, 116–17.
2 The exception was William Grey, bishop of Ely.
3 Brown, *op. cit.*, 117. The majority of lords were equally reluctant to attend parliament regularly: J. S. Roskell, 'The Problem of the Attendance of the Lords in Medieval Parliaments', *BIHR*, xxix (1956), 153–204.

Men like Gloucester or Northumberland in the 1470s and 1480s probably could not often spare the time to make the long journey from the north to Westminster, and indeed were not expected to. From time to time council meetings may have become a forum for contending factions amongst the nobility, notably in 1467–8, when the declining influence of the Warwick group was pitted against that of the 'king's men' over the issue of alliance with Burgundy.[1] Occasions of this kind were probably rare, for magnates, like other councillors, were summoned to advise and support the king, not to oppose his wishes.

By contrast with the magnates, some at least of the barons were regular members, amongst them some of the king's most influential councillors. This phenomenon, however, owes something to Edward's practice in the early years of the reign of ennobling his most trusted servants. Many of those most prominent in the council between 1461 and 1470 had been newly promoted from the ranks of the gentry.[2] A more significant change in the composition of the council is the increase in the numbers of men of gentry origin, many of them connected with the royal household, amongst them some of the king's most reliable servants. Their numbers rise markedly (from eleven to twenty-three) after 1471, and we should really add to this total four knights recently ennobled by Edward – Hastings, Howard, Dinham and Mountjoy.[3] These figures illustrate Edward's tendency to rely upon men of lesser rank in the government of the realm. Knights like John Fogge, John Scott, John Elrington, William Parr and Thomas Vaughan, all of whom held important posts in the royal household, were also much about the king at court and served him as ambassadors, military commanders and commissioners, as did Hastings and Howard.[4] Such men formed the core of Edward's personal 'establishment', and their conspicuous role in the council, especially after 1471, is evidence of his success in reasserting untrammelled royal control in government and high politics. His liking for laymen, however, did not include a marked preference for lawyers, who were to become so prominent on Henry VII's council. Edward was the first king to appoint a solicitor-general, and about one-third of the commoners on his council were lawyers, but the gentry of the household remained a majority.[5]

The functions of the king's council seem to have remained much the

[1] Lander, 'Council, Administration and Councillors', 159–60.
[2] They include Hastings, Herbert, Ferrers, Dinham, Mountjoy and Humphrey Stafford.
[3] Lander, op. cit., 151–2.   [4] See further below, pp. 324–6.
[5] E. W. Ives, 'The Common Lawyers in Pre-Reformation England', TRHS, 5th ser., xviii (1968), 154–5.

same under Edward as they had been earlier in the century, except that they were less executive and more advisory in character.[1] As a matter of convenience the king consulted his council on a wide variety of issues, from high policy decisions down to comparatively minor administrative matters, including the answering of individual petitions and the disposal of royal patronage. It is clear that major questions of war and peace were discussed in council. It was, for example, by a 'verdict' of the council, sitting in its usual meeting-place, the Star Chamber in Westminster Palace, that reprisals were ordered against Hanseatic merchants in London in November 1468, an act which led to commercial war with the Hanseatic League. It is also an example of the extent to which the private interest of individual councillors helped to shape an official policy decision.[2]

Major issues of foreign and domestic policy might also be considered before specially-summoned 'Great Councils', particularly when the king was anxious to obtain the advice and cooperation of the lords spiritual and temporal as a whole. In October 1469, after Warwick had been obliged to release him from captivity at Middleham, the king summoned all the peers of the realm to a series of great council meetings between November and February 1470, clearly in order to buttress his exercise of authority. In February 1476 the elaborate and compli-cated regulations for the Staple's relations with Calais were submitted to another great council. In February 1477 eighty-five great men were summoned by writs of privy seal to discuss the situation on the Conti-nent caused by the death of Duke Charles of Burgundy, and in Novem-ber 1480 another great council meeting at Westminster was assembled to support the king's intransigent line towards the Scots. The import-ance of great councils can, however, easily be exaggerated. Whilst some meetings were clearly 'extra-parliamentary sessions of the House of Lords', others styled as great councils, especially in unofficial sources, resembled specially large meetings of the regular council, reinforced by a number of lords and knights.[3]

It was, however, in the day-to-day conduct of government that the council was of the greatest value to the king – in implementing as well as formulating policy, in relieving the king of some of the burden of administrative and judicial decision, and generally in keeping the

---

[1] Brown, *op. cit.*, 115–17; Lander, 'Yorkist Council and Administration', 46.
[2] Below, pp. 365–6.
[3] Most of the evidence for great council meetings is brought together by Scofield, II, 376–8; for 1476, see Lander, 'Council, Administration and Councillors', 143. Cf. Myers in *English Historical Documents*, 356–7.

machinery of government working smoothly. Professor Lander's researches have shown how the council provided a continuous supervision of particular problems, for example, the many difficult issues involved in the garrisoning and financing of Calais and relations with the Company of the Staple. The council was also consulted and made proposals over the whole field of finance and general administration. Its advice was sought, along with that of the merchants, for the re-coinage of 1464–5; it was consulted about the reform of the royal household in 1478; it dealt with problems of customs evasion and restitution for piracy. It was active in the administration of the Crown lands. Its opinion was asked on questions like the summoning of parliament and convocation. But it had only a limited capacity for independent executive action. It was always the *king's* council, and its proposals needed the king's assent, even in times of emergency. In 1464, for example, when money was urgently needed to put down insurrection, the council in London proposed selling licences to trade in wool, but not until the patent had been sent to the king in Yorkshire, and signed by him, did any action result.[1]

One of the features of late medieval political development in Western Europe was the emergence of the court as a centre of power and influence. In part this was due to a greater sophistication of social life: the court became a centre of lavish display, and the king came to be surrounded by an elaborate and formal etiquette. This enhanced the importance of the courtier who was part of that ceremonial organization. Much more, however, was it a product of the concentration of patronage in the person of the ruler. The king was the *fons et origo* of reward and punishment, lord and master of the whole spectrum of grace and favour. The attraction of the court was the attraction of access to the person of the monarch.[2]

At the heart of the court was the royal household which performed the dual function of supplying the ruler's daily needs and of providing a suitably magnificent setting for his public person.[3] Many prominent courtiers were officials of the royal household, though for some their

[1] Scofield, I, 331; and for a detailed survey of conciliar work, Lander, 'Council, Administration and Councillors', 138–51; 'Yorkist Council and Administration', 35–46.
[2] On the functions of the court, see the stimulating discussion by P. S. Lewis, *Later Medieval France: The Polity*, 119–26, and also the remarks of B. Wilkinson, *Constitutional History of England in the Fifteenth Century*, 214–16.
[3] A. R. Myers, *The Household of Edward IV*, for a full description of household organization and reform during the reign.

functions had become honorific and their duties were handed over to deputies. But the court was thronged by many other people – relatives of the king and queen, the great officers of state on official business, foreign envoys and visitors, and a host of suitors and petitioners after favour. All, from the highest to the lowest, sought the king's grace.

The attitude of most Englishmen towards the government of the day has always been deeply influenced by self-interest. The Yorkist period was no exception. In particular, the politically-conscious propertied classes were much less interested in who advised the king on matters affecting the common weal than in who advised him – and whose advice he took – where their private interests were involved. Influence, properly applied, might help to avert retribution or penalties and open wide the doors of royal patronage. Hence the goodwill and good offices of those about the king were eagerly sought. 'Friends and influence at court were the key to most things in the fifteenth century.'[1] Men about the court were, therefore, focal points for intensive lobbying as petitioners sought to gain the king's prior attention for themselves. Contemporaries firmly believed that a word from the right people at the right time was essential to achieve or to speed their purpose. This need for lordship, patronage and 'well-wishers' in high places is one of the strongest themes in the surviving private papers and letters of the Yorkist age.

Even for highly-placed persons the normal method of access to the king was by written petition. These were often handed to the king personally, but even for those fortunate enough to get that far, the support of influential friends was thought highly desirable if a favourable response were to be obtained. For example, when the king was visiting Durham in 1461, the prior of Durham sought to obtain repayment of 400 marks, which, he claimed, his monks had been compelled to supply to Queen Margaret, 'money they might never worse have spared in all their days'. He was lucky enough to have the goodwill of both his bishop, Laurence Booth, and of the great earl of Warwick himself. As the king left the cathedral, the prior relates:

> my lord of Durham took me in his hand, and sat down upon his knee before the king, and so did my Lord of Warwick, and I beside him; and they prayed the king to be my good lord; and the king answered and said, 'Prior, I will be your good lord, and I shall remember your bill.'[2]

For those less well connected than the prior of Durham, it was a matter of keeping a careful watch on the political scene and then seek-

---

[1] Brown, 'Authorization of Letters under the Great Seal', 148–9.
[2] James Raine, *The Priory of Hexham*, I, ciii–iv. The prior did not, however, recover his money.

ing the good offices of those judged to be of greatest influence. For the Paston family, threatened by powerful and unscrupulous local magnates, the winning of suitable patrons was a constant preoccupation. In the first twelve years of the reign they sought the favour of over a dozen of the king's councillors and courtiers. In 1461 John Paston approached the treasurer, the earl of Essex. His response is an interesting indication of the constant pressure to which the king was subject from those around him.

> And now of late [writes Paston's son] I, remembering him of the same matter, enquired if he had moved the king's highness therein; and he answered me that he had felt and moved the king therein . . . beseeching him to be your good lord therein, considering the service and true part that ye have done and owe to him . . . he said he would be your good lord therein as he would be to the poorest man in England. He would hold with you in your right; and as for favour, he will not be understood that he shall show favour more to one man than to another, not to one in England.[1]

In other words, the intervention had failed, for it was essentially favour, and special favour, that the Pastons sought. Others about the king whose good offices the Pastons sought in this period included the two royal dukes, three earls (Warwick, Pembroke and Rivers), the archbishop of York, the bishop of Ely, Lords Hastings and Scales, Sir Thomas Montgomery, Sir John Woodville and Thomas Wingfield. In the end none of this lobbying won them redress against the dukes of Norfolk and Suffolk, and their failure to win the king's favour made them welcome the return of Warwick and fight against Edward at Barnet Field. Even the good offices of humbler men whose position gave them access to the king were not to be despised. In 1479, for example, John Paston sought to persuade the king to 'take my service and my quarrel together' by enlisting the support of 'Sir George Brown, James Radcliff and others of my acquaintance which wait most upon the king and lie nightly in his chamber'.[2]

The Yorkist court, rather than the council, was the main marketplace for those who wished to buy and sell influence. Even the great influence wielded by that prominent councillor, William, Lord Hastings, sprang more from his office of king's chamberlain throughout the reign, for in this capacity he controlled business brought before the king in

[1] PL, III, 301–2.
[2] PL, I, 259–61; VI, 28–9; Lander, 'Council, Administration and Councillors', 164 and n.

person, including the hearing of petitions.[1] In the second decade of the reign, however, even Hastings's influence seems to have been overtaken by that of the queen and her relatives, as Hastings himself admitted. Even before 1470, the support of the queen's kinsmen was thought well worth having. In 1469 the Pastons sought the good lordship of her brothers, Anthony, Lord Scales, and Sir John Woodville, although neither is known to have been a councillor at the time. We have already seen how anxiously the London Merchant Adventurers and Mercers lobbied the queen and her kinsmen; so too did the corporation of Bristol, when they wished to 'move' the king. The Woodvilles were the courtier group *par excellence* in Edward's later years.

Whether any of Edward's numerous mistresses exercised much influence at court is a question almost impossible to answer. Among the ladies who graced the royal court in Edward's later years there were many who attracted the king's attention, for there is no evidence that his licentiousness diminished with age. Dominic Mancini, writing in 1483, insists that[2]

He was licentious in the extreme; moreover, it was said that he had been most insolent to numerous women after he had seduced them, for, as soon as he grew weary of dalliance, he gave up the ladies much against their will to the other courtiers. He pursued with no discrimination the married and unmarried, the noble and lowly: however, he took none by force.

Edward's detractors could later dwell on the extent to which his lechery had become a source of public scandal and irritation. Richard III used his brother's womanizing to discredit his memory, and More echoes the phrasing of the act of settlement of January 1484:[3]

the king's greedy appetite was insatiable, and everywhere all over the realm intolerable. For no woman was there anywhere, young or old, rich or poor, whom he set his eye upon . . . but without any fear of God, or respect of his honour, murmur or grudge of the world, he would importunely pursue his appetite, and have her, to the great destruction of many a good woman . . . and all were it that with this and other importable dealing, the realm was in every part annoyed. . . .

The identities of almost all the ladies who shared the royal bedchamber are nowadays decently obscured from us, and probably few had much influence over him. The exception is perhaps the charming

[1] A. L. Brown, *op. cit.*, 149; and for what follows, above, pp. 101–2.
[2] Mancini, 67.
[3] More, *Richard III*, 72 (part of the duke of Buckingham's speech attacking Edward's reputation); *RP*, VI, 240.

Mistress Shore (whose real name was Elizabeth, not Jane), of whom
Sir Thomas More has left a touching portrait. The wife of a London
merchant, William Shore, she was still alive, though old and
impoverished, when More was writing his *History of King Richard
III*:[1]

> Proper she was and fair. . . . Yet delighted not men so much in her beauty,
> as in her pleasant behaviour. For a proper wit had she, and could both
> read well and write, merry of company, ready and quick of answer, neither
> mute nor full of babble, sometimes taunting without displeasure and not
> without disport. The king would say that he had three concubines . . . one
> the merriest, another the wiliest, the third the holiest harlot in his realm,
> as one to whom no man could get out the church lightly to any place, but
> it were to his bed. The other two were somewhat greater personages, and
> nathless of their humility content to be nameless, and to forbear the praise
> of those properties. But the merriest was this Shore's wife, in whom the
> king therefore took special pleasure. For many he had, but her he loved,
> whose favour to say truth . . . she never abused to any man's hurt.

More believed that she had considerable influence with the king,
though she did not use it for her own personal gain:

> Finally, in many weighty suits, she stood many men in great stead, either
> for none or small rewards, and those rather gay than rich: either for that
> she was content with the deed itself well done, or for that she delighted to
> be sued unto, and show what she was able to do with the king, or for that
> wanton women and wealthy be not always covetous.

However this may have been, Mistress Shore, unlike Edward III's
unattractive mistress, Alice Perrers, was not showered with rewards
which left their traces in the official records of the reign, and More
may have overstated her influence. In the absence of any other references to the king's mistresses, it seems reasonable to assume that, like
Philip the Good, duke of Burgundy, he altogether excluded his mistresses from state affairs, and there is no evidence that any exerted an
influence comparable with French royal mistresses of the fifteenth and
sixteenth centuries.[2] Queen Elizabeth may well have resented Edward's

---

[1] More, 55–6; Nicolas Barker, 'Jane Shore', *Etoniana*, no. 125 (June 1972), 383–91
('The Real Jane Shore').

[2] R. Vaughan, *Philip the Good*, 132–3. Unlike Philip, Edward did not legitimize his
bastards or introduce them to court. Only two of them are known to us by name:
Arthur Plantagenet (d. 1542), created Viscount Lisle by Henry VIII in 1523 (*CP*,
VIII, 63–8) and a daughter named Grace, who may have been brought up in the

womanizing: More tells us that she hated Lord Hastings partly because of his influence with Edward, but also she thought him 'secretly familiar with the king in wanton company', though Mancini reported that not only Hastings but also the queen's sons, Dorset and Richard Grey, and one of her brothers, Sir Edward Woodville, were the principal 'promoters and companions of his vices'.[1] But there is no good reason to suppose that the king's promiscuity in any way diminished the queen's influence over her husband.

For those who possessed it, influence at court was a highly marketable commodity, to be paid for in grants of office or fees, gifts in cash and kind, bribes and douceurs. Hastings's standing at court brought tangible rewards in the form of fees or annuities from an impressive list of English lords, ladies, bishops, abbots and gentry, especially some, like Lord Rivers, who felt their position to be politically dubious at the outset of the reign, and in the large pensions he was later to receive from Duke Charles of Burgundy and King Louis of France.[2] Unfortunately, we possess little similar information about the rewards accumulated by other prominent courtiers, but there is no reason to suppose that Hastings was in any way exceptional. Very probably John, Lord Howard, for example, benefited handsomely from his influence with Edward after 1475: Louis XI gave him presents worth 24,000 crowns in cash and plate as well as a pension of 1,200 crowns yearly, though these may well reflect Howard's importance as Edward's principal negotiator in his dealings with France.[3] What cannot be readily assessed is the flow of gifts of pipes of wine, venison and other dainties which an influential courtier might expect to receive wherever he went, and of which many examples survive, especially in the records of the English towns. Yet it would not do to over-emphasize the importance of such rewards, for they do not compare with the wealth and influence which these men acquired by the king's own gift. More than one of Edward's courtiers rose from comparative rags to riches through the patronage lavished on them by their royal master. But the typical Yorkist courtier was no pleasure-loving favourite, no idle fop-about-town. He was generally not only a courtier but also a

---

household of the dowager queen Elizabeth Woodville, and was present at her death in 1492 (B.M. Arundel MS 26, ff. 29v–30r). I am indebted to Miss M. M. Condon for this (the only known) reference to her.

[1] More, 10–11; Mancini, 67–9.

[2] Above, pp. 73–4.

[3] For examples of profits made by other courtiers, and for evidence on bribes and inducements, see Lander, 'Council, Administration and Councillors', 163–4; and for Howard's rewards, above, pp. 234, 255.

councillor, administrator, soldier and king's servant. Save for a few of the queen's kinsmen, Edward's grace and favour had to be earned.[1]

The fifteenth century in England was an age when educated laymen steadily penetrated into areas of government formerly monopolized by clergy. Nevertheless, the Crown still relied heavily on the higher clergy for the conduct of government at the centre. With the exceptions of Thomas Bourchier, William Grey and George Nevill, promoted respectively to Canterbury, Ely and Exeter during Duke Richard of York's tenure of power in the 1450s, Edward IV had inherited a Lancastrian-appointed episcopate, some of whose members had had close links with Henry VI or his queen. Seven bishops (apart from those mentioned above) chose to link themselves with Yorkist fortunes after the take-over of power in July 1460, and four of these appear at various times on Edward's council in the early years of the reign.[2] But only one Lancastrian bishop, Lawrence Booth of Durham, who was translated to York in 1476, was ever promoted to a higher see, and this not until he had proved his loyalty; and only Booth, as chancellor from July 1473 to May 1474, from this Lancastrian group was ever to hold high office in Yorkist administration. Richard Beauchamp, bishop of Salisbury from 1450 to 1481, claimed in 1462 that he was high in favour with the king, 'as the chief of the three to whose judgement all the most secret matters of the council are referred', but in default of other evidence his claim lacks substantiation. He was, however, prominent in the negotiations leading to the Burgundian marriage of the Lady Margaret, and performed the wedding ceremony, and in the 1470s, when he became chancellor of the Order of the Garter, he was closely connected with Edward's rebuilding of St George's, Windsor.[3] Otherwise, Edward had little confidence in the Lancastrian bishops, and they are not prominent in his government. This is in spite of the fact that vacancies on the episcopal bench were remarkably few in the first decade of the reign, except in the remote see of Carlisle. This was normally occupied by northerners who had little share in central govern-

---

[1] For some evidence on this, see below, pp. 324–8.

[2] This section is based on the biographical notices of bishops in the three volumes of A. B. Emden, *A Biographical Register of the University of Oxford* (1957–9), and his companion volume for Cambridge (1963), which are alphabetically arranged; for membership of the council on the lists in Lander, 'Council, Administration and Councillors', 166–75; and for the changes in the character of the episcopate, R. J. Knecht, 'The Episcopate and the Wars of the Roses', *University of Birmingham Hist. Journal*, vi (1958), 108–31, though my own conclusions differ from those of Dr Knecht on certain points.

[3] *CSP, Milan*, I, 64; Scofield, I, 412–15, 429–33, 442, 455, 463; and above, p. 275.

ment, and was of no political importance. Apart from Canterbury, three sees, two of them major – Winchester, London and Lichfield – were held throughout the reign by Lancastrian-appointed bishops, and (except at Carlisle) there were only four English vacancies and one Welsh in Edward's first decade. He had, therefore, little chance before 1471 to stiffen the bench of bishops with his own supporters.[1]

The three 'Yorkist' bishops, Bourchier, Grey and Nevill, stand somewhat apart from their fellows not only for their earlier political connections with the House of York but also in being men of high birth with powerful aristocratic affiliations. In 1461 Archbishop Bourchier was already a man of about fifty, and had been a bishop for twenty-eight years. His thirty-two-year tenure of Canterbury (1454–86) was to prove the longest in the long history of that see. He was an experienced administrator, and his close support as primate was of great value to the king. Though never appointed by Edward to a major office of state, he was active in the council chamber, officiated at state functions such as coronations and prorogations of parliament, lent considerable sums of money to the Crown, and occasionally served on local commissions. He also managed the convocation of Canterbury in the king's interest, and proved very willing to follow the king's line in respect to such matters as papal attempts to tax the clergy. His attitudes reflect clearly enough the general attitude of the English clergy to the pope, which has been described as 'the passive recognition of the pope's leadership of Christendom, the faint acknowledgement of his right to obedience, the dislike of taxation, and the effective dominance of the king who was close at hand'.[2]

The subtle and energetic personality of the young George Nevill is even more prominent until the breach between Edward and the Nevills made him suspect and disloyal. Chancellor of England until 1467, he proved an able servant, who was also active on the council and in the negotiations with France and Burgundy, and was probably the chief spokesman for the Nevill interest at court. He had been well rewarded for his services by translation to York in 1465, and was one of the few ecclesiastics to be given substantial grants of land at the king's disposal during the great share-out of the early 1460s.[3] Less well

[1] There were three vacancies at Carlisle, 1462–8, and one each at Bath and Wells, Exeter, Rochester and York, and at Bangor.

[2] F. R. H. Du Boulay, ed., *Register of Thomas Bourgchier, 1454–86* (Canterbury and York Soc., 2 vols, 1955–6), i–xxiii; Du Boulay, 'The Fifteenth Century', in C. H. Lawrence, ed., *The English Church and the Papacy in the Middle Ages*, 218–19. Judging by his neglect of his diocesan business, much of his time and energy must have been spent in the service of his sovereign.   [3] See above, pp. 71–2.

connected than the others, the scholarly William Grey, who had spent several years studying in Italy, was none the less a useful royal servant: a councillor at least from 1463, he was also the only cleric to hold the office of treasurer (1469–70). Edward himself, however, was careful not to choose his bishops from the families of the high aristocracy, as had often been the case under Henry VI. Until the appointment of his brother-in-law, Lionel Woodville, to the see of Salisbury in 1482, Bourchier and Nevill had no counterparts on the Edwardian bench. Three younger sons of peers were preferred (Richard Scrope to Carlisle, William Dudley to Durham, and Edmund Audley to Rochester), but none was of magnate origin.

The typical Yorkist bishop, as revealed in Edward's own promotions, owed nothing to birth or high connection. He was usually a man from the lesser gentry or of merchant background who had made his mark in some aspect of the royal service, and had risen through his proven abilities in the conduct of secular affairs. They were in general a competent and hard-working body of men. Almost without exception they were highly educated, graduates of Oxford or Cambridge, many of them with doctoral degrees. Some of the most successful had been trained in canon or civil law, and the number of lawyer-bishops increased significantly in Edward's reign. These also tended to command the more important and wealthy sees. Several were themselves respectable scholars, and most were patrons of scholarship and education. Some at least managed to combine active service to the king with conscientious, if not spiritually inspiring, government of their dioceses. Men like Bishop Robert Stillington of Bath and Wells, who visited his diocese only once in twenty-six years, were scandalous exceptions rather than the norm. They owed their advancement, however, less to personal piety, scholarship or pastoral devotion, than to their value to the king.[1]

Of the twenty-two men who became bishops in Edward's reign, only seven had no known close connection with the king. Four of these held the more obscure Welsh sees, and the other three were short-lived incumbents of distant Carlisle. Of the remainder, three had their start by serving the king as his secretary – which now became a firm stepping-stone to a see – and a fourth went on to serve Henry VII in the same capacity, and was promoted to Exeter in 1492.[2] But it is a sign of the times that the other two men who held this essentially 'clerical' office,

[1] Knecht, *op. cit.*, esp. pp. 108–10; A. Hamilton Thompson, *The English Clergy and their Organization in the Later Middle Ages*, 1–39.
[2] They were John Booth of Exeter, Peter Courtenay of Exeter, James Goldwell of Norwich and Oliver King.

William Hattcliffe (who had been Edward's physician) and William Slyfield, were both laymen. Three more of Edward's bishops, Robert Stillington of Bath and Wells, Thomas Rotherham of Rochester, Lincoln and York, and John Russell of Rochester and Lincoln, were rewarded with sees for their services as keepers of the privy seal, an office which between them they held throughout the reign, whilst Stillington and Rotherham together held the chancellorship of England for a total of fourteen out of twenty-two years. In these two major offices there was, therefore, a remarkable continuity of occupation. Other bishops were able chancery clerks, such as John Alcock, bishop of Rochester (1472-6) and of Worcester (1476-86), and John Morton, bishop of Ely (1479-86), the future cardinal-archbishop of Canterbury. Both of them, as successive masters of the rolls, had been the effective departmental heads of chancery. Richard Martin, who became bishop of St David's in 1482, likewise had chancery experience, but had also been one of the king's chaplains. Another royal chaplain was William Dudley, who was appointed dean of the chapel royal immediately after Edward's restoration, but he probably owed this, and his later promotion to the very wealthy see of Durham in 1476, partly to Edward's gratitude, for he had been one of the first to join Edward in 1471.[1] Thomas Milling, who was advanced to Hereford in 1474, likewise owed his progress to political services. As abbot of Westminster, he had sheltered the queen and her family in sanctuary during Edward's exile, and he was one of the only two members of religious orders to achieve an English see under Edward's rule.[2]

Such men served the king in a variety of ways. Apart from monopolizing the chancellorship and keepership, the great majority of the bishops, more especially Edward's own appointees, were active members of the king's council. All had experience in diplomatic work. Bishop Russell, for example, was heavily engaged as ambassador both before and after his promotion to Lincoln. In 1467-8 he had been prominent in the negotiations with Burgundy; between 1471 and 1473 he was a leading negotiator both with Burgundy and the Hansards, and after 1474 also served on embassies to Scotland and Brittany.[3] Bishop John Alcock, the founder of Jesus College, Cambridge, was another successful lawyer-administrator, who first appears in the 1460s

---

[1] Above, p. 164.
[2] The other was Richard Bell, prior of Durham (1464-8), bishop of Carlisle (1478-1495), and a member of the king's council from 1471.
[3] Emden, *op. cit.* (Oxford); Scofield, I, 430, 455, 507; II, 16-17, 30, 47, 51, 63-80, 102, 124-5, 251, 300.

as an expert appointed to hear appeals in the admiral's and constable's courts of England. In 1470 he was on embassy to Spain, and in 1471 was an envoy to the Scots. By then master of the rolls, he was one of those appointed to administer the lands of the prince of Wales, and in November 1473 he was made the prince's tutor and president of his council, and much of his work thereafter lay in Wales and the Marches. His close connection with the royal family is illustrated by the fine set of stained-glass portraits of the king, queen and some of their children which he installed in his newly-rebuilt priory church at Little Malvern in Worcestershire.[1] The civil lawyer, James Goldwell, acted as master of requests, as ambassador, as clerk of the council, and as Edward IV's agent in Rome at various times during the reign, becoming bishop of Norwich in 1472. The Franciscan Richard Martin of St David's was a councillor from 1470, chancellor of the earldom of March and chancellor of Ireland, a councillor of the prince of Wales from 1473, and an ambassador to Burgundy and Spain.[2] It is not surprising to find in view of this record of service that no fewer than nine of Edward's surviving bishops went on to find favour with Henry VII, some to hold high office, some to achieve further promotion within the episcopate.

If the clerical statesmen and civil servants still supplied invaluable traditional expertise in the work of diplomacy and administration, they were already being overshadowed in the political aspects of government by their lay counterparts. One of the characteristic features of Edward's choice of royal servants is the extensive use he made of laymen, especially those below the rank of baron. This was not wholly without precedent, for both Richard II and Henry IV, in special circumstances, had delegated important tasks to knights and gentry. Yet the process had not been continued under Henry V and Henry VI, and Edward's reign marks an important phase in the development which was soon to lead to the virtual monopolization by laymen of government office. The main reason for this phenomenon under Edward IV is the highly personal nature of his rule in an age when the reassertion of royal prerogative power and the maintenance of effective political control in the country at large were the ruler's main preoccupation. It also owes something in the early years of the reign to the circumstances of his accession; like Henry IV, Edward found that the political basis of his regime amongst the established peerage was slender, and he had to rely on the services of lesser men (some of whom he ennobled) to a

[1] Emden, *op. cit.* (Cambridge); *CPR*, I, 89; II, 169, 171, 184, 201, 283, 366, 379, 401.
[2] Emden, *op. cit.* (Oxford).

greater degree than had been normal in the previous half-century. Even when fully secure on the throne, however, he continued to rely on proven gentry servants, and the men of the royal household and the knights and esquires of the body are even more prominent in the second decade of the reign.

This is not to suggest that he did not still rely in many important respects on the goodwill and cooperation of the baronage. Yet the function of the aristocracy was seen as essentially the upholding of royal authority and the maintenance of order in the provinces. The driving-force of government came from the king at the centre, and it was the men of the royal household (among them some of the 'new Yorkist' peers like Hastings and Howard) who could best implement policies expressive of the king's prerogative and directly produced by his own decisions. In constant contact with the king personally, and enjoying his confidence and favour, they became the chief agents of the king's personal rule.

The royal household entourage (excluding the domestic departments 'below stairs') was never very large, numbering some 250–300 at the beginning of the reign, with a modest increase later. The inner ring of knights and esquires of the body, who were politically employed, expanded more noticeably. In 1468 there were ten knights of the body, in 1471 about twenty, and probably thirty by 1483, and there was a similar increase in the numbers of esquires, who totalled between thirty and forty at the end of the reign.[1] Above them in rank and importance were the senior officers of the household. Its official head was the steward, normally a nobleman. The first two stewards, William Nevill, earl of Kent, and John Tiptoft, earl of Worcester, were often absent from court on other duties, but their successors, the earl of Essex (1467–71) and Lord Stanley (1471–83), were probably much less involved in outside activities. In any event all were much in the royal confidence and prominent in the council. The office of chamberlain was held throughout the reign by Lord Hastings. The effective head of the household was its treasurer, whose official standing is illustrated by the fact that when the steward was absent he was to have the rank of an earl, and when he himself was away from court, he had a daily subsistence allowance of 20s, the same as the keeper of the privy seal. The treasurer, like the controller of the household, was normally a knight, like Sir John Fogge, treasurer from 1461 to 1467, and Sir

---

[1] Morgan, 'The King's Affinity', 4–5, 13, and see also generally Myers, *Household of Edward IV*.

John Scott, controller 1461–70.[1] With the development of the house-hold as revenue-collecting and spending department, the offices of cofferer and treasurer of the chamber became increasingly influential. These again were held by gentry or men of humble origin, such as Sir John Elrington, cofferer from 1471 to 1474, and Sir Thomas Vaughan, treasurer of the chamber from 1465 to the end of the reign. The ways in which these men served the king other than in their household duties varied considerably, but most were active outside the household, and their role may best be illustrated by example.

One of the most energetic, successful and well rewarded of the Yorkist administrator-politicians was Sir John Howard, of Stoke-by-Nayland in Suffolk. In his range of interests and versatility of talents he fore-shadows the Renaissance courtiers of Tudor England. Knighted after the battle of Towton, he became the first Yorkist sheriff of Norfolk on 6 March 1461, and in July was appointed to the privileged position of king's carver, with a salary of £40 a year, as well as being made constable of Norwich and Colchester Castles (offices which doubled his slender income from land). In 1463 he took part in the northern campaign at the siege of Alnwick and then held a naval command as deputy to the earl of Kent over the English fleet which raided the French coast. In 1467–8 he sat in parliament as M.P. for Suffolk. From 1467–71 he was treasurer of the royal household, combining this position with diplomatic work in connection with Lady Margaret's Burgundian marriage and membership of the king's council from February 1468. In 1470 he com-manded a fleet at sea against the Hansards and later against Warwick and the Bastard of Fauconbe:g. After lying low during Edward's exile, he emerged to join him in London in April 1471, and probably fought at Barnet and Tewkesbury. Soon after, he was Lord Hastings's deputy at Calais and went there with him to subdue the rebellious garrison. He played a leading part in the negotiations with Louis of France during the campaign of 1475, remained behind as a hostage, and thereafter became Edward's agent in the intensive diplomatic negotiations with Louis (with whom he was clearly in high esteem) right up to the final despairing attempts to stave off the Treaty of Arras in the autumn of 1482. In the previous year he had commanded the English fleet which ravaged the Firth of Forth.

All this was combined with a good deal of activity in East Anglia, where he frequently acted on commissions of array, commissions to

---

[1] For the principal officers of the household, see the lists in Myers, *op. cit.*, 286–97, and in *Handbook of British Chronology* (2nd edn 1961), 72–80.

arrest rebels and rioters, to bring men before the king and council, to seize men and ships for the king's fleets, and to investigate the evasion of statutes, and a number of major commissions of oyer and terminer; and in 1480 he was one of the six royal councillors deputed to investigate a major clash between the abbey and townsmen of Bury St Edmunds. Royal favour greatly increased his local influence, and in southern East Anglia, and especially along the Essex seaboard, he became a great power in the land. His local standing was of considerable military value to the king. Probably long before he inherited his share of the estates of the Mowbray dukedom of Norfolk, he could turn out a force approaching the thousand men he supplied in 1483 to Richard III. That king obviously thought his support worth buying at a very high price. Like Edward himself, Howard also owned and managed a considerable fleet of ships – at least fourteen can be identified as his during the reign – some of which were later sold to the king for service in the royal navy.

His loyal and active service to King Edward brought him rich rewards. The lands granted to him in East Anglia could scarcely have been worth less than £300 a year, and as early as 1464 his influence at court was earning him another £81 a year in fees paid to him by private persons, which were greatly augmented after 1475 by the favours shown to him by Louis of France. Towards the end of the reign he was obviously a very wealthy man. In 1481 he was able to afford £12 for a Christmas present to William, Lord Hastings, and could finance the education of four poor boys at Cambridge. His career illustrates the way in which personal service to the king might enrich a man and increase his influence, but it also shows how varied and continuous was the service demanded by his master. The successful Yorkist civil servant had to be a man of great energy and considerable ability.[1]

A similar lesson (at a slightly lower level of success) might be drawn from the careers of two of Edward's controllers of the household, Sir John Scott (1461–70) and Sir William Parr (1471–4 and 1481–3). Like his fellow Kentishman, Scott was one of the group of faithful servants who served the king throughout his reign. Between 1461 and 1470 he was especially active on commissions in Kent, where royal favour in the form of offices, grants of land, and wardships steadily

[1] For Howard, see the article in *DNB*; *CPR, 1461–85, passim*; and the large numbers of references supplied by Miss Scofield. On some points I am indebted to the researches of Miss Anne Crawford, notably the fact that he was not treasurer of the household as late as 1474, as is usually stated, and for information on his shipping interests.

increased his influence. In 1467 he was sent to negotiate the marriage of Margaret of York, and in 1468 he was one of those who accompanied the bride on her way to Bruges. From May 1469 until February 1470 he was away from court negotiating with the Hanse in Flanders. He also sat as M.P. for Kent in the parliament of 1467–8. He may have shared Edward's exile, certainly fought at Barnet, and played a leading part in suppressing the rebellion in Kent of 1471. Though he held no household office after 1471, he continued to serve the king actively as councillor, commissioner in Kent, marshal of Calais, where he was left in charge during the invasion of 1475, as a member of the council of the prince of Wales, and as a diplomat. His presence in the parliament of 1472–5 for the Westmorland borough of Appleby, with which he had no personal connection, shows the government using its influence to put reliable and substantial supporters into the commons when their backing was needed.[1]

His successor, Sir William Parr, from Kendal in Westmorland, performed local service like Scott's at the other end of the realm. Knight of the shire for Westmorland in 1467–8 and 1472–5, and for Cumberland in 1478, sheriff of Westmorland for life after 1475, and deputy to the duke of Gloucester in Carlisle and the West March, he was one of the government's chief supporters in the north-west, along with his brother, Sir John Parr, king's knight and master of the horse to Edward by 1472. Both were former connections of the earl of Warwick, who had committed their fortunes to Edward in 1471 soon after his landing, and had fought for him at Barnet and Tewkesbury; and William's appointment soon after as controller may have been connected with that fact. His diplomatic experience was specialized in extensive negotiations with the Scots, and it was perhaps his acquaintance with Scots and Border affairs which led to his reappointment as controller in 1481 when relations with Scotland were deteriorating into open war. He was one of the two household men – the other was Sir Thomas Montgomery – to be elected as a Knight of the Garter in the second half of the reign.[2]

Below the great officers of the household came a much larger group, all of whom performed services to the king. They included the king's carvers and sewers (together six in number), the knights and esquires of the body already mentioned, and the king's knights and esquires, who occupied slightly less honourable positions in the hierarchy, though

[1] Wedgwood, *Hist. Parl., Biographies*, 750–2.
[2] *Ibid.*, 663–4; and the many references in Scofield and the Calendars of Patent Rolls; Morgan, *op. cit.*, 15, 20.

only about a half would have been on duty at any one time.[1] These men had a dual function. In the household's domestic organization they carved the king's meat, poured his wine, helped dress and undress him, brought food to the royal table, and attended and watched his person by day and night, each according to his degree. But they also had a wider political function. According to the 'Black Book' of Edward's household, they were 'by the advice of his council to be chosen men of their possession [i.e. men of means], worship and wisdom; also to be of sundry shires, by whom it may be known the disposition of the countries' (i.e. shires or regions).[2] Their careers show that in practice they formed one of the chief links between court and country, more especially since the 'shift-system' allowed them to alternate between their duties about the king and their own local interests.[3]

Some of these men were relatives of the king, such as Thomas Bourchier and Thomas Grey, his cousins, and Thomas St Leger, his brother-in-law. Others were kinsmen of more prominent royal servants, like John, Lord Howard's son, Thomas, the future earl of Surrey, William, Lord Hastings's brother, Sir Ralph, and William, Lord Herbert's brother, Thomas Herbert, esquire. The majority of king's knights and king's esquires belonged to established landowning families. Men like Thomas Sturgeon, the son of a London mercer, who became master of the ordnance, or Thomas Prout, a man of obscure origin who rose from king's servitor to king's esquire but never sat in parliament, are rare. Most were members of the county establishment, who normally not only served as sheriffs and justices of the peace but also sat in parliament for shire rather than borough seats. Of the twenty-two men named in the household ordinance of 1471 as knights or esquires of the body or king's carvers or cupbearers, all but four can be followed through their careers: of these eighteen, fifteen were knights of the shire at one time or another.[4] At least thirty such men sat in parliament during the reign, and the number may well have been much

[1] A 'shift-system' allowing them to be away from court for half the year seems to be clearly implied in the provisions made by the Black Book of the Household for knights of the household, esquires of the body and esquires of the household (Myers, op. cit., 108, 111, 127). Of the twelve knights, for example, it provides that four should be 'continually abiding and attending upon the king's person in court' and elsewhere makes arrangements for the time when 'viii. of these knights be departed from court'. [2] Myers, op. cit., 127.

[3] For the political use of a similar system by the dukes of Burgundy, see C. A. J. Armstrong, 'Had the Burgundian Government a policy for the nobility?', in Britain and the Netherlands, ed. J. S. Bromley and E. H. Kossmann (1964), II, 9–32. Cf. Morgan, op. cit., 20–1.

[4] For the ordinance, see Myers, op. cit., 199–200, 262–4.

higher in fact, because so many returns of M.P.s are lacking. In the parliament of 1472–5 they represented between them as many as eleven counties. They were also prominent on commissions of array and other key commissions in the counties, especially in times of political crisis.[1] They were also important as providers of troops for the king's personal following, and made a most substantial contribution to the 1475 invasion army.[2] Rarely of sufficient importance to sit on the king's council, they nevertheless served Edward as constables of royal castles, stewards or officials in royal lordships, and commissioners to deal with a wide variety of business within their own areas of local influence.

As with others who served Edward well, their rewards were considerable. A typical example of a successful king's knight is Sir John Pilkington, of Chevet Hall near the royal lordship of Wakefield in Yorkshire. A member of a cadet branch of the important Lancashire family of that name, his services during the crisis of 1460–61 were rewarded with his appointment as an esquire of the body, in July 1461, with a fee of 50 marks a year, and he was made constable of Berkhamsted Castle and controller of tonnage and poundage in the port of London. Substantial grants of forfeited Lancastrian estates followed in the 1460s. Imprisoned in 1470 for his loyalty to Edward, he was knighted by the king at Tewkesbury, and enriched by further grants of land and office in the years which followed. Shortly before he died in 1478, he was wealthy enough to found his own chantry in the parish church of Wakefield, and to secure a licence to fortify his new-built hall at Chevet and three other North-Country houses; and his estates were valued after his death at £213 yearly, at least double their worth before Edward's accession.[3]

To the king the value of these men lay also in their political reliability. As a group, they showed a high degree of political loyalty to their master. Some shared his Burgundian exile, and an impressive number fought at Barnet and Tewkesbury.[4] Their loyalty survived his death, for

---

[1] E.g., the commissions to seize the lands of the duke of Clarence into the king's hands in March and April 1478 (CPR, 1476–85, 108–11), which were staffed almost exclusively by household men.

[2] Above, pp. 221–2; and for other examples, and the importance of Calais as an 'outward office' of the chamber, Morgan, op. cit., 16–17.

[3] A. Gooder, The Parliamentary Representation of the County of York 1285–1832 (Yorks Arch. Soc., Record Series, 1935), I, 204–7; and Calendars of Patent Rolls, passim. For the information about the value of his estates, I am indebted to my former student K. R. Dockray.

[4] At least nine were knighted after the battle of Tewkesbury (PL, V, 105; Shaw, Knights of England, II, 14–16).

they were also prominent amongst the leaders of the 1483 rebellion against Richard III, a king who had deposed, and was presumed to have murdered, Edward's legitimate heir.[1] It is to Edward's credit that he could inspire both loyalty and devoted service from all who knew him well. It is true that this was a mercenary age, and service was rewarded generously, but it would be unwise to ignore the importance of Edward's personal charm and leadership in extracting such hard work and devotion from his servants.

Yet events were to prove that there were serious weaknesses in the structure of this royal affinity which Edward built around his person. Knights and gentry in the king's service formed only a comparatively small group amongst the English gentry as a whole. By contrast with the earlier Lancastrian kings, Edward IV spent comparatively little money on retaining the services and the loyalty of gentry who did not come to court. There has survived 'a list of fees and wages granted out of the Crown to divers folk by king Edward IV, whom God pardon', reflecting his expenditure of this kind at the end of his reign.[2] Together they total £9,164. Much of it went on the salaries of the officers of state and the judges, such as the chancellor's £420, the keeper of the privy seal's £365, and the £215 paid to the chief justice of the king's bench; there were also the fees and rewards of a number of chancery and exchequer officials. There are a few payments which appear to be annuities, among them £107 17s 4d to the king's mother, Duchess Cecily, 300 marks to Earl Rivers, 200 marks to another royal brother-in-law, Thomas, Lord Maltravers, and 100 marks to John, Lord Dinham. Almost all the remainder is taken up by the wages and fees of the king's household staff, heralds and pursuivants, serjeants-at-arms, minstrels, trumpeters, yeomen of the Crown and of the chamber, and an occasional senior officer like the king's secretary, Oliver King. Another list gives the fees and wages of officers of the Duchy of Lancaster for 1482–3 totalling a further £1,391.[3] All this represents, however, essentially a *wages* bill, not expenditure on annuities. There is no sign of anything comparable with Henry IV's massive expenditure of £24,000 on *annuities alone* in 1400. Such retaining fees absorbed nearly

---

[1] Apart from Sir John Fogge and Sir Thomas St Leger in Kent (where the rising had strong Woodville connections), they were the real leaders of the Wiltshire–Berkshire sector of the risings of 1483: amongst these, William Norris, William Berkeley, William Stonor, John Cheyne and Giles Daubeney were attainted for their treason in the parliament of 1484 (*RP*, VI, 245–6).

[2] B.M., Harleian MS 433, fos 310–16.

[3] *Ibid.*, fos 317–21. Cf. the comments of Wolffe, *Royal Demesne in English History*, 185–6.

£9,000 of the Duchy of Lancaster revenues in the early years of Henry's reign.[1]

Consequently Edward IV did not command anything comparable with the great 'Lancastrian connection' recently analysed by Dr A. L. Brown, which included no fewer than two hundred retainers who normally stayed at home in their shires and had no close personal connection with the king.[2] Lancastrian expenditure on retaining, it has been argued, was justified because 'it created the political following which enabled Henry of Lancaster to usurp the throne and keep it in the upheavals which followed', and after 1399 the Crown became the centre of bastard feudalism 'because the king's own affinity was far greater and stronger than that of any of his supporters'.[3] The House of York had never had such a connection, and Edward IV as king did not seriously attempt to create one. In his first decade he used the extensive resources of his patronage to buy baronial support, particularly in his attempt to create a 'new Yorkist' peerage. But even after 1471 he was not much concerned to extend and expand the king's affinity amongst the substantial gentry of England. His affinity remained strongly court-centred, and in 1483 its members were not strong enough to control the dissensions amongst the Yorkist nobility.[4] Richard of Gloucester came to power at the head of a largely independent affinity, inherited from Warwick and the Nevills, and firmly rooted in the north of England.

[1] J. L. Kirby, *Henry IV of England*, 128; T. B. Pugh, in *Fifteenth-Century England*, 107–8; A. L. Brown, in *ibid.*, 19–20.
[2] A. L. Brown, in *Fifteenth-Century England*, 18–19.
[3] T. B. Pugh, in *op. cit.*, 107–8.
[4] Morgan, 'The King's Affinity', 24.

Chapter 15

THE KING AND THE COMMUNITY: NOBLES, COMMONS IN PARLIAMENT, AND MERCHANTS

(i) *Relations with the Nobility*

The skill with which a late medieval king managed his great men is the acid test of his ability, and often of his capacity to survive. Together the nobility commanded formidable resources of land, wealth and territorial influence, and the active cooperation of this group, or at least some substantial section of it, was essential if the Crown were to preserve the political peace and well-being of the realm. Without a standing army or an effective police force, the king lacked coercive power, and relied heavily on the local influence of magnates and barons to keep law and order and maintain the royal authority in the shires. Their capacity to raise troops was no less vital in times of war, invasion or rebellion. The king's problem was to win their goodwill and obedience without making excessive concessions to a class whose power had increased steadily during the previous century and a half.

Previous chapters have shown how closely Edward's security depended upon his handling of the nobility, but it will be convenient here to discuss his policy towards the peerage as a whole, especially since it has aroused widely differing opinions amongst modern historians. For E. F. Jacob he was a king who remained to the end very dependent upon a powerful faction amongst the nobility: Yorkist rule was a 'party experiment'. That view was rejected by S. B. Chrimes, who believed that Edward was so successful that 'by 1480 there was no over-mighty subject left in England'. J. R. Lander, more moderately, found in Edward's reign the serious beginnings of a policy of curbing baronial power in general, and 'breaking the teeth of the sinners'.[1] In fact, it can reasonably be argued that if Edward did not actually increase aristo-

---

[1] E. F. Jacob, *The Fifteenth Century*, 645, and the comments of Chrimes in *History*, xlviii (1963), 27; S. B. Chrimes, *Lancastrians, Yorkists and Henry VII*, 125; J. R. Lander, 'Edward IV: The Modern Legend', 52.

cratic power, he did little to diminish it. In his first reign his attempts to establish his regime on the support of a small group of established baronial families reinforced by a newly-created nobility of his own broke down when dissensions developed amongst them. Although his policies changed after 1471, the result was to produce an alienation between the majority of 'country peers' and the 'court peers', and Edward's death in 1483 was the signal for a power-struggle amongst the latter which brought ruin to the House of York within two short years. Certainly Edward never attempted the highly effective if highly unpopular methods whereby Henry VII reduced his nobility to a state of nervous subjection to the royal will, and it is in their treatment of the aristocracy that the contrasts between Edward IV and the first Tudor are most sharply and significantly defined.

The king had two major assets in his dealings with the peerage. First, he alone had the power to ennoble a man or to promote him from baronial status to one of the higher ranks of nobility. The mere conferment of a title did not in itself greatly increase a man's power, but it was a distinction much sought after in an age when English society was becoming more stratified at the top, and when a small class of fifty or sixty parliamentary peers were emerging 'in possession of rank and privileges which marked them off from lesser men'.[1] Edward IV made lavish use of his power of ennoblement. His reign began with the immediate creation of seven new barons, the promotion of two of his kinsmen, Henry, Viscount Bourchier, and William Nevill, Lord Fauconberg, to the earldoms of Essex and Kent, and the elevation of his brothers, George and Richard, to the dukedoms of Clarence and Gloucester. It may be argued that these early creations were necessary to fill the gaps in the parliamentary peerage caused by civil war, attainders, and the normally high rate of natural extinction, especially among the higher ranks of the nobility. Sixty-four lay peers had been summoned to the parliament of 1453, among them five dukes and twelve earls; only forty remained to be summoned to Edward's first parliament, if we exclude his new creations, and amongst the upper ranks there was only one duke and four earls. It was necessary, too, to reward his firm supporters and help establish their dignity as well as their power. Yet the flow of creations and promotions continued steadily up to 1471: one duke, eight earls and six barons received their titles during these years. After 1471 the king's policy changed. Promotion to the higher ranks of the peerage was almost entirely confined to members of the royal family: Edward's second son, Richard, became

[1] K. B. McFarlane, *The Nobility of Later Medieval England*, 122-5.

duke of York and Norfolk, Thomas Grey earl of Huntingdon and then marquis of Dorset, and Clarence's son, Edward, was recognized as earl of Salisbury. Two new viscounts (Berkeley and Lovell) and three new barons complete the list. Yet the total of creations remains substantial: thirty-two new peers, among them four dukes, two marquises, ten earls and two viscounts.[1]

The contrast with Henry VII is striking. He showed himself to be extremely reluctant to add to (or even replace losses within) the numbers of the hereditary peerage. He is often credited with nine new creations, but some of these were restorations, and others were based upon a personal summons which was not necessarily intended to create a barony. It has recently been claimed that only one of these nine (Giles, Lord Daubeney) was given a barony by charter, to him and his heirs male.[2] He was even more sparing in replenishing the higher ranks of the peerage, creating only one duke, two earls, one marquis and one viscount (and some of these were restorations to titles forfeited under the Yorkists). 'The English higher nobility numbered 20 families in 1485, but only half these titles survived when Henry VIII was crowned.'[3] For Henry VII, we are told, election to the Order of the Garter rather than a peerage was the ultimate mark of honour, especially for men who had climbed solely by service to the king.[4] Edward IV made similar use of the Order as a means of rewarding his friends and servants, creating only one fewer new knights than Henry, but significantly more were English noblemen.[5] But the fact that Edward was so obviously more generous in dispensing new titles of nobility and in promotion to the higher ranks of the peerage is surely indicative of his favourable attitude towards the baronage as a class. On balance it could serve only to strengthen the position of the aristocracy in English society.

Far more important than the distribution of dignities, however, was the use the king made of his royal patronage and the extent to which he was willing to strengthen the landed power and local influence of the aristocracy by the tangible rewards of grants of land, offices, wardships, marriages and cash pensions and annuities. The king controlled a vast reservoir of patronage which no private subject could match, and of which even the highest in the land were eager to obtain their due – and

---

[1] Edward's peerage creations are usefully listed by T. B. Pugh, in *Fifteenth-Century England*, 116–17; see also his comments, pp. 88–91.
[2] Chrimes, *Henry VII*, 138–40.
[3] Pugh, *op. cit.*, 115.   [4] Chrimes, *op. cit.*, 140.
[5] Edward created 36 knights of the Garter, of whom 21 were English noblemen, including members of the royal family; Henry created 37, including 16 noblemen; G. F. Beltz, *Memorials of the Order of the Garter*, clxii–vi; *CP*, II, App. B, 542–7.

often undue – share. Here Edward, at the beginning of his reign, enjoyed exceptional advantages. The series of attainders of Lancastrian
supporters in 1461, together with the deaths of others not attainted,
brought Edward, in the form of forfeited lands and wardships, surely
the most magnificent windfall of the entire middle ages. Within a few
years it had been almost totally dispersed. We have already seen something of the motives and methods which lay behind this dispersal, and
the consequences for the king's finances are examined below.[1] The
main point here is that the principal beneficiaries were a comparatively
small section of the baronage. He had done nothing to cure the problem of the over-mighty – or even the mighty – subject. He had created
several new magnates, and had strengthened the power of certain well-
established families, above all the Nevills. He had not won the backing
of the baronage in general, few of whom had benefited materially from
his rule.

After 1471 the king's treatment of the baronage changed significantly
only in one respect. In the 1460s an important part of his distribution of
patronage had been to create and delimit areas of territorial influence
in which his chosen great men should have the rule of the shires – the
Nevills in the north, Herbert in Wales and the Marches, Hastings in
the midlands, and Humphrey Stafford in the south-west. With this
scheme now largely in ruins, he turned instead to a similar territorial
re-ordering, but this time aimed at the endowment of members of the
royal family, including the queen's kinsmen. Between 1471 and 1475
Clarence and Gloucester were allowed to divide the Warwick inheritance between them, but for Gloucester this was only the beginning of
a steady build-up of power in the north, culminating in the great
hereditary franchise in the north-west and hereditary tenure of the
West March in 1482.[2] Having destroyed one over-mighty subject in the
north, Edward now created another. Political needs during the trouble
with the Nevills had meanwhile involved the restoration of the Percy
family to the earldom of Northumberland, thus reviving the power of
the most independent of all the northern magnate families. Room was
also found in this northern scheme for the new steward of the royal
household, Thomas, Lord Stanley, as master of the county palatine of
Lancaster, and his brother, William Stanley, with land and office in
north-east Wales.[3]

In Wales and the Marches Edward built up the nominal authority
of his heir Edward, even to the extent of virtually expropriating the

[1] Above, pp. 68 ff.; below, pp. 373–7.
[2] See above for details, pp. 199–203.   [3] Morgan, 'The King's Affinity', 19.

second earl of Pembroke. In form this new government might be conciliar, but politically it gave a large regional authority to a group of
Woodvilles and their associates, headed by the senior member of the
family, Anthony, Earl Rivers. There was no place in this scheme for the
greatest of the surviving Marcher lords, the young head of an old
magnate family, Henry Stafford, duke of Buckingham. He had been
allowed to enter on his inheritance, as a minor, in 1473, but soon afterwards was consigned to political limbo.[1] He was appointed as steward
of England at the trial of Clarence in 1478, and such few favours as he
received – the king's acting as godfather to his newly-born son, Edward,
and a grant of the royal manor of Cantref Selig, Co. Brecon – belong
to this period.[2] But he was mysteriously absent from the royal invasion
army of 1475, having contracted to go, and was given none of the
employments and responsibilities which a man of his position might
have expected: most remarkable of all was his exclusion from the commissions of the peace everywhere except in Stafford.[3] It was later
alleged that Buckingham resented having been married to a Woodville,
and he clearly wanted to recover that share of the inheritance of his
Bohun forebears which Henry V had claimed arbitrarily against a
poor exchange – a price Richard of Gloucester was willing to pay for
his support; but, these considerations apart, he may well have had
cause to resent his cold-shouldering by Edward IV.[4]

In the midlands Edward was already contemplating a territorial
rearrangement even before the death of the hostile Clarence. In 1474
Lord Hastings was given charge of various lordships recovered from
the duke under the act of resumption of 1473, especially the Honour
of Tutbury in Staffordshire, and in the following year provision was
being made for the infant Richard of Shrewsbury, the king's second son.
Lands formerly belonging to the Welles and Willoughby families were
settled on him in March 1475, and under his will drawn up before
leaving for France Edward seems to have planned for Richard an
appanage based on Fotheringhay, Stamford and Grantham and other
Duchy of York lands in the north-east midlands, combined with certain
Duchy of Lancaster honours in the same area.[5] Soon after, the death of
Duke John of Norfolk in January 1476 offered Edward the opportunity

---

[1] Above, pp. 194–8, for policies in Wales; for Buckingham, Morgan, *op. cit.*, 18.
[2] *CPR, 1476–85*, 63, 67, 69, 134; Scofield, II, 205 (Buckingham at the marriage of
Anne Mowbray, January 1477).
[3] Above, p. 230 n.; Morgan, *op. cit.*, 18 and n.
[4] Mancini, 75; More, *Richard III*, 89; Polydore Vergil, *English History*, 193; T. B.
Pugh, *op. cit.*, 111.
[5] Bentley, *Excerpta Historica*, 370–2; Morgan, *op. cit.*, 18.

to add the substantial Mowbray inheritance to Richard of Shrewsbury's projected endowment, by marrying him to the infant heiress, Anne. The death without issue three years later of the infant bride did not deter Edward from keeping the Mowbray inheritance for his son. A king who had already proved willing to disinherit the countess of Warwick for the benefit of Clarence and Gloucester, and the countess of Oxford on Gloucester's behalf, saw no problem in vesting the Mowbray lands in Richard and his heirs, an arrangement sanctioned by act of parliament. The principal sufferer was the heir-at-law, his own servant, John, Lord Howard.[1]

Meanwhile, similar methods were being used, presumably under pressure from the queen, to provide an endowment, chiefly in the West Country, for her two sons by her first marriage, Thomas Grey, who became marquis of Dorset in 1475, and Richard Grey. Her efforts to find Thomas a wealthy heiress in the 1460s proved abortive, for the young lady, Anne Holland, daughter of the attainted Lancastrian duke of Exeter and his wife, the king's sister, Anne, died young and without issue.[2] In 1474 the queen procured a second wealthy bride for Thomas. With the king's help, William, Lord Hastings, was persuaded to part with the marriage of his stepdaughter, Cecily, then aged thirteen: she was ultimate heiress of the Bonville and Harrington families, and had extensive estates in Somerset and Devon. If Thomas died before the marriage was consummated, she was to marry his young brother, Richard, and all this was confirmed by act of parliament.[3] After the death of Clarence, Dorset was given, for a payment of £2,000, the custody and marriage of his heir, Edward, earl of Salisbury, and the wardship of a substantial slice of his estates, mainly in Hampshire, Wiltshire and Gloucestershire.[4] But the queen had not abandoned hope of laying hands on the inheritance of the Hollands, dukes of Exeter. In 1472, after being allowed to divorce the duke, Duchess Anne had married her lover, Sir Thomas St Leger. Their infant daughter, also called Anne, was then contracted in marriage to Dorset's son and heir by

[1] See above, pp. 248–9. As there noted, the other co-heir to the Mowbrays, William, Lord Berkeley, had signed away his rights to Edward IV, but Richard III was able to win his allegiance by creating him earl of Nottingham (28 June 1483) and allowing him his share of the Norfolk lands.

[2] Following the forfeiture of the Holland lands in 1461, the king gave most of them to Duchess Anne and her heirs by the duke (22 December 1461) and then on 26 August 1467 vested them in her daughter, with remainder to the duchess and the heirs of her body (CPR, 1461–7, 104–5; 1467–77, 32–3).

[3] Ibid., 456–7; RP, VI, 106–8.

[4] CPR, 1476–85, 212, 263, 283–4. He had also been given, after his second marriage, a life-interest in some of the Holland estates (CPR, 1467–77, 582; 16 March 1476).

Cecily Bonville, Thomas Grey, and in 1483 the young Anne was declared heiress to all the Exeter estates. An act of parliament passed to legalize this unscrupulous arrangement also provided that part of the Holland inheritance, valued at 500 marks yearly, was to be set aside for the queen's second son, Richard Grey. For this substantial inheritance (again chiefly in western England) the queen paid the king the very modest sum of 5,000 marks. No regard was paid to the interests of the surviving descendants of the Holland family, chiefly Ralph, Lord Nevill, heir of the earl of Westmorland, who became an early and trusted supporter of Richard III.[1] Such repeated interference with the laws of inheritance for the benefit of the royal family gave several English magnates 'a vested interest in the downfall of the children of Edward IV and Elizabeth Woodville'.[2] In general also the concentration of royal patronage on members of his own family, and chosen lords within the court circle, tended to widen the gap between the smallish circle of peers who had close and rewarding connections with the king, and the much larger element of 'country' peers who were largely divorced from politics and government. That they respected and perhaps even feared the king is probable; that they admired the stable government he brought in the latter half of the reign is equally likely; but few had benefited personally from his rule after 1471 or had much direct stake in his regime. It may be that, after twenty years of civil war and rebellion, deaths in battle and execution, many of them believed with John Blount, Lord Mountjoy, that it was unwise 'to be great about princes, for it is dangerous'.[3] In 1483 few of them were prepared to risk involvement in the heady perils of the succession crisis which followed Edward's premature death.

Edward's attitude towards his nobles had certain important consequences for the government of the realm as a whole. Since he chose to place 'the rule of the shires' in the hands of noblemen whom he could trust, it follows that he was unlikely to do anything to erode or undermine their local influence. In Professor Dunham's words, 'Edward banked upon the allegiance of his own baronial clients and through them upon the fidelity of their retainers', to administer county govern-

[1] *RP*, VI, 215–18; *CP*, V, 212–15. Because of the attainder of the duke of Exeter, Nevill had no strict legal right to the inheritance, but Woodville greed undoubtedly prevented any chance of the attainder's being reversed in Nevill's favour as heir male. The fact that an act of parliament was felt necessary to legalize the arrangement (including the provision for Richard Grey, who had no claims at all) suggests that it was felt to be arbitrary.

[2] Pugh, in *Fifteenth-Century England*, 112.

[3] Cited by McFarlane, 'Wars of the Roses', 119.

ment and provide troops when needed.[1] This meant in turn that the legislation and proclamations of the reign against the abuses of the system of bastard feudalism were little more than pious verbiage so far as the aristocracy was concerned, and however much he might wish to present himself as the administrator of impartial justice, impartiality received short shrift when it ran counter to the interests of one of the king's great men.[2] The consequences for law and order could sometimes be serious, and there was little hope of redress at law against those who held the favour of the king. A further consequence of the king's indulgent attitude to the powers and privileges of the peerage as a class was that the programme devised in the later years of the reign to exploit certain aspects of the Crown's feudal rights lacked teeth in the enforcement, for Edward did not choose to enforce it against men whose goodwill he wished to retain. Recent research has shown that he often failed to employ existing powers to prevent tenants-in-chief evading royal rights of wardship, that in 1475 he had to allow his nobility almost complete freedom to settle the future of their estates (at the king's expense) before they would accompany him to France, and that his tentative effort to legislate against the practice of enfeoffments to use, which cost the Crown much in lost revenue, was emasculated before it reached the statute book. Admittedly, however, the problem of uses was difficult and intractable, as both Henry VII and Henry VIII were to discover when they in turn tried to attack this aspect of landowning privilege.[3]

Edward IV's reliance upon the local authority and influence of the baronage in the government of the different regions of his realm was only partly a matter of political necessity. It was also a matter of choice. That a less indulgent attitude was possible is strikingly revealed by the far more aggressive policies which Henry VII came to adopt. His notorious campaign to exploit royal rights of wardship and other feudal prerogatives of the Crown became not only a huge source of profit but also proved a means of humbling and disciplining the mighty of his realm.[4]

---

[1] W. H. Dunham, *Lord Hastings' Indentured Retainers*, 46.

[2] One or two injunctions concerning the enforcement of the statutes against livery and maintenance have survived in municipal records (printed by Myers, *English Historical Documents*, IV, 1108–9, 1132), and in 1479 the Bristol authorities said that a certain evildoer ought to be fined £2,800 for breaches of the statute of 1468, though no action was taken (*Great Red Book of Bristol*, IV, 72) but lords were a different matter: see further below, pp. 412–13.

[3] J. M. W. Bean, *The Decline of English Feudalism, 1215–1540*, 215–16, 238–42; C. D. Ross, 'The Reign of Edward the Fourth', in *Fifteenth-Century England*, 60–1.

[4] Chrimes, *Henry VII*, 208–16, for a general survey of these policies.

He made effective and extensive use, too, of other and even more arbitrary devices to cow and coerce the nobility. The manipulation of what may be called suspended sentences of attainder, and the extraction of bonds and recognizances in punitive sums of money, were erected into what Professor Lander has rightly called a 'terrifying system' whereby 'a majority of the peerage were legally and financially in the king's power and at his mercy', and his prime motive for doing so was not profit but to ensure political obedience and control.[1] The recently-discovered 'Petition' of Henry's chief agent of extortion, Edmund Dudley, drawn up just before he died, reflects the harshness with which King Henry treated his noblemen: 'Item the lord Dudley paid £1,000 upon a light surmise . . . Item the earl of Derby was often-tymes hardly entreated and too sore, . . . Item Richard [Lord] Hastings paid too much for the marriage of his wife.' There is ample evidence to support Dudley's claim that 'the king's purpose was to have many persons in his danger at his pleasure'.[2] The same could never have been said of Edward IV.

This marked contrast between Yorkist and early Tudor policy towards the nobility can be well illustrated in their approach towards the problem of the north in general, and the wardenships of the Marches towards Scotland in particular. Before 1461 it had become customary to grant the wardenship of the Marches to local magnates – usually the Percies in the east and the Nevills in the west – and these appointments were made for long terms and at generous salaries which enabled the wardens to maintain private armies at the king's expense: their troops were even allowed to wear their lords' private badges.[3] Edward continued this policy, and with the fall of the Percies, the Nevills came to dominate both Marches. But the destruction of the Nevills in 1471 gave the king an opportunity to pursue an alternative policy had he wished. Instead he carried the older system to extremes in his patronage of Gloucester, ending with granting him the wardenship of the West March on hereditary terms in 1482, and restoring the

[1] J. R. Lander, 'Bonds, coercion and fear: Henry VII and the Peerage', in *Florilegium Historiale: Essays Presented to Wallace K. Ferguson*, 328–67; 'Attainder and Forfeiture', 119–52.

[2] C. J. Harrison, 'The Petition of Edmund Dudley', *EHR*, lxxxvii (1972), 82–99. Lander was able to show that 'out of 62 peerage families a total of 46 or 47 were for some part of the reign at the king's mercy, and only 16 escaped . . . the system was so extensive that it must have created an atmosphere of chronic watchfulness, suspicion and fear' ('Bonds, coercion and fear', 347).

[3] R. L. Storey. 'The Wardens of the Marches of England towards Scotland, 1377–1489', *EHR*, lxxii (1957), 605–7.

Percies to the East March. The wardenships remained appendages of private power, the prizes of the most powerful lords of the region. In sharp contrast, Henry VII placed the West March under the control of a minor local peer, Thomas, Lord Dacre, who was allowed no security of tenure: his appointment was during pleasure only, and his commissions of appointment were renewed no fewer than six times in nine years. His salary was drastically reduced to a mere £100, in contrast to the £1,000 in wartime and £800 in peacetime which Gloucester had enjoyed in 1480. His obedience was further ensured by his being compelled to enter into no fewer than twelve bonds and sureties in large sums of money.[1] On the East March Henry had little alternative but to employ the earl of Northumberland, but even this mighty northern magnate was made to feel that his tenure was precarious and dependent on the king's goodwill, and he too was saddled with an enormous fine, respited as a condition of his good behaviour. The local influence of the Percies was checked and challenged: the power of the Crown became 'an active presence in the midst of the northern gentry communities . . . which it would be perilous to ignore'.[2]

It has recently been argued that the early Tudor kings, like the Yorkists, had to rely heavily on the nobility in government, and that in consequence the magnate had to be given a fairly free hand in his own locality.[3] It would be rash to deny that either Edward IV or Henry VII did not depend on baronial cooperation, however grudgingly given, but there are important differences in the spirit and the methods with which they approached the problem. It was Henry rather than Edward who began to 'break the teeth of the sinners', and who rejected their claim to special favour. No longer would the Crown admit that their loyalty must be purchased with lavish rewards. Rather the boot tended to be on the other foot – the nobility had to buy royal patronage by good service and proof of loyalty. For Edward, however, the dictum expressed by Bishop Russell in 1483 held good, that 'the politic rule of every region well ordained standeth in the nobles'.[4] He had done nothing to reduce the excessive local influence of the aristocracy. By the end of his reign, it is true, some at least of the more important magnate

[1] Storey, *op. cit.*, 608–9; for the appointments, *Rotuli Scotiae*, II, 472, 479, 486, 498, 501, 515, 518; *CPR, 1494–1509*, 213; and I am indebted to Miss S. S. M. Taylor's researches for information about the bonds.
[2] M. E. James, 'A Tudor Magnate and the Tudor State', 15–24.
[3] Lander, *Wars of the Roses*, 29; *Conflict and Stability*, 175–6; 'Bonds, coercion and fear', 348–51.
[4] Printed in *Grants from the Crown during the Reign of Edward V*, ed. J. G. Nichols (Camden Soc., 1854), xliii; reprinted by Chrimes, *Eng. Constitutional Ideas*, 172.

interests were those of his own family or of men whom he had raised to magnate status. Yet this placing of old wine in new bottles did little to reduce the political importance of the nobility or limit their capacity to cause political disruption, as the disorders which followed his death were to reveal.

(ii) *The King and the Commons in Parliament*

The reign of Edward IV has traditionally been regarded as one of the least constructive and inspiring phases in the history of the English parliament. If we employ the equally traditional yardstick – the degree of initiative and activity shown by the commons – this remains largely true. Parliaments were infrequent; the volume and importance of the legislation they produced dwindled noticeably; and a greater share of it was initiated by the government rather than by the commons as had been usual under the Lancastrian kings. The centre of gravity in government swings back to the Crown and parliament plays a comparatively minor role. The commons admitted the dominance of the king, and made little effort to oppose his will or criticize his administration.[1] Yet this very tractability has been seen recently by some scholars as a sign of the restoration of confidence between king and commons, and even as an indication that Yorkist government was in some sense 'popular'. Edward is said to have deliberately sought the cooperation of his people, and, by raising the status of the commons, made a great contribution to the unity of parliament. 'Perhaps for the first time here was a king more at ease with the Lower than the Upper House of Parliament.'[2] Such views do not carry conviction. The commons' docility seems to owe more to royal attempts to influence the composition of their house and to his skilful use of the arts of management rather than to any overt policy of cooperation. An overall impression emerges of a king who expected the commons to do his will without cavil, and was very much the dominant element in their relationship.

This is not to deny that Edward did not make considerable efforts to sell himself and his policies to the commons of the realm 'comen to this my court of Parliament'. In his first parliament in November 1461 he

[1] For these or similar views, W. Stubbs, *Constitutional History of England*, III, 273–6; J. E. A. Jolliffe, *Constitutional History of Medieval England*, 491–3; H. L. Gray, *The Influence of the Commons on Early Legislation*, 126–38; A. R. Myers, *English Historical Documents, 1327–1485*, 368.

[2] B. P. Wolffe, *The Royal Demesne in English History*, 143–4, following the views of A. F. Pollard, *Parliament in the Wars of the Roses*, 15 ff., and see also Wilkinson, *Constitutional History of England in the Fifteenth Century*, 142–6, 284–5.

made a gracious speech from the throne, thanking the commons for their 'true hearts and tender considerations', and their assistance in restoring him to his right and title, and promising that he would be their 'very rightwise and loving liege lord'. In response, the speaker, Sir James Strangways – a close connection of the Nevills, who was to be paid for his services as speaker – did what was expected of him and presented a congratulatory address to the king which was the longest recorded speech of any medieval speaker.[1] We are fortunate in possessing for this parliament a unique record, part of an incomplete *Lords' Journal*, the only one of its kind to survive until the series begins regularly in 1510. This suggests that the king was personally present at the lords' meetings for each of the eight days' business recorded in the journal, and on at least one occasion 'he put in a bill with his own hand'.[2] In June 1467 he again addressed the commons in person to assure them of his purpose to 'live of his own', and that he did not intend to charge his subjects except in 'great and urgent causes, concerning more the weal of themselves, rather than mine own pleasure', and again he thanked them for their goodwill and kindness towards him.[3]

Projecting the royal personality was not the only means of procuring a docile commons house. Modern historians have doubted whether the king or the lords were much concerned to influence or manipulate elections: it was not often necessary, it has been claimed, for 'no great political issue faced the electors at most elections', and Professor Dunham's researches suggested that even a powerful councillor like Lord Hastings did not usually bother to return his own men to parliament although able to do so if he chose; but these opinions have not gone unchallenged.[4] Certainly there is considerable evidence that Edward IV was very much concerned to influence the composition of the commons by installing royal servants in both shire and borough seats, and that at least on important occasions he expected his lords to support him with their own followers.

[1] *RP*, V, 462–3, 487; J. S. Roskell, *The Commons and their Speakers in English Parliaments, 1376–1523*, 80–1.

[2] W. H. Dunham, Jr, *The Fane Fragment of the 1461 Lords' Journal*, 57–8; Pollard, *op. cit.*, 5.

[3] *RP*, V, 372. It has recently been suggested (by G. L. Harriss in *EHR*, lxxxviii (1973), 172) that far from representing a conscious programme, as Wolffe believed, this famous statement was designed to soften up his subjects for taxation in the following year.

[4] H. G. Richardson, 'The Commons and Medieval Politics', *TRHS*, 4th ser., xxviii (1946), 38, 41–3; Dunham, *op. cit.*, 33–4; but cf. Patricia Jalland, 'The Influence of the Aristocracy on Shire Elections in the North of England, 1450–70', *Speculum*, xlvii (1972), 483–507.

The clearest evidence of a deliberate attempt to secure a docile lower house is provided by the parliament of 1478, summoned to bring about the attainder of the duke of Clarence. Of its 291 known members, no fewer than 57 – about 20 per cent of the whole house – had close connections with the central government, and thus supplied the highest proportion of what has been called 'the Westminster crowd' of the entire fifteenth century.[1] Of these, at least 43 were active members of the royal household, including its treasurer and controller, the keeper of the wardrobe, and the treasurer of the chamber, together with 17 knights or esquires of the body or of the chamber. 24 of these household men sat for the counties, making a substantial proportion of the 74 shire-knights, whose wealth and standing made them more influential than many of the parliamentary burgesses. Of the 37 English shires represented in parliament, no fewer than 23 drew one or both of their members from the staff of the king's household. Modern historians have mostly been at pains to stress that freedom of election in the shires was a reality in the fifteenth century;[2] but these figures show how much influence the Crown could exert on shire representation when it chose. Nor do these figures make allowance for king's servants whose connection with the Crown was local rather than central, though these sat chiefly for borough seats. It is well known that the changing character of borough representation in the half-century before 1478 had made possible the intrusion of many 'outsiders' into borough seats, especially in the smaller towns.[3] This development was often to the advantage of the Crown, for many boroughs were largely controlled by the king in one capacity or another. Thus the representation of Dover was often influenced by the warden of the Cinque Ports, then the earl of Arundel: in 1478 it returned Roger Appleton, royal surveyor of Eltham manor and counsel to the lieutenant of Dover Castle, and Thomas Hextall, clerk of Dover Castle and receiver of the duke of Gloucester. Cornwall was, like Wiltshire and Surrey and Sussex, grossly over-represented, and most of its borough seats were usually at the disposal of the Duchy of Cornwall officials. Here, in 1478, there is evidence not of mere in-

[1] Derived from Wedgwood, *Hist. Parl.*, *Register*, 433–46; for slightly different figures, see J. S. Roskell, *The Commons in the Parliament of 1422*, 136.

[2] Roskell, *op. cit.*, 27; K. B. McFarlane, 'Parliament and Bastard Feudalism', *TRHS*, 4th ser., xxvi (1944), 53–79. Both were considering primarily aristocratic influence on elections, but for a persuasive challenge to this opinion, see P. Jalland, *op. cit.*

[3] M. McKisack, *The Parliamentary Representation of the English Boroughs in the Middle Ages*, 44–6, as revised by Roskell, *Commons in the Parliament of 1422*, 125–44, and K. Houghton, 'Theory and Practice in Borough Elections to Parliament during the Later Fifteenth Century', *BIHR*, xxxix (1966), 130–40.

fluence or manipulation of elections, but of wholesale direct interference, all the returns having been blatantly tampered with. Not a single member dwelling in the Duchy was returned. Among the M.P.s for the Cornish boroughs, nearly all from Kent and the midlands, were a royal customs officer, an exchequer auditor, a legal counsel for the Duchy of Lancaster, and the keeper of the Common Bench writs, who was also joint chancellor of the Duchy of Lancaster.[1]

There are also clear indications that the king's great noblemen exerted themselves to secure the return of trustworthy men to this same parliament. No fewer than seven, and perhaps as many as ten, were followers of William, Lord Hastings. In East Anglia the influence of John, Lord Howard, seems likely to have been behind the election of his son, Thomas, for Norfolk county, and of his son-in-law, John Timperley, and his chief man-of-business, James Hobart. One of the M.P.s for the borough of Maldon, Essex, Robert Plomer, was a servant of the earl of Essex, and so, probably, was the other, William Tendring. One of the knights of the shire for Westmorland, Sir Richard Redman, was a close connection of the duke of Gloucester; his second son, Edmund, sat for Carlisle, a borough normally controlled by the duke as warden of the West March, and he was afterwards to become a prominent servant of Richard as king.[2] As Professor Dunham has observed, in connection with Hastings's men in this parliament, 'if a dozen peers, in league with king and court, contributed a like number of M.P.s', this would have been sufficient 'to direct, and probably carry through the government's policies'.[3]

It is probable that similar efforts were made for the long-lasting parliament of 1472–5, which was required to finance the invasion of France. Thirty-nine royal servants sat in the commons, forming about 14 per cent of the house, and again most of them were members of the royal household. Its controller and twelve knights or esquires of the body between them sat for twelve English shires. These proportions are certainly much higher than for the only assembly of the 1460s for which full returns survive: in 1467–8 only twenty royal servants were returned,

---

[1] Houghton, *op. cit.*, 136–8. He suggests that the Cornish M.P.s were largely returned by Lord Hastings, as receiver-general of the Duchy, and Sir John Fogge, as administrator of the Duchy lands for the prince of Wales. For the similar use of the prince of Wales's and the duke of York's electoral influence by Earl Rivers in January 1483, see Ives, 'Andrew Dymmock and the Papers of Anthony, Earl Rivers, 1482–3', 222–3.

[2] Wedgwood, *Hist. Parl., Biog., s.n.*; and for the influence of the wardens of the West March in N.W. England, Jalland, *op. cit.*, 495–501.

[3] Dunham, *Lord Hastings' Indentured Retainers*, 33–4.

fourteen of them household men, but forming no more than 5 per cent of the house. For 1461–2 and 1463–5 we know the names of less than a quarter of the M.P.s elected, but it is unlikely that for this important first parliament the government and their supporters would have spared their efforts to return likely men to Westminster, and in 1463 Edward cancelled all the elections on the grounds that they had been irregular, but his real reason may have been that he did not fancy the composition of the house they would have produced. The fact that three of his six parliaments sat for several sessions suggests that, having found the temper of a particular assembly to his liking, he preferred to keep it in being rather than risk facing a less sympathetic body. But although the influence of king and peers on the composition of the commons is likely to have been considerable, it should not be over-estimated: even in 1472–5 and in 1478 it is doubtful whether committed 'government supporters' were numerous enough to deprive the commons of all independence or initiative.

An increasingly important part in the management of the house of commons under the Yorkists was played by successive speakers of the house, who played a dual role, combining that of a modern speaker with that of a modern leader of the house. With the partial exception of Sir James Strangways in 1461–2, Edward's speakers were prominent royal servants and councillors, and all were rewarded handsomely for their 'diligence' in serving the king in that office. (This practice of rewarding speakers, like the similar one of large rewards to sheriffs to ensure their loyalty and good service, was largely a Yorkist innovation.)[1] Sir John Say, speaker in 1463–5 and 1467–8, had been under-treasurer of the exchequer and became chancellor of the Duchy of Lancaster. He is also an example of the group of competent Lancastrian servants who chose to take service under the House of York, for he had been speaker in 1449 and chancellor of the Duchy from 1450. Sir William Allington, speaker in 1472–5 and 1478, was a tutor and councillor of the prince of Wales, became a councillor of the king, and had links with the queen and Earl Rivers. The last speaker of the reign (January 1483), John Wood, had also been an under-treasurer of the exchequer. By this time the speaker had probably become largely a nominee of the Crown. At all events the willingness of the commons to choose as speakers such outright 'king's men' strongly suggests that their primary function was to present and direct the king's business before the assembled knights and burgesses.[2]

Apart from these methods of managing parliament, there were

[1] Roskell, *Commons and their Speakers*, 344.　　[2] *Ibid.*, 271–93, 333–6.

others of which we know comparatively little. The 'Fane Fragment' tells us something of behind-the-scenes operations by king and lords which could not be learnt from the official Rolls of Parliament. It shows, for example, that two bills, one concerning restrictions on the import of certain kinds of merchandise to protect native producers, the other a sumptuary law against 'excessive apparel', were discussed by the king and his advisers in 1461-2, and one was 'put in' by the king's own hand; but they were afterwards enacted in 1463 in the guise of 'commons bills' (preceded by the rubric 'Prayen the Commons . . .'). Government inspiration played a part in the amendment by the lords of commons bills: on one occasion in 1461 'it was thought that divers lords *should declare unto the Commons that the king's pleasure is* that he will not authorize their said franchises and liberties by authority of parliament . . .'.[1] Indeed, one of the features of Edward's reign is the effort which the Crown made to remove tension by itself promoting legislation on issues which in the Lancastrian period had had to be forced on government by the angry commons. Conspicuous amongst these were the three Acts of Resumption of 1465, 1467 and 1473, each more stringent than the last. At least in part these were intended to improve the king's finances and hence not to 'burden his poor commons'.[2] 'Most important business' (Professor Myers tells us) 'was initiated by the government and prepared in advance by his councillors, who were represented in both houses', a tendency which became still more marked in the early Tudor period.[3] But not all these devices of management quite served to ensure complete harmony between king and commons, for the latter could be stubborn where their own interests and pockets were involved, and their confidence in the king's honesty and fair dealing was by no means unbounded.

In all, Edward met six parliaments in the twenty-three years of his reign. Together they sat for a total of 84½ weeks. These may seem infrequent by comparison with the almost annual parliaments of the late fourteenth and early fifteenth centuries – Richard II, for example, summoned twenty-four parliaments in a similar length of time – but infrequency did not mean short duration. Three of Edward's assemblies sat for more than one session. That of 1472-5, with its seven sessions lasting a total of 44 weeks, was the longest parliament held up to that date and longer than any of its successors until the Reformation Parliament. As in many other matters, there is here a close comparison with

[1] Dunham, *Fane Fragment*, 65-78 (my italics).
[2] Discussed by Wolffe, *Royal Demesne*, 144-58.
[3] Myers, *op. cit.*, 368; Gray, *Influence of the Commons on Early Legislation*, 138-62.

Henry VII, whose seven parliaments in twenty-four years sat for a total of 70 weeks. In summoning a parliament, Edward had one or both of two main reasons – the need for a subsidy, and the desire to get the consent of the assembly for measures not usually held to be fully valid or lawful without it. These include a number of important acts of attainder and resumption, together with others sanctioning arrangements and endowments for the royal family. Several of these latter were clearly dubious under the common law, and could only be regarded as legal when blessed with the overriding authority of the high court of parliament.

'The king's business' in this sense formed the main concern of parliament, for the other legislation of the reign is not of great importance. Taking under review only those acts of parliament which were later enrolled as statutes (that is, measures which were of permanent importance and which were thought 'to modify the common law and to be applicable in the ordinary routine of the courts'),[1] the entire reign produced only fifty-four statutes. By far the largest group concerned commerce and industry, dealing with wages and prices, weights and measures, imports and exports, and bullion regulations: these numbered twenty-eight in all. Twelve more were primarily legal, four of which involved the office of sheriff, but only two of these were of any great significance. Two were sumptuary laws, three concerned with administration, and the remaining eight were of miscellaneous character, mostly dealing with minor matters such as the prohibition of unlawful games or regulations concerning swans.[2] A few more might have been added, if the king had not rejected the commons' bills proposing them; and some of these were of greater importance than those he accepted.[3] These Edwardian statutes form an unimpressive body of legislation, and it would be hard to refute the claim of Hallam that his reign was the first in our annals in which not a single enactment was made for increasing the liberty or security of the subject.[4]

Relations between king and commons in the first decade of the reign were far less harmonious than some historians have supposed, especially where matters of taxation were concerned.[5] Edward was heir to a tradition whereby the king was expected so far as possible to 'live of his

---

[1] The definition is by Chrimes, *Eng. Const. Ideas*, 248–9.
[2] *Statutes of the Realm*, II, 360–476.   [3] Gray, *op. cit.*, 127–8, 130–2.
[4] H. Hallam, *View of the State of Europe during the Middle Ages* (1860 edn), III, 198. Even the much larger body of legislation produced by Henry VII's reign (192 statutes) has been said recently to do little to justify Bacon's claim that legislation was Henry's 'pre-eminent virtue and merit' (Chrimes, *Henry VII*, 177–84).
[5] Cf. Wolffe, *Royal Demesne*, 145–7.

own' and not to levy taxation except for such 'great and urgent causes' as resistance to foreign invasion or war against France and Scotland. The commons of the 1460s showed no disposition to open their pockets for the benefit of the new king. His first parliament ratified his title to the throne and approved a massive act of attainder against the supporters of the House of Lancaster. Yet, though the king had a pressing need of money and was largely dependent on loans for immediate cash, it is noticeable that he did not ask his commons for a grant of taxation, presumably because he would have been unable to persuade them that the profits of these vast forfeitures were insufficient for his immediate livelihood. But it is worth observing that Edward had already started to collect the customs duties entirely on his own authority and without waiting for the usual sanction from parliament: they were said to be 'due to the king of his inheritance', a claim which represents a complete break with precedent.[1]

Not until two years later, in response to Edward's promise to lead an army against the invading Scots, did the commons make their first grant of money. The normal form of a parliamentary subsidy was a grant of a fifteenth and tenth of the value of movable property levied according to a very outdated system of assessment. This was calculated to yield £37,000, but in the Lancastrian period it had become usual to remit £6,000 of this sum from places too impoverished to pay. In the first session of the 1463 parliament, the commons promised the king what they called an 'aid' of £31,000, to be levied in the manner of a fifteenth and tenth, but they also undertook to raise a further £6,000 chargeable on those inhabitants of the shires and incorporated boroughs who could best afford to pay. This was to be the first of a series of experiments in Edward's reign to develop new methods of taxation, attempts largely frustrated by taxpayers' resistance. The commons specified that the money was to be used 'only for the said defence' of the realm. Edward, however, defaulted on his promises, and the widespread resentment which followed was reflected in the mood of the commons when next they met in November 1463.[2] In consideration of the great charges they had borne – such was the burden of their complaint – they now demanded that the £6,000 be remitted, and that collection of the second half of their grant should be deferred. Their mistrust of the king appears in a curious passage on the Parliament Roll in which they protested that they delivered their 'paper' only as 'a remembrance of their intent', reserving their right to alter it as they wished.[3] In the final session of this parliament (January–March 1465),

[1] CFR, 1461–71, 4, 6.   [2] RP, V, 497–8, and above, pp. 55–6.   [3] RP, V, 499.

however, they relented sufficiently, probably in response to the king's acceptance of a body of mercantilist legislation favouring native merchants, to grant him the wool-subsidy and tunnage and poundage for life.[1]

The experience of 1463-5 was repeated in the parliament of 1467-8. In its first session, Edward made his well-known declaration that he intended to 'live of his own', which effectively precluded any demand for taxation. Then in 1468 he appealed to them for money to finance his projected invasion of France, the only issue on which they could be expected to respond with enthusiasm. They answered, generously enough, with a grant of two fifteenths and tenths, less the usual remission. Again Edward defaulted on his promises, but continued nevertheless to collect the monies voted by parliament. In this parliament, too, the speaker made a pointed demand that the king should tackle urgently the abuses of livery and maintenance and the misbehaviour and 'heavy lordship' of his own great men. It is not altogether surprising that in 1469 the rebels could appeal to popular discontent on these counts, claiming that 'the laws were not duly ministered', that there were 'great maintenances', and that the king had taxed his subjects heavily, even though he had as great a livelihood as any king of England ever had.[2]

The 1472-5 parliament witnessed a legacy of this mistrust. The main reason for its extraordinary length was the king's wish to get sufficient finance for the planned invasion of France. After various unsuccessful attempts to raise money by new methods, the commons eventually granted the king four whole fifteenths and tenths, more than he had received from them in all the previous part of his reign; but they made a point of insisting that the money when collected should be delivered only when they were quite sure he was going to France. Such heavy taxation to be levied in so short a time as three years was certainly not popular with everyone, as John Paston put on record.[3] The commons also countered the bishop of Rochester's assurance that the laws would be put into execution by firmly reminding the king that disorder was rife and oppression by the powerful went unpunished. Eventually, the

---

[1] Wolffe (*op. cit.*, 146) claims that this grant, so early in the reign, reflects the commons' confidence in the king, by contrast with Henry VI, who had to wait thirty-one years for the same privilege. But Richard III and Henry VII were both granted the customs for life in the first years of their respective reigns, before much confidence could have been established, and, as noted above, the absence of a commons' grant had not stopped Edward collecting the customs on his own authority. For the mercantilism of this parliament, see below, pp. 359-60.

[2] Above, pp. 119-20, 124.   [3] *PL*, V, 178, and above, p. 214-16.

outcome of the 1475 expedition proved so unpopular that Edward thought it politic to remit to his subjects three-quarters of the last fifteenth and tenth they had voted, but which had not so far been collected.[1]

The king's improved finances after 1475 enabled him to go for several more years without seeking further subsidies from his reluctant commons, until the mounting costs of his war with Scotland made his needs urgent. How little he relished the prospect of once again confronting them with further demands is shown not only in his recourse to benevolences but also in his ill-judged demand in 1481 for payment of the three-quarters of the subsidy he had remitted after his return from France in 1475. The 'adverse turmoil' which resulted was one of the reasons for his postponement of the invasion of Scotland for that year.[2] However, by January 1483, his desire to continue the war with Scotland or to renew the war with France compelled him to summon his last parliament. Whether this assembly was as heavily packed as its predecessor in 1478 we have no means of knowing, since the returns of members are highly defective, but it proved compliant enough to grant him a further subsidy and a tax on alien merchants and to approve several bills highly favourable to members of the royal family. Yet before parliament was dissolved, the commons again returned to their persistent grievance, when the speaker in the final session most urgently (*instantissime*) requested the king to attend to the enforcement of a number of existing statutes for the maintenance of law and order.[3]

In all, Edward persuaded his lay subjects to vote him the equivalent of 6¾ subsidies, or about £272,000. Although this was less than half the yearly incidence of direct taxation enjoyed by Henry V and Henry VI, it may be compared with the sum of £282,000 raised by Henry VII over a similar period.[4] Both kings faced the same problem, the reluctance of their commons to vote taxes, even for foreign conquests. Both were therefore driven to seek as far as possible to raise money from other sources of income. For Edward this was perhaps the major problem of government with which he had to contend; but – as this survey of his relations with his commons may suggest – in the eyes of his subjects a no less urgent task was the better maintenance of law and order. Much depended on his finding solutions to both problems.

[1] Above, p. 236.   [2] Scofield, II, 304–5, 386.   [3] *RP*, VI, 198.
[4] Edward's figures include the tax voted by the parliament of January 1483, which he never lived to collect, but excludes the three-quarter subsidy remitted after his return in 1475. For Henry VII, see R. Lockyer, *Henry VII*, 55, citing the unpublished work of Dr R. S. Schofield, on parliamentary lay taxation. For the comparison with the Lancastrians, Wolffe, *Royal Demesne*, 146.

(iii) *Merchants and Commercial Policy*[1]

Edward IV has some claim to be regarded as the first 'merchant king' in English history. From the beginning of his reign he sought to improve his finances by indulging in personal trading ventures, an example followed by many of his great men. Already by the spring of 1463 he was actively engaged in the wool trade. Soon after he was exporting a variety of other merchandise, notably cloth and tin, and by 1470, if not before, he was active as an importer. Thus in May 1464 one of his Italian factors, James de Sanderico, was commissioned to ship no fewer than 8,000 cloths on the king's behalf, and 3,000 of these, exported soon after, were valued at £6,589. The tin trade was largely dominated by the king, especially at the trade's chief port of Southampton. In 1467–8, for example, the entire export of 160 mwt (a measure of 12,000 lbs) was shipped for the king by another Italian agent, Alan de Monteferrato, and was valued at £1,600. In February 1470 no fewer than twenty-five ships entering or leaving the port of London contained goods of the king, shipped by one or more of his various factors and their sub-agents. This activity continued throughout the reign. In his later years he also made use of the royal ships, when not engaged on other business, as commercial charter vessels. In August 1478, for example, the *Antony* was sailing to the Mediterranean with a wool cargo on behalf of the London alderman, William Heryot.[2]

Some scholars have expressed doubt as to the degree of the king's

[1] For English overseas trade in general during Edward's reign, see E. Power and M. M. Postan, *Studies in English Trade in the Fifteenth Century* (1933), esp. chapter I, 'English Foreign Trade from 1446 to 1482', by H. L. Gray; chapter III, 'The Economic and Political Relations of England and the Hanse from 1400 to 1475' by M. M. Postan; E. M. Carus-Wilson and O. Coleman, *England's Export Trade 1275–1547* (1963), which, despite its title, deals only with wool and cloth; E. M. Carus-Wilson, *Medieval Merchant Venturers* (1954, 2nd edn 1967), which reprints several important studies, including her 'Overseas Trade of Bristol' from Power and Postan, *op. cit.*, chapter V; E. E. Power, 'The English Wool Trade in the Reign of Edward IV', *Cambridge Historical Journal*, ii (1926), 17–35, reprinted and expanded in chapter II of Power and Postan; A. A. Ruddock, *Italian Merchants and Shipping in Southampton, 1270–1600* (Southampton, 1951); M. R. Thielemans, *Bourgogne et Angleterre*; N. J. M. Kerling, *Commercial Relations of Holland and Zeeland with England* (Leiden, 1954); and M. E. Mallett, 'Anglo-Florentine Commercial Relations 1465–1491', *EconHR*, 2nd ser., xv (1962), 250–5. What follows is closely limited to a discussion of royal impact on the commercial fortunes of England 1461–85.

[2] Scofield, II, 404–14, for Edward's trading activities in general; for information on the tin trade I am indebted to Dr John Hatcher, of the University of Kent, whose forthcoming study, to be published shortly, is entitled 'The English Tin Industry and Trade before 1550'.

direct interest in this trading activity. The late Eileen Power claimed that some at least of the shipments made in the king's name were in fact made by his factors on their own behalf. H. L. Gray believed that trading ventures from which the king, like any ordinary merchant, hoped to profit by the direct sale of goods abroad were uncommon, and that in general Edward made his profit by selling licences to alien or native merchants to export at a reduced rate of custom, or without paying customs at all.[1] But such scepticism about Edward's direct interest seems unjustified. Though his business was handled by a variety of factors, nearly all Italians, who bought, shipped and sold on his behalf, the fact that the king was a principal in these transactions is suggested not only by the constant references to the *king's* cloth, wool and tin in the English customs accounts, but also in foreign business records, like those of the Medici.[2] Nor should one disregard the very explicit statement of the Croyland Chronicler, whose author, Bishop Russell, was in a good position to know: his slight clerical sense of impropriety that a king should behave so comes through in his comment:

> This same king *in person*, having equipped ships of burden, laded them with the very finest wools, cloths, tin, and other products of his realm, and, *like a man living by merchandize*, exchanged goods for goods, both with the Italians and the Greeks, through his factors.[3]

Throughout the reign we have evidence of the king's intelligent and individual interest in the commercial affairs of his nation, and of his readiness to welcome innovation. In February 1483, for example, he granted a licence to John de Salvo and Antonio Spinola, two naturalized Italians, to introduce some twenty craftsmen into England from abroad in order to instruct the English in new methods of finishing and dyeing cloth. He was always anxious to promote the development of the English merchant marine. In 1474, when visiting Bristol, he offered rewards to any man in the town who would build a new ship, and in 1476 he rewarded a London mercer who had just built at his own expense a ship called *le George Cobham*. On one occasion at least, in order to promote long-distance commerce in English ships, he equipped a ship (not a galley) to sail to Porto Pisano, where it was known as 'the nef of the King of England'.[4] He was interested, too, in developing

---

[1] Power, 'Wool Trade', 22; Gray, 'English Foreign Trade', 326–8.
[2] Mallett, *op. cit.*, 260 and n.
[3] *CC*, 569; my italics and translation; the rendering given by Riley, *Ingulph's Chronicle*, 474, is misleading.
[4] *CPR, 1476–85*, 342; Scofield, II, 415–16; E. Miller, in *Cambridge Economic History of Europe*, III, 101.

new markets for English commerce. There are clear signs that in the 1460s he was encouraging his merchants to break into the trade of the Barbary Coast of North Africa, an area in which the Portuguese claimed a monopoly. Lions were being bought for him there by two English merchants, John Lokton and Richard Whitington, as early as 1465, and English penetration into this region in the 1470s provoked a Portuguese counter-reaction. In return, Edward attempted to undermine the Portuguese position by appealing to the pope to authorize English trade in Africa: this, in February 1481, refers to the Guinea coast of Africa. This interest in new markets also led him to encourage, even if he did not provide either the initiative or the finance, straightforward voyages of exploration. In the summer of 1480 he granted a licence to Thomas Croft and three Bristol merchants to trade for three years 'to any parts', and it has been suggested that this licence to explore may have resulted in the discovery of America in 1481.[1] Another innovation, sometimes claimed for Henry VII, which belongs to Edward's reign was the practice of 'wafting', or providing protection vessels for English ships at sea. Royal ships were in demand to convoy the wool fleets to Calais in 1474-5. The practice of privately hiring wafters to protect fishing vessels is known as early as 1473, but in 1482 it received official authorization and was extended to include ships of any nation fishing off the east coast of England.[2]

There were, however, a number of excellent reasons, other than private profit and personal inclination, why Edward took a close and direct interest in that important and wealthy section of his subjects who made their living from trade. The most compelling reason was his extreme dependence on both English and foreign merchants as a source of loans. Amongst the English by far the most important were the Londoners. We have seen that the support of London had done much to help Edward to win his throne, and the financial backing of the London patriciate was a major prop of the regime, especially in the first decade of the reign. In contrast with Henry VI, he was remarkably successful in persuading them to invest in his government.[3] In return, Edward courted, honoured, flattered and rewarded the leading London merchants more assiduously than any king before him. Under his rule London was the permanent centre of court and government, in

[1] D. B. Quinn, 'Edward IV and Exploration', *Mariner's Mirror*, xxi (1935), 275-84; 'The Argument for the English Discovery of America between 1480 and 1494', *Geographical Journal*, cxxvii (1961), 227-85.
[2] Richmond, 'English Naval Power', 10; *CPR, 1467-77*, 318; *1476-85*, 317.
[3] Below, pp. 378-9.

contrast to the neglect of his capital by Henry VI. On 9 November 1462 he gave the city a charter, which confirmed some useful privileges it had received in 1444 and added new ones, including the right to impose taxes on foreign merchants, except the German Hanse – a royal concession to the anti-alien prejudices of the London patriciate.[1] Between 1461 and 1471 he knighted no fewer than eighteen London citizens, a remarkable number when one reflects that only eleven had ever been knighted before, the last of them in 1439. Five London aldermen, including Sir Thomas Cook, were signally honoured by being made knights of the Bath at the coronation of Queen Elizabeth in 1465: it was, 'Gregory's Chronicle' remarked, 'a great worship unto all the city'. The remainder were knighted as a reward for London's gallant resistance to the Bastard of Fauconberg's attack in 1471.[2]

Quite apart from his intimate association with at least one London merchant's wife, Edward was far more socially accessible to the London patriciate than most of his predecessors had been, and in this too he was followed by many members of his court. In 1465–6 the mayor, Ralph Verney (afterwards knighted for his share in the defence of London), is said to have feasted 'the king, the queen, and the queen's mother, the lady of Bedford, and many other lords', and from the inclusion of this item in a London chronicle, it seems likely that it had not been a usual practice.[3] Social flattery of the leading merchants continued to the end of the reign. In 1482 the king invited the mayor, aldermen, and leading commoners out to a summer hunting party in Waltham Forest. A meal was served in 'a strong and pleasant lodge made of green boughs', where they were served 'right plenteously with all manner of dainties as if they had been in London', washed down with 'all kinds of Gascon wines in right plenteous manner'. Twice during the dinner, the lord chamberlain (Hastings) 'was sent to them from the king to make them cheer', and the king refrained from eating until he saw they had been served. In the afternoon they joined the king in his hunting – a highly aristocratic pursuit in which merchants rarely shared. As they took their leave, much gratified, the king gave unto the mayor 'good words and to them all favourable and cheerful countenances'. Soon after Edward despatched a gift of two harts, six bucks and a tun of Gascon wine to the mayoress and the aldermen's wives.[4] *Fabyan's Chronicle* adds the information that this bounty was to honour the mayor, William Heryot, because he was 'a merchant of wondrous adventures into many and sundry countries, by reason

---

[1] *CChR*, VI, 188.
[2] Above, p. 175; Gregory, 228.
[3] *Ibid.*, 232.
[4] *GC*, 228.

17a. Angel with a shield of arms of Edward IV, from Canterbury Cathedral (Royal window).

17b. One of Edward's daughters, from Canterbury Cathedral.

18. Coinage of Edward IV. The two upper panels show (obverse and reverse, left to right) a gold noble, groat, half-groat, and pennies from London and York, of the period 1461–4; in the centre is the gold noble of the recoinage, 1464–70; and below, the half-ryal, groat, penny, and half-groat, 1464–70.

19b. Continental imitations of Edward IV's rose noble (1464–5 recoinage). Flemish, sixteenth century.

19a. Coins of Edward IV: enlargements of the gold angel, 1464–70, and of the groat, post-1471, from the London Mint.

(a) Obverse   20. Great Seal of Edward IV.   (b) Reverse

21. Waurin's Chronicle: the author presents his manuscript to Edward IV. One of the manuscripts commissioned from Flanders by Edward, whose arms appear in the lower border. On the right a man in armour carries a banner with the motto of the Garter upon it. (*B.M., Royal MS. 15 E IV, fol. 14*)

22. A page from Edward IV's copy of Waurin's Chronicle (showing the court of Richard II). Edward's arms and his badge of the 'Rose en Soleil' appear in the border. (*B.M., Royal MS. 14 E IV, fol. 10*)

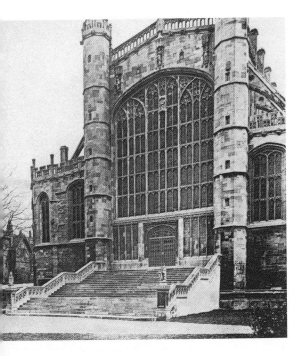

23a. Windsor: the west front of Edward's new chapel of St George.

23b. Windsor: St George's Chapel, with the stalls and banners of the Knights of the Garter.

24a. Windsor, St George's Chapel. The ironwork grille for the tomb of King Edward, executed by John Tresilian, *c.* 1481–3.

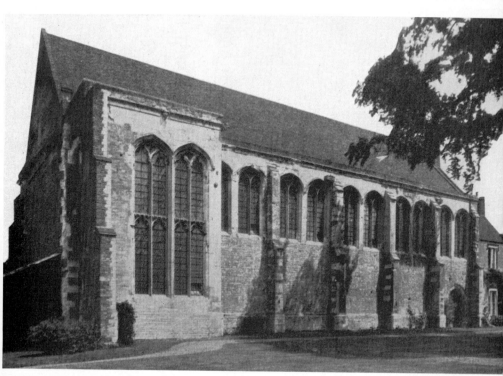

24b. Eltham Palace, Kent. Edward's Great Hall, built between 1475 and 1483.

whereof the king had yearly from him notable sums of money for customs, besides other pleasures that he had shown to the king before times'.[1] Sir Thomas More, commenting on this episode, pointed out the effects of the king's graciousness and friendliness: 'no one thing in many days before, got him either more hearts or more hearty favour among the common people, which oftentimes more esteem and take for greater kindness, a little courtesy than a great benefit'.[2] The connections between some of Edward's great men and the city of London is a subject which would repay closer investigation, but it is unlikely that they were any less close than their master's. John, Lord Howard, for example, was married to Margaret Chedworth, the widow of a former lord mayor of London, and through her was cousin to Sir John Crosby, who, as sheriff of London in 1471, had driven off the Bastard's attack on London Bridge and was knighted by Edward IV: he had recently built the splendid Crosby Hall which was later to serve Richard III as a London residence. Sir Thomas Vaughan, treasurer of the king's chamber from 1465 to 1483, married the widow of a London grocer. William, Lord Hastings, was closely connected with the Irish-born goldsmith, Hugh Bryce, a generous lender to the Crown, who for much of the reign was Hastings's deputy as master of the royal mint. Bryce was important enough to be able to name the archbishop of Canterbury as overseer of his will, and Hastings himself was overseer for the will of Sir John Plommer, K.B., one of the men accused of treason along with Sir Thomas Cook in 1468.[3] Such ties of self-interest and social connection ensured for the great London merchants ready access to the king and his great men. The records of the London mercers show how often they saw and talked with the king and many members of his council, and the intensive lobbying which they could apply in consequence. Some at least of the commercial legislation of the reign was prepared in advance between king, council and groups of merchants before being placed before parliament.[4] In the context of this otherwise careful and consistent wooing of the Londoners, Edward's persecution

---

[1] *Fabyan's Chronicle*, 667, and for Heryot as a royal factor, above, p. 351.
[2] *Richard III*, 5.
[3] Wedgwood, *Hist. Parl.*, *Biographies*, 241, for Crosby; Steel, *Receipt of the Exchequer*, 344, *CPR*, *1461–7*, 371, 475, and *1467–77*, 149, and S. Thrupp, *The Merchant Class of Medieval London*, 268, 278, for Bryce and Vaughan, and see her chapter V *passim* for further connections.
[4] *Acts of Court of the Mercers' Company*, 51–140 *passim*; Dunham, *Fane Fragment*, 65–7; and above, pp. 101, 304. In 1461 there is evidence that a bill to remedy the hurts of the merchandises of London was first lobbied by the London merchants and then put into parliament by the king's own hand.

of Sir Thomas Cook and his fellow-citizens in the trials of 1468 stands out as a singular lapse of judgement. Less influential, but still important as a source of loans, were the Italian interests in England. Pre-eminent amongst these were the Florentine merchant-bankers. The Medici founded an independent branch in London in 1466 – formerly their English affairs had been run from Bruges – and under their chief agent, Gerard Caniziani, Medici money played a large part in financing both the king and many of his nobles. Some at least of these loans were unwise, and Caniziani's wish to ingratiate himself with his English patrons overrode his loyalty to his employers, with the result that the affairs of the London branch had finally to be wound up and its business transferred to Bruges in 1478. Caniziani, who had become a naturalized Englishman in 1466, stayed on in London, and was still acting as a royal agent in financial matters at the close of the reign: he was, for example, receiving part of Margaret of Anjou's ransom from Louis XI in 1478, and two years later he was a joint custodian of the exchange at Calais and of the exchange in England for foreign parts.[1] Loans to the Crown were a means of obtaining licences to export wool, and help to explain Edward's relative tenderness towards Italian mercantile interests, as compared with the equally unpopular Hansards.

Within the general context of his financial needs, however, Edward was prepared to be responsive to native English demands for commercial advantage and encouragement. Yet these, too, were subordinate to his political and diplomatic objectives. It would be hard to find an occasion in the reign when he allowed commercial pressures to compete successfully with the demands of foreign policy and internal politics. Yorkist commercial policy, therefore, was formed from a series of pragmatic responses to conflicting and competing demands. If English interests often came out on top, it was largely because of their financial and political importance to the Crown.

Unfortunately for Edward, even the English mercantile interests rarely spoke with a united voice. The two main groups of English merchants, the Company of the Staple and the much more loosely-organized Merchant Adventurers, were constantly at odds with each other. The political importance of the Staple derived less from its share in the overall volume of English trade – which had been declining for more than a century – than from its place in the system of public finance. Wool exports were disproportionately heavily taxed, and the subsidy on them formed a major item in customs revenue. It was therefore important that they should be channelled as far as possible through the Staple system at Calais, where they could be controlled, and this need was increased when, in the early years of the reign, the Company was made responsible for the financing of the Calais garrison from the customs revenue it had collected.[1] The Company also had to bear the burden of repeated attempts by the English government to ease the chronic shortage of cash and bullion in the country by forcing the Staple to compel its foreign customers, mostly from the Low Countries, to pay for a large proportion of their purchases in cash, which could then be brought back to the Calais mint, and turned into coin of the realm.[2] For all these reasons, and aware too of their declining share of trade, the Staplers bitterly resented any expansion of alternative methods of exporting wool. The Italians, under royal licence, might export direct to Italy by sea through the 'Straits of Marrock' (or Gibraltar), and the merchants of Newcastle-on-Tyne were allowed to export the cheaper and coarser wools of the four northern counties directly to the Low Countries. The Italians competed with the Staplers especially for the highest quality wools, such as the clip of the Cotswolds and Herefordshire, and there was a danger that the Newcastle export might, if not properly regulated, allow good wool from other northern regions to evade the Calais Staple. Even more bitterly resented was the royal practice of granting licences to export wool other than by the Calais Staple to foreigners, native merchants and members of the royal family, often as a means of paying off debts.[3] The cloth export trade of the Merchant Adventurers was no less a danger to their interests, since it absorbed increasing quantities of English raw wool at source, whilst bearing a very small share of customs duty (only 2–3 per cent as compared with 25 per cent on wool for English merchants) and the Staplers were always attempting to restrict the Merchant Ad-

[1] For the rivalry of Staple and Merchant Adventurers, see G. Schanz, *Englische Handelspolitik gegen ende des Mittelalters*, I, 344 ff.; for the Staple in public finance, W. I. Haward, 'The Financial Transactions between the Lancastrian Government and the Merchants of the Staple', in Power and Postan, *op. cit.*, 293–321; and Power, 'The Wool Trade', in *ibid.*, 72 ff.; and above, p. 379.

[2] Power, 'The Wool Trade', 79–90; J. H. Munro, 'An Economic Aspect of the collapse of the Anglo-Burgundian alliance', *EHR*, lxxxv (1970), 225–44; Thielemans, *Bourgogne et Angleterre*, 349 ff., and the corrections suggested by Munro, 'The Costs of Anglo-Burgundian Interdependence', *Revue Belge de Philologie et d'Histoire*, xlvi (1968), 1234–6; and for the problem of English bullion shortage in general, H. A. Miskimin, 'Monetary Movements and Market Structure: Forces for Contraction in Fourteenth- and Fifteenth-Century England', *Journal of Economic History*, xxiv (1964), 470–90.

[3] Power, 'Wool Trade in the Reign of Edward IV', 18–22.

venturers in the interests of their own wool business. It has even been suggested that the Staplers encouraged the duke of Burgundy to ban the import of English cloth into the Low Countries in order to increase their own sales.[1]

The various companies or associations of Merchant Adventurers, which already existed or were coming into being in the major provincial towns, such as Bristol, York or Newcastle, and were particularly important in London, were not yet as tightly organized as the Staplers. But they represented a powerful commercial lobby, for by 1483 they controlled 38 per cent of English exports and more than 66 per cent of the import trade, as compared with the Staplers' 27 per cent share of the export trade, and already more than 50 per cent of the wool exported from England was in the form of manufactured cloth.[2] The interest of the Merchant Adventurers lay in an absence of restrictions on their export and import trade to foreign markets, and they deeply resented the competition of privileged aliens, above all the German merchants of the Hanseatic League. In the previous twenty years the Hansards had succeeded in excluding them almost entirely from any direct participation in trade with North Germany, the Baltic lands and Scandinavia, and, through their dominance over Denmark and Norway, were gradually forcing them out of the Icelandic trade also.[3] At the same time the Hansards had succeeded in maintaining a highly privileged status in England, including an extra-territorial status headquarters at their Steelyard in London, and exemption from the customs duty of poundage (an *ad valorem* levy of 12d in the £) on all their exports and imports, which all English merchants were required to pay.[4]

Alien merchants and residents in England – Italians, Hansards, Flemings and Dutch – were generally unpopular in England, especially in London. In the lax days of late Lancastrian rule, xenophobia had led to serious anti-Italian riots in London in 1456 and 1457, which carried over into Southampton. Anti-Italian sentiments led to violence again in London in 1463. After Edward's flight in 1470 the Kentishmen broke into the London suburbs and attacked the beerhouses owned by

---

[1] Kerling, *op. cit.*, 80; and for the customs duties, Carus-Wilson and Coleman, *op. cit.*, 22–3, 194–5.

[2] Carus-Wilson, *Medieval Merchant Venturers*, xxiv–xxv, xxviii–xxix, xxxiv; Edward Miller, 'The Economic Policies of Governments', being chapter IV of *Cambridge Economic History of Europe*, ed. M. M. Postan and E. E. Rich, III, 355.

[3] Postan, 'Economic and Political Relations of England and the Hanse', in Power and Postan, *op. cit.*, 120 ff.; Carus-Wilson, 'The Iceland Trade', in *ibid.*, 177–81.

[4] Postan, *op. cit.*, 98–9; Carus-Wilson and Coleman, 194–5.

Dutchmen and Flemings. But violence was for the most part restrained by the king, who intervened from time to time to protect the aliens. In May 1463, for example, he removed from office the anti-alien mayor of Southampton, John Payne, senior, whose attacks upon the Italians were jeopardizing the trade of the port. In January 1483 the London mercers were told that the king was displeased with affrays against the Dutch. But this did not prevent the Londoners from maintaining their anti-alien campaign in other ways, especially in the early years of the reign, when the Hansards were the prime target. Attempts were made to deprive them of their privileges in London, by pressure in parliament, and to persuade the king to impose a poll-tax on alien residents in England. The Hansards were unable to obtain anything more than a series of temporary renewals of their privileges.

Anti-alien campaigns, however intense, usually foundered on the rock of England's inability to dispense with their products. This was particularly true of the Hansards, whose imports of corn, timber, pitch, tar and ashes (used in the clothing industry) could not be replaced from other sources, and whose control of great north-European markets made them valuable customers of many English manufacturers, especially the cloth-producers.[1]

The influence of some of these conflicting and competing pressure-groups, especially the native merchants, and Edward's response to them, is reflected in the legislation of the reign. More than half the statutes enacted by Edward's parliaments deal directly with matters of commerce and industry, and form much the largest single area of parliamentary interest.[2] The parliament of 1463–5, in particular, produced a body of legislation which was markedly protectionist and nationalist in tone. In its first session in 1463, it re-enacted, in a modified form, some legislation of Henry VI's reign, which reflects the interests of the Staplers as well as Edward's concern with the drain of bullion from his realm. By severely restricting credit to foreign wool buyers, and requiring payment in cash for all sales from the Calais Staple, it was bound to be deeply resented by the merchants of the Low Countries, as it had been in the past.[3] At the same time the act prohibited any export of wool by alien merchants, which dealt a severe blow at the

---

[1] R. Flenley, 'London and Foreign Merchants in the reign of Henry VI', *EHR*, xxv (1910), 644–55; M. S. Guiseppi, 'Alien Merchants in England in the Fifteenth Century', *TRHS*, new ser., ix (1895), 75–98; Ruddock, *op. cit.*, 173–80; *Acts of Court of the Mercers' Company*, 140; Scofield, I, 196–7, 272–3; Postan, 'England and the Hanse', *op. cit.*, 91–3, 99–100, 132.
[2] Above, p. 347.
[3] See the works cited above, p. 357, n. 2.

Italian wool trade to the Mediterranean, largely conducted through London, Sandwich and Southampton. The act also incorporated a 'navigation' clause requiring all native merchants to ship their goods in English vessels whenever available.[1] Another act, which prohibited the import of foreign corn unless English prices reached a certain level in times of dearth, aimed at protecting the interests of English arable farmers. English silk manufacture, centred in London, was likewise protected by a prohibition of imports of foreign wrought silk, and earlier exceptions for certain Genoese silk goods were now dropped (3 Edw. IV, c. 3). To avoid the impoverishment of native artificers, another act (c. 4) banned the import of a wide range of 'fully wrought' manufactured goods from abroad, mainly articles of clothing and metalware.

In the second session (1465) the commons returned to the charge. The king accepted three statutes reaffirming and tightening the regulations controlling the wool export trade, which again reflect pressure from the Staplers. One of these criticized the king's free use of licences to export by channels other than the Staple, and another attacked evasion of the controls on the export of northern wool. Another statute, aimed at closer regulation of the wool trade, was also protectionist, and gave preference to native clothiers and yarn-makers in the purchase of their raw material. Meanwhile, the duke of Burgundy had responded to the provocative English legislation for the Staple by prohibiting the import of all English goods into his dominions, and parliament now riposted by imposing a total ban on all Burgundian imports, except victuals, into England. The king, however, refused to accept a demand for penalties on any man who accepted a royal licence in contravention of the act, and he retained freedom of action in his dealings with Burgundy by declaring that the ban should remain in force only during the royal pleasure.[2]

In all, this parliament produced no fewer than eleven statutes strongly favouring native mercantile and industrial interests.[3] Edward's acceptance of them reflects his extreme need of internal support. Part of his reward came in the grant to him for life in the 1465 session of the customs duties, though at reduced rates: he would not, however, accept a commons' demand that the Hansards should be deprived of their privilege of exemption from paying poundage.[4] The first session

[1] 3 Edw. IV, c. 1; *RP*, V, 501–3; *SR*, II, 392–5.
[2] *SR*, II, 403–13 (4 Edw. IV, caps 1–5). For the Burgundian embargo, see Myers, *English Historical Documents*, 1042–3.
[3] To those cited above should be added, 4 Edw. IV, c. 8, for the protection of the craft of horners.
[4] *RP*, V, 508–9.

of the parliament of 1467–8 passed an act in the interest of native clothiers, by banning the export of woollen yarn and unfinished cloth (7 Edw. IV, c. 3). But no later parliament produced any comparable programme of economic protectionism; though many statutes dealt with the regulation of trade, industry, customs, and bullion and currency matters, these were for the most part concerned with *internal* organization.[1] But for a variety of reasons even the programme of economic nationalism laid down by the 1463–5 parliament could never be enforced in full or maintained for long. The 'Navigation Act' of 1463 was little more than a well-meant aspiration, for although shipbuilding was already a growth-industry in England, the English merchant marine was not yet sufficiently developed to tackle the country's entire carrying trade, and in any case the act did not extend to the trade of alien merchants.[2] Edward was still much too dependent on Italian financial support to allow the anti-alien legislation to bear too hard on his foreign friends, and during a period of commercial feud with Burgundy he could not risk alienating the Hansards. Finally, the demands of Edward's foreign policy could override even the most pressing of commercial considerations.

When Edward achieved the throne, English trade had been in the grip of a severe depression for more than a decade. Anglo-French commerce, like the French economy generally, was still suffering from the period of prolonged war (renewed from 1450 to 1453), and although hostilities had now ceased, the two countries remained technically at war, with trade subject to a series of restrictions. English trade with Brittany, which had followed the hostile line of the French, was similarly affected. Commerce with both suffered from largely unrestricted piracy. Of greater importance were the unsettled relations between England and the Hanseatic League and England and the Burgundian Low Countries. In spite of a favourable treaty with the Hanse in 1437, the German towns had failed to make good their promises to provide trading privileges for the English in the Baltic and North Germany comparable with those long enjoyed by the Hansards in England. This in turn led to the rise of a powerful anti-Hansard movement in England, and major acts of piracy permitted by Henry VI's government against

[1] 7 Edw. IV, caps 1 and 2, worsted manufactures and Devon cloths; 8 Edw. IV, c. 1, Norfolk cloth manufactures; 12 Edw. IV, c. 3, customs regulations; c. 5, northern wools; 17 Edw. IV, c. 1, bullion regulation; 22 Edw. IV, c. 2, fishpacking; c. 3, silk manufactures; c. 5, fulling of hats and caps. In Edward's last parliament, January–February 1483, a poll-tax was imposed on alien residents, with exemption for Hansards, Spaniards and Bretons (*RP*, VI, 197–8).

[2] R. B. Wernham, *Before the Armada*, 64–5.

the Hanseatic Bay Fleet (carrying salt from Biscay for the fish-curing industry) had done little to improve matters. Relations with Burgundy were bedevilled by the competing bullionist policies of the English and Burgundian governments, as well as by shifts in ducal policy, for, like the king of England, the duke had to balance the demands of conflicting commercial interests amongst his own subjects. The result was a series of bans on the import of English cloth into the duke's dominions, but with exemptions for certain major markets like Antwerp and Bergen-op-Zoom. Nor was Duke Philip indifferent to the chance of capturing the Hanse market from English merchants in the interests of his own people.[1]

It could scarcely be claimed that, on balance, the new king's commercial policies in his first decade did much to remedy the ill-fortunes of English trade. Part of the blame may be laid on the subordination of economic to political interests, part on a certain impulsive inconsistency. It is true, however, that trade with some of the less important southern European markets, especially the denizen share in it, benefited from Edward's support and encouragement. The 1463 ban on alien wool exports was amongst the factors which frightened the Florentines into opening their port of Pisa to foreign shipping on equal terms, thus inaugurating a growing English trade with that port, culminating with the establishment of the English wool staple there in 1491. The cloth trade with Pisa was further encouraged by the lifting of an earlier ban on the import of certain types of cloth in 1466.[2] But at the same time Edward's generosity with licences to Italians to export English goods (many of them in his own name) helped to stimulate the flagging trade of the Florentines and the Venetians with England. In contrast, Genoese trade declined sharply. This was partly due to Genoa's losing to the Florentines her former monopoly of the supply of alum (a commodity vital to the English cloth-manufacturer), but it also reflects Edward's personal coolness towards the Genoese, which in turn was prompted by his good relations with the city of London, and by Genoese negotiations with the restored government of Henry VI in 1470–71.[3] But any

[1] Carus-Wilson, *Medieval Merchant Venturers*, 272–8; H. Touchard, *Le Commerce Maritime Breton au fin du Moyen Age*, 185–7; Carus-Wilson, *The Expansion of Exeter at the Close of the Middle Ages*, 8–9; Postan, 'England and the Hanse', Power and Postan, *op. cit.*, 130–1; Kerling, *Commercial Relations of Holland and Zeeland with England*, 76 ff.
[2] Mallett, 'Anglo-Florentine Commercial Relations', 254–8.
[3] Ruddock, *Italian Merchants . . . in Southampton*, 212–13. The Genoese were already unpopular for their destruction of the expedition of the Bristol merchant, Robert Sturmy, to the Mediterranean in 1457. This hostile act produced a great outcry in England, especially in London; Ruddock, 173–5.

improvement in Italian trade in general owed more to his financial dependence on Florence and (to a lesser extent) Venice than to any direct encouragement of Italian trade, and it certainly did not prevent a steady decline in its volume towards the end of the reign. A treaty concluded in 1468 with another Italian state, the kingdom of Naples, led to the appearance of Neapolitan galleys in the port of Southampton, but it is doubtful whether the trade was ever of significant proportions. With Castile, Edward, anxious for a political alliance, concluded a mercantile treaty in 1466 which gave Spanish merchants exceptional privileges, placing them on the same footing for customs purposes as denizen merchants; and this in turn led to a noticeable increase in Spanish participation in trade with England, especially with the western ports.[1]

All this, however, did little to offset the continuing difficulties with England's more important commercial neighbours. The volume of cloth export in the hands of native merchants continued up to 1465 to run at no more than half what it had been in 1446–8, and their trade in miscellaneous merchandise fell by a similar proportion.[2] With France, the valuable wine trade failed to recover, and between 1456 and 1462 was running at a rate of little more than 3,000 tuns, as compared with an average of 10,000 tuns imported into England in the years before 1449. English cloth exports to France as reflected in the trade figures of the southern and western ports show a fall from about 15,000 cloths a year in 1446–8 to 5,300 in 1459–62, and they sank even further to an average of only 3,565 in the troubled years 1469–71. Bristol's cloth exports had fallen by some 60 per cent in the 1460s as compared with the averages of the period 1440–50. The advent of Edward IV made little difference to this depressed branch of commerce. Continuing political differences brought interruptions and restrictions on trade, as in 1462 when Louis XI, then backing Margaret of Anjou, forbade the export of any merchandise to England, and Edward banned the import of all Gascon wines, even under safe-conduct. The strained relations of the two kings meant that there was little hope of substantial improvement here until the definitive treaty of 1475. Nor did the duke of Brittany's change of policy towards England, and the Anglo-Breton commercial treaty of 1468, do much to revive Anglo-Breton trade in the 1460s.[3]

[1] *RP*, V, 622; Ruddock, 67–8; Rymer, *Foedera*, XI, 571–2; G. Connell-Smith, *Forerunners of Drake*, 31–2.
[2] Gray, 'English Foreign Trade', in Power and Postan, *op. cit.*, 30.
[3] Carus-Wilson, *Medieval Merchant Venturers*, 275–8; *Expansion of Exeter*, 8–9; Gray, *op. cit.*, 28–9; J. W. Sherborne, *The Port of Bristol in the Middle Ages* (1965), 21–2.

With Burgundy relations were marred by the ill-advised Staple-bullion regulations of 1463, and by the embargoes on commerce which followed. These forced the English Merchant Adventurers to remove their Low Countries base from its natural centre in the great mart of Antwerp to Utrecht, and this most important sector of overseas commerce was severely depressed until 1467. Yet the renewal of good commercial relations with Burgundy was obviously essential to Edward's plans for a political and matrimonial alliance with the ducal house. In September 1467, therefore, Edward exercised his prerogative and unilaterally lifted the ban on Burgundian imports into England. This opened the way to a commercial treaty, concluded on 24 November, which restored free trade in general, whilst reserving certain unresolved differences for discussion at a diet to be held at Bruges on 15 January 1468.[1] Scofield believed that Edward did not succeed in persuading the duke to remove his ban on the import of English cloth into the Low Countries, and that, in spite of repeated diets, it was in fact maintained until 1478; but her argument does not seem to be supported by the evidence.[2] The treaty seems to have given a substantial boost to England's export trade. Cloth exports to the Low Countries, as reflected in the denizen export from London, almost doubled in the last three years of the decade, and there was a substantial increase in the volume of trade in miscellaneous merchandise. A further incentive to the cloth export trade had been given by the devaluation of the pound sterling during the re-coinage of 1464–5

[1] Scofield, I, 430–1; Rymer, *Foedera*, XI, 591–601, 605–13.

[2] Scofield, I, 467. Her claim does not appear to be supported by the terms of the treaty. The subject-matter of various diets at Leyden and Lille in 1469, 1473 and 1478 to discuss commercial differences between England and Burgundy was not the cloth ban but the Staple ordinances and matters of exchange. Both Maximilian's instructions to his ambassadors, 4 July 1478, on the eve of the treaty, and Edward's on 2 May, specifically state that these had been the subjects of the diets, and the treaty regulated them in great detail. (Power, 'Wool Trade in the Reign of Edward IV', 29–30; Rymer, *Foedera*, XII, 66–8, 76–86.) It is inconceivable that no reference would have been made during the discussions to a cloth ban had one still been in force, and a ban continued over ten years would have produced a much greater and more publicized protest among both English and Burgundian commercial groups. Bans of this kind were difficult to enforce and were often quietly allowed to lapse (Munro, 'An Economic Aspect . . . of the Anglo-Burgundian alliance', 227; Kerling, *op. cit.*, 80). Scofield also believed that the 1467 treaty was unpopular in England because of the continuance of the cloth embargo, but the only direct evidence of its unpopularity is Monypenny's report of gossip in the London taverns in January 1468, cited above, p. 124; and her reference to 'Gregory's Chronicle', 238, does not support this claim. Finally, her view is almost impossible to reconcile with the improved trade figures cited below. See also the comments of H. van der Wee, *The Growth of the Antwerp Market and the European Economy*, II, 83.

(English goods were now 25 per cent cheaper), and it was helped too by the reorganization of the Netherlandish market.[1]

Meanwhile, in response to the demands of the Londoners, Edward had been subjecting the Hansards to heavy pressure in an effort to compel them to make good their promises of reciprocal privileges for English merchants in their territories. His weapons were repeated threats to suspend their privileges or to impose poll-taxes on them. These were effective, for by 1467 a majority of the member-cities of the League was ready to come to terms and even the most obdurate opponent of England, Lubeck, was preparing to give way. Against this background the disastrous decision of 1468, the so-called 'verdict of the council', whereby all Hanseatic merchants in England were to be arrested and imprisoned and held to ransom in retaliation for the alleged share of the League in the seizure of four English ships by the king of Denmark, is altogether inexplicable. It may be that having recently reopened his trade with Burgundy Edward now felt he could proceed to extremes against the League, but the English action was universally condemned, even in England, and by the Merchant Adventurers in the Low Countries, as unjust and arbitrary, and was no way to bring the Hansards to terms. It succeeded only in alienating England's friends in the League, with the exception of the merchants of Cologne, who were so dependent on the English trade that they were now prepared to break with the League. It is not unlikely, as the Hansards themselves alleged, that Edward was altogether too willing to listen to certain influential members of the council, among them Warwick and his brothers, Sir John Fogge, and perhaps Sir John Howard, who had suffered directly from the Danish capture.[2] 1468 was a tense and nervous year, when the king showed a tendency to behave arbitrarily and was susceptible to undue influence, as the affair of Sir Thomas Cook demonstrates. By the end of the year there are signs that Edward was already beginning to regret his impulsive action. The imprisoned merchants were released; the fine demanded of them was largely remitted; English envoys would be sent to meet envoys from the Hansards and treat for peace. But by now it was too late. The League's attitude had hardened, and the negotiations in Bruges in the summer of 1469 broke down on the obstreperous and extravagant demands by the Hansards for reparations for their injuries, both new and long-standing. Even before the League officially closed the doors

---

[1] Van der Wee, op. cit., II, 83; Touchard, op. cit., 225.
[2] Scofield, I, 196–7, 271–2, 465; Postan, 'England and the Hanse', in Power and Postan, op. cit., 132–3; Hanserecesse von 1431–76, ed. G. von der Ropp, II, vi, no. 97.

on England in August 1470, Anglo-Hanseatic trade had come to a virtual standstill, and there was open war at sea. If the principal sufferers from this breakdown were the Hansards themselves – their trade with England now fell to the lowest level of the entire fifteenth century, whilst the English found alternative outlets for their cloth to a certain degree – England suffered also. The loss of the substantial Hanse export trade may explain the dissatisfaction expressed by cloth producers with this new development, and it may have been especially the breach with the Hanse which the chronicler, John Warkworth, had in mind when he reported that 'many men said that King Edward had much blame for hurting merchandise'.[1]

In one sphere of governmental action affecting the prosperity of commerce, Edward did, however, achieve considerable success. In the last decade of Henry VI's reign, English piracy had reached extravagant proportions, and the Crown had done little to curb it, indeed had often condoned it, with unfortunate consequences for England's relations with her trading partners. In contrast, Edward's government showed far more vigour in its efforts to deal with the threat. If few pirates were indicted on criminal charges, the government was at pains to provide a speedy machinery for investigating complaints and petitions for restitution or compensation, although, unfortunately, the surviving evidence does not permit us to say confidently that the victims were generally successful in obtaining restitution.[2] At the same time the number of recorded acts of piracy by Englishmen drops away sharply under Edward's rule. Excluding official arrests at sea, 120 piracies are known from the period 1450–61, as compared with only 58 between 1461 and 1483. The political upheavals of the years 1469–1471 saw a brief but dramatic revival of piracy, thanks largely to the activities of the fleets of Warwick and the Bastard of Fauconberg in the Narrow Seas, but Edward's restoration brought about a further reduction. Only four piracies a year are recorded between 1471 and 1475, and thereafter they are fewer still. By 1483 English piratical attacks had become very rare events. This achievement probably owed a good deal to more efficient keeping of the seas, both in the early years of the reign, and still more with the organization of the navy after Edward's recovery of the throne, and partly of the known willingness of the

---

[1] Warkworth, *Chronicle*, 12; Postan, *op. cit.*, 134–6; and for the effects on trade, see Gray in Power and Postan, *op. cit.*, 27.

[2] For this, and what follows, I am indebted to the work of my former student, Miss M. Meehan, 'English Piracy, 1460–1500' (unpublished M.Litt. thesis, Bristol, 1972). For a somewhat different view, see C. L. Kingsford, 'West Country Piracy', in his *Prejudice and Promise*, 78–106.

government to control piracy. As early as 1467 the king had attempted to regulate piracy by means of international agreement: his treaty of that year with Burgundy showed a more positive approach to the whole problem, and the clauses of the treaty dealing with piracy reflect an effort to tackle the problem in detail. They provided both a model and a starting-point for similar later treaties with other commercial powers.

These policies were continued into the 1470s, with the added stimulus of Edward's anxiety to achieve good relations with his potential allies or with neutrals as part of his preparations for the invasion of France. This led him to be generous in the matter of compensation to the victims of English attacks. The settlement of the Hanse involved a payment of £10,000 in reparations, part of it for losses due to piracy. In 1474 he granted the merchants of Guipuzcoa in northern Spain 5,000 crowns' compensation for attacks on their shipping committed before 1472, and a further 6,000 for later attacks. In both cases he was paying compensation in part for piracies committed during the Readeption period. Relations with Brittany were especially bedevilled by piracies committed by ships of both sides, and Edward and Francis II tried hard to control them. The pirates of Fowey in Cornwall were so notorious that they were excluded from the Anglo-Breton truce of 1471 and from the Treaty of Châteaugiron of 1472. Here again Edward was generous in providing compensation. Breton merchants were allowed to import goods into England without payment of customs, and against Portsmouth, whose ships had plundered two Breton merchants to the value of 10,000 marks, Edward issued letters of marque empowering the victims to recover the value from the townsmen. In 1474 the continuing misbehaviour of the Fowey pirates against Breton and Spanish commerce finally drove the king to drastic action. All masters, mariners, pirates and owners of ships in Fowey and its estuary were to be arrested, since they had not heeded royal orders and daily committed great depredations; all their ships, gear, goods and merchandise were seized and kept in safe-custody. This vigorous act of punishment had its effect, for little more is heard of Fowey piracy for the rest of the reign.[1]

One reason why Edward's sensible, consistent and vigorous policy in the repression of piracy enjoyed a considerable success is that he did not

[1] Meehan, thesis cited above; Kingsford, op. cit., 105–6; Pocquet du Haut-Jussé, François II Duc de Bretagne et l'Angleterre, 183–8; CPR, 1467–77, 492. It is, however, noticeable that Edward did not proceed to extremes against Henry Bodrugan (for whom see pp. 410–11), accepting an offer of 3,000 marks for himself and 3,000 for distribution amongst the victims of his piracy.

have to worry about any conflict between diplomatic and commercial advantage. It was not always so. In 1473–4 his diplomatic preparations for war with France required him to clear up his relations with the Hanseatic League, and at the Treaty of Utrecht, though only after much stubborn bargaining, the English ambassadors finally agreed to terms which represented an almost total surrender to Hansard demands, with no effective corresponding privileges for English merchants. Yet the king should not be overly blamed for his final concessions, for the Hansards, as Henry VII in his turn was to discover, were a very tough nut to crack.[1] There was rather less justification for his decision in February 1483 to prohibit English merchants from all trade with France. This reflects his deep chagrin at Louis's success at Arras, and the temporary collapse of England's most cherished policies, at a time when his own grasp and judgement were perhaps beginning to fail; but it does show how even at this late stage he was apparently prepared to sacrifice the manifold commercial advantages of the Picquigny treaty to assuage his injured dynastic pride.[2]

Yet in general Edward in his second reign was notably more success-ful in promoting favourable conditions for his country's commerce, mainly to the benefit of native merchant interests. Even the Treaty of Utrecht, though bringing the English no more than vague promises of reciprocity which were never to be executed, achieved a great and immediate boom in Hanseatic trade with England, which by 1479–82 had surpassed its previous highest total.[3] The commercial clauses of the Treaty of Picquigny in 1475 finally freed Anglo-French trade from the many tiresome restrictions which had saddled it during the previous two decades. Aided by the general economic recovery of France during a similar period, they made possible a vast expansion in com-merce with England, from which the western ports benefited especi-ally, as they did also from a considerable growth in Breton maritime activity. The cloth exports of the Devon ports jumped from an average of 1,000 cloths during the years of depression to 6,000 cloths a year in 1481–3; Bristol's cloth exports more than doubled by the end of the reign; and a similar increase took place in Gascon wine imports and in the volume of trade in miscellaneous merchandise.[4] The commercial

---

[1] Chrimes, Henry VII, 235–7.
[2] Acts of Court of the Mercers' Company, 145.
[3] Gray, in Power and Postan, op. cit., 27. Hanseatic cloth exports, which had averaged 6,000–7,000 between 1462 and 1468, fell to 3,000 in the years of war, mostly exported by the Cologners, and rose by 1475 to 9,133, and then to 13,907 a year in 1479–82.
[4] Gray, 31–2; Carus-Wilson, Expansion of Exeter, 8–9; Sherborne, Port of Bristol, 21–2; Touchard, op. cit., 225 ff.

treaty of 1478 with Burgundy eliminated some of the friction which had affected relations between the Staplers at Calais and their Netherlands customers, and saw the abandonment of the provocative monetary policies of the previous decade. With most of England's other commercial neighbours – Castile, Portugal and Denmark – the treaties of the seventies and eighties helped to maintain or improve trading relations.[1]

The consequences of all this may be seen in the steadily improving

Exports and Imports of Dutiable Commodities
in the later fifteenth century*

Years	Exports of wool (sacks)	Exports of broadcloths	Imports of wine (tuns)	Exports and imports of miscellaneous merchandise (in £)
1446–48	7,654	53,699	11,000	121,795
1448–50	8,412	35,078	9,432	91,456
1450–53	7,660	38,928	7,424	91,001
1453–56	9,290	37,738	6,826	82,533
1456–59	7,664	35,059	4,072	59,089
1459–62	4,976	31,933	4,190	65,503
1462–65	7,044	25,855	7,074	57,449
1465–69	9,316	39,664	5,492	93,942
1469–71	7,811	27,610	3,411	53,421
1471–76	9,091	43,129	4,729	115,475
1476–79	7,502	51,889	6,887	120,333
1479–82	9,784	62,586	6,927	179,340

* Annual averages in 3-year periods except 1446–8, 1448–50 and 1469–71 (2-year periods), 1465–69 (4-year period), and 1471–76 (5-year period).

(Reproduced from M. M. Postan, chapter IV of *The Cambridge Economic History of Europe*, ed. M. Postan and E. E. Rich (1952), II, 193.)

[1] Rymer, *Foedera*, XI, 775–6 (Denmark, 1473); XII, 145 (Portugal, 1482); XII, 148 (Castilian province of Guipuzcoa, 1482).

trade figures of the later years of the reign. Cloth exports first reached and then overtook the high levels of the late 1440s. There was an even larger expansion in the export–import trade in miscellaneous merchandise, a recovery in the wine trade, and even a temporary expansion in the volume of wool exports within the context of that trade's long-term decline.[1] Moreover, if we except the Hanseatic sector, a growing share in all this activity was in the hands of native English merchants: by 1483 those who made their living from commerce and industry had good reason to be grateful to their king. It is no surprise to find that the essential features of Yorkist commercial policy were pursued with equal vigour, but with no less risk of subordination to diplomatic and dynastic objectives by Henry VII.[2]

[1] See Table.
[2] Chrimes, *Henry VII*, 219–39; Wernham, *Before the Armada*, chapter V ('Sea Power and Trade, 1485–1509'), 62–76.

Chapter 16

THE KING'S FINANCES

Under the majority rule of Henry VI the revenues of the English Crown
had fallen to an unprecedentedly low level. The king's wasteful dispersal of royal lands and patronage; the decline in customs revenue
caused by a major trade recession; the reluctance of parliament to
grant taxes – all these conspired to worsen the state of the king's
finances. Real revenue – so far as it is revealed by exchequer sources –
fell to less than £24,000 a year in the last five years of Henry VI's
reign, as compared with about £90,000 under Henry IV. Meanwhile,
current charges and outstanding debts mounted from £225,000 in
1433 to £372,000 in 1450. Wages and salaries went unpaid for years,
and large debts accumulated even to important creditors like Duke
Richard of York. The government was forced into borrowing at
ruinous rates of interest, which may sometimes have been as high as
33 per cent. Yet as debts increased so lenders became more reluctant
to invest in an insolvent regime, and loans became more difficult to
find as confidence in the Lancastrian government ebbed away. The
financial weakness of the Crown reflected and exaggerated its general
lack of prestige. For the new king in 1461 the restoration of some
degree of solvency and financial credibility was a task of the greatest
urgency.[1]

Edward's approach to this problem during the first decade of his
reign was marked by that mixture of intelligence and inconsistency so
characteristic of his policies. He could not count on parliamentary
taxation for anything save 'extraordinary' expenses. Taxes voted by the
commons between 1461 and 1470 yielded a total of £93,000, but this
cannot be regarded as equivalent to £10,000 per annum of 'normal'
revenue. The larger part of it was necessarily spent on the repression
of rebellion and urgent defence needs. Even relatively small-scale and
isolated military operations could prove very expensive. Thus in
November 1468 Edward recognized a debt of £5,521 to William Herbert, earl of Pembroke, for his services in Wales, chiefly for the costs of

[1] Steel, *Receipt of the Exchequer*, 323–4, 344–5, 352; for the debts, Wolffe, *Royal Demesne*,
141; for the money owed to York, above, p. 12.

besieging Harlech Castle.[1] Lay taxation was supplemented by the fifteenths and tenths voted by the clergy, through the convocations of Canterbury and York, which produced a further £7,000 a year during the same period.[2]

But these sums were quite inadequate to meet even the regular demands on the royal purse. The royal household could not be effectively financed on less than about £11,000–£12,000 a year.[3] General administrative expenses, such as the wages and salaries of royal officials, both local and central, and the costs of diplomacy, absorbed a similar sum, quite apart from the unknown amounts paid out each year in annuities to royal supporters and servants.[4] The maintenance of England's regular military establishment accounted for even more. The major item here was the financing of the garrison and fortress of Calais, which cost about £10,000 a year in peacetime.[5] The policing of the northern marches towards Scotland also proved a heavy burden. When John Nevill, Lord Montagu, took on the wardenship of the East March on 26 May 1463, he was to be paid at the rate of £6,000 a year in wartime, and £3,000 in time of peace or truce, and by March 1465 he had already expended £8,000 on the wages and rewards of his troops.[6] On the West March his elder brother, Warwick, was serving from 1462 at rates of £2,500 in wartime and £1,250 in time of peace or truce.[7] Provision for members of the royal family was another unavoidable charge on the royal revenues. Though established on a smaller scale than was allowed to her queenly predecessors, Elizabeth Woodville's household in 1466–7 was costing her husband just over £4,500. Much land had been set aside for the dukes of Clarence and Gloucester, the former in particular with a guaranteed 5,500 marks a year, being generously provided for. 400 marks a year had to be provided for Edward's sister, Margaret of York, and after 1466 allowances made for his own children.[8] Together these regular charges involved

---

[1] P.R.O., E. 404/74/1, no. 129.   [2] Ramsay, *Lancaster and York*, II, 463.

[3] Myers, *Household of Edward IV*, 45. This does not allow for the expenses of the great wardrobe, which ran at about £2,000 a year in the early years (45, n. 3).

[4] J. L. Kirby, 'The Issues of the Lancastrian Exchequer and Lord Cromwell's estimates of 1433', *BIHR*, xxiv (1951), 143–5 (representing average expenditure on this head in the first twelve years of Henry VI's reign).

[5] Power and Postan, *Studies in English Trade*, 44–5 (arrangements under the act of retainer, 1466).

[6] R. L. Storey, 'Wardens of the Marches', 615; *CPR, 1461–7*, 426.

[7] P.R.O., E. 404/74/1, no. 1.

[8] Myers, *Household of Edward IV*, 38; 'The Household of Queen Elizabeth Woodville, 1466–7', 667, n. 9; for Clarence and Gloucester, above, pp. 117, 186; for Margaret of York, *CPR, 1461–7*, 142.

the king in an annual expenditure of some £50,000 a year. Even this makes no allowance for heavy if irregular charges for particular purposes. Thus the dowry of Margaret of York in 1468 was to cost her brother £41,666 13s 4d, of which £10,000 had to be paid on her wedding day, and a further £2,450 was spent on her trousseau, her cash-in-hand (£500), and the cost of transporting the bride and an appropriate escort across the Channel.[1]

To meet these heavy demands Edward had two steady sources of revenue. First was the customs duties, which he collected from the beginning of the reign without any specific authority until granted them for life in 1465. Unfortunately, this source of revenue was adversely affected by the continuing depression in English trade, largely due to war and to bad relations with England's commercial neighbours. For a time in the middle years the customs produced about £30,000 a year, but the average over the whole decade was some £25,000 a year, or about the same as in Henry VI's reign.[2] Not until trading conditions were improved by the commercial treaties of the 1470s and better foreign relations could much be done to boost customs revenue.[3]

Of greater immediate and potential value to the Crown were the royal estates, now swollen by dynastic change and forfeiture. The great array of forfeited estates after the act of attainder of 1461 included the lands of two dukes, five earls, one viscount and six barons, as well as several dozen gentry inheritances. Nor was this all. The king could now draw upon his own paternal inheritance – the broad acres of the Duchy of York and the Earldom of March – and on the Principality of Wales, the Duchy of Cornwall, and the Earldom of Chester, forfeited from the Lancastrian Prince Edward. In addition, he enjoyed the wardship of several baronial estates in the hands of minors, the most valuable being those of Duke Humphrey of Buckingham and John Talbot, earl of Shrewsbury.[4] No precise estimate could be given of the total annual value of all this, but £30,000 would be a conservative guess, or rather more than Henry VI's supposed revenue in his later years.

Much has been written recently in praise of the 'Yorkist land-

[1] P.R.O., E. 404/74/1, no. 35 (8 June 1468).
[2] My own calculations from the tables of total overseas trade printed in Power and Postan, *Studies in English Trade*, 403–4, confirm the figures given by Ramsay, *Lancaster and York*, II, 461. For Henry VI, see K. B. McFarlane, 'War, the Economy and Social Change: England and the Hundred Years War', *Past and Present*, no. 22 (1962), 6.
[3] Below, pp. 384–5.
[4] *RP*, V, 476–83.

revenue experiment', described at length in the writings of Dr B. P. Wolffe.[1] Basically, it involved removing lands in the king's hands, whether by reason of inheritance, forfeiture or wardship, from the control of the exchequer, which was ill-equipped to manage them efficiently. Its old-fashioned system of farming them out at fixed rates benefited the farmers rather than the king. Instead, they were now to be placed under the direct control of specially-appointed receivers and surveyors administering convenient and contiguous groups of properties, their duties and methods being modelled on the practice of the great private estates, including the Duchy of York itself. These men, Wolffe tells us, were no mere rent-collectors but officials of the highest responsibility and trust, and among them were a number of experienced estates administrators like Sir Richard Fowler, Sir Richard Croft, Peter Beaupie, Nicholas Sharpe and Nicholas Leventhorpe, who served the king throughout the reign. They were now made to account not to the exchequer but to the king's chamber within the royal household, and the revenues they brought in were now made immediately available for the king's use. This development coincided with the rise of the chamber as both a revenue-collecting and spending department, which long before the end of the reign had superseded the exchequer as the chief financial office of the state. Apart from land revenues, it began to receive such things as temporalities of vacant sees, the profits of the exercise of royal prerogative rights, the French pension, benevolences, even the proceeds of parliamentary taxation, including, it would appear, the war taxes of 1472–5. The exchequer was deprived of much of its control of the process of auditing accounts, now carried out in the chamber, and had to be content with verbal declarations from the king that accounts had been duly discharged. The exchequer was made to transfer large if irregular sums to the chamber of the household, especially in years of heavy spending like 1467–8 and 1471, when the transfers totalled over £21,000 in each year. By the end of the reign, however, the exchequer had become so starved of money that it became necessary for the chamber to subsidize it by transfers in the other direction.

The advantages of the scheme lay in its providing a more speedy and flexible system of getting and spending and in the fact that it was under the direct and immediate personal control of the king and trusted and experienced officials directly answerable to him. Once again it is worth

---

[1] 'The Management of English Royal Estates under the Yorkist Kings', *EHR*, lxxi (1956), 1–27; *The Crown Lands, 1461–1536*, 50–60; *Royal Demesne*, 158–79, on which what follows is based.

emphasizing the degree and continuity of the king's personal involvement. In 1469 he could tell the treasurer, Richard, Earl Rivers, that he should be discharged of all sums expended by him 'such as we *expressed unto you by word of mouth*' and 'of the which *we remember* that ye never had warrant nor discharge', without any need for further accounting in the exchequer.[1] In 1478 one of the estates officials, John Hayes, was said to be quit of monies 'paid and delivered unto our own person in the Chamber' and he made other payments 'by our commandment given by our own mouth'. It was here in the chamber that the king made bargains for the sale of forfeitures and wardships, appointed officials, often again by word of mouth, and supervised the financial business of the realm. It was probably also in his chamber, as well as in council, that some of the many administrative changes and innovations, especially affecting the king's finances, were decided upon and formulated. These included the programme of appointing commissions to enquire into neglected or usurped prerogative rights of the Crown, first attempted in the early years of the reign, but becoming more general from 1478 onwards; the series of economical reforms in the royal household between 1472 and 1478; changes in the exchequer, such as the overhaul of the system of enrolments, involving the abandonment of the Issue Rolls and the purging of extraneous and minor matters from the Foreign Rolls, leaving an orderly roll concerned exclusively with non-estate business; the careful scrutiny of fees and annuities charged on the exchequer and on local revenues, and the drawing-up of new lists of farms, wards and marriages at the king's disposal, both aimed at providing him with a more precise knowledge of the overall state of his revenues; and the series of measures to tighten customs control and port administration.[2] Here was a spirit of enterprise and reform under the guidance of a king for whom the accumulation of wealth became more important in his later years, and with the aid of a body of experienced and skilful administrators. Already by 1483 there had emerged a system of highly personal financial control, centred on the chamber, which anticipates in all essentials the structure once thought to have been created by the early Tudors.

These new methods have an obvious importance as a major step towards economical reform and good business management, but their importance should not be overestimated in the context of improving

[1] P.R.O., Warrants for Issues, E. 404/74/2, no. 36; and for John Hayes below, Wolffe, *Royal Demesne*, 168.
[2] Wolffe, *op. cit.*, 173–4; J. R. Lander, 'The Administration of the Yorkist Kings' (unpublished Cambridge M.Litt. thesis), esp. 227 ff., 257 ff.

the king's revenues, especially in the decade 1461–70. Wolffe believed that the revenues of the great landed acquisitions were brought under the new system of Yorkist estate management for the benefit of the king's finances.[1] But closer enquiry reveals that they were largely alienated from the Crown within a short space of time. The dispersal of the inheritance of that arch-enemy of the York family, James Butler, earl of Wiltshire and Ormond, provides a good example of the scale and speed of these alienations. In the late spring and summer of 1461 a number of receivers, surveyors and auditors were appointed to administer these estates, but immediately after the act of attainder of 4 November 1461 made it possible for the king legally to dispose of the estates, the partition began. By August 1462 almost all of the earl's fifty-one manors and lordships in England, spreading over twelve counties from the west of England to East Anglia, had been granted to beneficiaries like the earl of Kent, Hastings, Herbert and Howard, and lesser royal servants such as John Donne, esquire, Richard Fowler, and Fulk Stafford. By the end of that year it appears that no more than four manors were still under royal control. A similar fate overtook most of the other forfeited estates, and the new officials were left to administer a mere fragment of the lands originally entrusted to them.[2] Such royal open-handedness ensured that the king's finances benefited little from forfeitures and wardships during the first reign. Because of the disappearance of the chamber records, we have no means of assessing how much land revenues contributed to the king's coffers, but it was clearly very much less than it might have been had Edward chosen to adopt a different policy. Before 1471 he showed no consistent intention to accumulate or retain lands in his own grasp, in sharp contrast to the tenacity with which Henry VII clung to his landed acquisitions. With the partial exceptions of the childless Jasper, duke of Bedford, and John de Vere, earl of Oxford, Henry saw no need to endow and reward his supporters with land on anything like the scale adopted in the 1460s.[3]

---

[1] Wolffe, op. cit., 164, and also 157–8 for the suggestion that some forfeited lands may have been sold.

[2] For the Wiltshire lands, CPR, 1467–77, 12, 19, 29, 32, 34, 47, 72, 75, 77, 86, 95, 104–5, 111–12, 116, 118, 129, 139, 143, 186, 198, 212, 225. I am indebted to Dr Roger S. Thomas of the University of Swansea for evidence which shows that the lands of the earldom of Richmond had been similarly alienated by the summer of 1462. For other evidence on alienation of forfeited lands, see above, pp. 70 ff.

[3] See for example the list of lands worth £24,620 a year in Henry's hands in 1503–4, many of which had been under royal control since 1485, printed by Wolffe, Crown Lands, 142–6. For his grants to his supporters, see Chrimes, Henry VII, 54–8, though many of those there said to be in favour of the Stanleys were only confirmations of what they had gained under Richard III.

For Edward IV, his judgement of political expediency and his personal generosity overrode financial pressures.

All the sources of revenue so far discussed did not suffice to keep the government solvent. Financial stringency is reflected in the use of a variety of fund-raising devices, some distinctly arbitrary and of dubious legality. In March 1464, with the advice of his council, Edward ordained that all of his subjects to whom he had granted land, annuity, fee or office worth 10 marks a year or more, must pay one-quarter of their annual value to the king, in order to assist him in reducing the northern strongholds to obedience.[1] In the same year he put pressure on the clergy to grant a subsidy of 6d in the £, in response to Pope Pius's appeal for the launching of a crusade. Though called a 'gratuitous subsidy', it was clearly made under compulsion from the Crown, abetted by Archbishop Bourchier, and the proceeds were handed over to royal agents. Probably most, if not all, of this subsidy remained in the king's hands. There was at least sufficient suspicion of this for the rebels in 1469 to include it amongst their charges of royal mismanagement.[2]

A more legitimate, if scarcely more popular, device was the recoinage of 1464-5. The official proclamation on this measure gave as its reason the acute shortage of gold and silver in the realm (which was true), and claimed that all was being done for the weal of the realm, blandly ignoring the king's opportunities for profit from the operation. It was in fact the most drastic devaluation of the English coinage since the introduction of bimetallism in 1343.[3] Edward increased by 25 per cent the nominal value of the coin coined from a pound of metal, but without increasing the amount of alloy. Thus the face-value of the gold noble rose from 6s 8d to 8s 4d, and 1 lb of silver now produced 450 as against 360 pence. This decision 'many men grudged passing sore, for they could not reckon that gold not so quickly as they did the old gold'.[4] In April 1465, therefore, the government introduced a new gold coinage based upon a noble (often called a rose-noble or a royal) valued at 10s, a half- and a quarter-noble, together with two coins in money of

---

[1] CCR, 1461-8, 230.

[2] W. E. Lunt, *Financial Relations of the Papacy with England, 1327-1534*, 145-50; Warkworth, *Chronicle*, 49.

[3] A. Feaveryear, *The Pound Sterling* (rev. edn, 1963), 39-45; T. F. Reddaway, 'The King's Mint and the Exchange in London, 1343-1513', *EHR*, lxxxii (1967), 1-23; and, for the royal proclamation, *CCR, 1461-8*, 216.

[4] Gregory, 227. Feaveryear denied that the re-coinage was unpopular, but in 1469 the rebel manifesto charged the king with 'having changed his most rich coin' (Warkworth, *Chronicle*, 48).

account, an angel worth 6s 8d and an angelet of 3s 4d. The result was a handsome and much-copied gold currency.[1] But in the process the king gained a minting charge increased out of all proportion – 47s 8d instead of 3s 4d for gold, and 3s 4d instead of 3d for silver, less fees paid to the king's officers. This brought him a handsome profit of at least £17,500 in the two years between September 1464 and September 1466, and smaller amounts thereafter.[2] The re-coinage may not have been very successful in stimulating the amount of currency in circulation, but the consequent devaluation helped to stimulate demand for English goods on foreign markets.[3] By this time, too, Edward was also actively seeking to improve his finances by personal trading ventures. The records unfortunately do not permit us to discover how much profit the king derived from this source, but it seems likely to have been considerable, judging by the scale of royal commercial operations.[4]

Nevertheless, the government faced a constant shortage of ready cash, and this meant an equally constant recourse to borrowing. But it is a clear indication of a renewed confidence in the Crown's financial credibility that hard-headed men of business now showed themselves far more willing to lend to Edward than they had been to shore up the shaky galleries of Henry VI's finances. In particular, three important groups of lenders, who had been largely alienated by the Lancastrians, provided substantial backing. First, the Londoners, who had invested quite heavily in the Yorkists even before Edward's victory at Towton. Apart from the large corporate loan of £11,000 in 1460–61, London merchants, either as individuals or in syndicates, lent the Crown no less than £35,852 between 1462 and 1475, more than three times their investment in Henry VI in the last decade of his rule. The Company of the Staple had a strong stake in the survival of Edward's government, for only through him could they hope to recover the large sums they had advanced to the Lancastrians, and, in fact, between 1462 and 1475 they lent him £23,208. But the really dramatic rise in lending to the Crown comes with the third group, the alien bankers and merchants. These had lent only £1,000 to Henry VI in his last decade, but now proceeded to advance £38,128 to Edward before 1475. The principal

[1] C. W. C. Oman, *The Coins of England* (1931), 217 ff. C. E. Blunt and C. A. Whitton, 'The Coinages of Edward IV and Henry VI Restored', *British Numismatic Journal*, xxv (1945–8), 4–59, 130–82; and pp. 183–209 of the same journal, A. Thompson, 'Continental Imitations of the Rose Noble of Edward IV'.
[2] Feaveryear, *op. cit.*, 41–2.   [3] Above, pp. 364–5. See Plates 18 and 19.
[4] Two shipments of wool and cloth alone produced £1,872 in June 1463 (Steel, *Receipt of the Exchequer*, 288); for Edward's trading activities in general, see above, pp. 351–2.

source of loans was the Florentines, especially one of the king's chief factors, Gerard de Caniziani, who lent £24,705. The Medici bank provided a further £5,000 and smaller sums came from Genoese and Venetian bankers.[1] Edward was much more successful in winning the confidence of the Italians than any of his fifteenth-century predecessors, and, with the Londoners and the Staplers, they came to be the chief financial support of his government.

This success can be explained only by the fact that these lenders appreciated the real efforts the government was making to meet its obligations, despite its difficulties. It is true that wages and annuities often went unpaid for considerable periods. For example, John Convers, a king's serjeant, was one of many minor officials who in 1466 had not received any payment of his stipend since the beginning of the reign. In March 1464 Geoffrey Gate, lieutenant of the Isle of Wight, was owed £377 8s for his own and his men's wages, having served at his own expense from July 1461. Even the much more influential Walter Blount, Lord Mountjoy, was still awaiting payment in March 1468 of £3,436 spent by him on the king's behalf, although promised it three years before; and he was said to be greatly troubled by suits from his creditors 'if the king succour him not'.[2] But in general failure to pay, or long delay in payment, never reached the proportions common under Henry VI, and the government was prudent enough to avoid the accumulation of very large long-term debts to powerful men. Similarly, it tried to avoid the constant defaults on promises to pay which had been so disturbing a feature of late-Lancastrian finance, and creditors seem to have been confident that they would be repaid in due course. The Company of the Staple in particular benefited from the sensible rationalization of the system of financing Calais enshrined in the 'Act of Retainer' of 1466 and its later modifications. Under Henry VI the garrison had been unpaid and mutinous, and had retaliated by seizing the Staplers' wool and holding the Company to ransom. Now the Company was itself made responsible for the regular payment of the garrison and recovered the money from the profits of the customs duties on wool exports – an arrangement which suited all concerned.[3]

If Edward and his advisers could feel reasonably satisfied at having avoided the worst financial ineptitudes of the Lancastrians, it was not until 1475 and after that real solvency was achieved, royal debts were

[1] Steel, op. cit., 344–6, 351–3, 357.

[2] CCR, 1461–8, 343–4; CPR, 1461–7, 424; CCR, 1468–76, 9–10.

[3] Lander, 'Council, Administration and Councillors', 138–44; Power, 'The Wool Trade in the Fifteenth Century', in Power and Postan, Studies in English Trade, 74–5; RP, VI, 55–61, 101–3, for the modifications of 1473 and 1474.

finally discharged, and the king became normally independent of financial assistance from parliament, the first English ruler to do so for more than a century. How was this achieved? A contemporary analysis by the Croyland Chronicler, from his vantage-point within the government, provides a good starting-point. First, he tells us, the king 're-sumed possession of nearly all the royal estates, without regard to whom they had been granted, and applied the whole thereof to the support of the expenses of the Crown'. Tighter customs control was ensured through the introduction of surveyors of the customs, 'men of remarkable shrewdness, but too hard, according to general report, upon the merchants'. He continued to profit from his trading ventures. He began to enforce his feudal rights more sharply, and to draw revenues from vacant prelacies. Finally, he enjoyed the French pension of £10,000 from 1475 until the year before his death. 'All these particulars,' the Chronicler adds, 'in the course of a very few years, rendered him an extremely wealthy prince.'[1]

Though the Chronicler's assertions on almost all these points can be substantiated, they are far from providing a full picture of royal financial policies. It is doubtful whether even the third of Edward's acts of resumption, that of 1473, did much to increase the revenues. Its purpose was primarily political, to undo the arrangements for the Crown lands made during the Readeption, and to check the power of the duke of Clarence.[2] More important was a generally tougher policy towards retaining and exploiting lands under royal control. Though the gains of 1471 had been dispersed, Edward became notably less generous in his later years, as his avarice mounted.[3] Some wards' lands were now mainly kept in the king's hands, and their revenues paid into the king's chamber: thus portions of the estates of the earls of Shrewsbury and Wiltshire and of Lord Morley, during the minority of their heirs, provided up to £1,400 a year towards the rebuilding of St George's Chapel at Windsor.[4]

Even in his later years, however, Edward proved far less grasping in such matters than Henry Tudor was to be. For instance, the estates of the Talbot earldom of Shrewsbury in wardship produced no more than £450 for the king, although worth in excess of £1,000 a year, largely because of his indulgence to William, Lord Hastings, who paid only £300 for lands of twice that value.[5] Several lesser baronial inheri-

[1] CC, 559. [2] Wolffe, Royal Demesne, 154-6.
[3] For 1471, see above, pp. 185-7.
[4] Ramsay, Lancaster and York, II, 459.
[5] A. J. Pollard, 'The Family of Talbot, Lords Talbot and Earls of Shrewsbury in the

tances, among them those of Lords FitzWarin, Say and Berners, were allowed to be farmed out by the exchequer at fixed rates instead of being incorporated into the royal system of land management.[1] The first major estate to be appropriated and exploited directly for the king's benefit was Clarence's share of the Warwick, Despenser and Salisbury lands, which was worth about £3,500 a year in net cash.[2] It also appears to have been the only one.[3] In contrast, one finds Henry VII, after a similar period of eighteen years' rule, administering all or parts of more than a dozen forfeited or escheated estates, and drawing a further revenue of £6,264 from wardships. This explains why his land revenue towards the end of his reign was of the order of £42,000.[4] In comparing him with Edward IV, however, allowance must be made for his highly favourable family position, for by then his only dependent was his surviving son, Henry of York, who was not permitted to draw the revenues of the Principality of Wales. Edward, on the other hand, had to provide for his mother, his queen, his brother, Gloucester, and a large and growing family. According to the most recent calculation, lands under royal control at the beginning of Richard III's reign were worth between £22,000 and £25,000 in net cash, exclusive of annuities, but whilst Edward was alive at least half this sum was absorbed by provision for the royal family, and it is possible that his actual income from land was much less than £10,000.[5]

Fifteenth Century' (unpublished Bristol Ph.D. thesis, 1968). This was one of the wardships particularly mentioned by Wolffe as being part of the 'Yorkist land-revenue experiment', *Crown Lands*, 69.

[1] *CPR, 1467-77*, 593; *1476-85*, 48, 228; *CFR, 1471-85*, 142, 239.

[2] This is the estimate given by Wolffe, 'Management of the Royal Estates', 7. But about a dozen manors and lordships were afterwards given in wardship to Thomas, marquis of Dorset, in 1480; four Isle of Wight manors went to Earl Rivers; and a few alienations were made from those estates which Clarence held by royal grant. For guidance on this point I am grateful to my former student, M. A. Hicks, who is engaged upon a full-scale study of the career and estates of the duke of Clarence.

[3] It is not clear what arrangements were made for the Mowbray inheritance which Edward procured for his second son, Richard, duke of York. Sir Thomas Vaughan, treasurer of the chamber, was appointed 'surveyor and demiser at farm' in 1477, and Sir Robert Wingfield, controller of the household, was made steward of the lands (*CPR, 1476-85*, 10, 12), but no appointments of receivers have been noted.

[4] Wolffe, *Crown Lands*, 142-6; *Royal Demesne*, 219.

[5] Wolffe, *Royal Demesne*, 188-90, for Richard's income. For Edward deductions from this total must be made for the queen (£4,500), the prince of Wales (£5,600) and the duke of Gloucester (about £3,500). G. L. Harriss has recently suggested (reviewing Wolffe, *Crown Lands*, in *History*, lviii [1973]), that the Crown lands could yield only £4,500 of the £11,000 set aside for the support of the royal household in 1483, but this may have been only a matter of administrative convenience.

Alongside the new methods of estate management introduced earlier in the reign, Edward's later years saw a much increased concern with the exploitation of the king's feudal rights. From about 1478 there was what Sir Robert Somerville has called 'an intense activity over feudal dues'.[1] This involved enquiries into profits due from tenants holding of the king by knight service, demands for fines for respite of homage or for withdrawal of suit of court, and the concealment of wardships, reliefs and outlawries. At the same time efforts were made to increase the efficiency of estate management by sending out special groups of officials, notably on the Duchy of Lancaster estates, to survey and inspect the condition of lordships and manors and devise measures for their reform. They had instructions to examine closely the condition of buildings, parks, herbage, timber, to increase rents and revise rentals, and generally to tighten up on the work of local officials, often in minute detail.[2]

Clearly such activity might produce substantial results. Following the official 'progress' of the Duchy of Lancaster council through Lancashire and Cheshire in 1476, there was a sharp increase in the receipts of Thomas, Lord Stanley, as the duchy's receiver-general in Lancashire. From £347 in 1476–7, they rose to £800 in 1477–8, and finally climbed to £885 in 1481–2.[3] How far was such improvement general? In the present state of our knowledge this is a difficult question to answer. Although an exact comparison is not possible, the gross yields of the northern parts of the Duchy amounted to £7,391 in 1463–4; in 1478–9 it was £6,696. The net profits, including arrears, were £3,647 and £3,484 respectively.[4] Part of the reason for this state of affairs may have been the neglect and inefficiency of Duke Richard of Gloucester, as chief steward of the Duchy north of Trent, and local steward also of many northern Duchy lordships, since 1471. In 1482 the Duchy council roundly told him that he and his deputies, through sales of timber and other defects of administration, had brought his lordships into great decay.[5] This letter is a remarkably outspoken criticism of a powerful royal duke, but one doubts whether Henry VII would have tolerated such a situation over twelve years.

Evidence from other royal lands or estates in royal hands suggests

[1] Somerville, *Duchy of Lancaster*, I, 243.
[2] *Ibid.*, 250–1; A. R. Myers, 'An Official Progress through Lancashire and Cheshire in 1476', *Transactions of the Historic Society of Lancashire and Cheshire*, cxv (1963), 1–29.
[3] Myers, *op. cit.*, 5.
[4] P.R.O., Rentals and Surveys, D.L. 43/15/5; D.L. 43/16/1. Cf. Somerville, *op. cit.*, I, 238, whose calculations omit an item of £829 for 1463–4.
[5] Somerville, *op. cit.*, 254.

a similar conclusion. The lands of the Duchy of York in Somerset produced £348 in 1459–60 and £352 in 1477–8, whilst a group of Yorkshire manors which yielded £117 a year at the beginning of the reign was producing the same amount at its end.[1] All the efforts of Yorkist administrators did not succeed in raising the revenues of the southern parts of the Principality of Wales to the levels reached during Henry VI's minority. From about £2,000 a year in 1430–32 these had fallen to no more than £213 in 1456–7; under Edward they averaged between £700 and £1,000 a year. But Henry VII likewise had no great success in this region.[2] In administering the Talbot lordship of Goodrich in Herefordshire, the royal officials were notably less successful than William, Lord Herbert, who extracted from it a revenue of £115 a year in the 1460s compared with a yield of only half as much when it was in royal hands during the next decade.[3]

Too often there seems to have been a gap between theory and practice in royal estate management. Alongside 'the enterprising and reforming spirit' noted by Sir Robert Somerville in the administration of the Duchy of Lancaster, there are many striking examples of failure to get things done.[4] For example, in an effort to increase revenue from the Yorkshire honours, the Duchy council appointed commissioners to make new rentals in 1474, but found that nothing had been done when it visited the area in 1476, and the ministers' accounts show that nothing had been done two years after that. In Michaelmas 1480 the officials of the Honour of Pontefract were still largely working on rentals first compiled in 1424–5 or 1420–21.[5] One may well doubt whether Edward's government was much more successful in its efforts to exploit the king's feudal revenues. Here again the problem was recognized and remedies proposed, but the arrangements for enforcement lacked teeth. Thus in 1471 the escheator in Lancashire was particularly directed to enquire into the practice of tenants entering on their inheritances without livery or licence, but in 1479 the Duchy council noted that the practice continued. Similarly evasion of royal rights of wardship (admittedly an intractable problem) continued to be widespread.[6]

The idea that much slackness and inefficiency remained in Edwardian administration can be confirmed by the evidence of documents

---

[1] J. T. Rosenthal, 'The Estates and Finances of Richard, duke of York', 159–60.
[2] R. A. Griffiths, 'Royal Government . . . in the Principality of Wales' (unpublished Ph.D. thesis, Bristol University, 1962).
[3] A. J. Pollard, 'The Family of Talbot'.   [4] Somerville, op. cit., I, 255.
[5] Ibid., I, 250; P.R.O., D.L. 29/511/8261.
[6] Somerville, 245–6; Bean, Decline of English Feudalism, 215–16, 238–42.

drawn up in the reign of Richard III. Among them is a 'remembrance' proposing improvements in royal financial methods.[1] Among the faults it lists were the laxity and slowness of accounting procedures at the exchequer; the fact that stewards of royal lands were often self-seeking and ill-equipped for their positions; and the continuing practice of farming out royal estates, wardships and ecclesiastical temporalities in the king's hands at fixed and unprofitable rents instead of administering directly for the king's benefit. This final point is amply borne out by the evidence.[2] Similarly, a set of instructions issued by Richard III to Sir Marmaduke Constable, steward of the Duchy Honour of Tutbury, suggests that officials often failed to observe the standards of careful management laid down by the Duchy council.[3] As in other matters, it was left to Henry VII to make these fully effective.

The appointment of surveyors of the customs noted by the Croyland Chronicler was the climax of a series of efforts by Edward's government to improve customs revenue by preventing evasion. As early as 1466, Edward appointed powerful commissions in many ports to enquire into breaches of the statutes and to investigate customs administration in general. Similar commissions were appointed in 1473 and 1474, and in 1475 parliament approved an act increasing the penalties for fraud in the import of luxury textiles from a fine of double the subsidy to forfeiture of the smuggled goods.[4] Meanwhile, individual surveyors of the customs were appointed from 1471 onwards, and this became a general system in 1478. The powers of these new officials were very wide, and the importance attached to their work is shown in the high rates of pay (up to 100 marks a year) which they received. The stringency with which these men operated produced a large crop of prosecutions, as many as thirty-six cases being presented by the king's attorney in Trinity term 1478.[5] Stricter customs control was matched by a vigorous and on the whole successful offensive against piracy. In both these areas of administration the Yorkist government displayed far more energy and efficiency than its Lancastrian predecessor.

[1] B.M. Harleian MS 433, fos 271–2, in Gairdner, *Letters and Papers Illustrative of the Reigns of Richard III and Henry VII*, I, 79–85.
[2] Ecclesiastical temporalities were usually farmed to the incoming bishop, often before his election or provision, and sometimes without rendering anything to the king: e.g. *CPR, 1467–77*, 344, 597; *1476–85*, 105, 122, 131, 206, 344. Henry VII, in contrast, forced the incoming bishops to pay heavy fines for the restitution of their temporalities. For the farming of baronial inheritances, see above, p. 381.
[3] B.M. Harleian MS 433, fo. 270; Gairdner, *op. cit.*, I, 79–81.
[4] *CPR, 1461–7*, 530; *1467–77*, 427, 489–90; *RP*, VI, 154–5.
[5] *CFR, 1471–85*, 24, 42; *CPR, 1467–77*, 391–2; *1476–85*, 101, 225, 231, 236; J. R. Lander, 'The Administration of the Yorkist Kings.

More important than such measures in raising customs revenue was the gradual improvement in trading conditions after 1471. This owed something to greater political stability at home, but even more to the series of commercial treaties with all England's trading neighbours which marks the 1470s, particularly the Treaties of Utrecht (1473-4) with the Hansards, of Picquigny (1475) with France, and with Burgundy (1478). All this made possible an increase, gradual at first but markedly gaining in momentum by 1480, in the volume and value of England's foreign trade. In consequence, customs revenue rose to an average of about £34,000 after 1471, some £10,000 a year more than in the first decade of the reign.[1]

To these improvements in his most stable sources of revenue, Edward could add a total of £86,250 received from France, either as pension or the ransom payment for Margaret of Anjou, in the last seven years of his reign. Between 1471 and 1483 the clergy contributed £77,100 in taxation, and parliamentary lay taxation provided £93,000, although all of this latter sum was spent on the expedition of 1475.[2] The Crown derived further money from the proceeds of benevolences and Edward's private trading ventures, but we have no idea of the amounts involved.[3] Taken together, and in combination with the very modest expenditure on the royal household following the reforms of the 1470s, we have no reason to doubt the claims of contemporaries that in his later years Edward was an extremely wealthy prince. By the end of 1478 he had almost entirely paid off his debts, and had even managed to accumulate a substantial treasure.[4]

Any calculation of Edward's total annual revenue in the last eight years of his reign must of necessity be imprecise, by reason of the disappearance of the all-important chamber records. Disregarding taxation, the profits of benevolences, and unknown sums from trading ventures, it would appear that his revenue from regularly recurring sources was of the order of £65,000 to £70,000.[5] This may be compared

1 Ramsay, *Lancaster and York*, II, 461, 470, citing Enrolled Customs Accounts.
2 Ramsay, *op. cit.*, II, 463; and for the taxation of 1472-5, see above, pp. 214-17, 237.
3 The benevolence of 1475 produced at least £21,656 8s 3d, but the returns are far from complete.
4 Mancini, 67; *CC*, 559, 564, 567, 575, for his wealth; for the debts, see Scofield, II, 215-16, and Lander, 'Edward IV: the Modern Legend: and a Revision', 46-7. The treasure is mentioned by More (*Richard III*, 19), as well as Mancini and *CC*; but see the remarks of Wolffe, *Royal Demesne*, 223-5, on the subject of royal treasures.
5 For purposes of comparison with Henry VII, the joint income of Edward, his queen, and the prince of Wales from land may be taken at about £20,000; £35,000 a year from customs; and £12,000 from the French payments. Ramsay, *op. cit.*, II, 466, who included certain other sources of revenue, suggested £85,000.

with the income of £104,863 which (according to the most recent calculation) Henry VII enjoyed in the last few years of his reign.[1] The real measure of Edward's achievement lies in his ability to achieve solvency, pay off debts, and maintain an impressive royal estate without having any recourse to parliament between 1475 and the last months of his life. Yet it was success bought at a price. The risk of losing his French pension hampered his diplomatic freedom of movement, and solvency was immediately at risk by any involvement in warfare. For Scofield, his ability to finance the Scottish war of 1481-2 from his own resources was his 'most remarkable financial feat . . . it may even be considered the most remarkable fact of the king's career'.[2] But this exaggerated claim seems to ignore the fact that the war involved Edward in some highly unpopular measures and finally forced him to seek aid from parliament once again. A recent judgement on Henry VII's financial situation can be applied to Edward's with equal force: 'War is a terribly expensive business which no responsible king could face without the necessary ready cash in hand – and this he could never have saved from his ordinary revenue.'[3]

Historians' judgements on Edward as a financier have varied from the mildly dismissive to the moderately enthusiastic.[4] Certainly, his reputation has suffered from the inevitable comparison with Henry VII, the most money-conscious king in our history, who attacked the problem with a grinding application and a willingness to risk unpopularity for financial gain. By contrast, Edward was properly but not obsessively businesslike and often prepared to sacrifice financial to political advantage. He also managed to die a popular as well as a wealthy king, despite the fears of contemporaries that, given longer, he might have become 'an hard and severe prince'; but this, as Polydore Vergil observed, 'was prevented by the brevity of his life'.[5] He did, however, face a much harder task than Henry. To rescue the Crown from the financial abyss into which the Lancastrians had plunged it was no mean achievement. To die solvent was something no other English king had achieved for more than two hundred years. Henry VII had the great advantage of being able to build upon the foundations laid by his father-in-law. Indeed, the best testimony to the quality of Edward's financial policies is the degree to which the shrewd and calculating Henry held firm to them.

[1] Wolffe, op. cit., 217.   [2] Scofield, II, 386-7.
[3] G. R. Elton, England under the Tudors, 48.
[4] Cf. Elton, op. cit., 46; Ramsay, II, 457, 467; Wolffe, Royal Demesne, 174, 179-80.
[5] Polydore Vergil, English History, 168.

Some recent historians have seen both Edward IV and Henry VII as prisoners of what has been called 'the antiquated straitjacket of endowed monarchy', implying that their chief weakness was their inability to tax their subjects freely and that this in turn was a product of their political insecurity.[1] Their revenues, it is claimed, were pitifully low compared with the £800,000 commanded by the king of France or the £1,100,000 enjoyed by the Emperor in the 1520s. This comparison, however, overlooks the great differences in size, population and wealth between England and these continental states. It also ignores the fact that Edward and Henry were little less wealthy than their fourteenth-century predecessors, whose capacity to tax their subjects was offset by their constant involvement in expensive wars, and was paid for in political concessions. Edward relied upon his personal energy to maintain his affluence, and even more upon his will or ability to keep out of war, but he was also much less dependent, at least in his later years, on the reluctant cooperation of his subjects. Poverty had been one of the chief weaknesses of the Lancastrian regime. A relative affluence was part of Edward's strength.

[1] Lander, *Conflict and Stability*, 111; Lockyer, *Henry VII*, 31.

Chapter 17

LAW AND ORDER

To maintain effective order and to enforce his laws were among the more intractable problems confronting a medieval king. Violence was endemic in English society. This was scarcely surprising in a land where men normally carried arms, where there was neither police force nor standing army, and where the machinery of justice was cumbrous, slow-moving and open to corruption. The result was a crime rate of appalling proportions. Self-help was a constant temptation which few chose to resist.

If medieval men accepted a high level of violence as a normal feature of social life, they were a good deal less complacent about the ease and frequency with which so many criminals escaped justice. Complaints about lack of justice and failure by the Crown to enforce the laws were bitter and frequent and only too fully justified by the facts. Unfortunately, in the present state of our knowledge we have little statistical evidence to support generalizations about the efficiency with which the law was enforced under Yorkist rule. Occasionally, punishments could be condign and severe. The Hampshire peace roll for 1474–5 shows that of twenty people indicted for felony before the local justices of the peace, ten were tried and eight were convicted and sentenced to hang, whilst four others were kept in prison to await the justices of gaol delivery.[1] Such efficiency was probably exceptional, and may well reflect the presence of the king in the neighbourhood during his judicial progress to suppress disorder and discontent following upon his return from France in the autumn of 1475. But fuller evidence from the late fourteenth century and earlier fifteenth century suggests a very different picture. The rolls of the justices of the peace in Shropshire between 1400 and 1414, for example, show that of 251 persons indicted for felony, 156 were summoned into the king's bench, but only 14 actually stood trial and not one was convicted. At Lincoln in 1396, of 224 summoned before the king's bench only 54 could actually be brought

---

[1] B. H. Putnam, *Proceedings Before the Justices of the Peace, Edward III to Richard III*, 271. Both the date and the figures are incorrectly cited in Bellamy, *Crime and Public Order in England in the Later Middle Ages* (1973), 157–8.

to appear in court, none of whom was convicted; the other 170 were outlawed and none convicted. In the absence of more comparable evidence for the reign of Edward IV, it would be safe to assume that the number of criminals who escaped justice was much nearer this level than the small Hampshire sample would suggest. It has recently been calculated that only between 10 and 30 per cent of persons tried before the justices of gaol delivery were actually convicted.[1] A very large number of those indicted for felony never came before a court for trial.

There is a variety of reasons – legal, social and political – why so many wrongdoers escaped the clutches of the law. Contemporary English common law contained a number of devices to protect the accused, and many of these could be used improperly to delay or divert the course of justice. It was often very difficult to apprehend indicted men, and sheriff's officers sometimes went in fear of their lives. Forcing a messenger to eat the parchment writ of summons he carried was a not uncommon practice amongst those who thumbed their noses at the law.[2] The Northumberland knight, Sir William Lisle, who in 1528 declared 'By God's blood there is nother king nor his officers that shall take any distress on my ground or within my liberties', had many Yorkist predecessors.[3] In 1467 Lord Strange complained to the king against one Roger Kinaston, who was unlawfully in possession of estates belonging to Strange. Kinaston, he said, had ignored a board of arbitration appointed by the king, letters under the king's signet commanding him to appear before the council, and similar letters under the privy seal – the messenger carrying these was beaten nearly to death – and a commission of arrest under the great seal had failed to apprehend him.[4] That a series of *direct* royal orders could be so ineffective only serves to highlight the even greater difficulties which confronted the normal agents of the law in bringing offenders to trial.

A man who failed to obey an order to appear in court risked a sentence of outlawry and the forfeiture of his possessions. But outlawed men often disappeared successfully and led normal lives for years on

1 Bellamy, *op. cit.*, 158. For the Shropshire and Lincolnshire figures above, E. G. Kimball, ed., *The Shropshire Peace Roll, 1400–1414* (Salop County Council, 1959), 41. *Records of Some Sessions of the Peace in Lincolnshire, 1381–1396* (Lincoln Record Society, xix, 1955), liii–liv. No other J.P.s' proceedings for the reign of Edward IV are known to survive except those for Worcestershire, 1477–8 (printed Putnam, 424–34), and the results of the proceedings before them are not known.
2 See, for example, Storey, *End of the House of Lancaster*, 153.
3 Cited by M. E. James, *A Tudor Magnate and the Tudor State*, 11–12.
4 J. F. Baldwin, *The King's Council in England during the Middle Ages*, 430–1.

end. With the spread of education, the number of those able to claim benefit of clergy – and hence escape the jurisdiction of the royal courts and virtually go unpunished – increased, and became an obvious abuse of the system. Even for those not so privileged, the chances of escaping punishment when brought before a court were high. Juries were often reluctant to convict persons indicted for felony, which carried the death sentence, though noticeably more willing to bring in verdicts for lesser offences such as trespass or offences against the statutes dealing with wages and prices. Proceedings against a defendant might be discontinued if he could obtain a writ of *supersedeas*, either from chancery, the king's justices, the justices of the peace, or from the king himself under writ of privy seal, this last being a convenient device for the wealthy or well-connected offender.[1]

Many wrongdoers, even when tried and found guilty, escaped the penalties of their crimes by procuring a royal pardon. The Crown itself contributed to the problem of lawlessness by its readiness to grant pardons even for major crimes. Purchasing a pardon (it has been claimed) was a routine pecuniary transaction for many offences including murder. For those with influence at court, pardons could be obtained for even the most scandalous offences. Thus in 1456 the earl of Devon and his sons, Thomas and Henry, had been pardoned a variety of crimes, including the waging of private war, the terrorization of an entire county, and the most atrocious murder (of Nicholas Radford) of the fifteenth century. Henry VI was notorious for his excessive clemency, and his willingness to temper justice with mercy had done much to undermine the authority of the law.[2] More research is needed before we can say with any certainty how Edward IV, a king with a reputation for clemency, compares with his predecessor in this respect, but a recent enquiry into his use of pardon as revealed in the records of the commissions of oyer and terminer concluded that he was only slightly less generous than his predecessor had been, though men sometimes had to wait longer before a pardon was granted.[3] Many of his pardons, it is true, were given primarily for political offences, but since they covered felonies, homicides and riots as well as treason they often provided a cloak for men who were notoriously lawless in addi-

[1] Bellamy, *op. cit.*, 101–2, 151–6, 158–9; M. Hastings, *The Court of Common Pleas in Fifteenth-Century England* (1947), 216–17.
[2] Bellamy, *op. cit.*, 194–7; Storey, *op. cit.*, 37, 165–74 (for Devon), 210–16 (general pardons under Henry VI).
[3] Judith B. Avrutick, 'Commissions of Oyer and Terminer in Fifteenth-Century England' (unpublished M.Litt. thesis, London, 1957), p. 158.

tion to being politically disaffected. Success in obtaining pardons enabled even the most hardened and notorious lawbreakers to prove that the wages of crime were high.[1]

If these various legal devices to block the swift and impartial enforcement of the law did not succeed, men had recourse to a whole range of illegal methods. The sheriff was a notoriously weak link in the machinery of law enforcement at the local level. As the chief executive agent of the courts, his office was often a focal point for corruption.[2] By bribery and influence, he could be persuaded to make false returns to writs, or make no return at all, to empanel partisan juries, or fail to compel offenders to appear in court. A spectacular example of contumacy is provided by Sir Robert Wingfield, sheriff of Norfolk in 1454 and 1471, and his wife, Margaret. Together they neglected for thirty-three years to send a prisoner into the king's bench, in spite of repeated distraints.[3] Moreover, sheriffs held office for only one year at a time and could not be held accountable for the failures of their predecessors in arresting offenders.

Contemporaries believed that the remedy for misuse of the extensive powers vested in the sheriff's office lay in a steady increase in the responsibility and authority of the justices of the peace. In his first parliament Edward IV continued the process by transferring to them the criminal jurisdiction in the hundred courts formerly exercised by the sheriff in his tourn.[4] Like his predecessors, he continued to appoint reliable magnates to the commissions in the shires where they held land in the hope of extending government control and supervising their work. But magnates rarely served in person at the sessions of the peace, especially when, like the royal dukes or Warwick or Hastings, they had been appointed to the bench in a dozen or more counties. Yet even this remedy had its limitations, for on occasion even a whole bench of J.P.s could be intimidated into returning unjust verdicts. Thus in 1456 Edward's future lieutenant, Sir William Herbert, then a prominent servant of his father, seized the town of Hereford by force, arrested the mayor, emptied the prisons, and so overawed a session of the Herefordshire J.P.s that they condemned six citizens to death for their supposed share in the murder of Herbert's kinsman, Walter Vaughan, shortly before; and they were straightway hanged.[5] Even the justices of assize

---

[1] See, for example, the pardons obtained by Henry Bodrugan, below, pp. 410–11.
[2] Hastings, *op. cit.*, 224–9.
[3] M. Blatcher, 'Distress infinite and the contumacious sheriff', *BIHR*, xiii (1935–6), 146–50.
[4] 1 Edw. IV, c. 2: *Statutes of the Realm*, II, 389–91. [5] Storey, *op. cit.*, 180 *n.*

were not immune from intimidation. In March 1464, following a riot in which Sir John Butler had been slain, Edward IV found it necessary to direct that the forthcoming sessions in Lancashire should not be held, since great troubles might thereby ensue, and from the fact that he found it necessary to summon before him Thomas, Lord Stanley, and three of his kinsmen, three members of the Harrington family, and Thomas Pilkington, it would appear that some of the most powerful men in the county palatine were involved in the disturbances; clearly any attempt by the local justices to indict them would not have been feasible.[1]

Juries were even more vulnerable to bribery, pressure and intimidation. Straightforward bribery for bringing in a particular verdict – the often-condemned offence of embracery – was not uncommon; but frequently all that was needed to influence a jury in one's favour was to seek the protection of a great lord 'whose disfavour twelve men, however good and true, would hesitate to incur'.[2] Nor was there anything illegal in the practice of 'labouring' a jury, whereby one party made sure the jury was made aware of facts favourable to its case, especially when there was reason to suppose that the other party had influenced the selection of the panel. The king himself had recourse to the process at least on one occasion. In 1481 one John Tailour was paid 26s 8d as part of his expenses in labouring a Devonshire jury to return a verdict 'which passed with the king'.[3]

Juries could also be intimidated by an open show of force. In 1475 the commons in parliament petitioned against the acquittal of certain evildoers indicted for riot and felony in Herefordshire, in spite of the king's promise that they should be punished. The petition claimed that a jury of presentment consisting of no fewer than eighteen of the most notable knights and squires of the county had confessed to the king's commissioners that 'they durst not present nor say the truth of the defaults before rehearsed, for dread of murdering, and to be mischieved in their own houses, considering the great number of the said misdoers, and the great bearers-up of the same', unless they had 'especial comfort of the king's good grace, and the assistance of the lords there present'.[4] An even more scandalous demonstration of private

---

[1] P.R.O., E 28/89. In 1459 the commons in parliament alleged that amongst other offences twenty-five notorious malefactors denounced by them had disturbed and hindered both the justices of the assize and of the peace (RP, V, 367).
[2] Hastings, op. cit., 221.
[3] P.R.O., E. 28/92; Bellamy, 'Justice under the Yorkist Kings', 144.
[4] RP, VI, 159–60.

might and malice was the action of the duke of Clarence in 1477 in dragging Ankarette Twynho and two other innocent persons before the justices of the peace at Warwick and causing them to be indicted of murdering his wife, Duchess Isabel. He then forced the jury to return a verdict of guilty, which they did 'for fear and dread of great menaces, and doubt of loss of their lives and goods . . . contrary to their own intents, truth and conscience'. Ankarette and one other were hanged forthwith. Indictment, trial and judgement all took place within the space of three hours.[1]

With the commons' reference in 1475 to the 'great bearers-up of the same misdoers', with whom only the king and the lords could deal, we come to the very heart of the problem of law enforcement in fifteenth-century England. Most of the flagrant examples of open defiance of the law, ranging from bribery and intimidation, through murder and riot, to private war and general terrorism, were the work of gangs of men – 'riotous persons arrayed in manner of war' as the common phrase went – acting on behalf of powerful people, or at least afterwards able to claim their protection. In 1472 a widow petitioned parliament seeking justice against the murderers of her husband, and could plausibly allege that after the murder they had sought to get themselves accepted into the service of the duke of Gloucester, so that they 'should have been supported in their horrible felony, murder, and robbery'.[2] She was justified in her belief that there was small hope of redress against a powerful nobleman through the normal channels of justice. It is a striking fact that in the entire fifteenth century no nobleman ever appeared in court charged with offences which might cost him his life.[3] In some parts of the realm their authority counted for more than the king's. Even in Tudor times it could be said that the north of England had never known a king other than a Percy, a Nevill or a Dacre. In Edward's own day John Harding could write of the Percies that 'they have the hearts of the people by north and ever had'. R. L. Storey's researches have shown that for more than twenty years before 1461 the normal courts of law – chancery, king's bench, assize and gaol delivery – had become almost totally ineffectual in the counties close to the Scots border. Men no longer had recourse to them at all. Instead, they sought the protection of great lords powerful enough to 'maintain' their interests since the ordinary course of law

[1] *RP*, VI, 173.
[2] *Ibid.*, 39.
[3] Bellamy, *Crime and Public Order*, 200. Nobles, like M.P.s, enjoyed the privilege of freedom from arrest by the ordinary processes: Hastings, *op. cit.*, 170.

provided neither justice nor protection.[1] Only the king could bring such powerful persons to book. If, on the other hand, he chose to extend to them the same protection as they in turn gave to their retainers, servants and well-wishers, then the authority and prestige of the law was being choked at the very fountainhead. What was often lacking was the will to enforce the law. This was the tenor of a celebrated speech made to all the justices at Blackfriars in 1485 by Chief Justice Hussey, most of whose professional career had been spent in the service of Edward IV. It had been agreed that there were already excellent laws, very advantageous to the kingdom if they could be carried out. The question was, would they be carried out? Hussey observed that

> the law would never be carried out properly until the lords spiritual and temporal are of one mind for the love and fear they have of God, or the king, or both, to carry them out effectively. Thus when the king on his side, and the lords on theirs, will do this every one else will quickly do it, and if they do not they will be punished, and then all will be warned by their example.[2]

Some indication has now been given of the nature and magnitude of the problem of law and order in late medieval England. But it is also essential – with Hussey's remarks in mind – to see it in the right perspective from the standpoint of the king. His concern with the administration of justice and the enforcement of the law was at best a limited one – limited both by choice and necessity. Like his subjects he was prepared to suffer a high level of day-to-day violence provided his own interests and the security of his realm were not threatened. He was rarely concerned to right the wrongs of individuals or to take much care to see justice done in causes between private persons. The suppression of treason and insurrection was his first concern. When large-scale disorder threatened to involve a whole countryside or flagrantly defied the royal authority it could not be long ignored. Lawbreaking which deprived him of revenue, as with customs fraud, or affected his foreign relations, as with piracy, might attract close royal attention.[3] But his interest did not go much further. Even had he chosen to try to enforce penal statute law more widely and impartially his means of doing so were limited. He was hampered by dependence on unreliable

[1] Storey, 'The north of England', in *Fifteenth-Century England*, 132; *End of the House of Lancaster*, 118; John Harding, *Chronicle*, ed. Ellis, 378.
[2] Year Book 1 Hen. VII, Mich. no. 3, fol. 3, printed by C. H. Williams, *English Historical Documents*, V, 533.
[3] For customs control and piracy, see above, pp. 366–7, 384–5.

and often corrupt local agents, by ingrained social habits, or by more purely political considerations such as the need to retain the goodwill of his great men. The most recent enquiries have shown that even Henry VII, whose record of action by legislation, injunction and administrative device shows him to have been much more concerned with general law enforcement than his Yorkist predecessors, had remarkably little success in this sphere.[1]

Nevertheless, the problems inherited by Edward IV were formidable, even when allowance has been made for the restrictions of attitude and intent outlined above. The inherent difficulties of keeping the peace had been worsened by the severe deterioration in public order – never very high in late medieval England – during the twenty years of Henry VI's majority rule. The weakness and partiality of king and council had placed little curb on the misdeeds of powerful offenders. The growth of faction was accompanied by recourse to private war, recently documented by Storey, and the outbreak of civil war, which in one aspect at least may be seen as an 'escalation of private feuds',[2] had served only to make matters worse. Riot, oppression, vendetta and gangsterism flourished under the umbrella of civil strife and armed rebellion. The first few months of Edward IV's reign probably saw a higher level of disorder than any other period in the entire fifteenth century.[3]

How then did the new king propose to break the teeth of the sinners? The reign began promisingly with a public statement of his intention to take vigorous action against lawlessness. This pronouncement is of interest since it shows clearly that he already appreciated the close connections between a rising rate of crime and the practices of illegal livery and maintenance promoted by powerful men. On the king's behalf, the chancellor told his first parliament that because the giving of liveries and badges had led to the multiplication of maintenance of quarrels, extortions, robberies and murders, Edward had ordained certain 'articles'. These he had caused the lords of parliament to swear to observe, and they were now to be published throughout the realm. Further, it was the king's design to make progresses throughout the land, the better to inform himself about the state of public order. On their return to their constituencies, the M.P.s were to inform the people at large to prepare bills against evildoers in readiness for the king's coming. The 'articles' thus promulgated placed limits on the giving of signs and liveries, forbade anyone to give refuge and succour to known

---

[1] S. B. Chrimes, *Henry VII*, 191–3.
[2] Storey, *End . . . of Lancaster*, 27.   [3] Above, chapter 3, section i.

criminals, and commanded all the king's subjects to do their duty in bringing evildoers to jail. Nor should they be prevented from doing so by fear of any protector of malefactors, be he lord or any other person, 'for in that case the king will suffer no lord or other to make any quarrel or hurt any person so doing'.[1]

As we shall see, Edward's professed intention of making war on the abuses of the system of livery and maintenance turned out to be little more than a pious declaration. He was, however, and of necessity, concerned to act vigorously against treason, riot and major disturbances of the public peace. In this campaign he did not seek to strengthen the law-enforcement agencies by new legislation. Apart from transferring much of the remaining criminal jurisdiction of the sheriff to the justices of the peace, as noticed above, and the act against retaining and livery, the meagre body of statute law which emerged from his reign contains almost no reference to the problem of law and order. This was not to his discredit, for, as Chief Justice Hussey was to remark, there were already laws aplenty. Instead he preferred to make use of existing machinery, often infusing new life into it by the personnel he employed and his own personal backing for its work.

In the first decade of the reign especially, when the security of the realm was threatened by treason and insurrection as well as general disorder, he made extensive use of three weapons against lawlessness – the court of chivalry under the constable of England, commissions of oyer and terminer, both general and specific, and his own great personal activity in the enforcement of the law. The constable's court, whose savage penalties won for John Tiptoft, earl of Worcester, his unenviable reputation for ruthlessness, was roundly condemned by an earlier generation of scholars. It was a summary court, acting without indictment and without benefit of trial by jury, and it employed a law other than the common law of England. Its activities, in the words of Bishop Stubbs, 'condemned its agents to perpetual infamy'. He further regarded its summary jurisdiction over treason as a novel usurpation at the expense of the common law courts.[2] However, recent research has suggested that there was ample precedent under the law of arms for its use in treason trials. As a branch of civil law, the law of arms required neither indictments nor juries. Often Tiptoft as constable was merely pronouncing a sentence which had already been 'ordained' by the king in advance. The king could still 'record' a verdict based upon his

---

[1] *RP*, V, 487–8. Other articles prohibited dicing and card-playing, and made anyone who renounced his allegiance after being pardoned by the king guilty of high treason.
[2] W. Stubbs, *Constitutional History* (1878), III, 282–3.

knowledge of notorious treason without further justification. Most of the court's victims were men taken in battle, in open rebellion against the Crown, clearly guilty of the high-treason offence, under the great statute of 1352, of levying war against the king. Many too were men who had already reneged on royal pardons, and this in itself had been declared a treason by the articles of 1461. Faced by persistent insurrection, Edward can scarcely be blamed for using a summary tribunal which did away with the need for prompting or labouring juries.[1]

There is, however, some evidence that the jurisdiction of the constable's court was widened to include treasonable offences which had formerly been dealt with by the common law and which came under the other major category of treason, compassing and imagining the death of the king. Such was the trial of the earl of Oxford, his son, John de Vere, and Sir Thomas Tuddenham in 1462, when Tiptoft was accused by the chronicler Warkworth of improperly using 'the law of Padua', that is, the civil law. Similarly, in 1468 a Lancastrian secret agent, Richard Steres, a London skinner, was tried and sentenced to death before the constable. In the second decade of the reign the constable's court was much less active, but was still used to try cases of insurrection, and from as early as 1467 Edward appointed a special officer to act as king's promoter of all causes civil and criminal concerning the crime of *lèse-majesté* before the judges of the constableship and admiralty of England.[2]

Of wider scope and greater importance than the constable's court were the commissions of oyer and terminer. Such commissions might and often did try cases of treason, and some of the more famous treason trials of the reign were heard before them, such as those of Thomas Cook and his fellow-Londoners in 1468, of Henry Courtenay and Thomas Hungerford at Salisbury in 1469, and of Clarence's associates, Stacey and Burdett, in 1477. But they were also widely and frequently used as a weapon to deal with major disorders, especially large-scale riots involving powerful offenders, which the justices of the peace or the ordinary courts were often incapable of settling. They might be either general commissions, with wide powers over a group of counties, or specific to deal with a particular crime or group of crimes. They had the advantage of speed and efficiency and were notably more successful in terminating cases than either the king's bench or the justices of the

---

[1] M. H. Keen, 'Treason Trials under the Law of Arms', *TRHS*, 5th ser., xii (1962), 85–103; Bellamy, 'Justice under the Yorkist Kings', 139–43; Bellamy, *The Law of Treason in England in the Later Middle Ages*, 158–63.

[2] Bellamy, *op. cit.*, 158–63; Lander, *Conflict and Stability*, 100.

peace. But their chief advantage lay in the quality of their personnel. They could be staffed by royal councillors and household men, magnates and peers with local influence, and a number of judges and professional lawyers. Together this often gave them an authority which even the most defiant and well-protected offender could hardly ignore.[1] Thus the special commission appointed in 1469 to try Hungerford and Courtenay contained two dukes, three earls, four barons, ten justices and serjeants-at-law, including the chief justice of common pleas, three knights and the mayor of Salisbury.[2] The marquis of Dorset, four earls, twelve barons and six justices formed the commission which sat in judgement on Stacey and Burdett in 1477.[3] General commissions might be scarcely less impressive. Thus one appointed for six midland and Welsh Border shires on 13 February 1468, included the dukes of Gloucester and Clarence, the earl of Warwick and Earl Rivers, seven barons, all with local interests, twelve lawyers and three knights, all king's councillors.[4] It was often only by the appointment of such high-powered tribunals that results could be obtained, as may be seen from the misfortunes of a commission set up in 1463 to deal with disturbances in the county of Cambridge. Its first session was scheduled for January 1464, when only Peter Ardern, one of the justices of common pleas, and three local gentry were present from the members of the commission, but the perpetrators of the original crime with twenty supporters forcibly prevented the jury of presentment from appearing. They even went so far as to threaten the commissioners, saying that they would let the hearings start, provided that they were not indicted. Not until February, when the king himself, with the earl of Worcester and other lords and justices, arrived in Cambridge, could a greatly strengthened commission be appointed. Proceedings got under way and the cases against most of the accused were successfully concluded.[5]

On this particular occasion it was probably the personal presence of the king which guaranteed firm action in a difficult local situation. But when the king was not on the spot, it was the presence of magnate members of the commissions, especially in their early sessions, which proved a crucial element in their success. For magnates implied their

---

[1] Avrutick, thesis cited above, p. 390, n. 3; Bellamy, 'Justice', 147–8.
[2] *CPR, 1467–77*, 128. Six of the magnates were present on the bench when the jury presented their verdict: P.R.O., K.B. 9/320.
[3] *CPR, 1476–85*, 50.   [4] *CPR, 1467–77*, 69–70.
[5] Avrutick, 'Commissions of Oyer and Terminer', 66; and for the commissions, *CPR, 1461–7*, 279, 304.

retinues, and a coercive force capable of casting a deep shadow over even the tallest malcontent. Here, too, the oyer and terminer commissions held an advantage, for most if not all magnates appointed to them usually took an active part in their work, in contrast to rather occasional contributions to the sessions of justices of the peace. They were also a highly personal weapon for the king, for few commissions did not include a substantial element of councillors, household men, or lords close to Edward. Thus of the fourteen non-judicial members of the midlands commission of February 1468 mentioned above, each one was either a royal councillor at the time or appears as such before 1471.[1] There was also a close connection with the council itself in its judicial capacity, which played a part in preparing evidence and interrogations.[2] These various advantages help to explain why such extensive use was made of the commissions as a weapon against major disorder, in contrast with the J.P.s, who were usually ineffective except in dealing with routine crime. It is also characteristic of Edward's methods of government that he should rely upon an essentially *ad hoc* apparatus whose strength derived from the close connection between the men who worked it and the king himself.

The personal activity and support of the king was a vital element in the entire process of law enforcement. The Paston Letters reveal in detail how close an interest Edward took in the affairs of this particular corner of his realm, especially in the early years of his reign. In July 1461 Thomas Denyes thought it expedient 'that the king were informed of the demeaning of the shire'. The king's will and concern was made known through the mouths of his servants. Justice Yelverton said in December 1461 that 'the king had commanded him to say that if there were any man, poor or rich, that had cause to complain of any person he should put up his bill . . . the king would have his laws kept . . . he was displeased with the manner of their gathering, and would have it amended'. Sir Thomas Montgomery, sheriff of Norfolk and Suffolk from 7 November 1461, said a month later that 'he would neither spare for good, nor love, nor fear, but that he would let the king have knowledge of the truth'. The king's interest was shown too in his selection of men for local office, often men known locally to be close to Edward. Thus in December 1461 Yelverton could say that he and Montgomery had come down 'to set a rule in the country', and of Montgomery he remarked 'as for a knight there was none in the king's

1 Lander, 'Council, Administration and Councillors', 166–75; p. 398, n. 4 above.
2 See below, p. 403.

house that might worse a be for bore [i.e., ill-spared] than the Sheriff might at this time'. Shortly before, in October, Sir John Paston had failed to answer two royal summons to appear before the king, sent under the privy seal by two yeomen of the chamber. His disobedience provoked a royal outburst: 'we will send him another tomorrow,' said the angry Edward, 'and by God's mercy, if he come not then he shall die for it. We will make all other men beware by him how they shall disobey our writing.' When he did appear he found himself flung in the Fleet prison, along with Sir John Howard, the sheriff of Norfolk, whose dispute with him had occasioned the royal summons.[1] Edward's agents were at pains to present him as a king who was at once well informed, benevolent to the well disposed, but sharp to correct the wrongdoer. Thus Yelverton in 1461: 'he [the king] conceiveth that the whole body of the shire is well disposed and that the ill disposed people is but a corner of the whole shire . . . [the] misdoing groweth not of their own disposition but of the abbetment and stirring of some ill disposed persons which is understood and known to the king's highness'. If any complainant would not accept Yelverton and Montgomery's rule, then the king himself 'should set the rule'. Any false or malicious complaints would be sharply punished. Or Justice Peter Ardern in February 1464: 'the king wills that justice be had'.[2] In the second decade of the reign we hear less from the Pastons of such direct royal interventions, probably because the county had become more peaceful; but they were still forthcoming when needed. In August 1473, for example, orders were sent to the sheriffs of Yorkshire, Cumberland and Westmorland, to express the king's displeasure at the continued forcible occupation of Hornby Castle by Sir James and Sir Robert Harrington: it was in 'contempt of his laws, to the worst example of all his well disposed lieges; which his highness will not of his royal duty suffer to remain unpunished'.[3] Later still the king is to be found acting as arbitrator in one of those disputes about land which had caused so much trouble in the past. In October 1479, there having been 'great variance' between John, Lord Cobham, and his stepfather, Robert Palmer, esquire, over a group of manors in the West Country, both parties were summoned before the king, and bound over in the huge sum of 50,000 marks to stand by the king's award. This was made 'after great deliberation', and in witness of his action the king signed the letter close setting forth the terms of his decision.[4]

Edward's promise to tour the realm and deal with serious distur-

[1] *PL*, III, 284, 313; IV, 16, 19–20.   [2] *PL*, IV, 19, 94–5.
[3] *CCR*, *1468–76*, 315.   [4] *CCR*, *1476–85*, 221–2.

bances of the peace was no idle boast. Even before it was made, he had
visited the West Country and the Welsh Borders to show the majesty
of the royal person, to do justice, and assert his authority. In the early
years of the reign especially, the king, often in company with several
great lords and a group of justices, was as peripatetic as any twelfth-
century king. In 1462 he made a judicial progress to the east midlands.
In January 1464, with the two chief justices, Markham and Danby, he
descended upon Gloucester to deal with a local feud between the townsmen and the men of the shire, and his arrival saw the setting up of
a commission of oyer and terminer. This was appointed on 5 February
and after extremely swift action in summoning juries and hearing cases,
all was done by 10 February. Five days later he was on his way to Cambridge to deal with disturbances there, and soon after he was punishing
rioters in Dartford, Kent. In 1467 he went to the north midlands to
look into a feud between his own supporters, and in 1469 made a semi-
judicial progress through East Anglia. Others followed, though less
frequently, in the second part of the reign, in 1473, 1475 and 1476. In
Hampshire and Wiltshire in November 1475, where returning troops
were running amok, he acted ruthlessly, sparing no one, not even his
own ministers and servants, according to the Croyland Chronicler.[1]
How much people hoped from a royal visit to their locality may be
illustrated again from the Paston correspondence. In 1469, for example,
the Pastons hoped that if only they could persuade the king to see for
himself the devastation wrought by the duke of Suffolk, they at last
could get redress against this powerful enemy.[2] The personal appearance of the king was often the only answer men could think of to remedy
serious disorder. In 1475 the commons petitioned against major disorders in Herefordshire and Shropshire, committed both by the men of
those shires and from the adjacent Marches of Wales, whereof, they
said, no remedy could be had 'without your high presence there', or at
least 'great might and power sent by your highness into those parts';
and it was apparently in response to this that Edward sent the queen,
the prince of Wales, 'many great lords spiritual and temporal, and many
other notable persons, as well as your judges, as others of great honour
and discretion', to deal with the problem.[3] Even as late as May 1482
the council of the Duchy of Lancaster, sorrowfully surveying the continuing disorders within the county palatine, urgently hoped that
Edward would visit Lancashire in person to provide the necessary
correction.[4]

[1] CC, 559; Bellamy, 'Justice', 136–8.   [2] PL, IV, 30–1.
[3] RP, VI, 160.   [4] Somerville, Hist. Duchy Lancaster, I, 252.

Where treason was involved, the king was often at pains to supervise the proceedings personally. In autumn 1461 the rebel Sir Baldwin Fulford was brought before the king in Bristol before being tried. In 1468 the Lancastrian agent Cornelius was brought into the king's presence at the monastery of Stratford, and it was probably Edward's personal decision which three days later landed him in the Tower, there to be tortured in the hope of incriminating his confederates. In 1469 the trial of Hungerford and Courtenay was delayed until Edward arrived in Salisbury in time to hear the verdict pronounced. That very conspicuous villain, Henry Bodrugan, and his associates, were to be brought before the king in person when arrested in 1474.[1]

A limited but useful role in the investigation of treason and the repression of major crime was played by the king's council. Professor Baldwin believed that at least in the early years of the reign the royal council in its judicial capacity reached an ultimate point of weakness, largely because of its inability to compel offenders to appear before it, and that instead major cases were generally summoned to appear before the king in chancery. Only after 1468 does the council's authority seem to strengthen.[2] This, however, seems to be a mistaken view. Between 1461 and 1463 it is impossible to distinguish between the kind of cases considered by council and chancery, and although between 1463 and 1468 a majority of writs summoned men to appear before chancery rather than council, this was probably a matter of administrative convenience, reflecting an attempt to relieve the burden of work of a council much preoccupied with administrative and financial problems. The jurisdictions of the two were by no means mutually exclusive.[3]

In any event the council in its judicial capacity was not regarded as a major tribunal to enforce the law. It retained a residual authority derived from the king himself to do justice where other means were lacking, especially where persons of great might were concerned. But it did not initiate actions itself, nor did the king use it for this purpose. Its judicial business was usually on petitions from individuals or resulted from the work of informers. It did not pass judgements involving the loss of life and limb, and generally it merely referred complaints for action to the proper common-law authorities. Thus in 1482 a petitioner sought for justice against one William Idle, who with a large number of rioters had committed an act of forcible dispossession of property, and was being maintained in his quarrel by none other than

[1] Bellamy, *Law of Treason*, 164–5.   [2] Baldwin, *King's Council*, 430–2.
[3] Bellamy, 'Justice', 148–9, noting examples of men being ordered to appear before chancery, and the instructions altered for them to appear in council, and *vice versa*.

the king's brother-in-law, the duke of Suffolk – hence the appeal to the council. The case was simply sent by letter bearing the royal sign-manual to Sir William Stonor, a knight of the body, Humphrey Forster, esquire, and their fellow-justices of the peace in Oxfordshire.[1] Otherwise a commission of oyer and terminer might be appointed to deal with the matter. Edward's reign saw no serious effort to extend conciliar jurisdiction at the expense of the common-law agencies.

What the council could do in its judicial capacity – for this purpose it often sat in the Star Chamber, though there was as yet no *Court* of Star Chamber[2] – was to provide improved methods of investigation. Its evidence was presented in writing, and it could seek evidence on matters of fact from outside sources without reliance on juries. It could make use of informers, whose activities were encouraged in the Yorkist period – under the act against liveries of 1468, for example, an informer was to be rewarded with half of any property forfeited by the accused.[3] Parties summoned before the council could be subjected to inquisitorial interrogation, though this rarely involved physical duress. The use of torture to obtain information was almost unknown, and only two instances can be traced in Edward's reign, both in connection with a major treason enquiry.[4] But the new practice of examination, with the opportunity to obtain reliable information, to cross-check it and to re-examine, gave conciliar methods an obvious advantage in treason enquiries, where the council played an increasing part in collecting and preparing evidence. Thence it spread gradually into the common law. In November 1482, for example, Earl Rivers and other commissioners appointed to investigate a feud in Norfolk were instructed first to examine the parties and put their findings into writing: only then were they to proceed to enquire by jury into the alleged felonies.[5]

How effective was the Yorkist campaign against disorder? From the evidence of the Paston Letters, it has been argued that there was a great improvement in the level of public order. The vast difference in atmosphere between the letters of the 1460s, preoccupied by fear and violence, and those of the period after 1472, concerned with 'normal' politics, could not have occurred if life had not been more peaceful in

[1] I. S. Leadam and J. F. Baldwin, *Select Cases Before the King's Council, 1243–1482* (Selden Soc., xxxv, 1915), 116–17; Bellamy, *Crime and Public Order*, 135–6; Chrimes, *Henry VII*, 147–9.
[2] Chrimes, *op. cit.*, 147.
[3] 8 Edw. IV, c. 2; *Statutes*, II, 426–9.
[4] Bellamy, *Crime and Public Order*, 140, but cf. his 'Justice', 146.
[5] *CPR, 1476–85*, 343. For other examples of common-law use of examination, mainly in relation to mercantile offences, see Bellamy, *Crime and Public Order*, 137–8.

Edward's second reign.[1] Dr Bellamy reached a similar conclusion about the results of two decades of strong government. The Yorkists did not deserve their reputation for judicial ruthlessness, but 'even more praiseworthy was their success by established and even antiquated methods in reducing endemic disorder to manageable proportions and thereby setting the stage for the final assault on local disturbance'.[2] Elsewhere it has been suggested that the growing concentration of the commissions of oyer and terminer on cases of treason implies that a strong government was now more capable of dealing with serious crime other than treason through more regular tribunals.[3]

But there are a number of reasons and a variety of evidence for taking a more sceptical view. Clearly, in the suppression of treason and insurrection Edward had enjoyed a considerable measure of success. Until his premature death and the minority of his son provoked lethal dissensions amongst the Yorkist magnates, no sensible man could have predicted the overthrow of the dynasty only two years later. Much of the disorder of the early years of the reign, as we have seen, was linked either with treason or with the violence let loose by civil war, and once the Lancastrian–Nevill challenge had been defeated, some of the earlier violence was bound to disappear, as it does from the Paston correspondence. In any event the often-quoted Paston evidence must be used with the greatest caution. Much distortion has been introduced into our view of fifteenth-century English history by rash generalization from the particular conditions of the Pastons' East Anglia. This was a region where several great magnate interests – York, Mowbray, de la Pole, de Vere – had grappled with each other in the 1450s and 1460s. With York enthroned, de Vere removed in 1471, and Mowbray extinct by 1476, local competition amongst the magnates inevitably declined. East Anglia is arguably not a 'typical' area. But was English society in general more peaceful and law-abiding by 1483? And had the ability of the mighty and their minions to create violence and pervert justice been seriously reduced?

The commons in parliament evidently thought otherwise. In the early years they seem to have exercised a certain patience with a king still harassed by rebellion, and who had already promised in 1461 to take vigorous action against wrongdoing. Bishop Nevill's opening speech to the parliament of 1463 reaffirmed the royal preoccupation

[1] E.g., by J. R. Lander, 'The Administration of the Yorkist Kings' (unpublished Cambridge M.Litt. thesis, 1949).
[2] Bellamy, 'Justice', 155.
[3] Avrutick, 'Commissions of Oyer and Terminer', 170.

with its theme of how justice should be kept.[1] But in 1467 the commons called the king's attention to the increase of murders, riots and other outrages, and asked for urgent measures to enforce the laws; and the king in reply promised stern action. The second session of the same parliament (May–June 1468) saw the passing of the major act against unlawful retaining. That there was justification for the commons' concern is shown in the serious dispute amongst Yorkist supporters in Derbyshire at the end of 1467, in the reference to 'the great riots and oppressions done to our subjects' mentioned as the reason for commissions of oyer and terminer in six midland counties at the end of 1467, and in the king's own decision to surround himself with a bodyguard of two hundred chosen valets and archers when he went to Coventry to keep Christmas in that year.[2] But the 1472–5 parliament, which had before it a number of petitions for the redress of serious crimes, was still deeply concerned about the problem, especially abuses of the system of livery and maintenance which still went largely unpunished. They complained especially of,

> the great abominable murders, robberies, extortions, oppressions, and other manifold maintenances, misgovernances, forcible entries . . . affrays . . . committed and done by such persons as either be of great might or else favoured under persons of great power, in such wise as their outrageous demerits as yet remain unpunished . . . to the great discouraging of your well-ruled and true liegemen, and to the great emboldishing of all rioters and misgoverned persons . . .

and they went on to ask for the enforcement of existing statutes directed against these evils. They asked further that proclamation should be made throughout the realm of the relevant statutes and the penalties to be incurred under them. They also called attention to the special disorders in the Welsh Marches, where 'the outrageous demeaning of Welshmen' had been abetted by the keepers of castles. Later in this parliament they petitioned against the acquittal of evildoers indicted for riot and felony in Herefordshire, in spite of the king's pledge that they should be punished.[3] Finally, in the last parliament of the reign (January–February 1483), they returned to the charge, asking for the more vigorous enforcement of the criminal-law statutes and the legislation against labourers, beggars and vagabonds, and the granting of liveries.[4]

[1] *RP*, V, 496.
[2] *RP*, V, 618 (commons in 1467); *Annales*, 788–9; *CPR, 1467–77*, 55; *CCR, 1468–76*, 25–6 (Grey-Vernon and the bodyguard).
[3] *RP*, VI, 8–9, 159–60.   [4] *RP*, VI, 198.

Like most medieval petitioners, the commons may have been prone to exaggeration, but the government never questioned the truth of their complaints. Indeed, on more than one occasion it publicly admitted the extent of lawlessness and disorder in the country, although inclined to regard it as a consequence of civil strife. Thus in his address to the parliament of 1472 the chancellor advanced as one reason for an invasion of France that it would keep the 'multitude of misdoers' occupied elsewhere. He spoke eloquently of

the multitude of riotous people which have at all times kindled the fire of this great division [the civil war of 1469–71] is so spread over all and every coast of this realm, committing extortions, oppressions, robberies, and other great mischiefs, that if for them a speedy remedy be not found, it is to doubt that the prosperity, wealth and richesse, so greatly desired, can not be had nor purchased surely to the king's people.[1]

There was no doubt a certain truth in the suggestion that civil war gave a free rein to private vendetta, like the Berkeley–Talbot feud in Gloucestershire which ended in a pitched battle at Nibley Green in 1470, the Harrington–Stanley feud in Lancashire between 1469 and 1473, and the long-running quarrel in the midlands between the Harcourts and the Staffords of Grafton, which flared up again in November 1470, with the murder of Sir Robert Harcourt by the Bastard of Grafton and 150 of his retainers.[2] But there is also an air of resigned hopelessness in the chancellor's suggestion that only a foreign war could solve the problem by engaging the criminally disposed against the national enemy.

The misfortunes of the Paston family in the 1460s are a well-known case-history in the workings of 'bastard feudalism', and need be mentioned only briefly here. An air of constant crisis hangs over the correspondence as they struggled to fend off the armed attacks of powerful neighbours by enlisting the aid of equally powerful neighbours. What is striking is their inability to get any redress against their mighty enemies. Even when the king came to Norfolk in 1469 and surveyed the ruins of Hellesdon manor, devastated by the duke of Suffolk's men four years before, he would promise no action. They were told they should have put in bills to the justices of oyer and terminer when the king was at Norwich. Caister Castle, taken from the Pastons by the duke of Nor-

---

[1] *Literae Cantuarienses*, III, 274–6. See also Edward's privy seal letter to Salisbury of 11 February 1472, which dwells on 'the great wildness and indisposition' which followed upon civil strife (Benson and Hatcher, *Old and New Sarum*, 179–80).
[2] Above, p. 134; below, pp. 408–9.

folk after a veritable five-week siege in the summer of 1469, was not finally recovered until after Norfolk's death in 1476.[1] The support of men like Norfolk and Suffolk was far too important to Edward in these troubled years for the king to risk offending them. But if things improved for the Pastons in the later years of the reign, it would not do to assume that there was a similar level of improvement elsewhere in the country. There is ample evidence that private feuds, major disorders and a high level of violent crime continued to the end of the reign, and that they cannot be explained in terms of the licence given by civil war. Offenders with the right connections showed a remarkable capacity to defy the law openly over periods of years, often successfully ignoring repeated royal orders, and yet, despite their offences, were able to obtain royal pardons and retain the king's favour.

As might be expected, open defiance of the law was often most flagrant in the more remote parts of the realm. Cornwall was a chronically disturbed county – as it continued to be throughout the Tudor period – and the records of the 1472–5 parliament are full of the lawlessness of the Bodrugans, the Trethewys and Vyvyans, the Glyns and Clemens. These last had a violent feud over their claims to the deputy-stewardship of Cornwall going back to 1469, which culminated in 1472–3 in Thomas Clemens's killing of John Glyn, a murder so atrocious in its details as to recall the death of Nicholas Radford and the worst days of Henry VI. Yet three years later, Clemens and his two chief accomplices were still at large, for a commission including the ruffianly Henry Bodrugan was appointed to bring them before the king in council. It evidently had no success, for in February 1476 a further commission was needed. Thereafter Clemens disappears from the records, but, as Rowse remarks, 'if this was the kind of thing a leading person in the county . . . was responsible for, it may be imagined what was the deterioration of order, the disturbed state of those times'.[2]

In Wales, the Marches and the Welsh Border counties, conditions were no better. The government had persistent trouble with several members of the prolific Herbert–Vaughan clan, who were in open defiance of its authority by February 1474. A strong commission was then appointed to array all the king's lieges in the shires of Hereford, Gloucester and Shropshire against three bastard sons of William Herbert, 1st earl of Pembroke, and two sons of Roger Vaughan, who had refused to appear before the council for divers offences (probably including the intimidation at Hereford which the commons complained

[1] *PL*, I, 262–4.
[2] *RP*, VI, 35–9, 51–4, 133–43; A. L. Rowse, *Tudor Cornwall*, 106–8.

about) and had then withdrawn to Wales and were there stirring up insurrection. Yet they were all still at large in 1478 when they added to their misdeeds by seizing Pembroke Castle and holding it by force.[1] In Shropshire, near Oswestry, and further north at Chirk, there was extensive rioting and lawlessness in 1475, requiring commissions of array under the marquis of Dorset and Sir Richard Grey to suppress them.[2] The resort to commissions of array – normally used against rebellion or for defence against enemy invasion – emphasizes the scale of these disorders, implying the disruption of a whole countryside.

The county palatine of Lancaster was another chronically disturbed area. As late as 1479 the justices at Lancaster were ordered to proclaim publicly the king's intention to have an end to continued 'misrule and unrestful government', but three years later there had been no improvement, and the Duchy council pleaded with the king in May 1482 to visit the shire in the hope of ending disturbances which had caused its 'unrestful rule and governance . . . to the great impoverishment of the inhabitants'.[3] Earlier in the reign the county had been the scene of a violent feud between two leading families, the Stanleys and the Harringtons. The activities of the Harringtons provide a deeply instructive example of the government's reluctance to take decisive action against its own supporters. The Harringtons were a strongly Yorkist family. Sir Thomas and his eldest son, John, had fallen with Duke Richard of York, leaving as heirs John's two infant daughters, Anne and Elizabeth, aged five and four. Their wardship and marriage belonged to the king, who in November 1461 granted that of Anne to Geoffrey Middleton, esquire. This, however, reckoned without the desire of Sir Thomas's younger sons, Sir James and Sir Robert, to keep hold of the family inheritance. Together they took control of the heiresses and held them prisoner, 'contrary to their wills, in divers places, intending the utter destruction and disinheritance of the said complainants', as they later claimed. Without any semblance of legality they also seized and retained the girls' inheritance, including Hornby Castle in Lancashire. Not until 1468 did the king's attorney sue for them to appear in chancery to answer the charges against them, and both were temporarily placed in the Fleet prison. The king now gave the wardship

[1] CPR, 1467–77, 429; R. A. Griffiths, 'Royal government in the southern counties of the principality of Wales' (unpublished Ph.D. thesis, University of Bristol, 1962).
[2] Evans, Wales and the Wars of the Roses, 200.
[3] Somerville, Hist. Duchy Lancaster, I, 225, 252, for this and other evidence of lawlessness in the north parts of the Duchy; also CPR, 1467–77, 515, for power, 1 May 1475, to Lord Stanley to grant pardon to those who had been stirring up insurrection in the county of Lancashire.

and marriages of the girls to Thomas, Lord Stanley, who speedily supplied Stanley husbands, and sought to possess himself of their lands. Two successive attempts at arbitration, by Richard Nevill, earl of Warwick, met with no success, and the Harringtons held on. During the Readeption they held Hornby Castle by force against Lord Stanley, and may have had some help from the young duke of Gloucester, who had his own feud with the Stanleys in the spring of 1470.[1]

Nothing further was done in the matter until April 1472, when both parties were bound over in large sums to accept an arbitration award, and it is clear from the terms of the bond that the king was taking a personal interest in the affair. This time the decision went against the Harringtons, but they did not give up. A powerful commission headed by Gloucester, Northumberland, Shrewsbury and Hastings was appointed in June 1473 to eject them from Hornby Castle and the rest of the Harrington lands. But a proclamation of August 1473 shows that they were still holding Hornby, having 'stuffed and enforced it with men and victuals, and habiliments of war'. The king was now clearly very angry, and, faced with his wrath and the might of Gloucester and his fellow-commissioners, the Harringtons at last gave in. No penal action was taken against them, and they continued to prosper in the king's service. Sir James went on the French expedition in 1475, was M.P. for Lancashire in 1478, and was a knight of the body to Edward from 1475, and his brother, Robert, was M.P. for Lancashire in the 1472–5 parliament when they were still in open defiance of the Crown.

The explanation for their tender treatment is clear enough. Both were trusted Yorkist servants. James, for example, had been Edward's first escheator in Yorkshire in 1461, sheriff of the county in 1466–7 and again in 1475–6, and M.P. for Lancashire in 1467–8, had played a leading part in the capture of the fugitive Henry VI in 1465, and was one of the first to join Edward after his landing at Ravenspur in 1471. In the late 1450s and 1460s he had been a retainer and a member of the council of Richard, earl of Warwick, and then, like many other Warwick servants, passed into the service of Duke Richard of Gloucester, whose valued councillor he became. It is scarcely surprising that the king was unwilling to alienate such loyal and long-standing

---

[1] For this, and what follows on the feud, *CPR, 1467–77*, 426–7; *CCR, 1468–76*, 36, 71 244, 315; Rymer, *Foedera*, XI, 699; Whitaker, *History of Richmondshire*, II, 261; *Proceedings in Chancery in the Reign of Queen Elizabeth I, Calendars* (Record Commission, 1827), I, lxxxvi. I am indebted for information on this matter to my former student, K. R. Dockray. For the Stanley–Gloucester feud, see *CCR, 1468–76*, 138.

servants, especially when they had high-placed advocates to plead for them.[1]

The Harringtons' reason for defying the law had been no more criminal than an understandable desire to keep their father's inheritance for themselves. But there were others who exploited their position to pursue actively criminal careers and enrich themselves in the process. For example, Sir Gilbert Debenham of Little Wenham in Suffolk, whose record of violent misdoing extended back into the 1440s, was protected from reprisal by his position as steward of the duke of Norfolk. He survived to prosper under Edward IV, using the ducal influence to penetrate and corrupt the town governments of Ipswich and Colchester for his own benefit. He died peacefully in 1481, a wealthy and successful man, with his son, Sir Gilbert, already established as Edward's chancellor of Ireland from 1474.[2]

The most remarkable, and certainly the most impudently successful, of these licensed malefactors was the Cornishman, Sir Henry Bodrugan. He was one of those notorious wrongdoers denounced by the commons in the parliament of 1459, and his arrest had been ordered in June 1461. Saved by the revolution of 1460–61, he soon established himself as an important royal servant in Cornwall, and acted on a variety of royal commissions, including several to deal with Cornish piracy, a fine opportunity to be gamekeeper and poacher at the same time. By 1473 his misrule in Cornwall had reached such proportions that a whole flock of petitions against him reached parliament from half the gentry of Cornwall, at a time when he was suspected of collusion with the earl of Oxford's landing at St Michael's Mount, or, at the least, of turning the situation to his own account. One complaint from Thomas Nevill stated that he could obtain no remedy at common law 'for if any person would sue against the said Henry and Richard [Bonython] or against any of their servants, anon they should be murdered and slain, and utterly despoiled of all their goods, so that no man dare sue . . . whereby the said county is lawless and like to be utterly destroyed'. One especially nasty offence alleged against him was that without any authority he had taken upon himself to prove people's last testaments and 'change their last wills damnably'. He then administered their estates, taking for himself all their goods and chattels. The complaints

1 Wedgwood, Hist. Parliament, Biographies, 423–6; for his connections with Warwick, Gladys M. Coles, 'The Lordship of Middleham, Especially in Yorkist and Early Tudor Times' (unpublished M.A. thesis, University of Liverpool, 1961), App. B, 12, and p. 127.
2 W. I. Haward, 'Gilbert Debenham: a Medieval Rascal in Real Life', History, xiii (1929), 300–14.

in parliament produced a series of summons against him to appear
before the king, which he failed to answer. His lands were thereby
forfeited and he was attainted. Yet the following year he succeeded in
getting this sentence reversed and in 1476 was knighted by the king at
the creation of the prince of Wales. Thereafter he was twice outlawed
and pardoned, and yet contrived to continue for the rest of the reign as
the most powerful man in Cornwall, heading nearly all the local commissions of array, peace, subsidy assessment, and against piracy – and
all this in spite of a steady stream of complaints to the Duchy of Cornwall from those who had suffered, and continued to suffer, from his
misdeeds. Only an undue and uncharacteristic commitment to Richard
III finally brought about his downfall. His career is the more remarkable in that he seems not to have enjoyed the protection of a powerful
patron.[1]

There were many Debenhams and Bodrugans abroad in Yorkist
England. In the parliament of 1459 the commons denounced some
twenty-five persons as notorious malefactors, who had been favoured
and assisted by persons of great might: their misdeeds had been 'to the
universal grudge of all your true people' and if not checked were likely
to 'grow to great inconvenience and mischief irreparable'. These men
were not condemned, as has been assumed, because they were Yorkist
sympathizers, but because they were a universal nuisance to men of any
political sympathy.[2] Yet, of those whose careers can be traced, a surprising number were still at large, and apparently unharmed and
uncurbed, a decade or more later, among them the ineffable Bodrugan.[3]
Their immunity reflects the inability of the government to bring such
men to heel except by extreme efforts, and even more its unwillingness
to proceed against its own servants or the dependants of the mighty.
Until much more research has been done on the voluminous though
often incomplete legal records of the age, it is hard to support case-
histories with reliable statistics. Yet it is difficult to avoid the impression

[1] A. L. Rowse, 'The Turbulent Career of Sir Henry de Bodrugan', *History*, xxix
(1944), 17–26. Rowse, however, failed to notice his condemnation by parliament in
1459 as an already notorious malefactor (*RP*, V, 367–8).
[2] *Ibid.*; Wedgwood's assumption that they were Yorkists ignores the fact that several
were prominent Lancastrians, e.g. Sir William Tailboys, executed after Hexham,
and John Caterall, attainted 1461, *RP*, V, 477.
[3] E.g. Sir Robert Harcourt and John Cockayne, for whom see Storey, *End . . . of
Lancaster*, 57–8, 156–8: the latter was still alive in 1504. For a detailed and interesting
study of another rascal with a thirty-year record of crime – Sir Thomas Malory of
Newbold Revel, until recently thought to be the author of the *Morte d'Arthur* – see
William Matthews, *The Ill-Framed Knight* (Berkeley and Los Angeles, 1966), 13–33.

that treason, rebellion, and their incidental violence apart, England was not a noticeably more law-abiding country in 1483 than it had been in 1461, and there was still an alarming incidence of major disturbances of the peace.

The crucial failure of Edward's government was its reluctance to make any serious attack on the system of livery and maintenance. The system of retaining by indenture, and its extension into the giving of signs and livery, were the means by which a lord attracted men into his service. Good lordship, in return, implied his protecting his servants and maintaining their quarrels. A body of legislation dealing with these practices already existed by 1461. A distinction between lawful and unlawful maintenance had been made, and the giving of badges and livery of company had been prohibited, except for resident household servants or to a lord's council or counsel learned in the law, but the practice of retaining men by indenture, even non-resident knights and esquires – the basis of a lord's local influence – remained lawful.[1] Under the articles of 1461, Edward took action against the giving of signs and liveries, by prohibiting lords and all other persons to give liveries to any man, unless he had 'special commandment by the king to raise people for the assisting of him, resisting of his enemies, or repressing of riots within his land'.[2] In the statute of 8 Edward IV, c. 2 (1468), he went much further by declaring the practice of *retaining* itself to be illegal, except for resident household servants and legal counsel; and there is little doubt that it was meant to apply to lords as well as those of lesser rank.[3]

But there is no evidence that the act was ever enforced. It had probably been prompted by the Grey–Vernon dispute in Derbyshire, which had led to three lords – Shrewsbury, Grey of Codnor and Mountjoy – being indicted of having unlawfully given liveries, some as long ago as 1461. But no action was taken against them under the new law, although the case against them was being heard in king's bench after it had been enacted.[4] The statute may have been intended as a warning that retainer was there on sufferance, but it was little more than that. Indeed we have the authority of Chief Justice Hussey for the lords' casual indifference to it. He had seen (he told his fellow-justices) 'all

[1] W. H. Dunham, *Lord Hastings' Indentured Retainers*, 66–71.
[2] *RP*, V, 487–8.
[3] *Statutes of the Realm*, II, 426–9. Dunham, *op. cit.*, 73–7, argued that the statute did not extend to peers, but cf. the comments of Bellamy, 'Justice', 152–4, and E. W. Ives, 'The Common Lawyers in Pre-Reformation England', *TRHS*, 5th ser., xviii (1968), 162.
[4] Bellamy, 'Justice', 152.

the lords sworn to keep and execute that statute which they with others had just drawn up by command of the king himself. *And within an hour, while they were still in the Star Chamber,* he saw the lords making retainers by oath, and swearing and doing other things contrary to their above-mentioned promises and oaths.'[1] It seems likely that both for king and lords the passing of the act of 1468 was little more than a public-relations exercise in response to the importunities of the commons, and they had little intention of enforcing it. Certainly the practice of re-taining continued unchecked, often with the express knowledge of the king and the lords. An example is the well-known 'compact' about their retainers made by Gloucester and Northumberland in 1474 'according to the appointment . . . by the king's highness and the lords of his council'.[2] No evidence has so far come to light of prosecutions under the act, nor is it likely to (even though much primary material remains to be examined), given Edward's chosen policy of depending upon his lords and their retainers for the supply of troops, for 'the rule of the shires', for the staffing of commissions, and for the packing of parliament. Even under the much more suspicious and tyrannical Henry VII, retainer 'was regarded as a social evil only when it conflicted with the king's interests'.[3] Edward's attitude towards the nobility meant that his subjects had to learn to live with 'a great number of misdoers and the great bearers-up of the same'.

[1] Williams, *English Hist. Documents*, 533.
[2] Dunham, *op. cit.*, 74–82, and 140 for text of the 'compact'. It was precisely the frequency of retaining which led Dunham to believe that it could not have been meant to apply to lords. All but five of the sixty-nine indentures of retainer by Lord Hastings post-date the act of 1468, *ibid.*, 73.
[3] Chrimes, *Henry VII*, 191.

Conclusion

THE END OF THE REIGN:
ACHIEVEMENT AND AFTERMATH

King Edward kept his last Christmas at Westminster Palace with particular splendour. Although his health may already have been failing, he was still capable of making a vivid impression of royal majesty on the minds of his admiring subjects. Surrounded by his five daughters, whose beauty caught the attention of those present, the king himself, resplendent in a fashionable new wardrobe, presented 'a distinguished air to beholders, he being a person of most elegant appearance, and remarkable beyond all others for the attractions of his person'.[1] Apart from a brief visit to Windsor, the court stayed on at Westminster during the early months of 1483, until about Eastertide (28–30 March), when the king suddenly fell ill.

Contemporary sources are so imprecise and conflicting that the nature of this final illness cannot be more than a matter for speculation. The Croyland Chronicler, whose explicit testimony would have been of the highest value, chose to be deliberately enigmatic with his remark that the king took to his bed 'neither worn out with old age nor yet seized with any known kind of malady, the cure of which would not have appeared easy in the case of a person of more humble rank'. Polydore Vergil similarly speaks of death from 'an unknown disease', but elsewhere hints at poison. The Tudor chronicler, Edward Hall, believed that Edward had contracted an ague or malarial infection in France which suddenly turned from a 'tercian' or benign phase to a malignant 'quartan' fever, and the end was brought on by a surfeit of food. Malaria was still common in medieval Europe, and the marshes of the Somme valley in the wet summer of 1475 were a likely place to catch it, but it is doubtful whether Edward's contemporaries would not have recognized and recorded the disease, and no source before Hall mentions ague. Mancini, who was in London at the time of Edward's death and had contacts with the court, tells us that the king caught cold on a fishing-trip with some of his courtiers.[2]

[1] CC, 563.
[2] CC, 563–4; Polydore Vergil, *English History*, 171–2; Hall, *Chronicle*, 338; Mancini, 59.

Commynes twice asserts that Edward died of apoplexy ('quaterre') brought on by excess. This was soon to kill his own master, Louis XI, who like Edward lingered on for several days after a (second) cerebral haemorrhage on 25 August 1483.[1] This explanation certainly fits best with what we know of Edward's gigantic physical appetites. Mancini reported that 'In food and drink he was most immoderate: it was his habit, so I have learned, to take an emetic for the delight of gorging his stomach once more. For this reason, and for the ease, which was especially dear to him after the recovery of his crown, he had grown fat in the loins.' There is no evidence that his sexual extravagance had diminished with the years, as Mancini testifies. The Croyland Chronicler likewise refers to his corpulence, debauchery, extravagance and sensual enjoyments.[2] All this self-indulgence made Edward vulnerable to some form of stroke. Elsewhere, however, Commynes asserts that the king's death was caused by melancholy or chagrin at the news of the Treaty of Arras, a blow from which he never recovered. Bishop Russell seems to confirm that this contributed to his decline, for, in an address drawn up three months later, he asked: 'Was not his pensifous sickness increased by daily remembrance of the dark ways, that his subtle-faith friends had led him in?'[3] But it is unlikely that such concern could have overwhelmed a man of Edward's resilient temperament, and on the whole his death was probably more or less directly the result of continuous excess, which his wealth and station allowed him to indulge in, as the Croyland Chronicler's cryptic comment seems to suggest.[4]

The king's illness was serious enough for his death to be reported prematurely in York on 6 April, and a mass was sung for his soul in the Minster the next day. Yet in fact he lingered on, still clear enough in his mind to add several codicils to his last will, and to attempt to reconcile feuds amongst his courtiers, especially the quarrel between

[1] Commynes, II, 304, 344; and see the edition by B. de Mandrot, II, 63, for his use of the word 'quaterre'; Kendall, *Louis XI*, 368–9.
[2] Mancini, 67; *CC*, 564.
[3] Commynes, II, 231; *Grants of Edward V*, ed. J. G. Nichols (Camden Society, 1854), liii (for Russell's statement). Mancini, 59, also suggested that melancholy over the Treaty of Arras hastened the king's death.
[4] That his death was brought on by apoplexy following a surfeit is accepted by Calmette in his edition of Commynes, II, 231. For other modern views, see Ramsay, *Lancaster and York*, II, 452–3 (following Hall); Scofield, II, 365–6 ('anger and chagrin' about the Treaty of Arras combined with 'libertinism and high living'); Kendall, *Richard III*, 153 (following Mancini); Winston Churchill, *History of the English-Speaking Peoples*, I, 377 (who suggests appendicitis). The views of some foreign contemporaries are summarized by C. A. J. Armstrong in Mancini, 107.

Hastings and Dorset.[1] After an illness lasting ten days, he died on Wednesday, 9 April 1483, three weeks short of his forty-first birthday. The Croyland Chronicler tells us that as the end approached he repented sincerely of his sins, desired that all his debts should be fully paid, and was in devout reverence of the sacraments of the church. Such, he added wryly, was 'the most beseeming end of this worldly prince, a better than which could not be hoped for or conceived, after the manifestation by him of so large a share of the frailties inherent to the lot of mankind'.[2]

His funeral rites were carried out with all the panoply and sombre splendour which Edward would have wished (and at a cost of no less than £1,496 17s 2d).[3] First, his body, naked except for a loincloth, was laid upon a board in Westminster Palace, whilst the lords spiritual and temporal then in London, and the mayor and aldermen, came to gaze upon it. The corpse was then embalmed, wrapped in cerements of waxed linen, clothed, with a cap of estate on the head and the feet shod in red leather, and in this guise it lay in state for eight days in St Stephen's Chapel, Westminster, watched over by nobles and royal servants to the sound of requiem masses. On 17 April the body was placed upon a bier, covered with a large, rich cloth of gold, and carried into Westminster Abbey by fifteen knights and esquires of the body. Above it was a canopy of cloth imperial fringed with gold and blue silk, flanked at the corners by four banners of the Trinity, Our Lady, St George and St Edward. Before the bier walked Lord Howard carrying Edward's own banner. The chancellor, Archbishop Rotherham, nine bishops and two abbots led the procession into the Abbey, and behind the bier came a parade of the temporal lords and knights, among them many of his old friends and servants, like Hastings, Stanley and Ferrers, some of whom had attended his coronation twenty-two years before. A 'similitude' or life-sized image of the king had been constructed, and this now stood beside the bier dressed in the royal clothes, crowned, and equipped with orb and sceptre, as bishops, lords, judges, mayor, aldermen and household knights and esquires made their offerings.

The next morning (18 April) the funeral procession set out for Charing Cross and then to Sion Abbey, where it rested overnight. The

[1] More's circumstantial story of the deathbed reconciliation is supported in its essentials by Mancini, 69.
[2] *CC*, 564.
[3] What follows is based on the contemporary accounts by heralds in *Letters and Papers . . . Richard III and Henry VII*, ed. J. Gairdner, I, xvii, 3–10. For the expenses of the funeral, see *Registrum Thome Bourgchier*, II, 54.

following morning it moved on through Eton, where the bishops of Lincoln and Ely and members of Eton College censed the corpse, to Windsor and Edward's fine new chapel of St George. All that night the body was guarded by a great company of nine lords and many household men and the kings and pursuivants of arms. On 20 April the final masses were celebrated in the chapel by Archbishop Rotherham of York and Bishops Russell of Lincoln and Dudley of Durham. Offerings were then made of the accoutrements which were to rest upon the tomb – shield, sword and helmet – by those who had been close to the king by blood or service. After offerings made by 'the man of arms', Sir William Parr, controller of the household, clad in full armour, and bearing a battle-axe head downwards, the lords made their offerings of cloths of gold, 'each after his degree or estate', and the body was laid in the tomb. Following the usual custom, the great officers of the household cast their staves of office into the grave, and the heralds did likewise with their coats of arms. Given new coats, the heralds then immediately cried out 'Le Roy est vif! Le Roy est vif!' and offered prayers for the dead king.

Long ago Edward had left precise directions for the construction of his tomb. In the will he had drawn up in 1475 he had conveyed to trustees very extensive estates, mainly sections of the Duchy of Lancaster and Duchy of York lands, for the payment of his debts, to provide an appanage for his younger son and marriage portions of 10,000 marks each for his daughters, Elizabeth and Mary, and a similar sum for the child the queen was then carrying should she prove to be a daughter, and had made arrangements for the payment of the rest of the marriage portion of Cecily, then affianced to the heir of Scotland. He had also adjured his heir to make sure of the continuance of any grants he had made to 'divers of our Lords as well of our blood as other and also Knights, Squires and divers other our true and loving subjects and servants' who had 'faithfully and lovingly assisted us and put them in the extreme jeopardy of their lives, losses of their lands and goods in assisting us as well about the recovery of our Crown and Realm of England as other divers seasons and times of jeopardy'. A great deal of the will, however, consisted of elaborate injunctions for the carrying-through of his new works at Windsor, with his own tomb as its centre-piece. He was to be buried 'low in the ground, and upon the same a stone to be laid and wrought with the figure of Death with a scutcheon of our Armour and writings convenient about the borders of the same remembering the day and year of our decease'. Over this should be built a vault, and upon the vault a chapel with an altar and tomb, and 'upon the same tomb an image for our figure, which figure we will be of silver and gilt or at the least copper and gilt'.[1]

This chapel had been built at the same time as the choir, and was screened from the aisles by a pair of superb iron gates suspended from iron towers, which have been described as 'without doubt the most remarkable works of their period in that material remaining in the country'. These gates, now in the presbytery, were probably the work of John Tresilian, who had been employed on ironwork in the chapel since 1477. In the financial year 1482–3, thirty-three casks of touchstone, or black marble from the Low Countries, had been delivered for the construction of the tomb. Unfortunately, neither the 'figure Death' or cadaver nor the king's funeral effigy were ever completed, and the tomb remained unmarked until the present slab of touchstone was placed there in 1789, similar to that put above the tomb of Edward's old enemy and victim, Henry VI, whose remains were transferred to Windsor from Chertsey on the command of Richard III. However, some of the accoutrements placed on the tomb during the funeral rites were to remain there for over two hundred years. The king's coat of gilt mail, covered in crimson velvet with his arms embroidered on it in pearls, gold and rubies, and his banner of 'taffety' with the royal arms painted thereon, were finally removed from the tomb by Parliamentary soldiers in 1642.[2]

In the five hundred years since he died, Edward IV's historical reputation has suffered a series of vicissitudes. For early Tudor writers, like Sir Thomas More and Polydore Vergil, whose accounts were based upon the reminiscences of a wide circle of men who had known and served Edward, he was a king of considerable achievement and stature. He was seen as an active, businesslike king, who had done much to make his realm peaceful and prosperous and whose rule had been both firm and popular. This tradition was maintained throughout the sixteenth century by Hall, Holinshed and Stow, who largely reproduced More's balanced and respectful appraisal, and from whom Shakespeare obtained his material. Not until the eighteenth century, when the French historian, Rapin, published his *History of England* in 1723, did a different view emerge. Rapin, followed later in the century by David Hume, imported into his assessment of the king the critical and prejudiced views of Philippe de Commynes. Edward now appeared as

---

[1] *Excerpta Historica*, 366–79, esp. 366–7.
[2] Beltz, *Memorials of the Order of the Garter*, lxxiv; Hope, *Architectural History of Windsor Castle*, 418–19, 428–9; Colvin, *King's Works*, II, 887–8; *GC*, 229.

debauched, cruel, avaricious and lazy, capable of energy and decision only in times of crisis.[1] This characterization was repeated and in some ways exaggerated by almost all the historians of the nineteenth century, and Edward's reputation reached its nadir in the blend of grudging condescension and moral disapproval expressed by the most influential of Victorian medievalists, Bishop William Stubbs:[2]

> Edward IV was not perhaps quite so bad a man or so bad a king as his enemies have represented; but even those writers who have laboured hardest to rehabilitate him, have failed to discover any conspicuous merits.

Stubbs then credits Edward with personal courage, affability, a 'fairly good' education, a definite plan of foreign policy, skill as a merchant, and a readiness to enforce the law where it did not clash with 'the fortunes of his favourites or his own likes and dislikes', and he continues:

> But that is all: he was as a man vicious far beyond anything that England had seen since the days of John; and more cruel and bloodthirsty than any king she had ever known: he had too a conspicuous talent for extortion. . . . Edward far outdid [in fierce deeds of bloodshed] all that his forefathers and his enemies together had done. The death of Clarence was but the summing up and crowning act of an unparalleled list of judicial and extra-judicial cruelties which those of the next reign supplement but do not surpass.

Modern historians have moved a long way from this highly prejudiced and ill-informed assessment. Freed from Stubbs's preconceptions, concerned rather with the realities of political power than with Victorian theories of parliamentary sovereignty, and working from the hitherto unexplored records of the reign instead of chronicle and narrative evidence, they now see him in a far more flattering light. Here was 'a king of iron will and great fixity of purpose', 'an astute and able ruler', a monarch who possessed 'the ruthlessness of a Renaissance despot and the strong-willed ability of a statesman', who had the capacity to rescue England from the horrors of civil strife and replace them with order, wealth and prosperity.[3] Moreover, his

---

[1] J. R. Lander, 'Edward IV: The Modern Legend: and a Revision', *History*, xli (1956), 38–42.
[2] *Constitutional History of England* (1878 edn), III, 219–20.
[3] These are the opinions of, respectively, J. R. Lander, *op. cit.*, 52; A. R. Myers, *England in the Late Middle Ages*, 113; G. A. Holmes, *The Later Middle Ages*, 220; B. Wilkinson, *Constitutional History of England in the Fifteenth Century*, 144. A more sceptical note is sounded by K. B. McFarlane, 'The Wars of the Roses', 101, 114.

intelligent responses to the problems of late medieval government provided in all essential respects the foundations on which the early Tudors were to build. This modern estimate has been succinctly phrased by S. B. Chrimes:[1]

> He did much to consolidate the monarchy, to rehabilitate its finances, and to restore its prestige. He stopped the process of decay in monarchy and government . . . he went far to remedy the 'lack of politique reule and governance' which had brought Henry VI to disaster; he was not to be led astray by Henry V's martial dreams; he grasped firmly the financial nettles which Henry IV had either evaded or sown. He achieved much that Richard II had tried but failed to do. . . . Edward's achievements as man and king were not small. . . . The foundations of what has commonly been called the 'New Monarchy' were laid not by Henry VII, but by Edward IV.

To a large extent this re-appraisal was overdue and well deserved Yet it should not be carried too far. His failings as a politician can easily be overlooked among the general chorus of approval for his achievement in domestic government. He was at once more fallible, more impulsive, more inconsistent, and less far-sighted than the judgement quoted above might suggest.[2] It may also be argued that he was more self-interested and lacking in principle. For what were the principle. on which Edward based his government?

The answer to this question must lie in a consideration of the policies he adopted or further developed after 1475 when at last he had full freedom to rule as he wished. His first reign saw him largely on the defensive, concerned with the problem of survival in face of powerful opposition at home and the threat of foreign intervention, and with the urgent need to restore the royal authority with only a comparatively slender power-base on which to rely. After 1471 his rule was based much more firmly on the prestige of his own great victories, the overthrow of internal challenge to his authority, and the absence of any plausible claimant to the throne – for Henry Tudor became a serious contender only after the Buckingham-Woodville rebellion of 1483 further weakened an already divided Yorkist group at the centre of government. But not until 1475, when he had stabilized his foreign relations and shelved the schemes of overseas military adventure which

---

[1] S. B. Chrimes, *Lancastrians, Yorkists and Henry VII*, 111, 124–5; and see also his review-article, 'The Fifteenth Century', *History*, xlviii (1963), 27.
[2] These specific points are discussed in my article, 'The Reign of Edward IV', in *Fifteenth Century England*, 49–66.

had preoccupied him for three years, had he the means and the opportunity to develop his domestic policies without distraction or distraint. What use did he make of this power?

For both the Croyland Chronicler and Polydore Vergil the fall of Clarence brought more than a risk of despotism.[1] Yet to the former – an understanding, sympathetic, but by no means uncritical student of the king he served – the most conspicuous feature of the last eight years of the reign was Edward's sustained effort to accumulate personal wealth by all possible means in order to eliminate his dependence on his subjects.[2] Such emphasis on the pursuit of royal wealth serves to highlight an aspect of his rule which has not, perhaps, been sufficiently stressed – that is, the extent to which it was government by the king in the interests of the king.[3] Edward never escaped from the rather old-fashioned proprietary notion of kingship implied in his own claim to the throne. This monarch who spoke of taking *possession* and *seisin* of the realm of England was the son of a great private landowner who now saw himself restored to an even greater inheritance from which his immediate forbears had been unjustly excluded. Moreover, he had grown to manhood during a struggle for power when the greed and land-hunger of the English aristocracy had been permitted their most naked expression. In an age of partisan government the competition for the profits and perquisites of political power had largely obscured the older 'medieval ideal of government by the king for the good of the whole community.'[4] It is scarcely surprising that a king of such preconceptions and background should have approached his position in terms of marked self-interest.

Much has been written for and against the concept of the 'New Monarchy', of which J. R. Green originally saw Edward as the creator, and the arguments need not be rehearsed here.[5] In so far as there was novelty in Edward's rule, it can be claimed that it lay less in the extensive personal exercise of power by the king, in the use of 'new men' in

[1] *CC*, 562, quoted above, p. 245; Polydore Vergil, *English History*, 168.
[2] *CC*, 559, and above, pp. 380ff.
[3] Except by Dr G. L. Harriss in his two valuable contributions to the debate on 'A Revolution in Tudor History?' in *Past and Present*: see no. 25 (1963), 8–39, and no. 31 (1965), 86–94. These stressed the 'personal' as distinct from the 'household' character of late medieval government, and the self-interest of Yorkist and early Tudor rule.
[4] Harriss, *Past and Present*, no. 31 (1965), 91–2.
[5] See for example K. B. McFarlane, *Nobility of Later Medieval England*, 279–87, and *Past and Present* mentioned above. The original theory is in J. R. Green, *History of the English People* (1878), II, Bk V, and esp. 27–8; cf. his *Short History of the English People* (1876), 282–7, which shifts the emphasis from 1461 to 1471.

government, in a preference for working through 'household' agencies and servants, in the avoidance of royal dependence on parliament, than in the degree to which Edward governed for himself, his family and his friends. The public finances of the country were transformed into the king's personal finances, the requirements of which were given 'absolute, immediate, and automatic priority'.[1] Nor is it a coincidence that so many of the administrative reforms and innovations which have been closely associated with the notion of a 'New Monarchy' – chamber finance, household reform, the 'land revenue experiment', the beginnings of the exploitation of royal feudal and prerogative rights, effective exploitation of the customs system – were the direct and immediate product of the campaign to accumulate royal treasure, much of which was spent upon objects equally personal to the king.[2] Further, Edward was perhaps more concerned with the aggrandizement of his own kin by blood and marriage than any of his predecessors since Edward I. In the later years of his reign this led him to interfere extensively with the rights of the nobility, whose class-interests he had otherwise respected – in this, as in much else, he was not a very consistent king.[3] We have seen, too, how much his foreign policy was influenced by essentially dynastic ambitions – the wish to marry his children into the royal and princely houses of Europe. There was, however, nothing unusual or novel in this, except in the degree to which he allowed avarice to temper his dynastic schemes and in his stubborn pursuit of the proposed French marriage for his eldest daughter at the expense of diplomatic advantage.

It would not do to overplay this aspect of Edward's rule. A highly personal exercise of power was an obvious necessity after what K. B. McFarlane once called 'forty years of virtual minority' when 'the medieval kingship was in abeyance',[4] and the desired reassertion of royal authority could most readily be achieved by the use of royal servants and agencies directly and immediately responsive to the king himself. In part also his policies were imposed upon him by the prejudices and attitudes of his subjects, for Englishmen had become weary of underwriting the extravagance and insolvency of their rulers and were less than enthusiastic in their support of sustained wars of foreign conquest for dynastic ends. Unlike his brutal and ruthless grandson, Henry VIII, Edward did not choose to attempt the immense task of imposing on his subjects their forced cooperation in foreign policies

[1] B. P. Wolffe, 'Henry VII's Land Revenues and Chamber Finance', *EHR*, lxxix (1964), 227.

[2] Above, pp. 261ff, and chapter 11.   [3] Above, pp. 334-7.

[4] McFarlane, *Nobility*, 284.

involving heavy expenditure and taxation. Still his avoidance of major schemes of foreign conquest may have been partly a matter of temperament – for he was a rare example among medieval kings of a successful commander in the field who yet had little natural taste for warfare. In any event his reluctance to commit himself to foreign war in his later years (with the usual inconsistency of Scotland) was an essential condition of his search for royal solvency at home.

It remains open to question whether Edward had much disinterested or altruistic concern with the good of the whole community. His determination to be obeyed, his suppression of major disorders, his expansion of the prestige of monarchy – all these were conditions of survival. His concern for justice did not extend beyond his own interest and was not allowed to clash with those of his family and friends. Even his promotion of English commercial interests owed much to his dependence on London merchant pressure-groups and his own financial interest in improving trade and customs revenue. The very absence of constitutional conflict during the reign is largely due to the separation of the king's interests from those of the realm, especially in matters of finance.

Yet it is easy to see why his own contemporaries, and the early Tudor commentators (though for somewhat partisan motives) both admired and respected him. Whatever his motives, he had achieved much. He had put an end to civil conflict; he had brought a measure of political stability and order, if not impartial justice, into a divided realm; and he had given his people some years of respite from overseas war, trade conflict, and the burdens of heavy taxation. He had restored the prestige of the monarchy, and given England the reassurance of a strong hand at the helm of government. Until 1478, when a growing avarice and arbitrariness made Englishmen perhaps a little fearful for the future, his firm rule had been tempered by a natural generosity and clemency. His handsome kingly image, personal charm and affability, which continued to the end of the reign, and his avoidance of policies which exploited his subjects, combined to make him a king who was generally popular as well as respected. There can be little doubt that if he had lived a few years longer, he would have transmitted to his son a secure throne as well as a prosperous realm.

Still the inevitable questions remain. Why was a king so successful in his own lifetime unable to secure the peaceful succession of his heir? How far can he be held responsible for the upheavals which within two years overthrew his son and the House of York itself? There is an obvious and striking contrast between the sequence of events in 1422, when Henry V died at the age of thirty-four, leaving an heir of only nine months, twenty-two years after the House of Lancaster had usurped the throne, and those of 1483, when Edward's death at the age of forty left an heir of twelve, after a similar period of rule by a new dynasty. In 1422 a united aristocracy had no difficulty in defeating the aspirations of the infant king's younger uncle, Humphrey, duke of Gloucester, to an effective regency, and the question of replacing Henry VI was never raised, in spite of the prospect of the longest royal minority England had ever faced.[1] Why did things go so differently in 1483?

The real answer lies in the continued dependence of the Yorkist regime at the highest political level on a small group of over-mighty or mighty subjects. Politics had become the preserve of about one-third of the nobility, nearly all of whom were either Edward's kin by blood or marriage or had been raised by him to power and influence, and this group was seriously divided internally. In particular, there was an inherent conflict in the positions of the Woodvilles and of Duke Richard of Gloucester. In April 1483 Earl Rivers was at Ludlow with the prince of Wales, and his powers as governor of the prince's household had been revised and perhaps enlarged as recently as 27 February; he was also in a position to raise an army in Wales, and on 8 March had sent to London for a copy of his letters patent authorizing him to raise troops if need be.[2] The rest of the Woodvilles were in London, where Thomas, marquis of Dorset, as deputy-constable of the Tower, controlled Edward IV's treasure, and his uncle, Sir Edward Woodville, was soon to be placed in charge of part of the king's navy.[3] The family was in a position to secure its control of the young king and his brother by force if necessary, and evidently planned to do so. Yet Gloucester, through his own independent affinity and influence in the north, also had the resources to engineer a take-over of power by force, and could expect the support of several powerful people who had suffered materially from Edward IV's rule or stood to gain substantially if Richard came into control. Among them were the two leading representatives of the older nobility, Henry Stafford, duke of Buckingham, and Henry Percy, earl of Northumberland.

All this might have been less disastrous if the Woodvilles had not

[1] For 1422, see J. S. Roskell, *The Commons in the Parliament of 1422*, 98–100, 103–7; and for the equally sharp contrast with the succession of the nine-year-old Edward VI in 1547, see Mortimer Levine, *Tudor Dynastic Problems, 1460–1571*, 76. There are valuable remarks on 1483 by T. B. Pugh in *Fifteenth-Century England*, 110–14.
[2] Ives, 'Andrew Dymmock . . . and Earl Rivers, 1482–3', 223–5.
[3] *Ibid.*, 225; Mancini, 81 (who also refers to the division of Edward's treasure between the queen, Dorset and Edward Woodville).

been so unpupular with the ruling group as a whole, and on bad terms with Gloucester and Hastings in particular. Duke Richard had every reason to fear the jealousy and malice of the queen's family if once they were established in power.[1] Hastings was equally afraid of 'their most signal vengeance', and played a decisive part in persuading the council in London, meeting soon after Edward IV's death, to prohibit Earl Rivers's plan to bring Edward V to London at the head of an army.[2] Even the dead king's councillors, though ardently desirous that 'the prince should succeed his father in all his glory', viewed the prospect of a Woodville-dominated minority with unmitigated dismay.[3] Outside this court group the majority of the barons had neither the power nor the will to interfere, for the Wars of the Roses had wrought a change in their political attitudes, and few were anxious to commit themselves to this dangerous game,[4] certainly not in the Woodville interest. Even when the actions of Gloucester and Buckingham had begun to raise doubts about their intentions, the queen's family still could not rally much support. Mancini tells us that 'when they had exhorted certain nobles . . . and others to take up arms, they perceived that men's minds were not only irresolute, but altogether hostile to themselves'.[5] Lord Hastings's change of mind – a *rapprochement* with the Woodvilles to protect Edward V's position – came too late to deflect Gloucester from his almost involuntary march to the throne.

This situation was the direct outcome of Edward IV's policies in his later years. He can scarcely have been unaware of the unpopularity of the queen's kin, and of their jealousy of Gloucester and Hastings. Yet he had done nothing to reduce their power, and by placing the prince and his brother in their exclusive charge, had given them an entrenched position from which they could be removed only by force. At the same time he had built up Gloucester as the mightiest magnate in the realm, and provided him with potential allies by alienating others. As the only surviving adult male of the House of York, Gloucester was the natural protector or regent of England in the event of a minority. This was the insoluble dilemma which confronted Edward during his final illness. We cannot be certain what his intentions were, since his last will and the codicils which he added to it have not survived: it is probable, but not entirely certain, that these designated

---

[1] Pugh, *op. cit.*, 112–13; Ives, *op. cit.*, 225.
[2] *CC*, 564–5.   [3] *Loc. cit.*
[4] McFarlane, 'Wars of the Roses', 117–19, who describes their mood as 'chastened, indeed craven' by 1485.
[5] Mancini, 78–9.

his brother as protector of the realm.[1] Not to have appointed him was a recipe for disaster, since neither he nor many others would accept the queen's family. Equally, the Woodvilles could be expected to oppose any attempt to deprive them of control of the princes, which would expose them to the revenge of their many ill-wishers. The king's death-bed attempt to reconcile Dorset and Hastings did little to solve this central problem.

Edward IV's failure to make early and deliberate provision for the succession in the event of his own premature death is certainly con-sistent with his attitude to politics in general. His pragmatism persisted to the last, and he assumed too readily the influence of his own personal charm and his ability to cover all contingencies.[2] He remains the only king in English history since 1066 in active possession of his throne who failed to secure the safe succession of his son. His lack of political fore-sight is largely to blame for the unhappy aftermath of his early death.

[1] On this point, see the comments of C. A. J. Armstrong in Mancini, 61, 107-8; for the codicils, *CC*, 564.

[2] More (*Richard III*, 10) observes that whilst Edward was alive the dissensions amongst friends somewhat irked him: 'yet in his good health he somewhat the less regarded it, because he thought whatsoever business should fall between them, himself should always be able to rule both the parties'.

APPENDICES
SELECT BIBLIOGRAPHY
INDEX

Appendix I

NOTE ON NARRATIVE SOURCES

The reign of Edward IV was singularly ill-served by contemporary writers of history. It falls uneasily into a period of limbo between the voluminous monastic chronicles of an earlier age (a form of writing already moribund by 1450) and the developed 'humanist' or 'politic' histories of the sixteenth century and later. The gap thus left is only very partially filled by the vernacular city chronicles, mainly of London origin, which became 'perhaps the most important of all the original authorities for English history in the fifteenth century' (C. L. Kingsford, *English Historical Literature in the Fifteenth Century*, 70). Nor (with exceptions for the years 1470 and 1471) did the period produce in England the series of official and semi-official histories patronized by the kings of France, nor the 'memorialists' like Basin and Commynes, politically-conscious students of politics and government in their own time, who were intent on drawing upon historical experience for general rules of political behaviour (for whom see Denys Hay, 'History and Historians in France and England during the Fifteenth Century', *BIHR*, xxxv (1962), 111–27). The consequences of all this for the student of Edward's reign are serious indeed. For no other reign in English history since Henry III do we possess less strictly contemporary information, save perhaps that of Henry VI. It is often far from easy to establish a precise sequence of events, especially when these took place far from London, like the Lancastrian resistance of 1461–4, or the northern rising of 1469 (for which see Appendix IV). Still more difficult is any discussion of motive and the interplay of personality in politics, matters generally beyond the range of the unsophisticated and often ill-informed and parochial writers of the time. Too often the inner logic of high politics depends on inference from action and events, and, as G. R. Elton rightly observed, 'it is because no sound contemporary history exists for this age that its shape and meaning are so much in dispute now' (*England 1200–1640: The Sources of History*, 22).

The failings of contemporary narrative sources can be partly supplemented by the evidence of contemporary letters, notably the Paston correspondence, and from official records. The latter, however, apart from financial and legal records, fall primarily into the category of enrolments of official *acts*, and fall far short of providing the political insight to be derived by the student of sixteenth-century history from the great mass of memoranda, reports, instructions and correspondence known collectively as 'State Papers'. These, as Elton expressed it, 'add the dimension of individual personality to our knowledge of English history' (*op. cit.*, 66 ff.).

Whatever their obvious and manifold defects, however, the historian of Edward IV's reign remains heavily dependent on the available narrative sources, especially for its political history. For this reason, I append below brief historiographical notes, which also indicate the degree of reliance I have placed on individual sources or groups of sources.

1. The 'Croyland Chronicler'

By far the most important single source for the years 1471–85 is the account generally known as the 'Second Continuation of the Croyland Chronicle', cited here as *CC*. Despite the name, this was not a late survivor of the monastic chronicle tradition, although in form it survives as a continuation of two spurious chronicles associated with the Fenland abbey of Crowland. According to a marginal note, its author was a doctor of canon law and a councillor of Edward IV, who took part in an embassy to Burgundy in 1471, and elsewhere the author claims that he wrote and completed the narrative at Croyland within ten days, ending on the last day of April 1486. These claims were generally accepted (see Kingsford, *op. cit.*, 180–5) until challenged by Sir J. G. Edwards ('The second continuation of the Crowland Chronicle; was it written in ten days?', *BIHR*, xxxix (1966), 117–29), who threw doubt primarily on the date of the chronicle and, by implication, on the authority of the marginal note about authorship. His arguments must, however, be rejected on the internal evidence of the Chronicle itself, though detailed proof awaits the publication of N. Pronay's forthcoming edition of the text. More recently, M. M. Condon has assembled evidence, to be published shortly, which puts beyond all reasonable doubt that the author of the chronicle was in fact Bishop John Russell, himself a doctor of canon law, a royal councillor, and keeper of the privy seal to Edward IV (1474–83) and chancellor to Richard III (June 1483–July 1485). Even if this identification be not accepted, it can be shown from the internal evidence of the chronicle that its author was a clerk, a royal servant with knowledge of the chancery, who was present in a number of meetings of council, parliament and convocation, and accompanied Edward IV to France in 1475. He was on occasion at least an eye-witness of the events he describes, for example, the stormy council meeting when Clarence and Gloucester quarrelled over the Warwick inheritance, and the Christmas festivities at Edward's court in 1482. Moreover, he was clearly a man of intelligence and high education who possessed a considerable inside knowledge of affairs. Where his specific statements can be checked against other evidence (e.g., on Edward's financial policies) they are almost invariably correct. He must, therefore, be accepted as an authoritative witness in default of other evidence. In particular, it is worth noticing that (a) although a loyal servant of Edward IV, he was still capable of trenchant criticisms of his fallible master, and (b) that although not personally hostile to the Woodville family, he regarded them as a disastrous element in politics – this comes out especially in his account of the council meeting following Edward's death, at which he was probably present in person.

2. The London Chronicles

The identification, nature and value of the many surviving vernacular chronicles of London origin were first discussed by C. L. Kingsford in his *Chronicles of London* (1905), v–xlviii, a volume which contains *inter alia* the chronicle known as Vitellius A. XVI, which in its present form extends to 1509, apart from a few later jottings up to 1516. His views were developed in his *English Historical Literature* (1913), 70–112, and his conclusions are still accepted, apart from the revisions made by A. H. Thomas and I. D. Thornley in their edition (1938) of the more recently discovered *Great Chronicle of London*. Thomas and Thornley were able to show that the common author of both the *Great Chronicle* and Fabyan's *New Chronicles of England and of France* (ed. Ellis, 1811) was the London draper Robert Fabian, who was writing up to the time of his death in February 1513. Sheriff of London in 1493 and master of the Drapers' Company in 1495–6 and 1501–2, he had been an apprentice to Sir Thomas Cook in 1468, of whose disgrace he had personal memories. Amongst other sources on which he drew was Vitellius A. XVI, which, however, retains a certain independent value. Both the value and the limitations of this group of sources were determined by the way in which they were put together and by the audience which commissioned and read them. For the most part they were assembled by London citizens as a part-time hobby, with an eye to the interests and prejudices of their chief readers, the London merchant class. They remain essentially compilations, with the compiler using one or more existing versions and adding to them from his own knowledge as events neared the time he was writing. They were never national histories for general consumption, and remain parochial to London, showing much interest in civic affairs and events in the capital, but little knowledge of events abroad or elsewhere in the country. They are essentially annalistic rather than analytical, uncritical of their sources, and offering no explanation of the causes or significance of the events they describe. Sometimes the compiler injected a personal note into his account, as in 'Gregory's Chronicle' (*Collections of a London Citizen*, 58–239), which is of considerable value for the first decade of Edward's reign. Much the same might be said of the 'Short English Chronicle' (ed. Gairdner, *Three Fifteenth Century Chronicles*, 1–80), which ends in 1465, and was probably written very soon after. Although some of the London chronicles, especially the Great Chronicle, were finally put together at a comparatively late date, and therefore reflect some elements of Tudor prejudice and propaganda, their importance (apart from the lack of other narratives) lies 'in the fact that they, or the sources from which they were compiled, were written soon after the events recorded and thus reflect, to some extent, the popular opinion of those events' (Thomas and Thornley, introd. to *Great Chronicle*, xxxiv).

3. *Other contemporary English sources*

This body of material was surveyed at length by Kingsford, *English Historical Literature*, chapters VI and VII. Comparatively little has been written since to affect his assessment, except that the *Annales rerum anglicarum* printed by J. Stevenson (*Letters and Papers illustrative of the Wars of the English in France*, Rolls Series, II, pt ii, 756–92) from the text originally printed by Thomas Hearne, *Liber Niger Scaccarii* (2nd edn, 1771), II, 522–41, have been conclusively shown not to have been written by the antiquary, William Worcester (see K. B. McFarlane, 'William Worcester: a Preliminary Survey', in *Studies presented to Sir Hilary Jenkinson*, ed. J. Conway Davies (Oxford, 1957), 196–221, esp. 206–7). This collection (cited here as *Annales*) has more the character of a scrapbook than of a deliberately composed piece of work, and was compiled by a writer at work in 1491. Nevertheless, it contains material not found elsewhere, especially for the years 1460–68, and is of interest for its strongly pro-Nevill bias, a point not noticed by Kingsford. Another recent discovery was 'John Benet's Chronicle' (ed. G. L. Harriss and M. A. Harriss, Camden Miscellany XXIV, Royal Historical Society, Camden 4th ser., ix. 1972, 151–234). This valuable clerical chronicle is primarily useful for the period of Henry VI's majority rule but has much of interest for the years 1460–62.

Also of considerable value for the early years of the reign is the 'Brief Latin Chronicle' (*Three Fifteenth Century Chronicles*, ed. J. Gairdner, 164–85), which is of interest for contemporary reactions to Edward's policies, especially its critical comments on the military and naval operations in the north 1462–3. In the same context the 'Brief Notes' (1422–64) printed by Gairdner (*Three Fifteenth Century Chronicles*, 148–63) are of considerable use, not least for their highly contemporary character: they seem to have been a record of news written down from time to time as it arrived at Ely, where the collection was compiled. Information about events in the north of England is sufficiently rare to give a greater importance than it might otherwise have possessed to the work of John Warkworth, *A Chronicle of the First Thirteen Years of the Reign of King Edward the Fourth* (ed. J. O. Halliwell, Camden Soc., 1839). Master of Peterhouse, Cambridge, the author came from Northumberland, and the chronicle was written by or for him, probably by 1482 (see Kingsford, *op. cit.*, 171–3; Lander, 'Treason and Death of the Duke of Clarence', 20–1 and note); it is of special value for the events of 1470–71.

Very much apart from this miscellaneous material stand the examples of 'official history' produced in England during Edward IV's reign. The two most important are the *Chronicle of the Rebellion in Lincolnshire* (ed. J. G. Nichols, Camden Soc., 1847) which covers the events of three weeks in March 1470, and the *Historie of the Arrivall of Edward IV* (ed. J. Bruce, Camden Soc., 1838), covering the period from 2 March 1471, when Edward sailed for England, to 26 May, following the defeat of the Bastard of Fauconberg. Kingsford's discussion of the latter (*op. cit.*, 174–6) now needs to be supplemented by J. A. F. Thomson, ' "The Arrival of Edward IV" – The

Development of the Text', *Speculum*, xlvi (1971), 84–93. Their value lies in their immediacy – a short version of the *Arrivall*, for example, was completed within three days of the final event it describes, for distribution on the Continent – and in the fact that the author, a vigorous writer of English prose, was clearly in Edward's company during the course of these events and was an eye-witness of many. Their propaganda purpose is clear enough (e.g. the statement that Henry VI died in the Tower 'of pure displeasure and melancholy') but they are also often remarkably frank – the *Arrivall*, for example, makes no bones about the extent of the hostility to Edward on his landing in 1471 throughout the north of England. Both must be regarded as of the highest value for the events they describe.

4. Continental Sources

Foreigners, especially in France and Burgundy, but also as far afield as Italy, were much interested in the English civil wars, partly for the bearing which changes in England's attitude might have on the complicated structure of continental alliances. This interest was not generally supported by much first-hand knowledge of English affairs, and some continental authorities are chiefly of value precisely for the hearsay and rumour which they report, much of it quite ill-founded (e.g. the Milanese ambassador in France's report in March 1461 that Margaret of Anjou had persuaded Henry VI to abdicate and had then poisoned him, or his belief in 1471 that Edward IV had murdered Margaret as well as Henry VI). These ambassadorial reports, of which the most important are in the *Calendar of State Papers, Milan*, vol. I (1385–1618), ed. A. B. Hinds, are also of value for the French court reactions to events in England (especially in 1472–5) and for the occasional report on English affairs by correspondents who had visited or were writing from England.

The memoirs of Philippe de Commynes, as an early example of 'Machiavellian history', have an importance far greater than their bearing on contemporary English history, and have been the subject of many translations and commentaries. Commynes is unusual amongst contemporary writers in that he had personal acquaintance with high politics, and took part as a principal in many of the dealings he describes, especially the negotiations leading to the Treaty of Picquigny of 1475, for which he is an indispensable source. But his prejudiced view of Edward IV's character and ability has helped to distort historians' estimates of the king, and largely contributed to the decline of Edward's reputation in the seventeenth century and later (see Lander, 'Edward IV: The Modern Legend; and a Revision', and above, Conclusion). His reliability for particular statements has been considered in the footnotes, but it is worth noticing that his general historical reputation has recently been under severe attack from several quarters, notably in the works of Bittmann and Dufournet (for which see the useful short introduction to the translation of the *Mémoires*, for the reign of Louis XI, by Michael Jones, Penguin Classics (1972), and the less reliable introduction to the edition by S. Kinser and I. Cazeaux, *The Memoirs of Philippe de Commynes*, South Carolina, 1969). These criticisms, concerned with Commynes's explanations of events on the Continent, tend to strengthen suspicions of his reliability on English affairs.

A modern assessment of the historical writings of Jean de Waurin, the most important for our purpose of the Burgundian chroniclers of the time, is sadly overdue. Meanwhile, it is hard to assess his authority, especially in view of his confused chronology and tendency to elaborate his narrative by fictitious speeches put in the mouths of his characters. However, Sir Charles Oman's judgement that 'his domestic English annals are confused and often worthless' (*Political History of England*, 504–5), is too harsh. He was a man of affairs; he visited England in 1467, and in 1469 waited upon the earl of Warwick in the hope of obtaining material for his history; and his account of 1461–71 was written between 1465 and his death in 1474. Some of the information he acquired about England is unique to him, and occasionally I have ventured to depend upon him (for example, in relation to 1460 and 1467).

The valuable account of the revolution of 1483, written by an Italian visitor to England, Dominic Mancini, before the end of the year, has been the subject of a scholarly assessment in the edition by C. A. J. Armstrong, *The Usurpation of Richard III* (2nd and revised edn, 1969). Mancini's account is of particular interest for the importance it attaches to the influence of the Woodvilles in Edward's later years: even if exaggerated on some points, it may reflect what contemporaries believed. It also tends to substantiate Sir Thomas More's account on many points of detail (*op. cit.*, xx).

5. The Early Tudors: Polydore Vergil and Sir Thomas More

So much has been written about these two famous authors that little need be said. Polydore's *English History* has been thoroughly assessed by Denys Hay in his *Polydore Vergil: Renaissance Historian and Man of Letters* (1952) and again in *The Anglica Historia of Polydore Vergil, 1485–1537* (Camden Series, lxxiv, 1950), and More's *Richard III* in the splendid edition by R. S. Sylvester (Yale edn of the *Complete Works of Sir Thomas More*, II, 1963), where full bibliographies will be found. In spite of their differing qualities of bias and historical intent, the value of both men's works lies in their access to the oral information of contemporaries who had taken part in the politics of Edward's later years. Polydore's account of the reign, however, becomes really valuable only for the later years, when he could draw on the knowledge of men like Morton and Bray, and I find it hard to accept *in toto* Professor Hay's claim that 'from at latest 1460 to 1537 the *Anglica Historia* offers a narrative of the highest value'. So far as the decade 1461–71 is concerned, Kingsford seems to be nearer the truth with his comment that 'its value lies not in its description of events, but in its presentment of opinion fifty years later' (*op. cit.*, 254 ff.). Any assessment of the very flattering view of Edward IV presented by More must take into account the remarkable influence on More of his classical models, emphasized by Professor Sylvester (*op. cit.*, xciii–v), especially the contrast made by Tacitus between the 'good' Augustus and the 'bad' Tiberius, which is reproduced, and in part paraphrased, by More in his juxtaposition of Edward and Richard of Gloucester. Even the innocence of the Woodvilles in More's narrative owes much to Tacitus's picture of Augustus's sorrowing widow and her children.

Appendix II

EDWARD IV's GOVERNOR

The statement that Richard Croft, of Croft, in Herefordshire, was 'governor' to Edward and his next brother, Edmund, was first made by Sir Harris Nicolas in an article on the Croft family in *Retrospective Review*, 2nd ser., i (1827), 472–3, and was repeated by Scofield, I, 11, Ramsay, *Lancaster and York*, II, 268, and elsewhere. Nicolas admitted it to be an inference from the complaint made by the young lords, in a letter written to their father, probably in 1454 (Ellis, *Original Letters*, 1st ser., I, 9–10), against the 'odious rule and demeaning' of Richard Croft and his brother. Nicolas suggested that this was corroborated by a further statement in B.M., Cotton Charters XIV, 3, that Croft's wife, Eleanor, was 'Lady governesse unto the yonge princes at Ludlow'. This comes from a genealogical roll of the descent of Sir Thomas Cornewall, Knt. Baron of Burford, made *c.* 1600, and its reliability on a point like this seems doubtful, representing no more than hearsay or family tradition at best: it is perhaps worth noting that it wrongly describes Croft as controller of the household to Edward IV (instead of Henry VII). Croft was an extremely obscure person to act as governor to the sons of a royal duke; he does not appear on the Herefordshire commissions of the peace until 1474, which suggests that his landed estate was small, and in 1459, when pardoned, he is described merely as 'gentilman' (*CPR, 1452–61*, 539). Moreover, there is a difficulty about his age. He died in 1509 and unless he was unusually long-lived, was probably little older than Edward himself (who would have been sixty-seven at that date). It seems much more likely that Croft and his brother (and the boys' complaint was directed against *both* of them) were the sons of minor gentry of the neighbourhood who were being brought up in a great household, a practice very common at the time, and were just sufficiently older than Edward and Edmund to bully the pair. For Croft's later successful career under the Yorkists and Henry VII, see Wedgwood, *Hist. Parl.*, *Biog.*, 237. I am indebted to Mr G. R. C. Davis for help on this point.

EDWARD IV'S GRANTS TO WARWICK

On 7 May 1461, whilst the king was staying at Warwick's castle of Middleham in North Yorkshire, the earl was appointed Constable of Dover and Warden of the Cinque Ports (with a fee of £300 a year to support the office), steward of the manor or lordship of Feckenham, Worcestershire, and master forester of the king's forest there, master of the king's mews and falcons, and great chamberlain of England for life, and was given the custody of all the lands of his uncle, George Nevill, Lord Latimer (*CPR, 1461–7*, 45, 71). At the same time he was confirmed in his tenure of the wardship of most of the Stafford lordships in South Wales and the Marches, and of the Talbot lordships of Goodrich and Archenfield, Co. Hereford, which had already been granted to him on 4 November 1460 (*CFR, 1452–61*, 287; *1461–71*, 37, 40): but (as noticed above, p. 71) these were soon granted instead to William, Lord Herbert. Two days previously (5 May 1461) he had been given for twenty years all the offices, farms and custodies held by his father, Richard Nevill, earl of Salisbury (*CPR, 1461–7*, 95). On 31 July 1461 he was appointed warden of the East and West Marches towards Scotland during pleasure, and on 5 April 1462 this was converted into an appointment for twenty years (*Rot. Scotiae*, II, 402; Storey, 'Wardens of the Marches', 614–615). Though replaced on the East March by his brother, John Nevill, on 1 June 1463, he held the West March until 1470, in spite of the Act of Resumption of 1467. Meanwhile, he had been confirmed in his post as Captain of Calais (*CPR, 1461–7, passim*), was acting as Admiral of England by 14 December 1461 (*ibid.*, 89), and was appointed to act as Steward of England 'at the trial of Henry VI' and his associates, 3 December 1461 (*ibid.*, 63, 89). Having been appointed jointly with his father as Chief Steward of the Duchy of Lancaster, both north and south parts, on 1 December 1460, he was reappointed alone on 15 December 1461, and at the same time was made chief steward of the Duchy honours in Lancashire and Cheshire, and steward and constable of the honours of Pontefract, Knaresborough, Pickering and Tutbury, and constable and master forester of Needwood and Duffield. He had held the Tutbury offices from 4 November 1460, and was also from 18 November 1460 steward of the honour of Leicester and constable and master forester of Castle Donington, but was replaced in these latter offices by Hastings on 4 July 1461 (Somerville, *History of the Duchy of Lancaster*, I, 421–2, 429, 493, 514, 524, 534, 540, 564).

On 27 May 1462 he received a revised form of a grant of 27 April, of Topcliffe and a series of Percy lordships and manors in the North and West

Ridings of Yorkshire (*CPR, 1461–7*, 186, 189: of these Topcliffe alone was worth £90 a year in 1478–9; J. M. W. Bean, *The Estates of the Percy Family, 1416–1537*, 47). Together with these Percy lands he was given also in fee simple, the castles, manors and lordships of Pendragon, Brough, Brougham and Appleby, and all other Clifford lands in Westmorland, the manor and lordship of Newport Pagnell, Buckinghamshire, forfeited from the earl of Wiltshire, that of Strensham, Worcestershire, and three royal manors in Cos. Northampton and Warwick. In June 1463 he was allowed to convey lands worth £1,000 a year to a group of friends and councillors in order to execute his will, even though the reversions of the properties might belong to the king if he died without issue (*CPR, 1461–7*, 270), and on 12 December 1463 was given custody of the temporalities of the see of Carlisle during vacancy, which he held until June 1464 (*ibid.*, 292). On 11 April 1465 his fee simple grant of the lands given him in May 1462 was converted to one of tail male, and in addition he was given the important Percy lordship and castle of Cockermouth in Cumberland, and a third part of the lordship of Egremont, together with the office of hereditary sheriff of Westmorland, paying nothing to the king save a rent of £100 from Cockermouth so long as Richard Salkeld lived (*ibid.*, 434–5). On 21 November 1466 he was made justice and given custody of the king's forests north of Trent, with a fee of 100 marks a year, and on 13 November 1467 was granted the wardship of all the lands of John, late Lord Lovell – one of the wealthiest of peers below the rank of earl – and the marriage of the heir, Francis (*ibid.*, 540; *1467–77*, 51). He was appointed constable and steward of the Duchy lordship of Kenilworth on 14 February 1468 (Somerville, *op. cit.*, 560). With his brother, John Nevill, and Sir John Howard, he was given custody for forty years of all the king's mines, of gold, silver and lead north of Trent, taking most of the profits thereof (*ibid.*, 132). Finally, on 22 February 1469, the earl was granted in tail three further Percy manors in Cumberland (Papcaster, Aspatrick and Withall) and the manors of Solihull and Sheldon, Warwickshire, the reversion of three more manors in Cumberland, and a release from the charge of £100 a year he had been paying from the lordship of Cockermouth (*ibid.*, 137).

Under the Act of Resumption of 1467, all royal grants to Warwick were exempted, save those made to him for a term of years (*RP*, V, 579). From the list above, it will be clear that only the offices, etc., held by his father, and granted for forty years to the son, came under this heading, and the earl's losses could not have been substantial. They were probably more than made good by the grants of 1468–9. John Warkworth (*Chronicle*, 25–6) had every justification for his statement about Archbishop George Nevill, who was also very wealthy, that 'he and his brothers had the rule of this land, and had gathered great riches many years . . .'.

Appendix IV

THE NORTHERN
REBELLIONS OF 1469:
A NOTE ON SOURCES
AND CHRONOLOGY

The fullest and most elaborate account of these risings is by Polydore Vergil (*English History*, 121–3): it is also the most obviously contrived, and of very late date to be reliable for events of this character. It mentions only *one* rebellion, that in Holderness under a leader named 'Robert Hulderne' (Robin of Holderness?) and 'Robin of Redesdale' is nowhere mentioned. According to Polydore, after the leader had been executed by John Nevill, his followers moved on south, and this was the force which was to defeat Herbert (Stafford is not mentioned) at Edgecote Field. No indication of date is given. John Warkworth's *Chronicle*, the only contemporary source with North-Country associations, describes the rising of Robin of Redesdale, but on the other hand makes no reference to the rebellion of Robin of Holderness. This latter, in fact, is mentioned otherwise only in the contemporary 'Brief Latin Chronicle' (*Three Fifteenth Century Chronicles*, 183), where its purpose is described as being different from that alleged by Polydore (see above, chapter 7, p. 127,). The 'Brief Latin Chronicle', however, raises difficulties of dating by placing the Holderness rebellion *after* Redesdale's, which is said to have broken out 'about Trinity Sunday' (i.e., 28 May). Of the London chronicles, 'Vitellius A. XVI' (*Chronicles of London*, 180) barely mentions a rebellion, and the account in *GC*, 208–9, is uncertain and confused: it dates Redesdale's rising merely as 'in the summer time' and believes that the rebels (not Warwick) had the Woodvilles put to death. The chronicle known as 'Hearne's Fragment' (*Chronicles of the White Rose*, 24–5) adds some details, but is at variance with other accounts on many points, and is itself confused.

These difficulties are reflected in the confusion of modern writers. Oman, *Warwick the Kingmaker*, 183–4, believed that there was only one rising, led until his death at the hands of John Nevill by Robert Huldyard, and then by a new leader, Sir John Conyers; both these captains called themselves Robin of Redesdale. Ramsay, *Lancaster and York*, II, 338–9, speaks of two risings (Robin of Holderness followed by Robin of Redesdale), but explicitly has to reject the date (28 May) given by the 'Brief Latin Chronicle' as being much too early. To overcome these difficulties, Scofield (I, 488–90) proposed *three* risings: (a) an abortive rising under Redesdale; (b) Robin of Holderness; and (c) the revived rebellion of Redesdale. This version has been followed above, but it must be emphasized how very doubtful is the evidence, especially for the first rising of Redesdale.

Appendix V

WARWICK, CLARENCE, AND THE LINCOLNSHIRE REBELLION OF 1470

The notion that Warwick and Clarence were not implicated in the Lincolnshire rebellion (see above, chapter 7, p. 138), and that the king merely made use of it to brand them as traitors, was strongly argued by Sir Charles Oman in his *Warwick the Kingmaker*, 196–8. He claimed that the official narratives, more especially the 'Confession of Sir Robert Welles' (made in an attempt to save his life and therefore untrustworthy), were highly suspect. Why, he asked, should they have gone to a county where they had no influence, and used men like Welles with strong Lancastrian backgrounds? Why did they not call out their retainers in the midlands and South Wales, or raise Kent and Yorkshire? Why, having managed a successful rising in the previous year, did they display such insane bad management as the unsuccessful Lincolnshire rising displayed? For Oman, it was in keeping with Edward's deceitful character that, finding himself at the head of a successful and loyal army, he took the opportunity to fall on Warwick and Clarence, and revenge himself for the deaths of Pembroke and Rivers in 1469.

These arguments deserve respect, but must on balance be rejected. It seems, on the whole, unlikely that Warwick and Clarence initially stirred up the Lincolnshire rising, but they were clearly prepared to profit from it. Once the rebellion was under way, a connection between the duke and earl and the rebels is strongly suggested by the rebels' movements, aiming at a junction with them at Leicester. Both Clarence and Warwick were now somewhat discredited, and (as argued above) could now scarcely pose as champions of popular discontent with much conviction, and the rebellion they stirred up in Richmondshire in 1470 found little support. We also have the explicit statement of John Warkworth (*Chronicle*, 8), admittedly in a confused and contradictory account, that they (Warwick and Clarence) 'caused all this, like as they did Robin of Redesdale to rise afore that at Banbury Field'. If they were innocent, why did they ignore the king's repeated messages to join him in suppressing the rebellion? Finally, they can hardly have been innocent of a share in the risings in Richmondshire and the West Country (above, chapter 7, pp. 141–3 and notes). Nor does Oman's very hostile character-assessment of Edward seem to fit the facts. The king had gone to considerable lengths to avoid trouble and to show that he was prepared to overlook past offences. It seems most unlikely that a king who was prepared to trust them with commissions to array troops would not have accepted their declarations of innocence a few days later. It was their own behaviour which convinced him that they were not guiltless. Even then he waited until 23 March before making any official statement that they were rebels and traitors (in his letters to Ireland and Calais, above, p. 144). Clearly, the official versions of the rebellion must be regarded as possessing a substantial accuracy.

To those writers noted above (chapter 7, p. 138, n. 2) who regard the rebellion as being inspired initially by Lancastrian sentiments must be added Calmette and Perinelle, *Louis XI et l'Angleterre*, 109 ('les partisans de la Rose rouge conduits par Richard Welles'). But the only *direct contemporary* evidence that it was Lancastrian in character is Warkworth's statement (*Chronicle*, 8) that the rebels under Welles 'cried "King Harry" and refused King Edward', which he then proceeds to reject by the specific statement quoted above that Warwick and Clarence were behind the rising. The most recent discussion (by R. L. Storey, 'Lincolnshire and the Wars of the Roses', *Nottingham Medieval Studies*, xiv (1970), 64–83) suggests that the trouble arose originally from the resentment felt by older-established families in the shire for the rise of the 'Yorkist parvenu', Sir Thomas Burgh. He was Master of the Horse to the king, and had been richly rewarded for his services with land and office in Lincolnshire, as steward of the Duchy of Lancaster honour of Bolingbroke, constable of Lincoln Castle, and beneficiary of the forfeited lands of William Tailboys of Kyme. He had also sat as M.P. for Lincolnshire in the parliament of 1467–8. Morgan, 'The King's Affinity in the Polity of Yorkist England', also notes (p. 20) how Burgh was allowed to build up an ascendancy in Lincolnshire.

SELECT BIBLIOGRAPHY

The bibliography which follows is intended to provide details of printed works and unpublished theses cited in the footnotes to the book, and is in no sense designed to provide an exhaustive book-list. Very comprehensive bibliographies up to 1936 will be found appended to the chapters (XI and XII) by K. B. McFarlane and C. H. Williams in *Cambridge Medieval History*, Volume VIII, and much recent work is cited by A. R. Myers, *English Historical Documents*, IV, *1327–1485* (1969). To facilitate ease of reference from books and articles cited by short titles in the footnotes, primary sources and secondary authorities have been combined in a single alphabetical list.

Abbreviata Cronica, ed. J. J. Smith (Cambridge Antiquarian Soc. Publications, 1840).

Acts of Court of the Mercers' Company, ed. L. Lyell and F. D. Watney (1936).

Acts of Parliament of Scotland, ed. T. Thomson and C. Innes, 12 vols (1844–75).

ANGLO, S., 'Anglo-Burgundian Feats of Arms at Smithfield, June 1467', *Guildhall Miscellany*, ii, no. 7 (1965).

——, 'The *British History* in Early Tudor Propaganda', *Bulletin of the John Rylands Library*, xliv (1961–2).

——, *The Great Tournament Roll of Westminster* (1968).

——, *Spectacle, Pageantry and Early Tudor Policy* (Oxford, 1969).

'Annales rerum anglicarum', in Vol. II, pt ii, of *Letters and Papers Illustrative of the Wars of the English in France*, ed. J. Stevenson, 2 vols (Rolls Series, 1864).

ANSTEY, H., *Epistolae Academicae Oxon.* (Oxford Historical Society Publications, xxxv, xxxvi) (Oxford, 1898).

Antient Songs, ed. J. Ritson (1790).

ARMSTRONG, C. A. J., 'The Burgundian Netherlands, 1477–1521', in *The New Cambridge Modern History*, I, ed. G. R. Potter (1957).

——, 'Had the Burgundian Government a Policy for the Nobility?', in *Britain and the Netherlands in Europe and Asia*, II, ed. J. S. Bromley and E. H. Kossmann (1964).

——, 'The Inauguration Ceremonies of the Yorkist Kings, and their Title to the Throne', *TRHS*, 4th series, xxx (1948).

——, 'The Piety of Cecily, Duchess of York: A Study in Later Medieval Culture', in *For Hilaire Belloc*, ed. D. Woodruff (1942).

——, 'Politics and the Battle of St Albans, 1455', *BIHR*, xxxiii (1960).

——, 'Some Examples of the Distribution and Speed of News in England at the Time of the Wars of the Roses', in *Studies in Medieval History Presented to F. M. Powicke*, ed. R. W. Hunt, W. A. Pantin and R. W. Southern (Oxford, 1948).

AVRUTICK, J. B., 'Commissions of Oyer and Terminer in Fifteenth-Century England' (unpublished M.Litt. thesis, London, 1967).

BALDWIN, J. F., *The King's Council in England during the Middle Ages* (Oxford, 1913).

BARKER, N. and BIRLEY, R., 'Jane Shore', *Etoniana*, nos 125, 126 (June, December 1972).

BARNARD, F. P., *Edward IV's French Expedition of 1475: the Leaders and their Badges* (1925).

BARTIER, J., *Charles le Téméraire* (Brussels, 1944, 1972).

BATESON, E., *History of Northumberland*, I (1893).

BEAN, J. M. W., *The Decline of English Feudalism, 1215–1540* (Manchester, 1968).

——, *The Estates of the Percy Family, 1416–1537* (1958).

BEAUCOURT, G. DU FRESNE DE, *Histoire de Charles VII*, 6 vols (Paris, 1881–1891).

BELLAMY, J. G., *Crime and Public Order in England during the Later Middle Ages* (1973).

——, 'Justice under the Yorkist Kings', *American Journal of Legal History*, ix (1965).

BELTZ, G. F., *Memorials of the Most Noble Order of the Garter* (1841).

BENNETT, H. S., *Chaucer and the Fifteenth Century* (Oxford, 1947).

BENSON, R. and HATCHER, H., *Old and New Sarum*, 2 vols (1843).

BITTMAN, K., 'La Campagne Lancastrienne de 1463: un document italien', *Revue Belge de Philologie et d'Histoire*, xxvi (1948).

BLADES, W., *The Life and Typography of William Caxton*, 2 vols (1861).

BLATCHER, M., 'Distress Infinite and the Contumacious Sheriff', *BIHR*, xiii (1935–6).

BLUNT, C. E. and WHITTON, C. A., 'The Coinages of Edward IV and Henry VI Restored', *British Numismatic Journal*, xxv (1945–8).

BLYTH, J. D., 'The Battle of Tewkesbury', *Transactions of the Bristol and Gloucestershire Archaeological Society*, lxx (1961).

BOINET, A., 'Un Bibliophile de XVIème Siècle, Le Grand Bâtard de Bourgogne', *Bibliothèque de l'École des Chartes*, lxvii (1906).

'Brevis Cronica', in J. Pinkerton, *The History of Scotland*, 2 vols (1797).

'Brief Latin Chronicle', in *Three Fifteenth-Century Chronicles*, ed. J. Gairdner (Camden Society, 1880).

BROOKS, F. W., *The Council of the North* (Historical Association Pamphlet G. 25, revised edn, 1966).

BROWN, A. L., 'The Authorization of Letters under the Great Seal', *BIHR*, xxxvii (1964).

——, 'The King's Councillors in Fifteenth-Century England', *TRHS*, 5th series, xix (1969).

——, and WEBSTER, B., 'The Movements of the Earl of Warwick in the Summer of 1464 – A Correction', *EHR*, lxxxi (1966).

BROWN, P. HUME, *History of Scotland*, 3 vols (Cambridge, 1902–9).

BROWN, R. A., COLVIN, H. M. and TAYLOR, A. J., *The History of the King's Works: The Middle Ages* (1963).

BURNE, A. H., *Battlefields of England* (1950).

——, *More Battlefields of England* (1952).

Calendar of Charter Rolls, VI (*1427–1516*) (1927.)

Calendar of Close Rolls: Henry VI, VI, *1454–61* (1967); *Edward IV*, I–II, *1461–1468*, *1468–76* (1949, 1953); *Edward IV–Edward V–Richard III*, *1476–85* (1954).

Calendar of Documents Relating to Scotland, ed. J. Bain, IV, *1357–1509* (1888).

Calendar of Entries in the Papal Registers relating to Great Britain and Ireland, XIII, pts i and ii, ed. J. A. Twemlow (1956, 1957).

Calendar of Fine Rolls, XIX, *Henry VI*, *1452–61* (1940); XX, *Edward IV*, *1461–71* (1949); XXI, *Edward IV–Richard III*, *1471–85* (1961).

Calendar of Patent Rolls, *Henry VI*, VI, *1452–61* (1911); *Edward IV*, I–II, *1461–7*, *1467–77* (1897, 1899); *Edward IV–Edward V–Richard III*, *1476–85* (1901).

Calendar of State Papers and Manuscripts existing in the Archives and Collections of Milan, I, *1385–1618*, ed. A. B. Hinds (1913).

Calendar of State Papers and Manuscripts relating to English Affairs, existing in the Archives and Collections of Venice (etc.), I, *1202–1509*, ed. R. Brown (1864).

Calendarium Inquisitionum Post Mortem sive Excaetarum, ed. J. Cayley and J. Bayley (Record Commission), IV (1828).

CALMETTE, J., 'Le Mariage de Charles le Téméraire et de Marguerite d'York', *Annales de Bourgogne*, I (1929).

——, and DEPREZ, E., *Les Premières Grandes Puissances* (*Histoire Générale*, ed. G. Glotz, *Histoire du Moyen Age*, VII, pt 2) (Paris, 1937).

——, and PERINELLE, G., *Louis XI et l'Angleterre* (Paris, 1930).

CAMPBELL, J., 'England, Scotland and the Hundred Years' War in the Fourteenth Century', in *Europe in the Late Middle Ages*, ed. J. Hale, J. R. L. Highfield and B. Smalley (1965).

CARTE, T., *Catalogue des rolles gascons, normands, et françoises*, 2 vols (1743).

CARUS-WILSON, E. M., *The Expansion of Exeter at the Close of the Middle Ages* (Exeter, 1961).

——, 'The Iceland Trade', in *Studies in English Trade in the Fifteenth Century*, ed. E. E. Power and M. M. Postan (1933).

——, *Medieval Merchant Venturers* (2nd edn, 1967).

——, and COLEMAN, O., *England's Export Trade, 1275–1547* (Oxford, 1963).

CHANDLER, R., *The Life of William Waynflete, Bishop of Winchester* (1811).

Charters Relating to the City of Edinburgh (Scottish Burgh Record Society Publications), 1871.

CHASTELLAIN, G., *Œuvres*, ed. Kervyn de Lettenhove, 8 vols (Académie Royale de Belgique, Brussels, 1863–6).

CHOPE, R. P., 'The Last of the Dynhams', *Transactions of the Devonshire Association*, I (1918).

CHRIMES, S. B., *English Constitutional Ideas in the Fifteenth Century* (Cambridge, 1936).

CHRIMES, S. B., *Lancastrians, Yorkists, and Henry VII* (1967).
——, *Henry VII* (1972).
——, *An Introduction to the Administrative History of Medieval England* (Oxford, 1925).
——, 'The Reign of Henry VII', in *Fifteenth-Century England, 1399–1509*, ed. S. B. Chrimes, C. D. Ross and R. A. Griffiths (Manchester, 1972).
The Chronicle of John Harding, ed. H. Ellis (1812).
The Chronicle of John Stone, ed. W. G. Searle (Cambridge Antiquarian Society Publications, xxxiv, 1902).
Chronicles of London, ed. C. L. Kingsford (1905).
Chronicle of the Rebellion in Lincolnshire, 1470, ed. J. G. Nichols (Camden Society, 1847).
Chronicles of the White Rose of York, ed. J. A. Giles (1845).
CHURCHILL, W. S., *History of the English-Speaking Peoples*, I (1956).
CLOUGH, C. H., 'The Relations between the English and Urbino Courts, 1471–1508', *Studies in the Renaissance*, xiv (1967).
COLES, G. M., 'The Lordship of Middleham, especially in Yorkist and Early Tudor Times' (unpublished M.A. thesis, Liverpool, 1961).
A Collection of Ordinances and Regulations for the Government of the Royal Household, Society of Antiquaries (1790).
COMMYNES, PHILIPPE DE, *Mémoires*, ed. J. Calmette and G. Durville, 3 vols (Classiques de l'Histoire de France au Moyen Age, Paris, 1924–5).
——, ed. E. Dupont, 3 vols (Société de l'Histoire de France, Paris, 1840–47).
——, ed. B. de Mandrot, 2 vols (Paris, 1901–3).
——, *The Memoirs for the Reign of Louis XI, 1461–1483*, translated by Michael Jones (1972).
——, *The Memoirs*, ed. and translated by S. Kinser and I. Cazeaux, I (South Carolina, 1969).
——, *Memoirs*, ed. and translated by A. R. Scobie, 2 vols (1856).
Complete Peerage of England, Scotland, Ireland and the United Kingdom, ed. G. E. Cokayne: new edn by Vicary Gibbs, H. A. Doubleday and others, 13 vols (1910–59).
'Confession of Sir Robert Welles', in *Excerpta Historica*, ed. S. Bentley, pp. 282–4.
CONNELL-SMITH, G., *The Forerunners of Drake* (1954).
CONSTABLE, R., *Prerogativa Regis*, ed. S. E. Thorne (1949).
COOPER, J. P., 'The Social Distribution of Land and Men in England, 1436–1700', *EconHR*, 2nd series, xx (1967).
Coventry Leet Book, ed. M. D. Harris, 4 pts (Early English Text Society, Original Series, 1907–13).
CROTCH, W. J. B., *The Prologues and Epilogues of William Caxton* (Early English Text Society, 1928).
'Croyland Chronicle': 'Historiae Croylandensis Continuatio', in *Rerum Anglicarum Scriptores Veterum*, ed. W. Fulman (Oxford, 1684), pp. 449–592.
CURTIS, E., *History of Medieval Ireland from 1110 to 1513* (1923).
——, 'Richard, Duke of York as Viceroy of Ireland, 1447–1460', *Journal of the Royal Society of Antiquaries of Ireland*, lxii (1932).

DEVON, F., ed., *Issues of the Exchequer (10 Henry III to 39 Henry VI)* (1837).

DU BOULAY, F. R. H., 'The Fifteenth Century', in *The English Church and the Papacy in the Middle Ages*, ed. C. H. Lawrence (1965).

DUGDALE, W., *The Baronage of England*, 2 vols (1675).

DUNHAM, W. H., *The Fane Fragment of the 1461 Lords' Journal* (Yale, 1935).

——, *Lord Hastings' Indentured Retainers, 1461–1483* (Transactions of the Connecticut Academy of Arts and Sciences, xxxix) (New Haven, Connecticut, 1955).

DUNLOP, A., *The Life and Times of James Kennedy, Bishop of St Andrews* (1950).

EDWARDS, J. G., 'The Second Continuation of the Crowland Chronicle: Was it written in ten days?', *BIHR*, xxxix (1966).

ELTON, G. R., *England under the Tudors* (1962).

——, *England 1200–1640* (Sources of History Series) (1969).

EMDEN, A. B., *A Biographical Register of the University of Oxford to A.D. 1500*, 3 vols (1957–9).

——, *A Biographical Register of the University of Cambridge to A.D. 1500* (1963).

English Chronicle of the Reigns of Richard II, Henry IV, Henry V, and Henry VI written before the year 1470, ed. J. S. Davies (Camden Society, 1856).

English Historical Documents, IV: 1327–1485, ed. A. R. Myers (1969).

English Historical Documents, V: 1485–1558, ed. C. H. Williams (1967).

EVANS, H. T., *Wales in the Wars of the Roses* (Cambridge, 1915).

Excerpta Historica, ed. S. Bentley (1831).

FABYAN, R., *The New Chronicles of England and of France*, ed. H. Ellis (1811).

FAHY, C., 'The Marriage of Edward IV and Elizabeth Woodville: a new Italian Source', *EHR*, lxxvi (1961).

FEAVERYEAR, A., *The Pound Sterling: A History of English Money* (Oxford, 2nd edn, 1963).

Fifteenth-Century England, 1399–1509: Studies in Politics and Society, ed. S. B. Chrimes, C. D. Ross and R. A. Griffiths (Manchester, 1972).

FLENLEY, R., 'London and Foreign Merchants in the Reign of Henry VI', *EHR*, xxv (1910).

FONBLANQUE, E. B. DE, *Annals of the House of Percy*, 2 vols (1887).

FORTESCUE, J., *The Governance of England*, ed. C. Plummer (Oxford, 1885).

FOSS, E., *The Judges of England, 1066–1870*, 9 vols (1848–1864).

GAIRDNER, J., *History of the Life and Reign of Richard III* (Cambridge, 1898).

GOODER, A., *The Parliamentary Representation of the County of York, 1283–1832*, 2 vols, Yorkshire Archaeological Society Record Series (1935–8).

Grants from the Crown during the Reign of Edward V, ed. J. G. Nichols (Camden Society, 1854).

GRAY, H. L., 'English Foreign Trade from 1446 to 1482', in *Studies in English Trade in the Fifteenth Century*, ed. E. Power and M. M. Postan (1938).

——, 'The First Benevolence', in *Facts and Factors in Economic History Pre-*

sented to J. F. Gay, ed. A. E. Cole, A. L. Dunham and N. S. B. Gras (Cambridge, Mass., 1932).

GRAY, H. L., *The Influence of the Commons on Early Legislation* (Cambridge, Mass., 1932.)

The Great Chronicle of London, ed. A. H. Thomas and I. D. Thornley (1938).

The Great Red Book of Bristol, ed. E. W. W. Veale, 5 vols (Bristol Record Society Publications, Bristol, 1931–53).

GREEN, J. R., *Short History of the English People* (1876).

——, *History of the English People*, 4 vols (1878–80).

'Gregory's Chronicle', in *The Historical Collections of a Citizen of London*, ed. J. Gairdner (Camden Society, 1876).

GRIFFITHS, R. A., 'Local Rivalries and National Politics: The Percies, the Nevilles and the Duke of Exeter, 1452–1455', *Speculum*, xliii (1968).

——, *The Principality of Wales in the Later Middle Ages: The Structure and Personnel of Government: I, South Wales, 1277–1536* (Cardiff, 1972).

——, 'Royal Government in the Southern Counties of the Principality of Wales' (unpublished Ph.D. thesis, Bristol, 1962).

——, 'Wales and the Marches', in *Fifteenth-Century England, 1399–1509*, ed. S. B. Chrimes, C. D. Ross and R. A. Griffiths (Manchester, 1972).

GUISEPPI, M. S., 'Alien Merchants in England in the Fifteenth Century', *TRHS*, new series, ix (1895).

Gwaith Lewis Glyn Cothi, ed. E. D. Jones (1953).

HALL, EDWARD, *Chronicle*, ed. H. Ellis (1809).

HALLAM, H., *A View of the State of Europe during the Middle Ages*, 3 vols (12th edn, 1860).

Handbook of British Chronology, ed. F. M. Powicke and E. B. Fryde (2nd edn, 1961).

Hanserecesse von 1431–1476, ed. G. von der Ropp, 7 vols (Leipzig, 1876–92).

HARRISON, C. J., 'The Petition of Edmund Dudley', *EHR*, lxxxvii (1972).

HARRISON, F. L., *Music in Medieval Britain* (1958).

HARRISS, G. L. (with P. WILLIAMS), contributions to 'A Revolution in Tudor History?', *Past and Present*, nos 23 (1963), 31 (1965).

——, 'The Struggle for Calais: An Aspect of the Rivalry of Lancaster and York', *EHR*, lxxv (1960).

HARVEY, J. H., *Gothic England: A Survey of National Culture, 1300–1550* (1947).

HASTINGS, M., *The Court of Common Pleas in Fifteenth-Century England* (1947).

HAWARD, W. I., 'Economic Aspects of the Wars of the Roses in East Anglia', *EHR*, xli (1926).

——, 'The Financial Transactions between the Lancastrian Government and the Merchants of the Staple', in *Studies in English Trade in the Fifteenth Century*, ed. E. Power and M. M. Postan (1933).

——, 'Gilbert Debenham: A Medieval Rascal in Real Life', *History*, xiii (1929).

HAY, D., 'History and Historians in France and England during the Fifteenth Century', *BIHR*, xxxv (1962).

HAY, D., *Polydore Vergil: Renaissance Historian and Man of Letters* (Oxford, 1952).
HICKS, M. A., 'The Career of Henry Percy, 4th Earl of Northumberland, with special reference to his retinue' (unpublished M.A. dissertation, Southampton, 1971).
Historical Manuscripts Commission, *12th Report, Rutland Manuscripts*, I (1888).
——, *11th Report, App. VII.*
——, *15, App. Part X, Shrewsbury Corporation Manuscripts.*
——, *54, Beverley Corporation Manuscripts* (1900).
——, *55, Various Collections, IV, Salisbury Corporation Manuscripts* (1907).
——, *78, Manuscripts of R. R. Hastings*, I (1928).
Historie of the Arrivall of King Edward IV, ed. J. Bruce (Camden Society, 1838).
HOPE, W. H. ST JOHN, *Architectural History of Windsor Castle*, 3 vols (1913).
HOUGHTON, K., 'Theory and Practice in Borough Elections to Parliament during the Later Fifteenth Century', *BIHR*, xxxix (1966).
Household Books of John, Duke of Norfolk and Thomas, Earl of Surrey, 1481–1490, ed. J. P. Collier (Roxburghe Club, 1844).

Illustrations of Ancient State and Chivalry, ed. W. H. Black (Roxburghe Club, 1840).
IVES, E. W., 'Andrew Dymmock and the Papers of Anthony, Earl Rivers, 1482–3', *BIHR*, xli (1968).
——, 'The Common Lawyers in Pre-Reformation England', *TRHS*, 5th series, xviii (1968).

JACK, R. I., 'A Quincentenary: The Battle of Northampton, July 10th, 1460', *Northamptonshire Past and Present*, iii, no. 1 (1960).
JACOB, E. F., *The Fifteenth Century* (Oxford, 1961).
JALLAND, P., 'The Influence of the Aristocracy on Shire Elections in the North of England, 1450–1470', *Speculum*, xlvii (1972).
JAMES, M. E., *A Tudor Magnate and the Tudor State: Henry, fifth Earl of Northumberland*, Borthwick Papers, no. 30 (York, 1966).
'John Benet's Chronicle for the Years 1400 to 1462', ed. G. L. and M. A. Harriss (Royal Historical Society, Camden Miscellany, xxiv, 1972).
JOLLIFFE, J. E. A., *Constitutional History of Medieval England* (1937).

KEKEWICH, M., 'Edward IV, William Caxton and Literary Patronage in Yorkist England', *Modern Language Review* (1971).
KENDALL, P. M., *Louis XI* (1971).
——, *Richard the Third* (1955).
——, *Warwick the Kingmaker* (1957).
KERLING, N. J. M., *The Commercial Relations of Holland and Zeeland with England from the late thirteenth century to the close of the Middle Ages* (Leiden, 1954).
KINGSFORD, C. L., *Chronicles of London* (1905).
——, *English Historical Literature in the Fifteenth Century* (Oxford, 1913).
——, *Prejudice and Promise in Fifteenth-Century England* (Oxford, 1925).
KIRBY, J. L., *Henry IV of England* (1970).

KNECHT, R. J., 'The Episcopate and the Wars of the Roses', *University of Birmingham Historical Journal*, vi (1957).

LA MARCHE, OLIVIER DE, *Mémoires*, ed. H. Beaune and J. d'Arbaumont, 4 vols (Société de l'Histoire de France, Paris, 1883–8).
LANDER, J. R., 'The Administration of the Yorkist Kings' (unpublished M.Litt. thesis, Cambridge, 1949).
——, 'Attainder and Forfeiture, 1453–1509', *Historical Journal*, iv (1961).
——, 'Bonds, Coercion and Fear: Henry VII and the Peerage', in *Florilegium Historiale: Essays Presented to Wallace K. Ferguson* (Toronto, 1971).
——, *Conflict and Stability in Fifteenth Century England* (1969).
——, 'Edward IV: The Modern Legend: and a Revision', *History*, xli(1956).
——, 'Council, Administration and Councillors, 1461–1485', *BIHR*, xxxii (1959).
——, 'Henry VI and the Duke of York's Second Protectorate, 1455 to 1456', *Bulletin of the John Rylands Library*, xliii (1960).
——, 'The Hundred Years War and Edward IV's 1475 Campaign in France', in *Tudor Men and Institutions: Studies in English Law and Government*, ed. A. J. Slavin (Baton Rouge, Louisiana, 1972).
——, 'Marriage and Politics in the Fifteenth Century: The Nevills and the Wydevills', *BIHR*, xxxvi (1963).
——, 'The Treason and Death of the Duke of Clarence: A Re-interpretation', *Canadian Journal of History*, ii (1967).
——, *The Wars of the Roses* (1965).
——, 'The Yorkist Council and Administration', *EHR*, lxxxiii (1958).
LEADAM, I. S. and BALDWIN, F. J., *Select Cases Before the King's Council, 1243–1482* (Selden Society, xxxv, 1918).
LELAND, J., *Itinerary*, ed. Lucy Toulmin Smith, 5 vols (1906–8).
LESLEY, J., *History of Scotland from the death of King James I in the year 1436 to the year 1561* (Bannatyne Club, 1830).
Letters and Papers Illustrative of the Reigns of Richard III and Henry VII, ed. J. Gairdner, 2 vols (Rolls Series, 1861–3).
Letters and Papers Illustrative of the Wars of the English in France during the Reign of Henry VI, ed. J. Stevenson, 2 vols (Rolls Series, 1861–4).
Lettres de Louis XI, Roi de France, ed. J. Vaesen and E. Charavay, 12 vols (Paris, 1883–1909).
LEVINE, MORTIMER, *Tudor Dynastic Problems, 1460–1571* (1973).
LEWIS, P. S., *Later Medieval France: The Polity* (1968).
Literae Cantuarienses, ed. J. B. Sheppard (Rolls Series, iii, 1889).
LITTLE, A. G., 'Introduction of the Observant Friars into England', *Proceedings of the British Academy*, x (1921–3).
LOCKYER, R. W., *Henry VII* (1968).
LUNT, W. E., *Financial Relations of the Papacy with England, 1327–1534* (Medieval Academy of America: Cambridge, Mass., 1962).

MACGIBBON, D., *Elizabeth Woodville* (1938).

MALDEN, H. E., 'An Unedited Cely Letter of 1482', *TRHS*, 3rd series, x (1916).

MALLETT, M. E., 'Anglo-Florentine Commercial Relations, 1465–1491', *EconHR*, 2nd series, xv (1962).

MANCINI, DOMINIC, *The Usurpation of Richard III*, ed. and translated by C. A. J. Armstrong (2nd edn, Oxford, 1969).

MATTHEWS, W., *The Ill-Framed Knight* (Berkeley and Los Angeles, 1966).

MAXWELL-LYTE, *History of Eton College* (1911).

MCFARLANE, K. B., *Lancastrian Kings and Lollard Knights* (Oxford, 1972).

——, 'The Lancastrian Kings, 1399–1461', in *Cambridge Medieval History*, ed. C. W. Previté-Orton and Z. N. Brooke, VIII (Cambridge, 1936).

——, *The Nobility of Later Medieval England* (1973).

——, 'Parliament and Bastard Feudalism', *TRHS*, 4th series, xxvi (1944).

——, 'War, The Economy and Social Change: England and the Hundred Years War', *Past and Present*, no. 22 (1962).

——, 'The Wars of the Roses', *Proceedings of the British Academy*, l (1964).

——, 'William Worcester: A Preliminary Survey', in *Studies Presented to Sir Hilary Jenkinson*, ed. J. Conway Davis (1957).

MCKENNA, J. W., 'The Coronation Oil of the Yorkist Kings', *EHR*, lxxxii (1967).

MEEHAN, M., 'English Piracy, 1460–1500' (unpublished M.Litt. thesis, Bristol, 1972).

MILLER, E., 'The Economic Policies of Governments', in *Cambridge Economic History of Europe*, III, ed. M. M. Postan, E. E. Rich and E. Miller (Cambridge, 1965).

MISKIMIN, H. A., 'Monetary Movements and Market Structure: Forces for Contraction in Fourteenth- and Fifteenth-Century England', *Journal of Economic History*, xxiv (1964).

MITCHELL, R. J., *John Tiptoft* (1938).

MORE, SIR THOMAS, *The History of King Richard III*, ed. R. S. Sylvester (*Complete Works*, Yale Edition, II, 1963).

MORGAN, D. A. L., 'The King's Affinity in the Polity of Yorkist England', *TRHS*, 5th series, xxiii (1973).

MORICE, H., *Mémoires pour servir de preuves à l'histoire de Bretagne*, 3 vols (Paris, 1742–6).

MUNRO, J. H., 'The Costs of Anglo-Burgundian Interdependence', *Revue Belge de Philologie d'histoire*, xlvi (1968).

——, 'An Economic Aspect of the Collapse of the Anglo-Burgundian Alliance', *EHR*, lxxxv (1970).

MYERS, A. R., *The Household of Edward IV* (Manchester, 1959).

——, 'The Household of Queen Margaret of Anjou, 1452–3', *Bulletin of the John Rylands Library*, xl (1957–8).

——, 'An Official Progress through Lancashire and Cheshire in 1476', *Transactions of the Historic Society of Lancashire and Cheshire*, cxv (1963).

——, 'The Outbreak of War between England and Burgundy in February 1471', *BIHR*, xxxiii (1960).

MYERS, A. R., 'The Household of Queen Elizabeth Woodville, 1466–7', *Bulletin of the John Rylands Library*, l (1967–8).

OMAN, C. W. C., *The Coinage of England* (Oxford, 1931).
——, *Warwick the Kingmaker* (1891).
Original Letters Illustrative of English History, ed. H. Ellis. Three series, 11 vols (1824–46).
OTWAY-RUTHVEN, A. J., *A History of Medieval Ireland* (1968).
——, *The King's Secretary and the Signet Office in the Fifteenth Century* (Cambridge, 1939).

Paston Letters, 1422–1509, ed. J. Gairdner, 6 vols (1904).
Paston Letters and Papers of the Fifteenth Century, ed. N. Davis, Part I (Oxford, 1971).
PEAKE, M. I., 'London and the Wars of the Roses', *BIHR*, iv (1926–7).
PERINELLE, M. G., 'Dépêches de Nicholas de Roberti, ambassadeur d'Hercule I, duc de Ferrare, auprès du Roi Louis XI', *Mélanges d'Archaeologie et d'Histoire*, xxiv (1904).
Plumpton Correspondence, ed. T. Stapleton (Camden Society, 1839).
POCQUET DU HAUT-JUSSÉ, B. A., *François II, Duc de Bretagne, et l'Angleterre* (Paris, 1929).
POLLARD, A. F., *Parliament in the Wars of the Roses* (Glasgow, 1936).
POLLARD, A. J., 'The Family of Talbot, Lords Talbot and Earls of Shrewsbury, in the Fifteenth Century' (unpublished Ph.D. thesis, Bristol, 1968).
POSTAN, M. M., 'Economic and Political Relations of England and the Hanse', in *Studies in English Trade in the Fifteenth Century*, ed. E. Power and M. M. Postan (1933).
——, 'The Trade of Medieval Europe: the North', in *Cambridge Economic History of Europe*, II, ed. M. M. Postan and E. E. Rich (Cambridge, 1952).
POWER, E., The Wool Trade', in *Studies in English Trade in the Fifteenth Century*, ed. E. Power and M. M. Postan (1933).
——, 'The English Wool Trade in the Reign of Edward IV', *Cambridge Historical Journal*, ii (1926).
POWICKE, M. R., *Military Obligation in Medieval England* (Oxford, 1962).
Privy Purse Expenses of Elizabeth of York: Wardrobe Accounts of Edward IV, ed. N. H. Nicolas (1830).
Proceedings Before the Justices of the Peace in the Fourteenth and Fifteenth Centuries, ed. B. H. Putnam (1938).
Proceedings in Chancery in the Reign of Queen Elizabeth. Calendars, ed. J. Caley and J. Bayley, 3 vols (Record Commission, 1827–32).
Proceedings and Ordinances of the Privy Council of England, ed. N. H. Nicolas, 7 vols (Record Commission, 1834–7).
PUGH, T. B., 'The Magnates, Knights and Gentry', in *Fifteenth-Century England, 1399–1509*, ed. S. B. Chrimes, C. D. Ross and R. A. Griffiths (Manchester, 1972).

PUGH, T. B., 'The Marcher Lords of Glamorgan, 1317–1485', in *Glamorgan County History*, III, ed. T. B. Pugh (Cardiff, 1971).
——, *The Marcher Lordships of South Wales, 1416–1536* (Cardiff, 1963).

QUINN, D. B., 'The Argument for the English Discovery of America between 1480 and 1494', *Geographical Journal*, cxxvii (1961).
——, 'Edward IV and Exploration', *Mariner's Mirror*, xxi (1935).

RAINE, J., *The Priory of Hexham*, 2 vols (Surtees Society, 1864).
RAMSAY, J. H., *Lancaster and York*, 2 vols (Oxford, 1892).
Records of the Borough of Nottingham, 9 vols (1882–1956).
REDDAWAY, T. F., 'The King's Mint and the Exchange in London, 1343–1513', *EHR*, lxxxii (1967).
Registrum Thome Bourgchier, 1454–1486, ed. F. R. H. Du Boulay, 2 vols (Canterbury and York Society, 1955–6).
REID, R. R., *The King's Council in the North* (1921).
Reports from the Lords' Committee Touching the Dignity of a Peer, 5 vols (1820–29).
RICHMOND, C. F., 'English Naval Power in the Fifteenth Century', *History*, lii (1967).
——, 'Fauconberg's Kentish Rising of May 1471', *EHR*, lxxxv (1970).
ROBBINS, R. H., *Historical Poems of the Fourteenth and Fifteenth Centuries* (New York, 1959).
ROBERTS, A. K. B., *St George's Chapel, Windsor Castle, 1348–1416* (Windsor, 1947).
ROGERS, J. E. T., *Six Centuries of Work and Wages: The History of English Labour*, 2 vols (1884).
Rolls of the Warwickshire and Coventry Sessions of the Peace, ed. E. G. Kimball (Dugdale Society, xvi, 1939).
ROOVER, RAYMOND DE, *The Medici Bank* (1948).
ROSENTHAL, J. T., 'The Estates and Finances of Richard, Duke of York', *Studies in Medieval and Renaissance History*, ii (1965).
——, 'Fifteenth-Century Baronial Incomes and Richard, Duke of York', *BIHR*, xxxvii (1964).
ROSKELL, J. S., *The Commons in the Parliament of 1422* (Manchester, 1954).
——, *The Commons and their Speakers in English Parliaments, 1376–1523* (Manchester, 1965).
——, 'John, Lord Wenlock of Someries', *Bedfordshire Historical Record Society Publications*, xxxviii (1957).
——, 'The Problem of the Attendance of the Lords in Medieval Parliaments', *BIHR*, xxix (1956).
——, 'Sir Thomas Tresham, Knight, Speaker for the Commons under Henry VI', *Northamptonshire Past and Present*, ii, no. 6 (1959).
——, 'William Catesby, Councillor to Richard III', *Bulletin of the John Rylands Library*, xlii (1959).
ROSS, C. D., *The Estates and Finances of Richard Beauchamp, Earl of Warwick* (Dugdale Society Occasional Papers, 1956).

ROSS, C. D., 'The Estates and Finances of Richard, Duke of York', *Welsh History Review*, iii (1967).

——, 'The Reign of Edward IV', in *Fifteenth-Century England, 1399–1509*, ed. S. B. Chrimes, C. D. Ross and R. A. Griffiths (Manchester, 1972).

Rotuli Parliamentorum, ed. J. Strachey and others, 6 vols (1767–77).

Rotuli Scotiae, ed. D. Macpherson, J. Caley, W. Illingworth and T. H. Horne, 2 vols (Record Commission, 1814–19).

ROUS, J., *Historia Regum Anglie*, ed. T. Hearne (Oxford, 1745).

ROWSE, A. L., *Tudor Cornwall* (1941).

——, 'The Turbulent Career of Sir Henry de Bodrugan', *History*, xxix (1944).

RUDDOCK, A. A., *Italian Merchants and Shipping in Southampton, 1270–1600* (Southampton, 1951).

RYMER, T., *Foedera, Conventiones, Literae . . . et Acta Publica* (etc.), 20 vols (1704–35).

SCATTERGOOD, V. J., *Politics and Poetry in the Fifteenth Century* (1972).

SCHANZ, G., *Englische Handelspolitik gegen ende des Mittelalters*, 2 vols (Leipzig, 1881).

SCOFIELD, C. L., *The Life and Reign of Edward the Fourth*, 2 vols (1923).

SHAW, W. A., *The Knights of England*, 2 vols (1906).

SHERBORNE, J. W., *The Port of Bristol in the Middle Ages* (Bristol, 1965).

SIMON, J., *Education and Society in Tudor England* (Cambridge, 1966).

SIMONS, E. N., *The Reign of Edward the Fourth* (1966).

Six Town Chronicles of England, ed. R. Flenley (Oxford, 1911).

SKEEL, C. A. J., *The Council in the Marches of Wales* (1904).

SMITH, G., *The Coronation of Elizabeth Woodville* (1935).

SMYTH, J., *Lives of the Berkeleys*, ed. J. Maclean, 2 vols (Gloucester, 1883).

Some Sessions of the Peace in Lincolnshire, 1381–1396, ed. E. G. Kimball (Lincoln Record Society, xix, 1955).

SOMERVILLE, R., *History of the Duchy of Lancaster*, I, *1265–1603* (1953).

Statutes of the Realm, ed. A. Luders and others, 11 vols (Record Commission, 1810–28).

STEEL, A. B., *The Receipt of the Exchequer, 1377–1485* (Cambridge, 1954).

STOREY, R. L., *The End of the House of Lancaster* (1966).

——, 'Lincolnshire and the Wars of the Roses', *Nottingham Medieval Studies*, xiv (1970).

——, 'The North of England', in *Fifteenth-Century England, 1399–1509*, ed. S. B. Chrimes, C. D. Ross and R. A. Griffiths (Manchester, 1972).

——, *The Reign of Henry VII* (1968).

——, 'The Wardens of the Marches of England towards Scotland, 1377–1489', *EHR*, lxxii (1957).

STOW, J., *Annales, or a Generall Chronicle of England* (1615).

STUBBS, W., *Constitutional History of England*, 3 vols (2nd edn, 1878).

Studies in English Trade in the Fifteenth Century, ed. E. Power and M. M. Postan (1933).

THIELEMANS, M. R., *Bourgogne et Angleterre: Relations Politiques et Econo-miques entre les Pays-Bas bourguignons et l'Angleterre, 1435-1467* (Brussels, 1966).

THOMAS, D. H., 'The Herberts of Raglan as supporters of the House of York in the second half of the fifteenth century' (unpublished M.A. thesis, University of Wales, 1968).

THOMPSON, A., 'Continental Imitations of the Rose Noble of Edward IV', *British Numismatic Journal*, xxv (1945-8).

THOMPSON, A. H., *The English Clergy and their Organization in the Later Middle Ages* (Oxford, 1947).

THOMSON, J. A. F., ' "The Arrivall of Edward IV" – The Development of the Text', *Speculum*, xlvi (1971).

——, 'The Courtenay Family in the Yorkist Period', *BIHR*, xlv (1972).

Three Fifteenth-Century Chronicles, ed. J. Gairdner (Camden Society, 1880).

THRUPP, S., *The Merchant Class of Medieval London, 1300-1500* (1948).

TOUCHARD, H., *Le Commerce Maritime Breton au fin du Moyen Age* (Paris, 1967).

The Travels of Leo of Rozmital, ed. and translated by M. Letts (Hakluyt Society, 2nd series, cviii: Cambridge, 1957).

VAN DER WEE, H., *The Growth of the Antwerp Market and the European Economy*, 3 vols (The Hague, 1963).

VAN PRAET, L., *Recherches sur Louis de Bruges, Seigneur de Gruthuyse* (Paris, 1831).

VAUGHAN, R., *Philip the Good* (1970).

——, *Charles the Bold* (1973).

VERGIL, POLYDORE, *Three Books of Polydore Vergil's English History*, ed. H. Ellis (Camden Society, 1844).

——, *The* Anglica Historia *of Polydore Vergil, A.D. 1485-1537*, ed. and translated by D. Hay (Royal Historical Society, Camden Series, lxxiv, 1950).

VERNON-HARCOURT, L. W., 'The Baga de Secretis', *EHR*, xxiii (1908).

Victoria History of the Counties of England: Cambridgeshire, III (1959); *Leicester-shire*, III (1955); *Oxfordshire*, III (1954); *Yorkshire*, III (1913).

WARKWORTH, J., *A Chronicle of the First Thirteen Years of the Reign of King Edward the Fourth*, ed. J. O. Halliwell (Camden Society, 1839).

WARNER, G. F. and GIBSON, J. P., *Catalogue of the Western Manuscripts in the Old Royal and King's Collections in the British Museum*, 4 vols (1921).

WAURIN, JEAN DE, *Anchiennes Cronicques d'Engleterre*, ed. E. Dupont, 3 vols (Société de l'Histoire de France, Paris, 1858-63).

WEBSTER, W., 'An Unknown Treaty between Edward IV and Louis XI', *EHR*, xii (1897).

WEDGWOOD, J. C., *History of Parliament, 1439-1509: Biographies* (1936); *Register* (1938).

WEISS, R., 'Henry VI and the Library of All Souls College', *EHR*, lvii (1942).

456   SELECT BIBLIOGRAPHY

WERNHAM, R. B., *Before the Armada* (1966).
WHITAKER, T. D., *An History of Richmondshire*, 2 vols (1823).
WILKINSON, B., *Constitutional History of England in the Fifteenth Century, 1399–1485* (1964).
WILLIAMS, C. H., 'England: The Yorkist Kings, 1461–1485' in *Cambridge Medieval History*, viii (1936).
WILLIAMS, P., *The Council in the Marches of Wales under Elizabeth I* (Cardiff, 1958).
WOLFFE, B. P., *The Crown Lands, 1461–1536* (1970).
——, 'Henry VII's Land Revenues and Chamber Finance', *EHR*, lxxix (1964).
——, 'The Management of English Royal Estates under the Yorkist Kings', *EHR*, lxxi (1956).
——, *The Royal Demesne in English History* (1971).
WORCESTRE, WILLIAM, *Itineraries*, ed. J. Harvey (Oxford, 1969).
WROTTESLEY, G., 'A History of the Family of Wrottesley', *Collections for a History of Staffordshire*, vi (ii) (1903).

York Civic Records, I, ed. A. Raine (Yorkshire Archaeological Society, Record Series, 1939).
York Records: Extracts from the Municipal Records of the City of York, ed. R. Davies (1843).

INDEX

Abbeville, 24; governor of, 63n
Abergavenny, Lord, see Nevill, Edward; lordship of, 71, 76, 190n
Aberystwyth Castle, 81
Acaster, 268
Africa, North, 353
Agincourt, 228
Aire, 160; River (Yorks.), 36
Albany, duke of, see Alexander
Alcock, John, bishop of Rochester and Worcester, 102, 196, 222, 321, 349; master of the rolls, 332
Alençon, Jean, duke of, 84n
Alexander (the Great), 301; History of, 262
Alexander of Scotland, duke of Albany, 287–90, 293
Alford, —, servant of duke of Norfolk, 123
Alice, queen of Burgundy, 301
Alkmaar (Holland), 153
Allington, Sir William, 243; speaker of commons, 345
Alnwick Castle, 46, 50–3, 59–61, 324
Alphonso V, king of Portugal, 4n
Alsace, 210, 213
Amboise, 147
America, discovery of, 353
Amiens, 214, 231, 233
Ancenis, treaty of, 113
Angers, 147, 158
Anglesey, 120
Anglia, East, 35–6, 42, 81, 128, 161, 324–5, 344, 376, 401, 404
Angus, earl of, see Douglas
Anjou, king of, see Réné
Anne, daughter of Edward IV, 247, 249, 254, 283–4
Anne, sister of Edward IV, duchess of Exeter, 93, 336–7
Anne, daughter of Francis, duke of Brittany, 246–7, 249n, 285
Anne, daughter of Louis XI, 91
Anthony, Bastard of Burgundy, see Burgundy
Antwerp, 109, 362, 364
Appleby, 326, 438
Appleton, Roger, 273, 343

Aragon, 112; see also John II
Archenfield, lordship of, 78n, 437
Ardern, Peter, justice, 398, 400
Ardres, 228
Armagnac, house of, 214
Arras, 240n; Treaty of, 249, 291–2, 294–5, 324, 368, 415
Arrow Park (Warws.), 240
Arthur (Plantagenet), natural son of Edward IV, Viscount Lisle, 316n
Artois, 228, 250, 291–2
Arundel, 48; earl of, see FitzAlan
Arundell, Sir John, 183
Ashby de la Zouch, 73
Ashley, Sir John, 53n
Aspatrick, manor of, 438
Astley, Sir John, 274, 305
Atholl, 49
Audley, lords, see Tuchet
Audley, Edmund, bishop of Rochester, 320
Austria, see Maximilian, Margaret

Balloch, Donald, 46, 49
Baltic Sea, English trade in, 212, 358, 361
Bamborough Castle, 50–3, 57n, 58–9, 61–2, 65, 186n, 279
Banbury, 131, 165, 441
Bangor, bishopric of, 319n
Bar, duchy of, 147, 207, 229
Barbary Coast, 353
Barfleur, 147
Barham Down (Kent), 222
Barker, John, 263
Barking, All Hallows Church, 274n
Barmouth, 120
Barmston (Yorks.), 163
Barnet, battle of, 37, 79, 158, 167–8, 176, 183, 300, 314, 324, 326, 328
Bath, 169; and Wells, bishop of, see Stillington, Robert
Baynard's Castle (London), 34
Beauchamp, Anne, countess of Warwick, 17, 145, 169, 187, 190, 248, 336
Beauchamp, Richard, earl of Warwick, 189
Beauchamp, Richard, bishop of Salisbury, 27, 34, 37n, 275, 279n, 318

Beauchamp, Sir Richard, 170, 185
Beaufort, Edmund, duke of Somerset, 4, 5, 12–14, 16–18, 42
Beaufort, Edmund (d. 1471), styled duke of Somerset, 106n, 156, 164, 167, 169, 171–2
Beaufort, Eleanor, duchess of Somerset, 186n
Beaufort, Henry, duke of Somerset (d. 1464), 20–2, 25, 29 and n, 30, 38, 42–3, 51–2, 58–60, 62, 65, 66, 84–5, 186n
Beaufort, Joan, countess of Westmorland, 5
Beaufort, John, 172
Beaufort, Margaret, duchess of Somerset, 186n
Beaulieu Abbey, 169, 189
Beaumaris, 120
Beaumont, John, Viscount Beaumont, 24, 27, 42, 66
Beaumont, William, Viscount Beaumont, 66, 72n, 75, 164, 167–8
Beaupie, Peter, 374
Beauvais, 228; Vincent de, 265
Bell, Richard, prior of Durham, bishop of Carlisle, 321n
Bellingham, Sir Henry, 58
Bergen-op-Zoom, 362
Berkeley, 170–1; family, 89, 134, 138, 406
Berkeley, William, Viscount Berkeley, 248, 333, 336n
Berkeley, William, 329n
Berkhamsted Castle, 328
Berkshire, 5, 81, 329n
Berners, Lord, see Bourchier, John
Berwick-on-Tweed, 29, 46, 51, 53, 272, 279, 282, 287–8, 290, 293; castle, 289
Beverley, 126n, 201
Bisham Abbey (Berks.), 53, 168
Blackheath, 174
Blackness, 282
Blake, Thomas, 240
Blore Heath, battle of, 21
Blount, John, later Lord Mountjoy, 173n, 181, 337
Blount, Walter, Lord Mountjoy, 36, 73n, 80, 83n, 95, 110, 113, 119n, 133n, 135, 142, 150, 155, 157n, 274, 310, 379, 412
Blount, Sir William, 168
Bodrugan, Sir Henry, 367n, 391n, 402, 407, 410–11
Bohun family, inheritance, 335

Bolingbroke (Lincs.), honour of, 442
Bolingbroke, Henry, duke of Lancaster see Henry IV
Bollati, Christopher, 223
Bona of Savoy, see Savoy
Bonville, Cecily, 185, 336
Bonville, William, Lord Harington, 75
Bonython, Henry, 410
Bonython, Richard, 410
Booth, John, bishop of Exeter, 320n
Booth, Lawrence, bishop of Durham, archbishop of York, chancellor of England, 45–6, 213, 313, 318
Booth, William, archbishop of York, 54
Borselle, Henry de, lord of Veere, 160
Boulogne, 106; honour of, 75n; count of, and of Auvergne, 287
Bourbon, cardinal of, 232
Bourbon, duke of, 20
Bourbon, Isabel of, countess of Charolais, 107
Bourbon, Jean, bastard of, 108, 230
Bourbon, Katherine of, 20
Bourbon, Mademoiselle de, 84
Bourchier, Edward, 23
Bourchier, Fulk, 79
Bourchier, Henry, Viscount Bourchier, earl of Essex, 18, 20, 22, 26, 34n, 48, 54, 79, 82, 83n, 93, 101, 121, 135, 155, 157, 166, 173–4, 182, 192, 221, 253, 309, 332, 344; treasurer of England, 27, 79, 185, 314; steward of household, 323
Bourchier, Humphrey, Lord Cromwell, 72n, 79, 83n, 140, 155, 167–8, 372n
Bourchier, Sir Humphrey, 79, 168
Bourchier, Isobel, countess of Essex, see Isobel of York
Bourchier, John, Lord Berners, 23, 36n, 79, 381
Bourchier, Thomas, cardinal, archbishop of Canterbury, 18, 20, 26, 34, 79, 95, 115, 121, 155, 157, 161, 215, 222, 233, 309, 318, 355, 377; career of, 319
Bourchier, Thomas, 327
Bourchier, William, son of the earl of Essex, Viscount Bourchier, 83n, 93
Bourchier, William, Lord FitzWarin, 79, 141n, 381
Bourchier, Sir William, 182
Brabant, 109, 252, 291
Brackley, Friar, 24n
Brancepeth Castle, 46
Brandon, Sir William, 305–6
Brecon, 136n
Bretelles, Louis de, 235

Brézé, Pierre de, seneschal of Normandy, 43–4, 50–2
Brice, Hugh, 259, 267, 355
Bridget, daughter of Edward IV, 245, 249n
Bridgwater, 48n, 132; lordship of, 78n
Bristol, 34, 48, 132, 170, 218–19, 351n, 352, 363, 368, 402; corporation of, 102, 303, 315, 338n; merchants of, 353, 358, 362n; recorder of, see Twynho, John
Brittany, duchy of, 31, 91, 104–6, 111–113, 118, 147, 161, 182, 205–8, 214, 219, 221, 223, 232–3, 246–7, 249, 261, 284–6, 292, 295, 321, 361, 367–8; and see also Francis; Anne; Isabella; and Edward IV
Brook, Edward, Lord Cobham, 26, 34n
Brook, John, Lord Cobham, 400
Brough, 438
Brougham, 438
Browne, Sir George, 143, 314
Browne, Sir Thomas, 143
Bruges, 108, 111, 123, 160, 161n, 210–11, 218n, 259, 264, 266–7, 326, 356, 364–5; Louis of, see Gruthuyse
Brussels, 111
Buckingham, dukes of, see Stafford
Buckinghamshire, 70
Burdett, Thomas, 240–2, 397–8
Burford, 32, 165; baron of, see Cornewall
Burgh, Sir Thomas, 138, 222n, 442
Burgundy, 44n, 54, 63, 83–5, 91, 104–14, 124, 134, 146, 149–50, 205–15, 223–231, 235–8, 239, 242, 245–6, 249–56, 259–60, 278, 283–6, 294–5, 301, 310, 319, 321–2, 327, 357; Anthony, Bastard of, 95, 109–10, 116n, 259, 265; dukes and ducal family of, see Alice; Charles; John; Mary; Maximilian of Austria; Philip
Burton-on-Trent, 141
Bury St Edmunds, 128; abbey of, 325
Butler, James, earl of Ormond and Wiltshire, 18, 20, 22, 24, 31, 37, 42–3, 45, 66n, 72, 75, 80, 117n, 203, 376, 438
Butler, John, earl of Ormond, 160n, 203
Butler, Sir John, 392
Butler, Thomas, 203
Bygod, Sir Ralph, styled Lord Mauley, 68n
Bywell Castle, 61

Cade, Jack, rebellion of, 11, 24
Cadwallader, 300

Caerleon, lordship of, 5, 31, 76, 77n
Caernarvon, 49, 120, 194
Cagnola, Giovanni Andrea, 246, 254
Caister Castle, 134, 158, 406
Calabria, John, duke of, 106
Calais, 18–19, 20–2, 25, 29, 50, 55, 80, 90, 103, 116n, 130, 144–6, 148, 158, 222–3, 225–6, 228, 234, 250–1, 280, 283, 286, 353, 356, 442; captaincy of, 18–19, 70, 98, 149, 156, 324, 437; garrison of, 20–1, 173–4, 175, 181; treasurer of, 81, 122; marches of, 191–2; defences, 272, 276, 292; Staple at, 311–12, 353, 357, 369; marshal of, 326; finances of, 357, 372, 379
Cambridge, 59, 272, 401; university, 268, 304, 320, 325, 432; King's College, 269, 272, 276, 305; Queens' College, 270; Jesus College, 321
Cambridgeshire, 58, 80, 186n, 398
Caniziani, Gerard, 223, 356, 379
Canterbury, 25–6, 48, 120, 130, 150n, 181, 183, 222, 287n; Buttermarket, 181; mayor of, see Faunt
Canterbury, archbishop of, see Bourchier, Thomas; convocation of, 54, 216, 281, 319, 371
Cantref Selig, manor of, 335
Capgrave, Chronicle, presented to Edward IV, 266
Cardigan, 76n, 137n
Carisbrooke Castle, 96
Carlisle, 46, 151, 326
Carmarthen, 31, 58, 194
Carreg Cennen Castle, 49
Castile, 59, 85, 108n, 112, 114, 214, 219, 363, 369; and see also Ferdinand; Isabella
Castle Donington, 437
Castleford, 37
Castle Martin, 77n
Caterall, John, 411n
Catesby, Sir William, 68n
Catherine, daughter of Edward IV, 245, 249n
Catherine of Valois, queen of Henry V, 31
Caux, Anne of, nurse of Edward IV, 7
Caxton, William, 97, 264n, 266–7
Cecily, duchess of York, mother of Edward IV, 5–6, 21, 87, 329, 381; piety of, 9
Cecily, daughter of Edward IV, marriage plans for, 213, 247, 249 and n, 278–9, 287, 289–90, 293

Cerne Abbey, 169
Chamberlain, Sir Robert, 161
Champagne, county of, 207, 214, 228
Chancellor, Thomas, 275
Charles VII, king of France, 43, 54
Charles, dauphin of France, son of
  Louis XI, 223, 233, 247, 251, 253, 284,
  286, 291–2
Charles of France, duke of Normandy,
  brother of Louis XI, 106
Charles, count of Charolais, duke of
  Burgundy, 58, 74, 84, 104, 128, 146,
  153, 220, 222, 235, 274, 285, 294, 317;
  hostility to York, 106; activities
  against Louis XI, 106; marriage to
  Margaret of York, 107–12, 259;
  alliance with England, 111; warns of
  Warwick's invasion, 148, 151; aids
  Edward in exile, 154, 158–9; alliance
  with England, 206–14, 219; behaviour
  during English invasion, 222, 224–31,
  236, 238; consequences of his death,
  239–40, 249–53, 311; emulates heroes
  of antiquity, 301; commercial rela-
  tions with England, 364, 369, 385
Charlotte, queen of France, 109
Charolais, count of, see Charles; countess
  of, see Bourbon, Isabel of
Châteaugiron, treaty of, 207–8, 367
Chedworth, Margaret, wife of John
  Howard, 355
Cheltenham, 171
Chepstow, 77n, 182
Chertsey Abbey, 418
Cheshire, 45, 58, 70, 117n, 170, 196,
  382, 437
Chester, 28; castle, 305; earldom of, 20,
  117, 373
Chesterfield, 143
Cheyne, Sir John, 233–5, 329n
Chichester, bishop of, 184n
Chimay, count of, 290, 291n
Chinon, 50
Chipping Norton, 32
Chirk, 408
Christian I, king of Denmark, 214
Cinque Ports, 70, 149, 173, 182–3, 343;
  warden of, 437 and see FitzAlan
  William
Cirencester, 170
Clapham, John, 131
Clarence, duke of, see George; Lionel
Clemens family, 407; Thomas, 407
Clifford, John Lord, 20, 29–30, 36–7,
  59, 66n, 70, 156n, 200, 438
Clifford, Thomas Lord, 17–18

Clifton, Sir Gervase, 122, 172
Clinton, John Lord, 23
Cluny, Guillaume de, 107
Cobham, lords, see Brook
Cockermouth, castle and lordship, 438
Colchester, 410; castle, constable of, 324
Cologne, archbishopric of, 224; mer-
  chants of, 211–12, 365
Commons, see Parliament
Commynes, Philippe de, references to
  English affairs, 73, 98, 106n, 125, 153,
  166, 251, 255; hostile view of Ed-
  ward's character, 86, 148, 294, 307,
  418–19, 429, 433–4; on Edward's
  appearance, 10, 232; on invasion of
  France, 221, 223–6, 230–5, 237; on
  Edward's death, 415
Compostella, 98
Conflans, treaty of, 106
Constable, Sir Marmaduke, 384
Convers, John, 379
Convocation, see Canterbury; York
Conway, 77n
Conyers, Sir John, 128, 141, 144, 439
Cook, Sir Thomas, 44, 99–101, 116n,
  121n, 122, 262, 354, 355–6, 365, 397,
  431
Coppini, Francesco, bishop of Terni, 25,
  27, 28n, 33n
Cornazzano, Antonio, 87
Cornelius, 122, 402; the goldsmith, 263
Cornewall, Sir Thomas, 436
Cornwall, 57, 72n, 79, 169, 187, 192,
  196, 407, 410–11; duchy of, 75, 78n,
  343, 373, 411; M.P.s for, 343–4
Cotentin, 147
Council, the king's, 89, 121; functions
  and powers of, 308, 310–12; composition of, 308–10; prominence of gentry
  upon, 310; relationship to great
  councils, 311; and the crisis of 1483,
  103, 425; in Star Chamber, 303, 311,
  403, 413
Court, the king's; as a centre of political
  influence, 99, 102, 121–2, 165, 313–17;
  display and ceremony at, 258–62, 277,
  414; as a centre of patronage for
  architecture and the arts, 270; and
  courtiers, 317–18; and see also Household
Courtenay family, 81, 137, 141, 142n,
  184, 187, 188
Courtenay, Henry, 66, 122–3, 390, 397–
  398, 402
Courtenay, Sir Hugh, of Boconnoc,
  141n, 143

Courtenay, John, styled earl of Devon, 157, 164, 169, 172
Courtenay, Peter, bishop of Exeter, 320n
Courtenay, Sir Philip, of Powderham, 142n
Courtenay, Thomas, 5th earl of Devon, 390
Courtenay, Thomas, 6th earl of Devon, 29, 37, 66n, 390
Cousinot, Guillaume de, 58, 59n
Coventry, 20, 89n, 117–19, 129–30, 132, 145, 152, 154, 159, 165, 173, 183, 405; bishop of (and Lichfield), 184n, 319
Crickhowell, 77
Croft, Eleanor, 436
Croft, Sir Richard, 7, 374, 436
Croft, Thomas, 353
Cromer, 161
Cromwell, Lord, see Bourchier
Crosby, Sir John, 355
Crowland Abbey, 430
Croyland Chronicler, 78n, 430; on appearance of Edward IV, 10; on his love of pleasure, 86, 415; on the Woodvilles, 103; on Warwick's breach with Edward, 104n, 107n; on Edward and his brothers, 116, 188–9; on the French pension, 233n, 234, 236; on Clarence's attainder, 242, 243n, 245, 421; on Edward's patronage of learning, 268; on Edward's patronage generally, 277; on treaty of Arras, 292; on Edward's memory and grasp of business, 306–7; on his trading interests, 352, and finances, 380, 384; on law and order, 401; on Edward's death, 414–16
Cumberland, 16, 17, 29, 69n, 128, 141, 199, 200, 202, 279, 400, 438; M.P. for, 326

Dacre of the South, Lord, see Fiennes
Dacre, Humphrey, Lord Dacre of Gilsland, 30, 37, 47–8, 50, 66n, 69n, 200
Dacre, Sir Humphrey, 38
Dacre, Thomas Lord, 69n, 340
Damme, 112
Danby (Robert), chief justice, 401
Darell, George, keeper of the wardrobe, 258, 261
Dartford (Kent), 14, 401
Dartmouth, 147n
Daubeney, Giles, later Lord Daubeney, 329n, 333
Dauphin of France, see Charles

Daventry, 166
Debenham, Sir Gilbert, 161, 410–11; junior, chancellor of Ireland, 410
Delves, John 305
Denbigh Castle, 5, 23n, 48–9, 77n, 120, 137n
Denbighshire, 58
Denmark, 112, 358, 365, 369; see also Christian I; Frederick I
Denyes, Thomas, 399
Derbyshire, 42, 81, 119, 144, 405
Desmond, earl of, see FitzGerald
Devereux, Walter, Lord Ferrers of Chartley, 23, 31, 34, 36, 43n, 48, 73n, 74, 81, 83n, 133, 134n, 136, 144n, 157n, 182, 196, 274, 310n, 416
Devon, earls of, see Courtenay; Stafford
Devonshire, 21, 29, 72n, 78n, 79, 81, 145, 147, 153, 157, 169, 187, 336, 368, 392; sheriff of, 141n
Dieppe, 169, 284
Dinas, lordship of, 76
Dinham, Joanna, 21
Dinham, John Lord, 21, 73n, 79, 133n, 137, 141n, 155, 157n, 182, 192, 214, 219, 221n, 310, 329
Doncaster, 62, 142, 144, 152, 164
Donne, Sir John, 58, 136, 141, 251, 376
Dorset, 43, 80n, 169, 195
Douglas, Archibald, earl of Angus, 51–2
Douglas, James, earl of, 46, 57, 279, 281, 293
Dover, 55, 149, 219, 222, 288; castle of, 70, 273, 343; constable of, 437; and see FitzAlan; M.P. for, 343
Driver, Stephen, 160
Drogheda, 204
Dryslwyn, rebel defeat at, 58
Dudley, Edmund, 144, 339
Dudley, John Lord, 119n, 128, 155, 157n, 174, 215, 221
Dudley, William, dean of Windsor, bishop of Durham, 164, 185, 230, 320–1, 417
Duffield, 437
Dumfries, 287
Dunois, count of, 233
Dunstable, 166
Dunstanborough Castle, 46, 50–3, 61
Dunster, lordship of, 77; Lord, see Herbert
Duras, Gaillard Lord, 146, 192, 206, 214, 223
Durham, 45, 51, 58, 201, 313; palatine bishopric of, 198, 201; bishops of, 201–2, and see Booth, Lawrence;

Durham—*contd.*
Dudley, William; prior of, 201, 313, *and see* Bell, Richard
Dymmock, Andrew, 98n, 102, 344n, 424n
Dymmock, Sir Thomas, 138, 139n, 140–1

Eclusier, 228
Edgecote, battle of, 78, 128, 131–2, 439
Edinburgh, 287, 289
Edmund of Langley, duke of York, 4, 29
Edmund, brother of Edward IV, earl of Rutland, 7, 14, 21, 23, 30, 271
Edward I, 422
Edward II, 130
Edward III, 4, 10, 229, 238, 274–6, 281, 316
EDWARD IV
Career:
birth and parentage, 3, 5; education and upbringing, 7–9; as earl of March, 14, 18, 23; flight and exile (1459–60), 21–2, 24–5; attainted, 23; as hero of Yorkist propaganda, 25, 30–2; victorious at Mortimer's Cross, 31;claims the throne, 32–4; coronation, 41, 258
1461–70: on Towton campaign, 33–8; problems facing him, 41–5; and Lancastrian resistance (1461–4), 42–62; in north of England, 45, 50–2, 54–5, 62; abandons Scots campaign, consequent unpopularity, 55–7; progresses to deal with disorders, 48–9, 58–60; policy of conciliation (1461–4), 42, 64–8; his marriage: early plans for, 20, 84–5, 91; to Elizabeth Woodville, 60, 85–6; reasons for, 85–7, and political consequences of, 90–103; relations with Warwick and the Nevills, 63, 70–2, 83, 87, 91–4, 97, 104, 107–12, 114, 117–18, 120–2, 125, 437–8; reasons for their estrangement, 104, 116; Edward not to blame, 115–116; his attempts at conciliation, 118, 135–6; and Lancastrian plots and dissidence, 118–20, 122–3; and treason trials (1469), 123; loses popular support, his government criticized, 124–5; alleged hatred of common people, 125; complacent about Nevill loyalties, 122, 128, 131; at last suspects treason, 129; and the rebellion of 1469, 129–33; his inactivity, 131–2; largely to blame for *débâcle* of 1469, 132–3; a prisoner of Warwick, 132, 135; plans for

Clarence to replace him as king, 133; regains control, 135; attempts pacification, 135–6; and restoration of Percies, 136–7, 144–5; aware of threat from Warwick, 137–8; and the Lincolnshire rebellion, 138–44, 441–2; reasons for his success, 143–4; drives out Warwick and Clarence, 145; plans against invasion, 148–51; drawn away to north of England, 151–2; forced to flee the realm, 152–3; reasons for his overthrow in 1470, 153–4; attainted by Readeption parliament, 155; in exile in Low Countries, 153, 159–60
1471–83: plans invasion of England, 160; lands in England, 161–2; lack of popular support for, 158, 163; the 'Recovery of England', 163–77; at Barnet, 167–8; and the Tewkesbury campaign, 168–72; reasons for his success, 163–4, 176–7; guilty of death of Henry VI, 175–6; and settlement of 1471, 181–7; settles quarrel of his brothers, 187–91; arrest of George Nevill, 191–2; and Oxford's landing, 192–3; builds up Gloucester's power in the North, 199–203; resentful of Louis XI, 205, and dislikes Charles of Burgundy, 205, 206 and n; decides on war with France, 205–8; his intentions serious, 211, 223–4; his war aims, 208, 223–4, 238; financial and military preparations for war, 214–24; invades France, 222, 225–7; negotiates with Louis XI, 225–6, 228–9; and the meeting at Picquigny, 231–2; and English reactions to the treaty, 234–7; at the peak of his career in 1475, 239; and the French pension, 230, 238, 250, 253, 255, 283, 285, 287, 292, 380, 385–6; much attached to French alliance, 250, 251n, 253, 292; and his dilemmas in foreign policy after 1475, 250, 254–5; outmanœuvred by Louis XI, 250, 254, 294; and the fall of Clarence, 239–45; entirely responsible for Clarence's death, 244; his dynastic marriage diplomacy, 213, 245–7, 249; and the Mowbray inheritance, 248–9; and the Burgundian succession, 249–251; his itineraries after 1475, prefers south-east of England, 271–2; responsibility for war with Scotland, 278–80, and its implications for his continental policies, 281, 283, 285–6, 290–1; anger and chagrin at the

Treaty of Arras, 292, 294–5; general assessment of his foreign diplomacy (1475–83), 293–5; last months, 414; mystery of his final illness, 414–15; death and funeral, 415–18; his will, 385, 415, 417–18; his treasure, 264, 385 and n, 424 and n; narrative sources for his reign, 429–35, *and see also* Commynes; Croyland Chronicler; More; Vergil; London Chronicles; estimate of his achievement, 419–26; largely to blame for the crisis of 1483, 423–6

Government and Administration:
Personal nature of his rule, and constant personal activity in government, xi, 63, 299–307, 322–3, 341–2, 374–5, 387, 398–402, 421–2; concern for his own and his family's interests, 334–7, 420–2; determination to be obeyed, 399–400; opportunist methods, 196; policies a mixture of intelligence and inconsistency, 371, 420; his close interest in diplomacy, 63; pragmatic approach to kingship, 299; emphasis on legitimacy in Yorkist rule, 299–300; administrative reforms and innovations, 373–5, 422; enterprising and reforming spirit in government, 375, but also slackness and inefficiency, 383–4; innovations not translated into new institutions, 301; use of patronage, 69–83, 333–4; reliance on trusted servants, 301, 323, 399, and on gentry and lesser men, 309–10; his extensive use of laymen, 322, and of household officers, 332–9, 421; role of his affinity in government, not comparable with Lancastrian connection, 329–30; use of Order of the Garter, 274, 333; attitude towards overmighty subjects, 202–3, 334, *and see* Nobility; and prerogative and feudal rights, 338, 375, 382; use of clerical servants in government, 318–22; and episcopal appointments, 318–22; not concerned with impartial justice, 124–125, 338, 394–5; and the problem of law and order, 388–413, *and see* Law Enforcement; attitude to retaining, livery and maintenance, 119, 124, 330, 337–8, 395–6, 405–6, 412–13; personal interest in treason trials, 123, 402; judicial progresses, 401; use of secretaries and signet, 307, 320–1; financial policies, 371–87; subordin-

ated to political expediency, 377; early reliance on loans, 378–9; accumulation of wealth, 380, 385; use of benevolences, 217, 281, 385; abilities as financier, 386–7; meagre legislation of his reign, 341; relations with commons in parliament, 341–50; and creation of a royal navy, 280; use of naval power, 149–50; and the English merchant marine, 352; and the problem of piracy, 219, 312, 366–7, 395; relations with the English merchant class, 351–61, 370, *and see* London; his private trading ventures, 351–3; commercial policies, 105–6, 108–9, 111, 352–3, 365–70; policies towards Wales and the Marches, 48–9, 75–8, 120, 136, 182, 193–8, 334–5; and the North of England, 198–203, 339–40; and Ireland, 203–4; his achievement in government, 423; comparisons and contrasts with Henry VI, 257–8, 302, 353–4, 370, 378–9, 390; and with Henry VII, 295, 302, 310, 332–3, 338–40, 347n, 368, 370, 380–4, 386–7, 394, 413; *and see also* Council; Court; England; Household; Parliament

Foreign policies towards
Brittany, 106, 110, 112–13, 160, 205–8, 214, 246–7, 284–5, 361, 363, 367
Burgundy, 84–5, 104–14, 159–60, 205–11, 223–32, 239, 246–7, 249–56, 259, 283, 290–1, 294–5, 357, 359–62, 364–5, 367–9
France, 43–5, 56–7, 90–1, 104–14, 146–7, 205–11, 213–14, 223–39, 249–56, 284–6, 291–2, 294–5, 361, 363, 368
Hanseatic League, 121, 125, 149–50, 160, 192, 205, 209, 211–12, 219, 358–9, 361–2, 365–8
Scotland, 45–6, 48, 49–50, 52–4, 56–7, 62, 205, 212–13, 278–83 *and see also under respective countries*

Character and personality:
Contemporary opinions, 10, 307, 418–20; paradox of, xi, 305–7; intelligence, 9; excellent memory, 9, 232, 306; personal charm, 9, 52, 122; qualities of leadership, 9, 169–70, 176–7; generosity to former opponents and to servants, 52, 58, 67–8, 71, 143, 149, 185–6; clemency, 9, 42, 51–2, 65–8, 183–4; self-confidence, 9, 122, 176; knowledge of languages, 8–9, 232,

Edward IV—*contd.*
Character and Personality—contd.
268; conventional literary interests, 9, 268–9; as a collector of books and manuscripts, 264–8; not a patron of learning or religion, 268–9, 273–4; his extensive building schemes, 270–3, 275–6, and favourite residences, 271–273; his special interest in Windsor, 274–6; physical appearance, height, good looks, 10, 232, 423; licentious habits, 86–7, 98, 232, 315, 415; his mistresses, 315–16; debauchery and profligacy, 98, 306, 415; taste for ceremony and display, 9–10, 258; taste for clothes, 10, 258, 261–4, and for jewellery, 10, 263–4, and for personal comfort, 220, 271, 280–1; his alleged laziness, love of ease and pleasure, 49, 62–3, 223, 251n, 255, 283, 294, 307; complacency and inactivity, 132, 148–9, 153; political miscalculations, lack of political judgement and foresight, 51–2, 58, 62, 85, 124, 132–3, 244, 307, 420, 426; in later years, alleged loss of grasp, 244, 283, 290, 292, and despotic tendencies, 245 and n, 386, 421, 423; his growing avarice, 248, 380, 423, a feature of his diplomacy, 246–7, 284, 286, 294; ill-health, 287 and n; military qualities: boldness, 37; interest in artillery, 220 and n, 272; alleged distaste for campaigning, 49, 63, 223–4, 423; military reputation exaggerated, 176
Edward, prince of Wales, later Edward V, son of Edward IV, 8, 98, 102–3, 166, 199, 222, 322, 334, 344n, 381n, 411, 424–6; his council in Wales and the Marches, 196–8; resident at Ludlow, 197; marriage plans for, 246–7, 249n, 285; his governor, *see* Woodville, Anthony; his tutor and president of his council, *see* Alcock, John
Edward (of Lancaster), prince of Wales, son of Henry VI, 19, 29, 38, 54, 57, 76, 84, 147, 156, 164, 169, 171–2, 373
Edward, earl of Salisbury, son of George, duke of Clarence, 333, 336
Egremont, lordship of, 438; Lord, *see* Percy
Elfael, lordship of, 190n
Elizabeth, daughter of John of Gaunt, duke of Lancaster, 4
Elizabeth (Woodville), Queen of Edward IV, 73, 83, 85–93, 100–1, 166,

185, 199, 245, 260, 266, 269, 273, 316n, 381 and n; widow of Sir John Grey, 85; marriage to Edward IV, 85–94; coronation, 95; parentage and family connections, 85, 89; churching of, 258–9; dower and household, 96, 372; political influence, 73, 99–103, 315–17, 336–7; personality and character, 87–9, 97; and the affair of Sir Thomas Cook, 100–1; and London mercers, 101–2, 304; jealous of Gloucester, 103; and of Hastings, 103; and the death of Clarence, 244; much attached to French marriage alliance, 251n; patron of Queen's College, Cambridge, 270; promotes interests of her Grey sons, 336–7
Elizabeth of York, daughter of Edward IV, 93, 114n, 258; betrothed, 136; French marriage planned for, 230, 233, 247, 249 and n, 251, 253–5, 284
Elne, bishop of, 252–5
Elrington, John, treasurer of the household, 218, 310, 324
Eltham, Edward's palace at, 271, 273, 276, 343
Elvaston, 81
Ely, 432; bishops of, *see* Grey, William; Morton, John
Empingham, 141
Empire, the, 112, 387; *see also* Frederick III
England; admirals of, 70, 156, 437; chancellors of, 309, *and see* Nevill, George; Stillington; Booth, Lawrence; Rotherham; constables of, *see* Tiptoft, John; Woodville, Richard; Richard of Gloucester; Vere, John de; keepers of the privy seal, *see* Stillington; Rotherham, Russell, John; treasurers of, 309, *and see* Bourchier, Henry; Blount, Walter; Grey, Edmund; Woodville, Richard; Langstrother, John; Grey, William
Essex, 5, 57, 100, 121n, 174, 181–3, 184n, 187, 188, 325; earls of, *see* Bourchier
Eton college, 268–9, 276, 417
Eu, county of, 206, 207
Eure, Sir William, 183
Ewyas Lacy, lordship of, 76
Exchequer, superseded by chamber as financial department, 374; changes in, 375
Exeter, 48, 145, 169; bishopric of, 319n, 320; bishops of, *see* Nevill, George; Booth, John; Courtenay, Peter; King, Oliver

Fabyan, Robert, 85, 99, 431
Fairfax, Guy, 202
Fastolf, Sir John, 263, 305
Fauconberg, bastard of, see Nevill,
Thomas; Lord, see Nevill, William
Faunt, Nicholas, 174, 181
Fauquembergue, 228
Feckenham, manor of, 437
Ferdinand of Aragon, king of Spain,
213, 246, 274
Ferdinand I, king of Naples, 111n, 213, 274
Ferrara, Hercule, duke of, 108n, 246n
Ferrers of Chartley, Lord, see Devereux
Ferrybridge, 36
Fevre, Raoul le, 265
Fiennes, Joan, Lady Dacre, 69n
Fiennes, Richard, Lord Dacre of the
South, 69, 102, 221n, 226
Findern, Sir Thomas, 60
Firth of Forth, 282, 324
FitzAlan, Thomas, Lord Maltravers,
72n, 93, 95, 329
FitzAlan, William, earl of Arundel, 20,
69, 83n, 110, 123, 135, 140, 173, 182,
186, 221, 267; constable of Dover and
warden of the Cinque Ports, 149, 219,
343
FitzGerald, Gerald, earl of Kildare,
203-4
FitzGerald, Thomas, earl of Desmond,
101n, 203-4
FitzHarry, Thomas, 35
FitzHerbert, John, 306n
FitzHugh, Henry Lord, 67, 128, 151-2
FitzHugh, Sir Henry, 128
FitzMaurice, Thomas, earl of Kildare,
203-4
FitzWalter, Lord, see Radcliffe
FitzWarin, Lord, see Bourchier, William
FitzWilliam, Richard, 140
Flanders, 225, 242, 250-3, 265, 326; the
Members of, 291; and Flemings, 152,
160, 166, 264-5, 358
Fletcher, John, 305
Flintshire, 196
Flodden, battle of, 281
Florence, merchants of, 362-3, 379, and
see also Medici
Flushing, 160
Fogge, Sir John, 26, 35, 99-100, 121, 130,
185, 310, 323, 329n, 344n, 365
Forster, Humphrey, 403
Fortescue, Sir John, 38, 56, 81, 114n,
172, 184, 257, 261
Fotheringhay Castle, 5, 7, 53-4, 75n,
129, 140, 271, 272, 287, 293

Fowey, 367
Fowler, Sir Richard, 374, 376
France, 7, 12, 24, 31, 42-5, 53, 55-6, 63,
79, 90, 104-14, 120, 142, 151, 158, 162,
169, 182, 205-15, 219-20, 222, 227,
228-38, 239, 247, 249-56, 278, 283-86,
291-5, 319, 335, 348-50, 361, 363,
367-8, 385, 406, 414, 429-30, 433;
admiral of, 147; see also Charles;
Charlotte; Jeanne; Louis XI
Franche-Comté, 291
Francis II, duke of Brittany, 256; seeks
aid of England against France, 58,
106, 112-13, 206-8, 214; 30-year
truce with England, 110; Edward in
exile seeks his help, 160; included in
1475 truce with France, 233; proposed
marriage of daughter Anne to the
prince of Wales, 246-7, 284-5; commercial relations with England, 361,
363, 367-8
Frederick I, king of Denmark, 247
Frederick III, Emperor, 108n, 210, 213,
224, 246, 251
Froissart, 265
Fulford, Sir Baldwin, 48, 402
Fulford, Sir Thomas, 280

Gainsborough, 138
Gam, Sir Dafydd, 75
Gascony, 207-8, 223-4
Gate, Sir Geoffrey, 173n, 181, 379
Genoa, 263, 360; merchants of, 280, 362;
bankers of, 379
George, duke of Clarence, brother of
Edward IV, 119, 133-6, 149, 154, 160,
335-6, 381, 393, 397-8, 419; birth, 7,
21; character and abilities, 116-17,
188; endowment of, 117, 372; marriages projected for, 94, 107, 115, 117;
marries Isabel Nevill, 129-30; con-
spires with Warwick (1467), 116;
(1469), 129-31; to replace Edward as
king, 133, 137; lieutenant of Ireland,
117, 187, 204; and Lincolnshire
rebellion, 138, 140-4, 441-2; flees to
France, 145-6; an embarrassment to
Warwick, 147; returns to England,
147, 152; difficult position during
Readeption, 156-7; defects to Edward, 164-5; at Barnet, 167; grants
to, in 1471, 187; quarrel with Gloucester, 187-91, 430; suspected of treason,
191-3; and the invasion of France,
221, 230, 232-3, 236; reasons for his
overthrow, 239-44; arrest and trial,

George, duke of Clarence—*contd.*
241–3; death, 243, 419; not allowed
to marry Mary of Burgundy, 251 and n
George of Windsor, son of Edward IV,
204, 245, 271
Germany, 212, 358, 361
Ghent, 209, 251
Gibraltar, 357
Glamorgan, lordship of, 16, 31, 71, 76,
190n
Gloucester, 31, 57, 76, 170–1; dukes of,
see Richard; Humphrey
Gloucestershire, 57, 59, 134, 197, 336,
401, 406–7
Glyn family, 407; John, 407
Goddard, Dr John, 241
Golden Fleece, Burgundian order of,
274, 301
Goldwell, James, bishop of Norwich,
241, 274, 320n, 322
Goodrich, lordship of, 78n, 383, 437
Gower, lordship of, 77n
Graçay, Jacques de, 230
Grace, natural daughter of Edward IV,
316n
Grafton, Bastard of, 406
Grafton Regis, 85
Grantham, 30, 129, 138, 141, 335
Great Seal, 83, 110, 117, 302n
Greece, merchants of, 352
Greenwich, 112, 222, 248, 271, 273
Grene, Godfrey, 200, 201
Gresham, James, 57
Gresley family, 42
Grey, Anthony, son of the earl of Kent,
83n, 93, 95, 221
Grey, Edmund, Lord Grey of Ruthyn,
earl of Kent, 27, 34n, 69, 93, 110,
144n; treasurer of England, 54
Grey, Edward, Lord Ferrers of Groby, 85
Grey, Sir Edward, 143
Grey, Henry, Lord Grey of Codnor, 67,
119, 204, 303, 412
Grey, Sir John, husband of Elizabeth
Woodville, 85, 89
Grey, Sir Ralph, 50, 53, 61
Grey, Reginald, Lord Grey of Wilton,
31, 221n
Grey, Richard, Lord Grey of Powys, 23;
his estates, 77, 156n
Grey, Richard, son of Elizabeth Wood-
ville, 96, 98, 102, 336–7, 408
Grey, Thomas, earl of Huntingdon,
marquis of Dorset, 96, 98, 101–2,
221, 234, 280, 288, 333, 336–7, 381n,
398, 408; his feud with Hastings, 98,

416, 426; and the crisis of 1483,
424–6
Grey, Thomas, esquire of the body, 305,
327
Grey, William, bishop of Ely, 20, 27,
144n, 215, 314, 318; treasurer of
England, 136, 268, 320
Greystoke, Ralph Lord, 60, 67, 200, 202
Grimaldi, Luigi, 263
Grimsby, William, 35
Gruthuyse, Louis of Bruges, lord of
Gruthuyse, earl of Winchester, 153,
160, 185, 207, 260, 264–5
Guelders, duchy of, 209, 286, *and see also*
Mary of Guelders
Guinea, English trade with, 353
Guinegatte, battle of, 254
Guines, 106, 228; fortress of, 25, 173n,
272; lieutenant of, 70, 91, 173n, 181
Guipuzcoa, merchants of, 367
Guise, county of, 207
Guns, the king's, called *Newcastle, Lon-
don, Dijon,* 61; called *Messenger,
Edward, Fowler of Chester, Megge,* 220
Gwladys Ddu, 75

Haddington, 288
Hague, The, 153
Hall, Edward, 87, 131n, 414, 418
Hall, John, 154
Hammes Castle, 192; lieutenant of, 70,
173n, 181
Hampshire, 5, 43, 80–1, 96, 236, 336,
388–89, 401
Hampton Court, 273
Hanseatic League, Hansards, 128, 192,
351n; ships attacked by Warwick, 24;
council verdict against, 121, 311; un-
popularity in England, 125, 356, 358;
naval war against, 149–50, 152, 159,
161, 211, 324; negotiations with, 160,
212, 321, 326; settlements with, 205,
209, 219, 237, 368, 385; Mercers'
complaints against, 304; exempted
from tax, 354, 360–1; commercial
relations with, 358–9, 361, 365–7, 370
Hapsburgs, 295
Harcourt family, 406
Harcourt, John, 306
Harcourt, Sir Robert, 274, 406, 411n
Harfleur, 113, 226
Harlech Castle, 48–9, 53, 66n, 76, 114,
118, 120, 372
Harrington, Lord, *see* Bonville
Harrington family, 134, 164, 392, 406,
408–10

Harrington, Anne, 408
Harrington, Sir James, 164, 202, 400, 408–9
Harrington, John, 408
Harrington, Sir Robert, 400, 408–9
Harrington, Sir Thomas, 408
Hastings, Katherine, wife of William Lord, 75
Hastings, Sir Leonard, 74
Hastings, Sir Ralph, 75, 167, 327
Hastings, Richard Lord, 339
Hastings, William Lord, 23n, 31n, 36, 42n, 48, 50, 54, 63n, 66, 71, 73n, 82, 90, 95, 102, 110n, 119, 121, 132n, 140, 201, 232, 250, 267, 282, 287n, 310, 325, 336, 391, 409, 413n, 416; character and relationship with Edward IV, 73, 274, 317; family background, 74; grants to, 75, 133, 185, 376, 437; pension from Louis XI, 74, 234, 255, 317, and from Charles of Burgundy, 186, 317, and from English notables, 74, 317; captain of Calais, 98, 181, 251, 324, 335; his influence with Edward, 104, 314–15, 317; relations with Woodvilles, 98, 103, 317, 416, 425; diplomatic missions, 106–8, 209; his midland connection, 142, 334; in exile with Edward, 152–3, 155; at Tewkesbury, 171; entertains Gruthuyse, 260–1; chamberlain of the royal household, 75, 314–15, 323, 354; his role in government, 323, 342, 344; his relations with London, 354–5
Hatcliffe, William, physician and secretary of Edward IV, 224, 321
Haughley, honour of, 75n
Haverfordwest, 31n, 99, 137n
Hawkins (John), 100
Hay Castle, 136n
Hayes, John, 375
Hedgeley Moor, battle of, 59
Hellesdon, manor of, 406
Helmsley, 200
Henry II, king of France, 269
Henry III, 429
Henry IV, 162–3, 300, 304n, 322, 329–330, 371, 420
Henry V, 90, 166, 205n, 216, 224, 226, 229, 263n, 264n, 268, 273, 280, 300, 322, 350, 420, 423
Henry VI, 45–6, 64–5, 66, 68, 84–5, 107, 130, 134, 152, 163, 184, 194, 238, 241, 257, 300, 302, 307, 318, 320, 322, 349n, 350, 407, 409, 420, 424, 429, 437; potential heirs of, 4; misgovernment, 11–12; persuaded to create Edward earl of March, 14; breakdown in health and recovery, 17–18; efforts to reconcile lords, 19; at Ludford, 21; prisoner of Yorkists, 22; lords loyal to him, 22, 24; at Northampton, 26–7; his throne claimed by York, 28; at 2nd St Albans, 32; escapes to Scotland, 38, 41; on raids into England, 50–4; seeks help from Louis XI, 56; abandoned by Scotland, 57; escapes after Hexham, captured and imprisoned, 61 and n; plans to restore him, 109; his Readeption, 126, 143, 154–60, 166–7; his death, 175, 433; library of, 246n, 266, 268; patronage of, 268–9, 276; pilgrimages to his tomb, 304, 318; commercial policies of his reign, 354, 359, 361–2, 366; revenues, 371–3, 378–9, 383; his clemency, 390, 395; see also under Edward IV
Henry VII, 182, 198, 204, 264, 295, 299, 301–2, 310, 320, 322, 332–3, 338–40, 347, 349n, 350, 353, 368, 370, 376, 380, 387, 395, 413, 420, 436; as Henry Tudor, earl of Richmond, 77, 157, 173, 182, 193, 420; see also under Edward IV
Henry VIII, 198, 281, 333, 338, 381, 422
Henry, elder brother of Edward IV, 7
Henry the Impotent, king of Castile, 85, 111
Heralds: Bluemantle Pursuivant, 260, 261n; Falcon Herald, 223; Garter King of Arms, 142, 225–6, 230, 292n
Herbert, Sir Richard, 114, 131–2
Herbert, Sir Thomas, 132, 327
Herbert, Sir William, Lord Herbert, 1st earl of Pembroke, 22, 31, 34, 43n, 48–9, 62, 67n, 73n, 82, 83, 95, 97, 99, 110, 114, 118, 120–1, 129, 130, 136, 156, 186n, 193, 274, 310n, 314, 327, 383; Edward's chief lieutenant in South Wales, 71, 76, 133, 195, 199, 334, 371; family background, 75; early career, 76, 391; other grants and offices, 77, 376, 437; influence with the king, 78, 130; death at Edgecote, 131–2, 439, 441; his bastard sons, 407–8
Herbert, William, Lord Dunster, 2nd earl of Pembroke, earl of Huntingdon, 72n, 77, 83n, 93–4, 99, 136, 156n, 182, 197, 335; justiciar and chamberlain of South Wales, 195

Hereford, 28, 31, 48, 196, 391, 401, 407; bishop of, 184n; see also Milling, Thomas

Herefordshire, 7, 29, 76, 197, 357, 391, 392, 405, 407, 436

Héricault, 224

Hertford Castle, 273n

Hertfordshire, 5, 190n, 191

Heryot, William, mayor of London, 351, 354

Hesdin, 56

Hexham, battle of, 60, 122, 411n

Hextall, Thomas, 343

Heydon, John, 42

Hillyard, Robert, 127, 439; see also Robin of Holderness

Hobart, James, 344

Holderness, 163, 439; see also Robin of

Holland, 109, 158, 219, 252

Holland, Anne, daughter of duke of Exeter, 93, 102n, 336

Holland, Henry, duke of Exeter, 4, 12, 17, 29n, 30, 38, 42-3, 49, 66n, 106n, 123, 156, 164, 165, 167-8, 184, 336-7

Honfleur, 147, 161, 169

Hopton, Ralph, 23

Hornby (Yorks.), 128

Hornby Castle, 164, 400, 408-9

Horne, Robert, 26, 35, 38

Hospitallers, see St John of Jerusalem, knights of

Household, the king's, functions and size of, 313-14, 323, 326-7; costs of, 372; reform of, and ordinances for, 260, 312, 375; importance in government, 323-30; chamber of, as central financial department, 374-6; chamberlain of, see Hastings; officials of, 323-6; knights and esquires of, as links between court and country, 327-328; household men, as agents of personal rule, 323; in parliament, 326-7, 343-5; in diplomacy, 324-6; and the invasion of France, 328; political reliability of, 328-9

Howard, Elizabeth, countess of Oxford, 284n, 336

Howard, John Lord, 327, 400, 416; summary of career, 324-5; military services to Edward IV, 36, 50, 167, 181; grants and offices, 73n, 274, 376, 438; influence in East Anglia, 81, 344; role in government, 121, 310, 323, 355; during Readeption, 83n, 133, 152, 157n; naval services and shipowner, 146, 280-2, 365; diplomatic

missions, 209, 226, 230, 233, 234-5, 252, 255, 284, 317; and the Mowbray inheritance, 248-9, 336

Howard, Thomas, later earl of Surrey, 327, 344

Hull, 30, 163, 201

Humber, river, 162

Humphrey, duke of Gloucester, 4, 424

Hunden, John, bishop of Llandaff, 184

Hungary, king of, see Matthias Corvinus

Hungerford family, 186

Hungerford, Eleanor Lady, 66

Hungerford, Margaret Lady, 66

Hungerford, Robert Lord, 26, 52-3, 59, 60, 66, 79n, 122

Hungerford, Sir Thomas, 66, 79n, 122-3, 397-8, 402

Huntingdon, 305; earl of, see Herbert, William; Grey, Thomas

Iceland, English trade with, 358

Idle, William, 402

Ipswich, 410

Ireland, 5, 21-2, 31, 148, 203-4, 242, 322, 442; lieutenants of, 7, 18, 22, 80, 117, 144, 156, 187; chancellor of, 410

Isabel of Lorraine, see Lorraine

Isabella of Brittany, 246

Isabella of Castile, queen of Spain, 85, 213, 246

Isabella, infanta of Spain, 246

Isabella of Portugal, 240n

Islington, 175

Isobel of York, countess of Essex, aunt of Edward IV, 79n

Italy, 54, 80, 98, 220, 223, 268, 294-5, 320; bankers of, 259, and see Medici; merchants of, 351-2, 356-8; see also Florence; Venice; Genoa

James II, king of Scotland, 29, 45

James III, king of Scotland, 211, 225n, 240, 271n; supports Lancaster, 49, 53, 192; settlement with England and marriage alliance, 212-13; forced into war with England, 278-82; his brother Albany supported against him, 286; and the war with England (1482-3), 287-90, 293

James, duke of Rothesay, later James IV, 213, 279, 289-90, 293, 417

Janyns, Henry, 276

Janyns, Robert, 276

Jeanne of France, daughter of king Charles VII, 84n, 109

Jersey, attacked by French, 43; re-captured by English, 113
Jerusalem, 143n
John, king of England, 419
John II, king of Aragon, 11n, 114
John II, king of Portugal, 274
John, duke of Bedford, 85, 89
John, duke of Burgundy, 231
John of Gaunt, duke of Lancaster, 4–5, 28, 106n, 147n, 170, 240n
Justices of the peace, 301, 388–9, 391, 397

Kendal, 326
Kenilworth, lordship of, 438
Kennedy, James, bishop of St Andrews, 46, 50, 54, 56, 63
Kent, 24, 35, 44, 57, 60, 117n, 119, 128, 181–3, 222, 273, 325, 344, 441; earls of, see Nevill, William; Grey, Edmund; rebellions in (1450), 11, 23–4; (1469), 130; (1471), 152, 173–4, 326; (1483), 329n, 358; M.P.s for, 326
Kent, Thomas, 121
Kildare, earls of, see FitzGerald; Fitz-Maurice
Kilgerran, castle and lordship of, 77n, 137n
Kilpeck, 99
Kinaston, Roger, 389
King, Oliver, bishop of Exeter, 320n, 329
King's Lynn, 152, 154
Kingston-upon-Hull, see Hull
Kingston-upon-Thames, 174
Kirkham, Robert, 110
Knaresborough, honour of, 70, 200, 437; bailiff of, 200

La Hogue, 147
Lancashire, 45, 58, 69n, 70, 126, 134, 164, 170, 280–1, 328, 382, 392, 401, 406, 437, 438; M.P. for, 409
Lancaster, dukes of, see John of Gaunt; Henry IV
Lancaster, duchy of, 20, 75, 198, 200, 329–30, 335, 382–3, 401, 408, 417, 442; chief steward of, 70, 437; officials of, 344; chancellor of, 345; receiver-general of, 382
Lande, Sir Thomas de la, 138
Langstrother, Sir John, prior of the Hospital of St John of Jerusalem, 133, 136, 172
Langton, Thomas, 252, 255, 286
Lannoy, Jean de, 54, 59, 91n, 92n
Laon, 229
La Plesance, manor of, see Greenwich

Latimer, Lord, see Nevill
Latimer, Sir Nicholas, 143
Lauder, Bridge of, 288
Law-enforcement, problems of, 388–95; and the powerful offender, 393–6, 405–10; lack of impartiality in under Edward IV, 411–12
League of the Common Weal, 104, 106
Legh, Alexander, 279
Leicester, 18, 60, 62, 164, 305
Leicestershire, 57, 74–5
Leventhorpe, Nicholas, 374
Leyden, 364n
Lichfield, bishops of, see Coventry
Lille, 252, 364n
Lincoln, 304, 388; castle, 442; bishop of, 27, 184n; and see Russell, John
Lincolnshire, 61, 69n, 75, 150n, 152; rebellion of (1470), 138–42, 144, 187, 432, 441–2; M.P. for, 442
Lindisfarne, 51
Lionel, duke of Clarence, 5, 28, 33
Lisle, Viscount, see Talbot
Lisle, Sir William, 389
Llandaff, bishop of, see Hunden, John
Llanstephan, lordship of, 137n
Llewellyn the Great, 300
Loire, valley, 273
Lokton, John, 353
London, 18, 19, 22–4, 26, 28, 31, 41, 50, 53, 95, 108–11, 116, 120, 129–30, 133, 152, 159, 165–6, 167–8, 174, 181–2, 219, 234, 241, 253, 257–8, 266, 271, 282–4, 286, 304, 312, 324, 358–9, 414, 424–5; attitude to Edward IV, 32, 34–5, 101, 130, 166–7, 174–5, 304, 353–6, 362, 365, 423; bishop of, 27, 184n, 319; merchants of, 353; knighted by Edward, 354; courted by the king, 353–4; as source of loans, 26, 35, 111, 166, 223, 281, 353, 378; xenophobia of, 358–9; common council of, 166, 173; mayor of, 26, 116n, 135, 166, 175, 234, 241, 416, and see also Cook, Thomas; Stockton, John; Verney, John; Heryot, William; sheriff of, 34, 355, 431; treaty of (1474), 210–11; Tower of, 26–7, 65, 95, 123, 155, 166, 168, 174, 184, 241, 243, 272, 402; Chronicles of, 9, 14, 80, 99–100, 116n, 121n, 125n, 182, 217, 257, 354, 364n, 429, 431
Lorraine, 229
Lorraine, Isabella of, 237
Lorraine, René, duke of, 224, 228
Lose-Cote, Field, battle of, 141

Louis XI, king of France, 58, 63, 74, 124,
148, 182, 273, 284, 324, 356, 363, 433;
as dauphin, troops aid Edward IV,
35, 36n; supports Lancastrians, 44,
50; *rapprochement* with Edward IV, 56;
plans for marriage of Edward IV,
90–1; centralizing policy, 104; relations with Warwick, 105, 109;
attempts to form alliance with England, 108–11; hostilities with England,
113; reconciles Warwick and Margaret, 146–7; supports Readeption,
154, 158; declares war on Burgundy,
159, 161; aid to earl of Oxford, 192,
205; manœuvres against England,
Burgundy and Brittany, 205–8, 212;
and the English invasion of France,
223–38; his pensions to English notables, 234, 317, 325; and the Burgundian succession, 240, 242, 249–53;
and the English marriage, 246, 249,
253–6; fosters war between England
and Scotland, 278–9, 287; rivalry
with Burgundy, 284–6, 290–2; his
diplomatic skill, 294–5; death, 415
Louis of Bruges, *see* Gruthuyse
Lovel, Francis, Viscount Lovel, 115,
186n, 333, 438
Lovel, John Lord, 67, 438
Lovel, William, Lord Morley, 73n, 380
Low Countries, 357, 359, 361, 364–5,
418; *see also* Burgundy
Lowys, Henry, 184
Lubeck, 365
Ludford Bridge, 'Rout of', 21–2, 25n,
35, 74, 76, 79
Ludlow, 18, 20, 24n, 28, 49, 222, 424,
436; castle, 5, 7, 197
Lumley, Sir George, 46
Lumley, Thomas Lord, 73n
Luttrell, James, 77
Luxembourg, Jacques de, 95, 160
Luxembourg, Louis de, count of St Pol,
207, 214, 222, 226, 228–9, 231, 235
Luxembourg, Pierre, count of St Pol, 89
Luxemburg, Jacquetta of, dowager
duchess of Bedford, wife of 1st Earl
Rivers, mother of Queen Elizabeth,
85, 89, 96–7, 100–1, 121, 258–9, 270
Lyons, archbishop of, 233
Lyster, John, 160

MacDonald, John, earl of Ross, lord of
the Outer Isles, 46, 49, 281
Madeleine, daughter of Charles VII of
France, 84

Maldon, 344
Malmesbury, 170
Malory, Sir Thomas, 411n
Maltravers, Lord, *see* FitzAlan
Malvern, Little, portraits of Edward IV
and his family at, 322
Manchester, 143
Mancini, Dominic, on appearance of
Edward IV, 10; on Hastings' influence, 73; on Edward's love of
pleasure, 86–7, and of women, 315;
on the Woodville family, 97n, 98,
102–3, 434; on the death of Clarence,
116n, 244; on Edward's death, 414–
415; on the crisis of 1483, 425
Mansel, Jean, 265
March, earl of, *see* Edward IV; Mortimer
Marche, Olivier de la, 112n, 220, 243n,
260, 301
Marches towards Scotland, 16, 38, 57,
199, 279, 287, 301, 339–40, 372;
wardenships of: West March, 17, 46,
70, 202, 293, 326, 334, 339–40, 344,
372, 437; East March, 46, 53, 70, 145,
156n, 293, 340, 372, 437
Marches of Wales, 5, 14, 18, 20, 30–1,
41, 48, 70, 76, 81, 102, 157, 187,
193–9, 303, 322, 334, 398, 400–1, 405,
407, 437
Margaret of Anjou, queen of Henry VI,
29, 45–6, 49, 65, 66, 80, 89, 96n, 123,
183, 184, 266, 270, 273, 299, 313, 356,
363, 433; fears of regency under her
domination, 17; birth of her son, 19;
hostility to Duke Richard of York,
19–20; Yorkist towns sacked by her
troops, 30–2; escapes to Scotland, 38,
41; a friend of Pierre de Brézé, 43;
raises French force to invade England,
50–4; aid given to her by Louis XI, 106;
rapprochement with Warwick, 109, 118,
146–7; prepares to invade England,
113, 150, 156, 161, 165; lands in
England, 169, 176; and the Tewkesbury campaign, 170–3, 175; ran-
somed and disinherited by Louis XI,
237–8, 251, 385
Margaret of York, duchess of Burgundy,
sister of Edward IV, 224, 240, 266,
284; marriage of, 107–9, 111–12, 118,
120, 250–1, 324; and its costs, 259–60,
373; her piety, 9, 273; her visit to
England (1480), 271, 273, 283
Margaret, daughter of Edward IV, 245
Margaret of Austria, daughter of Maximilian and Mary, 249n, 291–2

Margaret of Scotland, sister of James III, 240, 278, 289–90
Margate, 112, 120
Markham, John, chief justice, 100, 401
Marney, Sir John, 123
Martin, Richard, bishop of St David's, 321–2
Mary, daughter of Edward IV, 115n, 230, 233, 247
Mary, duchess of Burgundy, 107, 117, 210, 240, 247, 249–56, 283, 291
Mary of Guelders, queen of Scotland, 46, 48–9, 53, 85
Mason, John, 305
Massey, Henry, 263
Matthias Corvinus, king of Hungary, 213
Mauley, Lord, see Bygod
Maximilian of Austria, archduke of Austria, duke of Burgundy; commercial relations with England, 364; marriage to Mary of Burgundy, 210; proposed marriage alliances with England, 246–7; seeks English aid against France, 249–56, 278; alliance with England, 283–6; and treaty of Arras, 290–2
Medici bank, 223, 233, 352, 356
Mediterranean, English trade with, 351, 360, 362n
Merchant Adventurers, 101, 315, 356–8, 364–5
Merioneth, 77n
Metcalfe, Miles, 202
Michelson, Robert, 185
Middleham, castle and lordship, 21, 60, 62, 135, 187, 200, 311, 410n, 437
Middlesex, 121n, 190n
Middleton, Geoffrey, 408
Milan, 91; ambassadors of, and their reports, 107n, 109, 113n, 133, 162, 175, 217, 221, 223, 236, 246, 254, 433; dukes of; Galeazzo Maria, 246, 275; Francesco Sforza, 274
Milewater, John, 31
Milford Haven, 152
Milling, Thomas, abbot of Westminster, bishop of Hereford, 185, 321
Monmouthshire, 75
Monteferrato, Alan de, 351
Montereau, 231
Montgomery, Sir Thomas, 234, 237, 314, 326, 399–400
Montgomery, lordship of, 77n; castle of, 120
Mont Orgueil, Jersey, 113

Monypenny, William, 56n, 118n, 124–5, 364n
More, Sir Thomas, his view of Edward IV, 434–5; on Edward's appearance, 10; on influence of Hastings, 73; on Edward's love of pleasure, 86–7, and of women, 315–16; on the Woodvilles, 98, 416n, 426; on Edward's attitude to common people, 355; on his reputation, 418
Morley, Lord, see Lovel
Mortimer, Anne, 4
Mortimer, Edmund, earl of March, 79n, 300
Mortimer's Cross, battle of, 31, 33, 35, 74, 76, 182
Morton, John, master of the rolls, bishop of Ely, 184, 213, 224, 230, 234, 251, 253, 309, 321, 417, 434
Mountfort, Sir Osbert, 25–6
Mountjoy, Lord, see Blount
Mowbray, Anne, wife of Richard of Shrewsbury, 248, 260, 335n, 381n
Mowbray, John, 3rd duke of Norfolk (d. 1461), 12, 22, 30, 34, 35–7, 305, 410
Mowbray, John, 4th duke of Norfolk (d. 1476), 58, 76, 121, 123, 129, 133n, 134, 142, 155, 157–8, 161, 172, 175, 186, 248, 274, 305, 309, 314, 335, 404, 407; earl marshal of England, 248

Namur, 229, 231
Nancy, 249
Naples, 108, 112, 213, 363; see also Ferdinand
Narbonne, archbishop of, 110; vicomte de, 235
Naworth Castle, 48, 50
Needwood, 437
Nele, Brian, 202
Nemours, Jacques, duc de, 214
Nene, river, 27
Netherlands, the, 250, 252, 369
Neuss, 224–5
Nevers, county of, 207
Nevill family, 14–15, 17–18, 28, 45–6, 53, 54, 62n, 82–3, 87, 95, 101, 115, 121, 127, 172–3, 330, 334, 339, 342, 393, 404, 432
Nevill, Alice, 67
Nevill, Anne, princess of Wales, duchess of Gloucester, 94, 147, 169, 187, 190
Nevill, Charles, 134–5
Nevill, Edward, Lord Abergavenny, 22, 26, 34n

Nevill, George, duke of Bedford, 93,
    136–7, 145, 182, 189
Nevill, George, Lord Latimer, 70, 128,
    437
Nevill, George, bishop of Exeter, arch-
    bishop of York, 20, 26, 34, 55–6, 59n,
    81n, 118, 121, 127n, 129, 132–5, 148,
    150, 201, 309, 314, 318, 438; chan-
    cellor of England, 27, 83, 404; grants
    from Edward, 72; fall from favour,
    110, 115, 120n, 144n; during Re-
    adeption, 166, 184n; arrest and im-
    prisonment, 191; death, 193; char-
    acter of, 193; patron of scholars, 268;
    career, 319–20
Nevill, Sir Henry, 128
Nevill, Sir Humphrey, 58–9, 61–2, 65,
    120, 134–5, 305
Nevill, Isabel, duchess of Clarence, 94,
    107, 115, 117, 129, 145–6, 188, 239,
    241, 393
Nevill, John, Lord Montagu, earl of
    Northumberland, marquis Montagu,
    16, 21, 23, 93, 148, 156n, 160, 183,
    189, 190, 305, 437, 439; helps subdue
    the North, 41, 53, 59–62; grants from
    Edward IV, 72, 115, 137, 438; con-
    tinues to support Edward in 1469,
    126–7, 136, 141, 143–5; loses his earl-
    dom, 144, 150; supports Warwick,
    151–2, 157–8; during Readeption,
    163–5, 167; death at Barnet, 168;
    as warden of East March, 372
Nevill, John Lord (d. 1461), 30, 37, 66n
Nevill, Katherine, duchess of Norfolk,
    93, 248
Nevill, Katherine, wife of William, Lord
    Hastings, 75
Nevill, Ralph, 1st earl of Westmorland, 5
Nevill, Ralph, 2nd earl of Westmorland,
    47, 221
Nevill, Ralph, later 3rd earl of Westmor-
    land, 337
Nevill, Richard, earl of Salisbury, 16,
    437; warden of West March, 17;
    wealth and estates in North, 17;
    marriage to Salisbury heiress, 17;
    chancellor of England, 18; at 1st
    battle of St Albans, 18; and Blore
    Heath, 20–1; flight and exile in
    Calais, 21–4; attainted, 23; invades
    England, 25–6; death at Wakefield,
    30; interred at Bisham Abbey, 53
Nevill, Richard, 'The Kingmaker', earl
    of Warwick and Salisbury, 13, 16, 30,
    42, 44, 62, 65, 69n, 74, 78, 81n, 83,

183, 186–7, 189–90, 193, 199, 200,
    223, 232, 280, 310–11, 313–14, 324,
    326, 330, 365, 366, 391, 398, 409, 434;
    marriage to Beauchamp heiress, 17;
    income, 17; at 1st battle of St Albans,
    18; captain of Calais, 19–20; in exile
    at Calais, 21–4; attainted, 23; emer-
    gence as Yorkist leader, 23–4; de-
    feated at 2nd St Albans, 32; and
    Edward's assumption of the throne,
    33; and Towton campaign, 36–7;
    warden of Scottish Marches, 46, 372;
    commands northern campaigns, 50–
    60; contemporary opinions as to his
    power, 63; grants of land and office
    from Edward, 70–1, 437–8; his
    marriage plans for Edward, 85, 87, 91;
    attitude to Woodvilles, 90–5; mani-
    festo, 97; estrangement from Edward,
    104–5, 114–25; diplomatic activity,
    106–11; challenge to Edward and its
    failure (1469), 126–35; apparent paci-
    fication of, 135–6; involvement in
    Lincolnshire rebellion, 137–44, 441–2;
    extent of support for him (1469–70),
    133–5, 142–4; flees the realm, 145–6;
    dealings with Louis XI and Margaret
    of Anjou, 146–7; returns to England,
    147, 152; and the problems of the
    Readeption, 154–9; outmanœuvred
    by Edward (1471), 164–6; death at
    Barnet, 167–8
Nevill, Thomas, Bastard of Fauconberg,
    128, 146, 161, 173–4, 176, 181, 324,
    354–6, 432
Nevill, Thomas, son of the earl of Salis-
    bury (d. 1460), 16, 21, 23, 30, 53
Nevill, Thomas, 410
Nevill, William, Lord Fauconberg, earl
    of Kent, 25–7, 35, 37, 46, 50, 72, 78,
    146, 324, 332, 376; steward of the
    royal household, 323
Newark, 129, 139, 164
Newbold Revel, 411n
Newbury, 24n
Newcastle-on-Tyne, 37, 46, 53, 55, 57–
    60, 357, 358
Newnham Bridge, 25
Newport Pagnell, manor of, 438
Nibley Green, battle at, 138, 406
Nobility, the English, Edward's rela-
    tions with, 34, 36, 41–2, 64–83, 94, 97,
    331–41; his peerage creations and
    promotions, 332–3; creates 'court
    party' and king's men amongst, 69–83,
    87, 121–2, 124, 130, 332, and over-

mighty subjects amongst, 202–3, 334; change in policy towards after 1471, 334–7; his reliance upon, in regional government, 72, 82–3, 323, 331, 337; their power not diminished by his rule, 331–2, 340; their privileges, 338; their interference in parliamentary elections, 344; affected by his disregard for inheritance laws, 190–1; dissensions amongst in 1483 the result of Edward's policy, 330, 337, 424–6; and livery and maintenance and retaining, 119, 124, 330, 337–8, 395–6, 405–6, 412–13

Norfolk, 42, 57, 161, 403, 406; sheriffs of, 324, 391, 399; M.P.s for, 324; dukes of, see Mowbray; Richard of Shrewsbury

Norham Castle, 53–4, 59

Normandy, 43, 146, 206–10, 222–5, 228, 284; duke of, see Charles

Norris, Sir William, 164, 329n

Northampton, 54, 58, 131–2

Northampton, battle of, 22, 25n, 26–7, 35, 66–7, 76

Northamptonshire, 5, 67–8, 74n, 75, 438

Northumberland, 17n, 35n, 45–6, 50, 55–6, 60, 72, 117n, 120, 279, 389, 432; earls of, see Percy; Nevill, John

Norton, Thomas, 102, 303

Norway, 358

Norwich, 129, 406; bishop of, see Goldwell; castle, constable of, 324

Nottingham, 129, 131–2, 145, 152, 154, 164, 165, 199, 272, 282–3; castle, 272, 276, 278; constable of, 185; mayor and aldermen of, 303; earl of, see Mowbray; Richard of Shrewsbury

Nottinghamshire, 271

Nutwell (Devon), 21

Observant Franciscans, order of, 273

Offaly, 204

Ogle, Robert Lord, 73n

Olney, 132

Orange, prince of, 285–6

Ormond family, 184

Ormond, Thomas, 172

Ormond, earl of, see Butler

Oswestry, 408

Oxford, earls of, see Vere; countess of, see Howard, Elizabeth

Oxford, university of, 240, 269, 272, 276, 320; colleges: All Souls, 264n; Balliol, 268; Lincoln, 268; Magdalen, 270

Oxfordshire, 271, 403

Oyer and terminer, commissions of, use by Edward IV, 301, 390, 397–9

Pakenham, Hugh, 101

Palmer, Robert, 400

Panicharolla, Johanne Petro, 236

Papcaster, manor of, 438

Paris, 107, 232, 235

Parliament, frequency and duration of, 341, 346–7; royal management of, 342–7; interference in elections to, 343–6; royal servants in, 342–5; speakers of, 345; legislation in, 346–7, 359–61; and taxation, 54–5, 207, 214–218, 348–50, 371; and problem of law and order, 404–5; mercantilism of, 359–61; parliament of 1459, 20, 22, 28, 67, 80; of 1460, 27–8; of 1461, 33, 103; of 1463–5, 54, 349, 405; of 1467–8, 111–12, 344–5, 348; of 1469, 133; of 1472–5, 190, 195, 205n, 214–218; of 1478, 241–3; of 1483, 405; of 1484, 329n

Parr, Sir John, 224n, 326

Parr, Sir William, 164, 185, 191, 202, 310, 325–6, 417

Paston family, 20, 37, 73–4, 118, 121, 134, 158, 192, 305, 314–15, 399, 401, 403–4, 406–7

Paston, Clement, 23n

Paston, John, senior, 37, 314

Paston, Sir John, 134–5, 151, 158, 169, 190–1, 400

Paston, John, the younger, 51n, 112n, 158, 216, 349

Paston, Margaret, 42

Payne, John, senior, 359

Pembroke, 31, 48; castle of, 49, 77n, 137n, 175, 182, 196, 408

Pembroke, earls of, see Tudor, Jasper; Herbert, William

Pendragon, 438

Penrith Castle, 29

Percy family, 14–15, 45–7, 70, 117n, 127, 145n, 187, 339, 393, 438

Percy, Henry, 2nd earl of Northumberland (d. 1455), 16, 18, 47

Percy, Henry, 3rd earl of Northumberland (d. 1461), 16, 29 and n, 30, 37, 47

Percy, Henry, 4th earl of Northumberland (d. 1489), 47, 140, 157, 310, 409; restored to his earldom by Edward IV, 136, 144–5, 151; aids Edward in 1471, 154, 160, 163–4, 173; warden of the East March, 156n, 340; grants

Percy, Henry, 4th earl—*contd.*
to, 186 and n; relations with Gloucester, 199–203, 413, 424; and the invasion of France, 232; and the war
with Scotland, 279, 282–3, 287–8, 293
Percy, Henry, 5th earl of Northumberland, 198n
Percy, Ralph, 16, 47, 51–3, 59, 62, 65
Percy, Richard, 16
Percy, Thomas, Lord Egremont, 16, 27
Péronne, 214, 226, 228–9; treaty of, 113,
159
Perrers, Alice, mistress of Edward III, 316
Peverell, honour of, 75n
Philip the Good, duke of Burgundy, 50,
84, 95, 301; Warwick's negotiations
with, 20; troops aid Edward at Towton, 35, 36n; French plans to poison
him, 44; urges Mary of Guelders to
aid Edward, 46; attempts *rapprochement* between Edward and Louis, 56;
his embargo on English cloth, 105;
death, 110; his library, 265, 268; his
patronage, 269; mistresses, 316; com-
mercial relations with England, 358,
360–2, 364–5, 367
Philip of Burgundy, son of Mary and
Maximilian, 247, 252, 283–4
Philip, Matthew, 263
Philippa, queen of Portugal, daughter
of John of Gaunt, 4n
Picardy, 91, 159, 225, 228, 250
Pickering, honour of, 70, 200, 437
Picquigny, 231; treaty of, 233–4, 236–8,
239, 245, 249, 251, 253, 255, 368, 385,
433
Pike, John, 154
Pilkington, Sir John, 328
Pilkington, Thomas, 392
Piracy, *see under* Edward IV
Pisa, 362
Plomer, Robert, 344
Plommer, Sir John, 101, 355
Plumpton family, 200
Plumpton, Sir William, 200–1
Pocklington, 127
Poitiers, Diane de, 269
Pole, John de la, 2nd duke of Suffolk, 64,
69, 119, 128n, 129, 133n, 135, 142,
161, 175, 186, 204n, 263, 274, 309,
314, 401, 403, 404, 407
Pole, William de la, 1st duke of Suffolk,
11–12, 42
Pontefract, 135, 271; castle, 29, 163;
honour and lordship, 70, 200, 383,
437; priory, 271

Popes: Pius II, 25, 28n, 115, 377; Paul
II, 269; Sixtus IV, 273–4, 282
Portaleyn, 101
Portchester Castle, 96
Porter, John, 149n
Portinari, Thomas de, 218n
Porto Pisano, 352
Portsmouth, 22, 367
Portugal, 98, 109, 161, 353, 369; Pedro
of, 107; *see also* Isabella; John II;
Philippa
Powderham, 142n
Poynings, 123
Prout, Thomas, 327
Puissant, Pierre, 291

Quint, a petty captain, 181

Radcliffe, James, 314
Radcliffe, John, styled Lord FitzWalter,
36–7
Radcliffe, Robert, 282, 288
Radford, Nicholas, 390, 407
Raglan Castle, 75, 182; lordship, 77
Ravenspur, 162, 409
Ravensworth (Yorks.), 151
Reading, 91; abbey of, 92
Recoinage, of 1464–5, 364–5, 377–8
Redesdale, *see* Robin of
Redman, Edmund, 344
Redman, Sir Richard, 34n
Réné, king of Anjou, 237
Rennes, 261
Retford, 142
Rethel, county of, 207
Rheims, 209, 228, 229
Richard II, 130, 299, 322, 346, 420
Richard, duke of York, father of Edward
IV, 53, 74, 84, 263, 271, 305, 408, 436;
descent and claim to the throne, 3, 5;
family connections, 3, 22–3; estates
and income, 5; in politics of 1450s, 11–
21; protector of England, 17–19; at
'Rout of Ludford', 21–2; flight to Ire-
land, and ruler of Ireland, 22, 203;
attainted, 23; in 1460, 25, 28–9;
claims the throne, 28–9, 33; killed at
Wakefield, 30; character and abilities,
13, 17–18
Richard, duke of Gloucester, later
Richard III, brother of Edward IV,
7, 21, 128, 132n, 135–6, 181, 255, 310,
334, 339, 343, 344, 372, 381 and n,
393, 398, 409, 430, 435; marriage of,
94, 109, 188, 190; constable of England, 136; offices in Wales, 136, 195;

loyalty to Edward, 187; trusted by Edward, 136; and rebellion of 1470, 143; in 1471, 152; in exile with Edward, 153; attainted, 155; on 1471 campaigns, 165, 167, 170–1; and the death of Henry VI, 175; chief beneficiary of Edward's restoration, 186–7, 199; his quarrel with Clarence, 187–191; becomes chief power in North of England, 202–3; relations with earl of Northumberland, 199–203, 413; and the government of the north, 201–3; king's lieutenant in north, 201, 279; his palatine lordship in northwest, 202, 293n, 334; and invasion of France, 221, 230, 233; not involved in Clarence's downfall and death, 244; and the war with Scotland, 279, 282, 287–90, 293; his northern affinity, 203, 330; and the crisis of 1483, 203, 335, 336n, 424–6; as Richard III, 336n, 337, 349, 381, 384, 418
Richard of Shrewsbury, earl of Nottingham, duke of York and Norfolk, 2nd son of Edward IV, 102, 247, 332–3, 381n; marriage to Anne Mowbray, 248–9, 260, 336; endowment of, 335–6
Richard, son of George, duke of Clarence, 238
Richmond (Surrey), 264
Richmond (Yorks.), honour of, 117n, 186–7, 200
Richmond, earls of, see Tudor
Richmondshire, 141, 441
Ripon, 152
Riviere, Barthelot de, 213
Roberti, Nicholas de, 246n
Robin of Holderness, 127, 439–40
Robin of Redesdale (or Mend-All), 119, 126, 129, 130, 134, 140–1, 439–41; see also Conyers, Sir John
Rochester, 174; bishop of, 27, 319n; see also Rotherham, Thomas; Russell, John; Audley, Edmund; Alcock, John
Rockingham Castle, 75
Rogers, Thomas, 280
Rome, 98, 110, 115, 117, 274, 322
Roos family, 184
Roos, Sir Henry, 184
Roos, John Lord, 200n
Roos, Margery Lady, 200
Roos, Thomas Lord, 17, 29–30, 38, 46, 59, 60, 66n, 75
Ross, earl of, see MacDonald
Rosse, William, 220
Rotherham, 268

Rotherham, Thomas, bishop of Rochester, archbishop of York, 161, 222, 232, 234, 268, 309, 417; chancellor of England, 232, 241, 321, 416
Rouen, 4, 109, 113n, 161n, 237
Rougement-Grey, Thomas Lord, 46
Rous, John, 116n, 270
Roux, Olivier le, 240n
Roxburgh, 29, 46, 279, 288
Roy, Pierre le, 286
Royston, 140
Rozmital, Leo of, 258
Russell, John, bishop of Rochester and Lincoln, 268–9, 295, 309, 340, 415–16, 430; keeper of the privy seal, 269, 295, 321, 430
Rutland, 74n, 75

St Albans, 166–7; 1st battle of, 18–19, 67; 2nd battle of, 22, 32, 68, 85
St Andrews, bishop of, see Kennedy, James
St Asaph, bishop of, 184n
St Bartholomew, Smithfield, prior of, 26n
St Briavels, 117n
St Bridget of Sweden, 9
St Catherine of Siena, 9
St Christ-sur-Somme, 228
St David's, bishop of, see Tully, Robert; Martin, Richard
St John of Jerusalem, Hospital of, knights of, 96n, 183; priors of, see Langstrother; Tournay
St Leger, Anne, 336–7
St Leger, Thomas, 154, 184, 230, 234, 327, 329n, 336
St Maur, treaty of, 106
St Michael's Mount, 176, 192, 410
St Omer, 55–6, 90, 228
St Osyth, 192
St Paul's Cathedral, 19, 34, 54, 166, 168, 258; Cross, 241
St Pol, 160, 228; counts of, see Luxembourg
St Quentin, 227, 228
Salisbury, 48, 55, 57, 66, 122–3, 154, 397–8, 402; bishop of, see Beauchamp, Richard; Woodville, Lionel
Salisbury, earls of, see Nevill, Richard; George; Edward
Salkeld, Richard, 151, 438
Salvo, John de, 352
Sandal Castle, 5, 30, 163
Sanderico, James de, 351
Sandwich, 26, 48, 109, 128, 130, 145, 149, 174, 181, 219, 222, 280, 282, 360

Savoy, duchy of, 213
Savoy, Bona of, 91, 246
Savoy, Charlotte of; *see* Charlotte, queen of France
Savoy, Philip of, 109
Saxton, 37
Say, Sir John, speaker of the commons, 345, 349; chancellor of the Duchy of Lancaster, 345
Say, William, Lord Say and Sele, 26, 152, 155, 168, 381
Scales, Lord, *see* Woodville, Anthony
Scales, Elizabeth, 96, 278
Scales, Thomas Lord, 96
Scarborough, 200
Scotland, 38, 45–6, 49–50, 53–6, 59, 62–3, 92n, 108n, 112, 152, 159n, 168, 192, 201–2, 205, 212–13, 247, 249, 272, 278–83, 285–95, 311, 321, 326, 348, 350, 386, 423; *see also* Alexander; James; Mary of Guelders
Scott, Sir John, 26, 121, 149, 173, 310, 324–6
Scrope, John, Lord Scrope of Bolton, 26, 36, 58, 141, 143n, 144, 150, 157, 200, 202
Scrope, Richard, bishop of Carlisle, 320
Scrope, Thomas, Lord Scrope of Masham, 67
See, Martin de la, 163
Seine, river, 44, 146, 150, 161
Severn, river, 170
Shakespeare, William, 418
Sharpe, Nicholas, 374
Sheen, palace of, 188, 271, 273, 303
Sheldon, manor of, 438
Sheriff Hutton, castle and lordship of, 118, 187
Sherwood forest, keeper of, 185
Ships: the *Trinity*, 128, 145; the *Anthony*, 160, 162, 185, 218, 280, 351; the *Grace Dieu*, 218–19; the *Mary Redcliffe*, 219; the *Margaret Howard, George Howard, Thomas Howard*, 219; the *Katherine Rivers*, 219; the *Falcon*, 280; the *Carvel of Portugal*, 280; the *Mary Howard*, 280; the *George Cobham*, 352
Shore, Jane (*rectius* Elizabeth), 269, 315–16
Shore, William, 316
Shrewsbury, 195; earl of, *see* Talbot
Shropshire, 5, 29, 197, 388, 401, 407–8
Silvester, Nicholas, 304
Sion, abbey, 416
Skelton, John, 270
Skipton-in-Craven, 59, 200

Sluys, 54, 112
Slyfield, William, 321
Snowdon, master-forester of, 77n
Sodbury (Glos.), 170
Solihull, manor of, 438
Somerset, 5, 42, 77, 80, 169, 170, 195, 241, 336, 383; dukes of, *see* Beaufort
Somme, towns of, 106, 207; river, 228, 231; valley, 227, 414
Sotehill, Henry, 123
Southampton, 143, 145, 149–50, 263n, 351, 358–60, 363
Southwark, 152
Spain, 24, 44, 98, 161, 295, 322, 367; rulers of, *see* Isabella; Ferdinand
Spicing, a petty captain, 181
Spinola, Antonio, 352
Stacey, Dr John, 240–1, 397–8
Stafford family, of Grafton, 406; Bastard of, *see* Grafton
Stafford, Anne, duchess of Buckingham, 81
Stafford, Fulk, 376
Stafford, Henry, 2nd duke of Buckingham, 70–1, 76, 93–5, 156, 175, 221n, 230n, 315n, 335, 420, 424–5
Stafford, Sir Henry, 37
Stafford, Humphrey, 1st duke of Buckingham, 12, 18, 22, 27, 137, 194, 373
Stafford, Humphrey, Lord Stafford of Southwick, earl of Devon, 31, 36, 66, 73n, 74, 78–9, 82–3, 97, 110, 118, 121, 123, 129–32, 137, 310n, 334, 439
Stafford, John, earl of Wiltshire, 137, 150, 155, 186, 380
Staffordshire, 335
Stairs, Richard, 123
Stamford, 30, 129, 140–1, 304, 335
Stanley family, 134, 406, 408
Stanley, George, Lord Strange, 389
Stanley, Thomas, Lord Stanley, 23, 53, 95, 134, 143, 150, 152, 156, 164, 226, 230, 280, 288, 334, 359, 376n, 382, 392, 408n, 409, 416; steward of royal household, 323
Stanley, Sir William, 23, 136, 164, 185, 334, 376n
Staple, Company of, 19, 111, 311–12, 356–60, 378–9
Star Chamber, *see* Council
Stephen, king of England, 171
Stepney, 174
Steres, Richard, 397
Stillington, Robert, bishop of Bath and Wells, 108, 112, 157, 208, 253, 268

320; keeper of the privy seal, 321; chancellor, 321
Stockton, John, mayor of London, 166, 175
Stoke-by-Nayland, 324
Stonor, Sir William, 329n, 403
Stony Stratford, 85
Stourton, William Lord, 123
Strange, Lord, see Stanley
Strangways, Sir James, 305; speaker of the commons, 342, 345
Stratford by Bow, abbey of, 120, 402
Stratford Langthorne, 120n
Strensham, manor of, 438
Sturgeon, Thomas, 327
Sturgeon, William, 224n
Sturmy, Robert, 362n
Sudeley, lordship and castle of, 136n
Sudeley, Lord, 166
Suffolk, 5, 57, 77, 186n, 217; M.P. for, 324; dukes of, see Pole, de la
Surrey, 80n, 117n, 121n, 174; M.P.s for, 343
Sussex, 57, 182; M.P.s for, 343
Swiss, the, 210, 224, 284
Swynford, Katherine, 4
Symondson, Mark, 185, 280

Tadcaster, 37
Tailboys, Sir William, 47, 61, 411n, 442
Tailour, John, 392
Talbot family, 134, 138, 249, 406, 437
Talbot, John, 1st earl of Shrewsbury, 266
Talbot, John, 2nd earl of Shrewsbury, 20, 24, 27, 67, 373
Talbot, John, 3rd earl of Shrewsbury, 67, 70, 76, 78n, 119, 134, 143, 150, 152, 156, 164–5, 182, 196, 380, 409, 412; justiciar of North Wales, 195
Talbot, Thomas, Viscount Lisle, 77, 138
Tattershall Castle, 140
Taunton, 169
Tendring, William, 344
Tetzel, Gabriel, 10, 258–9
Tewkesbury, abbey of, 172; battle of, 37, 68n, 131n, 170–2, 176, 182, 299, 324, 326, 328
Thames, river, 174; valley, Edward's liking for, 271, 273
Thomas, Sir William ap, 75
Timperley, John, 344
Tiptoft, John, earl of Worcester, 9, 54, 61, 80, 142–4, 152, 155, 156n, 268, 398; constable of England, 43, 80, 82–3, 95, 120, 150, 396–7; lieutenant

of Ireland, 204; steward of the royal household, 323
Topcliffe, 437
Tour, Anne de la, 287
Tournay, William, prior of St John of Jerusalem, 183, 215
Towton, battle of, 36–7, 43, 45–6, 62, 66–8, 74, 80, 89, 324, 378
Trent, river, 34–5, 186n, 193, 199–201, 382, 438
Tresham, Sir Thomas, speaker of the commons, 35, 67, 123
Tresilian, John, 418
Trethewys family, 407
Tretower, 77, 182
Trollope, Andrew, 20, 35, 37
Tuchet, James, Lord Audley, 21
Tuchet, John, Lord Audley, 26, 31, 34n, 80, 82, 83n, 97, 118, 121, 123, 130, 157n, 214, 221n, 223
Tuddenham, Sir Thomas, 42–3, 305, 397
Tudor kings, 300, 307, 375
Tudor, Edmund, earl of Richmond, 20, 157
Tudor, Henry, earl of Richmond, see Henry VII
Tudor, Jasper, earl of Pembroke, 20, 30–1, 42, 48–9, 56, 66n, 76, 78, 114, 120, 147, 152, 156–7, 170, 172–3, 175–176, 182, 376
Tudor, Owen, 31, 182
Tully, Robert, bishop of St David's, 184
Tunstall, Sir Richard, 184, 221n, 252
Tutbury, honour of, 157, 189, 335, 383, 437
Tweed, river, 53
Twt Hill, engagement at, 49
Twynho, Ankarette, 241, 293
Twynho, John, 303
Twynho, Roger, 241n
Tynemouth, 46
Tyrell, Sir James, 190

Urbino, Federigo, duke of, 213, 274
Ursula, youngest sister of Edward IV, Urswick, Thomas, 174–5
Usk, lordship of, 5, 31, 76, 77n
Utrecht, 211–12, 364; treaty of, 368, 385

Valenciennes, 231
Vaughan, Sir Roger, 58, 136, 182, 195, 407
Vaughan, Sir Thomas, 102, 183, 191, 196, 310, 324, 355, 381n
Vaughan, Walter, 391
Veere, 160; lord of, see Borselle, Henry de

Venice, merchants of, 362–3; bankers of, 379

Vere, de, family, 186

Vere, Aubrey de, 43, 65, 397

Vere, John de, 12th earl of Oxford, 43, 65, 397

Vere, John de, 13th earl of Oxford, 65, 72, 122–3, 130, 133, 135, 143, 147, 152, 156–8, 161, 164–5, 167–8, 176, 186n, 187, 191–2, 376, 404, 410; constable of England, 155; his brothers, 161, 168

Vergil, Polydore, 107n, 118, 135–6, 176, 292, 414; on 1469 rebellions, 127, 131n, 439; on Edward's despotic tendencies, 386, 421; general value for reign, 418, 434

Verney, Ralph, 354

Vernon family, 42, 119, 412

Vernon, Henry, 119, 160n, 164, 165n

Verona, Guarino de, 268

Vervins, 235

Vignay, Jean de, 265

Vyvyan family, 407

Wakefield, 163, 328; battle of, 22, 30, 35, 53, 271

Walcheren, island of, 160–1

Wales, 5, 12, 17, 19, 20, 23, 29, 30–1, 38, 41, 43n, 44–5, 48, 58–9, 62, 74, 76–8, 98, 102, 114, 120, 129, 131–2, 134, 136, 156–7, 159n, 170, 175, 182, 193–9, 203, 301, 322, 334, 371, 373, 383, 407–8, 424, 437, 441; see also Marches of Wales; Edward IV

Walsingham, 128

Waltham Abbey, 140

Waltham Forest, 354

Wardour Castle, 80

Warenne, Earl, see Mowbray; Richard of Shrewsbury

Warin, Richard, 144

Wark Castle, 29

Warkworth Castle, 51

Warkworth, John, on events of Edward's reign, 52–3, 123–4, 128n, 132n, 160n, 163, 183, 192, 366, 377n, 432, 438–9, 442

Warr, Lord de la, see West

Warwick, 165, 241, 393; castle, 132, 135, 239, 242; earls of, see Beauchamp, Richard; Nevill, Richard; George

Warwickshire, 57, 70, 75, 140, 164, 438

Waurin, Jean de, 89, 116, 265, 434

Welles, Lionel, Lord Welles, 37, 66n

Welles, Richard, Lord Welles and

Willoughby, 138, 139n, 140–1, 335, 442

Welles, Sir Robert, 138, 139n, 140–1, 144, 441

Wells, 145, 169

Wenham, Little, 410

Wenlock, John Lord, 26, 73n, 80, 83–4, 90–2, 95, 106–7, 109, 121–2, 146, 148–9, 172

Wensleydale, 141

Weobley, 81

West, Reginald, Lord de la Warr, 183, 221n

Westminster, 27, 49, 65, 73, 110, 139, 174, 198, 202, 217, 241, 248, 251, 279, 305, 310, 345; palace of, 34, 166, 273, 311, 414, 416; abbey, 266, 274n, 476; abbot of, see Milling, Thomas; St Stephen's chapel, 275, 416; Henry VII's chapel, 276

Westmorland, 16, 69n, 70, 128, 141, 199, 202, 400, 438; M.P.s for, 326, 344; sheriff of, 326, 438; earls of, see Nevill, Ralph

Weymouth, 169, 214

Whetehill, Richard, 91, 173n, 181

Whitington, Richard, 353

Wight, Isle of, 43, 96, 113, 120, 381; governor of, 379

Wigmore Castle, 31

Willoughby, Lord, 60, 67n; the younger, 67; see also Welles

Wiltshire, 5, 42, 80, 122, 169, 236, 329n, 336, 401; M.P.s for, 343; earls of, see Butler; Stafford, John

Winchester, bishop of, 184n, 319; college, 268

Windsor, 128, 170, 241, 261, 271, 273, 275, 414, 418; St George's chapel, 263, 269, 271–5, 318, 380, 417; canons of, 266

Winestead, 127

Wingfield, Margaret, 391

Wingfield, Sir Robert, 381n, 391

Withall, manor of, 438

Wood, John, speaker of the commons, 345

Woodstock, 270–2, 282

Woodville family, 78, 83, 87, 104n, 110, 116, 118, 120, 124, 128–9, 137, 420, 430, 434; interests promoted by Edward IV, 92–7, 335–6; marriages of, 91–4, 115 and n; denounced as evil counsellors, 130; essentially courtiers, 99, 315; unpopularity of, and reasons for, 97, 129, 244, 424–5;

concern for own interests, 102, 336–7; political influence, 99–101, 137, 315; and the death of Clarence, 244; and the Burgundian alliance, 105, 110; and the crisis of 1483, 103, 424–6

Woodville, Anne, sister of Queen Elizabeth, 93

Woodville, Anthony, Lord Scales, 2nd Earl Rivers, brother of Queen Elizabeth, 89–90, 95–8, 109, 113, 118, 128–130, 136, 145, 149, 152, 160–1, 186, 207, 225, 280, 282, 309, 314, 329, 344n, 381n, 403; character, 97–8; interest in humanism and learning, 9, 97–8, 267–8; governor of prince of Wales, 98, 102, 196; feud with Hastings, 98, 181; in exile with Edward, 155; defends London (1471), 174; replaced as lieutenant of Calais, 181; on Breton expeditions, 206; plans for his second marriage, 251, 278, 289–90; regional authority in Wales, 335, 424; and the crisis of 1483, 424–5

Woodville, Sir Edward, brother of Queen Elizabeth, 96–8, 207

Woodville, Eleanor, sister of Queen Elizabeth, 93

Woodville, Elizabeth, queen of Edward IV, see Elizabeth

Woodville, John, brother of Queen Elizabeth, 93, 95, 129–30, 132, 314

Woodville, Katherine, sister of Queen Elizabeth, 93–4

Woodville, Lionel, brother of Queen Elizabeth, dean of Exeter, bishop of Salisbury, 96, 270

Woodville, Margaret, sister of Queen Elizabeth, 93

Woodville, Mary, sister of Queen Elizabeth, 77, 93, 99

Woodville, Richard, Lord Rivers, 1st Earl Rivers, father of Queen Elizabeth, 85–6, 89–90, 95–7, 99, 102, 108, 116, 118–19, 121, 128–30, 133, 145, 314, 375, 398; pardoned, 89; treasurer of England, 95; constable of England, 96, 131n; and the Cook affair, 99–101; executed, 132

Woodville, Sir Richard, brother of Queen Elizabeth, 96

Worcester, 170, 173; bishop of, see Alcock, John; earl of, see Tiptoft

Worcestershire, 70, 140, 197, 271, 389n

Wrexham, 120

Wrottesley, Sir Walter, 143, 173n, 181

Yelverton, William, justice, 399–400

Yeovil, 170

York, 37, 45, 51, 55, 57, 59, 61–2, 133, 135, 144–5, 152, 163, 201, 271, 281–2, 288, 358, 415; archbishops of, see Booth, William and Lawrence; Nevill, George; Rotherham, Thomas; convocation of, 216, 372; dukes of, see Edmund; Richard; Minster, 415; recorders of, 202; St Leonard's hospital in, 127

Yorkshire, 5, 16–17, 29, 36, 38, 45, 55, 59, 70, 74, 117n, 118–19, 125–6, 128, 134, 139–41, 144, 150n, 152, 161, 163, 183, 193, 199, 201–2, 279, 312, 328, 383, 400, 438, 441; sheriff of, 409; see also Holderness; Richmondshire; Wensleydale

Young, Thomas, M.P. for Bristol, 5

Zeeland, 109, 158, 219, 252